1906- Food + Drug Act
1938- Food Drug + Com
(also forbade sale of any
unless FDA found it to be safe.

Dept of Agriculture
    Chemical Division
    Division of Chemistry
    Bureau of Chemistry
Food, Drug + Insecticide Admin
    FDA

Federal Trade Comm
Created 1914

Anacin - 1915
Bufferin - 1949
Tylenol - 1955
Excedrin - 1961
Ibuprofen - 1974

ALSO BY CHARLES C. MANN

The Second Creation:
Makers of the Revolution
in Twentieth-Century Physics
(with Robert P. Crease)

THE ASPIRIN WARS

THE ASPIRIN WARS

MONEY, MEDICINE, AND
100 YEARS OF
RAMPANT COMPETITION

by CHARLES C. MANN
and MARK L. PLUMMER

ALFRED A. KNOPF   NEW YORK   1991

THIS IS A BORZOI BOOK
PUBLISHED BY ALFRED A. KNOPF, INC.

Portions of this work were originally published in somewhat different
form in *The Atlantic*, *Best of Business*, *In Health*, and *Geo*.

Library of Congress Cataloging-in-Publication Data
Mann, Charles C.
The aspirin wars : money, medicine, and 100 years of rampant
competition / Charles C. Mann and Mark L. Plummer. — 1st ed.
p.   cm.
Includes bibliographical references and index.
ISBN 0-394-57894-5
1. Aspirin—Marketing—History.   2. Farbenfabriken vorm. Friedrich
Bayer & Co.   I. Plummer, Mark L.   II. Title.
HD9675.A72M36   1991
381'.456153137—dc20   90-28735   CIP

Manufactured in the United States of America

FIRST EDITION

To my family, with lots of love
—C.C.M.

To Cassie, Robert, and Elizabeth,
who all helped
—M.L.P.

CONTENTS

THE ASPIRIN WARS

P R O L O G U E

"HOW ON EARTH DID ALL THIS COME ABOUT?"

At ten o'clock in the morning of March 2, 1988, forty people filed into a conference room adjacent to the fourteenth-floor office of Frank Young, M.D., Ph.D., the commissioner of the U.S. Food and Drug Administration. Anything but the sort of august, wood-paneled study seen in the movies, the conference room had a Formica-topped oval table, the Stars and Stripes and a few other flags, two screens for projecting slides, and a window overlooking Parklawn, a big cemetery northwest of Washington, D.C. The meeting was crowded, uncomfortably warm, and, for many of the participants, rather glum. They were about to get a lesson in the way big business and big government interact, and they suspected they were not going to like it. Indeed, they feared they were about to lose a market worth hundreds of millions of dollars every year.

Affable, plump, bespectacled, Frank Young took his position at the head of the table. Despite his credentials as a conservative Republican and a born-again Christian, Young was the antithesis of the Reagan administration's professed hostility toward government. The FDA is the branch of the Department of Health and Human Services that oversees the food and medicine sold in the United States; because of its reputation for toughness, it serves as a bellwether to its sister bodies in governments across the Atlantic and Pacific. In keeping with this image, Young liked to describe his agency as the cop on the beat, patrolling the lucrative world of big drugs. Although the yearly sales of the firms represented in Young's office that morning dwarfed his agency's budget, the executives around the table took the commissioner seriously indeed. With little in the way of preliminaries, the FDA has the authority to declare that a drug company's products are "misbranded"—sold as something they are not—and order them pulled from store shelves. In addition to costing millions in sales, misbranding actions generate a black cloud of negative headlines that can take months to dispel. Moreover, many pharmaceutical companies believe, the agency is often not satisfied until it has seen a few heads roll.

The businesspeople—presidents, general managers, and sales directors—in Young's conference room came from a select group: Their companies sold aspirin.* Five weeks before, on January 28, the *New England Journal of Medicine*, perhaps the most important and certainly the most visible biomedical journal in the United States, had published a preliminary report that aspirin could greatly lower the chances that an adult male would fall victim to a heart attack. Heart attacks are the leading cause of death in the Western world. In the United States alone, they kill more than 500,000 people a year. Stroke, an allied syndrome, annually takes another 150,000 souls. If, as the study suggested, a tablet of aspirin every other day could prevent a fifth of these deaths, at least 130,000 lives a year would be spared. In terms of annual mortality, this would be equivalent to wiping out AIDS in this country three times over.

The aspirin manufacturers greeted the report as a godsend. Aspirin is the most widely taken drug in the world, and has been for decades. In the United States alone, thirty billion tablets are consumed every year. Worldwide the figures are less certain, but a plausible estimate is that one hundred million pounds of aspirin disappear annually in the course of relieving headaches, reducing fevers, and soothing rheumatic pains—a small mountain of little white pills. Nonetheless, aspirin makers had long been unhappy. The market for headache remedies was now dominated by newer products like Tylenol (made from a different drug, acetaminophen) and Advil (made from ibuprofen), whose corporate parents spent vast sums on television advertisements proclaiming that they were safer (Tylenol) or more powerful (Advil) than aspirin. In recent years, moreover, a deadly but extremely rare children's disease called Reye's syndrome had come to be associated with aspirin, and the FDA had required a stiff warning notice to be printed on the bottle. Fearful of Reye's syndrome, many families stopped buying aspirin—so many that the children's aspirin market collapsed.

All this seemed about to change. Evidence of aspirin's beneficial effects had been accumulating for years, and in 1984 the FDA approved its use by patients who had suffered a previous heart attack, as well as for victims of some types of stroke and angina pectoris (chest pains due to oxygen deprivation in the heart). The *Journal* report was qualitatively different. It was the first scientific evidence that aspirin could reduce the chance of heart attacks in healthy people. Aspirin, in short, was not just for those unlucky enough

---

* In some nations, such as the United States, the United Kingdom, and France, aspirin is the common name for the chemical acetylsalicylic acid, and any company may use that name to describe its product. But ASPIRIN® is a registered trademark of Bayer AG, Germany, in approximately seventy countries worldwide. And in Canada, it is a registered trademark used exclusively to identify analgesics manufactured and distributed by Sterling-Winthrop, Inc.

already to be sick but also for the millions upon millions of people who *might* get sick.

Aspirin companies envisioned their humble pill, in the language of marketing, "repositioned" as a high-tech heart attack preventive. If half the men in the United States took an aspirin tablet every other day, annual aspirin sales would go up by $600 million, a 75 percent increase. Add foreign sales to that and the figure grew even more pleasing to contemplate. Moreover, those hundreds of millions would not be a one-time gain but would roll in year after year until the distant day when someone invented a cure for heart disease. Only one obstacle stood in the way of this rosy future: the FDA, with Frank Young at its head.

Of the ten aspirin companies at the meeting, the one with the most to lose was Sterling Drug, a New York City firm that, when the *Journal* article appeared, was in the process of being acquired by Eastman Kodak. Sterling makes Bayer aspirin, for seventy-five years the most familiar brand in the United States. Constant promotion has made Bayer's name and slogans ("Pure aspirin, not part aspirin," "Nine out of ten doctors recommend") synonymous with the drug. "For better or worse, we have a lock on it," Sterling research director Earle I. Lockhart explained not long ago. "The Bayer name lives and dies by aspirin."

Sterling had long been interested in aspirin's effects on cardiovascular disease. Without explicit approval from the FDA, it had broadcast television commercials about aspirin and second heart attacks for much of the past year. As part of this campaign, the firm had just produced its first "Calendar Pak"—a month's supply of aspirin dispensed like birth control pills, in a container with pouches labeled for each day, meant to be sold directly to the public. As the first Calendar Paks appeared on store shelves, company executives were elated to learn that the *New England Journal of Medicine* was set to publish a major new study on aspirin.

Known as the Physicians' Health Study, the medical experiment was one of the largest ever conducted, involving some 22,000 volunteers. Half took an aspirin every other day; the other half took a placebo—a pill that resembled an aspirin tablet but had no effect. For four years, a committee of doctors monitored the participants' health, looking for anything unusual. In December 1987, they found it: The group taking aspirin experienced 40 percent fewer heart attacks than the group taking placebo. Faced with this amazing difference, the doctors halted the experiment three years early, rather than continue giving placebo to participants who should be taking aspirin. And they contacted the *New England Journal of Medicine* to arrange expedited publication of the results.

Because the *Journal* refuses to print any material that has been described elsewhere, newspapers, magazines, and television networks usually agree to hold their stories until the day subscribers receive their copies. The Physicians' Health Study was stopped in mid-December; the printing of the preliminary report by the committee could not take place before mid-January. Sterling thus had a month to assemble a promotional blitz before the aspirin report was trumpeted by the media. Working night and day, the company kicked off its campaign at the earliest moment that would avoid the *Journal*'s wrath: 6:00 P.M., Wednesday, January 27, 1988—just in time for the evening news.

The coverage was everything Sterling could have wanted. "One aspirin every other day," *NBC Nightly News* anchorman Tom Brokaw told millions of viewers. "This simple prescription . . . dramatically reduce[s] heart attacks in men." The network cut to science correspondent Robert Bazell. "Many health officials see the results of the aspirin study," Bazell said, "as some of the best news ever about preventing heart attack." He interviewed Bernard Kabakow, a doctor who participated in the study. "In theory," Kabakow said, "as many as a hundred thousand or more [people] per year may have their heart attack prevented by the administration of an aspirin tablet every other day." Similar coverage appeared on the other two major networks, and on local news programs across the United States.

The study was splashed over the front pages of the *New York Times* and the *Washington Post* the next morning. Bryant Gumbel put aspirin on *Today*, the most popular morning news show, asking the study's director, Charles Hennekens of the Harvard School of Public Health, if "every male over the age of thirty-five should be doing it [taking aspirin]." (They should ask their doctors, Hennekens said.) Extra Bayer commercials blanketed network news programs throughout the day.

On January 29 Sterling took out full-page ads in newspapers across the nation. "Good News for Heart Health in America," inch-high letters proclaimed. Below, in slightly smaller type, was an unadorned column of print:

> A major study sponsored by the National Institutes of Health showing that an aspirin taken every other day helped prevent first heart attacks was reported this week in the *New England Journal of Medicine*. . . . Although not yet reviewed by the FDA, [the study] is further evidence that aspirin therapy for cardiovascular disease greatly advances the progress of heart health in this country. The Bayer Company will continue to make major commitments to finding innovative ways to better the heart health of America. Ask your doctor about aspirin therapy to help prevent heart attacks.

As self-promotion, the advertisement was modest. It presented an accurate summary of the results, gave the source of the report, emphasized that it was not yet reviewed by the government, and told potential users to call their doctors. The tone was conservative, even cautious. "This is *medicine*," Lockhart said later. "We aren't selling toothpaste."

The FDA telephoned the next day. "Good News" had to stop.

Aspirin makers have a remarkable, perhaps unique, history of competition; they have been slugging it out over exactly the same ground since the end of the First World War. The market for pain relievers—analgesics, as doctors call them—is well worth the effort. In 1990, Americans bought about $2.7 billion worth of analgesics, fully a quarter of the over-the-counter drug market, and more than the total for shampoos, deodorants, toothpastes, or any other single category of health and beauty products. Because the price of a pill is roughly ten times the cost of its active ingredient, the $2.7 billion leaves a hefty chunk for packaging, distribution, advertising, and, of course, profit. To make that profit, some aspirin firms sell pure acetylsalicylic acid (ASA), the scientific name for the chemical known as aspirin; others add ingredients such as caffeine and antacids; still others wrap the ASA in a special coating. Because ASA has remained unchanged since its invention in 1897, however, all aspirin brands, no matter how new and improved, have the identical active ingredient, and medical science has yet to show that any of these fancy versions are better than aspirin alone for headaches, fever, and inflammation.

In capitalist societies, such a situation—companies selling equally effective products with big potential profits—virtually guarantees furious competition, the type Adam Smith had in mind when he wrote of the awesome powers of the "invisible hand," the free market. And, indeed, the ten firms at FDA headquarters that morning have a record of industrial warfare that could serve as a chapbook to the means, honest or unscrupulous as they may be, by which modern corporations vie for superiority. Their struggle provides a vest-pocket history of the mixture of marketing, litigation, technology, and competition that characterizes so much of business, and of life, in this century. Another way to put it is that the annals of aspirin give a glimpse of the incredible lengths to which people will go to put something in a box and sell it.

Given this history, Sterling's competitors were not going to let it steal a march on them. Most of them in the past had emphasized the difference between their products and unadorned ASA, which meant that their brand names were not clearly associated with aspirin. Now that aspirin was headline news, Sterling's rivals were pushed into making stronger claims than those made for Bayer to compete on this shifting ground. Inevitably, one of them went too far, which is why they all ended up in the office of Frank Young.

The culprit was Rorer Consumer Pharmaceuticals, of Fort Washington, Pennsylvania, maker of a little-known brand named Ascriptin, a mixture of ASA and Maalox, the latter being a popular antacid that is added to alleviate the irritating effects of aspirin on the stomach. Until the Physicians' Health Study, the brand had primarily been marketed to doctors with patients who took large doses of aspirin to relieve arthritic pain. When the aspirin–heart attack story appeared on the evening news, it occurred to Rorer that Ascriptin might be a winner. If people began using aspirin to protect their hearts, they might want to protect their stomachs at the same time.

On February 10, Rorer, like Sterling before it, took out a full-page ad in the *New York Times*. Under the headline THE ASPIRIN YOU CAN LIVE WITH, it depicted the front page of the January 28 *Times*, folded to show the article that reported the Physicians' Health Study. "This may be the most important ad you'll ever read," the copy declared.

A single aspirin tablet every other day can cut a man's chances of getting a heart attack almost in half, according to a major new study.

But it can also upset your stomach.

So ask your doctor about Ascriptin. The aspirin you can live with.

Beneath it was a coupon ("This may be the most important coupon you ever clip") for Ascriptin. This was Rorer's bid to seize a greater share of the market. The campaign, it declared, would go on for weeks and involve considerable expense.

Hours after the publication of the ad, Rorer received a call from the Federal Trade Commission, the agency that regulates most forms of advertising. Gamely describing the conversation as "cordial," the firm announced it would cut short the campaign, although ads would still appear in the next issues of *Time* and *Newsweek*. On February 11, the offices of the attorneys general for Texas and New York sent a joint letter to Joseph E. Smith, the president of Rorer Consumer Pharmaceuticals. The letter was not cordial; it demanded that Rorer "cease and desist from any further placement of this or any similar advertisement." To make matters clear, the attorney general of Texas publicly threatened to sue. Several days after that, Rorer and nine other aspirin firms were asked to meet with Frank Young.

In some respects, the FDA's summons was a minor victory in a fifty-year battle over what Young has described as "the nastiest four-letter word: turf." Drugs are divided into two categories: prescription drugs, which are sold only at pharmacies to patients with orders from doctors; and over-the-counter drugs, which are sold almost anywhere. The Food and Drug Administration regulates the advertising of prescription drugs, whereas the Federal Trade

Commission regulates the advertising of over-the-counter drugs. The labels and package inserts of both prescription and over-the-counter drugs, however, are under the purview of the FDA, which means that one agency (the FDA) oversees what firms may claim about over-the-counter drugs on the label, and another agency (the FTC) oversees what they may claim about over-the-counter drugs in the advertising. The FDA bristled for years at this division of labor. "What the agency did with that," Peter Rheinstein, FDA director of medical staff in the Office of Health Affairs, said recently, "is to say that products advertised in ways inconsistent with their labels are misbranded, because the label fails to bear adequate directions for the advertised use." This allows the FDA to yank the drug from the market—thus giving it a *de facto* control of advertising that it is denied *de jure*.

Unsurprisingly, the FTC has vigorously resisted this usurpation of its powers. But it has received less than enthusiastic support from the companies involved. All drug makers must gain FDA approval to market new medicines, which have to be tested for safety and efficacy in a process that takes years and millions of dollars to complete. "Few people want to risk getting in its bad graces," said one pharmaceutical executive whose company avoids struggles with the agency. "Nobody wants to find that it takes the FDA's scientists an extra five years to go through your drug applications."

Aspirin is a regulatory rarity, in that it is treated as both an over-the-counter and a prescription drug. For headaches, fevers, and minor inflammation, aspirin makers can tout their product to the public under the scrutiny of the FTC; heart attacks, though, are the type of serious ailment that usually places a drug and its promotion under the purview of the FDA. Advertisements about the Physicians' Health Study thus straddled the blurry dividing line between the FDA and the FTC. After a call from Young, the FTC reluctantly let its rival agency lead the way.

Aspirin might indeed be a winner, the FDA admitted, but it did not want the firms to blare the news to the public. The study's final report was not yet published or even written; questions about side effects still had to be answered. On this skimpy evidence, the FDA was loath to endorse the idea of aspirin as a heart-attack preventive. In addition, even if the Physicians' Health Study ultimately turned out to be convincing, the agency was not sanguine about companies advertising on television that taking a pill might cut the risk of heart attack almost in half. As far as Young was concerned, people were going to learn about aspirin from their doctors, who could give them accurate information on the risks, and not from the commercial breaks on *The Cosby Show*. And that was just what he intended to tell the assembled aspirin manufacturers, regardless of the legal niceties.

The aspirin companies thus found themselves in a predicament. Frantic to seize the opportunity to recapture a lost market, they were being warned not to publicize a scientific study that was already on the front pages of newspapers across the world. Moreover, this warning did not concern *false* advertising—the FDA was not alleging that the ads were incorrect in any way. In fact, much of the advertising was more accurate than the quick summaries of the medical data blared over the airwaves. That made no difference. Even though the findings were so striking that one branch of the Department of Health and Human Services, the National Institutes of Health, had concluded that continuing the study would be immoral, another branch, the Food and Drug Administration, did not think them certain enough to broadcast to the public, let alone change the label. And, as the aspirin manufacturers knew, they were not allowed to advertise medicines for conditions not on the label.

The companies were also horrified to hear the agency voice concerns about promoting aspirin for second heart attacks, an advertising theme that was slowly winning back some of aspirin's lost glory (and, perhaps, market share). The FDA was muttering now that even if the firms restricted themselves to claims about second heart attacks—claims that the agency itself had tacitly approved—the public might be incapable of understanding the information presented. The citizenry might hear "second heart attack" on television and somehow get the idea that aspirin applied to first heart attacks, especially if the news programs were saying that a huge scientific study showed that aspirin prevented first heart attacks.

Consequently, the company officials filed into the conference room—two representatives from Sterling, two from Rorer, two from American Home Products (the maker of Anacin), two from Bristol-Myers (which sells Bufferin and Excedrin), and so on—with a considerable degree of apprehension. They were faced by twenty government officials: sixteen from the FDA; three from the FTC; and Herbert Israel, a man from the New York State Office of the Attorney General, which had vowed to take action if the federal government did not act first. Government and business faced each other across the table. It was not a comfortable moment. The stakes were high, and the outcome unclear.

The meeting opened with Young thanking the participants for attending on such short notice. He noted that there was "considerable press interest" in the meeting, and said that afterward he would make a statement to the media. This last was a reminder of the power of the FDA; none of the companies, which depended on the goodwill of the public, wanted to be held up as examples of malfeasance. Describing the Physicians' Health Study as "promising," Young said he hoped that the scientists would soon submit their data to the FDA. Until then, he said, the agency staff would be "concerned about the promotion of this unlabeled use for aspirin."

Citing some questions about the study's results—the aspirin group recorded an unusual number of strokes—Young "strongly urged that aspirin manufacturers voluntarily refrain from promotion of aspirin" for first heart attacks. He looked about the table. Glumly, the industry executives agreed. If, Young added, he saw "inappropriate promotions . . . he would not hesitate to invoke the misbranding provisions" of the law. He was therefore delighted by the unanimous promise of voluntary cooperation.

The meeting had lasted just a few minutes, but it already seemed to be over. When Young asked if anyone had questions, there was only one, from a junior executive in the middle of the table. Jack Jordan, the associate general counsel of SmithKline Beckman, the makers of Ecotrin, a brand of coated aspirin tablets, asked if advertising for second heart attacks would also be "inappropriate."

"They all looked daggers at him," said Peter Rheinstein, who was there. "They couldn't *believe* he was bringing this up."

Herbert Israel took the question. In Israel's view, there was no way that the public was going to see and hear "second heart attack" on a TV commercial and understand that aspirin might really only be safe for that and had not yet been accepted for first heart attack. "The public won't distinguish between first and second heart attack," he said later. "I wanted to broaden the ban."

Surprised by the question, Young asked William MacLeod of the Federal Trade Commission whether advertising for second heart attacks was allowed. MacLeod replied that the subject was not on the agenda.

That was enough for Young. Deciding the matter quickly, he told the assembled aspirin makers that they could keep advertising second heart attacks, but that they should not touch first heart attacks.

"And then you could just *see* the lights clicking on in their eyes," Rheinstein recalled, laughing ruefully. Imitating the thought processes of a thunderstruck aspirin manufacturer, he said, " 'Wait a minute—these guys are saying that the public can't tell the difference between ads for second heart attacks and ads for first heart attacks? And ads for second heart attacks are still okay? Great! Bye!' And they practically *ran* out of the door. It was the shortest meeting I've attended in my life."

Soon afterward, Young told reporters that the aspirin manufacturers, acting safely and responsibly, had voluntarily agreed to halt promotion of the drug as a preventive for first heart attacks. The drug company representatives accepted his praise with modest shrugs. "Why not?" Rheinstein said. "Everybody got what they wanted. The FDA got to show it was tough, and the companies got to advertise."

"After the feds acted, we couldn't do anything," Israel recalled. "It was an incredible mess—a real tangle. I had to think, how on earth did all *this* come about?"

PART ONE

"JUST A BUSINESSMAN"

CHAPTER ONE

"UNSURPASSED BY ANY OTHER DRUG"

Laying the foundation for an epic international commercial battle was not on Carl Duisberg's mind when he traveled in 1903 from Germany to Albany, New York—or, more exactly, to Rensselaer, the village across the river from Albany. A stout man with rapidly thinning hair and a wide moustache, Duisberg looked like the exceedingly successful German businessman he was. He was feared by his American competitors, who hired private detectives to shadow him up the Hudson Valley. He had come to build what would become one of the biggest and most technically advanced chemical plants in the United States. The factory would be an amazing sight in Rensselaer, a town of fewer than 8,000 people, in which a major topic of civic discussion was whether to pave the main street. Seventy-five acres in size, Duisberg's factory would sit just south of the trolley bridge to Albany, on a plot of land kept from washing into the river by a dike. There, leaning into the curve of the New York Central and Boston & Albany rail lines, a score of workshops would rise, turning out carboys of disinfectants, sleeping draughts, and chemical dyes. In the center would stand the campus's tallest feature, a barnlike one-and-a-half story structure almost filled by two great reagent vessels made of pure silver. The vessels would produce the plant's most important product: Bayer Aspirin.

Duisberg wanted to establish the Bayer name and symbol—the Bayer Cross, *B-A-Y-E-R* spelled out horizontally and vertically, with the two *BAYER*s crossing at the central *Y*—in the United States. The Aspirin factory would do just that. But, to Duisberg's dismay, it did much more. Not long after its completion, the plant was lost to an American firm, and with it the Bayer name and the Bayer Cross. Both companies sold Bayer Aspirin. To put it another way, two different, competing enterprises used an identical name to sell an identical product. In the business world, this situation is anomalous, as shocking as a violation of natural law, and the two Bayer aspirins fought each other for more than seventy years. Ultimately,

Bayer versus Bayer became one of the longest, strangest, and most frustrating corporate feuds in the annals of twentieth-century capitalism.

Friedrich Carl Duisberg, Jr., did not invent Aspirin, but he built the industrial empire that ensured its presence in medicine cabinets across the globe. Today his renown has faded, but during his lifetime Duisberg was as much a member of the commercial pantheon as Rockefeller and Rothschild, eulogized by *The Times* of London as "the greatest industrialist the world has yet had." Duisberg masterminded the assembly of I.G. Farbenindustrie AG— I.G. Farben, the hydra-headed chemical trust which became so identified with the Nazi state that its directors were put in the dock at Nuremberg with Goebbels and Himmler.

He was born on September 29, 1861, to a middle-class family in Barmen, a prosperous town twenty-five miles from Cologne in western Germany. Duisberg, Sr., had a little ribbon-making business, not much more than a couple of looms and handymen to operate them; his wife, Wilhelmine, ran the family farm, milking the Duisbergs' three cows and selling the results in the market. Growing up in an atmosphere of thrift and quiet hard work, Carl reacted by becoming an active, headstrong, ambitious child. He ardently wanted something in life with more grandeur and scope than spinning braid for small-time dressmakers.

In secondary school he took chemistry. From the first class, he fell in love with the subject—it was his way out of Barmen. Duisberg, Sr., meanwhile, believed that his son had spent enough time at school, and should join the family business. Carl refused. He was backed by his mother, who had great expectations for her only son. Carl's future, she told relatives, "is my business." A family tussle ensued. With his mother's support, Carl was victorious. He raced through the rest of high school, graduating when he was just sixteen. He hoped to study chemistry at the renowned university in Göttingen, but again faced the opposition of his father, who thought his son too young to live away from home. As a compromise, Duisberg enrolled in a nearby technical school. Again he finished the year's work ahead of schedule. In contemporary terms, he was qualified to become a laboratory technician.

Giving in, Duisberg, Sr., agreed to send his son to Göttingen. In those days it was possible to go directly from high school—actually, an *Oberrealschule*, which in U.S. terms amounted to a combination of college and high school—into a doctoral program. Duisberg plunged into his studies, signing up for advanced courses and working with the combination of fervor and obsessive organization that marked his entire life. A year later he had bulled his way through a thesis, only to learn he could not complete his degree because he had gone to the wrong type of high school (he didn't have a classical education, and could not pass the Latin test). Quitting Göttingen in disgust, he went to the university at Jena, where he came under the wing of Anton Geuther, an important chemist. Far from sympathizing with Duisberg's desire to leave school ahead of his classmates, Geuther was appalled to discover that his talented student had almost been allowed to graduate from Göttingen without having taken basic courses. He insisted that Duisberg go through drills in laboratory technique. Despite the delay, Duisberg won his doctorate in June 1882, three months before his twenty-first birthday. He threw a party so raucous that he was fined for disturbing the peace.

Wanting to be completely independent of his father, Duisberg took the first job he could find, a poorly paid position at a state laboratory that analyzed food. Once again, his professor, Geuther, was appalled, this time by Duisberg's apparent intent to squander his potential. He made Duisberg his private assistant, giving him a room in the garret above the lab. Geuther insisted that Duisberg promise to stay until he found employment worthy of his talents. But Geuther could not pay Duisberg enough to live on; the young man still had to beg for aid from his father, who saw this as confirmation that he had been right all along about the uselessness of higher education. Distressed by his father's scorn, Duisberg abruptly joined the military—he believed no one would give him a good job until he had completed his service. The decision provoked a violent argument with Geuther. After much shouting, Duisberg closed the discussion by smashing a big glass flask at his mentor's feet and stalking out of the room.

After a year in the army, Duisberg once more cast about for work, and in 1883 obtained a fellowship at Farbenfabriken vormals Friedrich Bayer & Company, a small chemical concern that specialized in dyes. Unfortunately, the firm was located in Barmen, the small town Duisberg had been trying to escape from since childhood. He nonetheless thought he was finally in the middle of the action. Even before Duisberg was born, industrialization had driven Thoreau to Walden Pond and traumatized the young Dickens, who was forced to work in a blacking warehouse, tying labels on pots of primitive leather dyes. That was when the Industrial Revolution was in its relative infancy. Now great enterprises with mechanized factories and thousands of employees were common in Europe and North America. Railroads carried goods across continents, telegraphs sent orders for stock transactions between nations, and air pollution, the malign emblem of commercial growth, shrouded many cities. The pace of change was tumultuous, and Duisberg was exhilarated by it. He had always wanted to take part in the excitement; with the dye industry he had at last found the vehicle that would carry him into the future.

The growth of such a high-tech industry in Germany was scarcely predictable. Because of its peculiar history, Germany was, from a business standpoint, something of a late bloomer. In 1815, there were thirty-eight independent German states. Some were relatively large and powerful, like Prussia and Bavaria, but most were small, rural, and undeveloped. Trade between the states was governed by a rococo network of more than a hundred treaties. The move toward a unified Germany began in 1834, when most of the states banded together to form a single *Zollverein*, or customs union. By promoting a common commercial law and a uniform currency, the *Zollverein* laid the foundation for the Industrial Revolution to take hold, decades after it had transformed the United Kingdom.

Bismarck slowly welded the German states into a nation, finally succeeding in 1871. The new nation had a valuable resource: the best scientific educational system in Europe. Universities such as those at Heidelberg and Freiburg were the first to build academic laboratories and promote the teaching of science. Almost every important chemist of the day was educated in a German school or was taught by someone who had learned in Germany. (When Duisberg entered Göttingen, the entire United States had exactly eleven graduate students in organic chemistry.) As a result, German business was in an ideal position to take advantage of the explosion in chemical knowledge. Laboratory flasks were bubbling with fascinating, previously unknown substances like helium, saccharin, rayon, and liquid oxygen, and a significant percentage of the people who understood them were in Germany. These savants flocked to the burgeoning chemical industry, developing new fertilizers, explosives, soaps, glass, textiles, and—in Duisberg's case—dyes.

The dye trade was founded on a black, smelly, and unpleasant goo called coal tar, which is created when coal is heated to a high temperature in a vacuum. Burning coal in this way produces a flammable gas that was then used in lanterns; the coal tar was originally regarded as a useless residue. In the 1840s, however, researchers in Germany and Britain discovered that coal tar was a mélange of useful chemicals. Like the nuts, bolts, and metal flanges in an untidy toolbox, the substances in coal tar could be combined into all manner of interesting things by a scientist who didn't mind a bit of trial and error.

Many of the first coal-tar products were dyes. Dye making having progressed little since the days when the Romans made royal purple by crushing thousands of seashells, the luminous reds, yellows, blues, and greens that poured from chemists' retorts were enormously popular. Exhibited to the crowds attending the London International Exhibition of 1862, the brilliant hues made possible by coal-tar chemistry became a rage among the prosperous European middle class, fostering the growth of the modern fashion industry. Clothiers eagerly pressed for more and better colors. In the nature of things, such demand gives rise to supply; dye companies sprang up throughout England, France, and Germany.

One of the first German dye companies was established in 1863 by Friedrich Bayer and Johann Friedrich Weskott. Bayer was a successful dealer in natural dyestuffs who had built up a worldwide network of sales agents; Weskott, a good friend and a member of one of Barmen's oldest families, was the owner of a profitable factory that extracted natural dyes. They made their first synthetic dye, fuchsin, in their home kitchens—cutting costs but, according to company legend, infuriating their wives. They also produced their first chemical wastes, which Bayer dumped in a corner of his property. Unfortunately, the wastes included arsenic compounds, which seeped into the local groundwater. When the neighbors discovered arsenic in their wells, they demanded compensation. Bayer and Weskott were forced to pay; eventually a line of neighbors showed up once a week for their checks. The fledgling company decided to move. After several enforced shifts of location, the two men learned to solve the problem by burying the wastes out of sight, and Friedrich Bayer & Company, as the business was called, settled on the steep, narrow banks of the Wupper river.

Bayer and Weskott were not leaders in the race to develop new dyes. In those days, their company did more practical experimentation—shrewd dabbling, really—than scientific research, producing recipes for new dyes that did not depend on a full understanding of their chemical composition. One such recipe for aniline blue used forty-eight egg whites in every batch, an improvement supposedly devised to avoid red overtones; the yolks were used on the same stove to make pancakes for the workers. After the company contracted to sell the yolks to a local baker, the recipe was quickly "improved" again by eliminating the eggs.

Friedrich Bayer's most trusted assistant was his son-in-law, Carl Rumpff. The son of a German wine merchant, Rumpff had immigrated to the United States at the age of twenty-four. After building a business in the infant American coal-tar industry, Rumpff was hired by Friedrich Bayer as the company's New York agent. In 1876, he joined the headquarters staff in Barmen; he also joined the family when he married Bayer's eldest daughter. Weskott died that same year. When Bayer died in 1880, Rumpff became the guiding spirit of the enterprise, which by this time had moved yet again, to the neighboring town of Elberfeld. A year after Bayer's death, the company sold its stock to the public for the first time. In the process, it was officially renamed Farbenfabriken vormals Friedrich Bayer & Company, which meant the Dye Factory formerly known as Friedrich Bayer & Company.

Farbenfabriken Bayer was faltering at the time—one reason it needed to raise money by selling stock. For more than a decade its major product had been alizarin, an orange-red dye. When alizarin sales slowed, the firm needed to diversify. It hired academically trained researchers to develop new dyes, but they didn't come up with much. Rumpff hired some more; he had little choice. Using his own money, he arranged for three promising young chemistry graduates to acquire the equivalent of postdoctoral fellowships. Before formally joining Farbenfabriken Bayer, the chemists were given a year or two to conduct their own research, the results of which would, perhaps, benefit the company. This program, too, was a flop; it was canceled within a year. Indeed, Bayer might have gone under, as financial experts of the day predicted, had one of the three graduates not been Carl Duisberg.

Duisberg spent a year at Strasbourg in Rumpff's program, entering Bayer officially in September 1884. One of his first jobs was to copy Congo red, a competitor's popular new scarlet-colored dye for cotton. Congo red had actually been discovered at the end of 1883 by a Bayer employee, but instead of passing the discovery on to the company, as required by his contract, the employee had quit the firm, patented the dye himself, and sold it to the highest bidder. A peculiarity of the German patent law of the time was that an inventor could patent only the process for making a product, not the product itself. If a competitor could find a slightly different method of making the same dye, for example, the first inventor could do nothing. As a result, every innovation triggered a burst of technical activity, as imitators furiously tried to emulate the product with a slightly different process, and legal activity, as the inventor with equal fury tried to patent every permutation of the original method. Duisberg's job was thus to find a way to synthesize Congo red that its inventor had not yet discovered.

Duisberg set to work in a tiny room behind the bathroom of the dye department. To save money, he still lived with his parents in Barmen, an hour away by horse-drawn streetcar. Every morning before dawn he left for Elberfeld, returning to Barmen after dusk. For weeks he tinkered with the recipe for Congo red, coming up only with vials of brown mud. With his usual conscientiousness, he carefully saved and labeled each failure instead of dumping them. He was fortunate: A few days after mixing up one successful batch, he noticed that it had turned an intense scarlet. Startled, Duisberg realized that the ingredients melded together very slowly. He had achieved the ideal result—a dye effectively identical to Congo red, but a process just different enough to stay out of legal difficulties.* Benzopurpurine 4B, as the dye is known now, was a big money maker, endearing Duisberg to Rumpff.

In the next three years Duisberg created two new dyes, enough to save his technologically maladroit employer from collapse. Rather than have the firm's best chemist follow every invention with a spate of legal and technical work to protect the patent, Rumpff decided to hire people to work under Duisberg's supervision. The arrangement was institutionalized when Duisberg was made the head of Bayer's research and patent program. One of his

---

* *Almost* out of legal difficulties, at any rate. The manufacturer of Congo red sued to invalidate Duisberg's patent anyway. Eventually the court agreed. Duisberg came up with an innovative method of avoiding a long fight in appellate courts. In a foreshadowing of things to come in the chemical industry, he urged the two companies to share their patents, effectively forming a small cartel that controlled this type of red dye.

first tasks was to get the firm involved in something other than the horribly competitive field of dye making. News of a chance discovery in Strasbourg persuaded him to look into drugs.

In 1886, two Alsatian interns, Drs. Kahn and Hepp, ordered some naphthalene, a treatment for intestinal parasites, from a nearby pharmacist. The substance they received failed to have the expected effect on the parasites but managed instead to reduce the patient's fever. Startled, the two doctors requested more of the same. This time, however, they received a substance that got rid of intestinal parasites but did nothing for fever. Upon further analysis, Kahn and Hepp discovered that they had been the victims of a happy accident; the first material was acetanilid, a coal-tar derivative used in the dye industry, never before given to human beings. At a time when people routinely died from infectious diseases, something that prevented them from burning up with fever—what doctors call an antipyretic—was of incalculable value.

salicylic

Just three compounds with similar effects were then known: salicylic acid, quinine, and antipyrine. Salicylic acid was a modern version of an herbal potion made from the bark of the white willow, a pleasant, droopy-leaved tree that botanists call *Salix alba*. Used for thousands of years—Hippocrates recommended it, correctly, for the relief of fever and pain—willow bark has effects that were discovered, forgotten, and rediscovered many times by obscure savants. Its properties were firmly established only in the eighteenth century, when the Reverend Edward Stone, of Chipping Norton in Oxfordshire, England, experimented with ways of reducing fever. Stone began with the belief, then widely held, that Providence placed the cures to diseases not far from their sources—as if little bottles of penicillin grew on trees next to houses of unsavory reputation. Stone surmised that people were particularly susceptible to agues (fevers) in swamps. Willow trees grow in swamps. Other tree barks were known to reduce fevers. Stone decided to try willow bark. He pulverized a pound of dried willow bark and over several years mixed it with water, tea, or "small beer" and gave it to fifty feverish people. With few exceptions, their fevers went away. In 1763, the Royal Society of London published Stone's "Account of the Success of the Bark of the Willow in the Cure of Agues." The active ingredient in willow bark turned out to be a bitter-tasting yellow crystal now called salicin, which German scientists isolated in 1828; ten years later, French chemists synthesized a simpler version, salicylic acid. Both attacked fever and pain, and their partisans advocated the salicylates' use as antiseptics, mouthwashes, and water preservatives for ocean voyages; one important chemist further suggested (erroneously) that sodium salicylate, a chemical relative, would successfully treat scarlet fever, diphtheria, measles, syphilis, cholera, rabies, and anthrax.

The drugs were widely employed to alleviate rheumatic fever, a then-common syndrome in which a strep infection suddenly induces a condition much like crippling arthritis. Alas, both salicin and salicylic acid had side effects, among them nausea and ringing in the ears, inducing doctors to hunt for less noxious remedies.

Another tree-bark derivative, quinine, had been used to treat malaria since the seventeenth century. Extracted from the Peruvian cinchona tree, it proved to be an excellent antipyretic. Unfortunately, it too had unpleasant side effects; moreover, chemists could not figure out how to synthesize it, and the supply was limited by the availability of cinchona bark. (For a long time all attempts failed to transplant the cinchona tree to other regions.) Consequently, quinine was exceedingly costly and, as an antipyretic, medically unsatisfactory.

The newest of the three remedies was antipyrine, the name given to a drug discovered by a doctoral student named Ludwig Knorr in 1883. The drug went by the name antipyrine rather than the chemical name in part because there was some confusion over its exact chemical composition. (Scientists knew how to make it but were not sure what it was.) Knorr gave the rights to produce antipyrine to one of Bayer's rivals: Meister, Lucius & Brüning at Hoechst, the ancestor of the chemical and pharmaceutical company that today is known simply as Hoechst.

By the time Kahn and Hepp stumbled across the effects of acetanilid, quinine and salicylic acid were in wide use, and antipyrine sales were growing. Reasoning that a fourth drug might also win a substantial market, the two doctors approached Hepp's brother, a chemist at Kalle & Company of Wiesbaden, the company that had supplied the acetanilid, and told him what had happened. The processes for making acetanilid were well established; there was no hope of wringing a patent from it. Instead, Kalle & Company coined a new name for acetanilid: Antifebrin. They then promoted the drug under its brand name, which belonged exclusively to the company, rather than by its chemical or generic name, which could be used by anybody. The tactic was a radical break from the past.

Before Antifebrin, German pharmacists dealt with drugs that were prescribed by their generic names. (An exception was antipyrine, but this was because of the confusion over its chemical composition.) Patients brought in prescriptions for, say, salicylic acid, and the pharmacist used a mortar and pestle to prepare a little sachet of salicylic acid. Pharmacists sold the drug labeled only with its chemical name; the manufacturer remained unknown to the public. Antifebrin was one of the first medicines to be sold under a brand name though a generic version was available. The gambit was successful: Physicians unfamiliar with the chemical term ''acetanilid'' used Kalle's name instead. Suddenly able to distinguish itself from the competition, the firm enjoyed a booming business. Pharmacists were enraged, because Kalle charged much more for Antifebrin than other firms demanded for the chemically identical acetanilid. But there was nothing that druggists could do to stop it. Even when they knew that the doctor who wrote "Antifebrin" on a prescription did so in ignorance, they could not change the order, for it was illegal for them to tamper with a physician's instructions.

Carl Duisberg became the supervisor of Bayer's research and patenting in the year of Antifebrin's invention. Seeing its sales rise, he decided to pursue the market for fever and pain reducers. The company's dye making produced a multitude of by-products, one of which, para-nitrophenol, was piled up in old barrels in the factory yard. Realizing that para-nitrophenol was chemically similar to acetanilid, Duisberg told his research staff to develop a new drug from his thirty thousand kilograms of waste para-nitrophenol. Their efforts were successful, and in 1888 acetophenetidin became Farbenfabriken's first pharmaceutical product. Taking a page from the makers of Antifebrin, the company called the drug by a brand name: Phenacetin.

Duisberg's accomplishment was revolutionary. For the first time, a drug had been conceived, developed, tested, and marketed, all by a private company. It marked the creation of the modern drug industry, the marriage of science and business that has transformed this century, making huge profits even as it saves lives. Phenacetin was a perfect harbinger of the industry's future. The drug cost the consumer much more than Antifebrin, but was a considerable improvement. In big or continual doses, both acetanilid and acetophenetidin can cause cyanosis and methemoglobinemia, which is to say that they turn people's skins an alarming shade of blue and destroy red blood cells. But acetanilid is much the worse of the two. In 1889, the year after Phenacetin's invention, an influenza epidemic ravaged the Northern Hemisphere. Victims took Phenacetin in England, Italy, France, Russia, Bohemia, and the United States, enriching Bayer considerably in the process.

Rumpff died a year later, and the ambitious Duisberg assumed *de facto* control of every aspect of the firm. Sitting in his sumptuous office, he ground through a steady mass of meetings, memoranda, and reports, all of which had to be reviewed and carefully filed at the headquarters at Elberfeld. At home in his elegant clothes he was the picture of the bourgeois gentleman. He had marred Johanna Seebohm, Carl Rumpff's niece. Surrounded by his wife and four children, he hosted lavish afternoon soirées at which guests admired his collection of paintings and bronze statuettes. Despite his formal manner, he was an indulgent paterfamilias at home, correcting his children's homework while they ran noisily through the house. "The boys become wilder and more unruly every day," he wrote to a friend. "But I don't mind that, because taming someone is easier than making him come alive." When eleven-year-old Carl-Ludwig, his oldest child, was warned he might flunk out of school,

Duisberg told the boy only that from that point on, Father would no longer do his homework. At the factory he was less indulgent. He worked long hours and kept his subordinates on a short leash.

One of the first businessmen to understand how teams of scientists could worry at a problem like a dog with a bone, Duisberg kept stuffing workers into Bayer's crude, overcrowded research quarters. Lab tables were scattered everywhere in the facilities, with foul-smelling experiments being conducted in corridors, bathrooms, and an abandoned woodworking shop. Lucky researchers had access to sinks; unlucky ones worked outdoors, in the river fog. They wore clogs because the muddy ground was full of harmless-looking puddles capable of disintegrating leather shoes. They had no chemical storeroom, no technical library, and little equipment—nothing but a platoon of boys who cleaned retorts and vials. By 1890, the company was ready to build a three-story, 1.5-million-mark research laboratory. Within four years, Duisberg had crammed it with ninety full-time chemists—six times as many as had been at the company in 1881—and was looking for more. When it was snowing or raining, a thick trail of workers' footsteps could be seen in blue, yellow, violet, or green, leading right up to the middle of town.

Bayer was outgrowing its Elberfeld headquarters. In 1891 it bought land for a much larger factory twenty-five miles away in what is now called Leverkusen. The former property of a small dye firm, Dr. C. Leverkus & Sons, the site was just north of Cologne, on the east bank of the Rhine. Duisberg submitted to the board of directors a master design for the organization of the new dyestuffs factory. Raw materials would come in from the wharfs, pass through a grid of interlocking factories that changed crude chemical to finished product, and end up in railroad cars or back on the wharfs to be shipped around the world. By following his design, Duisberg said, Leverkusen would become "the perfect factory." Completed in 1912, the giant plant still works according to Duisberg's original conception, and even today visitors cannot spend ten minutes there without hearing his name.

Duisberg did not ignore the old facility at Elberfeld. There, he built a second set of research labs, devoted solely to the creation of drugs: new Phenacetins, so to speak. Finished in 1896, the labs began with eight full-time chemists. The list of new products quickly grew so long that Duisberg decided to promote the pharmaceutical division separately. Realizing that its customers were the doctors who prescribed Bayer drugs, Duisberg wanted to bring the Bayer name to them in a way that would be sufficiently low-key to avoid offending their professional sensibilities. Because physicians could not keep track of all the new drugs invented at companies like Bayer, Duisberg decided in 1898 to print a thick book that would neutrally and objectively describe all known pharmaceutical products. Each time doctors used it, however, they would see the name of Bayer. The "Bayer Bible" was mailed to every doctor in Germany. The first edition landed on doorsteps at about the same time that his new pharmaceutical laboratory developed what was to become the company's greatest success story: Aspirin.

Bayer's drug lab was split into two parts: a pharmaceutical section, which developed new drugs and was run by Arthur Eichengrün, a researcher with several successful products already under his belt; and a pharmacological section, which tested the drugs and was directed by Heinrich Dreser, a respected professor from the University of Bonn. The idea of a separate testing facility was Duisberg's. Fearful of incurring doctors' wrath by shipping drugs that didn't work, Duisberg wanted an additional check that would weed out all but the best remedies. Any drug developed by Eichengrün's lab would be passed on to Dreser's lab for his approval.

As one of the new lab's first projects, Eichengrün chose to search for a version of salicylic acid with fewer side effects. What happened next spawned one of the best-known legends in pharmaceutical chemistry: Eichengrün assigned the job to one of his chemists, twenty-nine-year-old Felix Hoffmann, whose father was nearly crippled by chronic rheumatism. The elder Hoffmann took sodium salicylate for the pain, and the treatment was almost as bad as the disease, for it had eaten out his stomach; he begged his son to find some way to neutralize its bad effects. On October 10, 1897, Hoffmann succeeded, describing on that date in his laboratory notebook a process for modifying salicylic acid to produce acetylsalicylic acid: ASA: Aspirin. After testing, ASA was an immediate hit with both doctors and the public.

Like many legends, the Aspirin story is not completely untrue. Hoffmann truly did synthesize acetylsalicylic acid. He may even have given some to his father. Alas, Hoffmann found ASA not so much in the laboratory as in the library: It had been created in a crude form back in 1853 by a French chemist, Charles Frédéric Gerhardt, and synthesized in a purer form sixteen years later by Karl Johann Kraut, a German. (Hoffmann's method of making ASA, however, was an improvement over that of his predecessors.) The lack of novelty did not discourage Eichengrün, who passed ASA to Dreser for testing. It was not a hit. Many doctors believed that salicylic acid had an "enfeebling action on the heart"; declaring that acetylsalicylic acid would necessarily share that enfeebling action, Dreser rejected ASA out of hand.* For more than a year, what was destined to be the most successful drug ever invented sat on a shelf.

Dreser's indifference—and, presumably, that of Duisberg, who insisted on knowing about every decision—may have been due to simple distraction. At

---

* The reason for this erroneous belief is hard to ascertain, although it may have come from the then-common use of salicylic acid in massive doses to ease the pain and swelling of rheumatic fever. Given what in modern terms would be regarded as an overdose of salicylic acid, patients pant for breath and feel their hearts race. From this, doctors apparently concluded that salicylates can exhaust the heart.

that time, Bayer was basking in the phenomenal worldwide success of another newly introduced drug product: Heroin. Like ASA, Heroin (technically, diacetylmorphine) had been invented years before by someone else, in this case an English chemist named C. R. Wright, who was experimenting with derivatives of morphine. Little attention was paid to his work for more than twenty years until morphine developed into a widely used treatment for the suffering of tuberculosis victims and scientists became interested in finding a nonaddictive substitute. Dreser rediscovered Wright's drug, and tested it on Bayer factory workers. They liked it—it made them feel "heroic," a sensation Dreser adapted into the drug's brand name, Heroin. After further clinical trials, Dreser proclaimed to the Congress of German Naturalists and Physicians in 1898 that Heroin was ten times more effective as a cough medicine than codeine, but had only one-tenth its toxic effects. Safe, non-habit-forming Heroin, he said, was the solution to the growing plague of morphine addiction. Heroin was tried out for all manner of conditions, including the colic attacks of babies. Initial reports were uniformly positive. Excited, Bayer mailed out thousands of free samples to physicians. The repeat business was incredible.

Acetylsalicylic acid remained among the drugs rejected by the pharmacological laboratory, until it was again brought to Dreser's attention late in 1898. How this occurred is a matter of dispute. Decades afterward, Eichengrün asserted rather angrily that it was only through his efforts that ASA was reconsidered by Dreser, and that he, Eichengrün, had believed from the start that ASA was the most promising medication yet developed by the lab. Dreser's contract gave him a veto over all clinical testing. His opposition to ASA, the irate Eichengrün wrote, had been a "death sentence" for the drug.

Vexed by Dreser's rejection, Eichengrün tested the new drug on himself. When his heart was not poisoned, he decided to examine it further. While ASA sat in Dreser's lab, Eichengrün surreptitiously passed it to doctors in Berlin, who administered it to their patients. ASA not only eased the discomfort of fevers and aching joints, they learned, it also soothed headaches. Significantly, it had many fewer side effects than salicylic acid or any of the variants of salicylic acid on pharmacy shelves.

One of the doctors, Felix Goldmann, was Bayer's representative in Berlin, the nation's capital, cultural center, and biggest city. He delivered an enthusiastic report on ASA to the company's management. Asked his opinion of Goldmann's memo, Dreser growled: "This is the usual Berlin bragging; the product has no value." At this point, according to Eichengrün, Duisberg himself came to the rescue. He insisted that tests be conducted by an outside pharmacologist. The results were glowing. Finally acceding, Dreser wrote a scientific paper extolling ASA. In it he neglected to mention Hoffmann and Eichengrün.

As with Heroin and Phenacetin, the company did not call the new drug by its chemical name, acetylsalicylic acid, but by a brand name: Aspirin. The name Aspirin had its genesis in the Latin name for the meadowsweet plant, then placed in the genus *Spiraea*. Meadowsweet contains salicylaldehyde, which can be oxidized to salicylic acid—*Spirsäure* in German. Acetylation produces *Acetylspirsäure*, acetylsalicylic acid, from which, in January 1899, "Aspirin" was coined. *June 1899*

Five months later, Dreser presented Aspirin to the world. Promoting a new drug in those days was a delicate operation. Bayer did not advertise its drugs directly to the public. Instead it shipped free samples of Aspirin to hospitals, doctors, and medical professors, encouraging them to publish any findings about the usefulness of the drug. If the drug was effective, as Aspirin certainly was, word of mouth, spread through patients and the medical community, became the major source of promotion. This was supplemented by medical-journal advertisements that featured little more than the company name and a list of drugs: Aspirin for headaches, Somatose for insomnia, Heroin for coughs.

By November 1899, just five months after Dreser showed ASA to Bayer's management, Aspirin was in widespread use. That month F. C. Floeckinger of Texas published the first English-language account of Aspirin. By 1902, according to one estimate, some 160 scientific studies had appeared on the drug, "a literature . . . ," the writer said, "so voluminous that it is scarcely possible to review it."

The studies being almost universally favorable, Aspirin sales soared. Like Phenacetin and Heroin before, it quickly appeared in pharmacies from Siberia to San Francisco, and physicians prescribed it for every malady under the sun. (One English doctor actually proclaimed Aspirin to be mildly effective for diabetes.) Enrico Caruso demanded that impresarios provide him with Aspirin, claiming it was the only thing that vanquished his headaches; later, Kafka explained to his fiancée, Felice Bauer, in the course of their tortured relationship that Aspirin was one of the few things that eased the unbearable pain of being. Soothing aches existential and physical, Aspirin was on its way to becoming a resounding commercial triumph.

The bulk of Aspirin sales did not come from the relief of creative anxieties, of course. Then, as now, most ASA was consumed by people with inflammatory complaints like arthritis or rheumatic fever. ("Eighty percent of your sales goes down twenty percent of your users," one drug company executive recently explained.) Most Aspirin users might have used it for headache, but most Aspirin was used for inflammation. Indeed, for arthritis, doctors sometimes prescribed a daily dose equivalent in contemporary terms to as many as twenty-five tablets. The mainstay of Aspirin's progress was therefore the steadily rising number of prescriptions of ASA for inflammation; headache

and fever sales were extra. As long as Aspirin stayed in the good graces of
the medical profession, profits would continue to rise. There was no reason
to imagine this would change, and hence no ceiling in sight for Aspirin.

Eichengrün watched Aspirin's success with mixed emotions. Dreser, his
nemesis, earned a royalty on all medicines tested in his laboratory. Eichengrün and Hoffmann, on the other hand, received royalties only for those
medicines that were patented. Although the German patent office initially
agreed to patent ASA, the agency subsequently reversed itself; German law
covered only new processes, not new products, and the patent office ultimately decided that ASA was neither. Dreser became so wealthy from the
sales of ASA that he retired early; Hoffmann and Eichengrün apparently
received nothing.

Duisberg, of course, was troubled by no such reservations. Aspirin was a
thunderous vindication of his stewardship of Bayer. In 1906, the firm gave
its own measure of Aspirin's success:

> Aspirin has in the decade since its introduction become so popular that
> it is unsurpassed by any other drug. Surely it is not an exaggeration to
> say that it is today the most used and beloved medicine we manufacture.

It was time, Duisberg decided, to take Aspirin to the United States.

Farbenfabriken Bayer began selling its wares in the United States soon after
the firm was founded. It engaged an American sales agent, Schieffelin &
Company; it also set up a New York sales office, known as Farbenfabriken
of Eberfeld Company, which employed Carl Rumpff before his return to
Germany. Both the U.S. office and Schieffelin & Company sold the same
Bayer products, an awkward arrangement made worse by the temperament of
Ido J. Reinhard Muurling, Rumpff's successor as head of Farbenfabriken of
Eberfeld Company. A longtime U.S. resident, Muurling was a touchy, stub-
born man who loathed the "old-fashioned, terribly petty, jealous" Schieffelins. In Muurling's eyes, the Schieffelins were too "dumb" to see that their
agents should spend more time pushing Bayer's products. "Those people,"
he complained, "mumbled, grumbled, and drank—and that's all they did."
In Muurling's view, the Schieffelins refused to *sell*. Certainly they didn't sell
like Muurling, a hyperkinetic huckster who filled his reports to Leverkusen
with slogans like "Success is a duty!"

"Farbenfabriken is making progress here," he told Duisberg, "and it will
be on top before I die." And, indeed, the company did well in the United
States. At times the United States was the biggest single market for Bayer
dye products—bigger even than Germany—with U.S. sales tripling from 2.5
million marks in 1894 to 7.5 million marks in 1900.

Duisberg expected equal, if not greater success for the pharmaceutical business. This proved hard to come by. Because the firm had been able to patent Phenacetin in the United States, it should have had a profitable monopoly on the drug. But the duties imposed by U.S. customs increased costs enormously. Worse, smugglers bought Phenacetin in Europe, where it was unpatented and hence much cheaper, and shipped the drug to Canada and Mexico, where it could be easily slipped across the U.S. border. Duisberg demanded that Muurling stop the illegal sales. Farbenfabriken of Elberfeld sued, won, and sued again. Still the drug smuggling continued. Exasperated, Duisberg asked Muurling to report more often to headquarters in Leverkusen and hire a brace of new salesmen. Impatient with the stream of commands from Germany, Muurling exploded, "For God's sake, leave those things up to us, and don't burden me with makework! We already have such a huge number of employees that I'm not in the mood to hire any more."

Duisberg persisted, and eventually Muurling capitulated, filling out the forms Leverkusen wanted, holding meetings in the style Leverkusen demanded, and even hiring the technical advisory board Leverkusen recommended. Still, the drug business lagged. In May 1896, Duisberg sailed for New York to see what could be done. Never having been across the Atlantic before, he prepared for the journey with his customary thoroughness, blizzarding Muurling with letters, cables, demands, and proposals.

Upon his arrival, Duisberg presented his U.S. agent with detailed instructions for reviving pharmaceutical sales. Then the two men went to Boston, where Duisberg got an inkling of the growing industrial might of the United States: wool factories with 5,000 employees, cotton mills with 2,400 great looms in one big shed, a thread plant with a building that covered more than three acres, an automated chemical works that made sulfuric acid in a room without a single person in it, a mill that took in raw fiber at one end and excreted dress shirts at the other. Everywhere was mechanization, organization, efficiency, planning—encouragement for the principles laid down the year before in Duisberg's master plan for Leverkusen.

Seven years later, in 1903, he was back. Hiring more salespeople had boosted Phenacetin sales, but high U.S. duties remained a problem. In addition, the drug's patent would expire in three years, ending the company's legal monopoly and forcing it to compete with domestic manufacturers. Because those manufacturers had their plants in the United States, they would not have to pay duties, giving them an edge. Bayer's board of directors wanted to build an American factory. Muurling resisted—he didn't want the hassle. Duisberg, for his part, was afraid of losing control over such a faraway facility. Nonetheless, he reluctantly convinced himself there was no other path. Bayer, he conceded, was not without manufacturing experience in the United States; in 1881, it had purchased one-fourth ownership in the Hudson River Aniline & Color Works at Rensselaer, and that had not proved to be a catastrophe. Indeed, the plant might serve as a base for the drug factory Duisberg intended to erect. In November 1902, he wrote to Muurling:

> The longer I think about it, the more I come to the conclusion that we have to build the factory over there for the production of pharmaceutical products—which is too bad, because decentralization in the production sector means higher costs and brings a lot of anger and tedious work.

Despite such forebodings, Duisberg, Friedrich Bayer, Jr. (son of the founder), and Ludwig Girtler (the firm's chief engineer) came to New York in mid-April 1903. Arriving at the north end of the Hudson Valley, Duisberg was pleasantly surprised by the conditions he found. A hub for rail and river traffic, Albany was hospitable to the chemical industry (the first U.S. dye company was started there in 1869) and to the German community associated with it (German Day, in honor of German immigrants, was a major local holiday). Rensselaer too was promising. Although it was anything but cosmopolitan—the town had twenty-seven saloons but only one restaurant—it was growing rapidly, and had trained workers available from its ice and shirt-collar factories. The Hudson River plant was close enough to town to be accessible, but far enough that its wastes would not raise objections.

Instead of starting from the ground up, Duisberg decided, they would simply remodel the Riverside Avenue plant of the Hudson River Aniline & Color Works. In addition, Duisberg bought another local dye firm, the American Color & Chemical Company, on nearby Rensselaer Island, which would be dismantled and moved to Riverside Avenue. All of this was to take place under the strictest control from Leverkusen, which would provide blueprints of the buildings, designs for the machinery, and instructions on how to locate each building and install each machine. By such careful planning, Duisberg thought, he could pare the costs to less than two hundred thousand dollars. Upon completion, the combined facility, by U.S. standards, would be huge—seventy-five acres of factories and shipping facilities. Its centerpiece would be the Aspirin foundry, with two great vessels made of purest silver, one of the few metals—the others were the even more costly gold and platinum—able to withstand the acetic acid used to acetylate salicylic acid. To celebrate the occasion, Duisberg, Muurling, Bayer, Jr., and Girtler held the ground-breaking ceremony traditional in Germany.

As he had done on his last visit, Duisberg toured factories. But this time the journey was more arduous—he went from Boston to New Orleans, a trek he later claimed had given him a "heart neurosis"—and American industrial facilities seemed less impressive. The managers appeared uncouth and incapable, the employees troubled by the itch to form unions. Altogether, Duisberg thought, things were better in Germany.

It was in this dissatisfied mood that he received an unexpected invitation to address the New York Chemical Society on the centennial of the birth of Justus von Liebig, a German researcher who played a major role in the discovery of coal-tar dyes. (As a teenage student, Duisberg had been inspired by Liebig's belief that chemistry was "one of the mightiest means to elevate the culture of the intellect.") Duisberg spoke on May 13, three days after his return to New York City. The lecture was not warmly received. "Americans are not yet able to perform the exact and exhausting work necessary to make the principles of chemical science fruitful for industry," he grandly explained. "The American laborer holds industry by its throat and will strangle it." Duisberg was heckled, especially by the embarrassed Germans in the audience, and his departure for Germany a week later was accompanied by denunciations in the papers. When two U.S. science journals refused to print the speech, Duisberg was forced to publish it in *Popular Science Monthly*. He shrugged off the insult. The Americans didn't like "my scolding," he told Muurling.

Still, Duisberg thought the trip had gone well. As a result of his journey to Rensselaer, Bayer Aspirin was rooted in the United States. True enough— but he had also set into motion the circumstances that made it possible for someone to steal Aspirin from his company, the opening salvo in the labyrinthine battle of Bayer vs. Bayer.

CHAPTER TWO

"RICH BEYOND THE DREAMS OF AVARICE"

1903 - Aspirin to U.S.

On December 12, 1918, a small crowd of well-dressed men gathered at the front gate of the Aspirin factory in Rensselaer. The United States, which was at war with Germany, was selling all U.S. assets of Farbenfabriken Bayer to the highest bidder. Although the fighting had actually stopped a month before, the American government, encouraged by American business, was methodically peddling German corporations to their domestic competitors. Bayer's property included one of the nation's biggest chemical plants, but the acres of sophisticated machinery were by no means the only reason these businesspeople showed up for the auction. Plants and machinery could be copied; what could not be duplicated was something altogether more valuable—the name of Aspirin, and of Bayer itself.

The United States was the only country in which Bayer had both a trademark and a patent on Aspirin. Patents and trademarks are classic illustrations of what lawyers call "intellectual property," a subject of consuming interest to people who engage in commerce. Intellectual property is knowledge or expression that is owned by somebody. It most often takes forms like patented inventions or copyrighted songs, but intellectual property encompasses such ineffables as turns of phrase, styles of lettering, and even the abstract designs on modish clothing.

Both patents and trademarks establish valuable rights. A patent gives the holder the right to control the production of a particular good for a given period of time. A trademark, on the other hand, gives the holder the right to control the use of a name, and hence the public's mental associations with it—which amounts to owning a little piece of their brains. When Bayer patented Aspirin, it gained legal authority over all U.S. production of acetylsalicylic acid for seventeen years. But when it trademarked the name Aspirin, it acquired something more elusive and powerful, the possibility of making a word, Aspirin, spring into people's minds when they thought of headaches, minor aches and pains, and fevers.

A patent's worth is obvious, for it guarantees a monopoly; the value of a trademark is more subtle, for it plays to the human tendency to esteem objects with familiar appellations. Buyers gravitate to the certain and the known; they are comforted by the illusion that behind every bottle of Heinz ketchup or box of Quaker oats stands an old friend whose name is a guarantee of quality. Illustrating this, Boswell cites a remark by Samuel Johnson, who once oversaw the sale of a famous brewery. Asked the value of the property, the lexicographer replied that its renowned name was paramount. "We are not here to sell a parcel of boilers and vats," he proclaimed, "but the potentiality [offered by the name] of growing rich beyond the dreams of avarice."

Bayer's first corporate symbol was a heraldic emblem based on the coat of arms of Elberfeld, featuring a lion with two tails. After briefly putting the lion on a throne, the firm dropped the extra tail but added wings; the beast's noble paws rested on Mercury's staff and the globe. In 1904, the company introduced the Bayer Cross—two perpendicular *BAYER*s, meeting at the central *Y*. The Cross was ringed at first by the firm's full name, but later simplified in several steps to unadorned letters on a white or black background. In addition to this emblem, a symbol for its overall business, the firm held innumerable trademarks for individual products. Aspirin was one of the most valuable, particularly in the United States.

Farbenfabriken zealously defended its intellectual property rights. But it faced daunting problems in the drug field. In the late nineteenth century, medicines were described as either ethical drugs or patent medicines. Ethical drugs were much like today's prescription drugs: products bought from a pharmacist under instructions from a doctor. Their contents were listed for all to see, so that doctors knew exactly what they were prescribing. Sold only in pharmacies, ethical products were not advertised to the public, because physicians believed such marketing to be irresponsible, and ethical-drug makers depended on the goodwill of the medical profession. Patent medicine manufacturers, on the other hand, dealt directly with the public and often kept the ingredients secret, claiming that the nostrum was protected by a patent (hence the term "patent medicine").* These remedies were promoted massively and sold anywhere their makers could find shelf space.

Because most patent medicines were simple quackery, ethical companies tried to distance themselves from patent medicine concerns. But accommodating the medical profession's dislike of patents, trademarks, and advertising implied eschewing three of the basic tools of capitalism. Ethical-drug

---

* The term was used in England as far back as the early eighteenth century, when many nostrums were actually granted patents. Because obtaining a patent requires the inventor to make the invention—in this case, the medical formula—public, patent medicines increasingly became a misnomer, as their makers opted to maintain the secrecy necessary to foster the illusion that the treatment might have some effect.

companies therefore balanced between pleasing the doctors they depended on and acting like businesses. Bayer and other producers of coal-tar medicines patented and trademarked their drugs whenever possible, but hung on to their ethical status by not promoting their products to the public and, in almost all cases, selling them only through pharmacies.

Aspirin was typical in this respect. Bayer tried to patent and trademark the drug wherever possible. It easily obtained trademarks throughout the world, because ''Aspirin'' was a genuinely new name. But the firm was only able to patent Aspirin in those nations that did not regard the fact that ASA had been invented decades before by someone else as an obstacle to a claim of discovery. As it happened, Bayer could find only two such nations: the

Bayer had *patent*
in only

United Kingdom and the United States. With its huge size, the latter became
an important potential market. Bayer wanted to reach U.S. consumers but
avoid the ire of the American Medical Association, the powerful doctors'
trade association. It promoted Aspirin only to the medical profession, inun-
dating physicians' offices with samples, flyers, article reprints, and personal
letters; sending salespeople to doctors' offices; and advertising in the *Journal
of the American Medical Association*, then the most widely read medical
publication in the country.

Because Bayer was the sole legal source of ASA in the United States, it
could—and did—charge higher prices than where it was but one of many
producers. With relentless promotion to doctors, Aspirin became a gold
mine. It was far and away the most important of the many products the firm
sold in the United States. By 1907, Aspirin accounted for 21 percent of
Bayer's total U.S. sales; by 1909, it was 31 percent.

Such spectacular sales figures elicited the most sinister form of flattery:
smuggling. Almost from the moment Aspirin was introduced, contraband
ASA flowed from Canada, where Bayer had no patent, to the United States,
where it did. Early in 1905, Farbenfabriken of Elberfeld, Bayer's New York
office, filed a patent-infringement suit against Edward A. Kuehmsted, a
Chicago pharmaceutical dealer who was the kingpin of bootleg Aspirin west
of Philadelphia. The company believed that a successful trial would both put
Kuehmsted out of business and endorse the validity of its patent, making it
easier to slap quick injunctions on other infringers. Kuehmsted's defense was
the standard one in such cases: The patent claims were invalid.

In many cases such a defense is successful. Patent examiners are not
infallible, and sometimes an "invention" turns out to be merely a twist on
a well-established, and therefore unpatentable, principle. A patent suit thus
carries with it the risk that the claims the plaintiff seeks to enforce will
instead be declared invalid, eliminating the patent holder's legal control over
the product.

Immediately after filing suit, Bayer learned just how big that risk was. A
year before, the firm's English branch had sued the English branch of Chemische Fabrik von Heyden, a German chemical manufacturer, for selling
ASA, infringing its British patent. The trial began in May 1905. Heyden
claimed the patent was invalid, because Felix Hoffmann, the Bayer researcher
who developed Aspirin, had only duplicated the work of Kraut, the chemist
who synthesized ASA back in 1869. Bayer responded that Kraut's method
did not produce pure acetylsalicylic acid, that Hoffmann's method did, that
this distinguished the two methods, and that its patent claims were therefore
valid. On July 8, 1905, Justice Joyce of the Royal Courts of Justice took
pains to disagree. To hide the similarities between the methods of Hoffmann
and Kraut, the justice noted, Bayer's patent was couched in language so
obscure that "none of the experienced counsel engaged in this case had ever

seen another [one] like it." Britain was thus opened to competition, although Farbenfabriken kept the Aspirin trademark and dominated the market until the First World War.

Handed down a few months after Bayer filed suit against Kuehmsted, the British decision appeared to be devastating. The company's U.S. patent attorney, Livingston Gifford, thought it left "only a possibility in favor of the American patent." Nevertheless, he managed to stretch out the case for another five years, during which time the patent still held. In August 1909, the circuit court in Chicago finally issued its decision. To everyone's surprise, it upheld the patent. When Kuehmsted complained that Farbenfabriken couldn't keep its patent anywhere else in the world, the judge merely observed that the United States was not like other countries. A higher court denied Kuehmsted's appeal in July 1910.

Just before the appellate decision, Bayer's managers estimated that counterfeit Aspirin had seized a staggering three-quarters of the U.S. market. Because striking at the many manufacturers of fake Aspirin was a task of Sisyphean dimension, the company decided instead to focus on the retail druggists who sold bootleg ASA to the public (not to mention cornstarch pills labeled as Aspirin). In a letter to three hundred state and local druggist associations, Bayer trumpeted the Kuehmsted decision, threatened to sue counterfeiters and smugglers, and demanded that pharmacy owners sign an enclosed pledge to sell only genuine Bayer Aspirin. Showing the velvet glove around the iron fist, the company offered amnesty from prosecution to any druggists who confessed their past sins, fingered their bootleggers, and solemnly promised never to cheat again. Fewer than ten pharmacists accepted this generous offer.

In September 1912, Anthony Gref, another American Bayer attorney, and Herman Metz, a sales agent for Hoechst, announced a final war on infringers. "Frauds are practiced on such an extensive scale," Metz told reporters, "that the lives of at least one hundred million people in the United States are placed in jeopardy month in and month out." (The U.S. population at that time was about ninety-five million.) A squad of detectives searched drugstores for counterfeit Aspirin and other drugs, eliciting the ire of the pharmacists whose shelves were rifled. Eventually the assault paid off. In February 1914 agents bought sixty packets of Aspirin in nine different cities. Only sixteen—not quite 27 percent—were bogus.

Unfortunately, protecting the patent took so long that by the time Bayer finally beat back the infringers it was close to expiring. On February 17, 1917, the counterfeiters would be able to sell ASA legally. To Bayer, the consequences were dire. Canadian Aspirin sold for one-third the U.S. price. In most of Europe, pharmacists paid less than one-tenth what they paid in the States. Competition in the United States would force Farbenfabriken to cut prices drastically.

To counter the loss of its patent, the firm turned to its trademark. Bayer would try to make consumers so thoroughly identify headache and fever relief with Bayer Aspirin that its rivals would have no chance. Here, the firm confronted two problems, both arising from its previous marketing strategy. Bayer manufactured Aspirin almost exclusively as a powder, selling it to drug firms and wholesalers, which in turn sold the powder in tablets or small packets to retail pharmacists. If a company such as Upjohn purchased Aspirin powder from Bayer, the packet label read:

> Aspirin
> Five Grains
> Upjohn

Because Bayer promoted the drug to doctors, pharmacists, and drug firms, they knew the Bayer name; but it was unknown to the public. This had to change if the company wanted to keep its profits high.

Making the Bayer name known to the public obviously involved advertising—which was the second problem. The AMA's opposition to consumer advertising was so extreme that it once complained to Bayer about some hand fans the company had printed with the names of its products. The AMA even attacked the very idea of selling branded or patented products instead of generic drugs, arguing that brand names and patents did nothing but drive up costs and mislead patients. (For instance, it had long asked physicians to prescribe ''acetanilid'' instead of Antifebrin.) Advertising a trademarked product, Bayer Aspirin, to the public would inevitably infuriate doctors, and Duisberg and the other directors in Leverkusen were unwilling to risk the disapproval of their fellow professionals. The American marketing staff, however, wanted to break with the past. If the company wanted fabulous Aspirin profits, they said, it was going to have to *sell*.

As a temporary compromise, both pro- and anti-advertising factions agreed to boost the U.S. production of Aspirin in tablet form. Each tablet was stamped with the Bayer Cross, and the tablets were put in Bayer packages, which for the first time let customers see the name of the company that cured their headaches. The switchover to tablets commenced in early 1914.

Meanwhile, the grim patent-expiration day approached, and it became clear that Americans fully intended to make ASA. (One of the first was Herbert Dow, founder of Dow Chemical, in Midland, Michigan.) Although Bayer feared the AMA, it feared losing money even more. In the fall of 1916, Aspirin ads appeared in newspapers across the United States. ''BAYER,'' read a headline above a picture of an Aspirin box, ''Tablets of Aspirin.''

"The Bayer Cross"
on every package and on every tablet
of Genuine Aspirin protects you
against all counterfeits and substitutes.

By the standards of hype, the ad was modest. It did not mention a single
condition Aspirin could be used for, or even describe it as medicine. It did
not urge the reader to buy anything. "Not a sentence, phrase or word is used
in the copy that might give offense to even the stickler for the niceties of
medical ethics," observed *Printers' Ink*, an advertising journal. "All that the
advertising attempts to do is link up the name 'Bayer' with Aspirin."

Nonetheless, the AMA reaction was everything Bayer had dreaded. The
Journal scoffed at the notion that one brand of ASA could be different from
any other, or that any could be "counterfeit." And it lashed out at Bayer.
"For seventeen years," the *Journal* complained,

> it has been impossible in this country for anybody except the Bayer
> Company to manufacture or sell acetylsalicylic acid. . . . Needless to
> say, the American people have been made to pay exorbitantly for the
> monopoly our patent office granted this firm. . . . Not content with the
> iron-bound monopoly which it had been granted through our patent
> laws, the company attempted further to clinch its exclusive rights by
> giving the preparation a fancy name, "aspirin," and getting a trademark
> on this name. . . . [As soon as ASA can be made by anyone, doctors
> should] prescribe the compound under its scientific name, acetylsali-
> cylic acid.

The rebuke fell on deaf ears. By the time the patent expired, the United
States was about to declare war, and Bayer's German managers had more on
their minds than pleasing American doctors.

The sudden onset of the First World War in the summer of 1914 caught the
company's U.S. employees unprepared. To their dismay, the pistol shots at
Sarajevo transformed them from foreign residents into suspicious aliens.
Adding to their difficulties, Britain blockaded Germany—severing the New
York management from Leverkusen's supervision. Its subsequent actions
proved the wisdom of Duisberg's belief in centralized control. With his hand
off the tiller, the U.S. wing of Bayer entangled itself in a farrago of bizarre
schemes, of which the most peculiar was the Great Phenol Plot.

The Great Phenol Plot was a by-product of this country's long hesitation
over whether to join the war, a time when pro-German, pro-British, and

pro-neutrality groups squabbled bitterly, and sometimes violently. In May 1915, the *Lusitania*, a British passenger vessel, was sunk by a German submarine. More than a thousand people died, and pro-German sentiment in the U.S. fell precipitously. Worried about a tilt toward London, Germany's ambassador, Count Johann Heinrich von Bernstorff, was entrusted with the diplomatic task of molding public opinion in favor of the kaiser. With a lieutenant, Heinrich Albert, an Interior Ministry official, Count von Bernstorff also handled the less diplomatic task of preventing U.S. chemical companies from supplying Germany's foes with munitions. For this latter purpose, the two men enlisted Hugo Schweitzer, the chief chemical adviser of Farbenfabriken of Elberfeld in New York.

A Prussian, Schweitzer earned a Ph.D. from the University of Freiburg specializing in coal-tar research. Immigrating in 1889 to work in the nascent American chemical industry, he became a naturalized citizen five years later. He was appointed head of the pharmaceutical department at Bayer's New York office in 1896 and soon impressed the management back in Leverkusen. On his first trip across the Atlantic, Duisberg told Muurling that he had learned more about the United States from Schweitzer in six weeks than he had from Bayer's sales agents, Schieffelin & Company, in a year. Like Duisberg, Schweitzer was a highly organized, technically minded man with a sense of propriety so rigid that he regarded advertising as uncouth. He was not overly fond of the United States, where the newspapers were chockablock with ads for dubious panaceas, and where pharmacists attacked drug companies for exercising their patent rights. Nonetheless, he was successful enough to leave Bayer, becoming an independent chemical consultant and exporter from his apartment on an expensive strip of Riverside Drive in Manhattan.

When the war began, the fifty-four-year-old industrial chemist acquired a new identity, as a spy—German Secret Service Code No. 963192637. Schweitzer funneled money from Albert and von Bernstorff to Walter Scheele, a chemist who was Germany's only paid industrial spy in North America at the outbreak of war. Schweitzer and Scheele plotted to smuggle desperately needed American oil to Germany by chemically changing its appearance enough to fool U.S. customs into thinking it was fertilizer. Later, Schweitzer funded Scheele's sabotage attempts, which involved placing tiny cigar-shaped bombs in English ships.

Schweitzer was anything but circumspect. Even as he doled out Albert's money to deserving conspirators, Schweitzer worked as a prominent member of a campaign to sway American public opinion. Day after day, Schweitzer lent his voice to German causes, delivering anti-British broadsides to meetings at Madison Square Garden, negotiating to buy U.S. newspapers, defending the attack on the *Lusitania* (by riding on an English ship, he scoffed, the passengers "committed suicide outright"), and arranging for the publication of a deluxe, illustrated twenty-volume set of German literary masterworks, several hundred copies of which he donated to public schools.

The Great Phenol Plot began in 1915. A coal-tar product otherwise known as hydroxybenzene, or, inexactly, carbolic acid, phenol was used as a disinfectant and germicide. It was also a major ingredient in the production of dyes, perfumes, flavors, photographic chemicals, and explosives, particularly an explosive known as trinitrophenol. Schweitzer knew phenol well, for large quantities of it were used to synthesize salicylic acid, the principal ingredient of acetylsalicylic acid, or Aspirin. Most of this phenol was imported from the United Kingdom.

When war was declared, Britain's Parliament commandeered most of that nation's phenol to make trinitrophenol. Phenol imports into the U.S. plummeted. The laws of supply and demand being what they are, prices shot up. Phenol that had sold for 10¢ a pound in August went for $1.25 a pound the next February. Although the Rensselaer factory did not use phenol directly, the availability of the chemical was vital: Bayer made its Aspirin from salicylic acid, which in turn was produced by other U.S. companies from phenol. By April 1915, Bayer's Aspirin plant was almost shut down—a disaster for a firm that wanted to spread its new tablets far and wide. Worse, other companies took advantage of the shortage to produce fake Aspirin from chemicals other than ASA. With reports spreading that Aspirin might disappear from the market, druggists stocked up heavily, and often bought the counterfeit article.

The domestic supply of phenol provided no relief for Bayer's problems. Nearly all of the compound was destined for trinitrophenol or committed under long-term contracts to other firms. Left in the cold with Bayer was Thomas Edison, the Wizard of Menlo Park, who needed phenol to make one of his most renowned inventions, phonograph records. A man of action, Edison decided to make phenol himself. He quickly built two synthetic phenol plants, each with a capacity of six tons per day, a big increase in the spot supply. Using money from Albert's propaganda funds, Schweitzer contracted with Edison's sales agent to buy every drop of phenol the inventor did not use himself. (It was a big contract: Edison's excess production amounted to three tons a day.)

In June 1915, Schweitzer met with George Simon, vice-president and general manager of the American branch of the Chemische Fabrik von Heyden. Although Heyden was the German firm that had destroyed Bayer's British patent on Aspirin, it had supplied Rensselaer with salicylic acid until the phenol dearth forced it to stop. Schweitzer asked Simon to buy the phenol Schweitzer had bought from Edison and convert it into salicylic acid. Part of the salicylic acid would be used to fulfill Heyden's contract with Bayer. The rest would be resold to Schweitzer, who wanted it for his export business. Simon agreed.

The arrangement benefited all sides. Simon got to restart his salicylic acid plant, which let Bayer restart its Aspirin plant—and its campaign to save the Aspirin market. Schweitzer's control of the only large available source of phenol in the nation enabled him to make a fortune. (Moreover, because the money to pay Edison came from Albert, Schweitzer's costs were subsidized by the German taxpayer.) In turn, Albert was happy. The phenol used to make aspirin was not used to enlarge the U.S. supply of trinitrophenol. In just a few months, Albert claimed, Schweitzer managed to divert a supply of phenol equivalent to four and a half million pounds of explosives—three long freight trains' worth.*

The scheme quickly came to an end. Suspicious of Albert, the U.S. Secret Service had him followed. On July 24, Albert fell asleep on the Sixth Avenue elevated in uptown Manhattan. Waking up at his stop, he rushed out of the train, leaving behind a briefcase full of secret papers. Realizing his loss, he ran back into the train, only to be told by passengers that a young man had absconded with the briefcase. (After this, Albert was mocked as the "Minister without Portfolio.")

The young man was a Secret Service agent, and he took the briefcase to his superiors. It was stuffed with incriminating information about sabotage, but not quite stuffed enough to indict Albert, Schweitzer, or anyone else. Anxious to expose Albert nevertheless, a high government official leaked the briefcase papers to the fervently anti-German *New York World*. On August 15, the *World* covered its front page with reproductions of Albert's "lost" documents.

Albert, Schweitzer, and Count von Bernstorff were accused of being masterminds of German subversion. In a tone of horror, the *World* recounted Schweitzer's speeches, efforts at sabotage and peculation, and attempts to buy pro-German newspapers and magazines. Prominent among the machinations was the phenol contract, which the *World* charged was part of a broader plot to steal American chemicals. Schweitzer was indignant. "The entire output of [phenol] in the United States was and is greedily sought by explosive manufacturers at fabulous prices, in order to be converted into [trinitrophenol]," he said. At the rate of one pound of phenol for every three of trinitrophenol, he said, "it needs no imagination to realize how many men would have been killed, wounded, and maimed by the use of this enormous

---

* Even Edison was pleased. Simon claimed to have talked to Edison in June 1915, at which time the inventor said he wanted to steer his phenol into peaceful uses, such as pharmaceuticals, rather than explosives. "It was more to his feelings," Simon explained. Edison's feelings did not translate into actions, however. After the scandal broke, he turned around and sold phenol to the U.S. military.

quantity of one of the highest explosives known. . . . How there can be any criticism in this matter is beyond my understanding.'' Neglecting to mention that his phenol was helping a German company keep its monopoly on Aspirin, Schweitzer claimed that it was only to be used as a disinfectant. At three tons of phenol a day, the *New York Times* calculated, Schweitzer would be able to make 240,000 pounds of disinfectant, enough to provide every man, woman, and child in the country with a new two-ounce bottle every seven weeks.

Despite the publicity, no charges were brought; the United States was not yet at war, and Germans could legally buy all the phenol they wanted. Nonetheless, after the exposé Albert said he would no longer pay for phenol. Schweitzer asked George Simon to be his new financial angel. When Simon refused, Schweitzer went to Richard Kny, Simon's wealthy father-in-law. Kny and Schweitzer signed an agreement in September, but backdated it to June 30 to hide Albert's initial involvement. Even after being branded a dastardly German plot, the phenol deal nevertheless managed to earn the two men nearly a million dollars over the next six months. Celebrating their success, Schweitzer and Kny took Albert to dinner at the Astor Hotel. Over a lavish dinner, they presented the German official with a loving cup.

Schweitzer's ebullience did not last long; he contracted pneumonia and died at the end of 1917. In his apartment police found a secret office full of German flags, coded ledgers, annotated chemistry texts, packets of notes on various means of concocting Aspirin, speeches accusing England of absurd crimes, and paeans to the grandeur of German science. An investigation ensued, but not much happened; Schweitzer being dead, he could not be indicted. In addition, the government was then preoccupied by a second Bayer scandal.

Bayer's U.S. president was Emanuel von Salis, who had been with the company since the building of the Rensselaer factory. Considerable authority also resided with the corporate vice-president, Hermann C. A. Seebohm, the brother of Carl Duisberg's wife, Johanna, and a nephew of Carl Rumpff's. If the United States declared war, von Salis and Seebohm realized, they would suddenly become enemy citizens running an enemy business. On the other hand, the English blockade made it impossible for them to go home. They couldn't stay, and they couldn't leave. Faced with an insoluble dilemma, they spoke to a lawyer, Charles J. Hardy. This proved to be a mistake.

Whenever one part of humanity wages war on another, business on both sides has property in what has suddenly become enemy territory. Until the Middle Ages, foes inside a country's borders were enslaved or killed, and their property confiscated. Ideas slowly changed. The Magna Carta included a clause to protect enemy traders from losses, provided that the other government did the same for English merchants. At the beginning of the First World War, combatant nations put enemy firms into a trust, planning to use them for the host country's benefit until the fighting ended, after which they would be returned intact. As casualties mounted, such treatment seemed too mild. On both sides, enemy properties were sold outright. There being no reason to suppose the United States would behave differently if it joined the war, Hardy, Seebohm, and von Salis looked for a way to hide Bayer's assets.

The corporate shell game began in 1915, when Bayer received an advertising circular from the Williams & Crowell Color Company, a new dye firm in Providence, Rhode Island. At first, Bayer was interested for purely commercial reasons. If the United States entered the fight, it would draft soldiers. These soldiers would have to wear uniforms. Uniforms are made with khaki dyes. Seebohm and von Salis might have been worried about being declared enemies of the United States, but they also saw a market in equipping its army. Unfortunately Bayer was cut off from its dye supplies in Leverkusen. Williams & Crowell, which made the right sort of sulfur colors, might provide a way of meeting the expected demand for khaki.

Christian Stamm, the Bayer sales manager in Providence, was sent to look at the firm. After considerable wandering, Stamm finally came to "an old shack of a building on South Main Street, . . . a rather poor section of the City. . . ." In the shack was Williams, an elderly man who proved to be the manager of the outfit. (Crowell was the chemist.) Williams, Stamm discovered, "was not able to furnish even a small dye house with sufficient quantity of colors—in fact, when he stated in his letter that he could deliver any quantity desired, he had almost no conception of the wants of a large dealer." Still, Stamm thought, Crowell's dyes were pretty good. He recommended a deal.

Bayer bought a lot of Williams & Crowell dyes. When its orders pushed profits at Williams & Crowell to twenty thousand dollars per month, Bayer became interested in buying its dye supplier. Stamm was told to sound out the firm. Both Williams and Crowell rejected the idea, and Bayer came up with a strategy to persuade them to sell. "The basis of this plan," a subsequent investigation recounted,

> was the knowledge on the part of the officials of the Bayer Company and [Stamm] of the physical condition and health of Mr. Crowell, the chemist, which indeed was very poor, and, therefore, they opined that if the Bayer Company continually ordered very large quantities of sulfur colors, which Mr. Crowell had to attend to the manufacture of personally, he would soon be in a position where he would be glad to retire.

In the remote chance that Bayer could not induce Crowell to work himself to exhaustion, the firm made backup plans. It suggested that Crowell hire an

assistant. Bayer's candidate was a Mr. Seibert, who, investigators later discovered, "was known by his employers to possess certain qualifications
necessary in the manufacture of sulfur colors and also possessing the qualifications of watching every step of Mr. Crowell, so that in a very short time,
Mr. Seibert could manufacture the same sulfur colors that Mr. Crowell
could."

In the end, Williams & Crowell was undone not by overwork or industrial
espionage but by the recently passed income tax. The dye makers' enormous
profits were accompanied by an enormous tax: In the spring of 1917,
Williams & Crowell paid $75,000 to the government. The two men took it
badly. There was no reason to go into business if you had to do this kind of
thing. The tax, along with Crowell's poor health, induced them to sell.

The United States entered the war on April 6, 1917. For months, nothing
happened to resident Germans. Seebohm, von Salis, Stamm, and Hardy
had time to negotiate the sale with Williams and Crowell. In October, however, Washington passed the Trading with the Enemy Act, which instructed
the newly created Office of the Alien Property Custodian to take over
enemy property and hold it in trust during the war. A later amendment to
the act enabled the custodian to seize enemy-owned patents, copyrights,
and trademarks.

The first alien property custodian was A. Mitchell Palmer, a Pennsylvania
lawyer, former congressman, and power broker who helped engineer the
presidential nomination of Woodrow Wilson. In return for this good service,
Wilson supported Palmer's run for senator. When Palmer lost, the president
made him a judge and, later, alien property custodian. Arrogant and bull-
headed, Palmer viewed the custodianship as a step toward bigger things. He
was right; his stewardship earned him appointment as attorney general,
an office he used in 1920 to launch the now-infamous Palmer Raids, in
which some three thousand allegedly subversive aliens were rounded up for
deportation.

The custodian had a daunting task, for the nation's enemies owned considerable property in the United States. As of July 1, 1914, German investment alone was $950 million. Much of this was concealed by dummy
corporations, falsified contracts, and stock reassignments. To ferret out such
secret arrangements, Palmer created the Bureau of Investigation, naming
Francis P. Garvan, an assistant district attorney from New York, as its head.
Palmer and Garvan worked tirelessly; the Office of the Alien Property Custodian became one of the biggest business concerns in the country. Chocolate
in Connecticut, rails in Pennsylvania, woolens and worsteds in New Jersey,
lumber in Florida, beer in Chicago—the custodian was the head of a conglomerate.

In October 1917 Seebohm and Hardy were interviewed by Garvan's agent,
Frederick Lynch, a wealthy, politically connected lumberman from Minne-

sota. Uneasy about Bayer's connections with the notorious Hugo Schweitzer, Lynch made the two men promise to dissociate themselves from the chemist. That was easy—Schweitzer died two months later. Lynch also demanded the company's capital stock, and formally obtained it in January 1918.

Meanwhile, Hardy put together an intricate plot to ensure that handing over the stock to the custodian did not amount to handing over the company's profits. Reduced to its basics, Hardy's scheme evolved from the continuing negotiations between Bayer and Williams & Crowell. Hardy suggested that Bayer not go on record as the buyer of Williams & Crowell. Instead, he wanted to form a new corporation, the Williams & Crowell Color Company of New York, which would be owned by Seebohm, von Salis, and the other German-born managers. (Or, more exactly, the nominal owners would be friends of the managers so that the new company's stock would be associated only with Americans.) Williams & Crowell (New York) would purchase Williams & Crowell (Rhode Island). To do this, Williams & Crowell (New York) would borrow the money interest-free from Bayer and pay it back from the profits of Williams & Crowell (New York). Seebohm and his associates could guarantee those profits, because in their roles as Bayer executives they promised to buy the entire output of Williams & Crowell (New York) at an inflated price, increasing the latter's profits to fifty thousand dollars a month. In this way the U.S. managers of Bayer would funnel almost all of the company's profits into the pockets of the new owners of Williams & Crowell: the U.S. managers of Bayer (technically, the friends who nominally owned the stock).

Williams & Crowell (New York) was incorporated in January 1918, a few days before Seebohm handed over control of Bayer. He did not worry about being caught by the alien property custodian, because he had taken care to bribe Lynch, who had been installed as chairman of the board. ("A machine that is oiled well runs well," Seebohm told Stamm.) With Lynch paid to look the other way, Bayer could continue its operations exactly as it had before, except that Seebohm and von Salis now would dump the profits into Williams & Crowell (New York).

The Germans had not counted on the fervor of A. Mitchell Palmer. Palmer had always chafed at the idea of returning the fruits of his work after the war to the original owners. Wanting to transform his holdings into a fighting force, he begged Congress to let him sell enemy property to Americans. In March 1918, Congress amended the Trading with the Enemy Act as Palmer had suggested. Now he could hold a series of auctions—everything would go!

Although the amendment was a disaster for all German companies in the United States, it was a special problem for Farbenfabriken Bayer because of an earlier, unrelated corporate restructuring. The company's U.S. branch was replaced on paper in 1913 by two new entities, the Bayer Company and the Synthetic Patents Company.* Instead of using licenses from Leverkusen, the Bayer Company now *owned* the U.S. trademarks, including that of Aspirin, and the physical assets, including the Rensselaer plant. Duisberg kept control because the company's stock was nominally held by Seebohm, von Salis, and the other managers of Bayer's U.S. branch, all of whom were fiercely loyal to the mother firm. The patents, meanwhile, were awarded to a new entity, the Synthetic Patents Company; the stock of this company also was owned by the Germans, and its president was Hugo Schweitzer.

The arrangement had made no difference in the day-to-day operation of the firm. Ownership of the trademarks and patents had merely been shifted from one entity controlled by Leverkusen to another. But when Palmer exercised his authority, taking over both the Bayer and Synthetic Patents, the consequences for Bayer were frightening. If Palmer sold the companies, he would not be selling mere licenses to the Bayer Cross and the Bayer and Aspirin names, which Leverkusen could presumably cancel or renegotiate. (The patent had expired, so it could not be taken, but the company had patents to many other pharmaceutical products.) With the U.S. companies legally separated from their German parent, the custodian's auction would rob Leverkusen of patents and trademarks themselves.

Seebohm and von Salis believed that they had covered this eventuality by setting up Williams & Crowell and bribing Lynch. Lynch would ensure that the Bayer Company and Synthetic Patents were bought by someone who would secretly agree to sell both companies back to the Germans. The profits accumulating at Williams & Crowell would finance the plan.

It didn't work out that way. In April a man who lived near the Williams

---

* In October 1912, Alfred J. Keppelmann, the manager of the Bayer sales office in Philadelphia, was indicted for bribing local dye workers to tell their bosses to buy only Leverkusen dyes. (Apparently, such suits were widespread in the dye industry, as were the practices that inspired them.) The prosecution's case depended on Keppelmann's stenographer, who was to testify about the bribes. Just as the case was about to begin, Keppelmann found a highly effective way to silence the witness: He married her. Because people cannot be compelled to testify against their spouses, the prosecution had to give up. "It's no use, boys, it's all off," moaned an assistant district attorney. "The defendant has married the evidence, and it is not admissible."

Angry textile manufacturers looked for another way to attack the bribery—and found it in a shrewd application of U.S. antitrust laws. Bayer was a member of many cartels in Germany, where there was no strong injunctions against them. In June 1913, twelve textile manufacturers sued Bayer and its American branch, Farbenfabriken of Elberfeld, saying that the membership of the former in a cartel overseas was against U.S. law. Bayer's New York attorney, Charles J. Hardy, consulted various experts and concluded that the charges were going to stick. Bayer settled out of court. To avoid further attack, the New York company was split into two: the Synthetic Patents Company, which would own (rather than license) the U.S. patents for dyestuffs and pharmaceuticals; and the Bayer Company, which would own the trademarks and manage the production of dyes and pharmaceuticals. Both were legally independent companies though in fact controlled by Leverkusen.

& Crowell factory wrote a letter to the Department of Justice, informing it that the firm was putting "dangerous germs" in uniform dyes, "so that when an American soldier is shot, the germs in the cloth would infect the wound." In addition, he said, the dye maker was a subsidiary of Bayer, not an independent entity.

The letter seems to have triggered the inquiry that resulted two months later in the arrest of Stamm, the Providence sales agent, on suspicion of espionage. At first, Stamm was unworried, for he had been told that Hardy had political connections sufficient to protect all Bayer's U.S. employees. After being detained for several weeks, Stamm observed that Hardy was providing no such protection. He soon learned why. On July 16, Hardy abruptly quit the Bayer Company board, announcing his intent to buy the enterprise himself from the custodian. Helping Germans avoid difficulties with the American government no longer seemed to be in his interest. Within forty-eight hours of Hardy's departure, Stamm decided to talk about Williams & Crowell.

Agents grilled Seebohm and von Salis, both of whom resigned on July 18. Palmer asked von Salis to remain as manager of the Rensselaer plant, because nobody else knew how to run it; Seebohm was asked to remain as the sales manager of the New York office for the same reason. Both men agreed. They had little choice; they were spending an increasing amount of time being interrogated by federal agents. Everyone pointed the finger at everyone else; Bayer's U.S. management team disintegrated in a welter of angry accusations. In August, the Justice Department arrested seven Bayer Company officials, including Seebohm, von Salis, and Stamm, for violations of the Espionage and Trading with the Enemy acts. (Hardy was not picked up; he testified against his former clients.) Within a few weeks, the entire Bayer Company management was in jail.

One of the few Germans at the Bayer Company kept out of the Williams & Crowell scheme, and therefore out of jail, was Ernst Möller, the firm's export manager. Heartily disliked by his comrades, Möller was in some sense a man ahead of his time. He seems to have relished the freedom in turn-of-the-century America; he saw vast, empty spaces, and dreamed of filling them up with billboards, posters, and handbills proclaiming the miracle of Aspirin. Möller's superiors instead followed Duisberg's instructions to keep ad outlays to a low, fixed percentage of sales. To Möller, this was all wrong. Advertising was not a *cost*, it was an *investment*. It was the seed from which grew tomorrow's sales.

Möller was sent to the United States just as the war began. He quickly became a staunch supporter of the plan to sell Aspirin in tablet form. And it was he who finally managed to extract approval from a reluctant Leverkusen to run newspaper advertisements before the patent expired. But his success came at the cost of alienating Seebohm, his boss, who treated him as a Johnny-come-lately. Relations worsened when Möller caught one of Seebohm's friends rifling his desk. Harsh words were exchanged; the friend complained to Seebohm, and Möller found himself cut out of the loop.

The war brought changes to Möller's export trade, which covered Latin America, the Caribbean, Japan, and China. After Schweitzer's phenol deal allowed the Bayer Company to renew its production of Aspirin, output expanded rapidly. Bottled up by the British blockade, Leverkusen asked New York to supply Aspirin customers in the rest of the world. Möller was delighted. Suddenly he was an intercontinental kingpin of Aspirin.

His greatest fear was that the United States might enter the fight. If that happened, Washington would cut off contacts between American and German firms. In an attempt to dodge the bullet, Möller arranged with Seebohm for the Bayer Company to buy Leverkusen's export division—essentially, the right to use the various trademarks and sell Aspirin in foreign countries—for three hundred thousand dollars. The contract was signed on March 31, 1917, one week before the U.S. declared war.

Möller lacked the legal authority to make the transaction. Nonetheless, until someone declared the sale invalid, Möller had the cover to run the Aspirin business outside the United States and Europe. In practice, this meant primarily Latin America, but Möller was more than satisfied. At last the foreign Aspirin trade was under his sole control. He doubled and even tripled spending on ads in Latin America; to his delight, sales surged. Aspirin ads blanketed Mexico, Argentina, Brazil. The war was good to him.

Meanwhile, Palmer decided to put the firm up for auction. After the bad publicity from the Williams & Crowell affair, U.S. Aspirin sales went into free fall (even as they soared south of the border). Competitors like Smith, Kline & French took advantage of the scandal to plug their ASA with slogans like "Made by Americans, owned by Americans, sold by Americans, and will not profit Germany after the war." Moreover, so much of the Bayer Company staff had been arrested or discharged that the firm could barely operate; only one dye salesman was left, and the custodian had been forced to let Stamm out of jail to help von Salis at Rensselaer. When rumors spread that Bayer Aspirin tablets were poisoned, Palmer was urged to get rid of the firm before its value fell to zero. The armistice of November 11, 1918, did not lessen the pressure. Businesses implored the custodian to sell enemy properties quickly, before a peace treaty was signed and the Germans had a chance to get them back. Palmer scheduled an auction for Thursday, December 12.

Interest in the sale was intense. Dozens of companies queried Palmer about the Bayer Company. Most of the inquiries came from the other drug and chemical manufacturers, but the auction also attracted interest from businesses that had no obvious connection to drugs or chemicals, and even from wealthy individuals hoping to pick up a bargain. The Office of the Alien Property Custodian printed a brochure that showed the Bayer properties, and had the firm carefully audited. Long lists of Bayer patents and trademarks were prepared. To receive the custodian's brochure and a tour of the premises, potential buyers had to post a $100,000 bond. About a dozen did, including Paine Webber, representing a consortium of banks, and Du Pont, the biggest chemical firm in the nation.

On auction day, the interested parties trooped to Rensselaer. One of them would acquire the names Bayer had built up and defended for the past twenty years. Bids began at $1 million, and quickly climbed. Surprisingly, Du Pont dropped out early, bidding only a bit more than $2 million. Paine Webber and the others kept going. Three million. Four million. Five million. At $5,300,000, only Paine Webber and one other company were still in the game. Paine Webber went to $5,305,000. Its rival went to $5,310,000. Paine Webber bowed out. The auction was over. If Carl Duisberg had been present on that dark day, he would have been staggered. The new master of Bayer Aspirin was Sterling Products, Inc.—a patent medicine outfit whose lavishly advertised laxatives, dandruff nostrums, and impotence cures were the exact opposite of everything that he and Bayer had ever stood for.

CHAPTER THREE

"THE **FAKE BAYER**"

Sterling Products was established in the spring of 1901, when pharmacists William E. Weiss and Albert H. Diebold concocted a new pain reliever, Neuralgine. The two men had been teenage friends in Canton, a medium-sized town in southeast Ohio. Tall, soft-spoken Diebold got his start, and at least some of his money, from Diebold Safe & Lock, founded by his father and still extant today. Short, assertive Weiss graduated from the Philadelphia College of Pharmacy in 1896—his thesis examined the chemical composition of coffee—and went to work for the retail drug trade in Sistersville, West Virginia, seventy miles south and across the Ohio River from his boyhood home. After a few years he decided to sell patent medicines with his old friend Diebold. They relocated to Wheeling, a much bigger West Virginia city up the Ohio Valley.

The turn of the century was the heyday of the American patent medicine trade. Stores were flooded with the likes of Radam's Microbe Killer (99.381 percent water), "radium-impregnated" Radol (made with quinine and alcohol, but no radium), and Dr. Johnson's Mild Combination Treatment for Cancer ("Have you a friend with cancer?" its advertisements asked. "Do them a favor you'll never forget by sending them this ad"). Hoping to cash in on the boom, Weiss and Diebold set up the Neuralgyline Company, with Neuralgine as its only product.* They sold it from horse-drawn carriages throughout the West Virginia countryside, the two men a Mutt-and-Jeff pair as they rode on the painted buckboard, hopping off to nail a Neuralgine placard to a tree or fence. They were most industrious, selling ten thousand dollars' worth of Neuralgine in their first year of business. All ten thousand dollars went to advertise Neuralgine in two Pittsburgh papers. The strategy worked; sales kept rising. More sales paid for more advertising, and more advertising brought in more sales.

---

* Because Neuralgine was a patent medicine, it apparently did not list its ingredients. In any case, all records of its constituents have vanished, and nobody at the present-day Sterling knows what Weiss and Diebold were selling in the West Virginia panhandle. More than likely, it was acetanilid or another coal-tar analgesic.

Driven by relentless promotion, the Neuralgyline Company grew at a dizzying rate. Founded with a capital stock of $1,000, it expanded that stake within five years to $500,000; by 1912, the company was worth $4 million. Exhibiting a business acumen decades ahead of their time, Weiss and Diebold gobbled up other patent medicine firms, including the Knowlton Danderine Company, makers of a dandruff nostrum; Sterling Remedy, makers of No-To-Bac, a nicotine cure that left users constipated; and the California Fig Syrup Company, producers of a laxative. (The pieces of the infant company were, one observes, synergistic.) The firm having grown into an enterprise of respectable size, Weiss and Diebold needed a more glamorous identity than that provided by Neuralgine. They borrowed the name of Sterling Remedy to become Sterling Products, Inc., a name they intended to make world-famous.

Sterling Products was an exception in the patent medicine trade. Most companies were like the corporate progenitor of Dr. Robinson's Man Medicine, a "lost manhood" cure—"Makes 'old men' boys again"—devised and marketed by one Edward D. Hayes of Detroit. ("Dr. Robinson" probably was fictitious.) Owned and operated by a single individual, these firms sold but one product, and frequently shifted location as one market after another was saturated or became wise to unfulfilled promises. Weiss and Diebold, by contrast, saw that patent medicines could be more than a quick buck. By promoting not one but dozens of brands, they intended to build the first patent medicine conglomerate.

The two men were delighted to learn that the Bayer Company was up for auction. In their view, Bayer was not just a chemical company but also a collection of drug trademarks, Bayer Aspirin being the most valuable. Having no interest in dye making, Weiss and Diebold arranged just before the auction for the Grasselli Chemical Company of Cleveland, Ohio, to pay $1.5 million for the non-drug business should Sterling manage to acquire Bayer's assets. Sterling outlasted the other bidders, as Weiss expected, and he set rapidly to work. He told his board of directors,

> It is the object of Sterling Products to popularize [Bayer Aspirin] to the laity by means of newspaper advertising and other mediums of publicity. Sterling Products is the largest advertiser in the world.* We believe we know more about [patent] medicine advertising than anybody else and, as far as Aspirin is concerned, we know that the field has been merely scratched on the surface and that there are tremendous possibilities ahead for this preparation.

With the purchase, he asserted, Sterling had become the biggest patent medicine maker on the planet. Weiss intended to use Bayer Aspirin to make Sterling even bigger.

* Weiss's claim was untrue. Some patent medicine firms spent huge sums on promotion, but Sterling was not a major U.S. advertiser until the early 1930s.

*   *   *

At the Bayer Company board meeting on February 4, 1919, the custodian's directors bowed out, and a new cast of characters took over. The incoming board consisted of Weiss, Diebold, two other long-term Sterling executives, and Earl I. McClintock, the only holdover from the Office of the Alien Property Custodian, who was hired by Sterling at triple his government salary. McClintock's role with the company was curiously imprecise; years later, as vice-president, he was unable to specify a single area of his responsibility. Within the firm, he was believed to have used his position with the custodian to steer Bayer to Sterling Products, and that the job was his perpetual reward. In any case, Weiss and Diebold kept all real power, with Weiss having near-exclusive control of day-to-day affairs.

The two men quickly fulfilled their contract with Grasselli, selling the dye business for the promised $1.5 million. In March, they bifurcated the concern a second time, into the Bayer Company and the newly incorporated Winthrop Chemical Company. The division was lopsided: Bayer sold Aspirin, Aspirin in combination with other drugs—and nothing else. Winthrop handled the sixty-three other medications formerly sold by the New York branch of Farbenfabriken Bayer. The creation of a separate firm to handle ethical drugs was a public relations move to protect those products from the AMA attacks on Bayer Aspirin ads. In addition, druggists disturbed by the residual Teutonic overtones in ''Bayer'' now had an unimpeachably patriotic alternative: ''Winthrop'' came from John Winthrop, Jr., son of the governor of the Massachusetts Bay Colony, three-time governor of the Colony of Connecticut, and one of the first to make chemicals in colonial times.

Sterling intended to sell Bayer Aspirin in all corners of the earth. Unfortunately, the original owner of the name, Farbenfabriken Bayer, already did that. Rather than competing under a different name, Weiss and Diebold decided to filch the rights to the Bayer, Aspirin, and Bayer Cross trademarks wherever they could. Wartime legislation in many nations cast doubt on German intellectual property rights. Sterling representatives put the trademarks under legal siege throughout the world.

Farbenfabriken Bayer had spent more than fifty years building the Bayer name into a global emblem of probity, quality, and technological prowess. Now, should Sterling succeed, a patent medicine outfit from Wheeling, West Virginia, would be able to sell many of the same products under the same name, using the same symbols, in the most important markets outside continental Europe. As the actions of Weiss and Diebold gradually became known in Leverkusen, Duisberg grew irate. Then, amazingly, Sterling asked him for help.

The approach occurred because Sterling could not figure out how to make the sixty-three drugs that were supposed to be the stock-in-trade of the

Winthrop Chemical Company. To the producers of Neuralgine and No-To-Bac, Rensselaer was a daunting technological wonder. The former German supervisors having been jailed or deported, nobody knew how to run the machines; and, in keeping with German tradition, the patents, which were supposed to specify manufacturing processes, were marvels of obfuscation. The firm would run out of inventory long before it deciphered them. Weiss and Diebold concluded that they could not keep Winthrop afloat without aid. The aid could come from only one source: Farbenfabriken Bayer, the very entity that Sterling's purchase was supposed to drive from the United States, the company whose trademarks Sterling was attacking on four continents.

What seemed a calamity to Weiss and Diebold seemed an opportunity to Ernst Möller, the head of the Bayer Company's pharmaceutical export department. Although other Leverkusen employees told Möller that working with the new owners of the firm was wrong, he was attracted to Sterling Products, Inc. He thought Leverkusen could learn about advertising from these people. Envisioning a marriage of European science and American marketing, he urged Weiss to make some arrangement with Duisberg. Weiss sent Earl McClintock to Holland in May 1919.

Negotiating with German drug concerns was not what the Office of the Alien Property Custodian had meant when it certified Sterling as "100 percent American" a few days before McClintock's departure. And with the United States still technically at war, trading with Germany was illegal without a license granted by the president. Sterling had no such license. It didn't matter. When McClintock contacted a Farbenfabriken Bayer representative in Amsterdam, he was brusquely rebuffed. Nonetheless, Möller continued to press Sterling to cut a deal with Leverkusen. Weiss decided to go to Europe himself and meet Carl Duisberg.

Duisberg had greatly changed Farbenfabriken Bayer since his voyage to America in 1903, partly because of what he saw on that trip. Despite his scorn for most U.S. workers and managers, he had been fascinated by the big American industrial trusts, especially the Standard Oil of John D. Rockefeller. Impressed by the power and efficiency of these combines, Duisberg spoke after his return with Gustav von Brüning, (director of Hoechst,) and Heinrich von Brunck of Badische Anilin- und Soda-Fabrik (B.A. & S.F.), the forerunner of today's BASF, about forming an American-style trust in the German chemical industry. In January 1904, Duisberg wrote a fifty-eight-page memorandum that envisioned several companies amalgamating their sales, purchasing, and research departments but otherwise retaining a degree of autonomy—an arrangement that he hoped would balance coordination and independence, retaining the desirable features of each.

It was a propitious time for such ideas. After decades of discoveries, scientists had exhausted nature's storehouse of dyes. The German chemical companies were still prosperous, but as patents expired, competition would grow and profits would shrink. Duisberg saw commercial bloodletting down the road. Like any business leader, he was appalled by corporate warfare. (When business extols the free market, it means the freedom to make money, not the freedom to compete.) A complete union of the industry might avoid strife.

Duisberg met in February 1904 at Berlin's Kaiserhof Hotel, the most elegant in the nation, with three other big German chemical firms: Hoechst, B.A. & S.F., and Aktiengesellschaft für Anilinfabrikation, the ancestor of the present Agfa company, which was then best known for its photochemicals. Duisberg's proposal was attractive to some, but Hoechst's Brüning rejected the very notion of a merger.

A few months later, Duisberg was thunderstruck to read in the newspapers that Hoechst had swapped its stock with Leopold Cassella & Company, a smaller chemical business, forming an *Interessengemeinschaft*: a community of interests, in which the directors of each company sat on the other's management board, and consulted each other at all levels of business. Fearful of being swept away by the new giant, Farbenfabriken Bayer, B.A. & S.F., and Agfa plunged into their own confederation, the *Dreibund*: the Triple Association.

Both the Triple Association and the Hoechst-Cassella *Interessengemeinschaft* fell short of Duisberg's original conception, because neither embraced the whole industry, and because their component firms remained independent. Nevertheless, the twin combines prospered. Avoiding destructive competition at home, they increased their hold on markets abroad. Everywhere there was clothing, agriculture, or headaches, there was somebody from one of the two giants to sell dye, fertilizer, or analgesics.

When the war broke out, export markets vanished. The great chemical plants saved themselves from ruin by filling the kaiser's demand for military supplies, including the clouds of poison gas that overwhelmed French and British troops at Ypres. (This ghastly innovation was quickly duplicated by the Allies.) The chemical industry kept the German war effort alive; without synthetic nitrates, the army would have run out of ammunition by 1916.

Knowing that wartime production levels could not possibly be maintained in peacetime, Duisberg once again foresaw the approach of harmful competition. In July 1915 he resurrected his dream of a grand fusion by calling for the Triple Association to join the Hoechst-Cassella *Interessengemeinschaft* in an even bigger *Interessengemeinschaft*. He admitted that the elimination of all rivalry might lead to complacency, and that the public might fear the new commercial titan. But these defects would be more than offset by lowered costs. The two combines agreed, signing a pact in January 1916 that called for coordination in research, manufacture, finance, sales, and purchases, with the firms sharing profits according to a fixed formula. Each company retained its individual corporate identity and control over its own affairs, but was obliged to consult with the others. A firm had to talk to its partners before building a new plant, for example, but the partners could not tell it to build one. The big trust was still not quite the complete fusion that Duisberg had dreamed of, but it was close. He became chairman of the board of what was now named the Interessengemeinschaft der deutschen Teerfarbenfabriken: the Community of Interests of the German Tar-Dye Factories, or I.G. Farben.

As long as the fighting continued, the I.G. increased in size, output, and profitability. But the last months of the war and the peace that followed brought disaster. In October 1918, the German navy refused orders to make a last-ditch stand against the British fleet. The mutiny spread through Germany, workers joining soldiers in the rebellion. A general strike in Berlin a few weeks later spelled the end of imperial rule. Rival governments sprang up; the streets were filled with riot; confusion reigned in place of the kaiser. Eleven days after A. Mitchell Palmer auctioned the Bayer plant, a second naval revolt erupted; it was brutally suppressed.

As the strikes and demonstrations mounted, Duisberg and the other I.G. directors reacted with exemplary calm, methodically planning the conversion to peacetime. Despite the plans, they were overwhelmed by events. The armistice came, and Leverkusen was occupied by troops from New Zealand. British officers moved into Duisberg's house, confining the family to two rooms and the cellar. He tried to keep the I.G. going, but it was hopeless. By 1919, production had fallen to 60 percent of its prewar level.

Worse, the I.G. faced serious international competition for the first time. Armed with German patents bought from the Office of the Alien Property Custodian, American firms were preparing to battle for the U.S. market. In Britain, the government took over German dye plants and patents and melded them into the newly created British Dyestuffs Corporation, Ltd. The French government too created its own dye combine, which lowered the nation's dependence on imported dyes from 80 percent of the market in 1913 to 30 percent in 1919.

All these threats were compounded by the Treaty of Versailles, which officially ended the war between Germany and the Allies (except the United States, which never signed it). The German delegation to the talks arrived at Versailles on April 29, 1919. Among its members was Carl Bosch, the brilliant chemist who succeeded Brunck as head of B.A. & S.F., who appeared as an expert on the chemical industry. With Germany in civil chaos, the delegation believed the Allies might be moved to send aid; Bosch hoped that seized patents, trademarks, and factories would be returned.

Instead what followed was an exercise in humiliation. For several days after the Germans' arrival, the Allies did not acknowledge their presence.

The delegation was blocked off behind wooden fences, ostensibly to protect its members from being attacked on the streets. After a week, the Germans received the agenda for the negotiations. It did not include what would seem to be a central feature of any such talks: face-to-face meetings between the opposing sides. Negotiations took the form of written notes. As a start, the Germans were handed the Allies' first draft of the treaty. Nowhere in its 80,000 words and 440 articles was there a call for the return of seized German assets. (At about this time, McClintock showed up in Holland to dicker with Farbenfabriken Bayer.)

The Germans made a counterproposal on May 29. In response, the Allies produced a second draft of the treaty: a copy of the first, with a few changes written in the margin with red ink. This was resubmitted to the Germans on June 16, together with the demand that it be signed within a week. On June 22, twenty-four hours before the deadline, the German parliament approved the treaty except for four clauses, among them an admission of guilt for starting the war and an agreement to extradite Kaiser Wilhelm II and his principal military advisers. The Allies rejected these reservations. The German parliament, which had scattered, hastily reassembled; on June 23, two hours before the Allies' deadline, it accepted the treaty without conditions.

In their original form, the reparations stipulated by the Treaty of Versailles harked back to the days when Rome plowed salt into the fields of Carthage—one reason that the U.S. Senate refused to ratify the treaty. (Congress eventually declared the war over in 1921.) Among other provisions, Germany was required to surrender one-half of its dyestuff and pharmaceutical stocks on August 15, 1919, the day the treaty went into effect. In addition, until 1925 the Reparation Commission could buy one-fourth of the production of any dye or drug product at a low price.*

Despite the onerousness of the treaty, the I.G. was still viewed as a threat by Allied nations. They had too long demonized the German chemical industry as the epitome of Teutonic ruthlessness to believe it was truly tamed. Congress considered legislation on banning coal-tar imports. A former British officer lambasted the I.G. in a popular book, *The Riddle of the Rhine*, as a "serious menace," "a monster camouflaged floating mine in the troubled sea of world peace." Duisberg saw the I.G. in another guise. It was a giant conglomerate without the power to stop a U.S. patent medicine company from stealing its name.

*   *   *

---

* The reparations were repeatedly scaled down during the next few years—fortunately, for the very punitiveness of the original plan helped foil the intended goal of keeping the German chemical industry at bay. The Reparations Committee's huge appetite for German goods retarded the growth of the chemical industries in Great Britain and France, which could not match the supply or the price.

Although employed by Sterling, Ernst Möller was still loyal to Leverkusen. In June 1919, he met with one W. Korthaus, a Leverkusen official who had just been released from a detention camp. Möller's takeover of the export trade, Korthaus said, had just served it to Sterling on a platter; rather than allowing the enterprise to fall into another company's hands, Möller should have let the whole thing fall apart. Upon returning to Leverkusen after the meeting, Korthaus doubtless reported his scathing evaluation of Möller.

A few weeks later, Möller wrote Rudolf Mann, the director of the pharmaceutical department at Farbenfabriken Bayer, suggesting a meeting between Wheeling and Leverkusen. A longtime acquaintance of Möller's, Mann had been on the company's supervisory board since 1907. He acknowledged receipt of the letter, but did not mention Möller's proposal for a meeting.

Dismayed by the cold response, Möller wrote again on August 15, the day that the I.G. surrendered half its inventory of drugs, dyes, and other chemicals. Möller claimed that he was one of the few U.S. employees who had the company's true interests at heart. Everyone else in the New York office, he said, had only been looking out for themselves. But, he told Mann, "after the catastrophe was unavoidable, Fate has still been kind to you, inasmuch as these businesses have been secured by two concerns [Sterling and Grasselli] with which satisfactory arrangements are possible." To prove his point, he was going to Holland with Weiss in September; perhaps Mann would care to meet them.

Six days later, Möller sent a third, much angrier letter. He denounced his former colleagues in New York, who he believed had poisoned Mann's mind against him. Schweitzer was a "swindler, a virtuoso of mendacity"; Seebohm was "a business zero of rare perfection"; the two men hated each other, living "like cats and dogs." Moreover, von Salis, "however clever he might be in his subject [chemistry], was not a businessman." The whole group, Möller wrote, "was a refreshing mixture of vanity, jealousy, and envy, of conceit, self-promotion, and incompetence."

Möller cheered up a bit when he described Sterling's marketing practices. The Americans did not hesitate, he wrote, to spend $100,000 advertising a product in South America and $300,000 in the United States. A union between the two firms—Farbenfabriken Bayer, with its technological prowess, and Sterling, with its marketing expertise—would be a happy combination.

The alternative—no agreement—was infinitely worse. If the two sides could not come to terms, *two* Bayers would sell Aspirin, and maybe other products, in many countries. The two Bayers would fight endless legal battles, the probable result being a crazy quilt of ownership. Once export restrictions were lifted, Leverkusen would be able to sell its acetylsalicylic acid wherever it wanted, but in many countries it would not be able to sell Bayer Aspirin. In some places it could not sell anything called "Aspirin"; in the

United States and Canada, it could not sell anything named "Bayer." And all the while, there would be the other Bayer, no doubt using the Bayer Cross to adorn such horrors as California Syrup of Figs or Pope's Diapepsin. It would be a nightmare. Möller begged Mann to hear him out. On September 3, he sailed for Europe with William E. Weiss.

The agitated Möller at his side, Weiss went first to The Hague, where he met Rudolf Mann. Photographs of the time show Mann as a stolid-looking upper-middle-class burgher with a walrus mustache—someone who could easily make his skepticism clear. Weiss, a crackerjack salesman, did not beg for the technical assistance he so desperately needed. Instead, he grandly offered to let Leverkusen use Sterling as its new sales agent in the United States. Bayer Aspirin's sales were already increasing, he said, because of his skillful promotion. The Bayer name and the Bayer Cross looked terrific in Weiss's advertising. Sterling, he proffered magnanimously, was even willing to make the German company's drugs in Rensselaer—with a little assistance, of course. Weiss would handle the marketing, and Leverkusen would rake off a percentage. Everyone would win.

Listening to a stranger talk about using the Bayer name did not sit well with Mann. He was impressed by Weiss's firm, but looked down his nose at the man himself; the American, he wrote afterward, "makes a good impression" but finally is "just a businessman." But Mann could not change the situation, which "condemned [him] to impotence." Absent an arrangement with Sterling, which now held all rights, the United States was effectively closed to Leverkusen. In Latin America, too, the German company would be at a disadvantage.

Mann held but one card: Patent and trademark rights meant nothing if Sterling could not manufacture the products. Leverkusen, Mann said, would be able to help Winthrop. But in return it wanted a piece of the action—a joint venture. When Weiss demurred, Mann said that talks should be postponed until people from Germany could come to the United States. Weiss closed the meeting by expressing a desire to meet Carl Duisberg.

The meeting took place a few weeks later in Baden-Baden. No record survives, but it is inviting to picture the scene: Duisberg, the heavy, cultured, bombastic European, bald as an egg now but still vigorous; Weiss, the brazen American dynamo, a rich man who still spoke with a poor-boy country accent; each sizing up the other according to his lights. Duisberg was proud not to be "just a businessman"; Weiss was "just a businessman" and proud of it.

Duisberg regarded Sterling's purchase of the Bayer name as a kind of theft and wanted his property returned. Many people had synthesized acetylsalicylic acid over the years, but only one firm had created Bayer Aspirin. Little wonder that Duisberg wanted part of the U.S. market; he was just trying to get back his company's name. Weiss was not going to give it up—hardly a recipe for a successful long-term relationship.

Nevertheless, Duisberg and Weiss warily struck a deal. Weiss had refused to discuss the U.S. Aspirin business, but he agreed to assign Leverkusen half the profits from the ASA market in Latin America. In return, Duisberg gave Sterling uncontested use of the Aspirin and Bayer Cross trademarks in Latin America. And the Bayer Company, Sterling's ASA subsidiary, was allowed to manage the business.

Back in the United States, Weiss asked Livingston Gifford, the New York lawyer who had advised Farbenfabriken Bayer before the First World War, to examine the pact. On December 15, Sterling sent Leverkusen a new version of the agreement, with a few minor changes recommended by Gifford. Duisberg's assent was all that was required. It didn't come.

Having thought about the matter, Duisberg hardened his position: Either Leverkusen got some of the U.S. Aspirin business, or there would be no agreement. Weiss refused—steadfastly, completely, unflinchingly. His attorneys assured him that Leverkusen was over a barrel. Weiss owned the Bayer trademarks and patents outright. "When you, a stranger," the attorneys told Weiss,

> bought the stock, the [Bayer] company continued with all its legal rights, and with all the advantages those rights gave it, and, of course, without the slightest legal or moral obligation to exercise those rights in the interest of Leverkusen. . . .

Only by making an agreement with Sterling could Duisberg regain control of his company's name and its primal symbol, the Bayer Cross.

When the Germans invited Weiss to Leverkusen, he readily accepted, setting sail on March 20, 1920. Möller, who accompanied him, was not happy about the trip; he was "fed up on Europe." Joined in France by Walter Rowles, Sterling's English representative, and Carlos Austin, one of Möller's assistants, the party arrived in Cologne on April 7. To Weiss, who was overwhelmed by the factory at Rensselaer, the complex at Leverkusen must have been a shock: It was more than eleven times as big.

At every step Weiss saw a reminder of Duisberg's immense achievement. Thousands of workers, bustling river traffic, company clubs and societies, the extensive technical library—all were reflections of Duisberg's will. He lived in imperial fashion on the grounds of the plant, as if the hundreds of buildings were part of his back yard, along with the pools he had caused to be dug and the groves he had caused to be planted and the formal gardens he, had caused to be imported from Japan. In the large, factory-like labs that he had set up, platoons of workers walked from beaker to beaker, methodically dipping skeins of test yarn into each dye mixture and tabulating the results— research on such a vast scale that it was like a military operation. To monitor the explosion in scientific knowledge, Duisberg had bought the seven thousand books owned by the important chemist Friedrich August Kekulé von Stradowitz, and expanded the collection into what would become the biggest privately owned special library in Europe. The meetings with Weiss took place in the Great Hall of Leverkusen, a neoclassical monument surmounted by a frieze in the Greek style; on the huge front doors were brass handles embossed with the Bayer Cross. Mann, Korthaus, Otto Doermer (Leverkusen's corporate counsel), Richard C. Hennings (the former head of the English business), and several other Farbenfabriken directors sat at the table with Weiss, but the real sign of the conference's import was the presence of Duisberg himself.

The discussions were even more contentious than they had been the year before. Weiss began by brandishing the wartime letters that authorized Möller to buy Farbenfabriken Bayer's export business. Weiss knew that Möller had no legal power to make the sale, but he claimed that it allowed Sterling to supply Latin America with Aspirin and other products under the Bayer name. Mann retorted that Leverkusen's rights to those markets were intact and could be "reconquered" through sales of the original German product. Any deal on Latin American Aspirin, he said, must be part of a larger settlement that included North America.

Weiss backed off. He had brought up the letters to Möller only to show that Sterling meant business. A contract on North America, however, was impossible. Because the United States had never signed the Treaty of Versailles, it was still officially at war, and trading with the enemy was still a crime. Incredibly, the Office of the Alien Property Custodian was still seizing enemy assets. Weiss simply could not make a deal.

Mann and another director, Edmund Kloeppel, brushed aside Weiss's objections. An agreement on North America must be reached *today*, Kloeppel said. The Latin American agreement was only a beginning.

"It cannot be done," Weiss said.

Doermer warned that the German company could re-enter the United States under its own name, Bayer, and develop new patents and trademarks, perhaps even making a deal with another American firm. "We are not afraid," he said.

In return, Weiss fell back on his pledge to the Office of the Alien Property Custodian. He had to keep the company free of German influence: 100 percent American. The Leverkusen men were unimpressed, not least because the Grasselli Chemical Company, which purchased the Bayer dyestuffs business, had already consented to similar proposals. From this, Mann concluded that the impediments to a U.S. settlement were not insurmountable.

Unhappy, Weiss appealed to Möller and Rowles for their recollections of the meetings at The Hague and Baden-Baden. North America, he told the Germans, was never part of the deal. Ask Rowles! Ask Möller!

Throughout the day, Duisberg had sat in sphinxlike silence. Now he spoke passionately:

> The absolute condition for any agreement in Baden-Baden [he said] was agreement on the U.S. Everywhere in the whole world, except in the United States, people will say that we are the *right Bayer*. Laws say what they want; this situation contradicts global morality. . . . They can't use our prestige for their advantage. . . . That can't be bought, just as I cannot buy Herr Weiss. No money is good enough! We will risk it. . . . It is not a matter of money, but of our prestige. We still have honor in our heart! In South America, you will be the *fake Bayer* if there is no agreement.

Duisberg had elevated the discussion from business to morality. It was not just that his company was handicapped by having lost the right to its name. Weiss's use of Bayer was wrong, plain and simple. The meeting ended with both sides expressing regret over their inability to reach any understanding.

Weiss returned to Leverkusen a week later. Again the sessions were unproductive. With the talks at a standstill, Weiss and Rowles decided on April 19 to leave the next morning for Holland. Just as the meeting was about to end, Mann hammered out a rough accord: (1) The Latin American Aspirin agreement would go through as planned at The Hague but would be expanded to include profit sharing on all pharmaceutical products in Latin America; (2) the profits from the Winthrop business in the United States would be split equally; and (3) Leverkusen would get a sliding percentage of any cost savings achieved by its special assistance to the Bayer Company and Winthrop, especially improvements in the production of Aspirin.

After shaking hands on the deal, Mann promised to submit the arrangement to his board of directors the following morning. The board's decision would be telephoned to Weiss's party in Holland. When the phone rang, Weiss heard instead a request for further negotiations. The Sterling party made its third trek to Leverkusen. There Weiss was handed "minutes" of the previous discussions, which upon inspection contained a version of the proposed compact that he found unfamiliar. Suddenly, the cost-savings scheme was said to allow Leverkusen to "participate" in the U.S. Aspirin business; it would be Leverkusen, not New York, that would manage the Latin America business; and the trademarks in those countries would remain entirely in

German hands, with Sterling allowed to use them in advertising, but not in sales.

Weiss reacted to this ploy by storming out of Leverkusen. Möller stayed behind to see if anything could be salvaged. On April 22 he met again with Mann. With the abrasive Weiss out of the room, Mann backed down from his insistence that Leverkusen run the Latin American Aspirin trade, and agreed to grant Sterling a full license to the Bayer trademarks in those countries. The amount to be paid to Leverkusen for cost savings remained unresolved, but Möller and Mann assured each other that the two companies would refrain from further skirmishes until the final issues were addressed. An agreement in sight, Möller returned to New York—only to have Mann renege again.

Exasperated, Weiss sent Rowles and Möller to Europe in mid-July with what he called "a proposal so liberal that there can be no question in Leverkusen's mind that, ultimately, matters will work out to the satisfaction of both Leverkusen and ourselves." Sterling offered to split the Latin American Aspirin market 75–25, instead of 50–50, with Farbenfabriken Bayer getting the lion's share. After studying the proposition overnight, Mann declared that the new proposal was problematic—it had too many new features. Pessimistic, Rowles was dismayed by the Germans' tendency to "make greater demands in every conference, just as long as we shall show a tendency to answer them civilly. . . ." Rowles left Leverkusen on Tuesday, July 27, with the talks deadlocked.

For the second time, Möller stayed behind. Sympathizing with the Germans' awful position, he understood their hurt pride, their "extreme irritability." They were important people, and the war had reduced them to shadows. The men in the Great Hall, he explained later, could not shake "the feeling that the purchase of seized property is morally wrong." They hated dealing with Weiss, whom they regarded as little more than a thief—which was why, perhaps, Leverkusen kept reneging on pacts to which it had agreed. Without Weiss, Möller hoped, the Farbenfabriken Bayer board might give him a more sympathetic ear. But the Germans were not friendly. As soon as Möller was alone, they berated him. By letting the business fall into enemy hands, he had failed his "patriotic duty." He should have left the American branch in ruins rather than handing it to Sterling, intact and thriving. And then, once again, he learned that the firm was concerned with more than business—it wanted his loyalty. *Insisted* on his loyalty. If negotiations broke down, the board asked him, which side would he be on? Leverkusen or Wheeling, where did he stand?

Much had changed for Möller since the beginning of the war. Then, his feelings lay clearly with Germany. A foreigner in a hostile land, he had plotted with Seebohm to preserve Bayer's export business, massively advertised in Latin America to keep the company alive in the marketplace, and urged Leverkusen to contact Sterling after the Americans bought the Bayer company. But over time his loyalty had shifted. He had begun to like America and the American way of doing business. He was "fed up on Europe." "In my opinion," he wrote afterward, "there was only one answer to be given. . . ." His allegiance, he said, was to the export business, which was now owned by Sterling. His answer enraged most of the board. Ready to give up, Möller was convinced to stay in Leverkusen by Hennings and Mann. One final try, they said. On that last day, Möller managed a small compromise about the length of the Latin American trademark license—and suddenly barriers tumbled down.

When the dust settled, Sterling got most of what it wanted. The contract said nothing about the United States; it was restricted to Aspirin and Aspirin compounds; it covered all of Latin America except Cuba, which was the subject of a later contract; Sterling received an exclusive license to Leverkusen's Latin American trademarks; and the term of the contract was fifty years. In Leverkusen's favor, the 75–25 split of profits was retained. Finally, the Bayer Company of New York would sell no products in Latin America other than those covered in the contract (Aspirin and Aspirin compounds) without German consent.

After a final round of bickering, the contract was signed on October 28, 1920. Both companies must have breathed a sigh of relief, looking forward to a new era in Aspirin. Neither had a clue as to what it was really getting into.

CHAPTER FOUR

"SAID PRODUCTS"

Carlos Austin, Möller's lieutenant, journeyed from Manhattan to Mexico City a year after the Bayer auction to seek out counterfeit Aspirin. He was amazed by what he found. The pharmacies were full of fraudulent Aspirin, or, rather, Aspirina, the Spanish-language brand name. Many of the fakes were excellent—the tablets were stamped with the Bayer Cross, and the packages were identical to Bayer packages. Far from being covert, the scam was so well known that when Austin requested Aspirina one druggist asked if he wanted regular or counterfeit.

Austin should not have been surprised. Möller's advertising had created a big demand for analgesics. Because few Latin American companies made headache remedies, Sterling was free to charge more for its Aspirina than it did in North America, where it was restrained by competition. Just as had happened in the United States ten years before, the high price encouraged the sale of phony Aspirina. Some of it was high-quality stuff; other pills contained a little ASA and a lot of starch or anything else that was white and powdery.

Confusingly, some of the phony Aspirina was genuine. Many smugglers bought real, Leverkusen-made Bayer Aspirin in, say, Holland, shipped it over the Atlantic, and illegally sold it in Mexico for less than New York–made Bayer Aspirin. Sometimes this illegal real Aspirina sold for two-thirds less than legal real Aspirina. (Leverkusen had no interest in stopping this traffic; the Aspirin contract would not be signed for another year, and the two companies were still slugging it out.) If these secondhand sales could not be stopped, Möller moaned, it would lead to the "absolute demoralization of our price policy"—in other words, Sterling would have to charge less.

Many reports of bogus Mexican ASA came from Sterling's sales agent in the country, Kurt Niemann. Niemann had been Farbenfabriken Bayer's Mexico sales agent until the auction. Möller had had little choice about keeping Niemann on board: The agent had registered the Aspirin and Bayer trademarks in his own name, rather than that of his employer, making him their exclusive owner in Mexico. Niemann had repeatedly offered to sue counterfeiters on Sterling's behalf, but each offer was accompanied by a demand for payment of up to five thousand dollars. Möller sent Austin to Mexico to assess the situation.

Niemann told Austin that his investigations had uncovered the identity of a major counterfeiter, Carlos Basauri. Indeed, Niemann had gained Basauri's confidence by the clever expedient of assisting him in the fake Aspirina trade. Niemann was just waiting for the right moment to spring his trap. Austin didn't want to wait. Accompanied by detectives, he raided Basauri's factory. They found only an empty house—Basauri had fled. Inside, however, Austin discovered a trunk of incriminating letters. By grilling Basauri's family, the detectives learned the site of his hideout and arrested him. In custody, Basauri claimed that he was not the ringleader. The real mastermind, he said, was none other than Kurt Niemann, who had supplied Basauri with his tableting machines and his first shipment of acetylsalicylic acid. All the time Niemann had been complaining to New York that smugglers were selling real Aspirina under a name they didn't own, he had been selling fake Aspirina under a name he did own. Austin was skeptical until he learned that Niemann had absconded to Europe. Sterling sued Niemann *in absentia* for robbery.

Meanwhile, Austin visited the local German attaché, who was widely rumored to be involved in the ring. Denying any involvement, the diplomat instead fingered a second group of Leverkusen sales agents, this one led by a man named Federico Ritter. Austin persuaded Ritter to promise that Leverkusen would stop counterfeiting Sterling's trademarks in Mexico until June 30, 1920. Sterling would reciprocate, and not go after Leverkusen in the same period. Before a formal pact could be signed, Ritter received a message from Germany. Niemann had arrived in Leverkusen; they would never surrender the trademarks. Ritter backed out, Austin left in fury, and the Mexican trademark situation remained confused for years.

The 1920 Aspirin agreement did not stop the battle between Farbenfabriken Bayer and Sterling over the other German patents and trademarks. While the two firms were supposed to be negotiating an agreement to divide up the world on friendly terms, Weiss conquered half of it without waiting for Leverkusen's permission. Being what Duisberg called the *fake Bayer* put him in a powerful bargaining position. Every trademark suit, every registration, every package stamped with a "phony" Bayer Cross—they were like pinpricks, small jabs that Sterling thrust in from all directions, wearying the giant until it surrendered.

But even as Weiss attacked Farbenfabriken Bayer around the world, he suffered a major loss at home: the U.S. Aspirin trademark. The culprit was the United Drug Company, a drug wholesaler. It first purchased Aspirin powder from the Bayer Company in 1913, compressing it into tablets and selling it as "Aspirin, 5 grains, U.D. Co." United Drug continued to buy Aspirin and manufacture tablets until 1915, when the Bayer Company chose to make tablets itself and cut back sales of Aspirin powder. When the Aspirin patent expired in February 1917, United Drug re-entered the business, buying ASA powder from other newly legal manufacturers. As before, it labeled its ASA as "Aspirin, 5 grains, U.D. Co.," bringing a quick complaint from the Bayer Company, which still owned the Aspirin name. On March 3, 1917, United Drug petitioned the U.S. Patent Office to cancel the Aspirin trademark registration; two weeks later, the Bayer Company sued United Drug for trademark infringement.

Bayer's lawsuit was suspended on October 30, 1918, no doubt because the firm was about to be sold by the Office of the Alien Property Custodian. In the following March, just three months after the auction, the commissioner of patents granted United Drug's petition, and canceled the Aspirin trademark. This did not make Bayer's suit moot. It merely denied Sterling the Aspirin trademark under the specific statute governing trademarks. Sterling could still establish a common-law right to the trademark. The trial opened on this basis on May 17, 1920. The main issue was whether the old Bayer's treatment of the name "Aspirin" had signaled a *brand* of ASA or a *generic name* for ASA. If the latter was the case, Sterling would lose.

After a six-day trial, Judge Learned Hand ruled that the trademark Aspirin was well known to manufacturers and wholesalers, and that to them it indicated the product of the Bayer Company and not other makers of ASA. For sales of ASA to manufacturers and wholesalers, he awarded Sterling exclusive use of the Aspirin trademark. In Hand's view, however, the *public* treated Aspirin as a generic name, indicative of any ASA. He thus struck down the trademark on the consumer level. This meant that pharmacists had to buy, say, "United Drug Company Acetylsalicylic Acid," but could re-label the bottle as "United Drug Company Aspirin" if the firm asked them to. Unsurprisingly, Judge Hand's two-tiered Aspirin trademark never caught on, and Bayer lost its exclusive use of the term "Aspirin" in the United States. Bayer Aspirin was now only the Bayer brand of aspirin.

Hand's decision instantly deprived Sterling of a principal reason for buying Bayer—the U.S. trademark on Aspirin. The battle elsewhere correspondingly became more important. Weiss attacked Leverkusen's trademarks in Bolivia, Brazil, Nicaragua, Panama, Paraguay, and South Africa. He gained title to the Bayer Cross, the primal symbol of Farbenfabriken Bayer, in South Africa and India. In Australia he tried to register the Bayer Cross, only to discover that a German representative was doing the same thing. (Both were turned down.) In Mexico, a Leverkusen subsidiary got the trademarks from Niemann and tried to reclaim the market from Sterling. In Canada, the American Druggists Syndicate, with Leverkusen's support, petitioned the Exchequer Court to expunge Sterling's Aspirin trademark. The case went to the Supreme Court, where Sterling won on a technicality—Canadian law at that time had no mechanism to void trademarks.

One of the fiercest battles transpired in the United Kingdom, where Farbenfabriken Bayer had conducted business since 1878. In 1895, its English agent put together the Elberfeld Farbenfabriken Company, Ltd., which later changed its name to the Bayer Company, Ltd. The Bayer Company, Ltd., did not manufacture or even package any of the products it sold, but merely bought them from Leverkusen and resold them to the public.

In 1910 the English government ruled that the Bayer Company, Ltd., was only a shell, that Farbenfabriken Bayer itself, not its subsidiary, was truly conducting business in the United Kingdom, and that the German company as a whole was therefore fair game for the tax man. As a tax dodge, Leverkusen then repositioned its English branch as an ''independent'' company operating only in the United Kingdom. In the process, Leverkusen made the mistake it later made in the United States: It sold Bayer Company, Ltd., the British rights to the Bayer Cross.

War wrecked Leverkusen's British franchise just as surely as it did its American one. The English Board of Trade canceled the Aspirin trademark on February 5, 1915, and a year later it ordered the company to wind up its British affairs. With the trademark voided, anyone could now sell ASA as ''aspirin.'' Indeed, it was a patriotic duty for British drug makers to sell it under that name. ''The large army of aspirin consumers will now receive a British product,'' gloated *The Prescriber*, a Scottish pharmaceutical journal, ''and another stronghold of the enemy be destroyed.''

Unfortunately, shutting down Bayer Company, Ltd., also shut down the nation's supply of ASA. Few British firms produced the primary raw material, salicylic acid. The wartime phenol shortage drove prices up, and the promised aspirin did not appear. ''After eight months [of war],'' grumbled *The Prescriber*, ''all we have heard of the English manufactured product is a statement by the chairman of one of the largest hospitals that they had received the first consignment of 56 lbs. of English sodium salicylate [a chemical cousin to salicylic acid]—the mountain conceived and brought forth a mouse.'' The head of the Pharmaceutical Society of Great Britain admitted that making a little salicylic acid in the lab was ''child's play,'' but synthesizing it ''at the rate of a ton or more a week, that is a man's job.'' All British industry produced was pinkish powders, dirty crystals, muddy solutions, and high prices. In short, the English market for aspirin was wide open. Just the place for a patent medicine outfit from Wheeling, West Virginia.

In August 1919, Sterling asked the Board of Trade to let it buy the U.K. rights to the Bayer Cross and all other assets of Bayer Company, Ltd. The sale was approved in March 1920, and two months later Sterling became the registered owner of the trademarks. It now had exclusive control of the

Bayer name in the United States, Canada, the British Commonwealth, and parts of Latin America. Despite the agreement on Latin America that October, Leverkusen refused to recognize the validity of the British sale. Indeed, the Germans deliberately violated Sterling's newly purchased rights by selling their Bayer aspirin in England. Sterling threatened legal action. The Germans refused to back off. They had to begin a counterattack somewhere, and saw this as a good test case. In February 1922 Sterling filed for an injunction.

Mann and Hennings met with Weiss that May to talk about expanding their cooperation to cover products other than aspirin, thereby settling the growing battle over the Bayer Cross. The two Germans chose to harp, however, on what was not a sore subject: granting Leverkusen a portion of the U.S. aspirin business. "You can sympathize with us," Mann told Weiss later. "How painful it must be to us to renounce a share in the sale of this product, which, until further notice, overshadows all other products." If Sterling cut a deal on other drugs Leverkusen would stay out of the American aspirin market, which, Mann said threateningly, "we could take up immediately . . . in the name of Bayer."

Weiss did not fully respond until October, when he rejected Mann's claim that Leverkusen was responsible for aspirin's success in the United States. The way to go, Weiss insisted, was to marry forces: Leverkusen's new products and New York's marketing.

Think of what we are proposing, he told Leverkusen. In return for Leverkusen's know-how, Sterling was promising

> to eliminate from all the world, except as agreed upon, the activities of a company fully endowed with the right to use the name Bayer, with pharmaceutical equipment supplied by you, with ability and experience as a manufacturer and seller of medicinals, and with no covenants, legal or moral, to prevent it engaging in business anywhere in the world (except South America, Central America, and Mexico [where the 1920 contract applied]).

Sterling, he reiterated, would never let Leverkusen enter the U.S. aspirin market.

Mann, Duisberg, and Doermer came to New York in March 1923 for what both sides devoutly hoped would be a final round of negotiations. The talks lasted nearly two weeks. Weiss proposed a solution for the British situation: a new company, Bayer Products, Ltd. Capitalized by Sterling, Bayer Products, Ltd., would own all the trademarks and sell all of Leverkusen's drug and photographic products. The Germans would be allowed to buy some Bayer Products stock as quickly as that was politically feasible. Profits would be shared equally, and Leverkusen would ultimately manage the firm. The Germans resisted. They wanted more than partial ownership in the future. Weiss was conciliatory. I can offer no more, he said. Sterling had acquired the British trademarks with the stipulation that they never fall into German hands. Weiss could get around the vow, but it would take time. In the long run, Duisberg would get everything he wanted.

Weiss was conciliatory about Britain because he was shooting for the moon in the rest of the talks, which covered the long-awaited worldwide settlement on pharmaceutical and other chemical products. These would be made by Sterling's Winthrop Chemical Company—if Weiss could get Leverkusen to show him how to operate the factory in Rensselaer. The most important issue was the list of goods to be covered by the agreement. Weiss wanted the U.S. sales rights to every Leverkusen product except dyestuffs, which were already represented by the Grasselli Chemical Company. Sterling had the Bayer name for aspirin, Weiss said. Sterling should therefore have everything else produced at Leverkusen.

Impossible, said Duisberg, Mann, and Doermer. Leverkusen made fertilizers, lubricants, plastics, photographic films, pesticides, synthetic rubber—the entire chemical cornucopia. Sterling's theft of the corporate name was not going to force them into letting a peddler of patent medicines have exclusive rights to the repertoire of the world's finest chemical company. Duisberg wanted to restrict the agreement to pharmaceutical, agricultural, and possibly photographic products.

In the end, they came to terms. On April 9, 1923, Duisberg signed two contracts, one with Winthrop and one with the New York Bayer Company, and accepted a letter of undertaking from Sterling. As Duisberg wanted, Weiss won rights only to German pharmaceutical, agricultural, and photographic products, and any chemicals or substances used to make them. This list of goods—the chief point of argument—was referred to by the inelegant legal term ''said products.''

The first of the two contracts, the Winthrop contract, allocated the right to manufacture the said products. Winthrop got to make them in North America, where Leverkusen would provide technical help in return for half of the profits. Everywhere else was Leverkusen's territory. This was not a victory for Duisberg, because Weiss was uninterested in manufacturing. He wanted only the right to *sell* the said products and to sell them under the Bayer name. This was the subject of the second, more important contract, the Bayer Company contract. That contract gave the Bayer Cross to Weiss in the United States, Canada, Great Britain, Australia, and South Africa—the ''Weiss countries''—and assigned the Bayer Company the exclusive right to sell the said products in those nations. (The deal was slightly more complicated in Britain, where the two firms agreed to set up the new, jointly operated company Weiss had proposed.)* Sterling ceded control over the Bayer Cross to its original owner in the rest of the world—"Leverkusen countries"— except to sell aspirin in Latin America, as per the 1920 contract.

Finally, Sterling promised not to (1) use any of the Bayer trademarks on Sterling's own products, such as Danderine; (2) contest or use any other Leverkusen trademarks; or (3) sell any of the "said products" under the Sterling name.

It was a great day for Weiss. He had given in a little on the list of said products but won everything else. With the Bayer name as his fulcrum, he had been able to lever the acquisition of a factory he couldn't operate into a lock on the output of an industrial colossus. What need did he have for a global network of huge chemical plants? With Leverkusen's production at his disposal, Weiss had all the products he wanted without the headache of making them. The co-founder of Sterling Products seems not to have appreciated, however, that his ability to wrest concessions from Duisberg was due less to his crafty dickering than the German economy's abrupt self-destruction in the months before the contracts were signed.

Wars are extremely expensive, and nations rarely have the means on hand to pay for them. Typically governments get the cash by raising taxes, taking out loans, and printing money. In the days when currencies were tied to the value of gold, this last method meant leaving the gold standard. The inevitable result was a rise in domestic prices, unless they were capped by regulation. When wars ended, governments sought to return to the prewar "gold price" of the nation's currency.† Because the currency had inflated, returning to the gold price involved a deflation—taking money out of circulation, which increased the value of the currency by making it more scarce.

The Allied governments did exactly this following the war. A worldwide depression was the result. Between 1920 and 1921, industrial output fell 20 percent in the United States, 18 percent in the United Kingdom, and 11 percent in France. Unemployment jumped in all three countries. In the United States, the contraction was one of the worst in history. Wholesale prices fell by almost one-half from May 1920 to June 1921.

* More or less as Weiss had envisioned, Bayer Products Ltd., was incorporated on May 26, 1923. Diebold held almost all of the company's shares. On September 1, it contracted to give Leverkusen 50 percent of the English profits, in exchange for the exclusive right to sell Farbenfabriken Bayer products in the United Kingdom. Because Duisberg wanted a more secure stake in the company, Weiss promised to sell Leverkusen half the stock as "soon as circumstances make it politic to do so."

† Under a gold standard, a nation's central bank pledges to reimburse in gold anyone who wants to trade in currency. The gold price of currency is the official rate of exchange between gold and currency. For example, before the United States left the gold standard in 1971, the rate was $32 per ounce of gold, or $1/32$ ounce of gold per dollar.

Germany, which lost the war, stood in astonishing contrast. In the same period, its industrial production increased by a fifth, and unemployment fell. All the while, the nation did its level best to meet the Procrustean schedule of reparations demanded by the Allies at Versailles. Was the nation enjoying a postwar boom similar to that of Japan after the Second World War? No. The recovery was built on staggering infusions of money by the German central bank. This, as economists say, stimulated demand—money poured into the economy, and people spent it like mad. But the money kept flooding in so fast that the German economy went beyond stimulation, and roared toward the surreal state known as "hyperinflation."

By January 1922, the nominal cost of living was twenty times the prewar level. Initially, wages and salaries increased as well, and families did not suffer. A house might cost twenty times as much as it had ten years before, but if a worker's salary also went up by a factor of twenty, the real cost of living was no different. When inflation rose from 20 percent a year to 20 percent a month, the situation changed—money itself began to lose value. If bills were worth less every second they stayed inside a wallet, people naturally spent their cash as soon as they got it. They spent it on practically anything, for anything was better than having money. Unlike a mark, a chair would still be a chair, and not 50 percent of a chair, after a month. Germans embarked on a spending spree, which simply added to the inflation.

At about the same time, the committee overseeing German reparations announced a shortfall in some of the scheduled deliveries. The most important was in coal, which came from the Ruhr valley, near Belgium. Under the authority of the Treaty of Versailles, French and Belgian troops marched into the Ruhr in January 1923. The German government ordered civil servants to engage in passive resistance, disrupting commerce in the area. France retaliated by cutting off the Ruhr from the rest of Germany and the world. Leverkusen was in the middle of the occupied zone.

Duisberg and the I.G. board were rocked by the combination of hyperinflation and occupation. Leverkusen considered the trademark fight in England to be of utmost importance; it was a necessary counterpoint to the negotiations with Sterling, a way of impressing Weiss with the seriousness of its intent to stop and reverse the American's global expansion. Yet the chemical combine was in such poor shape that it could not afford a long legal battle. The economic collapse, a Leverkusen attorney later admitted, "made it almost impossible for us to conduct a number of lawsuits in the currencies of foreign countries." Unable to prosecute, Duisberg, Mann, and Doermer had no choice but to capitulate to Sterling.

Worse was yet to come. In April, Sterling and Farbenfabriken Bayer wrapped up the 1923 agreements. In May, German prices doubled; in July, they quintupled. The mark was so unstable that German firms did their accounts in foreign currency. State and local governments, industrial associations, chambers of commerce, businesses, and anyone else who could get away with it issued private scrips, which circulated freely—they were just as worthless as real money. In July, inflation was nearly 1,500 percent. Thousand-mark notes were replaced by million-mark notes, and millions by billions. To keep up with the need for ever-higher denominations, the government used forty-one money presses, printing night and day at a rate of about seventeen billion marks an hour.

It was a time in which money had ceased to function. Ordinary transactions became absurdly difficult. Stores marked their prices on chalk slates, changing them hourly. People paid off mortgages for the price of a pack of cigarettes. A bag of money bought a loaf of bread; a trunk of money bought a bus ticket—unless, as happened in Berlin, the driver told one man with a suitcase full of currency that he needed to bring on a second suitcase of cash to buy a ticket for the first. A man named Laurent Meyer, living near Strasbourg, inherited two thousand marks during the First World War. At prewar rates of exchange, it was worth more than five hundred dollars. Because the estate was not wound up until September 1923, when prices were rising 24,000 percent a month, the inheritance had shrunk to the equivalent of 0.0036 cent. In early October, a single egg cost eighteen million marks; five days later, it cost seventy million. Armed robbers in Berlin accepted only dollars and pounds, in one case returning a walletful of marks with a scornful "Thank you! We don't bother ourselves with those anymore!" On November 11, 1923, the first trillion-mark note was issued, shortly followed by notes for two, five, ten and a hundred trillion. They were printed on one side only. What you could buy for 1 mark before the war cost 1,250,000,000,000 marks by the end of 1923.

The government finally controlled hyperinflation in the only way possible: It abandoned the mark and created a new German currency, the rentenmark. For a short period of time, the old and new marks circulated side by side, with the former vanishing in early 1924. The rentenmark was a bridge between the old mark and the establishment of stronger controls over the central bank. In the autumn of 1924, a second central bank, the Reichsbank, and a third currency, the reichsmark, were established. With this, the German economy returned to a semblance of normality.

The country awoke as if from a dream. Accountants at Leverkusen picked up their pens and started keeping the records they had abandoned in the time when money meant nothing. The Community of Interests in the German chemical industry resumed planning for the future. In April 1924, Duisberg became the chairman of the I.G. General Council, the so-called council of the gods. The year of confusion in 1923 had brought changes in German law that made a further union financially attractive. That October, he urged the creation of a central management company to coordinate sales and investments. He backed off from the idea of a full merger, thinking that the years had shown it was impossible. Carl Bosch, head of B.A. & S.F., argued instead for a complete fusion—Duisberg's original vision. To Duisberg's amazement, the General Council voted to support the plan it had rejected before. At a two-day meeting at Duisberg's mansion in November, Duisberg and Bosch fought over the form of the merger. Duisberg wanted every detail planned in advance; Bosch wanted the companies to sort out problems as they came. Tensions ran so high that after dinner with the Duisberg family, Bosch and his allies shut themselves up in the downstairs bar. Duisberg and his supporters stayed in the billiards room, and mediators ran up and down the stairs between them. When Bosch won the vote, Duisberg was shattered. He resigned his chair, and was succeeded by Bosch. Before leaving, Bosch made a gesture of reconciliation, offering an important job in the new I.G. to Duisberg's son, Curt. But the two men still didn't see eye to eye, and the merger was delayed for almost a year while they settled their differences. On September 15, 1925, the six companies of the old I.G. announced the union. The fusion was actually accomplished on December 12 when B.A. & S.F. bought the other firms' stock and changed its name to Interessengemeinschaft Farbenindustrie Aktiengesellschaft: I.G. Farben AG.*

Few companies have been more lavishly reviled than I.G. Farben. Accounts of its perfidy make up a measurable portion of the books on the Second World War, and there is even an informal society of scholars, the I.G. Farben Group, devoted to understanding its history. At its height, the I.G. made dyes, insecticides, munitions, drugs, fertilizers, electrochemicals, acids, glass, nitrogen, photographic materials, coal, lignite, synthetic gasoline, and thousands of other things. For years, trade magazines like *Chemical and Metallurgical Engineering* and *L'Industrie chimique* and *Swensk Kemisk Tidskrift* published bewildering charts of its structure, with dozens of branches splitting into categories ranging from banks and insurance to mining and explosives. The I.G. was based in Frankfurt am Main, but its regional offices and plants were scattered in scores of German towns, including Leverkusen, which remained the center of drug production. The capitalization of this myriad enterprise quickly grew from its original 646 million marks ($153.7 million) in 1925 to 1.1 billion marks ($261.8 million) in 1926. By then it was the biggest commercial enterprise in Europe and the fourth largest in the world.

*   *   *

Sterling had little understanding of the metamorphosis that was taking place in Germany. Weiss had never dealt with Leverkusen's confederates, and was

---

* Oddly, the merger changed I.G. Farben's legal status—it was no longer an *Interessengemeinschaft*. Its use of "I.G." was as if an unincorporated business insisted that "Inc." was part of its name. Under German law this was illegal, and the I.G. had to wrest approval for its name from the German Supreme Court.

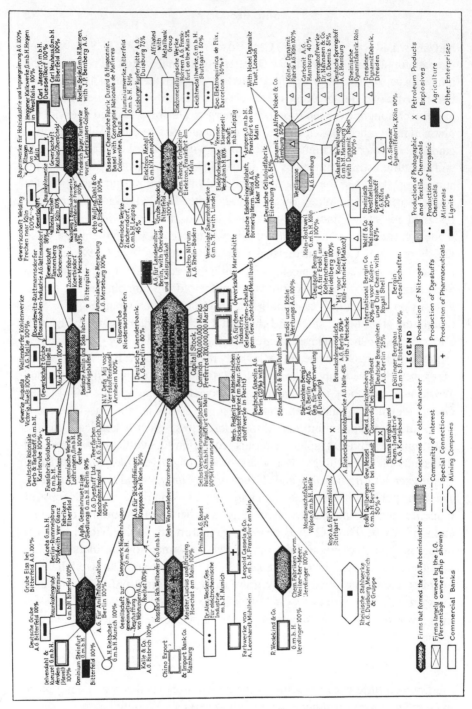

The sheer scale of I.G. Farben terrified its competitors. When *Chemical and Metallurgical Engineering*, a U.S. trade magazine, published this near-incomprehensible chart in January 1928, it only confirmed the American chemical industry's sense of foreboding. The chart was incomplete in one detail: it did not show the I.G.'s involvement with Winthrop.

even surprised when the combine as a whole had to pass muster on the 1923 contracts. In December 1925 he received a brief note informing him of the fusion. Wondering what this might mean, he consulted Edward S. Rogers, a renowned intellectual property lawyer. Rogers had little idea—he was unacquainted with the intricacies of German corporate law. One thing, he said, was certain: The old, familiar Farbenfabriken vorm. Fried. Bayer & Co. was no more. Aside from that, it was all a mystery. Rogers could only pose a series of questions concerning Leverkusen's new status:

> Was it [what] in the United States would be called a merger? Or was a holding company formed which acquired all the . . . capital stocks of the companies . . . , or was the plan one by which the plants and assets of all or some of the various companies were sold to the I.G.?

There seemed no doubt, Rogers thought, that the 1920 and 1923 covenants were still valid for Leverkusen products. The more interesting question was whether the contracts could be interpreted as applying to the products of the other I.G. firms and to new products developed by the I.G. If that was the case, Weiss would have parlayed his aspirin investment into a corner on the American sales of the world's fourth-largest company—an incredible return on his initial investment. It was, Weiss thought, an interesting notion.

Weiss and Rowles went to London in the first days of 1926 to confer with McKenna & Company, the solicitors for Bayer Products, Ltd. At about the same time, H. G. Bertram of Sterling visited Cologne to consult with a lawyer named Stroehmer, whom McKenna & Company had recommended to Weiss as one of the most eminent barristers in Germany.

Stroehmer's words were stunning. The entire I.G., he said, had inherited the legal obligations of its constituent parts. The "said products" therefore could not be subdivided into a group of "old," pre-fusion products and "new," post-fusion products. In other words, a gigantic plum had fallen into Weiss's lap: He had the legal right to "said products" from *all* the I.G. companies. What remained was to convince I.G. Farben of the correctness of this view.

Weiss, Bertram, Stroehmer, and Frederick A. S. Gwatkin of McKenna & Company went to Leverkusen that January to meet with Mann and Doermer. When Weiss demanded the right to sell "said products" from the entire combine, Mann made a counteroffer. If Sterling gave the I.G. complete control of Winthrop, he said, the combine might be willing to deal. Doermer argued that a recent German Supreme Court judgment threw doubt onto Weiss's position. Stroehmer scoffed at this suggestion. The two lawyers huddled—and Doermer came out admitting that Sterling, in fact, did have the I.G. over a barrel.

Back in New York, Weiss allowed himself the pleasure of gloating. "It seemed to us and still seems to us now," he told his board, "that Leverkusen and the I.G. have gotten themselves into a rather uncomfortable position."

As before, the Germans raised new demands when the agreement seemed settled. On May 19, Mann informed Weiss that the I.G. was having a few problems with the idea of giving Winthrop the full line of "said products." This could be resolved, Mann wrote, if New York agreed to grant the I.G. a share of the U.S. aspirin business. Weiss stood his ground. "As far as aspirin is concerned," he said, "there [can] be no consideration given to including it in any new arrangement. . . ." If Leverkusen continued to insist on it, he would cut off negotiations. Sterling would pursue its legal rights to the "said products" along some other avenue.

Mann backed down quickly. The pact was acceptable in its present form, although he still hoped Sterling could someday join with the I.G. In return for getting what he wanted, Weiss went out of his way to be magnanimous. At last breaking his pledge to the Office of the Alien Property Custodian, he awarded I.G. Farben 50 percent of Winthrop's stock, in place of 50 percent of Winthrop's profits. It was a fateful step. The change did not affect the I.G.'s balance sheet—it would receive Winthrop's dividends instead of its profits. But the German company now *owned* half of Winthrop. And that put Sterling in clear violation of the spirit, and perhaps the letter, of its agreements with the American and British governments. But to Weiss the game was worth the risk. On November 15, he signed a contract that opened a vast array of I.G. products to the former horse-and-buggy operation from Wheeling, West Virginia.

Aggressive and brash, Weiss was uncharacteristically hesitant in his relations with Germany—he may have outbargained the I.G., but he was still awed by the cartel. "He was always a guy from Wheeling, West Virginia," one of his co-workers said later. "You have to understand that about him—he was a small-town guy, suddenly playing in the big leagues." The more he went abroad, the more he treasured the respect of his German colleagues. He liked the Great Hall at Leverkusen, with its columns and gilt bas-relief. It was a treat to be surrounded by the fine china and high filigreed ceilings and silent waiters around the marble fountain in the Bayer guesthouse across the street. In an inevitable Balzacian process, he was seduced by the sheer respectability, social and intellectual, of that world; he measured himself against a man like Duisberg, and found himself wanting. He may have won the fight, but he was also being won over.

The contrast between the two headquarters was sharp. The river land bought by Duisberg three decades before had been almost filled up; every day, a stream of workers filled the broad avenues, and in hundreds of buildings products began their march to distant markets. Duisberg's taste for formal organization was everywhere. People met constantly, and memos, letters, and minutes were numbered, dated, and filed in a great archive. Every piece of correspondence issued by the company had to be signed twice; the writer signed on the right, and the left-hand signature belonged to the person charged with catching the flak if something went wrong. Only Mann and a few others could sign by themselves. Despite Duisberg's personal flair, the company lobbied rather than advertised, contacting establishment figures rather than marketing to the public; it did little to alert the citizenry to its presence, and always stressed its record as a responsible corporate citizen.

By contrast, Sterling's Manhattan headquarters consisted of an architecturally undistinguished twelve-story building in the factory area north of Wall Street. The executive suites were curiously empty. Weiss occupied a suite of rooms on the top floor, but spent much time at his old office in Wheeling—his family had never moved. Diebold worked separately, in an office on Park Avenue; people at Sterling hardly saw him. There were few meetings. When Weiss was out of town, his secretary, an imposing woman known only as Miss Briton, spoke for him. Hard-nosed and unforgiving, Miss Briton was regarded by some as Weiss's *éminence grise*. "Certainly she didn't do filing," one employee said later. "The place was always a mess."

It is little wonder that Weiss was gratified in August 1928 when the cartel notified him that he had been awarded an honorary doctorate from the University of Cologne. Three of the university's directors—Rudolf Mann, Otto Doermer, and O. van Höffer, all I.G. men—presented the degree at a champagne banquet in the Biltmore Hotel in New York City. The crepuscular banquet room was filled with the strains of *"Nach der Heimat Wieder."* Among the attendees were Diebold, McClintock, Emanuel von Salis, and Walter Duisberg (one of Carl's sons and a rising power in the company). Wearing black robes, Weiss made a speech in drugstore Latin. Otherwise the elaborate ceremony was entirely in German, a language in which Weiss remained obdurately incompetent until the end of his days. Nonetheless, Weiss grasped the main point: He insisted forever after upon being called "Doctor Weiss."

Max Wojahn had a big map of Latin America tacked to his office wall. Möller's lieutenant and successor as head of the Bayer Company export department, Wojahn was cut from the same stripe. A German emigré, he was a salesman first and foremost, with a salesman's drive and a salesman's optimism. Stuck into his map were tiny colored pins showing the location of the many local I.G. subsidiaries, which came to be known generally as the "Quimicas," because most had the words "Quimica Bayer" in their name. Because of the Sterling-I.G. contracts, Quimica employees served two masters: Under the direction of the I.G., they marketed German prescription drugs, the profits from which went solely to the I.G.; and under the direction of the U.S. Bayer Company—that is, Max Wojahn—they marketed aspirin under a variety of brand names and forms, the profits from which were split between the Bayer Company and the I.G. as set out in the 1920 contract. Though the Quimicas were only partly under his direction, Wojahn thought of them as his own. He was not discouraged by the sparseness of the pins on his huge map of Latin America. In the great forests of the Amazon delta and beyond he saw a continent full of people who did not yet buy aspirin.

The aspirin business in Latin America had faced formidable obstacles, especially from infringers. On the market was a single legitimate product: a tube of twenty tablets, each pill stamped with the Bayer Cross. These were sold to druggists throughout the continent by traveling salesmen, who rode on mules and horses to remote pharmacies to dispense the gospel of analgesia. Because many villagers could not afford the full tube, the *farmacistas* often sold the pills in bags of two or three. And often—or so Bayer salespeople believed—they stuck non-Bayer ASA in these packets.

To rectify matters, Sterling created its own packets of one or two tablets, which even the poorest headache sufferer could buy. And it concentrated on one of Leverkusen's less easily copied products, Cafiaspirina, a mixture, one Sterling employee said later, of "aspirin and a little caffeine to make you feel the whole thing was worthwhile." Most important, the firm increased advertising by every means available—newspapers, billboards, posters, newsreels, printed flyers, placards on streetcars, and, later, radio. It blanketed the continent with what the export department claimed was the biggest and most efficient traveling sales force ever assembled in Latin America. Advertising costs shot up to more than a fifth of total sales, a level unknown before the war.

What had taken place earlier in the United States happened again in the Southern Hemisphere: People saw the posters or heard the radio programs or watched the newsreels, thereby learning that a small white tablet could eliminate headaches, cure arthritis, and wipe out the flu. (In fact, aspirin cannot do the last two, but it sufficiently eases inflammation and fever to make people with arthritis or flu feel a lot better.) It is hard to imagine today what someone in a remote village must have felt like when, for the first time, a brain-killing headache was charmed away by a pill. As one Sterling memo later gushed, "Even the illiterates who formerly never would have thought of using a pharmaceutical product, became customers of the drugstores."

From the signing of the 1920 contract to the end of the decade, Latin American sales of Cafiaspirina and other Bayer aspirin products tripled, rising to more than $4 million per annum. Cooperation between the I.G. and Sterling lowered costs—after 1923 the two companies used a single sales force of Quimica employees. In addition, the export department constantly raised the price of Cafiaspirina. Still people kept buying. By 1929, Latin American consumers were swallowing 330 million tablets—100 tons of aspirin—each year, and the profit margin was a whopping 39 percent. Profits had outpaced sales, skyrocketing by a factor of eight during the decade. It was, Wojahn said, "an almost miraculous development."

The Latin American aspirin trade was of particular importance to I.G. Farben. In 1925 the I.G. companies earned a combined profit of $16.1 million, 5 percent of which—more than $800,000—came from Latin American aspirin; four years later, I.G. profits had grown to $24.9 million, of which Latin American aspirin brought in $1.25 million.* In the years that followed, aspirin sales did not quite keep up with I.G. sales, but ASA remained a cash cow for the combine. As a result, the trust found it frustrating to cede management of the aspirin business to the Bayer Company export department. The Quimicas marketed I.G. prescription drugs under the sole direction of the combine. The marketing of aspirin, however, was under the direction of Sterling. Gallingly, Mann was supposed to sit on his hands while Weiss and Wojahn dictated budgets, bought advertising, and hired sales personnel in this enormously profitable business—a business, moreover, that sold a product invented by his company using his company's trademark, the Bayer Cross. Little wonder that he could not resist filling memos about ASA shipments with suggestions and orders! Wojahn and Möller were annoyed, especially when Mann countermanded their instructions. Leverkusen's every action, Möller protested, had the object of "show-[ing] as often as possible that, on the basis of their 75 percent participation in the profits, the final decision rests with them at all times." He complained with such bile that late in 1926 Mann demanded that "the correspondence be conducted in the usual matter-of-fact way." In response, Wojahn apparently threatened to quit.

At an edgy conference in Leverkusen the following May, Weiss told Mann that the I.G. was "absolutely wrong in attempting to interfere with management by New York." The I.G., Mann said blandly, was not interfering. It was merely offering "helpful suggestions." He was unable to recall an example of actual *interference*. Wojahn retorted that Leverkusen was issuing orders to his agents. Mann "could hardly believe this to be the case." Another director at the meeting "could not recall a single instance where Leverkusen had written to agents in matters relative to aspirin." Wojahn offered to produce several such instances from his files. Mann promised not to do it again. But, of course, he did.

To Wojahn, the interference was all the more insufferable for the Germans' habitual timidity. In the mid-1920s, for example, the Quimica in

---

* The other contracts with Sterling were also important to I.G. Farben. In 1929 the total profits from all Sterling contracts were $2.69 million, or more than 10 percent of I.G.'s profits.

Argentina suggested that Wojahn stop pushing aspirin. The Argentine market was saturated, Buenos Aires said. Per capita consumption of the stuff having exploded, further growth was inconceivable. Leverkusen agreed—people could only consume so much aspirin. Wojahn was determined to prove them both wrong. He increased ad spending. And then increased it again. And then again. By 1930, business in Argentina had tripled. Moreover, the growth had occurred at the same time as the successful launch of a competitor, Geniol. The market was far from being glutted, Wojahn crowed to Weiss. Sterling should never ''make the mistake of being satisfied with looking back to what we have already accomplished and of believing that we cannot go much further.'' Their overwhelming success meant only that it was time to push deeper, into the few regions on Wojahn's map where the pins were still scarce.

CHAPTER FIVE

"A POSITIVE MENTAL ATTITUDE TOWARD THE PRESENT REGIME"

The night was foggy and cold. Bundled up against Leverkusen's winter chill, Carl Duisberg turned a switch—and a huge glowing circle sprang to life between two factory smokestacks. Two hundred and thirty-six feet in diameter, the circle was made from 2,200 light bulbs strung on wire. Inside, in letters twenty feet tall, the lights spelled out B-A-Y-E-R, once horizontally, once vertically, the two Bayers intersecting at the central Y. At night the sign was visible for miles, and instantly recognizable—the biggest advertisement in the world. "As the Southern Cross gives direction and hope to the mariner," a proud Duisberg told the assembled crowd, "may this 'Western Cross' in the heart of German industry shine out . . . as a symbol of our courage and our confidence."

Courage and confidence were sorely needed that evening. Just hours earlier, two I.G. executives had been among the elite corporate delegation that met with the nation's new chancellor, Adolf Hitler. Most German executives had long regarded Hitler and his Nationalsozialistische deutsche Arbeiterpartei—the NSDAP, or Nazis—as an annoyance. That changed when Germany was swept up in the worldwide slump that followed the crash of the U.S. stock market in October 1929; as banks failed, factories closed, and breadlines lengthened, the NSDAP attracted votes. After Hitler was appointed chancellor, business realized that it would have to deal with him, and arranged a meeting for February 20, 1933. The I.G. Farben deputation was led by Georg von Schnitzler, head of dye production. Like the others at the session, he was a powerful man, and expected to be heard out. Instead Hitler spoke for ninety minutes without interruption. The subject was recent German history, which he depicted as a struggle between the forces of creativity and decay. Only the NSDAP, he said, could save the nation from the Red peril. To the industrialists in the room, this was familiar stuff. The führer, however, added a new twist: If the Nazis did not win the parliamentary election on March 5, they would launch a civil war. Faced with this ultimatum, the businessmen attempted to leave. They were not permitted to depart. Hermann Göring, president of the Reichstag, the German parliament, wished to speak. The NSDAP, he said, was short of money to continue the campaign for decency. He suggested that business might bear a portion of the burden. In return, the Nazis would ensure the domestic tranquillity necessary for the orderly conduct of trade. The price of tranquillity was three million marks.

As countless rich, powerful people have done in similar situations, the industrialists caved in to the shakedown with a minimum of argument. Schnitzler had no authority to spend money, and so left without promising anything. He spoke to Carl Bosch, who gave the Nazis four hundred thousand marks on February 27 without informing the supervisory board.

The Reichstag building burned to the ground the next morning. With flames shooting out the windows, a Dutch vagrant was found alone in the building. The vagrant had been affiliated with the communists. Today it is assumed that the Nazis stage-managed the incident, but then the outcry against Reds was enormous. Angry mobs clamored in the streets. Shops were looted. Gunfire crackled. All in all, the environment was not conducive to long-term investment. After a coalition led by the NSDAP won control of parliament, Bosch gave another one hundred thousand marks to the party's allies. The I.G.'s total donation of half a million marks was the biggest made by any firm.

Bosch made his contribution warily. Hitler's social, political, and racial views had certain identifiable economic components, and Bosch did not think much of them. On the whole, Hitler thought, industrialization was bad, because it squeezed out the yeoman farmers he regarded as central to the nation. (His focus on agriculture was unfortunate for a land-poor nation that was heavily urbanized.) Foreign trade too was untrustworthy. Firms like the I.G. ended up swapping manufactured goods for foreign foodstuffs, a process that he thought left Germany at the mercy of bankers, most of whom, Hitler believed, were Jewish and therefore detestable. Moreover, sales to other countries would fall as those nations industrialized, foreign competition arose, and German companies established factories abroad. Decline was the ineluctable result for any country foolish enough to depend on foreign trade. Hitler had no intention of seeing Germany decline. Believing in the survival of the fittest, he naturally regarded economic competition as nature's way. But, as the historian Peter Hayes dryly put it, "a glance at Germany's industrial elite convinced the führer that the free play of economic forces did not unfailingly elevate the fittest to prominence." Rather than trust capitalists to return Germany to its former glory, Hitler thought that somebody should take charge. That somebody was himself.

Hitler moved to implement Nazi ideology with a speed that is startling even today. On May 1, he announced a Four-Year Plan—the first of two, neither of which lasted four years—that provided for a big public works program, a tax credit for business investments, and a bonus of one thousand marks for newly married couples, provided that the wife did not work. Quickly the country was militarized, with factories swept up into a civil defense program. The stock market, the bond market, and the market for foreign exchange were subjected to tough government control.

The NSDAP besieged Jews. In posters, newspaper articles, radio addresses, and official pronouncements, Jews were berated, ridiculed, demonized. Companies were not supposed to hire Jews, sell to Jews, buy from Jews, or borrow money from Jews. Nazi employees monitored their bosses' compliance, reporting foot draggers to the omnipresent NSDAP. The idea was to exclude the Jewish population from the rest of the nation's social and economic life—to reduce them to a status perhaps comparable with that of blacks under apartheid.

For I.G. Farben this atrocious policy had practical as well as moral difficulties; the combine had many important Jewish employees, including four members of the managing board. Moreover, anti-Semitic attacks had led to calls for boycotts of certain German goods—calls that alarmed the pharmaceutical department.* The I.G. could not, as Hayes remarked, "calmly contemplate the prospect of a cycle of persecutions and foreign reprisals." At the same time it did not want to pick a fight with the government.

Bosch was vulnerable to NSDAP pressure. Early in his career, he had helped invent an innovative process for turning coal into synthetic gasoline. After a pilot project showed commercial promise, he plunged the I.G.—over Duisberg's objections—into the construction of a huge synthetic gas plant in the town of Leuna, sixty miles southwest of Berlin. The project went hundreds of millions of marks over budget. At the General Council meeting in June 1929, Bosch reported a rate of production less than half what he had forecast at the beginning. In 1931, when Bosch's process won him a Nobel Prize, the Leuna plant finally achieved its production goal of one hundred thousand tons a year. In the meantime, new oil reserves had been found in the Middle East. The price of ordinary, nonsynthetic gasoline fell to five pfennigs a liter. Synthetic Leuna gas cost forty pfennigs a liter, eight times as much. Bosch had created one of the biggest industrial white elephants in Europe. The combine desperately wanted help from the government.

As a result, I.G. Farben responded equivocally to Nazi racism, at least in the beginning. Prodded by Hitler's minions, the I.G. continued to contribute

* Sterling held a special staff meeting on October 20, 1933, to deal with the rising number of questions about its German connections. It decided to stonewall. From that point on, questions would be answered by the simple statement that Winthrop was owned by Sterling Products, an American concern, and that its preparations were made in the United States.

to the party, giving more than nineteen million marks between 1933 and 1939. A few executives joined the NSDAP; others worked to ingratiate themselves with party moderates. They imagined themselves rewarded when Hitler's insistence on self-sufficiency led him to support the price of Leuna-produced gasoline. Bosch held his nose and accepted an offer that promised to salvage the fiasco that was the single biggest mark of his tenure at the top of the I.G. An agreement of Faustian import was signed in December 1933, when the Nazis promised to buy all of Leura's output at a high price. Three years later, Leuna was flourishing.

The I.G. did not completely give in to the Nazis. Bosch tried to protect Jewish employees, sending them abroad when possible. And he publicly assailed the attempt to Nazify science, which included Göring's bizarre campaign against vivisection (he thought testing drugs on animals was "Jewish science"). In 1933 the minister of justice proposed executing any German who "communicates abroad an invention . . . which is of essential value to the national defense." Heavy penalties would be levied on people who "pass on to others" matters "essential . . . to the preservation of trade or operational secrets of national importance." The I.G. pointed out that publishing a patent involved passing on information, and that the law therefore would make it impossible to patent discoveries. Ultimately the combine managed to delay the restrictions.

Wilhelm Mann, Rudolf's son, believed that I.G. Farben's only hope for survival lay in getting along with the Nazis. He was a First World War veteran, a patriot, a devoted husband, a passionate exponent of the moral obligations of the pharmaceutical industry. For twenty years he was a low-level I.G. functionary, never allowed to sign a letter alone. In 1929 he replaced his father as head of pharmaceutical sales, becoming one of the seven Leverkusen directors and Weiss's main contact. He liked the American's vigor and warmth, and the two men became friends. Seeing the depression rack his country, Mann flirted with the Nazi party, joining and resigning in 1932. He rejoined right after the election of March 1933. (Mann was just in time. In May, the NSDAP announced that it would no longer take new members.)

When Hitler warned that measures against the Jews would increase if complaints from overseas did not die down, Mann was one of many Germans who told foreigners that the NSDAP was not violent or anti-Semitic. Far from being chaotic, Mann wrote to Max Wojahn, Germany was "*one of the quietest countries of Europe.*" Some Jewish businesses had been attacked, he admitted, but

> the security of everyone is guaranteed in every way, and no one, including political opponents and Jews, suffers any injury. . . . We therefore urgently ask you, immediately on receipt of this letter, to contribute

to the spread of *information as to the actual facts* in a manner in which you deem best . . . either by personal visits to the leading personages of your country and to the editors of influential papers, or by circulars to physicians and customers . . . in all the lying tales of horror *there is not one word of truth*.

Mann told Weiss that the new government "was a clearly noticeable change for the better," because "prominent moderate elements" within it would "*desist from making commercial experiments*"—that is, the NSDAP would not interfere with business. But even as he wrote those words, Mann was struggling against Nazi interference with business.

In 1930 the I.G. had transferred its Winthrop stock to the American I.G. Chemical Corporation, a U.S. subsidiary set up the year before to handle products not covered by the contracts with Sterling. The I.G. sent no record of the stock transfer to Germany. Sterling then paid the I.G.'s share of Winthrop dividends to American I.G., which banked it in the United States or Switzerland, keeping the money from prying eyes in the NSDAP. In 1934 Mann decided that the arrangement was not secret enough. He asked Sterling to change the payments into a vaguely described "service fee" of fifty thousand dollars. (The correspondence was covert, with both sides mailing letters through the Danish consul in Cologne.) Reluctantly—the fee would be taxable at the American end—Sterling agreed. By 1936, Weiss was personally slipping checks to Mann during their semiannual conferences in New York. The check was handed over without a cover letter; Mann did not want the NSDAP to know that the same man who assured foreigners the party would desist from commercial experiments was making one of his own.

The Great Depression had a devastating effect on Sterling's money machine in Latin America. Aspirin sales fell by one-half from 1929 to 1933; profits sank to one-fourth their pre-depression level. It was a disaster.

To Max Wojahn, the solution was simple: *Increase advertising*. With sufficient advertising, he thought, the depression-wracked masses of Latin America could be persuaded to resume their purchases of Cafiaspirina—and Wojahn intended to provide sufficient advertising. Out into the countryside fanned a squadron, some eighty strong, of Quimica Bayer agents, each driving a truck equipped with loudspeakers blaring the wonders of Cafiaspirina. As time went by, the sound trucks were replaced by Junior Sound Cars equipped with sixteen-millimeter movie projectors. The sides of each truck unfolded into an improvised stage, onto which the agent climbed. A Cafiaspirina banner drooped above his head. Spectators gaped as the salesman played a gramophone, or perhaps sang some tunes; when the crowd was big enough, the agent propped up a movie screen and the show began. Almost anything might end up on the screen, because the audience, which had never seen the cinema before, was undemanding. Sometimes the programs featured Mickey Mouse, or out-of-date newsreels, or serials of the variety in which girls are tied to train tracks by sneering villains; mostly, however, the films were industrial documentaries made in Leverkusen to describe how the company made compounds like synthetic niacin. One element was constant: a set of commercials for Cafiaspirina, prominently featuring the Bayer Cross. In this way, aspirin salesmen introduced thousands of highland Indians to the age of mass media.

Cafiaspirina sales crept up throughout the decade, although because of changes in currency values they never quite reached in real terms what they had been before the depression. The Quimicas were constantly expanding; in Brazil alone the Bayer headquarters employed six hundred people. Wojahn was convinced that the rebound could continue. In a memo from which the sound of chortling and hand-rubbing is almost audible, Wojahn told Weiss that

> the Latin Americans are great consumers of prepared medicines, and for many of them the drugstore represents what the grocery stands for in other countries. It is claimed that in many parts of Latin America 20% or 25% of the average family budget goes for the purchase of medicines.

The huge sales effort brought the Quimicas an extraordinary amount of what accountants call "goodwill"—the propensity on the part of consumers to buy Bayer Cross products just because they were Bayer Cross products. The goodwill created by the Bayer aspirin sales force spilled over to sales of the I.G.'s ethical products, allowing the company to dominate the Latin American drug market.

It also made the I.G. worth investigating by the Nazi Foreign Organization, which was charged with extending the sway of the NSDAP abroad. Ernst Wilhelm Bohle, the head of the Foreign Organization, became the bane of the Quimicas' aspirin sales force. Short, dark, and unhandsome, Bohle was raised in South Africa by a family devoted to the splendor of the German nation. The lessons took hold; his high school nickname was "Kaiser Will." He attended university in Germany, joining the NSDAP in 1931. Fanatical in his hatred of communism, Judaism, and Christianity, Bohle impressed Hess with his youthful ardor. He welcomed the task of establishing party branches in German colonies abroad, believing they fit in with a national propensity for joining. ("Whenever three or four Germans get together," Bohle explained, "they think they must form some sort of a society or club. . . .") Such affiliates would provide the party with crucial political intelligence, especially in Latin America.

First switched on in 1933, the Bayer Cross towered over the Leverkusen headquarters of the German Bayer company until it was dismantled at the beginning of the Second World War. Some 236 feet in diameter, it was the biggest lighted sign in the world—a huge electric aspirin tablet. *(Bayer AG)*

Left: Felix Hoffmann (1868–1946), a German Bayer chemist, was the first to synthesize acetylsalicylic acid—aspirin—for commercial purposes. According to legend, he developed it for his ailing father, who was crippled by arthritis and unable to tolerate the treatments then known. The results were miraculous. *(Bayer AG)* *Right:* Hoffmann presented aspirin to his supervisor, Heinrich Dreser (1860–1924), the inventor of one of Bayer's most important products: heroin. Dreser looked over what was to be the most successful drug ever made—and rejected it. *(Bayer AG)*

Opposite: The relentless drive of Carl Duisberg (1861–1935), shown here with his wife, Johanna, and his son Carl Ludwig, pushed Bayer to enormous heights. He created the research system that in turn created aspirin, and was the godfather of I.G. Farben, the hydra-headed chemical trust that later was reviled as the symbol of Nazi evil. *(Bayer AG)*

Above: The facilities and staff of the Bayer pharmacological laboratory—then one of the most modern in the world—in about 1900. Dreser is second from right. The blur near his feet is one of the dogs that used to roam the lab. *(Bayer AG)*

Opposite top: Sprawling along the Hudson River, German Bayer's American aspirin plant was one of the biggest drug and chemical factories in the New World. When it was seized as enemy property during the First World War, Sterling Products, a small West Virginia patent medicine outfit, bought the plant at auction—setting off the Aspirin Wars. The picture dates from 1927. *(Sterling Drug, Inc.)*

Opposite bottom: Making aspirin tablets in the U.S. Bayer factory in the 1920s. Although Sterling learned how to produce aspirin in its newly acquired plant, its managers could not figure out how to manufacture the rest of the company's products—driving them into the arms of the Germans they had promised the U.S. government to avoid. *(Sterling Drug, Inc.)*

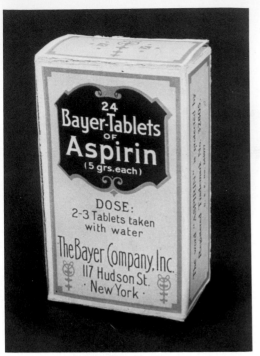

An aspirin box from 1914. Aspirin was originally sold in powder form to pharmacists, who mixed it into sachets for their customers. The side of the box proclaims: "The word 'ASPIRIN' is protected by Registered Trademark No. 32805." The notice was directed at America's legions of aspirin smugglers, who sold fake (and sometimes real) acetylsalicylic acid at a fraction of Bayer's price. *(Bayer AG)*

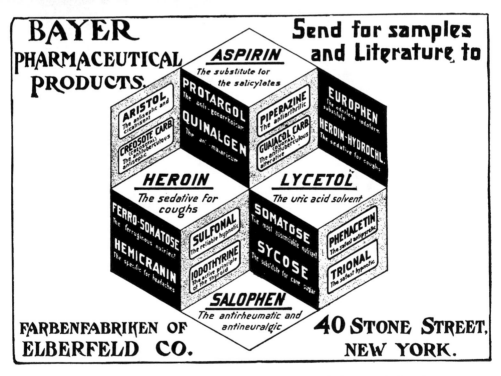

Ethical-drug makers like German Bayer did not advertise their prescription drugs, because they were afraid of offending the powerful American Medical Association, which loathed such promotion. Instead, such firms sent discreet flyers like this one to physicians, promoting Aspirin, Lycetol (a gout treatment), and Heroin.
(The Bettmann Archive)

Collier's
THE NATIONAL WEEKLY

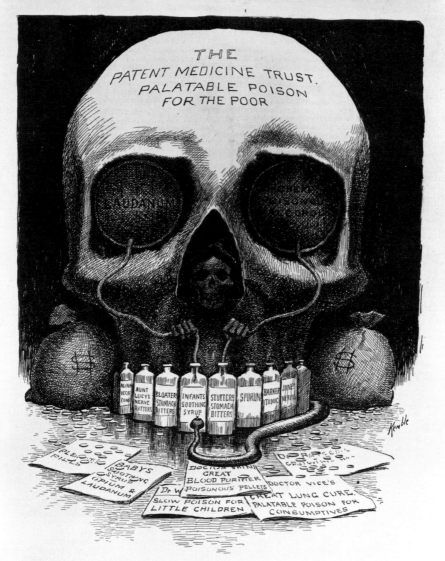

DEATH'S LABORATORY

Turn-of-the-century America was inundated with advertisements for the phony cure-alls known as patent medicines. Many of these, like the oddly named but popular Cuforhedake Brane Fude, were headache remedies. Muckraking journalists ceaselessly attacked patent medicines and their advertising, producing a public outcry that helped create the first food and drug legislation.

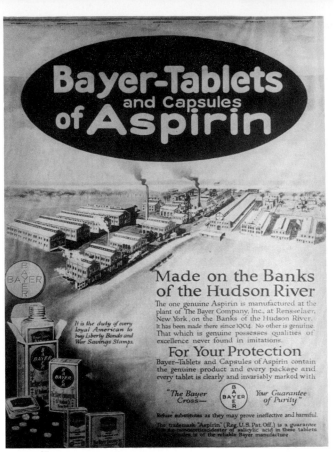

Just before the First World War, German Bayer's aspirin patent expired. To protect its market, it advertised aspirin to the public. The reaction of the medical profession to ads such as this one, from a *New York Times* Sunday magazine in April 1918, was immediate and extreme.
(Sterling Drug, Inc.)

In the 1920s and 1930s, aspirin advertising exploded around the world. Marvelously decorated Aspirin trucks such as this one became a familiar sight on European streets.
(Bayer AG)

The expatriate community in Latin America was large—southern Brazil alone had more than half a million people of German descent. It was a prosperous, conservative, and insular group; even after decades in Brazil, the populations of entire towns spoke only German. School curricula emphasized what novelist Robert Musil called the grand old Teutonic way of life, German managers hired the Germans they met in German associations, and there was considerable marching about in folkloric German costume.

A few Nazis emigrated to South America as early as 1924, but official contacts with the NSDAP did not begin until four years later. When Hitler became chancellor, more than 150 Nazi groups existed outside Germany—most of them small, some very small. Because the groups were powerless, almost anyone willing to devote the necessary time could be in charge; as a result, foreign NSDAP leaders tended to be drawn from the ranks of the unemployed, unpopular, and unsanitary. Bohle found them hard to work with. They spent all their time bickering, he complained, when they should be out subverting something.

Nonetheless, Bohle was convinced that these foreign party branches could induce Germans in Latin America to create a second Nazi state in the New World. A likely location was Brazil, whose 348 party members made it the world's center for expatriate Nazis. (The United States, by contrast, had 115; China had 83.) The party leader in Rio, Willie Meiss, led a clandestine effort to persuade forty thousand German families to move to south Brazil, which would then secede. When the Brazilian government got wind of the plot, it limited German immigration. There, perhaps, the matter would have rested, if the tale had not surfaced in British and American newspapers. The specter of Germans carving out a Nazi state in the Amazon jungle was irresistible; the "Nazintern," as Churchill called it, provided great copy for the tabloids, and was fodder for two generations of thriller writers.

The Quimicas were of particular interest to Bohle's forces. If he had seen Max Wojahn's Latin American map, with a pin in every locality that had a Quimica Bayer sales office, Bohle would have imagined a continent full of people who did not yet belong to the NSDAP. With a sales force dedicated to reaching even the farthest outposts of civilization at his command, Bohle could piggyback Nazi propaganda onto pitches for Cafiaspirina.

The I.G. did not welcome yet another partner in the Latin American drug trade. "We camouflaged [German ownership of the Quimicas] for the reasons of tax savings," I.G. manager Max Ilgner explained later. "The Foreign Organization, on the other hand, wanted to carry on decamouflage activities so that we could show the swastika flag. We wanted to keep our Jews because they were skilled people who knew their work. The Foreign Organization, on the other hand, had instructions to see that they be eliminated. The Foreign Organization wanted us to attend party meetings. We, however, neither had the desire nor the time to attend them. They wanted us to pay higher contributions to the Foreign Organization. We were not really keen on doing that.''

I.G. managers were among the more respectable figures in the expatriate German community—"people of good repute," Ilgner called them, "representatives of Germanism of the old coinage.'' They owned fine homes and large automobiles. They did not attend Nazi meetings, read Nazi newspapers, or march in Nazi rallies. They were less than enchanted by, say, the request of the German embassy in Montevideo, Uruguay, to use the company mailing list for a propaganda magazine. Or by the Brazilian party's insistence that the I.G. mail copies of Hitler's speeches to sixteen thousand Brazilian physicians. Or by Bohle's demand that the company stop advertising in newspapers that published "insulting and abusive articles" about Germany, even if those papers were read by Bayer customers.

The I.G. finally promised not to advertise in anti-Nazi newspapers. Wojahn seethed when he heard of the combine's capitulation—to him, it was another example of interference from Leverkusen. He paid absolutely no attention to the promise until January 1938, when he was informed by his brother, Kurt, who worked for the combine in Argentina, that the I.G. had ordered Bayer to advertise in *La Razón*, a tiny pro-Nazi paper whose readership was of little commercial value. A few days later, Weiss and McClintock learned that the Foreign Organization had joined the fray. Not only was *La Razón* being ignored, it complained, but Cafiaspirina ads inundated *La Crítica*, a lurid anti-Nazi scandal sheet. The *La Crítica* ads must be withdrawn immediately. Exasperated, Wojahn pointed out that if the combine refused to advertise in any paper that ran anti-Nazi articles, it would lose business to its competitors. And the loss would be bad for Germany, which needed foreign revenue to bolster its growing domestic military forces. Pumping up German profits, he said, was more important than being, so to speak, politically correct. As always, Wojahn's solution was simple: more advertising. "It pays to advertise," he lectured Leverkusen, "if you advertise where it pays.''

The I.G. brushed this aside. "Bayer advertisements must disappear from the pages of *La Crítica* . . . ,'' Kurt Wojahn was informed, "even if an important stratum of consumers can no longer be reached.'' Worried, Kurt met with his brother, who spoke with McClintock, who passed the buck to Weiss. Weiss stiffly informed Mann in March that mixing politics and promotion went against the purpose of any business: making money. Pro-Nazi propaganda would only annoy customers, driving away sales. Given his ultimate accountability to Sterling's stockholders, Weiss could not justify taking actions that he knew would lower the company's profits. Nevertheless, he compromised, promising to advertise Cafiaspirina in both papers.

Meanwhile, Kurt Wojahn was warned by Leverkusen that "the party in Germany was watching him and [he should] watch his step."

The Nazis continued to make demands on the I.G. Its response was one neither of resistance nor of collaboration. The firm tried to give party leaders what they wanted when this was compatible with making money, and dragged its feet when the demands were unprofitable. In the end, however, it always ceded. Leverkusen long resisted Bohle's orders to dismiss insufficiently fanatical workers, but in 1937 the Foreign Organization won; a number of I.G. reps were sacked, although some received generous pensions. The Nazis eventually succeeded in fully politicizing I.G. advertising. Posters and handbills showed the swastika. The Junior Sound Cars played pro-German propaganda movies. Standing in the Andean heights, an eyewitness later recalled, Cafiaspirina salesmen reminded their audiences that the wonderful show—and these wonderful pills—had come from a country called Germany, a faraway nation that loves you, a nation that is now surrounded by enemies.

By February 1938, Mann was proclaiming the pharmaceutical department's "unequivocal adjustment to National Socialist ideologies." The foreign branches, he said, were controlled by Germans, not foreigners, "as a *matter of basic policy*." (This meant that Sterling was not supposed to manage the aspirin business.) All advertisements in antifascist newspapers had been stopped, because "economic and propagandistic considerations must be subordinated to the higher political aspects." (This meant that the aspirin business should lose money if it was necessary to advance party goals.) The few remaining Jews were to be "systematically eliminated from our agencies." (This meant to fire them.)

Every employee, Mann warned, "should develop a positive mental attitude toward the present regime."

Seventy-four-year-old Friedrich Carl Duisberg, Jr., died on March 19, 1935. All Leverkusen turned out to honor his passing, and the great factory that was his legacy closed for the day. Industrialist, chemist, planner, philanthropist—Duisberg had left much behind. By his death, one British scientist said, "Germany is deprived of one of the greatest and most valuable citizens she ever had; in the legend of the future, he may well come to be considered the most efficient and effective industrialist the world has yet known. . . ."

Despite the eulogies in Leverkusen, Duisberg's empire was moving ever further from his original conception. In April 1935, Hermann Schmitz succeeded Bosch as chairman of the managing board. The combine's chief financial officer, Schmitz was exactly the sort of professional bean counter that Duisberg had always feared would end up in control. For all their disagreements, Duisberg and Bosch had always recognized each other as scientists and visionaries. Now the company was run by a man whose motto for dealing with problems was Wait, Reconsider, Then Wait Again. Schmitz was so cautious and secretive, a British historian wrote, that his official balance sheets "carried reticence beyond the limits of decency acknowledged even by trusts."

Schmitz was the wrong man at the wrong time. A striking example of his inadequacy is the snarl the I.G. got into over Geniol, the ASA brand that had risen to near parity with Cafiaspirina in Argentina. In addition to menacing what had been the best market for Cafiaspirina in Latin America, Geniol had expanded into Colombia, Peru, and Brazil. The brand's success was due to a simple strategy: It sold the same product as Bayer but at a lower price. Bayer had a simple response: It, too, would sell at a lower price, by introducing a new, less costly product. Called by another name, Instantin, to avoid weakening the image of Cafiaspirina, it would be sold in "a cheap, small packet of eight tablets," which would, Mann was sure, regain "the desired predominance" for Bayer. Instantin and Geniol would battle it out among the low-rent crowd, letting Cafiaspirina sail above the fray.

Although this strategy rooted out Geniol in most of the continent, the competition's base in Argentina proved resistant. Wojahn's response was automatic: He increased advertising. When that didn't work, he lowered the price of Instantin further. Still Geniol remained a thorn in Bayer's side. The brand had carved out a niche for itself, and even the dogged Wojahn could see that he was not going to dislodge it. Having failed to beat the other team, Wojahn had only one recourse: buying it. The competition had expanded the market in Argentina for both brands. If the two companies joined forces, he noted, "the fruits of all this labor" would "fall right into our lap." Together, they could exploit their market power "to the exclusion of everyone else."

Purchasing a company to create a monopoly was illegal in Argentina. Nonetheless Sterling and the I.G. agreed in October 1937 to make an offer for 51 percent of Laboratorios Suarry, the maker of Geniol. As usual, the Americans would run the business while the Germans took a three-quarter share of the profits. Sterling bought the company at the end of the year, expecting Leverkusen to chip in. But the Reichsbank refused to let the I.G. pay for Suarry, because it would be sending money out of the country to buy a firm managed by non-Germans—that is, Sterling. Mann asked Weiss to advance all the money for the purchase; the I.G. would pay back Sterling from the profits. Weiss demurred, because this put all the risks on his shoulders.

The impasse lasted for months. Meanwhile, Suarry asked Sterling to purchase another 28 percent of the stock. Sterling had to comply. The contract committed the new owners to buying any further stock that Suarry wanted to sell. By the spring of 1938, six months after the initial agreement, Sterling had sunk two million dollars into a project that gave three-quarters of the profits to a company that had not paid a penny. Wojahn was furious. The Reichsbank, in his view, was "trying to dictate terms and to impose burdensome conditions, and even penalize the aspirin business." Its interference was costing Sterling a fortune. The I.G. was only a little better off; it was forced to become a passive investor, watching Sterling manage Geniol. The Reichsbank was even hurting itself, by depriving Germany of needed foreign exchange.

At about this point, the German government learned of the existence of the 1920 and 1923 contracts. Because the I.G. had hidden the Winthrop payments by funneling them through its U.S. subsidiary, American I.G., to Switzerland, it looked like Sterling hadn't paid anything for the patents, trademarks, and procedures supplied by Leverkusen. The NSDAP was furious that Germans could have given them away to Americans. The I.G. had to come up with some explanations.

Earl McClintock, Sterling's vice-president, landed in the middle of the fracas when he came to Leverkusen for a routine discussion in March 1938. On his arrival he was suddenly whisked by Mann and Max Brüggemann, the corporate counsel, to Basel, Switzerland, where, in the manner of a spy novel, McClintock was sent alone on a mysterious and unwanted sightseeing trip. When he returned to his hotel he was confronted by Hermann Schmitz, whose penchant for secrecy had inspired the precautions. Schmitz told McClintock that Sterling must compensate the I.G. for the use of its products and processes.

Ridiculous, McClintock said. The I.G. had 50 percent of Winthrop's stock, and was being paid covert "service fees." If this arrangement had got them in trouble with the Nazis, that was their problem.

The I.G. proposed an alternative. Sterling would make a show of payment, presenting an annual check for $100,000. Eventually Leverkusen would find a way to send it back to New York. But, Schmitz said, Sterling had to pay $100,000—now. McClintock dodged the request.

He was escorted to Leverkusen. There, McClintock was invited to Mann's house. It developed that Mann's wife had been sick with cancer for seven months. She was dying in the bedroom. McClintock, rather a cold fish, watched at the bedside while Mann collapsed in tears. He managed to come up with flowers, claiming they were from Weiss. Mann was passionately grateful. The world seemed to be flying apart, he said. One of the few constants was his friends in New York.

On his return to the United States, McClintock spoke with Sterling's British attorney, Frederick Gwatkin. Incredulous that Sterling should be asked to shell out $100,000 for services it had already paid for, Gwatkin told McClintock "that the directors of Winthrop would have some difficulty in

justifying any such payment if the matter were enquired into.'' The payments
would cheat the stockholders, and thus be illegal.

That spring, the Reichsbank finally allowed Leverkusen to buy a three-
quarter interest in the original 51 percent of Suarry. However, the combine
could not get the Reichsbank to agree to either the extra shares bought by
Sterling or to Sterling's management of the company. Weiss was appalled.
His accountants were aghast at the irregularity of the Suarry purchase, and
he, as a Sterling director, was personally liable for fraud. But Mann said he
could not accept the debt ''as there was no permission obtained from the
government. . . .'' It was a standoff. Eventually, Weiss realized that there
was no place to go on the Suarry business but with the combine's original
offer. The extra shares would be held in trust for the I.G., which would buy
them whenever it could obtain permission; the money for the original shares
would be repaid through profits from the Latin American aspirin business.

Mann's wife died at the end of 1938. He was devastated; little work would
come from his office for some time. That November, Ernst vom Rath, third
counselor to the German embassy in Paris, was shot by an exiled German
Jew. Within twenty-four hours, the Nazis launched Kristallnacht, smashing
Jewish homes, stores, and synagogues across Germany. Three days later, the
NSDAP announced that all Jews were to be completely excluded from the
nation's economic life. It was the first big step toward Auschwitz.

Weiss went to Wheeling for the holidays. On New Year's Eve, a private
family party at his house was interrupted by a late-hour phone call from the
recently widowed Mann. The conversation was friendly to the point of unc-
tuousness, with Weiss's wife, son, and daughter-in-law trooping to the phone
to wish Mann a better year.

''I am, in spirit, forever clasping your hand in deepest gratitude for your
friendship,'' Mann wrote Weiss two days later. But, he said, ''new regulations have been issued.'' The I.G. needed its $100,000 check. The problem
had become ''urgent.'' Indeed, Mann said, the ''acute state that the matter
has reached . . . in the last analysis, *might possibly* not leave our original
agreements unaffected. . . .'' Which was, as Weiss had to know, a threat
from his dear friend to break the pacts of the last twenty years, and an
invitation to an all-out war over aspirin in Latin America.

CHAPTER SIX

"LET US KEEP THE SHIRT UNTIL IT IS ABSOLUTELY NECESSARY TO TAKE IT OFF"

The fate of Sterling Products and William E. Weiss had many harbingers, but one of the oddest was a telephone call received by Thomas R. Farrell, editor of the trade magazine *Drug Markets*, during the afternoon of Monday, August 22, 1927. For twenty-three years, *Drug Markets* had provided the trade with the sort of information about prices and products that is of obsessive interest to people in an industry but of no concern to anyone else. Farrell picked up the receiver to learn that someone named Ambruster was on the phone, and that this Ambruster wanted to know what ergot was selling for. A parasitical fungus that grows on rye plants, ergot was and is used in extract form to make many medicinal substances, including psychoactive drugs like LSD. Because ergot was perishable, of variable quality, impossible to synthesize artificially, and found only in Poland, Spain, and the Soviet Union, its price fluctuated wildly, rising to $7 a pound in mid-1920 and falling to thirty cents a pound in mid-1924. Farrell told Ambruster that it was currently being quoted at about eighty-five cents a pound. The quotes, Ambruster said, were wrong. He, Ambruster, had the only available ergot in the United States, and he was going to sell it for $1.75 a pound, just over twice the price. Ambruster had a corner on the market.

Farrell made a few phone calls. He discovered that yes, Ambruster had bought up the available ergot, but no, Ambruster did not have a corner on the market. Spanish ergot growers had pledged to deal only with Ambruster, but U.S. drug makers had enough stock to wait for later shipments from Poland and the Soviet Union. His claims drove up the price a little, but it soon retreated. "After the market position had resumed a tone of easiness . . . ," *Drug Markets* reported later, we left the subject alone. But this man and his associates had no idea of leaving it alone, to the great wonderment of many who did not—and who do not yet—understand what he has to gain.

The editors of *Drug Markets* were not alone in their bafflement. One of the great marginal figures in the history of pharmaceutical reform, Howard Watson Ambruster was a man who liked to do things because he thought they were right. A chemical engineer, Ambruster spent his early years as an obscure figure in the pesticide industry, and died an unsung kook; nonetheless his story remains an amazing, perversely inspiring example of the lengths to which some people will go to fight city hall.

Much of Ambruster's career has been lost to history. It is known that he began work at the end of the First World War in the American Dyes Institute; that he was then approached to help Leverkusen produce dyes; that he spent much time complaining to every conceivable governmental agency about abuses in the drug trade; that for years he campaigned against Bayer aspirin advertisements, writing at one point to every state medical society with the wild assertion that Bayer aspirin was violently dangerous to the circulatory system; that he testified frequently on Capitol Hill, denouncing representatives, senators, and officials of the Food and Drug Administration as incompetent and dilatory; that as early as 1931 he was waving incomprehensible charts about I.G. Farben in front of these same congressmen, senators, and officials of the Food and Drug Administration; that he lived in Westfield, New Jersey, just a little way from Earl McClintock, whom he taunted when they met in the train station; that he was the author of *Treason's Peace: German Dyes & American Dupes*, a 421-page exercise in surreal investigative journalism dedicated to ripping the lid off I.G. Farben, a "cabalistic organization" bent on "a world super-state directed by Farben"; and that, so far as can be learned, he went to his grave convinced that the United Nations was a creature of I.G. Farben, and "the consummation of the world conquest planned by faceless Farben figures to be consummated by Farben's faithless dupes."

In 1918, the young Ambruster went to work for Frank Hemingway, one of the organizers of the American Dyes Institute. The institute, a lobby for the nascent U.S. chemical industry, tried to prevent German companies from selling in the United States. Ambruster had great respect for Hemingway; one supposes that Hemingway's dislike of I.G. Farben had some influence upon his plant manager.

Ambruster's first recorded political foray began after he had left Hemingway to become an independent consultant. He learned that Spanish ergot was of considerably better quality than its Polish or Soviet equivalent. Unfortunately, it cost more to produce, and was being driven out of the market by its inferior competition. Ambruster undertook to drive up the price of Spanish ergot—hence the phone call to *Drug Markets*. Drug makers refused to buy his high-priced ergot, and Ambruster was left with a lot of rye fungus on his hands. He converted it into extract, which he then tried to sell. Still no one bought it. Worse, a warehouse fire destroyed his entire store. He was heavily in debt, and his credit dried up; the bank foreclosed on his home. "The only thing they haven't done is shoot me in the back," Ambruster said.

Here many people would have given up on saving Spanish ergot. Giving up was not the style of Howard W. Ambruster. He tried to buy advertisements in medical journals denouncing both the ergot importers and the Food and Drug Administration (known then as the Food, Drug, and Insecticide Administration), which in his view had permitted bad ergot to pollute American drugs. When the American Medical Association attacked Ambruster's ads, the journals refused to run them; Ambruster then turned on the AMA, as well as the FDA. He spoke before and mailed handbills to a wide variety of organizations, including some usually not thought of as being on the front lines of the debate over ergot standards, such as the Daughters of the American Revolution and the Federal Council of Churches of Christ in America. At the same time, Ambruster sued the secretaries of treasury and agriculture for permitting the importation of substandard ergot.

By June 1930, the furor was sufficiently loud that Burton K. Wheeler, a senator from Montana without previous interest in the drug trade, published a magazine article about the controversy. Its slant can be gathered from the title: "Profiteers in Poison." Irate, FDA Commissioner Walter Campbell demanded that the Senate investigate his own agency. The hearings took place in a spell of appalling summer weather. Ambruster testified at great length, showering invective on the FDA. The agency, he claimed, had entered into a vast conspiracy with the AMA, the Public Health Service, the Department of Justice, and most pharmaceutical companies to swamp the public with substandard drugs. Ergot was not the only problem; Ambruster mentioned ether, an anesthetic, and digitalis, a heart medicine, as others.

In the end, the FDA was completely exonerated. The hearings nonetheless launched the beaten Ambruster as a full-time gadfly. "These men," he said of the nation's drug makers, "can't conceive of a man becoming so damn mad about a thing that he is willing to push every other objective aside and pursue this one thing alone."

Ambruster was particularly infuriated by Sterling's advertisements for Bayer aspirin. In addition to its oft-repeated slogan that "Genuine Bayer Aspirin Does Not Harm the Heart," the company alleged that aspirin could cure flu, colds, and sore throat, all without any side effects. "Take one tablet—and go to sleep," Sterling said, for "aspirin not only relieves suffering, but acts as a sedative and induces rest at night.''* Certain that the advertisements were lies, Ambruster had lambasted Sterling at the FDA hearings; a few months later, in the fall of 1930, he took to the airwaves on a small radio station in New Jersey, informing listeners for some weeks that the owners of Bayer aspirin should be in jail. The station closed suddenly, and Ambruster was left without a pulpit. He sent angry letters to the heads of every state medical society; various publishing enterprises, including *Collier's, Time,* and the *New York Times*; many congressmen; the Federal Trade Commission; every radio station that carried *The Bayer Program*, source of the ''Does Not Harm the Heart'' campaign; the Public Health League of Washington State; and state governors, attorneys general, and boards of health across the nation. He at last struck pay dirt when former Judge and Congressman Ewin L. Davis of Tennessee was appointed commissioner of the Federal Trade Commission. The ex-chairman of the House Committee on Radio Legislation, Davis had corresponded sympathetically with Ambruster about aspirin ads. In September 1934, Davis's FTC ordered Sterling to stop claiming that aspirin did not upset the stomach, harm the heart, or hurt the body, no matter what the dose. The result was described by Ambruster:

Sterling did not give in immediately or graciously, and for some time the illegal advertising continued. It must have been impossible for the Sterling-Farben régime to believe that such an affront to its power and prestige could exist. Finally, one Sunday evening, my wife and I were listening to the radio to find out if [announcer] Howard Claney would repeat his unctuous statement, ''It cannot harm the heart.'' The program ended, and Mrs. Ambruster turned to me with, ''Daddy, he didn't say it! You've actually done it at last!'' But it was Judge Ewin L. Davis who had done it. For once Farben and Sterling had met their match.

Not resting on his laurels, Ambruster campaigned against Sterling and the I.G. with gusto, mailing so much material to the Justice Department that he earned the exasperation of Attorney General Homer Cummings. Despite Cummings's opprobrium, Ambruster believed that the true patriots on lower levels of the Justice Department approved of him. And he was sure that his hard work had paid off when Cummings's successor subpoenaed the records of Sterling Products, beginning an investigation that was to end the career of William E. Weiss in a flurry of scandal.

* These claims are false, except, unfortunately, for the one that Ambruster mainly attacked— that aspirin is not dangerous to the circulatory system. His beliefs about aspirin's toxicity probably stemmed from its effects in the massive doses given for rheumatic fever, the same symptoms that likely made Farbenfabriken Bayer almost refuse to market ASA.

*   *   *

Always, as Rudolf Mann had said, Weiss was just a businessman. His life passed in a happy tumult of meetings and travel and vacations and charities. Although he worked hard, he found time to be a member of two golf clubs in Florida; country clubs in Wheeling, Quebec, Miami, and Indian River, Michigan, near the Straits of Mackinac; the Shriners, Elks, and Masons (Weiss was a thirty-second-degree Mason); and civic organizations in Wheeling, Detroit, and New York City. He had a big home, Elmcrest, outside of Wheeling; an apartment in Manhattan's tony Biltmore Hotel; and a summer home, Bide-A-Wee Cottage, on the shores of Lake Michigan. In Wheeling, he was a celebrity: William Erhard Weiss, general manager of Sterling Products; director of General Aniline and Film (the new name of American I.G.) and Bayer-Semesan (a joint venture among Sterling, I.G., and Du Pont); holder of an honorary doctorate from the University of Cologne; and, not insignificantly, father of William E. Weiss, Jr., president of Alba Pharmaceutical, a growing Winthrop-I.G. venture dedicated to marketing drugs that fit neither the Winthrop nor the Sterling line. ("Alba" comes from the Latin for "white," which is rendered in German as "*weiss*.")

Weiss was not without worries. For example, he had begun to wonder whether Germany would start a war. If that happened, its foes might seize German property, as the United States had in the First World War. In Britain, the I.G. would lose its half of Bayer Products, Ltd. to the English custodian of enemy property; Sterling's share would be unaffected, but the firm would be disturbed. Prospects were darker in Latin America. Because the trademarks and patents were vested in the Quimicas—Sterling had only a license—they could be seized outright, thus ending the Latin American aspirin business.

The answer, Weiss thought, was to mask German ownership of the Latin American business and, in particular, the aspirin trade. His first plan was to ask each Quimica to sign a "declaration of ownership" claiming, untruthfully, that it was American property. In August 1938, Max Wojahn and James Hill, Jr., the company treasurer, made a trip to Latin America to investigate the legality of this measure; they learned that it would hoodwink nobody. They concluded that the Quimicas instead should actually become American property.

Knowing that such measures would not please the I.G.—not to mention its NSDAP supervisors—Weiss moved deliberately. But the growing war fever could not be ignored. By March 1939, Sterling was having to explain what it was doing in Latin America. Queries came from both the State Department and the Securities and Exchange Commission, which monitors the activities of American companies. The British too were on the case; Frederick Gwatkin, Sterling's London solicitor, was pressed to produce sample labels for all Sterling products in Latin America.

In May 1939 Weiss asked Gwatkin to examine the Latin American situation. Two sets of negotiations began. In one, Sterling begged the I.G. to sign over its Latin American agencies; in the other, Sterling and the I.G. talked with Imperial Chemical Industries, the giant British chemical trust, about taking over a third of Bayer Products, Ltd., which would insure majority control by non-Germans in case of war. With Leverkusen reluctant to cede any power, progress was slow. When Germany started the war on September 1, Weiss had accomplished nothing.*

Bayer Products, Ltd., was in trouble from the moment that Hitler's troops crossed the Polish border. The company was half owned by the I.G.; two of the four directors were German, including its managing director, Richard C. Hennings. Within days, the custodian of enemy property seized the I.G.'s shares. The English company used the confiscation to advertise that it was "neither controlled by nor in communication with any company in Germany." Meanwhile, Mann, Weiss, and Gwatkin discussed how to save the I.G.'s shares, and whether the Sterling half would get confiscated as well. It was just like the First World War. Only this time Weiss might not win a company, but lose one.

The second set of negotiations, concerning Latin America, was also galvanized by the war. Ten days after the invasion of Poland, Weiss told Leverkusen that they had to separate the Latin American aspirin trade, which was run by Sterling, from the ethical trade, which was not. Otherwise Sterling would lose the aspirin business if Latin American nations declared war and seized I.G. assets. Weiss wanted to set up new companies, owned by Sterling, to take over the aspirin business. To safeguard the goodwill built up over the past two decades, Weiss intended to take control of the Bayer Cross and the various aspirin trademarks in Latin America, giving the Quimicas a license to use them for their ethical products. Wilhelm Mann curtly rejected the plan: Leverkusen would never give Sterling any more jurisdiction over the Bayer name than it now had. Instead, Mann suggested, Sterling could pay Leverkusen in advance for Latin American aspirin, which would let Weiss claim the "goods as American property. . . ."

Exporting Leverkusen's ASA to Latin America became difficult when England imposed a naval blockade of Germany. By mid-October 1939, six weeks after war began, ocean freight rates had doubled, and shippers had to take out costly war risk insurance to transport German goods through the blockade. The I.G. suggested sending its ASA to Italy, which was not yet at war with England. Sterling could then repackage it and ship it to Latin America as an American drug. In Wojahn's view, this would never work. With imports required to carry country-of-origin stamps, Sterling would

---

* When war was declared, I.C.I. became, technically, an enemy of every German citizen. The Nazi government's penalty for trading with the enemy was death. This caused a slowdown in the talks among I.C.I., Sterling, and the I.G.

either have to admit the ASA was of German manufacture or explain why American-made drugs were supposedly being sent from New York to South America via Italy.

To Wojahn the solution was obvious: send New York's own Rensselaer-made aspirin to Latin America. Codicils in the 1920 contract allowed Sterling to take over manufacturing ASA for the Latin American market if its costs fell below those of Leverkusen. ASA powder from the factory in Albany was coming in at 45 cents a pound, whereas Leverkusen was producing it at 51 cents a pound. Because Sterling sold more than fifty tons of aspirin in Latin America every year, the savings could run into thousands of dollars. Even if there was no blockade, Wojahn thought Sterling should be shipping its own ASA. That it could bypass the blockade only added to the need to switch suppliers. Weiss was loath to proceed without Leverkusen's approval. On October 18, he cabled Mann, asking permission to send Rensselaer aspirin. In a second cable two days later, he exhorted the I.G. to act instantly. Five days after that, he again demanded an immediate reply. On October 26, Mann responded. His cable thanked Weiss for his concern and agreed that the problem needed to be addressed in the best possible way—an answer that said nothing. That day, the *New York Times* printed a British blacklist of firms with German connections; many of Leverkusen's Latin American agents were on it. That was it for Weiss. He sent two more telegrams. New York and Leverkusen must separate their assets; the deliveries from Germany had to stop.

Mann reluctantly endorsed the idea of creating new companies to take over the Quimicas' aspirin trade. But he insisted that Sterling's ownership be the thinnest of veils, and that Germany continue to supply ASA. With the NSDAP eyeing its every move, Leverkusen did not want to cut production. It would not consider letting Sterling send its own aspirin.

Weiss didn't know what to do. In its present grandeur, Sterling couldn't survive without the I.G. But if the United States went to war with Germany, as seemed likely, Sterling couldn't survive with the I.G.—it would be taken over by some latter-day A. Mitchell Palmer. To keep the Latin American business profitable, Weiss would have to ship Rensselaer aspirin. Yet that would antagonize the Germans with whom he had worked for twenty years. He couldn't dismiss those two decades, but neither would the federal government. Weiss looked at the black ring binders that kept the I.G. contracts— the bible that he carried with him everywhere—and saw years of successful negotiation. The Justice Department, however, would see years of successful cartelization, if not collaboration.

He telephoned Mann on November 5, 1939. No record exists of the conversation, but it was one of the most momentous in Weiss's life. Mann finally agreed to let Sterling ship its own aspirin. (He still refused, however, to surrender the trademarks.) Weiss then offered a fateful *quid pro quo*. He volunteered to take over and preserve the I.G.'s ethical trade in Latin America—a business in which Sterling had no contractual role whatsoever. Winthrop would manufacture the I.G.'s products and send them to Latin America along with the aspirin.

Doubtless Weiss made his proposal out of friendship. Sticking up for the Germans was, he told Mann later, "very gratifying to me personally." His "constant aim" was to help the "common welfare." But the move established him as a *de facto* arm of I.G. Farben, which by then was almost coterminous with the Nazi state. The new aspirin arrangements could be excused as the fulfillment of a long-term contract; offering to make the I.G.'s ethical products could not. With the United States edging toward war, the proposal was an act of folly.

Winthrop was hardly prepared to take over the ethical-drug market in Latin America. I.G. Farben had more than $275 million invested in plant and equipment, whereas Sterling had less than $10 million, and much of that was tied up in the Rensselaer aspirin factory, which had originally been built by the Germans. (Weiss planned to put up new buildings; construction crews were rushed to upstate New York, and the work began.) Pharmaceutical products often cannot be synthesized without special intermediate chemicals; Winthrop didn't know how to make them. (Leverkusen arranged to ship the intermediates to Sterling via the Trans-Siberian Railway and a Pacific steamer.)

Above all, Winthrop lacked the know-how to make many of the drugs. Obtaining the formulae from Leverkusen in wartime would plunge Weiss into skullduggery of a sort rarely encountered by patent medicine makers from West Virginia. Identifying himself by the code name "Syntent," Weiss cabled Mann ("Richter") in January 1940 at a dummy address in Amsterdam to arrange a conference in Italy. When "Richter" agreed to be there, McClintock sailed for Genoa. The meeting opened on February 6, 1940, in Florence's Hotel Excelsior, a magnificent nineteenth-century pile not far from the Duomo. McClintock sat with Mann and two of his closest advisers, Brüggemann the lawyer, and an I.G. director named Mentzel. The Germans were extremely nervous. Once McClintock had the formulae, it would be impossible to take them back. What if Sterling used them to strike out on its own? Worse, what if Sterling gave the formulae to Bayer Products, Ltd.? If the Nazis somehow learned that Mann had provided an American with technical information that ended up at an English company—the consequences were terrifying. Mann would be shot. After McClintock assured Mann, Mentzel, and Brüggemann of his continued love for Germany, the I.G. men said that "things are just the same as heretofore." (They may have been helped to this conclusion by McClintock's frequently expressed belief that Hitler would win the war.) Then everyone got down to business.

The plan to ship ethical drugs from New York to Latin America complicated the process of splitting the ethical business from the aspirin business
and putting the latter in new companies under Weiss's control. To secure
Sterling's aspirin interests against seizure, there had to be no connection
between them and Leverkusen; to protect the I.G.'s ethical interests, the
Germans demanded ironclad agreements between Sterling's new companies
(which would import the Winthrop-manufactured products into Latin America) and the old, Leverkusen-owned Quimicas (which would buy the products from the new companies and sell them to the public). Moreover, in case
the host nations declared war on Germany, the new companies had to have
contracts in hand that gave them legal title to the Quimicas' assets, especially
trademarks and patents. All of this was subject to intricate dickering. Eventually, nervously, both sides came to an agreement. Handing over the long
list of formulae must have been unnerving for the Germans; to preserve the
Latin American business, Sterling and I.G. Farben were committing themselves to alarming measures.

By the summer of 1940, Winthrop factories were churning out products for
the I.G. Using the technical data brought back by McClintock from Italy,
Winthrop functioned for the first time as a real pharmaceutical company.
Trucks loaded with freshly manufactured products drove out of the plant; the
workers talked of great expansion and of greater profits. The plant was so
busy it actually turned away orders. As the system evolved, Winthrop shipped
the drugs through a special, independent branch of the Bayer Company
export department, which also handled the American end of the Cafiaspirina
traffic.

Wojahn asserted control over the Latin American business with increasing
confidence. To hide the arrangements from the British, all correspondence
went through the United States, a neutral country not subject to the blockade.
The Quimicas sent all statements for Leverkusen in unmarked envelopes to
Hermann Kaelble, head of the Quimica in Brazil, who mailed them to an
office in Lima, Peru, which transported them to Mexico, where they were
mailed to Wojahn, who decided what to pass through to Leverkusen. When
Mann tried to contact Argentina independently, Wojahn was furious. In what
must have felt like an act of sweet revenge, he severed the connection
between the I.G. and the Quimicas. It was too dangerous, he said. They were
flouting Nazi regulations, and the German government read the mail.

Thus Mann and Brüggemann had only hints of Sterling's slow efforts to
create the new and supposedly independent corporate entities in Latin America. Despite Weiss's urgency, these companies—Farma Continental was the
name eventually chosen—took an incredibly long time to establish. As
France fell and bombs rained on London, Sterling fought Latin American red

tape to create the Farma Continentals. In October, eight months after the Italian meeting, McClintock went to Brazil to find out why the separation of the Quimicas' assets was taking such a long time. During his visit, Kaelble called Mentzel, the I.G. director. In a conversation marked by the shouting and frequent misunderstanding of the day's poor transatlantic connections, Mentzel too tried to find out from Kaelble why everything was going so slowly. Setting up a subsidiary of a foreign company in Brazil "takes at least six months," Kaelble explained. The books had to be made public, and massive numbers of governmental approvals had to be obtained.

"And so what happens with the company?" Mentzel asked. "Who owns the stock of the company?"

"Of the new company?" Kaelble said, confused.

"Yes."

"Bayer of New York would have the stock."

"All of it?" Mentzel asked, shocked. With Wojahn's blackout on communication, it was apparently the first time he had realized that the I.G. was being completely shut out.

"Yes, of course. All of it. And Bayer will send down a manager, and we must work closely with him. I am totally in favor of setting up this [company] this way."

"Kaelble," Mentzel said, "we have to talk this over." Eventually, though, he swallowed it. Leverkusen had no other choice. "But, listen, Kaelble," Mentzel said, "the stipulation for the entire operation . . . is that we get the profits put in safekeeping."

"I'll tell McClintock that he's to take this up in New York, okay?"

"Yes, Kaelble. That *is* the stipulation, isn't it? And put it in Swiss francs."

But the stipulation was not easily satisfied. Because Leverkusen could no longer get money shipped from Latin America, the I.G. decided to borrow the money in advance from a U.S. bank, having Sterling repay the loan from the profits.* (A similar method was employed in the Suarry purchase in 1938.)

A month later, Wojahn was flabbergasted to learn that Kaelble was not, after all, working to complete the arrangements for the new companies. Despite having told both McClintock and Mentzel that he was "totally in

* In December 1940 the Swiss representatives of I.G. Farben contacted the Chemical Bank & Trust Company in New York, which indicated it would make a million-dollar loan—provided that somebody in the United States would guarantee it. The I.G. asked Sterling. In a phone conversation on December 16, Weiss tried to get Mentzel to realize that he would be mad to countersign a loan from which Sterling received nothing. Weiss did promise that Chemical would be repaid from the I.G.'s share of the profits, but the bank still demanded a countersignature. Mann asked again that Weiss provide it. On February 25 Weiss cabled Mann: "NEGOTIATIONS DISCONTINUED STOP WE CANNOT LEGALLY GUARANTEE." Mann, evidently annoyed, cabled back: "COMPLYING WITH YOUR REPEATED WISHES NO GUARANTEE SHALL BE REQUIRED FROM YOU." The loan fell through.

favor" of setting up the subsidiary, Kaelble meant something quite different: He favored creating the new companies as legal entities, but wanted them actually to take over the aspirin business only after the United States declared war on Germany.

Wojahn thought it was crazy to leave such complex financial maneuvers to the last second. Although the plan called for a convoluted shift in the legal title to the businesses, he reminded Kaelble that "these measures do not entail any actual change." The day-to-day operation would hardly be altered; except for the name, nobody would be able to tell the difference between the old Quimicas and the new Farma Continentals. Only a few employees—paper shufflers and bookkeepers—would be affected. The Brazilian Farma Continental would even be located on one floor of the I.G. office in Rio.

"You must have forgotten that down here there are no secrets," Kaelble scoffed. "You cannot seriously believe [the new system] will go unobserved." In a letter that testified to the bitterness I.G. employees felt as they watched their business slipping into Sterling's hands, Kaelble explained that he was willing to give over the business completely, but only when he was up against the wall.

> You are in possession of a sealed, water-tight contract, you have all the trump cards in your hands, you are assured of our willing cooperation—of that there can be no doubt—and I fail to see what would disturb the picture. We have declared our willingness to undress for you down to the shirt if necessary, and I have but one request, i.e., that you let us keep the shirt until it is absolutely necessary to take it off, and then we shall do that, too.

From Kaelble's point of view, he was losing his business forever to Wojahn, and Wojahn should not be in such a hurry. "Even if the pace of developments should become accelerated," he wrote, "I cannot understand how you or the business would be in danger."

Others at Sterling understood all too clearly. In September, a committee led by Nelson Rockefeller, the son of John D. Rockefeller and a future vice-president, began collecting information on the operations of American companies in Latin America; Sterling was asked to send information. A month later, the Department of Justice began investigating U.S. businesses with Nazi connections. At the same time, the Senate announced plans to investigate whether German patents gave German industry a dangerously powerful role in the United States. On January 3, 1941, Burton K. Wheeler, the powerful anti-business senator who had supported Ambruster's ergot campaign, appointed a subcommittee to investigate American business relations with German firms. At the end of the month, I.G. Farben, Dow Chemical, the Aluminum Company of America (Alcoa), and two other firms were indicted for price fixing. All the while, the Federal Bureau of Investigation produced a stream of lurid—and, in truth, not terribly accurate—reports that Latin American subsidiaries of American firms were riddled with Nazi sympathizers. Sterling was a favorite target.

These actions greatly alarmed David M. Corcoran, the manager of Sterling's recent acquisition, the Sydney Ross Company, which sold patent medicines to Latin America (a trade not covered by Sterling's contracts with the I.G.). Hired in 1939, Corcoran came from a political family. His older brother was Thomas G. Corcoran, the renowned wheeler-dealer whose consummate political skills had pushed much New Deal legislation through hostile congressional committees. The very success of "Tommy the Cork" led to accusations by disaffected former presidential aides that he was the string-pulling manipulator of the president. He was pushed out of government before the election of 1940, in which Roosevelt won an unprecedented third term. Days after the election, his brother, David, asked him to come secretly to Mexico City. Tom wangled an appointment as an observer to the inauguration of Mexican President Manuel Ávila Camacho, and the two Corcorans met in the Hotel Reforma.

The brothers were vigorous, charming, toughly practical men. The sons of a politician in Rhode Island, they came from a home that was lace-curtain Irish, down to the family musical sessions around the piano. Both were star high school football players; both went to Ivy League schools; both got advanced degrees from Harvard, Tom in law, David in business. While Tom went on to clerk in the Supreme Court for Justice Oliver Wendell Holmes and then into politics, David, who craved travel and adventure, became a sales agent for U.S. automobile companies in Japan. Yielding to family pressure, he returned to the United States to work for Sterling, where, in 1939, he took over Sydney Ross. The firm had been started by Clarence Riker, a New Jersey man who wanted to peddle laxatives to South America. Believing that medicines sold better when they were associated with the medical profession, Riker looked for a doctor to lend his name to the enterprise. Ultimately he settled for a dentist, and Sydney Ross and Dr. Ross's Life Pills were born. Before he died, Riker sold the whole Ross line to Weiss, who was thinking of starting his own international drug business, just like the I.G. ("Weiss was sort of a puppet of the Germans," David Corcoran said later. "He was very, very jealous of them, and he wanted to have a worldwide business instead of just this little picayune Bayer business in the United States.") Weiss put Corcoran in charge. But Corcoran had hardly begun building up the business when he realized that Sterling was in great danger. That was why he met his brother in the lobby of the Mexico City Hotel, sitting beneath a brace of famous Diego Rivera murals.

Only a couple of sentences were necessary to make Tom understand the situation. He saw the problem in his own terms: "People with superior political connections appeared ready to legally steal [David's] company." The people likely included Senator Wheeler, who had quarreled with Tom in 1937. In Tommy the Cork's opinion,

> there was a fabulous motive for seizure: political venality. According to law, when the Alien Property Custodian confiscates foreign assets, he must dispose of them through their sale to private American interests— presumably on a highest-bidder basis. But how easy it is to arrange for a government insider to effectively fix a competitive auction. It would all look like it was on the up and up. But these deals were usually simple payoffs to the needy political faithful. That's to say the auction wouldn't be fixed for a simple financial kickback; the winner would be a corpo- ration whose future earnings would finance some trusted candidate's expensive campaign for national office. It didn't particularly matter who the beneficiary would be. . . . There were a number of well-connected potential candidates who'd willfully embarrass a Corcoran while feath- ering their electoral nests. What mattered was the possibility that Dav- id's company might be seized. Returning to New York from Mexico City, I knew I'd have plenty to do. . . . I must protect my brother.

Quickly he became Sterling's lawyer and assembled a defense team. Among his choices was John Cahill, a law school classmate and former colleague who was the U.S. attorney in New York. Cahill had been supervising the Department of Justice's investigation into Sterling. On February 10, 1941, Cahill resigned to go into private practice. His first client was Sterling Prod- ucts.

Dismayed by Kaelble's turnabout on the Farma Continentals, McClintock took a ship south that February within days of Cahill's resignation. Landing in Trinidad, McClintock found his name on the British blacklist. The au- thorities confiscated all papers in his possession, returning them only at five o'clock the next morning. He left in a hurry. Blasted in Trinidad for being insufficiently anti-German, he was made uncomfortable in Brazil for being insufficiently pro-German. The government censored films that supported England; the minister of justice openly cheered Hitler. Even the I.G. head- quarters was alarming: Kaelble worked in a palatial office with a huge por- trait of Hitler on the wall above his desk.

McClintock, Kaelble, and Mann conferred over the phone. In the end, the two I.G. officials convinced Sterling's vice-president that the Quimica trade- marks did not yet have to be transferred. War was far off. Nothing had to happen. Nothing need change. Business could go on as before. Everybody in Rio, Kaelble said, felt positive. Right now, in fact, he wanted Sterling to send down a year's supply of most I.G. drugs.

Bearing this cheery message, McClintock returned in early March to find that the Department of Justice had discovered dangerous German influence in the fields of housing, food, and drugs—indeed, a grand jury had already convened to look at pharmaceuticals. This seems to have been the impetus for Weiss to take action. Within days of McClintock's appearance in New York, Weiss demanded that the transfer of trademarks from the Quimicas to the Farma Continentals be finally shoved through—as well as the big Winthrop order that McClintock had picked up from Kaelble. Kaelble finally consented. After two decades, Weiss was about to get his hands on the Latin American trademarks to Cafiaspirina, Aspirina, and the Bayer Cross.

He had little time to savor the prospect. On April 10, the *New York Times* reported that the Department of Justice suspected American corporations of preserving "the South American market for German companies now cut off from that trade by the British blockade." The article's accuracy was confirmed within hours, when Justice Department subpoenas arrived in the offices of Sterling, Winthrop, and General Aniline and Film (the renamed American I.G.). The demands were exhaustive; eventually the firms would have to turn in thousands of documents, including, sadly, the black ring binders in which Weiss kept the I.G. agreements. Appalled, he told Wojahn to cancel all ethical shipments to Latin America. Corcoran, meanwhile, was exerting his considerable talents in a different effort: trying to keep Weiss out of prison. Sterling was under siege.

CHAPTER SEVEN

"FORCE MAJEURE"

It was time for Weiss to meet his chief nemesis, Thurman Arnold, the assistant attorney general in charge of the Sterling investigation. Accompanied by McClintock, he went to Washington, D.C., on May 4, 1941 for what today would be called a power breakfast with Arnold. It was not a pleasant encounter. A former Yale professor and an expert on constitutional law, Arnold regarded most federal regulation of commerce as a charade. He thought government should get tough with business, and didn't mind grandstanding to do it. Over eggs and bacon he bluntly informed Weiss that the contracts with I.G. Farben amounted to nothing more than illegal promises not to compete—the formation of an aspirin cartel. He conceded that there might be some extenuating circumstances. But Arnold was hearing complaints from Capitol Hill about Sterling, and assistant attorneys general cannot ignore such complaints.

Barraged by legal proceedings, Weiss pinned his hopes on the formidable political dexterity of Tommy the Cork. Arnold's staff also regarded Corcoran with awe. As one investigator recalled, they

> redoubled their efforts when they learned that Tommy Corcoran represented Sterling Products; they worked overtime at night in a determined drive to advance the investigation as rapidly as possible to a stage so complete that the sheer force of the facts revealed would defeat Tommy Corcoran's efforts. Tommy Corcoran was engaged in a race with time to (1) stop the investigation before it reached such a conclusive stage and (2) get the cases filed on a civil basis with consent decrees merely restraining further violation of the antitrust laws, and above all things, (3) prevent the presentation of the evidence [gathered from the subpoena] to a grand jury.

Corcoran and his team seemed to be everywhere at once. He was always on the phone, always scratching notes, always getting on the train for a quick meeting in a town three hours away. Up in the Sterling offices at 170 Varick

Street, Corcoran's partner, Cahill, was in charge of releasing files to Justice Department lawyers. Down in Washington, Corcoran camped in the office of Hugh Cox, Arnold's assistant, assuring him that the company would bend over backward to establish its good intentions. When McClintock balked at a Justice Department request to find some ancient employment files, Corcoran told him to get cracking. When Sterling deposited the I.G.'s share of the Latin American aspirin profits in the combine's American bank, Corcoran helped Attorney General Robert Jackson, Arnold's boss, impound the $250,000 payment. (The dramatic press accounts of the action cannot have annoyed Jackson, who obligingly did not mention Sterling to reporters.)

The seizure stunned Leverkusen. With the war on, it was difficult for Mann and his lieutenants, Brüggemann and Mentzel, to learn why a neutral nation had commandeered the money. Mentzel called Kaelble two days afterward, hoping that he might know what was the matter with New York. "Telegrams have gone out all over the world about the fact that I.G.'s property has been confiscated in the States . . . ," Kaelble told him. "Pamphlets here are going around with the headline BLITZKRIEG AGAINST GERMAN TRADE. Speaking of this, I have to tell you that our situation has made quite an impression on local officials. . . ."

"What kind of impression?" Mentzel asked.

"Unpleasant." Leverkusen, Kaelble said, had lost prestige. If the authorities pulled off this kind of trick in the States, wasn't Mentzel afraid that the same thing would happen in Germany? What if the German government got tired of the pharmaceutical department dallying with Americans? What if, Kaelble asked, "someone one day says to you, 'It can't go on like this'?"

Mentzel was noncommittal.

"In any case," Kaelble said, "we have the trademarks. They are positively ours." He had never finished all the paperwork necessary to give them to Weiss. If worse came to worst, he told Mentzel, the Quimicas could simply hide the profits in a trusted person's bank account until the war was over.

You can't pull off that kind of trick, Mentzel said, at five minutes to midnight.

"Not usually," Kaelble told him, "but you can still try it." Word of the idea may have got around; three days later, Corcoran asked McClintock to inform him about any new schemes to dispose of I.G. profits.

Corcoran had his own plan. Why not let Sterling keep all the aspirin profits for itself, and use them to offset the I.G.'s $1.2 million debt left from the purchase of Laboratorios Suarry? Corcoran presented this idea to Cox of the Justice Department on May 27 as a means of reducing the "danger that this money would get into Germany." Cox agreed. It was an amiable session. (It might have been considerably less so had Cox known that Sterling's treasurer was at that moment in Kaelble's office, discussing the transfer of the aspirin business.) Cox said that the investigation would finish by the end of June. "That," Corcoran later informed Cahill, "is the time when the fun will really begin."

Meanwhile, the press continued to denounce Sterling. On May 29 the *New York Herald-Tribune* splashed a lengthy account of the Latin American drug trade over its front page. Inside were big pictures of German- and American-made Cafiaspirina. Dozens of similar exposés followed in the next few months, as newspapers picked up the story of the evil conspiracy hidden in the medicine cabinets of America. "Listening on the radio to the lovely voice of Vivian della Chiesa," *Graphic Picture Newsmagazine* asked, "who would suspect that The Bayer '[American] Album of Familiar Music' was only part of a still bigger program—*a German program for the conquest of America?*" Most alarming was the muckraking tabloid *PM*, which filled its entire front page on June 1 with the words

These Firms Earn Money For Hitler

"Hitler gets millions for war chest through links with American firms," the article charged. Sterling, it said, was fulfilling Goebbels's "boast" that "Americans would help Hitler win the Americas"; Weiss and McClintock were described as active soldiers for the Nazi cause; Howard W. Ambruster was quoted to Sterling's detriment. A second story finished by exhorting the president to freeze Sterling's assets—denying it access to its bank accounts, which would be tantamount to shutting down the firm.

Weiss was horrified. Never intending to be more than just a businessman, he had worked himself into a situation where his name was becoming a synonym for "Nazi collaborator." His company was under the scrutiny of Wheeler's Senate committee, the Securities and Exchange Commission, the Treasury Department, the State Department, and the Justice Department. Thousands of documents from New York, Rensselaer, and Wheeling sat in Washington offices; investigators pored over accounting statements from 1919 to the present, conference minutes from the day Weiss first met Rudolf Mann, stockholder records from the time of Neuralgine, even the tyrannical memos of Weiss's secretary, Miss Briton.

The business, meanwhile, was a shambles. In the United States, the fusillade of negative publicity was sure to drive down sales, as it had in the First World War. In the United Kingdom, the custodian of enemy property was forcing Bayer Products, Ltd., to hand over its trademarks and patents (they were registered in the I.G.'s name). In Latin America, the painfully established Farma Continentals had been cut off before they started. In Al-

bany, the big investment in the Winthrop plant was threatened, because it
could no longer ship drugs overseas. Only the aspirin market in Latin America remained to him, and Corcoran was making noises about giving that up
too. The shaken Weiss pushed Sterling's lawyers into producing a twenty-
six-page statement defending the firm's conduct as "wholesome" and its
officers as ruled "by their sense of complete loyalty and devotion to the
United States of America." The statement was never released.

A hopeful sign came just when prospects seemed darkest. On June 2, the
day after the first *PM* exposé, Attorney General Jackson was nominated to
the Supreme Court. The new acting attorney general, Francis Biddle, was an
old friend of Corcoran's—they had both been law clerks for Justice Oliver
Wendell Holmes. Arnold's staff was sure that Corcoran would use his influence with the president to ensure Biddle's nomination as attorney general,
and that the payoff would be quashing the Sterling investigation. But any
celebrations by Sterling were premature. The Treasury Department froze the
firm's assets less than two weeks later.

Freezing assets may not be the worst thing that can possibly befall a company, but it is high on the list. A business without access to its liquid capital
cannot buy supplies, deposit profits, or even pay its workers. If its managers
want something, they can only promise that somehow they will pay for it
later; if customers want to buy something, the managers can accept payment
but must deposit it into a bank account that has become a sort of financial
black hole (money can go in, but it can't come back out). Trade becomes
infeasible. A firm that cannot trade soon ceases to exist.

The Treasury Department's action was not a total surprise. A few days
before, President Roosevelt had announced that all financial transactions in
the United States by firms from continental Europe would be blocked. Because Winthrop was half-owned by the U.S. branch of I.G. Farben, which in
turn was owned by a Swiss holding company, its transactions were theoretically included in the order.* Even with that warning, Sterling treasurer
James Hill, Jr., was shocked by the telephone call he received on the evening
of Friday, June 20. A big, bearish, moon-faced Midwesterner, Hill first met
Weiss when he inspected Sterling's taxes for the Internal Revenue Service.
Because Weiss made a habit of acquiring the services of those government

---

*This arrangement evolved after 1930, when the I.G. transferred its Winthrop stock to the
American I.G. Chemical Corporation, later renamed General Aniline and Film. Control of
General Aniline was then nominally assigned to I.G. Chemie, a Swiss firm that was secretly
owned by the I.G. The whole intricate charade was intended to keep the I.G.'s stake in
Winthrop hidden from both the U.S. and German governments—the United States because of
Sterling's promises to the alien property custodian, and Germany because the NSDAP wanted
to oversee all foreign subsidiaries.

officials who examined his affairs, Hill became the firm's accountant and then treasurer. Like Weiss, he never moved to New York City, preferring for his family to remain in Washington, D.C. He was, one executive said long afterward, "a truck-driver type who could hardly speak English," but he was also "a whiz with figures." Hill had always gone along happily with Weiss's deals in Germany—it was his boss's business. The phone call shocked him out of his complacency. It came when he was closing up the office and preparing to take the night train to Washington. He picked up the phone to hear his assistant, E. M. Mulhern. One of Sterling's bankers had just told Mulhern that he had cut off the firm's bank accounts on instructions from Washington, D.C. Faced with this appalling prospect, Hill contacted Tommy the Cork. Then, because there was nothing else to do, Hill took the train to Washington. He was going there anyhow.

The next morning, he drove to a conference at the Treasury Department that Corcoran had arranged. Waiting for him were officials from the departments of State, Justice, and Treasury, including Edward H. Foley, the general counsel of the Treasury Department. The only friendly face was Corcoran's. It was the first time Hill had met any of the men who held the company's fate in their hands. Surprisingly, they knew little about the freezing order—they hadn't heard of it before Corcoran's phone call. Nobody seemed to know from where the command had emanated.

Curiously absent from the proceeding was Weiss, whom Corcoran had cut out of the loop. While the fate of his company was being decided, Weiss was in Wheeling, West Virginia. (His brother, Fred, was sick, as was his daughter.) From a powerful man who singlehandedly ran an ever-growing corporation, he had become, almost overnight, an irrelevant, ghostly figure, someone who was fed information in dribbles by Tommy the Cork when it seemed necessary. The conqueror of Carl Duisberg had been bested himself. Utterly undone, he was now a man who existed at the mercy of circumstances. And what circumstances they were—the six prosecutors poring over Sterling's subpoenaed files were slicing the company's history into sets of criminal actions.

The deals of the past two decades appeared in a new and unflattering light in the rush of approaching war. The contracts in Weiss's black ring binders looked very much to Arnold's staff like agreements not to compete; the careful comparison of costs promised evidence of price fixing; the friendly correspondence with Wilhelm Mann appeared to show that Weiss had worked hand in glove with Nazi provocateurs. The Justice Department was being urged to indict; lawyers were talking to Ambruster, who was burying them beneath the records of his jeremiad against Bayer aspirin, Sterling Products, and I.G. Farben. If the investigators were listening to Ambruster, it was time to think about cutting a deal.

A wide man with a shiny honest face, Hill made a convincing witness. The

whole affair, he told them, was crazy. The press was vilifying them. Imagine
reading those headlines on your way to work. Justice Department investigators were crawling all over 170 Varick Street, but they would find nothing.
There was no real German interest in the company.* The Treasury Department, he said, should declare that Sterling was an American outfit, that it
couldn't be affected by an order freezing foreign assets, that it was completely cooperating with the government. Look how they had helped the
Justice Department on the matter of the I.G. payments.

Foley agreed to suspend the order for a week while Sterling came up with
proof that it was not controlled by Hitler. Hill and one of the Sterling
lawyers, Charles Guthrie, retired to Guthrie's office on K Street to write an
explanatory letter to Foley. In view of the uncertainty at the meeting, they
said, they were not sure that the secretary of the treasury had actually "declared Sterling and all its subsidiaries to be Nazis," but if that was the case,
the firm wanted time to explain its side of the story.

On Monday, Hill and Corcoran brought the memo to another meeting with
Treasury, State, and Justice. It developed that Sterling was not, after all,
frozen. Then, to Hill's irritation, they grilled him about the background of
the people he worked with. But Corcoran and Cahill and Guthrie were
running everything, and Hill wearily answered the questions. "They wanted
to know," he said later, "where they worked before and where they were
born and where they were raised and where they went to school and what
nationality they were, what their religion was and what their color was and
every damned thing you wanted to know about them they wanted to know."
Then, the emergency apparently over, he went back to work.

By the beginning of July, Corcoran was thinking about replacing the top
management at Winthrop or even selling the company. If that was done,
much of the export business could be put into Sterling's small export subsidiary, Sydney Ross, where his brother, David, would take charge. Once
David, an expert marketer, had the aspirin and pharmaceutical accounts,
Sydney Ross could go head to head with the I.G. in Latin America. This
way, Tommy the Cork told Arnold, Sterling could redeem itself by taking the
I.G.'s markets.

There was one small problem. Competing in Latin America was exactly
what Weiss had promised Leverkusen he would not do. If Sterling earned
Arnold's favor by engaging the I.G. in economic warfare, the company could
be sued by Leverkusen after the war for reneging on its contracts. Corcoran
wanted Arnold to indemnify Sterling against future legal action. Arnold told
him that Sterling should get whatever it had coming from whatever source
chose to give it. Still, Corcoran was optimistic. For the first time, he said,

---

* Technically, this was true. Despite the I.G.'s convoluted half-ownership of Winthrop and
the cooperation with Weiss, Sterling had kept its central corporate identity legally apart from
the I.G. contracts.

Arnold and Cox were listening to his story without "getting the problems entangled with anti-Hitlerism." It was time to "keep driving into them."*

Late one stormy night in the middle of July, Corcoran went looking for Arnold in Washington, D.C., finding him at a cocktail party. He told Arnold that he had the solution to the whole awful mess: An unsigned, undated memo, prepared by himself, in which Acting Attorney General Biddle, Arnold's boss, would declare that Sterling Products should be immune from prosecution because it was important to national security to fight the I.G.'s domination of the Latin American aspirin trade. To get Biddle off the hook for this preposterous claim, Corcoran proposed to obtain a similar declaration from the secretary of commerce, an unsigned, undated copy of which he brought with him. If Commerce accepted, Biddle could claim the decision was out of his hands. It was necessary to begin by getting Biddle's signature. Biddle was at his country house ninety miles outside the city. The phone lines were down; Corcoran, who had a flair for the dramatic gesture, wanted Arnold to accompany him there. The weather was appropriate for such skullduggery: a terrible thundershower.

Arnold was dragged out of the party around midnight. Two hours of Corcoran's hair-raising driving later, the two men arrived at Biddle's house. They banged on the door and were let in. It is easy to imagine the scene: Arnold in crumpled evening dress, Biddle in a bathrobe, Corcoran with a merry and expectant gleam in his eyes. Biddle was presented with the two memos that Corcoran thought would resolve everything. He read the papers carefully. He gave them back to Corcoran. The idea was silly, he said. The Commerce Department would never agree to such a thing. He would not sign anything. He was a friend of Tommy the Cork, but he would not sign.

History does not record the conversation between Corcoran and Arnold on what must have been a very long return trip. It was now certain that Sterling would not get off scot-free. Most of the Justice Department staff, including Arnold, wanted the evidence brought before a grand jury, preliminary to obtaining a major criminal indictment. These Justice employees believed that Weiss had violated antitrust laws; some thought, as one man in the attorney general's office later put it, that "Sterling Products had in fact become an agent of Nazi Germany, carrying out policies aimed at the United States." If true, this demanded charges of conspiracy, jail sentences, and large fines.

Corcoran counteroffered with what is called a civil information. The company would accept civil rather than criminal charges, which reduced the penalty it could face. Moreover, an information, unlike an indictment, bypassed the grand jury, which removed the risk of exposing Sterling's dirty laundry to public view. In exchange for receiving an information, Corcoran

---

* Corcoran would have been less sanguine had he known that Arnold had conferred with Foley at Treasury, and that both men had balked at giving Sterling immunity from future prosecution.

promised, Sterling would sign a consent decree that committed it both to canceling the I.G. contracts and to denying that it had thereby lost any rights to the I.G.'s U.S. patents. In South America, it would give up the old I.G. trademarks like Cafiaspirina. (This required absorbing a multimillion-dollar loss; in 1940 Sterling valued its trademarks and goodwill at $17.4 million, almost a third of the company's entire net worth of $57 million.) Furthermore, Corcoran's proposed consent decree called for Sterling to wage an aggressive campaign to sell its own new brand of aspirin in Latin America. It would wipe out Leverkusen's share of the aspirin market from Tijuana to Tierra del Fuego. It would be willing to face lawsuits from the I.G. It would be willing to lose a lot of money.

Enraging Arnold's investigators, Corcoran went over their heads by pushing his consent decree through the Interdepartmental Committee, the *ad hoc* group of Treasury, State, and Justice officials coordinating the different departments' investigations of Sterling. Early in August, Corcoran staged a dog-and-pony show for the committee. The star of the show was his younger brother, David, who was trying to sell the audience on the notion that his small subsidiary, Sydney Ross, was capable of mounting an aspirin war. The Corcorans arrived with a gigantic map of South America—"the biggest map anyone had ever seen," David said later—covered with swastikas and little photographs of Hitler representing the evil forces of Cafiaspirina. With every I.G. branch office getting a swastika and every head office getting a picture of Hitler, the map radiated menace. (It was a perverse echo of the sales map in Wojahn's office.) David had spent hours sticking on the Nazi symbols, and hours more pasting on little red, white, and blue flags that stood for the offices, factories, stations, and sound trucks of plucky Sydney Ross. As the map grew, it became necessary to roll it up like a carpet, and David spread it over the floor of the conference room. Crawling over the map with an aspirin tablet in his hand, he explained that the Ross forces would sell a Cafiaspirina clone called Mejoral, which, translated loosely, might be rendered in English as "Better-ol." Mejoral, David promised, would fight Cafiaspirina head to head throughout the continent. Blessed with the preternatural vigor that ran in the family, David had the glib charm of a born salesman. In a relatively short time he convinced the crowd that he was not merely Tommy the Cork's junior brother but also a marketing general capable of mounting an assault on the entrenched sales positions of I.G. Farben. "Finally," David's then secretary said, "it was agreed that Sterling would be let off the hook if David would go down . . . [and] beat the Germans out of South America. He would do it with a little tablet—Mejoral, a Bayer Aspirin copy."

The Corcorans asked only one thing in return for this selfless enterprise. If Sterling signed the consent decree, committing itself to the Mejoral scheme, the firm wanted Foley to certify to Arnold that Mejoral should be given "the fullest support of all branches of our government,'' and that the ''quality and degree of that governmental support may well determine the success or failure of this attempt to promote Latin American trade.'' Which meant that if Arnold's staff caused trouble, he alone would bear the onus.

Hill and Corcoran took the Mejoral idea in early August to Biddle, who had spent the summer waiting for the president to nominate him to be attorney general. In addition to working for Sterling, Corcoran had been pushing for Biddle to receive the job; then, he hoped, Biddle would appoint him solicitor general, the department's second-highest position. With all the wheeling and dealing, Justice Department staffers complained, Corcoran was practically living in Biddle's office. Now, speaking with Hill and Corcoran, Biddle gave his okay. In return for waging analgesic war, he said, Sterling could get a civil information and a consent decree.

Biddle's decision, Hill later recalled, caused an ''insurrection'' at the Justice Department. Arnold exploded. His staff threatened to quit en masse, which would heap scandal on Biddle at precisely the time he least wanted it. A week later, Corcoran and Hill met with Arnold, the source of the problem. I won't accept the Mejoral deal, Arnold said. Absolutely not. Selling aspirin was not enough penance. They would have to change things at Sterling. Corcoran and Arnold hammered away at each other. Finally, in Hill's recollection, Corcoran said, ''Mr. Arnold, it's understood we aren't going to have a criminal [indictment], we're going to have an information.''

''Yes,'' Arnold said.

''I'll prove I'm not the biggest bastard in the world,'' Corcoran said cheerily. ''I'll let you have it on a *criminal* information.''

The next day, August 13, Hill and Corcoran met with the Interdepartmental Committee. Hill was confident enough that he had brought in Weiss from Wheeling to shake hands on the deal. Instead Foley handed him a statement and said that the company had to sign it. Foley said, Hill recalled, '' 'This is what you have got to do or we freeze you.' . . . There was no comment allowed. 'This is it.' Just that cold 'This is it.'. . . We were prepared to discuss it, but we weren't allowed to discuss anything. . . . 'Here it is. Sign it or else.' ''

Eight pages long, the statement consisted of sixteen ''representations''— actions Sterling promised to perform. The representations would be the basis of a future consent decree. They were not substantially different from the promises in the draft consent decree that Corcoran had prepared two weeks before, except that the company received no protection from future I.G. lawsuits. It was still a discouraging picture. The Latin American trademarks would be lost. They would give back Sterling's share of the Cafiaspirina business. They would have to swallow the remaining $859,000 debt on Laboratorios Suarry. All that was left to Weiss from his years of effort on the continent was a few unimportant brands like Dr. Ross's Life Pills.

Nonetheless, Weiss agreed to sign. It was better than having the funds frozen. His company would survive in some form. And at least nobody would to go to jail.

Because the first representation abrogated the German contracts, Weiss sat down after the meeting for the dolorous labor of writing a cable informing Mann that he was handing back the aspirin business. After the telegram was approved by the Interdepartmental Committee, Weiss returned to New York for a *pro forma* meeting of the board of directors. On August 15, the board accepted the representations. That day, Weiss sent a cable to Leverkusen. "THE AIM AND PURPOSE," it began, "IS TO DISSOLVE ALL CONTRACTS AGREEMENTS UNDERSTANDINGS PARTNERSHIPS. . . ." The party was over.

Even in the midst of war, Weiss's message was a shock to Leverkusen. A lawyer, probably Mentzel, examined the telegram carefully. Whereas Weiss worried that the consumer's familiarity with the Bayer name would lead Leverkusen to dominate the playing field effortlessly after the war, Mentzel was sure that Weiss planned to use the I.G.'s inability to supply Latin America to build up a monopoly of his own with Geniol. It appeared to him that Weiss was going to come out on top. "Doubtless Weiss made this proposal under pressure from the U.S. government," Mentzel remarked dryly. "But he and his advisers are also not going to miss this opportunity to be 'smart businessmen,' which is reminiscent of their behavior at the fusion of the I.G. in 1926."

Bearing this in mind, Mann wired back:

AFTER CAREFUL CONSIDERATIONS FROM ALL ANGLES CANNOT FOR GENERAL REASONS ACCEPT YOUR PROPOSAL LATIN AMERICA MANN

Weiss had enough trouble without Mann refusing to end the contracts. He sent another, more apocalyptic telegram:

WE HAVE NO ALTERNATIVE EXCEPT TO INSIST THAT YOU RECONSIDER OUR CABLE AUGUST 15TH IMMEDIATELY OTHERWISE FORCE MAJEURE WILL ABROGATE AND DESTROY ALL LATIN AMERICAN BUSINESS ARRANGEMENTS AND UNDERSTANDINGS WEISS

The Justice Department staff still did not relish the prospect of a company's avoiding full prosecution for illegal contracts to sell aspirin in Latin America by promising to sell aspirin in Latin America. With Biddle and the Treasury Department supporting the consent decree, the investigators saw the case closing up before them, and Weiss, McClintock, and Hill getting away almost scot-free. Because the criminal information was already laid out, they could not press for stiffer charges. But they could make the representations tougher. At the least, they said, no consent decree should be signed until Sterling forces the I.G. to sell its half of Winthrop. Otherwise, they would be doing nothing other than asking Leverkusen to compete with itself in South America. For that reason alone, one investigator argued, the consent decree should be delayed.

The Interdepartmental Committee met late in the afternoon of August 19. Held in the office of Assistant Secretary of State Dean Acheson, the session was a crowded affair, with four people attending from Justice and six each from State and Treasury. The only Sterling representative was one of its lawyers, George S. Hills. Not to be confused with Sterling treasurer James Hill, Jr., Hills was a longtime colleague of Edward S. Rogers, Sterling's trademark lawyer in the I.G. contract negotiations.

The discussion focused on the twelfth representation, which empowered Washington to remove any Sterling employee engaged in actions "contrary to the national interest." A Justice Department delegate, Edward Levi, mentioned that the investigators wanted to use that representation to remove Weiss. Hills was staggered. Nobody had said anything about this before— not a word! The request was a breach of faith; if the government insisted on it, he said angrily, Sterling would revoke its signature on the representations. Everything would go back to square one.

The Treasury delegates were almost equally surprised by the Justice staff's hostility. Nobody seemed to have told them of the near-revolt in Thurman Arnold's office. At Treasury's request, a show of hands ensued. State and Justice wanted Weiss out, and Treasury wanted him to stay; the score was two to one, and Weiss was out. Hills was told to bring Corcoran and Hill to a meeting in two days. At that meeting they were to tell the Interdepartmental Committee the name of Weiss's replacement.

In those two days, the Justice Department demanded another body. Weiss and one other big name had to go. An exceedingly uncomfortable meeting took place at Sterling's temporary headquarters in a Washington, D.C., hotel. Diebold, McClintock, Hill, Corcoran, Hills—the whole crew was there, except Weiss, who was back in Wheeling with his sick brother and daughter, and had not yet been told of the Justice Department's demand. The question was who would accompany the managing director off the plank. "Nobody wanted to go," Hill recalled later. With a mixture of anger, cowardice, and embarrassment, all eyes turned to McClintock, who had been Sterling's senior vice-president for almost twenty years. Despite being involved with the I.G. since his trip to Europe before the Treaty of Versailles, McClintock bluntly refused the honor. There was no way to make him do it, Hill said. "So they talked Mr. Diebold into it." Diebold agreed to take the hit.

The group then turned to picking a new chairman of the board and president to replace Weiss and Diebold. McClintock badly wanted the president's spot. He was the logical candidate, but the decision had to be left to the next chairman of the board. The new chairman of the board had to be a figurehead of unimpeachable respectability, which of course left McClintock out. But whom to choose? After considerable discussion, Hill said, the group "of us in Washington came to the conclusion that the best man to propose [for chairman], providing Mr. Weiss was willing to quit—on which nobody had consulted him yet—would be Mr. Rogers. . . ." At that time, Edward S. Rogers was in semi-retirement after a distinguished legal career; he was unlikely to give offense to the government. Satisfied, they could now do the hardest part of the job: telephoning Weiss in Wheeling.

Weiss, Hill recalled, was furious. It was difficult for Hill, an easygoing man, to tell his boss that he had been fired. "I'll tell you right now, he didn't take it easily. He wasn't the type of man to take these things easily." At the same time, everybody knew that finally Weiss would have to do it. If he did not quit, the government would freeze Sterling's access to cash, and Weiss knew, as Hill said, that "you can't run the company without it."

Weiss did not agree to quit until well past midnight on August 21, less than eighteen hours before the final meeting with the Interdepartmental Committee. Now Hill had to call Rogers, who was avoiding the summer heat at his vacation home in Maine.

A measure of the Sterling group's frantic, harassed state is that they telephoned this seventy-three-year-old man at two o'clock in the morning to explain the offer. Despite the hour, Rogers apparently accepted the job on the spot. But he laid down a condition: Under no circumstances was McClintock to be appointed president. Rogers wanted Hill instead. One can only imagine McClintock's reaction. He was ten years older than Hill, and had been with Sterling for twenty years, twice as long as Hill. Nevertheless, he put a brave face on the loss. That morning he went with Hill to the committee meeting and announced the new lineup. The final consent decree was sent to the Justice Department three days later. Weiss and Diebold were each barred for life from Sterling and ordered to pay fines of, respectively, five and one thousand dollars. The changes were ratified by President Hill at a special board meeting on August 29.

Three days before, Mann sent the I.G.'s final response to Sterling's proposal to abrogate the contracts: No dice. The company felt so strongly about it that the cable was signed by the entire supervisory board. "THE ONE-SIDED ABOLITION OF THE LATIN AMERICAN CONTRACT IS NOT ACCEPTED," the directors said. They finished on an imperiously angry note: "WE DEMAND THE FULFILLMENT OF OUR CONTRACTUAL RIGHTS." It was the last time that Weiss heard from the people in Leverkusen who had given him so many things. His successors did not bother to respond.

*   *   *

On September 4, Biddle was at last nominated as attorney general. The next day, he announced the consent decree. Sterling's enemies in the press were irate—it looked like just another display of inside baseball by Tommy the Cork. The attack was led, as ever, by the indefatigable Howard W. Ambruster. Although Sterling was under the thumb of the Treasury Department, the Federal Bureau of Investigation, the State Department, and two Senate committees, Ambruster remained convinced that, as he put it in November, "Hitler still has his bloody hand clenched at the heart of the American drug industry." Even at the end of the war, with I.G. Farben taken over by the Allied military government, Ambruster was sure that the combine was plotting world domination. He went to his grave convinced that the shadow of Nazi aspirin was creeping over the heartland of America.

Weiss was not present when Biddle gave the consent decree to the press—his brother had died the day before. Then, dreadfully, his daughter passed away on September 13. The losses in business and family were devastating; Weiss disappeared from the scene in New York and Washington. After the consent decree, he telephoned his subordinates, promising that he would be back, and that he would restart the arrangement with the I.G. after the war. He held to what he could of the company in which he had invested four decades of his life. He did not resign until forced to in December, and he often visited the Sterling office in Wheeling. According to one possibly apocryphal story, he refused to clear out his office. Instead he suggested that the company build a separate entrance so that he could come and go without embarrassing anybody. By February 1942, Hill was furious; if Weiss kept showing up in the Wheeling building, Hill could not say that Sterling had severed all ties with the past. When Weiss went on vacation in March, Hill ordered the plant superintendent to toss the belongings of the company's founder into the parking lot.

His company snatched from beneath his feet, Weiss drifted around the Midwest. Though bereft of power, he had all the perquisites of wealth—houses in the country, a chauffeur-driven car, the respect of his neighbors. He spent time with his daughter's children, who moved in with him upon their mother's death. He was a local volunteer for the Chemical Warfare Board. That summer, he went with his wife and grandchildren to Bide-A-Wee Cottage, his summer place on Lake Michigan. Driving him home after a shopping expedition, his chauffeur slammed into another car. Weiss was fatally thrown into the windshield. He was sixty-three.

The funeral was held at Weiss's house in Wheeling on September 5, 1942, one year to the day after the consent decree. Rogers, Wojahn, and Walter

Hiemenz, the director of the Albany plant, came to the service; Hill and Diebold were pallbearers. McClintock did not show up. In Wheeling, the death was front-page news, the newspaper obituary one to honor a longtime civic leader.

At the end of the war, Mann and twenty-two other senior I.G. executives were tried as war criminals. The charges were various; the trial, lengthy; the verdict, troubling. Ten of the defendants, including Mann, were acquitted on all charges. They had become involved in such acts as proselytizing for the Third Reich, but the court at Nuremberg ruled that they could not be held responsible for what they were forced to do. Mann, with others, had been induced to supervise the slave-labor camp in Auschwitz. It is true, as Mann said, that the I.G. treated its unwilling employees with comparative humanity; true, too, that resistance by the I.G. executives would have been futile: If Mann had refused to work at Auschwitz, he would have been shot and replaced by someone who would do the job.

The I.G. had missed its chance. In 1933, when the opposition of the nation's biggest conglomerate might have done some good, the very executives who had been most contemptuous of Hitler had kept silent. Their accommodation came in part from the terror of the times and the lack of credible political alternatives to the NSDAP, but most important was the Nazis' promise to put the disastrous Leuna synthetic fuel plant in the black. Management thought of the shareholders and went along with the Nazi takeover. They had their responsibilities to the company.

In the end, when it counted, they had all been just businessmen.

PART TWO

"POUNDING HAMMERS"

CHAPTER EIGHT

"I AM NOT IN THE JAILBIRD CLASS"

On March 12, 1908, Judge Ivory G. Kimball of the police court of Washington, D.C., charged the jury after a trial unlike any other ever heard in his courtroom. For that matter, it was unlike any other ever heard in the United States. The case had alarmed Americans from Wall Street to the White House; the courtroom buffs who were usually the only spectators in the sleepy courtroom had been displaced by a mob of reporters, defenders of the accused, and worried representatives of pharmaceutical concerns. All had voiced their opinions. Now, Judge Kimball said, it was up to the jury. The central question was one that the jury, and only the jury, could resolve—what ordinary people understand when they read a label or an advertisement for a drug.

Their decision was vital, Kimball said. This case was the government's first attempt to enforce the nation's new food and drug law. As its sacrificial lamb, it had chosen not a street-corner vendor of patent medicine, but Robert N. Harper, president of the American National Bank and of the Washington, D.C., Chamber of Commerce. Described by the *Washington Herald* as "one of Washington's best known and progressive citizens," Harper was a handsome man with dark wavy hair above a high forehead and an aquiline nose. He earned a degree in 1885 from the Philadelphia College of Pharmacy, from which Weiss was to graduate eleven years later. Harper got a job at John Wyeth & Brother, a Pennsylvania drug firm that was the ancestor of today's Wyeth-Ayerst Laboratories. In the John Wyeth laboratory he experimented with a common coal-tar analgesic, acetanilid. After testing different mixtures on himself and friends he came up with something that seemed to do the job. His work at Wyeth attracted some attention in Washington, and Harper was asked to come down to the capital as the city commissioner of pharmacy. On the side he began selling his home-brewed analgesic. (Conflict-of-interest laws not being then what they are today, nobody protested that the commissioner of pharmacy was in charge of regulating his own business.) He earned enough respect to be awarded the honorific ''Colonel,'' and enough money to start his own bank. By the time of his arrest, Harper had sold more than two million bottles of his pain reliever at twenty-five cents apiece. In big capital letters each and every one of those bottles carried the name of his brand: CUFORHEDAKE BRANE FUDE.

Cuforhedake Brane Fude was but one of the analgesics that crowded store shelves in turn-of-the-century America. Aspirin then being under patent and available only by prescription, three other drugs—acetanilid, antipyrine, and acetophenetidin—were the analgesics most easily available to the public. All three could be made by any manufacturer; all three were the active ingredient in patent medicines by the score. Antipyrine, the first to be developed, was originally marketed by Hoechst, the German chemical firm that later joined Farbenfabriken Bayer in forming I.G. Farben. Acetanilid followed and spread across the globe with astounding speed; indeed, Harper was tinkering with it just two years after its discovery. Acetophenetidin, developed by Farbenfabriken Bayer at Duisberg's behest, was initially sold under the name Phenacetin. After the U.S. patent for Phenacetin expired in 1906, sales of the generic version, acetophenetidin, flourished. Because Aspirin was effective, had fewer side effects, and was marketed in the way M.D.'s preferred (only to them), doctors almost stopped prescribing acetanilid and antipyrine, which had the worst side effects (acetophenetidin was less affected). Nonetheless the three drugs sold heavily in patent medicine form. Quack cure-alls made of acetanilid, antipyrine, and acetophenetidin were stacked in pharmacy windows and trumpeted in newspaper advertisements across the land. People bought them by the bushelful.

Bayer Aspirin entered the over-the-counter market reluctantly and late. When Ernst Möller persuaded his superiors to let him promote Aspirin to the public, the result was a staid printed announcement that only stated the company's name and listed its products. After the aspirin patent expired and other companies could legally sell it, Bayer's competitors advertised in a similar fashion. The gloves came off when Sterling acquired the rights to the Bayer name. Promotions for Bayer aspirin went from simple advertisements recommending the brand for colds and headaches to claims that Bayer aspirin worked faster than a bobsled speeding down the course at Lake Placid or a hockey player's shot on goal. The cycle spiraled upward as other aspirin companies, and then the makers of other, newer analgesics, fought back. Eventually the distinction, so carefully preserved by Duisberg, between the fine products of a legitimate pharmaceutical house and the hyped-up nostrums of a patent medicine maker was obscured. Aspirin became the target of a two-pronged attack by the government, which assailed its labeling and its advertising so fiercely and so often that ASA became the bureaucracy's leading foil. The result was an endless skein of lawsuits, corporate shenanigans, and federal investigations that lasted for decades and involved otherwise sober businesspeople in feuds of the most raddled Hatfield-McCoy variety.

Harper's trial was the beginning of this imbroglio. The most serious count against Cuforhedake Brane Fude, Judge Kimball told the jury, was that the label claimed it contained no poisonous ingredients. Cuforhedake Brane Fude combined acetanilid and antipyrine in a solution of alcohol; caffeine; and sodium and potassium bromide. The prosecution contended that aceta-nilid's side effects meant that it was a poison. Kimball's instructions were straightforward: "If you find that the drug contained a poisonous ingredient, then your verdict must be guilty, because that is the plain issue."

The other major count against Harper concerned the claims implicit in his product's trademark. Here the issue was knottier, but here, too, Kimball was blunt. "With regard to this 'Cuforhedake,' " the judge said, "you can take it to mean what an ordinary man would take it to mean—the meaning which it conveys to an ordinary person when he gets a remedy said to be a cure for a headache." Would average people, he asked the jury, take Cuforhedake to mean the drug actually cured headaches, eliminating them for all time, or merely relieved them until the drug wore off and they came back again? And would someone seeing Brane Fude expect to get what the judge described as "a known and distinct kind of food that feeds and nourishes the brain as distinguished from a food that feeds and nourishes the whole body"? Le-gally, Kimball said, the entire trial could be decided by a single decision, one that would reverberate for years to come, and would shape the development not only of headache remedies but of the entire pharmaceutical industry.

"If you find that 'Brane Fude' means brain food . . . ," he solemnly explained, "your verdict shall be guilty. . . ."

U.S. v. *Harper* was a landmark in the long struggle to rein in the promotion of drugs. Patent medicines were introduced in the United States during colonial times, and quickly drew a chorus of complaints from doctors about the immorality of patenting medicines and selling them to the public. The opprobrium did not prevent Samuel Lee, Jr., of Connecticut from taking out the first U.S. drug patent in 1796, thus protecting his Bilious Pills, a blend of aloes, soap, potassium nitrate, and gamboge, an Asian tree resin, from duplication for seventeen years. Or so he thought: Another Samuel Lee of Connecticut patented *his* very similar Bilious Pills three years later. The original Samuel Lee yowled in protest, and the battle of the Bilious Pills was joined.

The majority of these potions were worthless; some were dangerous; all were extensively promoted. The spread of public education actually worked to the benefit of the industry, for it created a nation of readers. These readers needed something to read, and hundreds of newspapers were born. News-

papers needed something to advertise, and the maker of proprietary medicines was ready with tales of glorious cures and extraordinary effects.
(Knowing of doctors' dislike of patents, nostrum sellers preferred the term
"proprietary remedy.") Drug ads filled the penny press, and America's
credulous new readers responded. At a time when science seemed to produce
new miracles every day—the telegraph, the electric trolley—people readily
believed that those miracles could also be found in medicine bottles. In 1859
patent medicine sales totaled $3.5 million; by 1904, they had grown to $74.5
million.

Patent medicines created a great American industry: promotion. Jacob's
Antikink, Aunt Fanny's Worm Candy, Palmer's Hole in the Wall capsules—
each needed a slogan, a claim, a disease to cure, a colorful label, a testi-
monial to shout to the heavens. Advertising fed sales, which fed more
advertising. When William Weiss earned $10,000 from the first year's sales
of Neuralgine, he reinvested the money not in a new factory but in more
advertising. He did it again and again—and saw the value of his company
increase in eleven years from an initial stake of $1,000 to more than $4
million. The relentless marketing of patent medicines drove American advertising to its current pre-eminence; as late as 1927 a prominent ad executive
could observe that the greatest copywriters he knew "were schooled in the
medicine field."

The very success of such promotion fueled demands for reform. Patent
medicines, cried one House of Representatives report in 1849, are "an evil
over which the friends of science and humanity can never cease to mourn."
Reformers called for changes in two aspects of drug marketing: labeling
(claims on the packaging) and advertising (claims made everywhere else).
Although drug makers regarded both labeling and advertising as part of a
single effort to foster demand for their nostrums, the reformers ended up
treating them separately. When the government finally stepped in, rules
controlling labels appeared in advance of rules governing advertising—with
far-reaching, even absurd consequences. The division was not planned, or
even fully understood, at the time it occurred. Indeed, it came largely as an
unintended by-product of the beliefs of one man, Harvey W. Wiley, the
longtime chief chemist of the U.S. Department of Agriculture.

Dedicated to the point of fanaticism, Wiley spent decades in a solitary
quest to rein in the wild market in food and drugs that flourished in nineteenth
century America. A big-featured man with the massive shoulders of a professional athlete, Wiley walked so heavily that the floorboards squeaked in
protest. "His hair never stays in order," one acquaintance recalled, "but
masses itself forward on both sides of the forehead, giving him at times a
somewhat uncouth appearance. The penetrating glance of his rather small
eyes, the large and roughly modeled nose, and the severe lines of his mouth
add to this [unruly] impression." His wild demeanor was accompanied by a

pugnacious, informal style that set him at odds with his superiors. Nonetheless, Wiley's energy, quick mind, and gift for conviviality allowed him to become the Ralph Nader of his day. From the list of vitamins on the side of a cereal box to the rules for describing juice as ''natural'' or ''fresh,'' today's regulatory strictures on the sale of medicines and foodstuffs had their genesis in his career.

Born in 1844, Harvey Washington Wiley was raised on a farm in southern Indiana by fundamentalist parents. He was late to start school, but ended up at Harvard. He acquired an M.D., but never practiced. At thirty, he became a professor of chemistry at Purdue University, where his practice of riding around the campus on a bicycle scandalized the faculty. Rebuked by the board of trustees for his behavior, he threatened to resign. The trustees backed down. While at Purdue, he was asked to become the Indiana state chemist. He prepared himself for the job by a summer of study in Germany, where he came to admire that nation's strict food and drug laws. As state chemist, he campaigned against the then-common practice of mixing chemical additives into food without telling consumers. Wiley loathed secret adulteration, which he viewed as a betrayal of a public trust. His campaign went with him to Washington, D.C., in 1883, when he was appointed the nation's chief chemist. So did his penchant for vehicular innovation; he was the third person in the capital to own a car, and the first to get into an accident.

The Chemical Division of the Department of Agriculture had a professional staff of ten. (Later it was renamed the Division of Chemistry, and then the Bureau of Chemistry.) Using this modest base, Wiley systematically investigated the purity of the nation's food supply. In sixteen years he conducted thousands of tests and produced an eight-part report on food adulteration in America. Its conclusion was simple: Food producers had used the advances of science to doctor nearly everything on the family supper table. Wiley began a campaign to reform America's foods.

Such crusades were ideally suited to his talents. ''Wiley had the knack of eliciting tremendous loyalty,'' an historian reports, ''and his personal associations, tending toward the conspiratorial, were as important as his public speaking in creating organized pressure for a food and drug bill. Endowed with tremendous energy, he could operate without tiring on several fronts.'' As a bachelor, he could flit among the many men's clubs in Washington, always with a smile, a slap on the back, a word about the terrible need for legislation. He stumped women's associations across the nation, alternating between passionate attacks on frauds and sudden, charming lapses into doggerel:

> We sit at a table delightfully spread,
>   And teeming with good things to eat,

And daintily finger the cream-tinted bread,
    Just needing to make it complete
A film of the butter so yellow and sweet,
    Well suited to make every minute
A dream of delight. And yet while we eat
    We cannot help asking "What's in it?"

A rationalist, Wiley thought that the food business could be cleaned up easily. If companies were required to list the ingredients of their wares clearly, the public would know what it was buying, listen to the advice of nutritionists, and avoid bad brands. Wiley opposed banning products outright, which he saw as an infringement on the rights of the public and the manufacturer. "It is not for me," he said, "to tell my neighbor what he shall eat, what he shall drink, what his religion shall be, or what his politics. These are matters which I think every man should be left to settle for himself." He simply wanted to ensure that the labels were not, as he said, "misleading in any particular." Detesting adulterants himself, he was sure that once Americans learned about the strange chemicals on their dinner plates, the industry would be forced to change its ways or collapse.

Spurred by Wiley, Congress considered legislation in 1897, but did nothing. Two years later, the Senate Committee on Manufacturers held hearings on the status of the nation's food supply. Wiley was the committee's scientific adviser. In this role he analyzed more than four hundred food samples, helped question witnesses, and testified as the hearing's first witness. Congress failed to follow up, and the session ended with no bill being passed. The next few years saw a repetition of this pattern—interest, but no action—although some form of legislation managed to edge forward a little further each time.

Wiley had always loathed the malodorous promotion surrounding patent medicines. But he emphasized his primary concern, pure food, until 1903, when he established a drug laboratory in the Bureau of Chemistry and began to attack patent medicines publicly. Wiley's shift came just as Congress was considering the latest round of food and drug legislation, and lawmakers were fighting over the definition of "drug." The choice was between a narrow definition, which would restrict the law to prescription drugs listed in *The United States Pharmacopeia* or other official lists, and a much broader one, which would bring patent medicines under the authority of the government. The Proprietary Association, the patent medicine trade group, led the fight against the broader definition. The association's fear was not that patent medicines would be banned; following Wiley's beliefs, none of the legislation under consideration went to this extreme. The nation's drug makers feared instead the requirement that products list their ingredients, forcing them to reveal their formulae. This, the Proprietary Association charged, "would practically destroy the sale of proprietary remedies in the United States." Wiley pressed on, spurred by the abrupt revelation of a loophole in the one federal statute—a mail fraud law—then able to attack quackery.

The revelation involved an organization known as the American School of Magnetic Healing, the brainchild of one J. H. Kelley, who showed up in the small town of Nevada, Missouri, in November 1897. Soon after his arrival, Kelley established the school: a large secretarial pool supervised by several men whom one observer described as possessing "only to a limited degree even the rudiments of education." These men placed advertisements in newspapers around the nation. The ads explained that Magnetic Healing could instantly cure ailments of any sort from a distance of thousands of miles because Kelley and the other Magnetic Healers had powers like those of Jesus Christ. Thousands of letters poured into Nevada, Missouri. Many contained checks. The secretaries opened the letters, extracted the checks, and mailed back a circular describing the school's amazing "absent treatment." At an hour specified in the circular, patients emptied their heads of thought. The Magnetic Healer turned his mental powers on the faraway patient, and the sickness vanished. In this way the school treated hundreds of people at the same time—an extremely efficient process.

The School of Magnetic Healing did land-rush business. Two years after its founding, it was receiving three thousand letters a day, and earned about half a million dollars annually. On May 15, 1900, the U.S. postmaster general instructed the Missouri post office to stop delivering mail to the school. Letters were stamped "fraudulent" and returned to their senders. The school sued the postmaster of Nevada, Missouri. Legal battles ensued, in which the school was able to muster testimony from dozens of satisfied users of the absent treatment. Eventually the case made its way to the Supreme Court, which acquitted Kelley and his Magnetic Healers.*

Wiley was outraged but helpless. According to the Supreme Court, the school's claims could not "be proved as a fact to be a fraud," because medical opinions varied on the worth of such treatments. In areas of medicine where doctors strongly differed—areas, in the court's words, "still in the empirical stage"—the post office had no power to prosecute frauds. The decision did not completely defeat efforts to combat patent medicines sold through the mail. It did, however, force the post office to pick its cases more carefully, and to bolster them with the overwhelming medical evidence

* When a Missouri newspaper called the Magnetic Healers "miserable charlatans," Kelley sued for libel. At the trial, Kelley was informed that if the circular told all patients across the nation to empty their minds at, say, 3:00 P.M., he would have had to schedule several different sessions, because 3:00 P.M. occurred at different times in different time zones. Kelley, the judge wrote, "gave no clear explanation on that point." Nor was he able to explain how he had healed patients when he was on a summer vacation in Colorado, and had not even seen the letters they sent in. The newspaper won, which meant that the government could not prosecute people who could not be slandered by the epithet "charlatan."

needed to show that the fraud was beyond "the empirical stage." Most important, the case underscored the need for reforms—reforms that, given the ability of special interests to paralyze Congress, could only come through public pressure.

In early 1905, Wiley was contacted by Samuel Hopkins Adams, a young journalist with an interest in health issues. On assignment for the muckraking *Collier's*, Adams bought patent medicines, had them analyzed by one of his old college professors, and asked experts if the ingredients could possibly have the advertised effect. He obtained advertising contracts between newspapers and patent medicine makers, complete with "red clauses," which said the contracts would be canceled if the paper attacked patent medicines. (The name came from the red ink used to print the clause in the first such contracts.) And he looked for honest manufacturers—a lonely and unproductive search. Wiley spent a lot of time with Adams, lending him clippings, and even correcting early drafts of his articles.

"The Great American Fraud," the first of a ten-part series, appeared in October 1905, lashing out at dozens of remedies and creating a storm of reaction that was everything Wiley had hoped. The next *Collier's* article ripped into what Adams called "The Subtle Poisons"—cough syrups that contained cocaine and opium, and headache remedies that contained acetanilid. Selling cough syrups, Adams wrote, was a "shameful trade . . . that stupefies helpless babies, and makes criminals of our young men and harlots of our young women." His scorn for acetanilid was equally fierce: "Acetanilid will undoubtedly relieve headache of certain kinds; but acetanilid, as the basis of headache powders, is prone to remove the cause of the symptoms permanently by putting a complete stop to the heart action." (Adams did not rap Bayer Aspirin because it was available only through pharmacists.) He listed twenty-two victims of acetanilid overdoses and presented a ghastly parade of symptoms from surviving users. Worst, he claimed, acetanilid was addictive; its widespread use raised the specter of a nation of analgesic junkies.

Adams's articles induced President Theodore Roosevelt to speak out in December 1905 in favor of food and drug legislation. The Proprietary Association was bitter. "If the Federal Government should regulate interstate traffic in drugs on the basis of their therapeutic value," its Committee on Legislation asked, "why not regulate traffic in theology, by excluding from transportation all books which Dr. Wiley and his assistants . . . find to be 'misleading in any particular'?" Roosevelt having entered the fight, Congress no longer dared to bury the issue. After two months of rough debate, the Senate surprised reformers by actually passing a bill in February 1906; in the House, however, similar legislation languished, for reasons that were too familiar to Wiley:

[Washington, D.C.] has been full of lobbyists with plenty of money, indomitable energy and unceasing push, and it appears that they have the poor little food bill by the throat and are administering to the infant a lethal dose of soothing syrup.*

The law would have died once again had not chance intervened, in the form of the then obscure left-wing writer Upton Sinclair. The day after the appearance of the last part of "The Great American Fraud," Sinclair published *The Jungle*, a Zolaesque novel documenting the disgusting conditions in Chicago stockyards. It was a huge best-seller. Learning that the novel's portrayal was accurate, Roosevelt insisted that Congress ensure that American meat was fit for human consumption. The result was the Meat Inspection Amendments to the Agriculture Appropriations Act, signed into law on June 30, 1906, the last day of that session of Congress. As the amendments made their way through Congress, the House revived the stalled food and drug legislation. Despite attempts by lobbyists to wrap themselves in the flag— "Where liberty reigns," cried the Proprietary Association's president, "there you will find proprietary medicines"—Roosevelt signed the Food and Drug Act into law on the same day. Reflecting on the moment nearly twenty-five years later, Wiley unabashedly took credit for the law's passage: "How does a general feel who wins a great battle and brings a final end to hostilities? I presume I felt that way on the last day of June 1906."

Despite such words, the law was far from what Wiley had hoped. It covered the adulteration and misbranding of drugs and food. A drug or food was adulterated if its ingredients were in *The United States Pharmacopeia* or *The National Formulary* but did not follow the standards established in those official lists; they were misbranded if their packages or labels bore any statement "which shall be false or misleading in any particular." Lastly, the law forced drug labels to reveal the amount, as well as the presence, of such substances as alcohol, morphine, opium, cocaine, heroin—and acetanilid.

Most of Wiley's attention was occupied by the act's food provisions. Nevertheless, he wanted to test the rules covering the misbranding of drugs; the Magnetic Healing decision was still fresh in his mind. Wiley thought the best arena for the test would be Washington, D.C.: It would conserve his enforcement resources, and the law imposed greater penalties for drugs manufactured in the District than drugs shipped through interstate commerce. (Congress can pass laws governing the internal affairs of the nation's capital, but not of the states.) He found what he was looking for in Harper's Cuforhedake Brane Fude.

---

* "Soothing syrup" was a type of patent medicine. The most infamous example was Mrs. Winslow's soothing syrup, a mixture of cocaine and opium sold as a cough suppressant for infants.

*   *   *

On August 27, 1907, Henry C. Fuller, an assistant chemist in the Department of Agriculture, entered the Stone & Poole pharmacy in downtown Washington and bought nine bottles of Harper's analgesic. Analyzing the bottles in the department laboratory, he found that Harper was selling acetanilid, as the label reported. What concerned Wiley and his assistants was the circular that accompanied the bottle. It said that Brane Fude contained no poisonous ingredients, which was at odds with Wiley's views on acetanilid. And in Wiley's opinion, the name of the remedy—Cuforhedake Brane Fude— suggested that Harper's drug did not just confer temporary relief for headaches, but provided a permanent cure.

In October 1907 the Department of Agriculture notified Harper of its concerns about Brane Fude. He replied that the circular and the name of the product did not violate the Food and Drug Act, but he offered to change whatever the government wanted him to change, if it then guaranteed that he would not be prosecuted. The department refused. On the advice of his lawyer, Harper changed Brane Fude to Brain Food, and dropped the "no poisonous ingredients." It was not enough. He was arrested in January. Agents from the Department of Agriculture stormed his lab, seized bottles as they were being filled, confiscated tons of Brane Fude (old bottles) and Brain Food (new bottles), and filed criminal charges against him—the first made under the act.

The trial began on February 20, 1908, and attracted extraordinary interest. As one editorial put it, "A class of men who are not given to hysteria— bankers, commercial men, food and drug manufacturers, lawyers, government officials, and in an especial manner wholesale and retail druggists—are watching the precedent-making case now on trial with an eagerness we believe has seldom been equalled." After the government's opening statement, it called witnesses to establish that Harper sold the drug, and that it contained acetanilid. Wiley then took the stand to address a collateral issue, the meaning of "Brane Fude." "There is no food that nourishes the brain that does not also nourish other parts of the body," he said. Therefore, "brain food," however it was spelled, was misleading, and Harper was guilty. In Wiley's view, it was as simple as that.

U.S. Attorney D. W. Baker asked the chief prosecution witness, Reid Hunt of the Marine Hospital Service, to explain the effects of acetanilid. Was acetanilid a food? Baker inquired. "No." Either to the body or to the brain? "No." What, Baker asked, is its effect? "Well," Hunt said, "upon the brain it produces . . . a deadening effect, a sedative effect. Upon the motor part of the brain and the spinal cord, it is irritating and tends to cause a certain amount of convulsions. The most marked effect is upon the temperature in case of fever." How about the heart? When acetanilid use "is continued for any length of time, [it causes] a very extensive destruction of the blood, and as many as four-fifths of the red corpuscles may be destroyed.'' Once again, U.S. Attorney Baker asked if anything in the formula built up the brain. ''Nothing whatever,'' Hunt replied. The prosecution rested.

The defense took up the cudgel with surprising vigor. Chief defense attorney C. C. Tucker introduced Virgil Coblentz, a professor of pharmacy at Columbia University and a German-educated expert on acetanilid. After tracing Coblentz's lengthy academic résumé, Tucker asked, ''Would you or would you not say that this preparation was a poisonous preparation or otherwise?''

''I would not consider it a poisonous preparation,'' Coblentz said.

''Suppose a person who is free from idiosyncrasies should take the entire contents of this bottle . . . , would or would not that poison him?''

''I think not,'' Coblentz said. In any case, he said, calling acetanilid a poison was naïve. Almost any substance was toxic in large amounts. Describing something as dangerous without reference to dose was simply foolish. If buyers followed the regimen suggested by Harper, acetanilid was perfectly safe.

The defense matched the government expert for expert, hoping that the court would find the Magnetic Healing standard persuasive. (If experts differed on the dangers of acetanilid, the issue was still in the ''empirical [*relying upon observation or experiment*] stage,'' and Harper could not be found guilty.) Tucker also called prominent people to testify that they were satisfied Brane Fude users, including the treasurer of the National League of Base Ball Clubs, an editor of the *Washington Times*, an attorney for the Interstate Commerce Commission, and a Census Bureau administrator. After countering the government's case on nearly every point, the defense rested.

Judge Kimball's instructions returned the momentum to the prosecution. He did not mention that reasonable doubt could be created by a difference of scientific opinion, or that the size of the dose could affect the toxicity of a drug. Instead he asked the jury to determine the poisonous nature of acetanilid without regard to the actual likelihood that the dose in the bottle would cause harm. If Brane Fude contained a poisonous ingredient in any measure, he said, the verdict must be guilty. If ''Brane Fude'' meant ''brain food,'' it had to *be* brain food, its nutritional action centered on the brain. Otherwise, the verdict must be guilty. After Kimball explained that the law said the label could not be false ''in any particular,'' the jury took but twenty-five minutes to decide that ''Brane Fude'' meant ''brain food.'' The label was therefore false, and Harper, guilty.

The elated prosecution faced one last hurdle. To set an effective precedent, Harper had to be punished to the limits of the law. Unfortunately, the maximum fine of $700 was less than the costs of the trial. Because the charges had been criminal, the government demanded the one-year jail term provided by statute. To add muscle to the request, Department of Agriculture and Department of Justice officials approached President Roosevelt, asking him to call for a jail sentence. Although the executive branch usually hesitates to interfere with the judiciary, the impetuous Roosevelt issued a public appeal to punish Harper severely. Only at the last moment was he dissuaded from personally approaching Judge Kimball. U.S. Attorney Baker was instead summoned to the Oval Office on March 16. There, the president explained his wishes:

> It is your duty to make an example of this man and show to the people of this country that the pure food law was enacted to protect them. He has been convicted after a fair and impartial trial, and you should use every argument in your power to convince the judge to impose a jail sentence. To a man with his wealth, a fine as the penalty for his violation of the law would be little less than ridiculous.

Lawyers across the city spluttered with rage at the president's meddling with the judicial process; crowds of sympathizers thronged Harper's office. "I am not in the jailbird class," Harper declared, smiling. Two days later, he resigned his bank presidency, saying the notoriety would harm the institution.

A month afterward, he was sentenced in a crowded courtroom; Wiley was in the audience. Kimball ignored the Brane Fude issue almost completely, although it had convicted Harper. Instead he stated his belief that Brane Fude, food for the brain or not, was mislabeled; Harper was a trained pharmacist, and acetanilid was a dangerous drug, even if only in amounts above the recommended dose. On the other hand, Harper had shown himself willing to change the label. Defying the president, Judge Kimball did not mete out a jail sentence. Instead he imposed the $700 fine.

Wiley was disgusted. Harper had made $2 million from Brane Fude; with the fine, Wiley said, he "was just $1,999,300 ahead." In his view, the drug industry had triumphed.

Wiley was only half correct. In the wake of the Brane Fude decision, Harper stopped selling analgesics.* But the promotion and sale of headache powders and other patent medicines continued unabated. Surprised by the medical dispute at the Harper trial, Wiley ordered a thorough study of the harmful

---

* Harper went on to an even more distinguished career as a Washington, D.C., banker active in Democratic politics. He eventually became the treasurer of the Democratic National Congressional Committee and the chair of President Wilson's Inaugural Committee. At the behest of President Coolidge, he served as an honorary economic adviser to China in 1928, along with Henry Ford and two other industrialists. He died in 1940 at the age of 79.

effects of acetanilid, antipyrine, and acetophenetidin. Published in 1909, the report detailed the frightening liver, kidney, and gastrointestinal damage caused by big doses of analgesics, especially acetanilid. In response, some analgesic makers switched from acetanilid to acetophenetidin, which is safer. Bromo-Seltzer removed its acetanilid, as did Laxative Bromo-Quinine. Antikamnia, once a leading acetanilid brand, put "No Acetanilid" on its label.

Nevertheless, acetanilid continued to appear under dozens of peculiar sobriquets: U-Re-Ka Headache Powders, Telephone Headache Tablets, Falck's One-Minute Headache Cure, Funny-How-Quick Headache and Neuralgia Cure ("Does not stupefy, but braces one up"), and The Infallible Headache Tablet, which styled itself an "infallible cure" for the condition of "bighead." One Bureau of Chemistry report complained that the legion of analgesics seemed to be "increasing daily. It is true here and there a certain brand is discontinued, but new ones are introduced." A 1910 survey covered no fewer than 252 brands of headache remedy, of which 72 were found by the bureau to be misbranded or adulterated.

The Bureau of Chemistry filed hundreds of cases under the 1906 act. For the most part, accused drug merchants did not resist; it was easier to pay the $700 fine. But ultimately even that small sanction was nullified by the maker of Dr. Johnson's Mild Combination Treatment for Cancer, who hobbled the Bureau of Chemistry as thoroughly as J. H. Kelley and Magnetic Healing had impeded the post office.

A Kansas City M.D., Johnson made Cancerine tablets, Antiseptic tablets, Blood Purifier, Special No. 4, and Cancerine Nos. 1 and 17, the totality of which constituted Dr. Johnson's Mild Combination Treatment for Cancer. "This is an effective tonic and alterative," the Blood Purifier label claimed. "It enters the circulation at once, utterly destroying and removing impurities from the blood and entire system. Acts on bowels, kidneys, and skin, eliminating poisons from the system, and when taken in connection with the Mild Combination Treatment gives splendid results in the treatment of cancer and other malignant diseases." In 1909 the Bureau of Chemistry indicted Johnson on six counts of false labeling and misbranding.

At the subsequent trial, the judge followed the Pure Food and Drug Act with absurd literal-mindedness. He pointed out that Johnson's labels were accurate and that therefore the drugs were not adulterated or misbranded in terms of the amounts or composition of the ingredients. Even if, as the judge frankly admitted, the claims for the drug's effect were fraudulent, Johnson had not violated the Food and Drug Act. Wiley appealed to the Supreme Court, which upheld the initial decision, vindicating Dr. Johnson.

Wiley was left with an empty law. He could not convict a charlatan who preyed on the dying with phony cancer remedies so long as the ingredients of the worthless cure were accurately stated. Maybe the Supreme Court could understand why there was no connection between making phony claims on a label and being mislabeled, the devastated Wiley told a reporter. "I don't. All I can make out is that it gives anyone the right to lie about drugs whenever he feels like it." President Taft, Roosevelt's successor, deplored the ruling, and complained that more than 150 food and drug cases would be overturned. Congress promptly amended the Food and Drug Act to permit prosecution of "false and fraudulent" claims. But the term "false and fraudulent" was, in Wiley's words, a "joker." As interpreted by the courts, it required the government to prove fraudulent intent, and all quacks were willing to swear to their good intentions. The Food and Drug Act had been gutted.

A better crusader than an enforcer, Wiley came under fire for following his truth-in-labeling beliefs to petty extremes. Because he took the label literally, one of Wiley's superiors mockingly complained, the Bureau of Chemistry spent its time on such crucial questions as whether "boneless cod strips" must be from cod with *no* bones or if ladyfinger cookies were misbranded because they were not "actually the result of mayhem." Wiley's enemies seized their opportunity in 1911 when he was accused of hiring an outside consultant improperly. Not the most serious of charges, it was enough to allow his opponents within the Bureau of Chemistry to seek his dismissal. Although he was cleared of any wrongdoing by a congressional committee, Wiley resigned in March 1912 from the Bureau of Chemistry to write a column for *Good Housekeeping*. Becoming a muckraker himself, he churned out articles such as "The Inherent 'No-Accountness' of Patent Medicines." He was often asked his opinion of headache powders, once by a Wisconsin woman who wanted a list of the unsafe ones. "Dear Madam," Wiley wrote. "It is not necessary for me to send you a list of headache powders that are not safe. All headache powders belong to the unsafe class. . . . There is, therefore, only one safe rule: Avoid all headache powders." Still, he was a bitter man. Despite constant demands for change, headache remedies continued to flourish, as did patent medicines. Wiley spent the next eighteen years railing against what he saw as the evisceration of the Food and Drug Act.

Wiley's last fight was on behalf of another disappointed reformer, Howard W. Ambruster. This was the early Ambruster, importer of crude ergot, rather than the later Ambruster, sworn enemy of Sterling Products. In 1930, one recalls, Ambruster sparked a congressional inquiry into the regulation of imported drugs by the Food, Drug, and Insecticide Administration, the bureaucratic successor to the Bureau of Chemistry. When the hearings opened before the Senate Committee on Agriculture and Forestry, Wiley, though seriously ill at the time, spoke on his behalf. His testimony covered the history of the 1906 act, illustrating the need for tight regulation by the Food, Drug, and Insecticide Administration. Just as he steeled himself to recount the many ways his administration of the law had been thwarted, Senator

Charles McNary of Oregon, chairman of the committee, interrupted him. The hearing was an inquiry into substandard imported drugs, the senator reminded him, not Wiley's personal history. Wiley replied that he was not prepared to speak on that subject.

Later that month, his wife appeared before the committee on his behalf, delivering a message from her ailing husband. He had testified under a misapprehension about the nature of the hearings. "I am a very ill man at the present time," he wrote, "and I can not prepare what I wanted to say, even if it were in order for me to do so." One week later, at the age of eighty-six, Harvey W. Wiley died, convinced that his reforms had done no more than prick the quacks and adulterers he hated.

CHAPTER NINE

"AS MUCH BITE AS A CANTON-FLANNEL DOG"

L ess than ten years after its passage, the Food and Drug Act was in tatters. Wiley had believed that consumers who knew the ingredients of a food or drug would be able to distinguish between good and bad products, and their native intelligence would lead them to avoid the bad ones. But as experience with the law accumulated, it became obvious that truth in labeling was not enough. Patent medicines continued to sell, and another reform movement rose to decry both quackery and Wiley's law. One of its most notable members was George Creel, a journalist who later gained a measure of infamy as the head of a wartime propaganda committee charged by President Wilson to whip up "the people's righteous wrath" against Germany. In 1915 Creel wrote a series in *Harper's Weekly* much like the *Collier's* articles by Samuel Hopkins Adams ten years before.

Over the years, Creel wrote, the Food and Drug Act had "its teeth drawn one by one, until now it has about as much bite as a Canton-flannel dog [the contemporary equivalent of a teddy bear]." It was foolish, he said, to depend on the education and wit of the citizenry:

> The ultimate goal will not be reached until the public is afforded a protection that does not rest upon the initiative of the individual. Disclosure of ingredients will kill the sale of injurious compounds to persons of intelligence, perhaps, but it will not do to forget the large percentage of ignorant, careless or reckless purchasers, who will still persist in the use of health-destroying preparations. This is the problem.

Acetanilid was a prime example: "What proportion of headache sufferers know that it is a heart depressant that possesses fatal potentialities?"

The greatest problem with the law, Creel said, was that it did not cover advertising. Wiley used the act to clean up drug labeling, which included any accompanying literature such as the circular that came with Harper's concoction. A few nostrum makers, such as Dr. Johnson, fought this approach; most complied, not by stopping their outrageous claims but by moving them from the label to their consumer advertising. Through newspapers and magazines, they bombarded customers with soothing messages of safety and brazen claims of cures. Hope for self-regulation by the press had "grown old and decrepit," Creel said. As a result, Creel thought, Wiley's act was "a joke." "The Food and Drug law," he declared, "cannot be anything but a circling of Robin Hood's barn as long as the patent medicine liar has the daily press at his disposal." Something had to be done, he said, about advertising.

Advertising is the action of bringing something, usually a good or service, to the attention of the public. It provides information, though with no guarantee that it is accurate or complete. Sometimes the information consists of detailed claims about price or performance; often it is nothing more than the name of the brand. In its most benign form, advertising describes a product (aspirin, for example) and says something of interest about it (aspirin can prevent heart attacks). With data provided by truthful advertising, people make "good" choices (asking a doctor whether to use aspirin). But if the information in an advertisement is misunderstood, misleading, or simply false, people make "bad" choices (deciding that a more expensive brand of aspirin is better for the heart than a cheaper one). In both cases, the idea is the same: Companies use advertising to influence consumers in their economic choices, and consumers use advertising to make decisions about their economic life.

In many cases, the truthfulness of an advertisement is not difficult to ascertain. A claim that the price of a can of Campbell's soup is 99 cents, for example, can be confirmed or refuted on the next trip to the grocery store; a claim that a particular car is available in green can be tested by sight; even a promise that an analgesic will relieve a headache in twenty seconds can be verified with a stopwatch. But if the claim is that the price is "low," that the paint has a special undercoat, or that the relief is faster and more gentle than that provided by other brands, truth becomes harder to establish. And if the claim is for a product with capabilities (or shortcomings) beyond the understanding of the average person, determining the veracity of an advertisement becomes next to impossible.

Faced with an ad that is difficult to evaluate, people may try indirect means to weigh its reliability. Did the previous appliance bought from this company last a long time? Has the company produced other products that I've been happy with? Was the service my neighbor received with her purchase as good as was claimed? If a company was truthful before, people may choose to believe it a second time. Similarly, they may shun firms with a history of lies.

("Fool me once," the adage goes, "shame on you; fool me twice, shame on me.") In this way reputations are built.

Good reputations keep businesses going; bad reputations bring unpleasant consequences, as consumers abandon product lines after a disappointment. Consistent lying should therefore be the sole province of flimflam artists—a favorite example is the door-to-door peddlers of aluminum siding—who make their sales through high-pressure talk and appeals to emotion, not reason, and then move on, furious customers in their wake. To say otherwise would be to argue that people have no memory, or are stupid—dispiriting sentiments in a democracy.

Yet false advertising is as old as commerce itself. When J. H. Kelley established the American School of Magnetic Healing, thousands of people every year cleared their minds at the appointed time and calmly waited to be healed. And thousands believed that they were cured by Magnetic Healing, at least for a while. It seems incomprehensible that so many people willingly suspended rationality long enough to part with the required money—and yet they did. Were they unable to perceive the fraud? Were they powerless to be suspicious of absurd claims? Or were they merely stupid?

In the United States, these questions are the province of the Federal Trade Commission, a regulatory agency that opened its doors for business one month after George Creel decried the lack of such a body. The commission's role as the sheriff of advertising came as a surprise to its founders, for it had been created to fight "unfair methods of competition in commerce," not false advertising. And, in fact, the agency exerted relatively little control over advertising, let alone analgesic advertising, in the first years of its existence. But by the 1930s, the FTC was going after aspirin brands and headache remedies with a vengeance, beginning a history of analgesic false-advertising litigation which is, as Madison Avenue might say, unsurpassed for length and complexity. It culminated in a *Bleak House*-style legal battle that began in the 1960s and lasted well into the 1980s, when the first replacements for the first lawyers had long since been replaced and few indeed could recall exactly why and how the first complaints had been brought.

The FTC was a reaction to the huge trusts that Carl Duisberg so admired on his visits to the United States. But far from sharing Duisberg's esteem for U.S. Steel and Standard Oil, Congress and the American public were appalled by the companies' economic might. Even before Duisberg's visit, the Sherman Anti-Trust Act of 1890 had been passed to stifle cartels and monopolies. It didn't work. Twenty-two years later, Woodrow Wilson campaigned for president with the promise that he would do something about trusts. He found a receptive audience in Congress. Business leaders also wanted a new law, one that unlike the Sherman act would spell out clearly the practices from which they were supposed to refrain. Satisfying both, Wilson asked Congress for a law with a specific list of illegal business practices and methods of competition. In addition, he urged the creation of an interstate trade commission to collect information about fair business practices.

In June 1914, Congress passed two laws derived from these proposals. The Clayton Antitrust Act, as Wilson had envisioned, contained a specific list of practices declared illegal: price discrimination, exclusive-dealing contracts (restricting a buyer to a single seller), corporate mergers that reduced competition, and interlocking directorates that achieved the same end. The Federal Trade Commission Act created a new agency with the power to act against "unfair methods of competition." George Rublee, who wrote the act, served as one of the first commissioners; he took "unfair methods" to mean that the commission's powers were limited to attacking only those monopolistic practices that could not be controlled by the Justice Department through the Sherman or Clayton act. But, as seems to happen to bureaucratic organizations, the commission quickly expanded its reach. Rublee was dismayed to find his commission taking stances he had never imagined when he brought it into being. Many of these stances involved false advertising.

Advertising reform was in the air. Influenced by Adams, Creel, and Wiley, trade organizations such as the Advertising Men's League and the Associated Advertising Clubs of America had campaigned in favor of honesty for some years. Advertising-vigilance groups arose in Atlanta, Denver, Des Moines, Milwaukee, Minneapolis, Seattle, and other cities. The trade magazine *Printers' Ink* published a model state law covering truth in advertising in 1912. Within a year the statute had been introduced in fifteen state legislatures and passed in Ohio. (Twenty-three states passed it by 1921.) Even the Proprietary Association cooperated, unanimously endorsing the *Printers' Ink* approach in 1915.

Sensing the zeitgeist, FTC chairman Joseph P. Davies asked the Associated Advertising Clubs of the World to speak before the commission in November 1915. The group urged the agency to treat false advertising as an unfair method of competition. The FTC, a bureaucracy in search of a mission, was happy to comply: The first two legal actions it undertook were against false advertising.

It soon ran into a question: Should the commission root out each and every instance of a false claim, no matter how ludicrous and transparent, or should it suppress only the most sly and dangerous forms of deception? An example of the agency's quandary comes from its struggle to clean up door-to-door encyclopedia sales. Such peddlers commonly promised "free" multivolume sets—customers had only to buy expensive quarterly or yearly supplements. When the supplements arrived, they proved to be cheaply printed loose-leaf folders; buying the supplements, of course, was how consumers paid for the "free" encyclopedia.

The FTC sued several encyclopedia companies for these practices. Faced with a novel form of litigation, the courts looked for a standard by which to judge the unfairness of the practices, and found it in the notion of the "reasonable man." In cases of pornography, for example, judges try to decide whether average people, applying contemporary community standards, would find material prurient; libel, too, depends on the messages ordinary readers would derive from a book or magazine. Publishers cannot be punished for offending the overly puritanical; similarly, they cannot be sued for libel because confused readers might derive impressions that are actionable. In the "free encyclopedia" cases, the courts at first ruled that a consumer would have to be, in the words of one appellate decision of 1925, "a very stupid person [to] be misled by this method of selling books." Therefore, "by ordinary standards of the intelligence of traders, we cannot discover that it amounts to an unfair method of competition within the sense of the law." Eleven years later, another judge told the FTC that he could not treat "seriously the suggestion that a man who is buying a set of books and a ten years' 'extension service' will be fatuous enough to be misled by the mere statement that the first are given away, and that he is paying only for the second." The FTC, in short, could not go into the business of protecting nincompoops from their own stupidity.

Soon the pendulum swung the other way. The judge who could not conceive of customers being "fatuous enough to be misled" was overturned by the Supreme Court in 1937. "Laws are made to protect the trusting as well as the suspicious," the Court wrote. "The best element of business has long since decided that honesty should govern competitive enterprises, and that the rule of *caveat emptor* should not be relied upon to reward fraud and deception." With such august support, the commission began to insist, Wiley-fashion, on the most literal truthfulness in advertising. The barest possibility that some dolt might misinterpret a claim was enough to get a company dragged into court. In 1939 the FTC sued the maker of a facial cream for the outrageous claim implicit in its name: Rejuvenescence. No cream could actually replace one's complexion with a younger model, the commission charged. The company fought—and lost. People might be fooled, the court declared, into thinking that Rejuvenescence was a "perpetual fountain of youth." Perhaps the agency's most forceful protection of community standards of idiocy came in a 1944 case against a hair dye company for saying that it could "color hair permanently," which the FTC argued might dupe people into thinking that the dye could color hair not yet grown in. Although an appellate court admitted that it "seems scarcely possible that any user . . . could be so credulous," the judges refused to overturn the commission's determination, leaving the FTC primed to insist on the most literal truth in advertising, "clear enough so that, in the words of the prophet Isaiah, 'wayfaring men, though fools, shall not err therein.' "

That it took thirty years for the commission's advertising standard to evolve did not mean that the FTC was idle in the meantime. Actions against misrepresentation, the legal category that includes false advertising as its major component, occupied a growing fraction of the agency's time. In 1918 only 10 of 154 complaints filed by the FTC involved misrepresentation. Ten years later, 36 of 62—more than half—fell into that category. By 1933, when the commission launched what was to be the first of more than a dozen cases against aspirin makers, it was up to its neck in false advertising.

When Sterling Products acquired the Bayer name, William E. Weiss claimed that the company was the biggest advertiser in the world, and vowed to spread the name of Bayer aspirin through every newspaper and magazine in the United States. In fact, Sterling was slow to advertise Bayer aspirin in the United States, though the firm went all out on promotion in Latin America. Its discreet U.S. ads promised to cure "colds, pain, toothache, neuritis, headache, neuralgia, lumbago, [and] rheumatism," and counseled consumers to buy the genuine article. ("Warning! Say 'Bayer' when you buy Aspirin," the company told magazine readers in 1922.) But because the accumulated power of the Bayer name was enormous, the brand continued to prosper despite its high price and minimal promotion.

All this changed in the 1930s, when Sterling did in fact become the huge force in U.S. advertising that Weiss had promised. It had to—the competition was catching up. From Asper-Lax, an aspirin-laxative-stimulant ("No waiting for results. . . . No need to stay indoors"), to American Purest aspirin ("Registered U.S. Patent Office") and Lord's aspirin (which touted, incredibly, its high melting point, because "the lower the melting point the more opportunity for aspirin to form that same substance in your stomach which is sold over drug counters to remove corns"), drugstore shelves groaned with what one Bayer executive later estimated was a thousand competing brands of aspirin.

Many of Bayer's imitators were soluble or effervescent. The most well known of these was Alka-Seltzer, developed by Miles Laboratories, of Elkhart, Indiana, on the basis of what might be called anecdotal research. During a 1928 flu epidemic, Miles president A. H. "Hub" Beardsley visited the offices of the *Elkhart Truth*, the local daily. To his surprise, none of the staff was sick. Inquiring further, he learned that the paper's managing editor dosed his staff with daily drinks of aspirin and bicarbonate of soda. Impressed, Beardsley asked his head chemist, Maurice Treneer, to make a tablet of the two compounds. Both men had talked about the possibility of making a soluble aspirin pill; soluble, fizzy aspirin pills seemed a logical extension. In January 1929, the Beardsley family went on a Mediterranean cruise, accompanied by a gross of the new tablets. The passage was unpleasant; everyone was seasick, and there was a flu virus aboard. Beardsley passed out his tablets, and the passengers felt better, except for the two that died of pneumonia. After Miles improved the tablets to prevent them from exploding in the package, he marketed them in 1931 under the name of Alka-Seltzer. A few years later, Beardsley was chagrined to discover Alka-Seltzer had been paid the sincerest commercial compliment: It had more than two hundred imitators.

Sterling fought to maintain its dominance by jumping into a new medium, broadcast radio. Broadcasting began in the 1920s, when radio manufacturers put out news briefs to give their customers something to listen to. No one thought of putting advertisements on the air. That was the brainchild of American Telephone and Telegraph, which announced it would rent a transmitter to anyone who wanted it. Companies used the time to inform the public of their virtues. In 1926, the National Broadcasting Company was formed, and sold airtime to programs like *The Maxwell House Hour, The Palmolive Hour,* and *The General Motors Family Party.* Most featured concerts, and all were introduced by words from the sponsors. For some time, NBC was small; its 1931 advertising revenues of $25.9 million were less than the $35 million in ad sales of the *Saturday Evening Post.* Almost two-thirds of all radio programming was put on by stations themselves, with no advertising or sponsorship at all.

The relatively small initial ad sales did not reflect the programs' popularity, for radio won a loyalty that seems astonishing today. In the isolated small towns of depression-era America, the voice on the crystal set promised contact with the rest of the world. Destitute families forced to give up beds and kitchen tables clung to their radios, and the programming on them— including the ads. Listening to the radio, one critic moaned, Americans had come "to speak, think, feel in terms of this jabberwocky."

Sterling certainly hoped so. It and other aspirin companies were among the first to see the new medium's potential. By 1932, about one-fifth of national radio advertising featured drug and cosmetic products such as aspirin. With the ever-rising profits from the I.G. pouring into its coffers, Sterling paid for songs, programs, and news shows, and even put out a record, "American Album of Familiar Music," featuring singer Frank Munn. It sponsored the *Bayer Cavalcade of Song,* with an announcer who continually assured listeners that genuine Bayer aspirin did not affect the heart. With cheerful disregard for the truth, Sterling laced into other aspirin brands as dangerous impostors.

> Take Care! Counterfeit Aspirin! Thousands of boxes of counterfeit aspirin have been put on the market. Watch out. Take no chances and flatly refuse to accept any box not marked "Genuine Bayer Aspirin." Don't put any tablet not marked "Bayer" into your stomach. Tell your

family and your friends this. Refuse any preparation offered you as the "same" or "like" Bayer Aspirin.

By 1936, Sterling was the nation's fourth-biggest radio advertiser—astonishing, considering that the leaders were selling expensive goods such as cars. It spent almost half a million dollars in that year to broadcast Bayer aspirin commercials; it added another three hundred thousand dollars to promote the brand in magazines. And Sterling was by no means alone; its competitors were on the air too, each trying to outdo the others for listeners' attention and pocket change. Laymon's aspirin led "all competitors in quality," but Burton's aspirin did not "nauseate," and Everfresh aspirin was "fresher" than both.

As the claims escalated, the FTC became more active. Between September 1934 and April 1938, the agency found thirteen aspirin makers guilty of false advertising. Bayer aspirin, Best aspirin, Burton's aspirin, Cal-Aspirin, St. Joseph aspirin—all were admonished by the commission, most for saying that their aspirin was somehow different from that of their rivals. After a bit of protest, all promised not to claim this anymore. (Some companies forgot their promises, and had to be admonished again; St. Joseph was sued twice in this period.)

The pattern was considerably altered when the Federal Trade Commission sued a now-forgotten preparation called Aspirub.* Aspirub was aspirin with a difference: It was an ointment and came in a jar like a facial cream. Made by the Justin Haynes Company, of New York City, Aspirub consisted of petroleum jelly, camphor, menthol, pine oil, eucalyptus oil, oil of lavender, oil of spearmint, methyl salicylate, and aspirin. To relieve a cold, purchasers were supposed to apply it to their chests and throats and insert dabs in their nostrils. Like other brands, Aspirub was advertised heavily.

Get a jar of ASPIRUB today! Snuff it through your nostrils! Inhale its vapors when dissolved in hot water! Rub it on your chest overnight! . . . And see if ASPIRUB isn't the nicest, quickest-acting cold treatment you've ever used. Get a jar from your druggist today!

Unlike other brands, Aspirub fought the FTC.

In 1937 three expert witnesses testified before the agency that the ingredients of Aspirub could not treat colds effectively. They pointed out that aspirin cannot be absorbed through the skin, and that even if it could the dose in Aspirub—a two-and-a-half-ounce jar contained the equivalent of two regular tablets—would be too small to do anything. Putting aspirin on, say, a

---

* This brand should not be confused with today's Aspirub, an aspirin salve made by Aspi-Rub Laboratories, of Hackensack, New Jersey.

sore elbow was foolish, one witness argued, because aspirin acted on the central nervous system, not the elbow.

Justin Haynes's defense was both odd and effective. It pointed out that the commission's experts had never tested Aspirub, and indeed that two of them did not even know how much blood was in the body. It countered the charge of ineffectiveness with its own medical theory. When ordinary aspirin is eaten, the firm said, the ASA is "hurried to all parts of the body . . . and its local effect thereby dissipated," whereas Aspirub is concentrated in the "definitely stagnant" blood beneath the skin. Moreover, Justin Haynes's lawyers argued, Aspirub was such a new means of using aspirin that it was not in competition with ordinary aspirin. It was thus outside the purview of the FTC, whose authority was limited to actions that hurt competition.* Finally, the company adduced clinical evidence of its own, in the form of a study conducted by Fortunato A. Diasio, M.D., of New York City.

A specialist in the treatment of syphilis and skin diseases, Diasio had received from Justin Haynes a hundred jars of something labeled "aromatic ointment." The ointment was, of course, Aspirub. Diasio performed an *ad hoc* clinical trial—he smeared the aromatic ointment on fifty randomly selected patients, ranging from a man with a toothache to a woman with menstrual cramps. The work was innovative: It was undoubtedly the first time that anyone had ever treated a sprained ankle by rubbing the leg with aspirin. The experimenter also subjected his patients to measures ranging from iodine and pituitary injections to surgical drainage and footbaths. In all fifty cases, the patients reported less pain. Diasio took this as proof of the ointment's efficacy, apparently not realizing either that the other treatments might be responsible for the improvement or that most pains will go away after a while on their own, and that therefore the mere lessening of discomfort is not evidence of an analgesic's efficacy.

The FTC scoffed at Diasio and demanded that Justin Haynes stop intimating that Aspirub had the analgesic power of aspirin, a virtual death sentence for the product's trademark. Justin Haynes appealed but found the appellate court unsympathetic. Aspirub was discontinued.

Despite the victory, the Justin Haynes case illustrated the utter inexperience of the FTC in evaluating the sort of scientific claims on which drug manufacturers rely. The Food and Drug Administration (the new name for the Food, Drug, and Insecticide Administration, which was the successor to the Bureau of Chemistry) had exactly this kind of expertise. One might expect the two agencies to cooperate in a crackdown on a rowdy industry

* This restriction had been emphasized in 1931 when the FTC sued the Raladam Company, makers of an obesity cure consisting of "desiccated thyroid" and other substances that would, the company claimed, safely melt away excess flesh. Although the medicine was bogus and even dangerous, the FTC's decision against it was overturned in court, because the agency had failed to demonstrate that the company had any competitors to harm.

such as the aspirin trade. And, in fact, this might have happened, to the great cost of aspirin makers, if the FDA and FTC had not been occupied just then by a brutal turf battle.

In the first days of 1933, Rexford G. Tugwell, the assistant secretary of agriculture, met with Walter G. Campbell, chief of the Food and Drug Administration, to discuss fruit insecticides. Many sprays left toxic lead compounds on the fruit, but the FDA set standards for labeling only the lead content on the insecticide can. If lead got on the fruit, Tugwell asked Campbell, why didn't the agency just ban it? The reason, Campbell said, was that the Food and Drug Act of 1906 did not give him the power to ban ingredients, even if they were as poisonous as lead. Tugwell couldn't believe it. He went directly to the office of President Franklin D. Roosevelt. Roosevelt too thought the law was crazy. Before the afternoon was over, Campbell was back in Tugwell's office, listening to Tugwell declare that it was time for a new act. The proposed law's scope quickly expanded from insecticides to all food and drugs.

That November, the FDA pushed Congress to enact Tugwell's statute. Because the agency was prohibited from lobbying Congress about legislation, it had to make its desires known indirectly. It mounted an exhibition of photographs depicting the horrible effects of the patent medicines that the Food and Drug Act of 1906 had failed to remove from the marketplace. One set of pictures showed an attractive woman before and after her eyes had been seared by an aniline eyelash dye; another recorded the ghastly death of a Pittsburgh businessman after drinking four daily doses of a "lost manhood" cure made from radium, mesothorium, and distilled water. Dubbed the Chamber of Horrors, the exhibition was displayed at the FDA and sent on an informal tour around the country. Senate hearings on Tugwell's bill opened the next month, initiating what proved to be a long and hard-fought political tussle over food and drug advertising.

Conditions were even less propitious for the new law than they had been for Wiley's. Tugwell's bill sought to resolve many of the Food and Drug Act's shortcomings by expanding the FDA's supervisory powers to cover both labeling and advertising. Once again, industry charged that the statute would take away the public's right to self-medication. Unlike thirty years before, however, no muckrakers created an upswell of public indignation to steel congressional resistance to lobbyists. Moreover, the bill's likely backers were divided. Consumer organizations and public health agencies supported the bill, but the AMA did not testify. And Consumers Research, a progenitor of the present Consumers Union, actually attacked it, because its Senate champion, Royal S. Copeland, frequently spoke on radio programs sponsored by a company that would be affected by the legislation, Fleischmann's

Yeast. The bill failed to gain any support in committee; neither did a second, redrafted version.

A third attempt occurred in February and March of 1934. This time a new player appeared: the Federal Trade Commission. Not bound in those days by any restriction on lobbying, the commissioners had wide latitude to influence Congress. The FTC saw the Tugwell bill as an FDA attempt to take away some of its power, and strenuously fought the usurpation. In a dexterous performance, Ewin L. Davis—Ambruster's ally, the former judge who had become FTC chairman—endorsed the idea of allowing the FDA to sue for false advertising—as long as the FTC remained the arbiter for those suits. Hobbled by the FTC's "endorsement," the bill died on the Senate floor in May.

In January 1935, with Roosevelt's support, a fourth version of the bill was introduced. Presidential backing ensured the Senate's passage of a bill giving power over food and drug advertising to the FDA. The House held its hearings on the bill in the summer. Judge Davis testified again, as did Ambruster. After explaining why the FTC should keep its power, Davis reminded the House of the fourteen marvelous years he had spent in its chambers. He begged his fellow representatives, his oldest friends, not to fail him in the hour of his agency's need. The House stalled until June of the following year, when it passed a law awarding the FTC custody of food and drug advertising—exactly what Davis wanted, and exactly the opposite of the Senate bill.

Partisans for both agencies fought in the House-Senate conference committee to resolve the differences between the two versions. They deadlocked over the advertising issue. Finally, the Senate conferees bullied their House counterparts into giving the FDA control over advertising that had health claims. Returned to the House for approval, the compromise bill instead provoked angry denunciations of senatorial arrogance. "If you want to place the advertising under Dr. Tugwell," thundered Representative B. Carroll Reece of Tennessee, "and give him a whiplash not only over business, but over the press of this country, vote for the motion made. . . ." Representative Sam D. McReynolds, another Tennesseean, appealed to House patriotism: "Are you not tired of the Senate saying to this House, 'If you do not agree to what we say, you shall not pass a bill'?" To applause, he demanded, "Gentlemen, it is time to stand up and demand your rights. Let us send it back to them and say: 'If you do not agree with our amendment, you kill the bill.' " The compromise was overwhelmingly rejected.

In March 1937, the Senate passed Tugwell's bill yet again. The House sat on its hands for months, during which time FTC supporters prepared a flank attack in the Senate. The major objection to retaining FTC control over advertising was that the agency lacked the power to fine or imprison anyone for false advertising. Instead, it could merely issue a cease and desist order, which told the guilty party not to do it again. (If a company violated the order, it could then be fined, but it always got "one free bite of the apple.") To reformers a cease and desist order was not much of a penalty for people who preyed on the sick. Senator Wheeler of Montana, Ambruster's ally in the ergot battle, introduced a bill to give the FTC a wider range of sanctions.

The House version of Wheeler's FTC bill ended up in the same committee that oversaw the House version of Tugwell's FDA bill. Each addressed the issue of food and drug advertising; each gave authority over such advertising to a particular agency. Whichever was passed by the House would settle the battle. Unfortunately for supporters of the FDA, the chairman of the committee, Representative Clarence F. Lea of California, was on Wheeler's side. The FTC bill flew out of committee; the FDA bill lagged. Sensing defeat, FDA supporters tried to amend the FTC bill by giving the commission power to impose even greater penalties. Incredibly, the agency fought the idea—one of the few cases on record of a "cop on the beat" turning down a bigger nightstick. Turning the FTC act into a criminal statute, Lea argued, was "not the practical way to deal with businessmen." The FDA-supported amendment failed, and the House and Senate quickly passed the Wheeler-Lea amendments to the FTC act in March 1938.

The FDA bill might have continued to languish in Lea's committee except for the scandal created by a drug called Elixir Sulfanilamide. Sold by the S. E. Massengill Company, of Bristol, Tennessee, Elixir Sulfanilamide was a liquid form of sulfanilamide, a treatment for streptococcus infections. Unfortunately, the solvent used to make the drug liquid, diethylene glycol, was lethal. The company performed no tests whatsoever before marketing it, checking the product merely for appearance and smell. At least seventy-three people died. The FDA was able to seize the drug, but only on the narrow technical grounds that the product was misbranded, since "elixir" was defined to mean a product dissolved in alcohol. If Elixir Sulfanilamide had been called something else, the government would have been powerless to intervene.

After Elixir Sulfanilamide political resistance melted and food and drug reform became a certainty. On the last night of the congressional debate, Royal Copeland, who had stuck by the FDA for five years despite the attacks from consumer organizations, collapsed on the Senate floor. He died the next day. One week later, on June 25, 1938, the Food, Drug, and Cosmetic Act was signed into law.

What today is regarded as the most important aspect of the law was added at the last moment, without serious discussion: a codicil that forbade the sale of any new drug unless the Secretary of Agriculture (through the FDA) found it to be safe. The rule was further admission that the stern but limited approach to regulation championed by Wiley was inadequate. At last the government would tell the public what drugs it could and could not buy.

Taken as a package, the Wheeler-Lea amendments and the Food, Drug, and Cosmetic Act left drug regulation in the hands of the FDA, except for advertising, which was awarded to the FTC—a division of labor that the food and drug industry treated as a victory. "Despite the apparent stringency of [the Wheeler-Lea amendments'] provisions," *Business Week* reported, "business is relieved that the control of advertising reposes finally in the FTC and not the [FDA]; it does not anticipate any big crackdowns from its old friends in the commission offices."

For many businesses this sentiment has proved correct. The aspirin industry was a notable exception. With the rise of television, the aspirin industry became involved in an advertising war of such dimension that even business's "old friends" in the Federal Trade Commission were drawn into the conflict. The result was an industry-government battle that fell smack in the middle of the still-simmering turf battle between the FTC and the FDA. It didn't happen immediately, though, because the FTC, like much of the rest of the federal bureaucracy, was distracted by the Second World War, and federal attention to aspirin was reserved for Sterling Products and its efforts to subdue I.G. Farben in Latin America.

C H A P T E R   T E N

"FAST, <u>FAST</u>, FAST RELIEF!"

Carlos Mulvaney, a salesman for Sydney Ross, Sterling's export division, was making his rounds through rural Mexican drugstores. As he checked the shelf displays of his employer's new headache remedy, Mejoral, one drugstore owner tapped him on the shoulder. The *farmacista* pointed to a well-dressed man standing outside in the plaza. "There he is," the *farmacista* muttered. "He works for I.G. Farben."

Mulvaney strode out of the store and cheerfully introduced himself to the I.G. agent. "What do you sell?" he asked, all innocence.

Flushing with rage, the German pulled a bottle of Cafiaspirina from his pocket and shook it in Mulvaney's face. "It is an insult for you even to speak to me!" he cried, turning on his heel. "Traitor!"

Mulvaney laughed. "*Mejoral es mejor!*" he shouted at the I.G. agent's retreating back. "*Mejoral es mejor!*"

The German had no need for translation. The same words were on the posters Mulvaney had pasted up all over town. *Mejoral is better*.

It was early in 1942. While Americans and Germans fought with guns and tanks in Europe, Sterling and I.G. Farben aspirin salesmen fought a marketing war in Latin America. As part of the consent decree that ensured Sterling's survival, the new management promised to challenge Leverkusen's Cafiaspirina with Mejoral. Freed from regulation, inflamed by patriotism, stoked by favorable exchange rates, the blitz for Mejoral in Latin America was probably the most unbridled advertising campaign the world will ever see. Advertising has never been wilder, more flamboyant, and more appalling; it was the last hurrah of the old patent medicine hype artists.

Sterling faced a formidable adversary: its own past. Before the war, it had splashed the Bayer name in the most remote corners of the continent. Indeed, the last sign of Western culture voyagers saw going up the Amazon was a placard with the Bayer Cross. Now Sterling had to displace that symbol with the Mejoral logo. <u>David M. Corcoran,</u> president of Sydney Ross, spent as if the company's life depended on it—and it did, for success with Mejoral was the premise of Sterling's survival.

With Corcoran urging on the troops, Sydney Ross salespeople handed out eighty-one million handbills, twenty-seven million samples, and four million posters. Almanacs, saint's cards, religious posters, paper airplanes—all were given for free and by the millions, and all were plastered with the names of Mejoral and the other new Sterling products. In the first eight months of the campaign, Sydney Ross lavished $1.7 million on the promotion of Mejoral, a staggering sum in a place where radio stations charged as little as $100 to put on a hundred commercials a day for a month. At this rate the company theoretically could have run more than 76 *million* radio spots in a year. It didn't put on that many, of course, but quite a few stations put on sixty-five ads during the twelve-hour broadcast day—more than five an hour. Although most people did not own radios, café and barbershop sets blared the jingles out into the streets at top volume, ''making headaches,'' as one Sterling executive noted, and thus ''helping our Mejoral sales.''

Equipped with microphones and sixteen-millimeter movie projectors, more than a hundred ciné trucks climbed to the furthest reaches of the Andes with an updated version of the Wild West medicine show. Coming upon a village, the Sydney Ross sales force fanned out to stock the *farmacias* with the brands featured in that night's entertainment. Meanwhile the head agent bribed the mayor to turn off the town generator at nine. At the appointed hour, the town was suddenly plunged into blackness—except for the Sydney Ross truck, which used its own generator to power a spotlight and the head salesman's megaphone. Following the lights and noise, villagers flocked to the central plaza, where they were invited to sing and dance in an amateur show. Afterward, the mayor received his payoff: the opportunity to make a speech. Then the stage darkened, and the picture show began. Music swelled, and across an improvised movie screen a little red airplane spelled out *MEJORAL* in cartoon skywriting, gray smoke lettering against a blue sky. Applause from the crowd. The first film was *Ágiles Patinadores* (Agile Skaters)—not a brilliant cross-cultural choice. A Sterling salesman recalled the crowd's reaction:

> The peons of Colombia stare, amazed. They've never seen ice. They can't understand a chunk of lake or prairie on which folks can go slithering around like that. They listen, enthralled, as the sound truck chats about what's going on. But the most that can be conveyed is a vague impression that *norteamericanos* are just very peculiar dancers.

A commercial follows. Several boys and girls play happily around a swimming pool. In a corner sits one sad tyke, a headache victim. A nice girl hands him a Mejoral; five minutes later, from the highest of the diving boards, he sails majestically into the pool. "The point can't be missed," the Sterling man rhapsodized. "Mejoral is magical. Take a tablet and learn to dive!"

The Mejoral airplane flies again, signaling the next feature. The choice of material here is haphazard. Sometimes it is a film on Yellowstone, a less than exhilarating subject for people in the middle of a wilderness of their own; sometimes it is wartime propaganda, Orson Welles touring a munitions factory. In any case, it is followed by another commercial, this one featuring a pool player who can't make a shot. It's that headache again. He takes Mejoral. Five minutes later, he clears the table. Another miracle for Mejoral!

The next film: a day at Coney Island. The Indians stare, baffled, at the incomprehensible gringos leaping from the Parachute Jump. A final round of commercials takes the town late into the night. Then, in areas where demand for Mejoral has been less than fervent, the Sterling forces make their final attack. Customers who buy a three-pack of Mejoral, they announce, will receive a poster: the Virgin Mary, pictured inside a golden frame, and below, a big but respectful Mejoral logo. " 'One Virgin for a tablet of Mejoral— step up, step up, come on in!' " Joan Corcoran, David's wife, said later. " 'Buy a tablet for a Virgin!' And you know, at night we'd walk around the villages . . . and see these flickering lights in the distance in the different houses, always with a Virgin on the wall, and it was generally our Virgin."

Because most American men of eligible age were drafted, David Corcoran had to assemble his sales team from misfits, and keep them under constant supervision. "He thought a lot of them didn't have quite what it takes," chuckled Ed Landreth, one of Corcoran's lieutenants. "They'd stay with him in some dreadful shack where the meat pulsated on your plate, and he'd notice that for some reason they didn't like it." Even his few reasonably fit sales agents, like Landreth, were a problem—they were secretly inducted into the American Intelligence Service, an equivalent of the Office of Strategic Services that covered the Americas. Landreth, who spoke Spanish, was sent to AIS spy school early in 1944. Traveling under the code name "Harry," he checked into the Firestone estate in Miami, which had been taken over as a training center. "You were always supposed to refer to people by their code names to preserve absolute secrecy," he said. "Except that the first person I saw there was someone else I knew at Sterling."

With little in the way of actual Nazi activity to investigate, the Sydney Ross spies tended to spend their time in Latin America performing such mundane tasks as writing down the membership lists of the Rotary Clubs (thought to be German-influenced), following around I.G. Farben agents (thought to be plotting subversion), and, mainly, selling Mejoral in every way possible. Landreth was part of a Sydney Ross group that went into Argentina to recruit squads of jingle singers. These choirs spent the day in radio stations, singing "*Mejoral le quita el mal*" (Mejoral makes the pain go away) live during the brand's dozens of daily commercials. On one occasion, they gave an unknown chanteuse named María Eva Duarte her first professional singing job. Duarte was fired when she got sick and didn't show up at the station. Corcoran quickly learned an alarming lesson in Latin American politics. "Suddenly they shut up the radio station and threatened to close us up," Landreth said. "That was when we learned who she was." They had hired "Evita," who was to become infamous as the wife of demagogue Juan Perón. David and Tommy Corcoran went together to apologize personally. "They were practically on their knees," Landreth said, "begging her forgiveness." Evita relented, and the Mejoral show went on. With Evita singing the jingles, Landreth said, Argentina became the biggest per capita consumer of aspirin in the world. Almost all of the sales went to Mejoral; Geniol, which Sterling had bought with the Germans, but given up as part of its deal with the government, was barely able to survive.

"We did things for Mejoral that nobody ever did in their lives," Landreth recalled. "We printed up tin street signs with Mejoral logos and replaced every street sign in Buenos Aires. All the One Way signs had Mejoral on them—the mayor was furious! We practically owned the state radio station. Sometimes one out of every three commercials on the air would be Mejoral. In one town we stenciled half the dogs with Mejoral. In another we painted the cows. We would hook up speakers and make it so that you literally could not walk around a town without hearing our commercials. In Argentina all the salespeople dressed up as Chinese, don't ask me why, and sold Mejoral as the treatment of Dr. Fu Manchu. I'd been an actor, and one of the reasons I joined Sterling was to get away from the theater. And here I found myself singing and dancing on the sound trucks. It was like nothing anybody has ever done since."

In Mejoral's first year, James Hill, Jr., Sterling's new CEO, claimed the brand had snatched away 80 percent of Cafiaspirina's sales. (Edward S. Rogers, installed as chairman after the consent decree, died in 1949; Hill succeeded him.) Mejoral sales continued their climb. By the early 1950s, Landreth said, "we *owned* Latin America." Even after the war ended, and the German aspirin business could revive, the Latin American market was more of a money machine than it had ever been. The furiously competitive Corcoran defended it against all comers with Hill's wholehearted approval. Which makes it all the more peculiar that in the same period Hill surrendered the U.S. aspirin market without a fight. The challenger was an analgesic called Anacin, which, oddly enough, had once been a sibling of Bayer's.

A mixture of aspirin, acetanilid, caffeine, and quinine sulfate, An-A-Cin, as it was first called, was invented in 1915 by William M. Knight, a Minneapolis pharmacist. He marketed it to dentists as a remedy for the pain and inflammation of tooth extraction. Four years later, Knight sold the brand;

several changes of ownership later, Anacin landed in the lap of the Van Ess Company, manufacturers of a Liquid Scalp Massage that the *Journal of the American Medical Association* once attacked as "twenty cents' worth of kerosene and coal tar sold for forty-eight dollars." Van Ess, too, marketed Anacin to dentists, asserting that its blend of ingredients was more effective than plain aspirin. The claim attracted the wrath of the American Dental Association, which complained that Anacin ads took advantage of the common but incorrect belief that two drugs are always stronger than one. Anacin, it said, was "simply a mixture of well-known drugs, irrationally compounded and representative of the days when therapeutic prescribing was not so scientific as it should have been." Despite such cavils, sales rose from less than $20,000 in 1926 to almost $700,000 in 1930. That year, Van Ess was bought by American Home Products, a firm that, like Sterling Products, consisted of a group of brand names, mostly in the drug and household fields. The similarity to Sterling was no accident, for American Home was set up in 1926 by Albert H. Diebold, co-founder, with William E. Weiss, of Sterling Products.

For years a sister company to Sterling, American Home originally consisted of those firms that Diebold, the money man, thought were good financial opportunities, but that Weiss, the operating man, thought were not right for Sterling. "American Home was a pleasant, quiet little game for Mr. Diebold," Knox Ide, a former president, recalled. "He just sat in his office and shuffled these little companies around." From the beginning, Diebold looked for merchandise that was easy to manufacture, easy to distinguish from the competition, and easy to market. Jad Salts, Petrogalar, Hills Cascara bromide quinine, Wyeth's Sage and Sulfur—he picked up no fewer than twenty-one firms for American Home within a few years of its founding. Diebold told the subdivisions to promote their products like mad, but otherwise left them alone. His laissez-faire attitude stopped when American Home took a beating in the depression. In 1935, Diebold installed a new chairman, Alvin G. Brush, with a mandate to shake up the firm. One of the first products Brush shook up was Anacin, which had been under American Home's corporate roof for five years.

Born in 1897, Brush had a broad forehead and a long nose that dropped straight down between the small, deep-set eyes of an auditor. Raised on Long Island, he graduated from New York University in 1921 with a bachelor's degree in commercial science. He worked as an accountant before college, and later founded his own firm, Smith, Brush & Company of New York. In 1925 he married the daughter of a Congregationalist minister, and afterward had a daughter. Hardworking and ambitious, Brush, according to Aaron Weinstein, an ex–corporate counsel, "was very fair, but very tough, and he didn't like inefficiency. He was a great administrator, but he came from accounting, and he was a little deficient in human qualities." Late at night in his office, young Brush would talk with his associates about how he would run the companies they were auditing if he only had the chance. Somewhere along the line, Diebold hired Smith, Brush to examine his books. In 1933 Diebold persuaded Brush to jump to the other side of the ledger—"not that he needed much persuasion," Ide said—as president of R. L. Watkins, manufacturer of Dr. Lyon's tooth powder. Brush was so successful that a year later Diebold named him president of a slightly bigger firm, Affiliated Products. And a year after that, he was appointed president of American Home Products.

American Home was in bad shape, and Brush responded with character-istic efficiency. "For the first few weeks all he did was call people into his office and fire them one by one," Ide said. "It was all very capably and very cold-bloodedly done. And when all the junk was gone, he built on what was left." In large part, the remainder was Anacin. Brush continued Diebold's rush to acquire, buying small firms right and left. But he also decided to take on Bayer aspirin, the flagship brand of his sister company.

Competing with Bayer was a daunting prospect. Bayer was the Tiffany of analgesics; doctors may not have liked its advertisements, but they disliked the naked hucksterism of its competitors even more. It was also an adver-tising colossus. In 1935, American Home spent just $200,000 on radio and magazine advertising for Anacin. By contrast, Sterling was the sixth-largest radio advertiser in the United States, expending more than $750,000 on Bayer ads. Magazines were full of the illustrated adventures of Ambitious Smith:

Ambitious Smith Saves the Situation by Stopping His Cold in a Hurry

[SMITH:]   Mary, I'm catching a terrible cold, and we've got the meet-ing on that big deal tomorrow. Throat sore, too. What can I do?

[MARY:]   Listen, your mother's doctor told her of the surest way to get rid of a cold quick today. . . .

[She instructs him to swallow two Bayer tablets, then gargle three more, and repeat this every two hours, resulting in the consumption of dozens of aspirin tablets.]

[The next day:]

[SMITH:]   Well, dear, I put over the big deal. Yes, cold was practically gone when I got to the office. . . . That *Bayer aspirin* treatment for colds is certainly *fast*. . . .

DOES NOT HARM THE HEART

Brush decided to change American Home's also-ran status. In two years, he quadrupled Anacin's advertising budget. He patched fences with the medical profession by sending sixty-five thousand monthly samples to doctors and dentists, having his representatives visit six to seven hundred physicians a day, and setting up booths at conventions. By 1941, Anacin's ad budget had surpassed Bayer's; if Anacin had been a separate company, it would have been the fifteenth-largest radio advertiser in the nation.

Brush put a man named William F. Laporte in charge of this relentless promotion. Cut from Brush's mold, Laporte was taciturn, efficient, ruthlessly competitive—"cold as ice," Ide said, "and just as talkative." A man of extreme frugality, Laporte was to become renowned for his refusal to pay for such "inessentials" as headhunters, executive moving expenses, extra phone lines, company cars (American Home's corporate fleet reportedly long consisted of one used school bus), and even toilet paper in women's rest rooms. Laporte's credo, according to his 1932 prep school yearbook, was "Silence is more eloquent than words." True to this image, he instructed his switchboard operators to say only the telephone number when outsiders called, declined to hire a public relations staff, and rejected all interviews with the media. ("I don't talk to press-titutes," he once growled to a reporter before hanging up the phone.) He joined the company in 1938 as an assistant to the president of Whitehall Pharmacal, the subsidiary that made Anacin, analyzing Anacin radio commercials. The next few years saw him shuffled between American Home's ethical and proprietary divisions; eventually he became president of Whitehall and then, succeeding Brush, of American Home itself.

Laporte, like Brush, did not care whether the public knew the name American Home, or even Whitehall. All that was important was the brand name Anacin, and he poured money into that. (Advertising was one thing he was never thrifty about.) Blunt and humorless as Laporte himself, Anacin ads slammed home their point with a minimum of style, and did it over and over again. "Anacin is compounded on the prescription principle," radio announcers said many times a day, "meaning it is a combination of medically proven and tested ingredients—not just one."

Ads for Anacin never revealed that its principal active ingredient was aspirin. American Home did not actually deny that Anacin was made of aspirin. The firm simply failed to alert consumers to the identity of its product's ingredients, a practice that proved useful when the company quietly dropped the acetanilid in its recipe in favor of the less dangerous acetophenetidin, and again when it dropped the acetophenetidin and replaced it with more aspirin—but continued to advertise Anacin as though it were the same product.

Sales rose through the war, but slowed afterward. By 1954, Anacin was stalled. It could not inch farther ahead, no matter how much money Laporte

poured into promotion. Worried, Laporte met with a man named Rosser
Reeves.

Tall, round-faced, and boyishly enthusiastic, Reeves is a central figure in
advertising history. One of the original "hard-sell boys" of advertising, he
began his career in 1934, serving as a copywriter for Cecil, Warwick &
Cecil, a New York agency. After moving through a succession of jobs, he
went to work in 1940 for Ted Bates, an account executive who had just
started his own office. Having built up a notable reputation, Reeves was
installed as the new agency's star copywriter. Bates and Reeves ran the firm
for the next twenty-five years much as Diebold and Weiss had run Sterling.
Bates was the quiet executive, eating lunch by himself, minding the financial
matters; Reeves was the flashy creative genius, glad-handing new clients,
staging wild publicity stunts, inventing advertising slogans with *punch*. Advertising, to Reeves's way of thinking, was not a subtle art. Because it had
to compete with the rest of the world for the consumer's interest, it had to
deliver its message fast. It had to shout and be quick about it. And it had to
feature a special claim to attention, or, in Reeves's terminology, a Unique
Selling Proposition. To find the Unique Selling Proposition that Reeves was
sure lurked within every product, no matter how mundane or derivative, he
favored empirical research—of a sort. To find the U.S.P. for Minute Maid
frozen orange juice, for example, Reeves sent out twenty people to buy fresh
oranges, squeeze them by hand, and compare the juice with Minute Maid. A
Ted Bates technical squad analyzed both types of juice and found that the
fresh-squeezed had thirty-seven different types of bacteria and traces of orange peel oil, which is toxic when consumed in huge amounts. From that
came the Unique Selling Proposition: Minute Maid orange juice is better for
your health than oranges squeezed at home. "When we first proposed using
that copy line, the FTC climbed a tree," Reeves said to Thomas Whiteside,
a writer for *The New Yorker* magazine. "We showed them the research, and
they shut up."

Reeves had written copy for Anacin during a previous stint at another ad
agency, Blackett-Sample-Hummert. Frank Hummert, Reeves's boss, had
created the slogan "Like a doctor's prescription—not one but a combination
of ingredients." The combination of ingredients, Reeves believed, was
Anacin's Unique Selling Proposition. The line about the doctor's prescription was still good, he told Laporte when they met, but the current advertising didn't use it to its best advantage. Anacin's Unique Selling Proposition
had to be linked with something the eye would never forget.

Reeves was thinking, of course, about the new medium of television. In
1947, the first year of commercial TV in this country, Americans owned just
fifteen thousand television sets, and the medium was publicly derided by
radio magnates like William S. Paley, owner of the Columbia Broadcasting
System. Television nonetheless grew like mad. Wherever it appeared, movie

theaters shut their doors: 55 closed in metropolitan New York, 70 in eastern Pennsylvania, 134 in southern California. Bob Hope's hugely popular radio show lost three-quarters of its audience. By 1954, 32 million television sets were in the land, almost one for every five Americans, and their owners watched the tube more than they did anything else except working and sleeping. Early that year, an NBC executive named Sylvester ("Pat") Weaver figured out that advertisers could buy individual spots on a program, rather than paying for the entire broadcast, as had generally been the case in radio. This allowed smaller companies to have commercials, and vastly increased the chance for bigger firms to spray their message across the dial. For television, it was a revolutionary change.

Many ad executives would have agreed with Reeves that American Home could not afford to stay away from television. Early TV advertisers had reported extraordinary successes. Hazel Bishop lipstick had switched its advertising to the small screen and seen sales rise from $50,000 in 1950 to $4.5 million in 1952. Television was king, Reeves thought. But not everyone knew what to do with it. Reeves had a few ideas for Laporte about effective use of the medium.

At their meeting, Reeves sketched a silhouetted human head with lines dividing the brainpan into three boxes—an image that was to become an unavoidable part of the American scene. A hammer pounds in the first box. A spring coils and uncoils in the second. The third has a jagged lightning bolt zapping between two terminals. One by one, the boxes light up as a hyperactive announcer bellows out Anacin's powers. "Stops headache!" The hammer stops pounding. "Relieves tension!" The coiled spring relaxes. "Calms jittery nerves!" The electricity is grounded. Moments later, the screen splits. Suddenly there are two silhouetted heads, each with the three boxes, attached to two silhouetted bodies, each with the outline of a stomach. From one stomach quickly rises three lines of bubbles, representing the three ingredients of Anacin; from the other slowly dribbles a single stream of bubbles, representing the one old-fashioned ingredient of plain aspirin. Tellingly, the aspirin bubbles halt the pounding hammers but do nothing for the coiling spring or the lightning bolt. The Anacin bubbles stop harmful activity in all three sectors. "Relieves headaches fast!" shouts the announcer. "Relieves tension fast! Calms jittery nerves fast! For fast, _fast_, FAST relief, take Anacin!"

With their simple imagery, their continuous repetition, and their crude animation, the "Pounding Hammers" commercials were not easily forgotten, and even less easily liked. Laporte poured money into them, and the nation's new TV audience could not escape the bellow of "fast, _fast_, FAST relief," no matter where the dial was turned. Anacin's pounding hammers became symbols of everything false and irritating about Madison Avenue; critics savaged them as if they were the end of Western civilization. To

Reeves's undisguised satisfaction, a group of advertising experts rated "Pounding Hammers" as one of the worst ads in recent years. The "Pounding Hammers" spots, he said proudly, were "the most hated commercials in the history of advertising."

They were also one of the most successful. "It was a fifty-nine-second motion picture that cost eighty-four hundred dollars to produce," Reeves told *The New Yorker*, "and it made more money for the producers of Anacin in seven years than *Gone With the Wind* did for David O. Selznick and MGM in a quarter of a century."

At the same time a third player, Bufferin, entered the market. Incredibly, Bufferin, too, owed its existence to Diebold. In 1928 Diebold merged Sterling Products with the United Drug chain of retail pharmacies and a batch of small nostrum manufacturers into a conglomerate named Drug, Inc. A marriage of the nation's biggest maker of home remedies and the nation's biggest drugstore chain, Drug, Inc., was a holding company that tried to coordinate the production and sales of two independent fiefdoms. The intended cooperation never really came about—Sterling's membership in Drug, Inc., had almost no impact on its operations. When United Drug was hurt by the depression, Weiss at Sterling didn't want to share its losses, and the combine split up unceremoniously in 1932. One of the pieces was Bristol-Myers, a patent medicine maker that Diebold had incorporated, almost haphazardly, into the colossus of Drug, Inc. (It was founded in 1887 by William McLaren Bristol and John R. Myers, two graduates of Hamilton College, in upstate New York, to make bulk drugs for doctors.) Spun off from the combine as an independent entity, Bristol-Myers entered the aspirin market in 1949 with Bufferin.

Bufferin, like Anacin, said that it was better than aspirin. And, like Anacin, Bufferin neglected to tell consumers that it *was* aspirin, with a few added ingredients. In this case, the added ingredients were two antacids. The company originally intended Bufferin as a convenience to hangover sufferers, who frequently took aspirin for their headaches and antacids for their dyspepsia. When Bristol-Myers researchers tested the combination to make sure the aspirin and antacids did not interfere with each other, they discovered that antacids speed up the rate at which aspirin is absorbed into the bloodstream. Eureka, thought Bristol-Myers. It was aspirin, but even better. "Acts twice as fast as aspirin," said the 1949 advertisement in *Life* that introduced Bufferin, the "new, remarkable product for the relief of pain."

Bufferin, too, took to television. "Headache throbbing like a drum?" asked a singsong voice, as a cartoon stick beat a drum.

Don't let it last and last!
Get quick relief with Bufferin,
It's fast . . . fast . . . fast!

The scene changed to a cartoon of two human torsos, represented Rube Goldberg–style as a mass of pipes. One torso was labeled "aspirin," the other, "Bufferin." Into the aspirin stomach dropped a lot of little *A*s. Into the Bufferin stomach, a lot of little *B*s. The *B*s left the stomach through a sort of trapdoor, turning into bubbly *O*s as they traveled through the pipes. Meanwhile, the *A*s sat in the stomach like so many lumps.

Bufferin's formula combines aspirin with two special antacid ingredients which get the pain reliever out of the stomach into the bloodstream twice as fast as aspirin. That's why Bufferin acts twice as fast as aspirin.*

Sterling was slow to fight back. Its chief executive officer, James Hill, Jr., was an accountant by training. Not being a marketing man, he did not have Weiss's drive to *sell*. In a company run by one man, Hill's character meant everything. Perhaps he was convinced that the company's years on top could continue with little extra effort. Perhaps he wanted to control costs. Perhaps the company had just grown used to effortless superiority in the U.S. aspirin market. In any case, Hill made a fateful choice.

While ad budgets for Mejoral, Corcoran's quasi-independent fiefdom within the firm, soared, those for Bayer aspirin actually *dropped* by more than one-half between 1949 and 1954. By contrast, Anacin's advertising budget doubled in the same period. Then Reeves took over the account, and in the next two years it doubled again, to more than $15 million. Bufferin too heaped money on promotion. Beginning with expenditures of less than $350,000 in 1949, it was up to more than $13 million by 1956.

In 1949 Bayer had spent more on advertising than its two rivals combined. Seven years later it spent less than half as much as Bufferin, and less than one-fourth as much as Anacin. (The trend applied to all of Sterling's U.S. products: From 1949 to 1956, the company cut its total advertising expenditures by almost half.)

Bayer's market share plummeted. Anacin almost caught up with it in the early 1950s, grabbing on to one-fifth of the market compared with Bayer's fast-sinking one-fourth. The arrival of Bufferin made the aspirin market a three-way race, as the newcomer jumped from an initial share of 2 percent in

---

* Only at the beginning did the then-unsophisticated Bristol-Myers reveal that Bufferin's principal ingredient was aspirin.

1950 to claim 15 percent of all sales in 1957. Anacin felt the effect—it dropped to 18 percent—but found solace in the fact that it was now the leading brand of aspirin. Bayer had lost almost half of its share of the market. In Weiss's day, Sterling had proclaimed that it knew "more about proprietary medicine advertising than anybody else." Under Hill, the firm scrapped it all in a few years.

Smelling opportunity, Anacin stepped up its hard sell, presenting a new affliction of modern life, the tension headache. "Tense nervous headaches—get faster relief with stronger yet safer Anacin." According to "the highest medical authorities," American Home Products declared,

> the Anacin way—a formula combining smaller quantities of a *number* of highly effective pain relievers—gives faster, more effective and safer relief than a large dose of one *single* drug. This is one of the first fundamentals of medicine taught in all schools of medicine and dentistry.*

Eventually Bayer counterattacked. "Don't pay twice the price of Bayer aspirin for *Aspirin 'in disguise'!*" Bayer warned in 1957 about Bufferin and Anacin. "Why pay more for extra ingredients that can't relieve pain?"

In the past, a blow from Sterling could have flattened its rivals. But now its competitors sold as much as Bayer, and the race was a dead heat. Checkbooks in hand, Anacin and Bufferin were ready to take on Bayer; each was ready to claim, loudly and in perpetuity, that it was faster, safer, more effective. The Aspirin Wars had begun.

In May 1953, Andrew Graham, a Sterling attorney, wrote to the Federal Trade Commission about Bufferin's twice-as-fast ads. Bufferin might release ASA more quickly into the bloodstream, Graham said, but its makers had never proved that the speed had any relationship to driving away pain. (His argument was not illogical. The human body is complex, and the relationship between dose and response is often surprising.) In the past, Graham charged, the FTC had slammed aspirin makers for much more innocuous advertising. Now the agency was just sitting on its hands. The FTC made no response. Graham complained again in July 1956. And then again. And yet again. Four years after Graham's first letter, the FTC's Division of Scientific Opinions, which evaluated technical data for agency actions, finally allowed Sterling to present its case against Bufferin ads.

George Dobbs of the Division of Scientific Opinions told the firm that

---

* In fact, the opposite is true; doctors try to give few drugs at any one time, because they might interact in some unpleasant way.

despite his personal belief that Bufferin's claims were false, the burden of proof was on the FTC, and the agency would be hard-pressed to come up with solid evidence. To prove an ad false, the Division of Scientific Opinions had to establish what was true, and show that the ad varied from that standard. In the past, the division had simply reviewed scientific journals or consulted with experts. But now consumer drugs and cosmetics were covered infrequently in the medical literature. Nobody was going to get a Nobel Prize comparing Anacin and Bufferin to aspirin. The experts available to the FTC thus could testify to the properties of drugs in general, but they usually had no laboratory experience with the product in question, which inevitably threw doubt on their judgment.

The obvious solution, Dobbs conceded, was for the agency to conduct its own clinical tests, but it had little ability to do so. In 1957, the division had just six people on its staff: two doctors, two chemists, and two secretaries. Its budget was minuscule: two thousand dollars for tests by the Food and Drug Administration, two thousand for medical witnesses, and just under thirteen thousand for purchasing and testing commodities in the areas of medicine, therapeutic devices, wool, fur, and flammable fabrics.

Evaluating drugs was hard for the FTC, but evaluating analgesics in particular was almost impossible—not only for the government, but for anybody. Researchers can't put "pain meters" on people to get objective measurements of how bad they feel or how quickly they recover. It is even harder comparing one analgesic with another. To test whether Bufferin relieves headaches twice as fast as plain aspirin, for example, would require giving Bufferin and aspirin to people with identical headaches and somehow determining which one worked faster. Sterling had not done this; nobody had. On that basis, Dobbs said, the division "could not and would not recommend" that the FTC attack Bufferin advertising.

Despite his words to Sterling, the frustrated Dobbs in fact asked the National Institutes of Health to perform clinical studies on aspirin brands. When the NIH said no, the division contacted the Veterans Administration, which also declined. In 1960 the agency finally managed to inveigle two research physicians in Baltimore, Louis Lasagna and Thomas J. DeKornfeld, into comparing the efficacy of five aspirin brands: Anacin, Bayer, St. Joseph (made by Plough), Bufferin, and Excedrin, another product then being test-marketed by Bristol-Myers. Lasagna and DeKornfeld randomly distributed the five brands to 298 women who had just given birth. None had received general anesthesia, and from this Lasagna and DeKornfeld hypothesized that they were in physical distress. After fifteen minutes, the two men asked the women if they were feeling very severe pain, severe pain, moderate pain, slight pain, or no pain. After another fifteen minutes, the women were asked the same question again. After another fifteen minutes, they were asked a third time. Fifteen minutes later, they were asked a fourth time. After that, they were asked on the hour. Lasagna and DeKornfeld counted a drop from, say, very severe to severe as a score of $+1$. Correspondingly, a rise from one level to another was tabulated as -1. These figures were then used to compute a "mean pain-relief score." (The two scientists left unsaid what postpartum pain has to do with headache, the condition most commonly treated by aspirin, or whether women who have just gone through hours of labor are in a state to make fine distinctions about their current levels of agony.) The five brands ended up with almost identical mean pain-relief scores. One brand did not seem to work faster or longer than the others. Considering that they had the same active ingredient, this was not entirely surprising. Nevertheless the FTC was delighted to have scientific evidence in hand. Now it could bring order to the overheated aspirin market. It filed complaints against all four companies in March 1961.

The response was not what the commission expected. The companies fought—hard. They filed every imaginable type of opposing legal brief. Stunned, the FTC put the cases on "suspense" in June 1962, which stopped all action but left them alive, to be prosecuted later. It then revealed a plan to investigate the advertising practices of the entire industry, not just those of the four companies. Before the investigation could garner any results, the one medical study the FTC had blew up in its face.

Lasagna and DeKornfeld published their aspirin study in the December 29, 1962, issue of the *Journal of the American Medical Association*. The article caught the FTC by surprise: Somewhere down the chain of command, someone had mistakenly given the two men permission to go into print. The commission's major evidence against the aspirin companies was now out in the open, where the companies could pore over it to their hearts' content.

Sterling immediately confirmed the commission's worst fears. Less than forty-eight hours after the *JAMA* article's official release date, Sterling radio spots broadcast the study's conclusion that Bufferin and Anacin were no better or faster than Bayer. By the middle of January, advertisements in newspapers and national magazines were proclaiming that a "government-supported medical team" had revealed in a "highly authoritative journal" that "Bayer Aspirin brings relief that is as fast, as strong, and as gentle to the stomach as you can get."

Retribution was swift. Already embarrassed by the publication of the study by Lasagna and DeKornfeld, the commission was infuriated beyond measure by the Bayer ads. The study it had wanted to be a weapon against aspirin ads was now being used to support an aspirin ad. Sterling was going to pay for this. On January 17, 1963, a few days after the "government-supported medical team" ads appeared in print, the FTC issued a formal complaint about Sterling's use of the *JAMA* report. Then, in an act of bureaucratic vengeance, it filed for what, in a fit of irony, it called "fast relief"—a preliminary injunction to prevent Sterling from broadcasting or publishing its advertisements until the commission could rule on the complaint.

This was an unusual move. An FTC case begins when the commission's staff attorneys decide there is sufficient evidence to charge a company with some violation. The five commissioners then act as a grand jury, either quashing the case or giving the lawyers permission to proceed. If the commission approves, a complaint is issued, detailing the offending business practices. At this point, a company has two choices. It can negotiate a consent order, which is an agreement to stop behaving badly and a promise not to do it again. Or it can fight, in which case a trial is held in front of an FTC hearing examiner, a quasi-independent employee of the commission who evaluates the evidence from both parties and renders an initial decision. (Although the same body acts as grand jury, prosecutor, and judge, contacts among the various parties are strictly regulated, and criticisms about conflict of interest are surprisingly few.) If either the FTC attorneys or the company choose to appeal the initial decision, the case goes before the full commission, which now acts as an appellate court and renders a final decision. That decision can then be appealed outside the FTC to a federal appellate court, and on to the Supreme Court.

With such a labyrinthine procedure, FTC suits can stretch out for years. In the case of food and drug advertising, however, the FTC has the additional power to seek a preliminary injunction, which halts the offending ads while the case is proceeding. To obtain an injunction, it must convince a judge outside the FTC that the ads will injure the public in some way if allowed to continue. This is what the agency tried to assert in the "government-supported medical team" case.

As a judge in a New York district court considered the request for a preliminary injunction, the angry FTC went yet one step further. It asked for a temporary restraining order, a legal ban on the advertisements that goes into effect even faster than a preliminary injunction. Given one hour's notice, Sterling's lawyers argued for forty minutes with the commission's lawyers until both sides were cut off by the judge. In a ruling that set the tone for the next year of litigation, the commission was turned down cold.

Even if instantaneous relief was not to be had, the commission was still determined to go after the preliminary injunction. Held before a different New York district court judge, this hearing, too, did not go well. Although the FTC lawyers admitted that Sterling had presented the results of the *JAMA* study accurately, they argued that the overall impression of the ad was misleading. Exasperated, the judge told the FTC it was "picking at a fly." Maybe the agency didn't like it, but a "government-supported medical team" had, in fact, reported in a "highly authoritative journal" that "Bayer Aspirin brings relief that is as fast, as strong, and as gentle to the stomach as you can get.'' That was what Sterling had said, and that was what had happened. Adding to the FTC's humiliation, the judge chastised it for seeking to suppress information of value to consumers. "The advertisement is definite and precise," he wrote. "The Court cannot find on the papers submitted that it was a false statement."

Armed with a judicial declaration that the commercial was not false, Sterling petitioned the full five-member commission to dismiss the complaint. The commission declined, and the case proceeded along two paths: outside the FTC to a higher court, where the agency appealed the lower court's denial of the preliminary injunction; and inside the FTC to a hearing examiner, before whom the agency opened the trial based on its initial complaint. Neither pathway was easy footing for the government.

The Court of Appeals for the Second Circuit—the outside pathway— upheld the lower court's rejection of the FTC's request for a preliminary injunction. Three days after the decision was made public, Sterling further infuriated the agency by beginning a new advertising campaign: "She Learned about Bayer by Reading *JAMA* in Her Doctor's Office." Aghast, FTC lawyers watched as the *Perry Mason* and *Dr. Kildare* shows were interrupted by a commercial featuring two mothers sitting in front of a television set. In a modernist conceit, the two women discuss pain-reliever commercials. "Those [ads] . . . give me a pain," says one, disgustedly. "Ha," the other cries. "All I need to know is what it said in an article in the *Journal of the AMA* that I read in my doctor's office." She gives a ten-second summary of the Lasagna-DeKornfeld study, noting that the analgesics with "extra ingredients" were no better than Bayer, and that Bayer was as gentle to the stomach as its competitors. "And that includes your modern buffered products," she concludes. "*Ha!*"

All the while, the FTC gathered data for the hearing examiner—the inside pathway. True, agency lawyers conceded, the outside judge had found no lie in the ad. But that didn't matter. The important question was whether the consumer, not some judge, was deceived. The FTC called upon the greatest expert on consumer behavior: consumers themselves.

Twenty-one ordinary Americans in and around Washington, D.C., found themselves on the wrong end of a subpoena when they were told to appear before the FTC hearing examiner in the role of typical consumers. Bookkeepers and mechanical engineers, homemakers and repairmen—all were forced to discuss the meaning of "government-supported" and "highly authoritative journal" before a bank of lawyers. Many of the witnesses were reluctant, one mother furiously objecting to "being dragged up here" to testify. FTC lawyers asked them if they could recall reading the disputed Bayer advertisement in a Washington, D.C., newspaper. None remembered it. Undaunted, the attorneys then asked the consumers to read the ad on the witness stand and interpret its claims on the spot. Aircraft mechanic James

Clear hazarded the opinion that the words "government-supported" meant that the FDA (not the FTC) believed that Bayer aspirin "is as gentle to the stomach as a plain sugar pill." A sugar pill was just like a piece of candy, he said, and he wouldn't take either one.

After the consumer testimony ended, *Food, Drug, and Cosmetic Reports*, an industry newsletter known, because of its distinctive paper, as the "Pink Sheet," dispatched a reporter to the subdivision where more than half the witnesses lived. "Here's what I can't understand," witness Juanita Nelson said. "We're all for Bayer—we use Bayer aspirin—and then they do this to us, and we get stuck with these subpoenas." When the "Pink Sheet" knocked on the door of Dorothy Lytle, who had been forced to make two trips downtown to testify, she covered her head at the very mention of Bayer and shouted, "No questions, no answers, nothing—No! No! No!"

A few months after it had been turned down by the Second Circuit Court, the commission's miseries continued: The hearing examiner threw out the charges against Sterling, saying the testimony of the twenty-one consumers had little value. The agency lawyers appealed, bringing the case before the full commission. Sterling's lawyer, Thomas Mason, suggested that the commission dismiss all charges because Sterling had modified its advertising campaign, removing much of the offending language. The commission grumbled but gave in, terminating the action in February 1964, a year after it had promised "fast relief" from Sterling's audacious advertising.

The FTC turned its attention back to the investigation of the aspirin trade that it had ordered after the 1961 complaints were put on "suspense." In September 1964, commission lawyers, using the general powers of the FTC to investigate an industry without issuing any complaints, demanded all medical studies used by the aspirin companies to support their advertising. The four companies named in the 1961 complaints objected on the grounds that the commission was asking them to reveal the defense's evidence while charges were pending.

Conceding the point, the FTC dismissed the original complaints against the four companies in April of the next year. The industry was forced to send reams of technical data to Washington, knowing they would be providing new grounds for more legal action. Three years into the battle, the FTC had just begun to fight.

CHAPTER ELEVEN

"ASPIRIN: HOMEY, FAMILIAR, TIME-TESTED ASPIRIN"

It was the Summer of Love. While Richard Nixon campaigned for president, young people flocked to San Francisco, Pope Paul VI issued an encyclical forbidding birth control, and Lyndon Johnson maneuvered at the Vietnam peace talks in Paris, seven Ivy League law students worked without pay in the nation's capital, on what amounted to an extended field trip. They roamed the halls of the Federal Trade Commission, gossiping with the staff, chatting with attorneys about their cases, and familiarizing themselves with the agency's fight against false advertising. In the fall the students wrote about their summer vacation in a 185-page report, which was released with the imprimatur of Ralph Nader, inheritor of the mantle of consumer activism once worn by Harvey W. Wiley. Nader first drew attention by critiquing automobile companies that shortchanged the safety of their customers, but had recently shifted his focus to regulatory agencies that he believed served the industries they were supposed to control. To launch the campaign, Georgetown University Law Center professor Robert Pitofsky said later, Nader and his associates quite naturally "picked the biggest, fattest target they could find. They picked the FTC, which may actually have had the honor then of being the worst, slowest bureaucracy on Capitol Hill."

Released in January 1969, the Nader report found little to praise, and much to condemn. The FTC's record in seeking strong penalties was "abysmal"; it had spent great sums of money pursuing "trivial matters"; and the upper management was rife with "alcoholism, spectacular lassitude and office absenteeism, incompetence . . . and lack of commitment." The students had harsh words for FTC chairman Paul Rand Dixon, who had "trundled along and institutionalized mediocrity" to the point where his best course "would be to resign from the agency he has so degraded and ossified."

Dixon did not appreciate the suggestion. The Nader report, he said, was a "hysterical, anti-business diatribe and a scurrilous, untruthful attack on the career personnel of the commission. . . ." The student authors, in his view, were "young zealots . . . with a self-granted license to criticize a respected government agency by the use of a type of invective and 'smear technique' that . . . is unusual even for Washington." Nader's group in turn dismissed Dixon's defense as "a plea for support by the business community and by President-elect Nixon to keep him" in his post.

In March 1969, four of the students widened the attack to include the advertisers policed by the FTC. Testifying before a Senate subcommittee, they claimed that advertising produces "a glut of information about what are in reality contrived distinctions between identical products, but no information on the drawbacks of any particular product type." The students cited analgesic commercials as perfect examples. Inflicting a screening of Bayer, Anacin, and Bufferin spots on the attending senators, one student pointed out that all three products claimed to be the best, and that this was a logical impossibility. "Somebody must be lying," he said. "In fact, all are."

Now on the defensive, Dixon could do little but reassure Congress that the FTC had not gone soft. "We are going to have some hard-fought litigation, I will guarantee you that," he told a House committee in June. "There are going to be some cases that will ring around the halls of Congress."

Dixon never got to fulfill his promise. In September, the American Bar Association issued its own white paper on the FTC. Although less strident in its language than the Nader report, its conclusions were no less harsh. "The agency's performance," it said, "must be regarded as a failure on many counts."* A new chairman was needed—someone who, unlike Dixon, hadn't been at the FTC since before the Second World War. President Nixon replaced Dixon as chairman with an outsider: Caspar W. Weinberger, finance director for Governor Ronald Reagan of California, a man who had spent his entire political career in California Republican politics. To reformers, Weinberger's first statements about the job did not sound encouraging: He had to study the entire history of the FTC, he said, before proposing any new policies—a stalling technique of ancient vintage.

Except that Weinberger didn't stall. He turned the agency upside down. The cop, he let it be known, had returned to the beat. No more could advertisers count on sleepy, complacent supervision. The FTC was going to zero in on bad companies. Underscoring this point, William Rogal, assistant director of the FTC's Deceptive Practices Bureau, declared in Feb-

---

* ABA panelist Richard Posner, a University of Chicago law professor (and now a Seventh Circuit Court judge), went further. In a separate statement, he argued that the FTC "has done so badly continuously over so long a period of time that it is difficult any longer to regard its failings as accidental and remediable." Unless the agency found a new *raison d'être*, Posner thought, its budget should be frozen, which would let it be killed naturally by "the forces of inflation."

ruary 1970 that the agency was going to ''put down the shotgun and pick up the rifle.''

The agency's new enthusiasm did not fade when Nixon abruptly shifted Weinberger in June 1970 to the newly created Office of Management and Budget. He was replaced by another outsider, Miles Kirkpatrick, a Philadelphia antitrust lawyer and the head of the ABA commission that reported on the FTC. Kirkpatrick in turn asked the ABA commission counsel, Robert Pitofsky, to be the head of the Bureau of Consumer Protection, a branch of the FTC recently established to take over false advertising litigation and other consumer matters. Pitofsky accepted with alacrity. ''The incentives for advertisers to lie then were very great,'' he said later. ''The government was doing practically nothing, self-regulation didn't exist, and comparative advertising wasn't allowed by the networks—the advertisements were a free-fire zone. One oil company was claiming that if you used its gasoline, your car would pull a locomotive up a hill. The airwaves were full of the most blatant lies.''

Kirkpatrick and Pitofsky told their increasingly activist staff to drag in some of the big boys. They did. America's corporations were stunned by the fury of the new, demonic Federal Trade Commission. FTC lawyers worked day and night, and scores of companies found themselves having to defend advertisements they had run for years without regulatory flak. The lawyers reserved special ire for the analgesic firms. What better targets than American Home, Bristol-Myers, and Sterling, companies that the agency had wanted to get its hands on for years?

Aspirin commercials represented everything that consumer activists and the new, awakened FTC hated about advertising. The list of irritations was enormous. How could Anacin say it had a ''fortified formula'' when the product consisted solely of aspirin and caffeine, which no research had ever shown to be synergistic? How could Bayer argue that minute variations in its manufacturing process gave it noticeable pharmaceutical superiority? How could Bufferin claim that it was ''faster to your headache'' when nobody had ever developed a way to measure headaches? Why were Anacin and Bufferin allowed to pretend that they were not made from aspirin? Most of all, how could each of three slightly different versions of the same drug be allowed to claim that it was vastly superior to the others? It was an offense to logic, the FTC attorneys thought, and it had been on television night after night for years upon end.

''They were bad ads, and everybody knew they were bad ads,'' said David Bickart, an FTC lawyer during that era. ''The investigation had taken long enough.'' In December 1970, the commission ordered its lawyers to gather evidence that could be used to support charges against the big three aspirin companies. A new spirit invigorated the agency; rubbing its collective hands with zest, it was ready to get the analgesic makers once and for all.

*   *   *

Despite its determination, the commission faced the same problem that had haunted it for the past two decades: It had no evidence that aspirin advertising was false. The legal burden of proof in such cases was on the FTC. Unable to persuade other government agencies to investigate the analgesic companies, it had paid for the study by DeKornfeld and Lasagna. Not wishing to repeat *that* experience, the agency attempted to turn the burden of proof around—and ended up changing the face of advertising law forever. The proceeding through which the FTC moved ostensibly had nothing to do with the analgesic investigation, but it ultimately had alarming consequences for Sterling, Bristol-Myers, and American Home.

Early in 1970 the agency sued Pfizer, a pharmaceutical company, for claiming that its Un-Burn ointment could "anesthetize nerves" in sunburned skin. Un-Burn's active ingredient was benzocaine, a topical anesthetic that had been on the market for more than thirty years. Touting such compounds is a way of life for consumer products firms, and scrutinizing that promotion was something the agency had done for decades. What was unusual about the Un-Burn case was that the new, more aggressive breed of FTC lawyers attacked Pfizer not because Un-Burn failed to perform—benzocaine does, in fact, anesthetize nerves—but because Pfizer did not have its own scientific studies to *prove* that Un-Burn anesthetizes nerves. The agency was trying to change the meaning of "false" in the case of false advertising. An advertisement would no longer be "false" only if it was erroneous, incorrect, or wrong; it was now "false" if the company didn't have the evidence to back it up.

Agency lawyers had a complex rationale for this argument. When an advertiser makes an affirmative claim for a product ("Acts twice as fast as aspirin"), they said, the claim is implicitly paired in the public's mind with a claim of substantiation ("It acts twice as fast as aspirin, *and* we have tests that show this to be true"). If an advertiser does not have adequate substantiation, the implicit claim is not true, and the public is misled—exposing the company to charges of false advertising.

The FTC saw clear advantages in the Pfizer approach. Using this novel legal strategy, the agency retained the legal burden of proof but in practice shifted that burden to the companies it policed. Its job suddenly became much easier: The agency merely had to demonstrate that companies did not have their own tests, or that the tests they had done were inadequate.

Business interests were not slow to point out a bizarre implication of the Pfizer approach. In theory, a company could be convicted of false advertising even if upon later investigation the commercial turned out to be true.*

---

* Three months after the FTC issued its complaint against Pfizer, the company tested Un-Burn on the sunburned skin of 21 subjects. The results supported Pfizer's advertising

"Weinberger and Kirkpatrick told the lawyers to be innovative and come up with new ideas," a sardonic Bristol-Myers lawyer said later. "They sure did! They were full of piss and vinegar, but the thing that lasted was this idea that even if a claim is true, without evidence there is deception at a secondary level. A true ad can be declared false—very innovative! I say there's something about that which can't line up with the First Amendment, not to mention logic."

When the hearing examiner handed down his decision in the Pfizer case, the FTC lawyers earned a victory in their effort to reverse the burden of proof—even though they lost. The examiner noted that the commission had the power to decide what business practices were unfair or deceptive, and that the lawyers' theory of adequate substantiation was a legitimate exercise of this power. Unfortunately, he concluded that Pfizer had adequate substantiation for its Un-Burn claims. Worse, he rejected the attorneys' narrow definition of "substantiation"—"adequate and well-controlled scientific studies"—but gave them nothing to replace it. The lawyers appealed the decision to the full commission, but for the time being were left without any guidance as to what constituted adequate substantiation.

Into the vacuum stepped David Bickart, a young lawyer plucked from a job as a Supreme Court clerk. Bickart arrived at the FTC in September 1971, a few months after the hearing examiner's decision in the Pfizer case, and was asked to take charge of the analgesic investigation. Bickart was intrigued by the Pfizer approach, but also saw that it was not enough to snare Bayer, Bufferin, and Anacin. Aspirin firms had bushelfuls of scientific studies, some of which showed, purely by the play of chance, that one brand was faster or stronger. By choosing the right studies, firms could easily claim adequate scientific evidence for their ads, even though they had other studies with contradictory conclusions. The failure to reveal the existence of these other studies (when they did exist), Bickart and his colleagues decided, was deceptive.

In effect, the lawyers were turning the Pfizer approach up one notch, arguing that commercials with affirmative claims made not two but *three* claims: the original claim ("Twice as fast as aspirin"), an implicit collateral claim ("We have tests that show it acts twice as fast as aspirin"), and a second implicit collateral claim ("There are no other tests that show it *doesn't* act twice as fast as aspirin"). By failing to disclose that there was a "substantial question" about the evidence for their claims, the argument went, the aspirin companies were misleading consumers, and hence engaging in an unfair business practice that was illegal under FTC law. The regulation of advertising had come far: In the Magnetic Healing case, the

---

claims, but the commission eventually ruled that the test did not get the company off the hook because it came *after* the ad campaign began.

scientific uncertainty over the school's claims meant that the government was forbidden to intervene; now, seven decades later, the FTC lawyers were arguing that the scientific uncertainty meant that the government *must* intervene.

Under this theory, if American Home had clinical tests to support a statement like "Anacin is more effective than aspirin in the relief of pain," the firm's ads would still have to say "although the matter is open to question, we believe that Anacin is more effective than aspirin in the relief of pain" if other scientific studies did not agree. In a practical vein, the commission's attorneys viewed the new approach as time saving: To win the prosecution, they would need only to prove that medical opinion was divided, avoiding protracted quibbling with the advertiser's experts.

While the full commission was pondering their appeal of the Pfizer decision, the agency lawyers announced plans to bring charges against American Home, Bristol-Myers, and Sterling on the basis of this new theory. (In those days, the legal staff publicly proclaimed its intention to file complaints before actually filing them as a means of badgering companies into settlements.) The proposed complaints accused the firms both of failing to possess adequate substantiation (which the lawyers defined as "competent and reliable scientific evidence") for their ads *and* of failing to reveal the substantial question (defined as scientific controversy, the new, extended Pfizer doctrine) about their claims.

The three firms were hit with other charges too. Anacin and Bufferin were denounced for not revealing they were made of aspirin, important because of its potential side effects. ("We were going to make them finally come out of the closet and admit they were made of aspirin," Bickart said.) For the same reason, Anacin was attacked for neglecting to mention its caffeine.* The agency also assailed Bristol-Myers's other major brand, Excedrin. Introduced in 1961, Excedrin was first composed of aspirin, acetophenetidin, caffeine, and salicylamide (yet another cousin of salicylic acid). Two years later, in the face of growing doubts about the safety of acetophenetidin, Bristol-Myers replaced it with acetaminophen (the ingredient in Tylenol); Anacin also removed its acetophenetidin, but replaced it with more aspirin. This allowed Excedrin to best Anacin and Bayer in a contest of numerical superiority: "Four ingredients. Not just one or two. That's Excedrin." The FTC attacked this and other claims, arguing that more ingredients did not necessarily mean more pain relief.

Unlucky Sterling was accused of the novel offense of engaging in mutually inconsistent advertising campaigns. After complaining about Anacin and Bufferin for nearly two decades, Sterling at last had decided to cover all the

* The failure to reveal the side effects of caffeine was dropped during the hearings on the charges, and did not play a role beyond the initial complaints.

bases. It created two new products: Vanquish, which was basically Excedrin with added buffers, and Cope, which was basically a mild sedative and, depending on your point of view, either Anacin with buffers or Bufferin with caffeine. Sterling continued to promote Bayer aspirin as the equal of all other pain relievers, yet the ads for its two new brands intimated that they were better than aspirin. Sterling could not have unambiguous support for both claims, the FTC said. Logically, one had to be false, and the company guilty of false advertising.

The proposed complaints covered an enormous number of commercials. Bayer ads emphasized its pharmaceutical superiority over 220 other brands of aspirin. (''We had an ad that showed a rocket taking off and a bunch of astronauts taking Bayer aspirin to the moon,'' one Sterling lawyer said later. ''So we called it 'the world's best aspirin,' and they went after us.'') Anacin touted a survey of doctors that showed twice as many preferred Anacin over the other leading extra-strength brand. Excedrin noted how much medical science had progressed since the days when Lasagna and DeKornfeld could find no significant differences among pain relievers; now, it said, a study had turned up scientific evidence of the superiority of Excedrin over aspirin. A series of Bufferin ads claimed that it was better for ''sensitive people.'' A typical example of the series, ''New Housing,'' depicts a minor housing official about to tell an old couple that they must leave their condemned rental apartment in less than a week. Upset at the confrontation, the official gets a headache, the kind that afflicts ''sensitive people.'' He pops two Bufferins. In moments he is calm and smiling. He is able to give the old folks the straight story.

HOUSING OFFICIAL: That's the way it is. So you'll have to be out by Thursday.

OLD MAN: You know, our kids were born right here.

That's their tough luck. Our man has survived this scene, thanks to Bufferin. The commercial continues.

ANNOUNCER: Bufferin. For sensitive people. It's much better than plain aspirin.

(The claim in the last sentence is what irritated the FTC; there is no law against bad taste.)

Using the proposed complaints as a bargaining tool, the commission lawyers sat down with their counterparts from the three companies and tried to work out a consent order, which would avoid the lengthy process of formal complaint, hearing examiner trial, and full commission decision. American

Home and Sterling stuck together, maintaining cordial relations with the other side; Bristol-Myers, on the other hand, adopted what the Sterling lawyer called a "scorched-earth policy," refusing to give an inch in the belief that the collapse of discussions would win the case.

The scorched-earth policy bore the imprint of Gilbert H. Weil, Bristol-Myers's chief litigator since 1938. A short, large-featured man with quick hands, Weil had gone to law school almost accidentally, and discovered that he loved the give-and-take of litigation. It was a particular pleasure to fight clean and hard, and to tie his adversaries into knots over side issues—Weil was, as one FTC lawyer put it, "a master of the collateral suit." Weil always worked alone or with a few associates in an office that was shabby by the opulent standards of corporate law firms in Manhattan. But he gradually acquired a reputation as one of the finest and toughest attorneys in the field of drug advertising.

In 1961, when the first FTC complaints were issued, Weil was Bristol-Myers's champion in the struggle. Fighting every request for information as overly onerous, the acerbic Weil finally agreed to provide the FTC with some company data—and inundated the understaffed agency with a stack of photocopies more than twenty-three feet tall. His first major battle came in 1967, a few years after the original complaints were dropped, when the commission attempted to restrict the advertising claims of all analgesic brands, not just those of a few companies. The FTC can accomplish this with what is called a "trade regulation rule," which declares whole classes of advertising to be unfair or deceptive.

The proposed rule, one staff attorney noted, was "marked by industry opposition heretofore unknown." Leading the charge was Weil. "The agency was just trying to get up from the image of being little old ladies in tennis shoes," he said years later. "We managed to get them off track with procedural moves, which were essentially efforts at discovery, efforts to learn the basis of their case. And at that point [in the mid-1960s] the commission really didn't *have* a case. They had the Lasagna-DeKornfeld study, which showed no difference, but the failure to prove a difference doesn't mean there is no difference. And they knew that, so they finally tried a trade regulation rule, which was not subject to the same burden of proof. Well, I went after them with the Freedom of Information Act."

In November 1967, Bristol-Myers demanded under the Freedom of Information Act that the agency disclose all its sources for the regulation. Again, the commission was stunned into inaction. On February 1, 1968, it ordered its staff to stop working until the suit was resolved. Weil intended to use the Freedom of Information Act to explore the commission's "state of mind" when it came up with the proposed trade regulation rule (if the action was inspired by malice, as he believed, the rule was invalid). Exploring the agency's mental state necessarily involved laboriously examining its files—

at the very least subjecting it to the same onerous task of photocopying documents that Weil had griped about for years. The FTC balked at allowing its potential victims to go through its papers. Ultimately, however, an appellate court granted Bristol-Myers's request to rummage through FTC files to determine its "state of mind." As a result, the analgesic trade regulation rule was dropped. Now, with the new complaints, Weil was back at the agency doors.

The talks with the three companies hit an obstacle over the FTC's demand for corrective advertising. Believing that twenty years of bad commercials had planted false beliefs in the minds of the public, the FTC insisted that the companies spend 25 percent of their advertising for two years *retracting* their former claims. In response, Weil petitioned the commission for the power to subpoena advertising and sales records from twelve of its competitors during the consent negotiations. Only by knowing intimate details of the other companies, he said, could his client evaluate the impact of its past advertising and the FTC's demands. On June 26, 1972, the commission denied Bristol-Myers's request. Three days later, Weil sued the FTC, seeking a preliminary injunction to prevent the complaints from being issued until the subpoenas were granted, bringing the whole process to a screeching halt. (The suit was dismissed in August.)

At this point, the commission went through another changing of the guard. "That's something people don't realize about government," Bickart said. "You have to prepare the cases to reflect the ideas of one set of commissioners, but by the time you actually try it, half the commissioners have been replaced by people who may have totally different ideas." Reportedly unhappy with the invigorated Federal Trade Commission, Nixon wanted Kirkpatrick out of the chairman's seat. Kirkpatrick resigned. He was replaced in February 1973 by Lewis Engman, an assistant director of the White House Domestic Council under John Ehrlichman. The appointment was too late to save the analgesic makers. The next month, twelve years after the first round of aspirin complaints, the FTC finally climbed back into the ring.

Issued on March 12, 1973, the formal complaints against American Home, Bristol-Myers, and Sterling were not greatly changed from those floated in the press the year before. Written largely by Bickart, the complaints still contained the same charges, and still called for massive advertising retractions. The case was assigned to Judge William K. Jackson—FTC hearing examiners had become administrative law judges by this time—who was known for being tough on government prosecutors. He would have ample opportunity: Of the thirty-two lawyers in the FTC's National Advertising Division, eleven were assigned to the aspirin cases.

Jackson lived up to his reputation. The first order of business was a pretrial hearing in June 1973. Jackson—"a relic from the fifties," Bickart said—professed himself unable to comprehend by what route the lawyers had arrived at this "substantial question" business.

> I have no yardstick by the Commission or any court as to what a substantial question is. In these other cases you have yardsticks; you have precedents; but here you have dreamed up a phrase, "substantial question." And we don't know what it means. Now, who is going to define that?

Medical experts, the FTC lawyers said, would explain whether there was a substantial question about certain claims in analgesic advertising. Jackson asked what legal standard he should apply if there was conflicting testimony—a substantial question, so to speak—over the existence of a substantial question.

"Judge," Bristol-Myers lawyer Weil said, "I think your probing has brought to the surface what Complaint Counsel are trying to do in this case—to revive a horse that was sent to the slaughterhouse on [past] occasions by the Commission."

Jackson agreed, deriding agency counsel for not relying on the reasonable basis standard of the Pfizer case. "Why do you bury your head in the sand," he wondered, "and refuse to follow Commission-announced policy?"

The commission lawyers expostulated vainly that the Pfizer decision had been unclear.

Jackson cut them off.

"I think it has been shown on the record here," he said, "that you are not quite certain of what your theory is and you haven't precisely defined it or enunciated it and you can't tell me whether it falls under [the old FTC cases] or it doesn't."

He ordered the FTC lawyers to submit an explanation of the substantial question charge. In addition, Jackson slapped a protective order on the three proceedings that guarded the company's trade secrets by forbidding the agency lawyers working on one case to talk to those working on the others. The order split the FTC case staff into three malfunctioning parts and brought work to a standstill. Furious, Bickart and his subordinates decided to wait until Jackson's retirement, at the end of 1974, and hope for a more supportive jurist. "We played four corners for eighteen months," he recalled. "It was galling."

Meanwhile, the staff endured yet another change in the commission chair—its fourth in the past eight years. Unlike Engman, whose appointment signaled a reprimand, Michael Pertschuk was picked by Jimmy Carter as a sign of the new president's interest in an active FTC. Pertschuk was the Senate Commerce Committee's chief counsel under Senator Warren Magnuson of Washington, whose book, *The Dark Side of the Marketplace*, played a big role in the rise of the consumer movement. In his four-year tenure as chairman, Pertschuk would bring the FTC to the forefront of consumerism, and perhaps beyond. He launched so many cases against so much of American marketing that under his tenure the agency went beyond anything Kirkpatrick ever dreamed of, earning the nickname of "The Nation's Nanny."

The aspirin cases plodded along in relative obscurity. After Jackson retired, they were assigned to Administrative Law Judge Montgomery K. Hyun. Hyun lifted the protective order and consolidated the evidentiary hearings, allowing the FTC staff to proceed as originally planned. These hearings lasted through the summer of 1977, and prepared all sides for the coming trials. And, strangely, now that the actual courtroom battles were set to begin, the agency found itself downplaying the substantial question standard and proceeding mainly from the Pfizer doctrine—the firms had to have a reasonable basis for their ads.

American Home went first. Its claim of greater effectiveness for Anacin was based on a chain of logic: Anacin had more aspirin per dose than regular-strength aspirin; more aspirin means more pain relief; therefore Anacin provides more pain relief. Strong evidence existed that doubling the amount of aspirin significantly increased pain relief. Unfortunately, American Home had never tested to see if greater relief was observed in the much smaller difference between Anacin (400 mg per tablet) and regular aspirin (325 mg). Clearly, the FTC said, it had no reasonable basis for its assertions.

For its assertion that caffeine added power to aspirin, the company was forced to admit that it had no adequate support; for claims about tension relief, it had nothing. Moreover, there was ample evidence that the public did not know what was in Anacin. In 1964 only 17 percent of those interviewed in a Gallup poll could name aspirin as an ingredient in Anacin, and 78 percent could not name any ingredient; even when asked directly about aspirin, only 65 percent guessed that it was in Anacin. Another survey in 1972 showed that consumer ignorance had changed but slightly: A bare 23 percent could name aspirin as an ingredient in Anacin, and 71 percent had no notion of Anacin's ingredients.

In September 1978, Judge Hyun ruled against American Home on nearly every issue, including the necessity of corrective advertising. He required American Home to disclose the ingredients in its analgesic products and the existence of a substantial question in the medical evidence when such was the case; he also ordered the company to spend twenty-four million dollars to advertise that "Anacin is not a tension reliever." American Home was appalled. One company vice-president spelled out why:

If we go out there and tell people what we told them before was not true and that there was no substantiation or proof that we are any more effective than aspirin, I think we are going to raise further questions . . . [and] many consumers might agree we are not as effective as aspirin.

Rather than comply, American Home considered dropping regular Anacin altogether and putting its considerable marketing resources into a new brand, Maximum Strength Anacin, which, being new, could not be covered by the corrective advertising order. But it decided not to move until it appealed Hyun's decision to the full commission.

Bristol-Myers's trial began immediately after the American Home verdict, with Weil and his wife setting up camp in a Washington hotel and both sides settling down for a long fight. "We didn't move down there until mid-August," Weil recalled. "They told us the hearings would go on until Thanksgiving, but they didn't tell us *which* Thanksgiving. We were down there eleven and a half months, with no more than two or three interludes. I don't know how much it cost Bristol-Myers, and frankly I never wanted to know."

Weil assembled scores of three-ring binders and filled them with computer printouts. Working mostly by himself, he had catalogued every issue of fact and law, then listed the witnesses, documents, and exhibits for both sides on a computerized data base. "The incredible thing is that [in all this labor] you're not dealing with automobiles or refrigerators, where ads get somebody to buy something that costs thousands. You're dealing with items that were selling at the time for twenty-five cents. Suppose a consumer invests twenty-five cents in Bufferin. 'Yeah, I want twice-as-fast relief.' He spends twenty-five cents and finds it takes two hours. So—he never buys Bufferin again. At the very worst, he's out twenty-five cents. You have to wonder, what is the gain in all this? Legal action of unprecedented scope, legal action lasting a generation—for twenty-five cents?"

Unlike American Home, Bristol-Myers had evidence for its claims, especially a study conducted in 1969 at the Philadelphia General Hospital. The results were employed in an aggressive advertising campaign starring David Janssen, who had played a doctor in *The Fugitive*, a popular mid-1960s television drama. (Commercials often feature actors who have played doctors, because companies believe that the audience transfers the aura of respectability around the medical profession to the actor.) The ads showed Janssen at a medical convention in Atlantic City, where doctors had just learned of an amazing new experiment. "In this study," Janssen told viewers, "it took more than twice as many aspirin tablets to give the same pain relief as two Excedrin. . . . Not three aspirin, not even four aspirin."

FTC lawyers scoured the Philadelphia study for flaws, and they found one.

The group of patients that had taken Excedrin began with a higher average level of pain, effectively giving that analgesic a greater opportunity to provide relief. In addition, the *Journal of Clinical Pharmacology and Therapeutics* had refused to print the study, because the editor questioned whether the effects of Excedrin on the type of pain—pain following childbirth—covered by the experiment would carry over to other types of pain.* Even so, the agency case seemed weak. It was merely niggling over the protocol of Bristol-Myers's experiments.

Great was the glee of the agency lawyers when they discovered more evidence to counter Bristol-Myers's case. Hidden in the company's own files was a big, expensive clinical study at Massachusetts General Hospital that, Judge Hyun later concluded, could not "reject the hypothesis that aspirin is more potent than Excedrin. . . ." Further, the experiment was, the judge wrote, "more precise and reliable" than the Philadelphia study that supposedly substantiated Bristol-Myers's advertising. In other words, the company had evidence all along that its Excedrin ads might be wrong, and had hidden it from the public.

The trial then took up Bufferin's longest-running and, to Sterling, most irritating claim: "twice as fast as aspirin." In a corporate decision of questionable intelligence, Bristol-Myers had gone on record during the fight over the commission's trade regulation rule as saying that an analgesic claim such as "acts faster on tension headache" must be supported by evidence of faster pain relief, not just evidence from blood levels. Yet when asked to present its reasonable basis for its Bufferin claims, the company admitted that it had no clinical data of this sort. It offered only the testimony of its own medical director, Ben Marr Lanman, who argued that in a given amount of time Bufferin produced higher blood levels of aspirin than did regular aspirin, and that therefore it must work faster, even if he couldn't exactly say why. Oh, really? asked the FTC. It developed that Lanman had expressed skepticism about this line of reasoning in a 1969 memorandum:

> It is quite true that aspirin is more readily absorbed from Bufferin than from ordinary aspirin tablets. Unfortunately, it is a much more difficult thing to correlate clinical relief with Bufferin. In fact, we have no such correlation between clinical and laboratory tests and the explanation is a very complex one.

At the trial, Bristol-Myers was unable to explain its medical director's change of heart.

* Left unmentioned by the FTC was the fact that its sole analgesic study, conducted by Lasagna and DeKornfeld in 1960, had covered the same type of pain, and that the agency then had considered evidence from it reliable enough to use the Lasagna-DeKornfeld data as the basis for its original complaint against the analgesic companies.

Despite Weil's valiant efforts, Hyun ruled against Bristol-Myers. Like American Home, Bristol-Myers was required to disclose the existence of a substantial question (if such was the case) and the ingredients of its analgesic and other consumer drug products. The only difference was that this time Hyun did not demand corrective advertising.

Finally, Sterling had its day in court. After years of waging a silent war against Anacin and Bufferin advertising—it had pleaded with the FTC to intervene, and welcomed the trade regulation rule—Sterling had gone over to the other side just in time to be nailed by the FTC complaint. Sterling's trial began in October 1979 and lasted until the following August. By now the FTC attorneys had a lot of practice slicing up analgesic studies, and the testimony was devastating. They ripped apart the experiments that supported the Cope and Vanquish ads, demonstrating at length that the supposed benefits were statistically insignificant. As for Bayer's vaunted superiority to other brands of aspirin, the FTC shredded the firm's major evidence, a report comparing Bayer with 220 other brands of aspirin. Sterling had tested all the brands against thirty standards of pharmaceutical purity and performance, and appeared to win hands-down. But a closer look revealed curious lapses in the experimental procedure. Whereas half the Bayer samples were gathered fresh from the factory and sped to the lab by company courier, samples of the other brands were picked up from store shelves across the country and thrown in the mail. It was impossible to tell, the FTC lawyers argued, whether the differences technicians observed came from Bayer's superior quality control or from the fact that the other brands had sat for weeks in store warehouses and post office basements. Trying to establish a link between superior pharmaceutical quality and greater pain relief, Sterling resorted to the justification that Bayer aspirin was better because it reached the bloodstream faster, despite the firm's twenty-five-year opposition to Bufferin's use of such reasoning.

On January 30, 1981, the Sterling decision came out. The overall conclusions and remedies embedded in Judge Hyun's opinion were similar to those in the Bristol-Myers case; he also declined again to impose any corrective advertising. But, to the disbelief of the FTC attorneys, he rebuffed what they had viewed as an airtight argument—that mutually inconsistent advertising claims (Cope and Vanquish are better than aspirin; nothing is better than Bayer aspirin) are inherently illegal. Despite its logical appeal, Judge Hyun noted, strict enforcement of this "novel theory" might have a chilling effect on commercial speech. Suppose two sets of adequate, well-controlled studies existed for two associated products, each set sufficient to establish a reasonable basis for the product's advertising claims—except that the results of the two sets of studies were contradictory. If separate companies sold the two products, both would be able to use their set of studies as substantiation for their advertising. But under the FTC theory, if a single company sold both products, it would not be allowed to use the studies in this way, placing it at a competitive disadvantage. Sterling, for its part, was not particularly encouraged by this small victory: Both Cope and Vanquish were market flops, and the company never invested more than a token amount in their subsequent advertising.

All three cases were appealed to the full commission by both sides. Years more had passed, and the Carter era was drawing to a close. Pertschuk's reign as chairman had drawn the wrath of Congress: In October 1980, the House Appropriations Committee held up the agency's funding and shut down the FTC for a day. (It was in the middle of the Sterling hearing, and one of the company's most important expert witnesses was scheduled to testify; his appearance canceled by Congress, he refused to go to Washington again.) The unbowed Pertschuk still sat in the commissioner's chair when the first of the three cases, American Home, was presented to him in 1981. Disagreeing with Hyun only on the issue of corrective advertising, the final order addressed directly the central problem faced by analgesic makers for the past thirty years:

> Aspirin: homey, familiar, time-tested aspirin has long been an honored staple in the American family's arsenal against common maladies. So homey is this ingredient that it evokes no aura of mystery or magic, though indeed its therapeutic properties are significant; . . . so commonplace that a maker of one aspirin-based pain reliever seeking to differentiate its product from the rest faces a formidable marketing task. What better way to meet this challenge than to establish a new identity for the product, disassociated from ordinary aspirin, and then to represent it as special and more effective than its competitors? That effort may solve the marketer's marketing problem—but if the representations of specialness and superiority are not adequately supported, they can be, simply put, deceptive. That is the heart of the case before us.

American Home was saved the embarrassment of proclaiming its inability to relieve tension, but the remainder of the order was left intact.

The other two cases came before the full commission only after Pertschuk was succeeded as chairman by James C. Miller III, a Reagan appointee who stood in relation to Pertschuk as matter stands to antimatter. After years of being run by consumer activists, the cases were now in the hands of a man who often wore a tie adorned with small portraits of Adam Smith.

The final orders imposed on Bristol-Myers and Sterling, in February 1983, were considerably less onerous than the one given to American Home. Despite Pertschuk's vehement protest, the commission dropped the accusation that the companies had failed to reveal the presence of a substantial question. Commissioner David Clanton, the author of both opinions, candidly admitted that the FTC was retreating from the principle laid down in the American Home decision.

In the meantime, American Home had been seeking to modify its order. It succeeded—three times. The last modification, in June 1984, made its order equivalent to those given the other two companies. Appeals by the companies to higher courts went unheeded. The cases were over. Years after the commission had decided to move against the outlaw analgesic advertisers; years after Rosser Reeves, the brains behind the brazen Anacin ads, had retired from Ted Bates; years since the consumer movement had revitalized the FTC; years after every niggling detail of the last round of charges had been hashed over—the cases were finally over.

It no longer mattered. In one of its many appeals to the commission, American Home had captured the problem now facing the three aspirin companies:

> Developments in the [over-the-counter] analgesic market have simply overrun this and the other two cases. Tylenol, a non-aspirin (acetaminophen) product of Johnson & Johnson Company which has been promoted to consumers only since 1973 and has not been the subject of any Commission proceeding, has become the dominant product in the market.

Homey, familiar, time-tested aspirin was in a fight for its commercial life.

CHAPTER TWELVE

"LET YOUR RIVALS PAY THEIR OWN ADVERTISING BILLS"

In his later years, Claude Hopkins, one of America's most prominent advertising men, liked to tell the story of his visit early in this century to the Schlitz brewery in Milwaukee, Wisconsin. Hopkins began his career by writing advertising copy for Liquozone, a "germ killer" exposed by Samuel Hopkins Adams as 99 percent water and 1 percent sulfuric and sulfurous acid. The revelation did nothing to slow the sales of Liquozone or Hopkins's rise in the advertising world, and by the time of his stroll through the brewery, he was near the top of his profession. Schlitz desperately needed his help. It was mired in fifth place in the hotly competitive beer market. At the time, all beer advertisements played upon a single theme: Purity. "They put the word 'Pure' in large letters," Hopkins recalled in his memoirs. "Then they took double pages to put it in even larger letters. The claim made about as much impression on people as water on a duck." Another, better advertising theme, Hopkins thought, would get Schlitz on the move. In search of inspiration, he wandered amid the pumps, pipes, vats, and filters of the brewery. Sure enough, he found it: *"Our bottles are washed with live steam!"*

His client hooted. *Every* brewery cleans its bottles with steam, Schlitz's managers told him. No one makes beer any other way. Hopkins didn't care. No brewery talked about steam washing, which meant that it was brand new to the public. With lovely, foggy photographs illustrating the miraculous sanitary process of steam cleaning, Schlitz's "Live Steam" campaign lifted the brand into a commanding position.

Hopkins had invented a new type of advertising, one that subtly elevated the image of one brand in a market where all brands were more or less the same. "Again and again I have told simple facts, common to all makers in the line—too common to be told," his memoirs proclaim. "But they have given the article first allied with them an exclusive and lasting prestige.'' His ads did not puff his client at the expense of other brands, nor did they exaggerate the product's qualities. The key was to be the first to advertise an elementary truth. Others might follow, but none could claim it was first. (Even if other brands actually had done it earlier, they hadn't advertised it first.)

Rosser Reeves superseded Hopkins's approach. The man who was to become the master of the hard sell decided that modern advertising needed hard facts to sell. If it was good to state a fact about a product and quietly allow customers to think it was unique to that product, it was better to affirm something about the product that actually *was* unique, and say it out loud. Hence the Unique Selling Proposition, which provided a base for advertising campaigns throughout the 1950s and 1960s. The Unique Selling Proposition found special resonance in aspirin advertising. All aspirin was the same, and its makers were desperate to distinguish themselves from each other. What did it matter that the tiny differences in pharmaceutical quality found—or, perhaps, allegedly found—by Sterling in its test of 220 aspirin brands would make little or no difference to users? They existed, and nobody else could claim them, and that was enough. The other aspirin makers trumpeted their claims to specialness, too, and aspirin commercials became such a cacophony of Unique Selling Propositions that the Federal Trade Commission stepped in.

When the battle with the FTC was over, the aspirin market had been stood on its head by an advertising campaign that was a throwback to the days of Hopkins. The analgesic was Extra-Strength Tylenol; the campaign was ''You Can't Buy a More Potent Pain Reliever Without a Prescription.'' For most types of pain, the claim is factually correct: Nothing is more potent than Extra-Strength Tylenol, because all nonprescription analgesics have the same potency at the recommended doses. The claim thus could have been made by any of Tylenol's competitors. But it wasn't. And being first made all the difference in the world.

Tylenol is not made from aspirin but from another drug, acetaminophen. The name derives, tortuously, from the drug's chemical name, N-ace*tyl*-para-aminoph*enol*. As a further anagrammatic exercise, one can pull out ''acetaminophen'' from the same term. The drug is also known as APAP. Acetaminophen was first synthesized in 1878, well before acetanilid, aspirin, or acetophenetidin were on the market. Joseph von Mering, a Strasbourg biochemist and physiologist, noted its analgesic and antipyretic—fever-reducing—powers fifteen years later but reasoned that it would have the same deleterious side effects as a related compound, para-aminophenol. He recommended against using either drug. In 1894 another study of acetaminophen found it to be a somewhat better treatment for fever than acetophenetidin, but interest remained low, and N-acetyl-para-aminophenol was forgotten for many years.

The lack of interest was not surprising. When a company discovers a new drug, the years of work that go into its development are rewarded through the patent protection afforded the drug. Without the prospect of a patent, the incentives for basic research evaporate; as a result, companies almost never plow money into investigating old, unpatentable drugs, like acetaminophen, because anyone can profit from that research. Often this doesn't matter, because new drugs tend to perform their functions more safely and effectively than their predecessors. But sometimes old drugs have unsuspected new uses, and these may well remain undiscovered.

In the late 1930s, Walter Ames Compton of Miles Laboratories decided to plug this hole in the system. A graduate of Harvard Medical School, Compton joined Miles, the makers of Alka-Seltzer, in the depression. By 1939 he had become a member of the board and the company's research director. Although Miles conducted research of its own, Compton thought that company-sponsored studies would be viewed with skepticism. Tests by scientists from outside the company, on the other hand, would be viewed as independent and therefore reliable. With the help of the Proprietary Association, Compton persuaded ten headache-remedy and sleeping-potion firms to finance the Institute for the Study of Analgesic and Sedative Drugs, which would arrange for independent research. Experimentation would be sponsored by all, for the benefit of all.

Incorporated in August 1939, the institute had a roster that initially included Miles, Emerson Drug (Bromo-Seltzer), B.C. Remedy (B.C. headache powder), Stanback (Stanback powders and tablets), Dow Chemical (bulk analgesics), and American Home Products (Anacin). When the institute decided in 1941 to cover the salicylates, Sterling and other aspirin makers joined. The institute did not investigate individual brands. Instead it looked at the basic qualities of analgesics themselves. The need, many analgesic makers agreed, was apparent. As Charles Beardsley, a member of the family that founded Miles Laboratories, admitted, "These old drugs have been going on for years and years and years, and the question of how useful they are has never actually been obtained."

As its first projects the institute chose acetanilid and bromides. Acetanilid was, of course, the early coal-tar analgesic; the bromides were bromine compounds used as sedatives and anticonvulsants; the two were often combined in products like B.C. headache powders and Bromo-Seltzer. (The latter was sold, like Coca-Cola, at soda shops, and the image of the harried businessman rushing in with the words "gimme a bromo" was part of the folklore of the day.) These were selected as objects of study not least because five months before the institute was founded, the FDA seized a number of acetanilid-bromide compounds, B.C. headache powders and Bromo-Seltzer among them, because of the agency's concern about their side effects.

The institute hired scientists from leading medical schools to write monographs on analgesic and sedative drugs. The first monograph, on acetanilid, was published in 1946; more followed, including one on acetophenetidin in 1956, and two on salicylates in 1948 and 1966. It also sponsored conventions, of which the most important was a symposium on N-acetyl-para-aminophenol in 1951.

The symposium was indirectly spawned by the institute's attempt to learn why acetanilid occasionally damaged the blood. Two institute-sponsored researchers, Leon Greenberg and David Lester of Yale, discovered in 1946 that acetanilid quickly broke down in the body into a number of substances, including acetaminophen. Greenberg and Lester hypothesized that the latter drug, not the former, was responsible for the analgesic effect. Another institute-backed team, Bernard Brodie and his colleagues at New York University, showed in 1948 and 1949 that acetophenetidin too was metabolized to acetaminophen. A prominent neurochemist, Brodie pushed further into the question, observing that acetaminophen seemed not to have the serious side effects of acetanilid and acetophenetidin. Instead, the damage was due to other, more toxic compounds that appeared alongside acetaminophen when the digestive system broke down the two drugs. Further research showed that acetaminophen possessed the analgesic and antipyretic powers of both drugs.

As scientific backing for the drug mounted, the Sumner Chemical Company, a Miles subsidiary, began making small amounts of acetaminophen in April 1948. In July 1950, Squibb Pharmaceutical, a big drug firm in New York City, became the first to sell it, offering a prescription-only blend of acetaminophen, aspirin, and caffeine called Trigesic. (Squibb had been selling an aspirin-acetophenetidin-caffeine mixture, and substituted acetaminophen for acetophenetidin.) Late in 1950, Monsanto and American Cyanamid, two giant chemical companies, also started production. Observing that the price of acetaminophen had dropped from $3.00 a pound to $1.50, the trade magazine *Chemical Week* predicted in January 1951 that this "new" drug would probably come into wide use. Nonetheless, it prophesized, acetaminophen "will never threaten the aspirin tablet."

Five days after *Chemical Week* made its prediction, two Trigesic users developed agranulocytosis, a blood affliction that results in high fever, chills, swollen neck, and sore throat. Not only was the condition serious, but it was associated with other coal-tar drugs, although not acetanilid or acetophenetidin. After the initial incidents were followed by a third, Squibb pulled Trigesic from the market. Although subsequent investigation absolved acetaminophen of responsibility for the condition, the withdrawal was accompanied by considerable negative publicity.

By coincidence, the institute's symposium was held only three months after Squibb yanked Trigesic off the market. More than fifty members of the analgesic industry and scientific community gathered to evaluate the medical evidence concerning acetaminophen. The news was good: Study after study underscored the safety of the drug, and in no case did a researcher find evidence of agranulocytosis or any other blood disorder. As exciting as these results might have been to the scientists, the marketers had another question: Would another analgesic make new profits or simply steal sales from a firm's current line of analgesics?

One firm, Bayer Products, Ltd., a British subsidiary of Sterling, found the question easy to answer. In 1949 Sterling bought the half of Bayer Ltd. formerly held by I.G. Farben. It shaved off the parts of the company that sold drugs directly to consumers, creating two new enterprises: the Charles H. Phillips Company, with its Milk of Magnesia, and Scott & Turner, with its Andrews Liver Salts. The now shrunken Bayer Products, Ltd., dealt only in ethical products, except for Bayer aspirin. Although no prescription was needed to buy aspirin, Bayer Ltd., mindful of the doctors it served with its other medicines, marketed ASA like an ethical drug, refusing to advertise it to the public. This, of course, hurt its competitive position. In addition, Bayer Ltd. had many rivals in the aspirin trade, including the U.K. subsidiary of American Home Products, which sold Anadin (trademark conflicts prevented the use of the Anacin name), and Rickett, which sold a brand of soluble aspirin called Disprin, popular because it passed through the gastrointestinal tract quickly, thus providing less opportunity for stomach upset. Neither of these two companies had scruples about advertising. Unsurprisingly, Bayer Ltd. could not make headway against its adversaries; its annual sales were a bare £300,000. The company had nothing to lose by introducing a new analgesic.

Laurie M. Spalton, a pharmacist, joined Bayer Ltd. as sales manager in June 1950. A year later, Spalton became the managing director, and, he said afterward, "realized quickly that the company badly needed a new product." While doing some journal reading at home, Spalton ran across an article by Brodie and Julius Axelrod about acetaminophen. The drug was, he said, "acetophenetidin without the side effects. It ought to be safer, and could be used in higher doses." Intrigued, Spalton asked Ripley Oddie, medical director of Bayer Ltd., to concoct some acetaminophen in his lab. After initial tests on animals, Bayer Ltd. commenced clinical trials in 1953. The preliminary results convinced them that the drug was equivalent to aspirin in analgesic power.

Because acetaminophen was considered "old" in the United Kingdom, Bayer Ltd. could sell it without a doctor's prescription. But the company was an ethical-drug firm, unlike its namesake in the United States, and could not advertise to the public without permission from its overlords in New York. More important, Spalton felt it unethical to sell a drug to the public without amassing more clinical evidence, even if the active ingredient had been around for seventy years.

At the time, the most widely used prescription analgesic was a mixture of aspirin, acetophenetidin, and codeine called "compound codeine." Compound codeine was under fire by doctors worried about the side effects of aspirin and acetophenetidin. In addition, codeine induced constipation.* Seeing an opportunity in compound codeine's problems, Bayer Ltd. introduced its brand of acetaminophen, Panadol, to British consumers in 1956. (The first choice for a name was Banadol—"ban pain," from *dolor*, the Latin—but trademark problems interfered.) Panadol's Unique Selling Proposition was that it had all of the power of compound codeine but none of the side effects.

Getting doctors and hospitals to buy Panadol required an independent demonstration of acetaminophen's efficacy. Bayer Ltd. turned to D. R. L. Newton and J. M. Tanner, two London medical researchers, who pitted acetaminophen against compound codeine in a clinical trial. The results were disappointing. Although a few of the patients found acetaminophen to be the better analgesic, the doctors concluded that compound codeine was more powerful. Spalton was puzzled—why didn't the outside trial show what his team had found in the lab? (The explanation emerged only later, when it was learned that acetaminophen has little ability to reduce inflammation. Almost half the patients in the trial—nineteen of forty-two—were taking analgesics for rheumatoid arthritis, a condition for which compound codeine and aspirin are superior to acetaminophen.) Later studies turned out better for the company. Now backed by lab science, Spalton put all of his company's promotional resources into Panadol. "We did detail men, direct mail, medical journal ads," he said. "We threw in everything we could afford."

The theme of the pitch was Panadol's unambiguous advantage over aspirin in terms of stomach upset. Aspirin interferes with the ability of the stomach to protect itself from its own acids. Only a few people actually get upset stomachs, but almost everyone experiences a minuscule amount of gastrointestinal bleeding. Acetaminophen, by contrast, rarely causes stomach upset, and almost never causes bleeding. As a marketing device, Bayer Ltd. highlighted this difference by calculating the total amount of blood lost from aspirin ingestion by the population of Great Britain, expressing the answer in terms of "swimming pools of blood." Britain's lurid tabloids picked up on "swimming pools of blood," splashing the grisly metaphor across their pages and thoroughly alarming the populace. The savagery of the attacks on aspirin shocked John Baruch, then U.S. marketing director for Winthrop, when he saw them on his occasional trips to Europe. "If you were in Britain in the fifties," he said, "and asked for aspirin, it would be 'Good God, are you trying to kill yourself?' Aspirin was not only a poison, but it would burn a hole in your stomach!"

Sterling's foreign division was split into "Corcoronia" in Latin America

---

* Although codeine in large and continual doses can be habit forming, the amount in compound codeine was small enough to avoid this problem.

and Asia, run by David Corcoran, and "Spaltonia" in Europe, run by Spalton. Both operated with little supervision, which allowed Spalton to attack aspirin—the foundation of the American firm—without regard to sensibilities in New York. Once a year, Sterling president James Hill, Jr., and vice-president Earl McClintock—"a coaster," Spalton said of the latter—would visit Europe to discuss the business. Invariably they met in Paris, where, to Spalton's amusement, Hill stayed in Paris's elegant Hotel George V and ordered Blue Nun. "Hill was a burly man with a short haircut," Spalton said. "He *rolled* up to you in a peculiar way." But Spalton was delighted that Hill let him run Bayer Ltd. without interference. As long as the balance sheet remained positive, Hill saw no reason to change anything. He pushed Spalton a little to re-enter the aspirin market, but accepted it when Spalton stuck to acetaminophen.

Bayer Ltd. continued to promote the drug only to doctors, but took the path pioneered decades earlier by Duisberg: emphasizing the brand name, Panadol, but not the chemical name, N-acetyl-para-aminophenol. "I thought it might work," Spalton said, "but I never had any idea how well." Within a few years Panadol profits were re-energizing Bayer Ltd. Indeed, Panadol was so often prescribed that it caught the attention of the National Health Service, Britain's state-supported medical system, because the drug's increasing use and relatively high price was driving up the budget. The NHS preferred generic drugs to branded drugs, because the former usually cost less. Unfortunately, it could do nothing about acetaminophen. Though old, the drug was sufficiently new to doctors that it was not in *The British Pharmacopeia*, and hence had no official generic name. Doctors were therefore unable to prescribe it generically—they couldn't write "active ingredient of Panadol" on the prescription pad. *The British Pharmacopeia* was still a few years away from the next scheduled revision, the first opportunity to add a generic entry for acetaminophen. In January 1963, the NHS took the nearly unprecedented step of suddenly publishing standards for acetaminophen in the *London Gazette*, the official government record. In so doing, it coined a new name, paracetamol, which, like acetaminophen, is taken, but even more tortuously, from the chemical name N-a*cet*yl-*para*-a*mi*nophen*ol*. "With that," Spalton said, "every Tom, Dick, and Harry started to make it."

Panadol had been alone for long enough, however, to establish a firm base. Its sales continued to grow. In 1967 the consumption of aspirin was three times that of acetaminophen; by 1973, three years after Bayer Ltd. first advertised Panadol to the public, acetaminophen had nearly caught up.

Eventually Panadol's success caused Sterling to think about introducing it in the United States. By this time, Hill had died. "McClintock thought he was going to get the job," said Ed Landreth, one of David Corcoran's lieutenants. "Well, that made the other candidate, [J. Mark] Hiebert, look good. And Hiebert turned out to be a jerk." At an emotional meeting in

Hiebert's plush, bomb shelter–equipped country home in Rensselaer, Spalton and Corcoran urged the company to give acetaminophen a serious look. Hiebert was frightened by the thought of launching a potential competitor to Bayer aspirin. Bayer was the American franchise, he said. It was the base of the company. Panadol should stay across the Atlantic. "It was," Landreth said, "an unbelievably stupid decision in a company that had made its share of them."

In the mid-1950s, Laurie Spalton was shown a new American drug product. It was a little red plastic firetruck full of liquid acetaminophen. Spalton was appalled. He thought a drug should not be packaged in a toy; nor should it be mixed, as this product was, with a sweet elixir, and marketed as a product for children. The firetruck, in his opinion, was a "sick joke." It was his first encounter with Tylenol.

The 1951 symposium on acetaminophen had caught the attention of another pharmaceutical company without an analgesic in its product line: McNeil Laboratories. A small outfit in Fort Washington, Pennsylvania, McNeil began in 1879 as a drugstore in Philadelphia's mill district. The company attended the symposium; afterward, its interest was heightened by a report from two scientists at the respected Karolinska Institute in Stockholm, Lars-Olof Boréus and Finn Sandberg, who found that acetaminophen equaled acetophenetidin in pain- and fever-relieving power and was clearly superior in freedom from side effects. Of the two drugs, Boréus and Sandberg believed, acetaminophen was "the analgesic of choice." In addition, acetaminophen could be manufactured as a liquid—unlike aspirin, which breaks down in that form. The lack of side effects and solubility meant that acetaminophen would make an ideal fever remedy for children.

McNeil submitted a New Drug Application to the FDA for acetaminophen. When approval was granted on April 13, 1955, Tylenol was born. McNeil marketed no other consumer products, and thus sold Tylenol to children purely as an ethical drug. In 1958 McNeil decided to seek FDA permission for an adult version of Tylenol, planning to market it to that small minority of people who are allergic to aspirin. Before the agency acted, however, something unexpected happened: McNeil was bought by Johnson & Johnson, one of the nation's biggest and most ubiquitous consumer and health products companies.

Johnson & Johnson got its start in 1887, when three brothers—Robert, James, and Edward Mead Johnson—jointly invested $100,000 in making antiseptic surgical dressings. James was clever at production; Mead was a shrewd marketer; and Robert, the eldest, was an entrepreneur and manager. Their talents meshed, and the firm expanded fast. After two years its work force had grown from 14 to 125 employees, and the factory occupied two big buildings in New Brunswick, New Jersey. Like Duisberg, the Johnson brothers recognized the value of a corporate symbol for its products. Alas, its chosen symbol, a thick red cross, was already taken by Clara Barton's American Red Cross. To Barton's dismay, the use of this symbol had grown into a cottage industry: There were Red Cross cigars, Red Cross whisky, Red Cross churns, and even Red Cross dog collars. After unsuccessfully asking Congress to protect her right to the symbol, she licensed it to the Johnson brothers. Mead Johnson left in 1897 to start his own eponymous firm; under Robert and James, Johnson & Johnson continued to grow. Its baby powder first saw the light in 1890; in 1920, ten years after Robert Johnson's death, the firm introduced Band-Aid, its brand of adhesive bandage; Modess sanitary napkins followed in 1934. By 1954, its sales totaled nearly $245 million. It had operations throughout the world and a carefully guarded reputation for probity. It had established a distinctive manner of operation: a relatively small headquarters in New Jersey, and scores of almost completely independent subsidiaries that made products ranging from analgesics, bandages, and dental floss to computerized tomographic scanners, blood analyzers, and contraceptives. Each subcompany had its own president and management; the entity called Johnson & Johnson consisted of little more than a Johnson family–dominated executive board that set overall direction. Looking over the growing Johnson & Johnson empire at the end of the 1950s, the management realized that the one area of health care unexplored by the firm was pharmaceuticals. In 1959 Johnson & Johnson bought two small drug firms: Cilag Chemie of Switzerland and McNeil Laboratories. As usual, the parent firm let McNeil continue to manage and promote Tylenol.

A year later, McNeil received approval to sell adult Tylenol. Constant promotion to doctors ensured that they recommended it to the small number of people who can't take aspirin and the much larger number of people who think they can't. Sales inched upward. By 1965 Tylenol had made it onto the list of the two hundred most frequently prescribed drugs. Aspirin makers did not worry; as one trade magazine noted, their drug was "out in front of the pack for as long as any one in the trade can see." A main reason for aspirin's advantage was that acetaminophen cost almost two and a half times more in its chemical form, and was no bargain on the store shelf.

Although Tylenol was not a prescription drug, McNeil continued to sell it like one, investing almost nothing in consumer advertising. "There was argument for years within Johnson & Johnson about how to market Tylenol," remembered William Lynch, the former national sales manager of the company's health care division. "McNeil thought doctors would abandon the product if they put it on TV. Most people at headquarters, including [Johnson & Johnson chairman James E.] Burke, thought Tylenol should be marketed like a traditional consumer product, because somebody was going to come along and do it. And he was right." McNeil's pokiness exasperated

Johnson & Johnson's consumer division to the point that it brought out its own brand of acetaminophen, Truce. "The name Truce," Burke later told *Forbes*, "was kind of funny, because there was plenty of warring between our companies when we did it." Truce did not survive.

As Burke had predicted, others made forays into acetaminophen. In 1968 Bristol-Myers tested Neotrend acetaminophen in Connecticut and Massachusetts. The commercials had a straightforward theme: "We replaced aspirin." After a frank discussion of aspirin's potential side effects, the advertising insinuated that "even if aspirin never bothered you before, that doesn't mean it never will. With aspirin, you never know." They ended ominously: "Why take a chance when you can avoid aspirin altogether?"

Unfortunately for Neotrend, the ads hit the airwaves in the middle of a minor revolution at McNeil: After spending next to nothing for so many years, the company poured more than $700,000 into consumer advertising for Tylenol during 1967 and 1968. (In contrast, American Home spent almost $37 million on Anacin ads in the same two years.) McNeil used the theme it had been expounding to the medical community for fifteen years: "Many doctors have long recommended Tylenol, and your drugstore has it without a prescription." Battered by Tylenol's unexpected promotion, Neotrend disappeared from sight after less than two years.

In 1969 annual sales of Tylenol stood at less than $10 million, and the brand had a 2.5 percent share of the nonprescription analgesic market. Anacin was the leader, with more than 17 percent; Bayer was on its heels, one bare percentage point behind; and Bufferin was third, followed by its sister brand, Excedrin. The four top brands dumped almost $65 million into consumer advertising in that year; Tylenol, after its previous year's record budget of $453,000, spent no money on consumer advertising in 1969.

The years passed, and all the while McNeil continued its constant low-key pitch to hospitals about Tylenol's equal effectiveness and superior safety. Doctors responded: In 1975, Tylenol received 921,000 recommendations from physicians. Bufferin, its nearest rival, got 543,000. Anacin and Excedrin, by contrast, received none. Despite McNeil's spending less than $200,000 advertising to nondoctors between 1969 and 1974, Tylenol's share crept up to a bit more than 10 percent. It was now the leading brand in drugstores, although not in grocery and convenience stores. Bayer, with ad expenditures of $83 million during the same period, had a 12.3 percent share. Little wonder that several aspirin makers began looking seriously at acetaminophen. One of them, again, was Bristol-Myers.

In early 1975 Tylenol was selling a hundred tablets for a highly profitable $2.85. Bristol-Myers decided to vie for some of that profit by reintroducing Datril, another previous, unsuccessful acetaminophen product. What followed has become a legendary debacle in the annals of drug marketing. Bristol-Myers chose to promote Datril by a method that would have made

Rosser Reeves cry out in pain had he not been long retired. It selected what might be called a Non-Unique Selling Proposition: price. Because nobody had ever heard of "acetaminophen," the company introduced Datril by explaining that it was the same as Tylenol but cost a dollar less. Consumers in the two test markets, Albany, New York, and Peoria, Illinois, flocked to buy Datril.

Stunned McNeil executives watched Tylenol's share in the two cities fall by half. When a pleased Bristol-Myers announced that a national Datril campaign would begin in June, Johnson & Johnson sent out an army of price cutters—four hundred from McNeil and more than three hundred from other Johnson & Johnson divisions—to reduce the price on every Tylenol package they could find. On June 3, 1975, Johnson & Johnson chairman James Burke telephoned Richard Gelb, his opposite number at Bristol-Myers, to inform him that Tylenol's price had been slashed 30 percent that very day. Bristol-Myers, he said, was about to run a lot of false Datril ads.

Bristol-Myers didn't get where it was by backing down in the face of a little competitive heat. It ran the ads anyway. During the next three months, the company spent $3 million promoting Datril. Johnson & Johnson headquarters didn't think McNeil was ready for a major marketing war—the year before, Tylenol's budget for national media advertising had been a paltry $83,000. The mother corporation issued an ultimatum: Either it would take over the brand completely, or McNeil would allow a marketing team from New Jersey to come to Fort Washington and run the brand from there. McNeil chose the latter. On July 1, 1975, Wayne Nelson arrived.

A silver-haired, handsome man, Nelson is often described by the term "marketing genius." He began his adult life in journalism school but decided he'd rather do things himself than write about other people doing things. He joined Johnson & Johnson in 1971. By 1975, he had risen to become the director of product management for Johnson & Johnson's health care division. When he arrived at McNeil, he changed the atmosphere from the subdued ambiance of ethical marketing to one more suited to the tough days ahead.

Nelson's first action was to hector the networks about Datril's price comparison. Bristol-Myers was forced to change its claims to different, weaker formulae. By mid-July, the ad copy had become "Datril can cost less than Tylenol. A lot less." After more griping from Nelson, it became "Datril can cost less." Further complaints brought "Datril can cost less depending on where you shop." By October, Nelson had sent Bristol-Myers's Non-Unique Selling Proposition to the museum of failed advertising campaigns. Datril ads now urged consumers to shop around and "buy the one that costs less."

Remarkably, not a single new national ad appeared for Tylenol in all this time. Nelson didn't need them. People who had never heard of Tylenol now saw it featured in television and magazine advertising for Datril. That the advertising was for an imitator didn't stop them from trying the original. Bristol-Myers plugged away at how great Datril was because it was just like Tylenol—which told people that Tylenol was also great, and that it had been there for a longer period of time than this upstart with the shopping advice. Datril violated a rule of marketing that has been quoted to students of advertising since the turn of the century: "Let your rivals pay their own advertising bills."

Bristol-Myers persisted. In October 1975, it brought out Datril Elixir for children. The advertising campaign stressed . . . price. Datril Elixir bombed too.

Bristol-Myers launched yet another attack against Tylenol in the spring of 1976. Its commercials opened with a split screen showing two women, one with a bottle of Datril, the other with a bottle of Tylenol. This time, however, the Datril user declared that Datril has "a new, faster formula," and that it "delivers more pain relief faster than Tylenol."

Datril's greater speed, too, turned out to be a Non-Unique Selling Proposition. Nelson's technical team took Datril apart, seeking to find any reason, no matter how small, that Bristol-Myers could make the claim. They found that the powder in a Datril tablet was compressed more loosely than that in a Tylenol tablet, allowing Datril to dissolve faster in the stomach. There was no proof that faster dissolution meant faster analgesia. But Nelson didn't care. By the time the new Datril campaign was in full force, McNeil had reformulated its Tylenol tablets, packing them more loosely. Nelson then objected to the Datril ads, saying they were based on Tylenol's old formulation. Bristol-Myers was again forced to give in.

At this point, Nelson was handed a new weapon. In the early 1970s, McNeil's main rival in the prescription sale of mild analgesics was Darvon, made by Eli Lilly, of Indianapolis, Indiana. (The active ingredient is propoxyphene, a relative of codeine.) In 1971 McNeil developed a version of Tylenol that changed the per-tablet dose of acetaminophen from 325 mg to 500 mg. It then paid for a medical experiment that established that a 1,000-mg dose of acetaminophen (two 500-mg tablets) was superior to Darvon for the pain of episiotomy, a common surgical procedure performed during childbirth. The study in hand, it sought permission from the FDA to sell the bigger version of Tylenol as a prescription drug. The application was accepted a short time later. In 1974—this was still before Datril and Wayne Nelson's arrival—the company returned to the FDA, seeking approval to make the 500-mg version of Tylenol available without a prescription. The FDA acquiesced in July 1975, as the Datril battle was in full heat.

By May 1976, almost one year after Datril's campaign had begun, Nelson was ready to advertise Tylenol. Not all the delay had been due to his desire to take advantage of the free publicity from Bristol-Myers. In part, he had waited because he had been puzzling over how to present Tylenol. For two decades, McNeil had stressed the safety of acetaminophen for people who could not tolerate aspirin. But many consumers equated safety with lower analgesic power, and thought that if Tylenol was safer than aspirin, as it claimed, it must not be as powerful. How could the company make people believe that a safe drug could also knock out raging headaches? Nelson's answer was to devote nearly all of McNeil's promotion efforts for the Tylenol brand to the new 500-mg version, which he christened Extra-Strength Tylenol. He didn't have to spend a dime talking about safety, because twenty years of promoting that theme to doctors had created a halo of safety about Tylenol. The larger version of Tylenol should be positioned, he concluded, not as a larger non-aspirin brand, but as an extra-strength analgesic. Wayne Nelson was about to fuse the non-aspirin and aspirin markets, and create a single *analgesic* market.

Whipping up the fervor of his sales force, Nelson set up training sessions for them on the wonders of Extra-Strength Tylenol. Like General Patton on the night before a military offensive, he primed his troops for the assault on aspirin. Things had changed at McNeil, he told them. Now they had a killer product and they were going to go out there and *sell*. "There was one session down in Dallas," recalled Lynch, who arranged many of them. "The room full of people selling consumer products was suddenly invaded by this scientific professional from [the old-style] McNeil. He got into the pharmacology of the drug. The salespeople were totally lost. I said, 'Wait, here's the message you got to learn. It's a non-aspirin aspirin that sells like hell. That's it.' "

Extra-Strength Tylenol debuted in May 1976. Suddenly newspapers, magazines, and television were filled with Nelson's carefully crafted message: *"You can't buy a more potent pain reliever without a prescription."* This is an example of what is known, in the advertising trade, as a "parity claim." A favorite marketing device, parity claims are, as one drug company executive dryly put it, "attempts to take advantage of the imprecision of the language—you claim parity but imply superiority." Parity claims about drug strength are especially effective. "What's lovely about this is the element of danger," a drug company lawyer said later. "Everybody is convinced that their own personal headache is the worst in the world, right? So everybody wants the absolutely most potent thing out there. So every product except baby aspirin already pushes the maximum. But the public doesn't know that, and only Tylenol claimed it." Parity claims are an offense to Rosser Reeves's theory of advertising: A Unique Selling Proposition has to be based on a *real* difference—and Tylenol was saying it was just the same as other pain relievers! But it was a perfect example of Claude Hopkins's philosophy: State a simple fact, common to many producers, *but be the first to do so*. The public responded as Hopkins would have predicted, giving Tylenol "exclusive and lasting prestige." Tylenol sales, already rising quickly, shot off the charts.

In November, Tylenol passed Anacin as the leading analgesic brand. By then Bristol-Myers had spent more than eleven million dollars on Datril ads. Datril had 2 percent of the analgesic market but had helped to increase Tylenol's share by more than a third, to 14.5 percent.

Moreover, Extra-Strength Tylenol contained half again more acetaminophen than regular Tylenol at half again the price per pill. But because people took two tablets of both versions, Extra-Strength Tylenol was much more profitable. Its introduction recouped much of the money Johnson & Johnson had sacrificed by cutting the price of regular Tylenol to match that of Datril.

By the beginning of 1977 Tylenol was well on its way to becoming the biggest-selling health and beauty product in the nation—most of its growth due to advertising, and much of it due to someone else's advertising. In the ten years that had passed since 1967, its share of the analgesic market had grown from less than one-hundredth—so small that market analysts didn't even include it in their totals—to nearly one-fifth. In those same ten years, each of three leading aspirin brands—Anacin, Bayer, and Excedrin—had seen its market share drop steadily. Wayne Nelson had won; Tylenol was on top of the analgesic market. But getting there was only half the battle; the other half was staying there.

CHAPTER THIRTEEN

"SHAME ON YOU!"

S terling chairman W. Clark Wescoe saw himself losing ground on many fronts. A former chancellor of the University of Kansas, Wescoe had been selected by his predecessor, J. Mark Hiebert, a Kansas alumnus of unimpeachable loyalty. Wescoe, who had a scientific background, was first asked by Hiebert to join the Sterling board, conferring upon it some intellectual respectability. Gradually the enthusiastic Hiebert drew him into Sterling, but not enough to prevent alarm when Wescoe became chairman. ("There was no big fat cat who held all the stock," said John Baruch, former U.S. marketing director for Winthrop. "Nobody could tell Hiebert not to act as if he owned the company.") Almost bereft of sales experience, Wescoe now had the unenviable task of reversing Bayer aspirin's twenty-five-year slide. In 1977, Bayer had 10 percent of the analgesic market—10 percent for mighty Bayer! It was not just time to fight back. Sterling had been trying that for years. It was time to think creatively. It was time to find a whole new arena for battle, and after several false starts the company stumbled across it.

Bayer's first response to Tylenol had been imitation. In 1976 Sterling brought out its own acetaminophen brand, Bayer Non-Aspirin. Bayer Non-Aspirin was a big flop. After decades of hearing that Bayer was "pure aspirin, not part aspirin," consumers were befuddled to learn that Bayer was now not aspirin. Massive advertising failed to clarify matters. After an onslaught of TV commercials, Bayer Non-Aspirin topped out with a market share of 0.3 percent—barely discernible from zero. The brand was withdrawn.

Giving up the attempt to create a new product, Sterling returned to Bayer aspirin. In late 1976 it launched a new campaign to dispute Tylenol's charge that aspirin irritates the gastrointestinal tract, and to play up aspirin's chief advantage, that in large doses it has superior anti-inflammatory power. (The takeoff point was an NIH-backed study that found 99 percent of the people who took aspirin did not feel stomach upset.) Not only does aspirin pass easily through the stomach, Sterling commercials said, but by taking aspirin substitutes consumers "sacrifice an important therapeutic action," meaning its power to reduce inflammation. Johnson & Johnson promptly complained to the National Advertising Division of the Council of Better Business Bureaus, a self-regulatory group sponsored by American business. The NAD investigates campaigns and judges the veracity of their claims. If any are deemed to be false, it asks the sponsor to withdraw or modify its advertising. Although the NAD has no power to enforce its decisions, few companies choose to defy them.* The NAD ruled in the following spring that the phrase "important therapeutic action" was accurate. On the other hand, it said that the stomach-upset claim was misleading, because aspirin damages the gastric system, even if the harm is so slight that people can't feel it. Sterling and Johnson & Johnson both disagreed, but the entire matter was moot. The campaign was unsuccessful, and Sterling had already deep-sixed it.

Its replacement came in June 1977. This time Sterling let out all the stops—it caterwauled with the corporate outrage it had repressed for more than two decades. What triggered the fury was an ad that showed a doctor's black bag above the headline WHY DOCTORS RECOMMEND TYLENOL MORE THAN ALL LEADING ASPIRIN BRANDS COMBINED. (Tylenol, the copy said, is "safer than aspirin.") The "doctors recommend" slogan, like other Tylenol slogans, was completely true. Doctors recommended Tylenol more than all leading aspirin brands combined. Sterling was enraged because the medical profession rarely advocated the use of aspirin by brand but instead told patients simply to "take aspirin." Indeed, doctors suggested aspirin, as a drug, more frequently than acetaminophen. Johnson & Johnson's jiggery-pokery, Sterling said, was inexcusable. Big black accusatory headlines filled full-page advertisements in *Time* and *Newsweek*:

Makers of
Tylenol,
Shame on you!

Beneath a photograph of the offending Tylenol ad was the oddly school-marmish injunction, "Tylenol ads could fool people!"

Seeing Sterling raise the stakes, Johnson & Johnson matched and raised them again. In a letter that somehow managed to find its way into the press, it demanded that Sterling stop the advertisements immediately—or else the two companies would wind up in court. ("One of the things people remember about Wayne Nelson was that he fought tooth and nail *any* attempt to get in," said William Lynch, the former national sales manager of the company's health care division. "You name it, he sued.") Johnson & Johnson

* This record is deceptive, because a case is dropped if the campaign under investigation is stopped. Given the frequency with which ad campaigns change, this provision ensures that many investigations will become irrelevant before the NAD grinds to a conclusion.

assured Sterling that it had no desire to engage in a litigious duel. But if
Tylenol were to find itself before a judge, its lawyers might be forced to note
that many more people died from aspirin overdose than from acetaminophen
overdose. (This too was true, although doctors thought it was partly because
more people took aspirin, and partly because acetaminophen overdose, a
newer phenomenon, was vastly underreported.) Ultimately, Nelson knew, he
could not easily sue—Johnson & Johnson was making too much money to
demonstrate harm from the Bayer campaign. In mid-August, two months
after Bayer began shouting "Shame on you!," Tylenol had one-fifth of the
market, a share held in the past only by Bayer and Anacin. But by that time
Sterling was seeing the fruits of another strategy. It had journeyed to the final
recourse of any desperate business: the government.

The recipient of Sterling's pleas was the Food and Drug Administration,
which had embarked upon a lengthy review of the safety and effectiveness of
over-the-counter drugs. ("Over-the-counter," one recalls, is the trade word
for "nonprescription.") The OTC drug review, as it was known, had already
stretched over many years, much like the FTC analgesic cases. It grew out
of the thalidomide tragedy in 1961. An over-the-counter sedative sold by
Hoechst, thalidomide caused dreadful birth defects. Thousands of blighted
children came into the world before thalidomide was banned. Although the
tough standards of the FDA kept the drug out of the U.S. market, the law let
firms give samples to doctors. The awful results appalled a public already
angered by high drug prices. In 1962 Congress passed the first major amendments to the 1938 Food, Drug, and Cosmetic Act. Until then, the FDA
concerned itself with the safety of new drugs, but not their effectiveness.
Now the industry would be required to prove both to the agency's satisfaction. Moreover, the legislation did not apply only to new drugs. It charged
the FDA with evaluating all drugs, prescription and over-the-counter alike,
that had been introduced into the market after 1938. The task was daunting,
especially on the OTC side. Not only did thousands of different brands jam
store shelves, but each of those brands came in many different dosage forms
and sizes. Tablets, capsules, creams, salves, suppositories, gargles, sprays,
elixirs, powders, infusions—the agency hadn't a clue how many OTC products were out there to test, except that the number was enormous. Plausible
estimates, it said later, "range[d] from 100,000 to 500,000 separate items."
For the ulcer-creating job of counting them all, agency wags joked, drug
makers produced more than eight thousand antacids.

Although the legislation instructed the FDA to evaluate over-the-counter
drugs, it did not say how. The agency hired two independent scientific
bodies, the National Academy of Sciences and the National Research Council, to perform preliminary tests. The NAS/NRC team broke the drug market
into thirty categories and convened a panel of recognized experts to examine
a sample of products in each. More than four thousand drugs were ultimately

examined, of which about five hundred were over-the-counter. Reports were issued in May 1969.

"From what I can tell," Peter Rheinstein, director of medical staff in the Office of Health Affairs, said later, "the results were quite a shock. The prescription drugs were okay, but half the OTC drugs didn't work." (In fact, the proportion was closer to three-quarters.)

Reeling from the news that thousands upon thousands of products were probably ineffective, the FDA realized it would have to undertake the horrendous job of slogging through the entire over-the-counter market. (It also had to evaluate ethical drugs, but this was more easily subsumed into its current functioning.) After mulling over this unappetizing prospect for two and half years, the FDA announced its plan to forge order out of OTC chaos in January 1972. Rather than make decisions on a product-by-product basis—at one per day, the job would take 273 years—it decided to look only at the active ingredients, which were thought to number around five hundred. These were then parceled into twenty-six classes, each of which was the purview of a panel of medical experts similar to those convened by the National Academy of Sciences and the National Research Council. After requesting information from manufacturers, the panels would issue a list of recommended ingredients, dosages, and labeling for the products in their categories. When the recommendations became public, industry would again be allowed to weigh in. Then, balancing the concerns of the industry and the expert panel, the FDA would issue its own preliminary summary of permissible and forbidden drugs. Another round of comment would follow, and then each class would be covered by a final report called a monograph.

The monograph restricted the industry's freedom but also saved it money. When the monograph for a drug class was finished, companies could market a new product in that class without FDA approval, as long as it replicated the dosage and label information listed in the monograph. Anything outside the monograph—a new ingredient, size, recommended use, or warning—would require a New Drug Application, long and expensive laboratory tests, and endless bureaucratic delay.

Much industry attention focused on the monograph's system of categorizing drugs and drug labeling. Safe and effective ingredients and uses were put into Category I. Ingredients and uses not generally recognized as safe and effective were relegated to Category II, and banned forthwith. Drugs on which the state of scientific knowledge was uncertain were supposed to be left for later in Category III, but a lawsuit by a public interest organization made this impossible, and Category III was effectively outlawed. Although a brand might conceivably extricate itself from Category II, it would take much effort, and the product would inevitably reenter the market in a fog of suspicion. Category II thus meant commercial oblivion, and firms did everything in their power to avoid it.

The FDA predicted that the first draft monograph—on antacids—would be ready by May 1972, and that all twenty-six would be ready in draft form by the end of 1974. It was wrong. The Advisory Review Panel on OTC Internal Analgesic, Antipyretic, and Antirheumatic Products, as the board of experts that looked at aspirin and acetaminophen was called, did not even publish its first request for data and information until well after the project was supposed to be launched. In response to its request, the panel was promptly inundated by the volumes of clinical studies the analgesic companies had prepared for their battles with the Federal Trade Commission. The panel waded through these, and was treated to more, and then still more. Before the OTC review was over, analgesic firms would inundate FDA headquarters with comments, complaints, threats, inquiries, memoranda, legal briefs, meeting transcripts, summaries of phone conversations, and, above all, poorly photocopied journal articles in the thousands—an Alexandrian library of analgesic lore that all sides admit cannot possibly be comprehended, and that staffers jokingly call the Hall of Aspirin.

During the hearings, the analgesic companies learned that the Advisory Review Panel was no pushover. Composed of eminent specialists from across the nation, it was exactly the sort of august medical body that had savaged over-the-counter drug advertising since the days when the American Medical Association published a catalogue of patent medicines entitled *Nostrums & Quackery*. In addition, the panel's meetings began just after the widely publicized filing of the analgesic complaints by the Federal Trade Commission. The doctors in the FDA could hardly allow themselves to appear less stringent than the lawyers in the FTC.

Bufferin's troubles were typical. Since its introduction in 1949, Bufferin ads had claimed in every conceivable medium that it was "twice as fast as aspirin." The panel put questions to Bristol-Myers the company had apparently never thought of in all that time. If Bufferin puts aspirin into the bloodstream faster, the panel asked, shouldn't Bufferin also *leave* the bloodstream faster, leading to a shorter period of relief? Wasn't a faster drug inevitably more transient in its effects? Bristol-Myers pointed to studies that found no difference in analgesic duration between Bufferin and aspirin. But those studies also failed to find any difference in the onset of relief, Bufferin's major claim to superiority. Bristol-Myers was left to splutter that the experiments were reliable for measuring the duration of relief but not its onset, an opinion not shared by the panel.

American Home faced even harder grilling. In 1962 a flurry of reports about the dangers of acetophenetidin caused the firm to drop that ingredient from the Anacin recipe, leaving only aspirin and caffeine. The panel asked American Home to justify its current formula. Why had it chosen that particular dosage and combination, and not some other? In addition, why did Anacin contain caffeine, a mildly addictive substance with no proven ability to enhance the effects of aspirin? Anacin medical director Arthur Grollman admitted that the inclusion of caffeine was based on his personal "impression" that "there is a portion of the population who gets more relief" from an aspirin-caffeine mixture. The exact dose, 60 mg, was because . . . because . . . well, Grollman said vaguely, any more might act as a stimulant. In other words, the dose had been picked because it would have no discernible effect? That was not exactly the point, Grollman allowed. He hadn't really come prepared for this line of questioning anyway. Of one thing he was certain: No scientific studies whatsoever had been performed.

Because American Home emphasized the use of Anacin for "hours of gentle relief from . . . arthritis and rheumatism," it was subject to review both by the OTC Analgesic Review Panel and the Arthritis Advisory Committee, a standing committee that scrutinized ethical drugs for the other, prescription half of the drug review. (The official description of these two bodies—Advisory Panel and Advisory Committee—differs for reasons known only to the federal bureaucracy.) Both boards doubted the wisdom of letting Anacin call itself an arthritis treatment. The problem, as they saw it, was that the recommended maximum daily OTC dose for aspirin—650 mg, four times per day—was not enough to palliate arthritis and rheumatism. Aspirin was the drug of choice for those ailments, to be sure, but in such high doses that doctors wanted to supervise its use. If arthritis was mentioned on the label, it might lead people to take dangerous amounts of aspirin.

American Home argued that dropping a reference to arthritis on the label would damage aspirin's image, because it would appear that the FDA had decided that the drug was ineffective at any level for this use. The Arthritis Advisory Committee members said they were concerned about people's safety—it was not their job to worry about whether Anacin's image remained polished enough to let American Home keep sending its shareholders fat dividend checks. But the question was more than image, American Home responded. Aspirin *is* good for arthritis, and Anacin should be allowed to say it.

The fight over the label came to a head at a memorable Arthritis Advisory Committee meeting in 1975. A rheumatologist from Cleveland, Irving Kushner, testified before the committee with remarks that bore special relevance to American Home. "What concerns me about this problem," he said, "is a philosophic issue. That is the question of how much ought people to be allowed to know, and with how much knowledge can you really trust them? Are people too dumb to be permitted to make some sort of decisions about their health and the kinds of things that they take, or do you have to put up every conceivable safeguard so that nothing could possibly go wrong?

"Obviously, this is not a problem limited to aspirin. . . . It becomes a question of your concept of democracy, based on how dumb people really are and how much you can trust them. . . . I think in general most people would agree that there is no question about the efficacy of aspirin for arthritic types of complaints. I think most people will agree that the frequency of significant toxicity is relatively minimal. It is not a question, therefore, of how good it is or how bad it is, but, really, should people be allowed to know about it?''

On July 8, 1977, the Arthritis Advisory Committee's sister board, the OTC Analgesic Review Panel, provided an answer: No. In a 164-page report, the first step toward the final monograph, the analgesic panel recommended that all references to arthritis and rheumatism be relegated to Category II, making them taboo for over-the-counter drugs. That wasn't all. The panel wanted to increase the number of safety warnings. Aspirin users would be told not to take the drug if they had asthma, ulcers, stomach distress, or ringing in the ears, if they were pregnant or allergic to aspirin, or if they were taking medications for diabetes, gout, arthritis, or coagulatory problems. Moreover, the panel urged the establishment of ingredient standards stringent enough to put Excedrin into Category II and dose standards low enough to put all extra-strength products, such as Extra-Strength Tylenol, into Category II with it; refused to accept caffeine as an active ingredient, thus placing Anacin's formula into Category II; balked at putting aspirin into a treatment for stomach upset, thus dumping Alka-Seltzer into Category II; and said that Bufferin's stomach-upset claim was "unproven, and unlikely"—and hence fit for Category II. If it were to be given its way, the panel would have made illegal every past advertising claim and every form of labeling for Extra-Strength Tylenol, Alka-Seltzer, Bufferin, Cope, Excedrin, Vanquish, and Anacin, both regular- and extra-strength. They would be stripped.

The analgesic makers were horrified—except Sterling. Sterling alone sold pure aspirin. Bayer, like the other brands, would be stung by the added aspirin warnings. Unlike the other brands, however, Bayer was unaffected by the rest of the strictures. For the first time in years, its mundane theme ("Pure aspirin, not part aspirin") had found a sympathetic hearing. Now it could stand back, calmly twiddling its thumbs, and watch the ruin of the advertising identities its competitors had spent decades building. But that was not all. To Sterling's gloating satisfaction, the analgesic panel also took on Tylenol.

At the last pre-report panel meeting, Sterling's representatives suddenly grasped the cardinal business rule that freedom from regulation for oneself is good, but binding regulation for one's neighbor is better. Why should Bayer aspirin spend money to advertise that it is just as good as Tylenol when it could get Uncle Sam to force Tylenol to admit that it is no better than Bayer? Better yet, the admission would not come from a short-lived TV commercial featuring a huckster in a white coat, but from a federal rule that would last forever and be promulgated by a panel of incorruptible academics. Sterling had fought government encroachment in the form of the FTC for more than a decade; now it decided to embrace it in the form of the FDA. In the fall of 1976, as Tylenol was rising to primacy in the market, Sterling decided to assist the overworked drug agency. The company's representatives helpfully submitted evidence to the panel that acetaminophen had little anti-inflammatory power, which meant that it should not be treated as equivalent to aspirin. That in turn meant that "You can't buy a more potent pain reliever without a prescription" should be viewed as Category II.

"Think of the situation," said John Baruch. "The very company that destroyed the aspirin market in the U.K. [with Panadol] ruled the roost in the U.S. They turned down the chance to market acetaminophen here. Then, when Tylenol comes up, what do they do—they savage it! They say it practically shouldn't be sold!"

The panel's reaction was everything that Sterling hoped. It was not just that the panel reported that acetaminophen was "considered to be equivalent to aspirin in its analgesic effects," though that was doubtless pleasing. Buried deep within the pages of fine print in the *Federal Register* was something else—a warning to be inserted into the label of all acetaminophen products.

Do not exceed recommended dosage because severe liver damage may occur.

The early accounts of acetaminophen's freedom from side effects were over-optimistic. As the use of the drug grew, reports of liver damage were heard with increasing frequency. The OTC Analgesic Review Panel turned up almost forty studies on the subject and speculated that, like acetanilid, acet-aminophen breaks down in the body to create a compound that is toxic to the liver and kidneys. The damage may possibly be worsened by heavy drinking. Most worrisome, the damage occurs without overt symptoms, meaning that overdosers may not notice the harm until it is too late. (Aspirin overdose, in contrast, is accompanied by nausea, vomiting, and ringing in the ears, which are unpleasant but give the victim plenty of warning.)

Initially, Johnson & Johnson put a brave face on the matter. On July 7, 1977, the day before the panel released its report, the company held a press conference to say that it agreed with the new recommendations, and that it would voluntarily place a liver-damage warning on each and every box of Tylenol.

(Meanwhile, Gil Weil of Bristol-Myers attacked the panel for its inadequate footnotes and asked for an extension of the time allowed to comment. In December, he wrote a long, closely reasoned attack on the FDA drug review, which he believed had overstepped its bounds. The panel said that firms should not be allowed to advertise cures for fanciful conditions like "tennis elbow pain," because consumers might be misled. In Weil's view, this was just a "classically elitist justification for censorship," and contrary to free speech.)

For its part, Sterling geared up to capitalize on the analgesic report in its Bayer ads. The first one on the air asserted that the FDA panel had found no evidence for the claim that acetaminophen was safer than aspirin. (In truth, the report did not directly compare the two drugs in this way.) The FDA, like the FTC before it, did not appreciate Sterling's use of its research. In a letter to company chairman Wescoe that December, FDA commissioner Donald Kennedy threatened that if the advertising continued, "we will find it necessary to set the public record straight ourselves." Amazingly, Kennedy also wrote FTC chairman Michael Pertschuk to request that he open an investigation of analgesic commercials.

Sterling deleted the reference to the panel report in its ads. But it did not stop going after Tylenol. On December 2, 1977, Sterling sent seven volumes of scientific studies to the FDA, which was turning the panel's recommendations into a legally binding monograph. Much of the submission was devoted to negative scientific data about acetaminophen, a product it did not sell in the United States. Included was Sterling's notion of a more appropriate acetaminophen warning, printed in properly alarming capital letters.

DO NOT TAKE THIS PRODUCT IF YOU ARE ALLERGIC TO ACETAMINOPHEN. IF YOU HAVE ASTHMA OR ARE SENSITIVE OR ALLERGIC TO ASPIRIN, CONSULT YOUR PHYSICIAN BEFORE USING THIS PRODUCT. DO NOT EXCEED RECOMMENDED DOSAGE OR TAKE FOR MORE THAN 10 DAYS, BECAUSE SEVERE LIVER DAMAGE MAY OCCUR. IF YOU HAVE EVER HAD LIVER DISEASE, CONSULT A PHYSICIAN BEFORE TAKING THIS PRODUCT. IF YOU ARE TAKING ANY PRESCRIPTION MEDICATIONS, CONSULT YOUR PHYSICIAN BEFORE TAKING THIS MEDICATION.

Three days later, Johnson & Johnson's response arrived at the FDA. Tylenol was not, after all, going to cooperate. The promised warning labels would not appear. Hunkering down for a fight, the company charged that the liver damage notice was unfair because it described a "specific consequence" of overdose—damage to the liver—whereas the aspirin warnings didn't mention any individual organs. Johnson & Johnson, too, had thoughtfully prepared its own list of suggested warnings—for aspirin.

DO NOT EXCEED RECOMMENDED DOSAGE BECAUSE SERIOUS, POTENTIALLY LIFE THREATENING BODY CHEMISTRY CHANGES, RESPIRATORY FAILURE, COMA, CONVULSION, AND CARDIOVASCULAR COLLAPSE MAY OCCUR.

DO NOT TAKE THIS PRODUCT DURING THE THIRD TRIMESTER OF PREGNANCY SINCE PROLONGATION OF LABOR, INCREASED BLEEDING AT THE TIME OF DELIVERY, AND STILLBIRTH MAY OCCUR.

THIS PRODUCT CONTAINS ASPIRIN. DO NOT TAKE THIS PRODUCT IF YOU
HAVE A HISTORY OF BRONCHIAL ASTHMA, NASAL POLYPS, OR ALLERGIC
RHINITIS SINCE POTENTIALLY LIFE THREATENING REACTIONS INCLUD-
ING CARDIOVASCULAR COLLAPSE AND RESPIRATORY FAILURE MAY OC-
CUR.

CAUTION: DO NOT TAKE THIS PRODUCT IF YOU HAVE STOMACH DISTRESS,
ULCERS OR BLEEDING PROBLEMS, AS MASSIVE, POTENTIALLY FATAL GAS-
TROINTESTINAL HEMORRHAGE MAY OCCUR.

If a liver warning had to be inserted on Tylenol, Johnson & Johnson had
some suggestions.

DO NOT EXCEED RECOMMENDED DOSAGE. INGESTION OF MORE THAN 40
[REGULAR STRENGTH PILLS] OR 24 [EXTRA STRENGTH PILLS] TAKEN AS
A SINGLE DOSE MAY RESULT IN LIVER DAMAGE.

Richard Moriarty, director of the National Poison Control Network, was
enraged by the company's behavior. In a January letter to the FDA, he blasted
Johnson & Johnson's refusal to admit that acetaminophen could have dangerous side effects. As to the plaint that the "specific consequence" warning
was unfair, Moriarty said, "Would the acetaminophen industry be happier
with a 'non-specific consequence' label such as 'Do not exceed recommended
dosage because this drug may severely damage some organ in your body but
we can't tell you which one' . . . ?" Worst, he said, was Johnson & Johnson's
version of the liver warning. Telling would-be suicides not to take more than
forty tablets was "akin to providing a person who has just purchased a gun
with which to commit suicide with a detailed diagram indicating the best spots
on the body to place the muzzle." Johnson & Johnson was providing a
target—take more than forty, and you'll be sure to die.

Johnson & Johnson didn't care. On February 6, 1978, it mailed another
volume of studies to the FDA. A point-by-point rebuttal of Sterling's submission, the report frequently had recourse to what it asserted was a most
authoritative source on acetaminophen: a Sterling (U.K.) handout that lavishly extolled the safety and superior benefits of Panadol-brand acetaminophen. Mailed to British doctors and pharmacists, the brochure claimed that
Panadol "does not normally cause [liver disease] when used in normal therapeutic doses." Indeed, it said, "the literature only contains one possible
case of [liver disease] following normal therapeutic use and this probably
represent[s] an idiosyncratic reaction." Which, Johnson & Johnson commented, was pretty much in line with what it had been saying about Tylenol.

The FDA did not have time to be amused. Its doorstep was covered almost
daily by new studies, new memos, new comments. The other firms had

discovered Sterling's gambit. In the past, each had churned out impartial scientific evidence to defend the virtues of its own product. Now the science machine was in high gear, and the companies' labs produced another product, studies attacking their rivals. The overworked agency found itself caught in a crossfire of data as the analgesic companies attempted to regulate each other through the FDA. The Hall of Aspirin grew—and grew. And grew. Its computer-printed catalogue, each entry a single line ("86-11-06 C Bio Prods Inc [Reichertz, P] 18 Vols"), swelled to more than forty pages. Ten years passed. Meanwhile the analgesic firms discovered another battleground.

In late 1976 Wayne Nelson saw an Anacin commercial and became unsurpassingly annoyed.

SQUARE-JAWED SPOKESMAN: Your body knows the difference between these pain relievers [brandishes bottles of Datril, Tylenol, and Extra-Strength Tylenol] and Adult Strength Anacin [brandishes Anacin]. For pain other than headache, Anacin reduces the inflammation that often comes with pain. These [acetaminophen products] do not. . . . Anacin reduces that inflammation as Anacin relieves pain fast. These do not. Take Adult Strength Anacin.

The ordinary listener might have been struck by the near-incomprehensible syntax; one can read the sentence "For pain other than headache, Anacin reduces the inflammation that often comes with pain" several times without causing it to discharge its informational content. But Wayne Nelson's attention, and subsequently that of the federal judiciary, was drawn less to the syntax of the advertisement than to its grammar. "Anacin reduces that inflammation as Anacin relieves pain fast," said the American Home spokesman. "These [the acetaminophen products] do not." Do not *what*? To Nelson, it sounded as if American Home was saying that Tylenol did not relieve pain fast. And that, Nelson said later, "was just plain false, and they knew it." American Home Products, in Nelson's considered opinion, would "say or do anything to get an extra buck."

As before, Nelson protested to newspapers, the networks, and the National Advertising Division of the Council of Better Business Bureaus. ABC forced American Home to change the ad to "Anacin relieves both pain and inflammation fast. These do nothing for inflammation." But NBC and CBS let the commercial stand. Nelson kept up the drumbeat of complaint—loudly, constantly, publicly. On March 21, 1977, American Home made a big mistake. It sued Johnson & Johnson, seeking a court order to make Nelson shut up.

American Home was in its seventeenth year of rule by William Laporte. The company's strong record of profits had given him near-absolute control, and over time he molded American Home in his grasping, secretive, tight-fisted image. It relentlessly acquired subsidiaries, which Laporte kept independent of one another. Anacin, for instance, was made and marketed by Whitehall Laboratories, with almost no input from any other branch of American Home. Laporte kept control, it was widely reported, by personally authorizing all checks of more than five hundred dollars. Because Laporte refused to pay headhunters, moving expenses, or competitive salaries, the firm's hiring pool long consisted of those people in New York City who were willing to work in tyrannical conditions for substandard wages. "Unsurprisingly, the offices were full of Caspar Milquetoasts," said Jack Shapiro, a former marketing director for one American Home subsidiary. "Morale was terrible, and they were always telling you that you couldn't *do* something or other." Laporte, Shapiro said, did not believe in long-range planning. "He only cared about squeezing out every nickel for the next quarterly statement—the antithesis of what we now think is good management. As a result, when any problem came down the pike, it was completely unexpected, and the company reacted by massively flailing around until it hit on a response that worked."

Flailing around was exactly what American Home had done in its response to the rise of Tylenol. Like Sterling, it brought out its own acetaminophen pill. At first the brand was called Trilium, but later the name was changed to Extranol. Johnson & Johnson thought the similarity between Tylenol and Extranol a bit more than coincidence—"The packages were virtually identical," Wayne Nelson said later, "it was really a cheap trick"—and sued for trademark infringement on March 15, 1976. The court slapped a temporary restraining order on American Home, and Extranol was dead. American Home persisted. It changed the name to Extramed. That didn't fly. So the firm turned to one of its most valuable trademarks, Anacin, for help. Unlike Bayer, Anacin was not closely associated with aspirin. Indeed, Whitehall Laboratories had spent years trying to foster the opposite impression. Why not use the Anacin name on a new brand of acetaminophen? Even better, why not add that "special Anacin ingredient," caffeine? It would be as if this new Anacin were not a different drug, but simply another version of an old favorite. Whitehall settled on the mysterious monicker of Anacin-3. ("Nobody had a clue what had happened to Anacin-2," Shapiro said.) Despite a blitz of familiar American Home–style advertising, Anacin-3 was not a success, although it stayed on the market.

Giving up on acetaminophen, American Home turned back to regular Anacin. In December it started advertising "Your Body Knows the Difference" between Tylenol and Anacin, the commercial that so exercised Wayne Nelson. When Nelson's carping got on its nerves, American Home sued to have the court affirm "its right to broadcast the commercial free of interference from defendants" McNeil and Johnson & Johnson. Nelson reacted with his usual vigor. Three weeks after American Home filed its papers, Johnson & Johnson countersued under Section 43(a) of the Lanham Trademark Act of 1946.

Chiefly written by Edward S. Rogers, the intellectual-property expert then standing in as chairman of Sterling Products, the long and complicated Lanham Act governs the acquisition, use, and loss of trademarks in the United States. Deep within the act is Section 43(a):

> Any person who shall . . . use in connection with any goods or services . . . any false description or representation, including words or other symbols tending falsely to describe or represent the same . . . shall be liable to a civil action . . . by any person who believes that he is or is likely to be damaged by the use of any such false description or representation.

Section 43(a) had hardly been noticed in the three decades since Rogers penned its words. Johnson & Johnson's countersuit would change that. Indeed, it would create a new legal subspecialty, Lanham act advertising litigation.

Johnson & Johnson's countersuit charged that "Your Body Knows" constituted a "false representation or description" of Anacin "calculated to deceive the purchasing public into believing that Anacin is a superior analgesic to Tylenol." Johnson & Johnson did not accuse American Home of outright lies, although it characterized the commercial as a "prime example of adapting nineteenth-century patent medicine show tactics to modern day mass media marketing." Much like the FTC, Johnson & Johnson argued that no matter what the literal truth of the Anacin ad, it produced deceptions in viewers' minds, and thus was false.

The stakes were high. Not the least reason for Nelson's ire was that "Your Body Knows" was effective. While the campaign ran, Tylenol's share of the analgesic market dropped from 17 percent to 15.6 percent. With total analgesic sales running at perhaps $750 million a year, that small decline translated into more than $10 million in lost sales. And American Home had no intention of stopping. That summer it planned to spend an additional $5 million on "Your Body Knows"—almost half its promotional budget for Anacin, and enough, Tylenol's ad agency calculated, to expose the average American household to its message about once every two days.

Issues in many legal squabbles become bogged down in semantics. In the Anacin/Tylenol trial, the issue *was* semantics. What, precisely, did the advertisement *mean*? Considering that its language had been crafted at considerable expense by professional communicators, its specific message was oddly difficult to establish. "Anacin reduces that inflammation as Anacin relieves pain fast. These do not." What did that mean? Was the implication, as Johnson & Johnson believed, that Anacin relieves pain fast and the others do not? And that therefore American Home was professing that Anacin was faster and better than Tylenol for pain relief? Or was it, as American Home said, that Anacin eases arthritic inflammation and the others do not? And that therefore the commercial said nothing about faster relief of pain but only about the existence of relief from inflammation? If so, did it matter, given that the OTC Analgesic Review Panel had concluded in the very month the countersuit was filed that aspirin in the small over-the-counter doses contained in Anacin was ineffective against inflammation?

Circuit Court Judge Charles Stewart, Jr., of the Southern District of New York, refused to answer these questions himself. The year before, in another Lanham act suit, a different federal judge had concluded that his own interpretation of a commercial was irrelevant. "The question in such cases is," that judge wrote, "what does the person to whom the advertisement is addressed find to be the message?" The person to whom the advertisement is addressed is, of course, the consumer. Stewart asked the companies to learn what the average American thought of the commercials. The FTC had tried a similar approach when it subpoenaed people in Washington, D.C., and dragged them into court to interpret Bayer commercials. Stewart employed another method, and found himself plunged into the ramose, confusing thicket of consumer-survey statistical analysis.

American Home hired ASI Market Research of New York City to evaluate the meaning of "Your Body Knows." ASI paid people in an upstate New York shopping mall to sit in a special theater and watch a jumble of television shows and advertisements. One of the commercials was "Your Body Knows." During and after the screening, the company asked spectators what they remembered of the programs and commercials, and what implications they had drawn from them.*

The results provided an unwitting case study of the paradox of advertising. Although known to be an essential ingredient of commercial success, advertisements such as "Your Body Knows" pass through people's minds almost unnoticed. After the session was finished, a full fifth of the participants could not remember "Your Body Knows" in a single particular, despite having watched it in a darkened theater minutes before. Not quite two-thirds both recalled the commercial and thought it was trying to sell them something (ASI did not record what the other people thought it was trying to do). Of the people who recalled the spot and realized it was trying to sell them some-

---

* A few additional participants were asked to sit in chairs with a special dial on the armrest. As they watched the program, these people turned the dial left or right, depending on whether they were bored or interested at that moment. In this way, ASI tried to track their attention from moment to moment. Charts and graphs were prepared. A commercial of "average" interest was assigned a score of 500, with higher and lower scores indicating, respectively, ads of lesser or greater interest. Midway through, the Anacin commercial had a score of 420.

thing, about one-half mentioned "symptom relief," an answer they might have guessed from the mere knowledge that they were dealing with an analgesic commercial. Almost a third mentioned "competitive superiority," another reasonable hypothesis. Only 1 percent recalled any claim of "faster relief"—the stated point of the ad, and the lawsuits that sprang from it. In other circumstances, American Home might have regarded these results as sobering. Here ASI's figures were presented to the court as evidence that consumers had not drawn an incorrect message of analgesic superiority from its promotion, because they had not actually drawn any message at all.

Johnson & Johnson used a different research firm, Gallup & Rubenstein, which conducted its survey by telephone. The day after a "Your Body Knows" spot appeared on television, the firm asked a representative selection of households if anyone had viewed it. In contrast to the ASI survey, almost half the people who saw the commercial reported that it left them with the impression that Anacin was "fast acting," and a full 39 percent felt that the commercial included the message that Anacin was better or best.

Which survey was right? Like impartial scientific research, Stewart learned, impartial consumer surveys were capable of freely generating contradictory results. In both surveys, however, the survey respondents seemed to be reporting what they thought commercials *should* say, rather than what they actually *did* say. Television commercials worked their magic, the judge suggested, "by triggering the viewer's past association with the product as well as hooking the viewer's interest in the particular new advertising copy being aired." In other words, Anacin's present commercials mainly brought to mind memories of what it had claimed in the past, when it had made many superiority claims. Did that mean that the present spot was liable for the sins of past advertisements?

In August 1977, the judge rendered his decision. The law, he concluded, could treat only the advertisement in question, not commercials from the past. Therefore, Stewart's task was to determine what impressions a single ad would foster if viewed by people who had never seen an Anacin commercial before—circumstances that he admitted were unrealistic. This conclusion gave pre-eminence to the ASI survey, which tested viewers' reactions to "Your Body Knows" more directly, although it provided a less accurate picture of the actual impact of the ad, which was, one presumes, the issue of the suit. *Pace* ASI, Stewart ruled that "Your Body Knows" did not implicitly claim that Anacin relieved pain faster than Tylenol.

American Home drew little comfort, for the rest of the decision slammed the company. Even though the spot did not claim that Anacin was faster, Stewart ruled, it did suggest that Anacin was *better*.

"You should've seen the American Home guys after that," one Johnson & Johnson lawyer chuckled years later. "It was this big shock—'My God, how could he *say* that? How could anyone have got the idea that we would put on an advertisement to get people to think that Anacin was better than the competition?' ''

Having settled the implicit meaning of the ad, Stewart turned in his decision to the next question: Was this claim true? That is, is Anacin truly a better pain reliever than Tylenol? Here, again, were two issues: pain in general and the pain of inflammation. Virtually conceding that aspirin and acetaminophen were equivalent for pain in general, American Home staked its defense on aspirin's edge in reducing inflammation. Testimony delved into a host of medical issues, including the mysteries of cellular biochemistry, the standards of clinical trials, and the equivalence of tendonitis and "tennis elbow." As in the FTC and FDA proceedings, eminent scientists trooped through the courtroom. Again, they disagreed on nearly every issue, except that the evidence was clear. Acetaminophen had less impact on arthritis than aspirin, but did that mean it had *no* value as a treatment for inflammation? Even if it showed a smaller effect in the laboratory, what if real people took it and felt satisfied? "These lawyers are very smart," said witness Gerald Weissmann, a prominent rheumatologist at New York University Medical Center. "They had learned the science, and grilled us in a way that most scientists aren't used to. And I suspect many of the witnesses did what most people do when confronted by a very clever person who is determined to confuse them—they got confused, and contradicted themselves."

Faced with a jumble of conflicting testimony, Stewart declared the inflammation issue to be a toss-up: American Home failed to prove Anacin was better for inflammation, but Johnson & Johnson failed to prove it wasn't. The outcome was decided by the second issue: Was Anacin a generally superior analgesic for pain other than inflammation? Here Johnson & Johnson easily prevailed, because American Home had more or less admitted their equivalence. As a result, Stewart directed American Home to stop advertising, now and in the future, that "Anacin is a superior analgesic generally or a superior analgesic for conditions that are associated with inflammation or inflammatory conditions."

This was a shock. Aspirin's one clear advantage over acetaminophen—its action against inflammation—had been lost as an advertising theme. Johnson & Johnson hailed its victory. If it wanted, Johnson & Johnson could use Stewart's decision against other aspirin firms if they continued their attempt to press ASA's edge over Tylenol in reducing inflammation. American Home appealed, and lost in the Second Circuit Court of Appeals.

American Home Products v. *Johnson & Johnson* was a landmark case in Lanham act law. When the appellate court upheld Judge Stewart's decision, it established the precedent that Section 43(a) had jurisdiction over more than literal falsehoods and covered implied claims. The litigation floodgates were opened. Now the analgesic companies themselves could go directly after one

another for the faintest whiff of a false or misleading claim. No longer
limited to the literal interpretation of an advertisement, a firm could delve
into the psyche of the consumer, pull out an assortment of representations,
and sue under the Lanham Act for the one most at odds with the evidence.
American Home had no one to blame but itself—it had gone to court first.

Worse, it was back in litigation with Johnson & Johnson. Four months
after Stewart's opinion, Anacin put out new Anacin commercials. Like
"Your Body Knows," they emphasized aspirin's ability to reduce inflammation. This time, however, they carefully eschewed any comparison to
Tylenol or other drugs. Johnson & Johnson nonetheless objected, suing over
a commercial that did not even hint at Tylenol's name. The rationale was
convoluted. According to Judge Stewart, such ads inevitably created associations with Anacin's past campaigns, including "Your Body Knows."
Because Stewart had declared that campaign was illegal, Johnson & Johnson
said, American Home could not make *any* inflammation claim.

Johnson & Johnson hoped it was arguing the case before a sympathetic ear:
Judge Stewart. Anacin II, as the second case was called, dragged on until
July 1979, when Stewart refused to dismiss either the original charges against
American Home or the countercharges American Home had leveled against
Johnson & Johnson. Faced with a second long trial, the two companies
settled out of court. It was the last time they would come to such an amicable
agreement.

All in all, these were dark days for Anacin. Between January and September
1978, American Home was sued by Johnson & Johnson for the second time,
lost its appeal of Stewart's decision in the first Anacin trial, and was told by
the FTC to expend $24 million informing television viewers that Anacin was
made out of aspirin. After flirting with deep-sixing the Anacin trademark
altogether, American Home instead decided to make one final assault on
Tylenol. It created a bigger version of Anacin, Maximum Strength Anacin,
with 500 mg of aspirin per tablet. (A standard dose is 325 mg.) "The idea,"
said the Johnson & Johnson lawyer, "was to create a whole new category—
maximum strength—that would be beyond everything else. The whole
strength business was a little silly, considering that two tablets of regular old
Bayer have more aspirin than one of Maximum Strength Anacin. But that
was what they came up with."

New Maximum Strength Anacin is here, in the pain reliever doctors
recommend most.
Maximum Strength goes beyond regular strength.
Beyond extra strength to Maximum Strength.

Aspirin makers eagerly introduced the peoples of Asia, Africa, and Latin America to the wonders of modern marketing. Taking advantage of cheap currencies, the firms inundated the most remote hamlets with placards, handbills, posters, recordings, radio jingles, and, especially, "sound trucks"—vans with makeshift stages on which aspirin peddlers performed the twentieth century equivalent of a Wild West medicine show. One of the most vigorous promoters was the Australian brand Aspro, shown above with a sound truck at a Pakistani village in the early 1960s. Sterling's Mejoral was even more energetic, especially in Latin America. Below, its Brazilian sales staff poses for a group portrait, holding the Brazilian equivalent known as Melhoral. *(Above, Nicholas Kiwi, Ltd.; below, Joan Corcoran)*

¡tres puntos en que debe apoyarse Ud. siempre para estar seguro!

CAFIASPIRINA

1° Que no existe sino una **CAFIASPIRINA** y que ella es el remedio por excelencia para los dolores y las consecuencias de los abusos alcohólicos. las trasnochadas y el excesivo trabajo mental. porque proporciona alivio inmediato, levanta las fuerzas y **NO AFECTA EL CORAZON**

2° Que para defenderlo a usted contra el peligro de un substituto. la cajita en que va el tubo lleva la Estampilla fiscal amarilla, con la famosa **CRUZ BAYER**, que es el mas respetable signo de pureza y legitimidad.

3° Que para evitar equivocaciones. deterioro y desaseo, las tabletas de **CAFIASPIRINA nunca se venden sueltas.** Por tanto, cuando sólo quiera comprar una dosis. debe pedir el limpio, cómodo e higiénico **SOBRE ROJO BAYER.**

Si quieren darle cualquier mixtura de cafeína, en vez de la irreemplazable **CAFIASPIRINA**, o si le ofrecen tabletas sueltas. niéguese rotundamente a recibirlas. e insista en el producto legitimo, que es el único digno de confianza.

Mejoral's nemesis was Cafiaspirina, an aspirin-caffeine blend aggressively pushed by German Bayer. Millions of handbills, like this one from 1925, thundered out the warning: "If someone wants to give you some other caffeine mixture instead of the irreplaceable CAFIASPIRINA, or if he offers loose tablets, flatly refuse to take them, and insist on the legitimate product, which is the only one worth trusting." *(Half Brick Images)*

Taking advantage of an upsurge of nationalism in Egypt in the 1930s, Aspro proclaimed itself on the side of the rising masses. Its advertising tried to foster the impression that the hallmark of the truly progressive citizen of Cairo was the dedicated consumption of medical miracles like Aspro. *(Nicholas Kiwi, Ltd.)*

in fast-acting Anacin.

Anacin gives you the pain reliever doctors recommend the most. In fact, tablet for tablet, Anacin gives you *more* of this pain reliever than you can get in an aspirin, buffered aspirin or the 'so-called' extra-strength tablet. No pain reliever you can buy has the special combina-

Minutes after taking Anacin, your headache pain is gone — also its tension and depression. You experience remarkable all-over relief. Remember, *only* Anacin has this special formulation to relieve nervous tension headaches. See if Anacin Tablets do not *work better* for you.

Because all aspirin products have identical effects, drug makers had to resort to ingenious methods to make their brand stand out from the crowd. Anacin, as shown in this 1964 magazine ad, went to great lengths to avoid mentioning that it, like its rivals, was made from plain old aspirin. Instead it was described as being made from "the greatest pain fighter ever discovered."

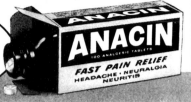

Contains what 2 out of 3 doctors call the GREATEST PAIN FIGHTER EVER DISCOVERED

Competition among aspirin makers reached a frenzied height in the 1950s, with the appearance of Bufferin, a blend of aspirin and two common antacids. The antacids do, in fact, speed aspirin more quickly into the blood, but the company has never been able to prove to the government's satisfaction that this has anything to do with speed of pain relief, or even that antacids protect people against the specific type of irritation associated with aspirin.

What kind of headaches do YOU have?

Your physician will tell you there are many different kinds

Tension—Do you pay the price of headaches as the result of the tensions of today's living? Then you should discover Bufferin, the modern, faster-acting headache remedy.

Over-indulgence frequently causes headaches. When this happens, it's the perfect time to take Bufferin because Bufferin acts *twice as fast* as aspirin to bring prompt relief.

Cold miseries are apt to hang on and often require prolonged treatment. That's why you need Bufferin, the modern antacid pain-reliever—and you can keep taking it as long as those painful cold miseries last without fear of upset stomach.

If you take aspirin for any of these ailments, remember

BUFFERIN ®

acts twice as fast as aspirin!

... and won't upset your stomach the way aspirin often does

1. Medical science knows that a pain reliever must go through the stomach and into the blood stream to relieve pain.

2. Bufferin combines aspirin with two antacid ingredients. These speed the pain reliever out of the stomach and into the blood stream twice as fast as aspirin. So . . .

3. Bufferin acts twice as fast to relieve pain. And it won't upset your stomach the way aspirin often does.

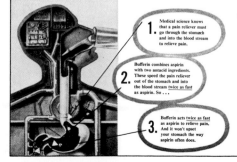

ANOTHER FINE PRODUCT OF BRISTOL-MYERS

IF YOU SUFFER FROM PAIN OF ARTHRITIS OR RHEUMATISM, ASK YOUR PHYSICIAN ABOUT BUFFERIN

Don't Pay Twice The Price Of Bayer Aspirin For ASPIRIN "IN DISGUISE"!

What is aspirin "in disguise"?...a pain relieving product that attempts to belittle straight aspirin yet combines aspirin with such non-pain relievers as aluminum compounds, magnesium carbonate, or baking soda—and it costs *you twice the price* of Bayer Aspirin!

Why pay more for extra ingredients that can't relieve pain? Instead, get Bayer Aspirin. It's *all* pain reliever—100%—and medical science has never discovered a safer and more effective pain relieving agent!

Sterling's Bayer, saddled with its plain-Jane identity, struck back at Bufferin and Anacin with this series of ads in 1957. But it was too late. The advertising strife had got out of hand, and the Federal Trade Commission was already beginning what would become some of the longest battles between industry and government in U.S. history.

For decades, aspirin was plagued by rumors that it somehow attacked the heart—a myth that Sterling denied (right) with the slogan "Does Not Affect the Heart." In the 1930s the government objected, and the company was forced to stop making this claim. So it was all the more surprising when, in the 1980s, Sterling advertised (opposite) that aspirin *does* affect the heart—and the government objected.

DEMAND BAYER ASPIRIN

Unless you see the "Bayer Cross" on package or on tablets you are not getting the genuine Bayer Aspirin proved safe by millions and prescribed by physicians over twenty-seven years for

Colds	Headache
Neuritis	Lumbago
Toothache	Rheumatism
Neuralgia	Pain, Pain

DOES NOT AFFECT THE HEART

Each unbroken "Bayer" package contains proven directions. Handy boxes of twelve tablets cost few cents. Druggists also sell bottles of 24 and 100.

Aspirin is the trade mark of Bayer Manufacture of Monoaceticacidester of Salicylicacid

Good News For Heart Health In America

. . . A message from the Makers of Bayer® Aspirin.

A major study sponsored by the National Institutes of Health showing that an aspirin taken every other day can help prevent first heart attacks was reported this week in the New England Journal of Medicine.

In 1985, as a result of research pioneered, compiled and submitted by the Bayer Company, the government approved the indication of one aspirin a day, under a doctor's supervision, for the prevention of second heart attacks and unstable angina.

We at the Bayer company were very proud of this important development and began communicating the news to the medical community and the American people.

Since then, we estimate that 30,000 to 50,000 lives have been saved and a quarter of a billion dollars cut from health care costs.

This newest study, although not yet reviewed by the FDA, is further evidence that aspirin therapy for cardiovascular disease greatly advances the progress of heart health in this country.

The Bayer Company will continue to make major commitments to finding innovative ways to better the heart health of America.

Ask your doctor about aspirin therapy to help prevent heart attacks.

The Bayer Company, Division of
Sterling Drug Inc.
Makers of Bayer Aspirin

BAYER. ® ASPIRIN
THE WONDER DRUG THAT WORKS WONDERS ™

The Aspirin Wars. In the late 1950s and early 1960s, rival aspirin makers deluged the airwaves with mutually contradictory commercials. Every brand was the fastest, the strongest, the most scientifically advanced.

Bufferin spots (top left) claimed the product was "twice as fast as aspirin"— startling, given that its active ingredient *was* aspirin.

Fighting back, Bayer (top right) asserted that it, not Bufferin, provided "fastest relief," though it too was nothing but aspirin.

TV ads for Excedrin (bottom left) said it was "50% stronger"—which meant only that each tablet had half again as much of the active ingredient, at considerably more than half again the price.

Anacin (bottom right) trumpeted its "combination of ingredients," two of which were "missing from aspirin." One of these two ingredients, acetophenetidin, was later banned by the FDA; the other was caffeine, which the agency has refused to agree adds potency to aspirin.

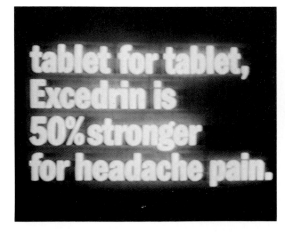

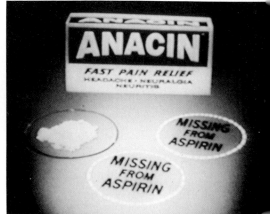

Battered by the rising sales of aspirin substitutes like acetaminophen (which is most widely known under the brand name Tylenol) and ibuprofen (such as Advil), aspirin makers hoped the increasing aura of medical respectability for their product would bring back sales. Secretary of Health and Human Services Margaret Heckler announced in 1985 that an aspirin a day helps prevent second heart attacks. *(Sterling Drug, Inc.)*

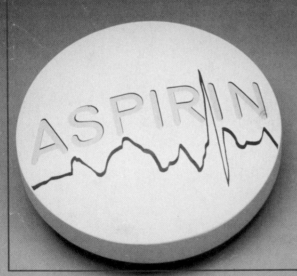

BUSH VS. RATHER
Running Against the Media

Newsweek

February 8, 1988 : $2.00

What You Should Know About

Heart Attacks

- **The Aspirin Breakthrough**
- **The Latest on Cholesterol, Diet and Exercise**

The excitement over the extraordinary new discoveries about aspirin rose in 1988, when the combination of aspirin and another old drug, streptokinase, was shown to increase survival from acute heart attacks by almost 50 percent. *(Newsweek)*

Get Maximum Strength Anacin.
Maximum Strength allowed without a prescription.

Silly or not, Johnson & Johnson didn't like the comparison to "extra strength," words that it had spent millions to associate with Tylenol. "When they said 'beyond extra strength,' what do you think they meant?" asked the Johnson & Johnson lawyer. "They meant Extra-Strength Tylenol, that's what they meant!" A consumer survey found that many Extra-Strength Tylenol users indeed got the message that Maximum Strength Anacin was a better pain reliever than Extra-Strength Tylenol—the impression Johnson & Johnson had already gone to court to fight. This time Johnson & Johnson didn't bother complaining to the networks. It went straight to Section 43(a) of the Lanham act. In August 1979, it launched Anacin III.

Despite having the opportunity to argue before a new judge, Morris E. Lasker, American Home had had a bellyful of the Lanham act. It changed "extra strength" to "added strength." Johnson & Johnson was unmoved. Nelson had got his back up, and the trial proceeded. In court, American Home claimed that it couldn't possibly have meant Extra-Strength Tylenol when it used the words "extra strength." Maximum Strength Anacin competed solely with other aspirin brands. For the fight with Tylenol, American Home had its own acetaminophen product, Anacin-3. To Johnson & Johnson, this reasoning was "the latest in a series of lame excuses," especially coming from a brand that had just lost a lengthy court battle over its right to take on Tylenol directly.

As before, the case hinged on the hermeneutics of advertising. Both companies presented consumer surveys, and both companies said that the rival's explication of those surveys was wrong. Johnson & Johnson claimed that American Home's own surveys backed its case, because respondents drew illicit messages of superiority from the commercials' very existence. ("I can't remember those Anacin commercials," a typical respondent admitted to American Home. "It probably said that it does better than any other pain reliever"—including Tylenol.) In reply, American Home accused Johnson & Johnson of misinterpreting its own studies. The results, American Home said, did not demonstrate that the Maximum Strength Anacin commercial was misleading, but that it was a "terribly poor" commercial—a remark with which the court fully agreed.

Handed down in July 1980, Judge Lasker's opinion went out of its way to scold American Home for deliberately blinding itself to the potential interpretations of its commercials. Adding insult to injury, the judge also noted that Maximum Strength Anacin was apparently branded improperly, because 500 mg per tablet was a bigger dose of ASA than that currently approved by the FDA. Maximum Strength Anacin, he said, was not the maximum strength allowed without a prescription. Maximum Strength Anacin was not allowed at all.*

Johnson & Johnson had triumphed again. Not content to rest on its laurels, the company introduced yet another marketing ploy: capsules. Easier to swallow and perceived as somehow stronger than the tablet version, Extra-Strength Tylenol capsules fueled the brand's continued growth. By the beginning of 1981, its share of the analgesic market stood at 30 percent—30 percent for mighty Tylenol!—and the aspirin companies were on the verge of throwing in the towel. Bufferin began an advertising campaign attacking Bayer, whose market share had sunk to less than 9 percent; other aspirin brands positioned themselves to fight their aspirin competitors, not Tylenol.

Tylenol's ascendancy was derailed, however, by a tragedy that would unfold in the following year. And shortly thereafter, Johnson & Johnson's nemesis, American Home, would be back, hoping to do unto acetaminophen what Johnson & Johnson had done unto aspirin: beat it with a new analgesic.

---

* One year later, Johnson & Johnson was back in court, this time against Bayer aspirin. "Nothing gives you more relief than Bayer," the Bayer ad said. "Nothing." It touted a new study to support this claim. Johnson & Johnson requested a look at the study. Sterling refused; Johnson & Johnson sued. In January 1983, as the two parties readied for trial, Sterling introduced a new product: Maximum Strength Bayer. As before, Sterling was conducting two mutually inconsistent advertising campaigns: Nothing is better than regular Bayer; Maximum Strength Bayer is better than regular-strength Bayer. Johnson & Johnson squawked. Sterling caved in, withdrawing the offending advertisements.

CHAPTER FOURTEEN

"SMALL NATIONS"

On September 30, 1982, the Cook County Medical Examiner's Office reported the deaths of three people from cyanide poisoning. In all cases the cyanide came from capsules of Tylenol. When the news hit Johnson & Johnson headquarters, the first reaction was disbelief—it must be a hoax. No one could imagine how cyanide had infiltrated the sophisticated Tylenol production system. But as reports, inquiries, and confirmations flooded in, the company's management realized that the unthinkable had happened. Three people had died horribly with Tylenol capsules in their stomachs.

James Burke had never confronted a greater crisis. Hired in 1953 as the product manager for Band-Aids, Burke had become chairman just as Tylenol began its domination of the analgesic market, and had watched Tylenol profits grow ever more important to Johnson & Johnson. The brand accounted for about 8 percent of the company's worldwide sales and more than 15 percent of its profits. Corporate profits had grown by one-sixth during Burke's turn at the helm—from Tylenol alone. (Johnson & Johnson in the 1980s was in the same situation as I.G. Farben in the 1930s: A tiny over-the-counter pill was absurdly important to the balance sheet of a vast and technologically sophisticated organization.) That fall Tylenol's share of the analgesic market was more than one-third, and market analysts saw no reason why it couldn't go up to one-half. Now Burke's greatest success seemed likely to become his greatest disaster.

Investigators proved quickly that the Tylenol had not been tampered with at McNeil's factory in Fort Washington. One of the victims had eaten capsules manufactured at McNeil's other plant in Texas, which suggested that the tampering occurred at the retail level, probably in the Chicago area. That didn't mean anyone could relax. Three people had died, and nobody knew how many more had poison in their medicine cabinets.

Burke pulled all Tylenol ads off the air. Then, after hours of frantic meetings with the FBI and FDA, he recalled all Extra-Strength Tylenol capsules, which accounted for 40 percent of the brand's sales. The FBI and FDA initially counseled against such a recall, because it would send the wrong message to terrorists. But after a copycat poisoning with strychnine occurred in California, the government agreed. The recall directly cost the company $50 million, but that was nothing compared with the indirect costs. Johnson & Johnson's stock price dropped through the month of October, and shareholders suffered a paper loss of $2 billion. Meanwhile, Tylenol's market share plummeted to 8 percent.

Pundits predicted that the Tylenol era was finished. Tylenol's name, they said, would be forever associated with the deaths. ''McNeil will definitely have to start all over,'' one drugstore buyer told *Business Week*. Johnson & Johnson would have to come up with a new brand name and millions of dollars to promote it. Then it would have to wait patiently while it worked its way back into consumers' hearts. Other analysts thought the Tylenol name might survive, but the company would be lucky to recoup more than half of its old market share.

The crisis did not let up. Four more people died. Meanwhile, competing acetaminophen brands jumped into the vacuum, among them Datril, which before the tragedy had a market share of perhaps one-hundredth of 1 percent. Sterling, on the other hand, remained above the fray, saying that to take advantage of the situation would be ''ghoulish.'' Sterling may have had another reason for hesitating. Panadol, its brand of acetaminophen, sold in seventy countries but still not the United States, generated about $100 million in annual sales, which compared favorably with Bayer aspirin's U.S. sales. According to one report, Sterling intended to introduce Panadol in spring 1983 with a major advertising campaign, and was not about to monkey with its carefully conceived plan.

American Home too announced its preference for the high road, sanctimoniously declaring to a *Wall Street Journal* writer that it would never try to profit from the tragedy. ''I read that report in the *Journal* on the eight o'clock train to work,'' recalled Jack Shapiro, the former American Home marketing executive. ''At nine o'clock, I was in a meeting where we were trying to figure out how to take advantage of [Tylenol's] problems to relaunch our own acetaminophen. People were walking around saying, 'Now's our chance to get those bastards!' ''*

Amazingly, Tylenol recovered. Of immense help was Johnson & Johnson's decision to remove the capsules from the market and individually examine each one—a move that cost the firm yet more millions. In addition,

---

* Ultimately American Home chose to attack the popular prescription-only mixtures of Tylenol and codeine by making its own mixture of codeine and acetaminophen. Tylenol Codeine came in four numbered strengths, of which the most popular was Tylenol Codeine 3. American Home's brand of acetaminophen was, one recalls, sold under the name of Anacin-3. The company's imitation of Tylenol Codeine 3 was called, absurdly, Anacin-3 Codeine 3. ''If you put in only one three,'' Shapiro said, ''it was misprescribed. I remember one poor Cuban-American doctor staring at our detail man in utter bafflement. 'Anacin-3 Codeine 3? *Qué? Qué?*' '' Anacin-3 Codeine 3 did not do well.

Burke kept the public informed, holding frequent news conferences that opened the curtain of secrecy that usually enveloped the company. Most important, perhaps, was his decision to offer 76 million $2.50 coupons for any Tylenol product, which made a bottle of thirty tablets just about free. Within a year of the poisonings, Tylenol's share of the analgesic market had bounced to 30 percent. Reports of its demise had been premature.

The tragedy that struck seven people in Chicago brought changes in the over-the-counter drug market—triple-sealed, tamper-proof packages—that will always be a reminder of the fear and distrust that the incident engendered. (The victims' lawsuits were not settled until May 1991.) It also serves a more banal purpose, as a lesson on the power of a name and on how people do not readily erase that piece of their brain latched onto by a familiar trademark or a trusted product.

For seven years, Tylenol had struck a responsive chord in consumers' minds. Hospitals trust Tylenol, you can't buy a more potent pain reliever, nothing is more effective than Tylenol—all these marketing themes hammered home the point that the competition could not be better than Tylenol. When, after a decent interval, Tylenol returned to the airwaves, it continued those themes, and people continued to believe them, and to buy Tylenol. As long as the analgesic playing field was level, and as long as Johnson & Johnson continued to promote the brand, Tylenol would maintain its edge. And then the playing field changed.

The change began in the front room of a small Victorian house on the outskirts of Nottingham, England, where a man named Stewart Adams spent many hours examining sunburned guinea pigs. The house contained the pharmacological research department of the Boots Company, an English retail drug chain. After the death of the firm's founder, Jesse Boots, in 1921, the U.S. drugstore magnate Louis K. Liggett bought the six hundred Boots Chemist's Shops. Liggett merged them into Drug, Inc., the short-lived over-the-counter drug combine assembled by A. H. Diebold. When Drug, Inc., fell apart, Boots returned to British ownership. Its new management set out in 1949 to find a drug with the analgesic powers of corticosteroids—drugs, such as cortisone, that are similar to the hormones produced by the adrenal glands—without their side effects, which include hypertension, ulcer, and diabetes. Adams was given the job. The sunburned guinea pigs were part of that effort.

After getting his doctorate at the University of Leeds in 1952, Adams became one of Boots's handful of medical researchers. The company put him on the steroid search. He faced a daunting task, because the technology for measuring a drug's analgesic ability was primitive. While exploring different ways to rate this effect, Adams stumbled across an obscure American dental journal that had an article connecting aspirin's analgesic capability to its effect on inflamed tissue. At the time, aspirin was used to reduce the pain that comes with inflammation, but it was not widely understood that it could actually reduce the inflammation as well. Adams became convinced that the reduction of inflammation was the central feature of aspirin. He was sure that if he found a drug with a strong anti-inflammatory capacity, it would, like aspirin, also have strong analgesic powers. And so he thought of himself as on a quest for another aspirin.

In 1955, chance favored Adams again. He stumbled across a German article about inducing a sunburn-like inflammation in guinea pigs by shaving their backs and exposing them to ultraviolet light. The degree of the burn could be measured objectively on a five-point scale. If Adams administered a drug to the guinea pig, he could assess whether the inflammation went down. The technique was simple in principle but difficult in practice. It took Adams more than a year to perfect it. But once he did, he was finally able to commence the intimidating job of identifying potential new drugs, evaluating their anti-inflammatory powers, and then testing for relative freedom from side effects. He requested additional assistance from Boots. John Nicholson, a biochemist, joined the effort in 1957.

Finding the new compounds involved sojourning in the wilderness of organic chemistry. Almost all molecules in living creatures are made from simple atoms like carbon, hydrogen, nitrogen, and oxygen, which are combined in the most extraordinarily various ways. Carbon, for example, has the ability to form a circle of six linked atoms called a benzene ring, each corner of which can be tied to a group of other atoms, including other benzene rings. (The need to describe the geometry of the molecule as well as its chemical makeup is one reason why organic compounds have such peculiar scientific names. In N-acetyl-para-aminophenol, or acetaminophen, the *N* is chemist's shorthand for the molecule's chainlike structure, and the *para* tells scientists where on each benzene ring the rest of the molecule is attached.) Because slight variations in the makeup of these compounds can make huge differences in their effect on the body, Nicholson was essentially being asked to create an entire chemical library of potential anti-inflammatory drugs, each volume of which was a slightly different version of the others.

At first, the researchers found a distressing but predictable tendency for the more powerful drugs to have more serious side effects. They reduced sunburn on guinea pigs, but also made the animals sick. Finally, the two men tested a compound previously used as a weed killer, and the results were promising. Nicholson prepared six hundred chemical siblings of the original weed-killer. The strongest reduced inflammation six times more readily than aspirin, apparently without aspirin's side effects. Eagerly, they passed the drug on for clinical testing—and found, to their amazement, that this potent drug had no effect whatsoever on patients' rheumatoid arthritis. The test

Adams had labored to perfect—the sunburned guinea pig—was giving false signals for the effects of the drugs in humans.

Adams turned to a newly developed animal test that directly evaluated a drug's analgesic power. According to this test, the drugs they had passed on for clinical testing had little ability to relieve pain. Adams was forced to reject his fundamental hypothesis—that the reduction of inflammation also signals analgesic power. By this time, Boots was interested in new fever-reducers, and so they changed their protocol to test for all three effects: analgesic, anti-inflammatory, and anti-pyretic.

Nicholson finally stumbled upon a group of chemicals that fit the bill. The first to be tested on human beings was 4-tert-butylphenylacetic acid—Drug 10335, as it was called in their laboratory notes. In the experiment, Drug 10335 was effective against rheumatoid arthritis but produced a rash. Adams thought this side effect was caused by an impurity in the batch used for the trial. After Nicholson prepared a very pure batch of Drug 10335, three Boots colleagues took it themselves. One came down with an even worse rash, and Drug 10335 was consigned to oblivion. Adams and Nicholson moved on. A variant of 10335, isobutyl phenylacetic acid, proved more successful. Effective against arthritis, it did not produce a rash. Ibufenac, as it was called, went on the market—only to be withdrawn when it was discovered to cause liver problems. (The drug remains on the market in Japan, however, because it does not have the same side effects in Japanese people.)

Understaffed but never actively discouraged by Boots, Adams and Nicholson kept looking. In 1961 Nicholson came up with another group of chemicals—phenyl propionic acids—that seemed to strike a balance between potency and safety. For the next three years, Adams and Nicholson made many slightly different phenyl propionic acids and tested them in the laboratory. The best of the lot was 2-(4-isobutylphenyl)propionic acid: ibuprofen. In animal studies, ibuprofen had more than sixteen times the analgesic power, more than eight times the antipyretic power, and twenty times the anti-inflammatory power of aspirin. Clinical trials, conducted in 1966, showed no evidence of serious short-term side effects. Boots was granted a patent on ibuprofen in England and, in 1968, the United States. After further toxicological tests and clinical trials, the drug went on the English prescription market in 1969. It was called Brufen, and marketed as a pain, fever, and inflammation reliever.

Years of research and testing had gone into Brufen. That did not stop the drug from flopping at its debut. The first paper published on Brufen showed no advantage over a placebo—a sugar pill. The major problem was the low dosage: Adams preferred (and Boots agreed) to introduce a new drug with a dosage on the low side, to avoid possible side effects. Eventually, doctors cautiously experimented with larger doses and found their greater power was not accompanied by greater side effects. Slowly the drug grew more popular.

By the mid-1970s, Brufen was successful indeed. Adams was happy, and Boots was even happier.

The Upjohn Company, of Kalamazoo, Michigan, had an option on any pharmaceutical product developed by Boots. Upjohn exercised its option for ibuprofen and in 1974 brought out its version in the United States under the name Motrin. Peddled in distinctive orange pills, Motrin was a smash. Doctors prescribed it for menstrual cramps, arthritic pain, toothache—anything that involved pain and inflammation. By 1983, eight billion doses had been sold, and it was the fourth most popular prescription drug in the United States.

As these numbers made their way through pharmaceutical circles, drug makers looked closely at ibuprofen. Like acetaminophen, it was familiar to doctors and hospitals; their patients knew its brand name, Motrin, and its easily identifiable orange pills. Like acetaminophen, ibuprofen was effective, and had an excellent safety record. All in all, people realized, Motrin looked like another Tylenol.

There is, Wayne Nelson has said, an old marketing rule of thumb, the "65 percent rule." In the long run, the first firm into a new market gets at least 65 percent; the second gets maybe half that; the rest fight over the remaining scraps. Tylenol was a more than perfect example of Nelson's rule; even after the poisonings, nine-tenths of acetaminophen sales went to Tylenol. Arguably, Nelson admitted, many Tylenol consumers did not know that it was made from a drug called "acetaminophen," and so did not know they could buy an identical competitor. They regarded "Tylenol" in the way Anacin users regarded "Anacin," as if it were the name of a drug in its own right. As long as that perception continued, nobody else would be able to, as marketers say, crack the Tylenol franchise. Bristol-Myers spent almost twenty million dollars on Datril in its first four years and ended up with nothing.

These lessons were not lost on those in the drug world who were interested in ibuprofen. Boots had licensed Upjohn to sell its products in the United States, but it had not awarded an *exclusive* license. The British firm wanted to wring out more money from ibuprofen before May 1985, when its U.S. patent expired. After spending eight years carefully introducing American doctors and hospitals to ibuprofen, Upjohn found itself competing with the drug's inventor when Boots debuted Rufen, its U.S. brand of prescription ibuprofen. "Boots will get some business, but we don't intend to have them walk away with the market," said a philosophical Upjohn vice-president. But that wasn't all. Much to Upjohn's horror, Boots put the over-the-counter rights up for grabs in late 1982. Upjohn had acquired prescription rights to ibuprofen, but had not taken over-the-counter rights—selling just a few OTC drugs, it was uncomfortable with the rough-and-tumble world of consumer sales. Now anyone could buy the license. The winner would have the right to introduce the drug to consumers while the patent was still valid, at once cracking the Motrin prescription franchise and giving it priority on the consumer level—and, if Nelson was right, a guaranteed 65 percent of the market.

The eventual licensee was a firm that was looking to settle a score: American Home. It set out to switch the drug from prescription status to over-the-counter. Upjohn was swept along, reluctant to do anything that would upset the ethical sales of Motrin's little orange pills, but unwilling to let American Home produce the next Tylenol by itself. It too bought over-the-counter rights to ibuprofen.

In potential, the payoff was huge. According to some analysts, ibuprofen was expected to take 10 to 15 percent of the analgesic market within a year of its appearance. Each percentage point being equivalent to sales of fourteen million dollars a year, people stood to gain or lose a lot of money.

But the money would only flow in if the companies acted quickly. The patent on ibuprofen was set to expire in two years. In that time—short, by bureaucratic standards—Upjohn and American Home needed to gain the approval of the FDA. But as part of the switchover process, the two companies had to justify themselves before a board of medical experts that had seen American Home in action before: the Arthritis Advisory Committee.

Both firms touted ibuprofen to the committee at a meeting on August 18, 1983. Upjohn made what most observers considered a curiously lackluster presentation. Wanting to protect the profits it made from prescription Motrin, it argued that ibuprofen should be sold over the counter only in a low and therefore relatively ineffective dose. American Home, by contrast, vigorously pushed the need for a larger dose, making the highest OTC dose equal to the lowest prescription dose of ibuprofen. The committee did not dwell long on this difference, settling the matter in favor of American Home.

The main concern was that people who can't tolerate aspirin—a condition that doctors call hypersensitivity—would be among those most likely to buy a new non-aspirin headache remedy. Any promotion of ibuprofen would therefore have to be careful and responsible. Committee members were not sanguine that American Home, purveyors of the notorious Anacin, could be trusted to market a drug carefully and responsibly. The discussion grew tense when Michael Weisman of the University of California at San Diego Medical Center asked American Home sardonically whether the promotion of ibuprofen would "break tradition" and "mention . . . the actual ingredient? Can we get an answer to that question?"

American Home spokesman Garrett Swenson refused to provide one.

"I think if the drug comes out, we are all concerned that it come out cleanly, advertised for what it is, and we have almost no examples of that on the market now in this general drug class," said Bonnie Hepburn, the chairperson of the committee.

"Your concern," Weisman asked Hepburn a minute later, "was that the promotion of [ibuprofen] will disguise the ingredient as the other two comparison drugs [aspirin and acetaminophen] that are marketed by the myriad of companies that advertise. Is that correct?"

"That is a major concern," Hepburn said. She wanted to know what the company was going to do about it.

Again Swenson said nothing.

The real problem, said John Harter of the FDA, was that over-the-counter drug advertising was monitored by the FTC. Then run by James Miller, a Reagan appointee, the FTC had resolved the aspirin cases six months before in a manner not calculated to endear itself to its federal colleagues in the FDA. The FTC's laxity, Harter said, "is why the Anacin, the aspirin, and the other ads on TV are . . . more flagrant examples of misdirection than the stuff you [doctors] see in your journals. . . ."

The committee was in a bind. Its members were acutely aware that drug costs were spiraling upward, and that switching ibuprofen, a safe and effective drug, to OTC status would cut its price drastically. At the same time, they worried that American Home, a corporation with an unsavory reputation, would fail to advertise that ibuprofen should not be taken by the approximately one million Americans who are allergic to aspirin. Nonetheless, the committee swallowed its misgivings and unanimously voted to send ibuprofen over the counter—with one catch. In an unprecedented proviso, it tied the recommendation to a request that advertising for ibuprofen "be controlled to an acceptable level."

There was one problem with this request. Ever since the struggle to create the Food, Drug, and Cosmetic Act back in 1938, the FDA had been denied authority over OTC drug advertising. "Technically, we do not regulate advertising," Harter reminded the committee. "We do not have the authority to. However, companies can voluntarily enter into agreements with us . . . for them to voluntarily let us monitor their advertising." The two companies agreed. American Home was eager to get going. Upjohn was not.

Upjohn had only sought OTC approval because American Home was doing it. Now it promised to match American Home's ad spending dollar for dollar because, according to Upjohn executive vice-president Lawrence Hoff, "we have to." But as the launch date approached, the company had second thoughts about competing with the makers of Anacin. It was like an Ivy League boxer getting into a street fight with a gun-toting thug. Taking a dive, Upjohn licensed its right to sell over-the-counter ibuprofen to Bristol-Myers.

Two established aspirin makers now had a chance to try their hands at a new analgesic. After watching Tylenol clobber aspirin, they were delighted at the prospect of returning the favor. A new day in over-the-counter analgesics was dawning.

Meanwhile the FDA grappled with the committee's recommendation. In January 1984, FDA officials met with their counterparts at the FTC, who pledged constant vigilance. The FDA was not encouraged—after decades of such vigilance, Anacin had yet to admit it was made of aspirin. Nonetheless, the FDA released ibuprofen for over-the-counter sale on May 18, 1984. The agency squeezed two promises out of the companies: that Bristol-Myers and American Home would not advertise in a manner that counteracted the label warnings, in particular that for aspirin hypersensitivity, and that the companies would allow the FDA to monitor their advertising. Bristol-Myers's ibuprofen was to be called Nuprin; American Home's was Advil.

The peace lasted less than a week. Six days after the FDA cleared ibuprofen for over-the-counter sales, Johnson & Johnson sued the agency, charging that it had "no authority to supervise, regulate, or control the consumer advertising of OTC drugs." Piously disavowing any desire to "interfere with the launch" of Advil and Nuprin, the makers of Tylenol argued that the FDA's action, if unchallenged, might open the door to sweeping illegal regulation by the FDA of the over-the-counter drug advertising. The case was quickly dismissed by what one Johnson & Johnson lawyer described as a "patsy judge."

Meanwhile, both Advil and Nuprin raced to the market, with American Home employees working round the clock, sleeping in their offices until the millions of Advil boxes were on drugstore shelves that June. The effort paid off, and Advil got there first. It quickly took a commanding lead over Nuprin. Bristol-Myers was aghast; it had committed millions and fallen completely on its face. Nuprin, advertising wags said, was the Datril of the 1980s.

Trying to hang on to its Motrin franchise, Upjohn was appalled to see American Home commercials featuring little orange Advil pills that looked remarkably like the distinctive little orange Motrin pills. In fact, as American Home apologetically explained, Advil pills were brown, but TV cameras inadvertently changed their color. But Upjohn was far from satisfied. One Advil print ad claimed, "It's so effective that doctors have already prescribed it over 130 million times." "It" was Motrin, and it sounded to Upjohn like American Home was claiming credit for that drug.

On July 3, Upjohn sued American Home, a company that had now been in court over one analgesic ad or another for more than ten years. Unwilling to get into a legal tangle at the outset of the Advil launch, American Home quickly made some changes in its advertising, ensuring that the pills' brown color came through and stating that Motrin was the product of another company. Unsatisfied, Upjohn persisted and won a partial victory in November.

The decision enjoined American Home from using any of the old advertising material, but not the modified ads.

American Home and Bristol-Myers were granted additional time in September 1984 to solidify their marketing positions. A set of amendments to the Food, Drug, and Cosmetic Act passed that month gave special status to drugs that had recently gone through the New Drug Application process, but were not new (ibuprofen had been approved for prescription use in 1974). Effectively, this category consisted of prescription drugs that were switched to OTC status. The amendments granted the companies that sponsored the switch— usually the patent holder or a company with a license from the patent holder— temporary exclusive rights to market the drug over the counter, even past the time of patent expiration. Upjohn and American Home now had the OTC ibuprofen market to themselves until September 1986.*

On June 4, 1985, Stanley Barshall, president of Whitehall Laboratories, proudly announced that Advil's first-year sales were $60 million, and that the new brand had a 4 percent share of the analgesic market. In drugstores, Advil outsold Bayer, Bufferin, and Excedrin. Confirming Nelson's 65 percent adage, Advil, the first to arrive, had two-thirds of all ibuprofen sales. Advil had yet to show a profit—American Home spent more than $35 million on advertising in that period—but that was soon to come. Most of its sales had come at the expense of aspirin, which now claimed less than half the analgesic market. But some, inevitably, had been taken from acetaminophen. The analgesic market was a three-way race.

Although they are chemically distinct entities, aspirin, acetaminophen, and ibuprofen do not have significantly different effects at over-the-counter doses. All three drugs relieve fever and pain; none reliably does it any better or faster. Acetaminophen does not have much, if any, impact on inflammation—but neither does aspirin or ibuprofen, except in large, doctor-ordered doses. In addition, acetaminophen does not foster bleeding or upset the stomach—but the great majority of people who take aspirin or ibuprofen will never feel discomfort from them, making the three drugs effectively alike in this circumstance too. One person may swear by acetaminophen; another may say that only aspirin cures his headache. Both will quite likely be right. Far more important than the objective differences among the drugs are the individual idiosyncrasies of the person taking the analgesic.

Pondering these facts, Johnson & Johnson worried that the nation's doctors might not be sufficiently informed about the relative advantages of the three analgesics. It decided to help, sending doctors a mailing in 1985 that

---

* Johnson & Johnson launched its own ibuprofen brand, Medipren, as soon as the extension was over.

suggested the appropriate drug for a number of indications and compared a judicious selection of the side effects of aspirin, ibuprofen, and Extra-Strength Tylenol. "Every non-[prescription] analgesic has its place," the mailing explained. Three boxes listed the appropriate uses for each drug. Not surprisingly, the longest list of uses was for Extra-Strength Tylenol, which was recommended for the treatment of a staggering range of human ailments. Aspirin, on the other hand, was confined to rheumatoid arthritis; ibuprofen was given severe dysmenorrhea—menstrual cramps—as its sole use.

The facing page listed seventeen side effects, with an adjacent column for each of the three drugs. A check in a drug's column signaled the possible occurrence of that side effect; an asterisk indicated relative freedom from that side effect. The final tally was clearly in Tylenol's favor: Its column contained a single check and six asterisks. In contrast, aspirin had thirteen checks and four asterisks. Ibuprofen had sixteen checks—a near-perfect negative score.

Now it was American Home's turn to become unsurpassingly annoyed. On June 24, 1985, it charged Johnson & Johnson with what would eventually become more than one hundred counts of false advertising, the most important of which featured the checklist. The objective of that mailing, American Home said, was to "tar ibuprofen products with the same stomach upset and other side effect safety concerns that McNeil has heretofore directed against aspirin-based analgesic products."

The company also objected to Tylenol's long-standing claim that it was the overwhelming choice of hospitals. This implied that Tylenol was better than other brands of acetaminophen and other analgesics, American Home argued, when in fact

> McNeil never informs consumers in its advertising that the reason Tylenol is chosen by hospitals over other brands of acetaminophen has nothing to do with any alleged superiority of Tylenol over other acetaminophen brands but rather the low price at which Tylenol is offered by McNeil to hospitals for purchase or other considerations unrelated to safety or effectiveness.

(American Home's complaint is true, as Nelson has cheerfully admitted. "We made damn sure that nobody was going to beat us on the price," he said. "Making money was not the point—I didn't care if we had to give it away.")

After it filed the lawsuit, American Home was further exercised by a Tylenol ad that appeared in medical journals from July to October 1985. It depicted a lush, rosy-cheeked Red Delicious apple. Closer inspection, however, reveals a flaw: a wormhole surrounded by a dark, rotten-looking region. "Aspirin and Ibuprofen—The Closer You Look . . . ," said the caption. "Up to ⅓ of newly diagnosed gastric ulcers may be related to aspirin therapy." Although the scientific study cited as the source for this assertion linked the ulcers only to aspirin, American Home believed the implication was that ibuprofen could produce similar effects. It wanted the mailings and advertising stopped. And, in a break from its past battles with Johnson & Johnson, it wanted $167 million in damages.

Johnson & Johnson replied with a shopping list of counterclaims, ranging from unfair competition—it charged American Home with building its Advil marketing division by raiding McNeil's personnel and stealing trade secrets—to false advertising. For example, one medical-journal ad claimed that Advil "interacts" (which doctors take to mean interacts unsafely) with fewer drugs than acetaminophen does. Accompanying the claim was a footnote: "Data on file, Medical Department, Whitehall Laboratories." Upon further investigation, the "data on file" turned out to consist mainly of a few pages in a textbook from Whitehall's library. Unfortunately, as American Home's own expert witness conceded, even these scraps of data failed to support the claim.

The most serious counterattack concerned Reye's syndrome, a serious but rare illness that strikes children in the aftermath of a viral infection, such as the flu or chickenpox. In the early 1980s, studies established a possible link between Reye's syndrome and the aspirin often taken by young flu or chickenpox sufferers. In January 1985, makers of children's aspirin began to put warning labels on their products; in June of the following year, the FDA mandated them for all aspirin products. The publicity, however, had long since altered the market for children's analgesics. In 1979 Children's Tylenol had more than 40 percent of the market, followed by Bayer's 20 percent and St. Joseph's 17 percent. Five years later, Tylenol had almost two-thirds of the market; the combined Bayer and St. Joseph share was less than 15 percent.

Johnson & Johnson claimed that American Home should have acted long before 1985, when it put a warning on Anacin. If the warning had been printed in 1980, when the first studies came out, Tylenol's share of the market would have increased much sooner than it actually had. Johnson & Johnson wanted its lost profits, as calculated by the company using econometric-style projections. The single delayed warning, it said, cost Tylenol $1.1 *billion*.

The lawsuit quickly reached such dizzying proportions that in August 1986 District Court Judge William C. Conner split it into three separate parts: a trial on the allegations of false advertising (which might be called Tylenol I-A); a separate determination of the Reye's syndrome issue (Tylenol I-B); and, after determining who was responsible for what false advertising, a resolution of the two parties' damage claims (Tylenol I-C).*

* That same summer Johnson & Johnson was in court with Bristol-Myers, suing Nuprin for advertising that "two little Nuprin are stronger than Extra-Strength Tylenol." Although

Conner ruled on Tylenol I-A in February 1987. His introduction revealed a flair for dry humor that the contending lawyers did not always appreciate.

Small nations have fought for their very survival with less resources and resourcefulness than these antagonists have brought to their epic struggle for primacy in the OTC analgesic market.

The simplest explanation of the long, complex, rather exasperated opinion that followed is that both sides lost—most of their ads were declared false. American Home was slapped for misleading comparisons between ibuprofen and acetaminophen and for false claims about Anacin-3. Johnson & Johnson was chided for its misleading checklist and other comparisons between ibuprofen and aspirin. More important, it lost the right to make the *unqualified* statement that nothing was stronger than Extra-Strength Tylenol, because the judge ruled that the highest over-the-counter ibuprofen dose, 400 mg, has slightly more analgesic power than the highest over-the-counter acetaminophen dose, 1,000 mg. This advantage only shows up for severe pain, however, and so Tylenol was still allowed to claim that nothing was stronger than Tylenol for mild to moderate pain, modifying its decade-old advertising theme.

The second trial, Tylenol I-B, centered on Johnson & Johnson's charge that all aspirin labels, including Anacin's, should have carried warnings about Reye's syndrome before 1986, when the FDA asked aspirin makers to add them. The judge ultimately dismissed the suit in November 1987, in part because Johnson & Johnson, as a member of the Proprietary Association, an over-the-counter-drug manufacturers' trade group, had vigorously argued from 1983 to 1985 against precisely the same warnings on the label that it later sued American Home for failing to add. Johnson & Johnson explained that it had opposed the warning requirements on "philosophical grounds." Conner noted with disapproval, however, that American Home had failed to clear store shelves of pre-1986 packages of Anacin that lacked the Reye's syndrome warning. He suggested that American Home correct this situation immediately or he would entertain a motion to reconsider the entire issue. Johnson & Johnson's $1.1 billion damages claim was thrown out with the decision in Tylenol I-B, Tylenol I-C never came to trial, although both sides blustered for a few years about the damages they would seek for Tylenol I-A.

Judge Conner's troubles by no means ended with Tylenol I. Eight weeks after his final decision on Tylenol I-A, Johnson & Johnson again sued Amer-

Johnson & Johnson admitted that two tablets of ibuprofen were stronger than two tablets of Extra-Strength Tylenol, the company argued that the FDA had recommended *one* tablet as the proper dosage, not two. If it could prevail on this issue, the playing field would be level again. The case was dismissed in September 1986.

ican Home under the Lanham act, this time for claiming that Advil, "like Tylenol," does not upset the stomach, thus creating Tylenol II. When the overworked Judge Conner granted Tylenol's request for an injunction in December 1987, American Home appealed, losing the following May.

Still, the two adversaries were not finished with the legal system. Like participants in a classic feud, they couldn't seem able to avoid a fight, and quickly embroiled themselves in *another* Lanham act suit, Tylenol III, which Conner described as "the latest skirmish" in the war between American Home and Johnson & Johnson. After the resolution of Tylenol I-A, Johnson & Johnson launched a new advertising campaign, "apparently attempting to go as far as the injunction allowed" (to quote Conner) in claiming effectiveness for Tylenol against headaches. Citing "the largest headache study ever conducted" as proof, the company continued its theme of "Nothing is stronger," amending the claim only to say "for headaches." Taken literally, as parity claims had been for years, the advertising was squarely within Conner's previous decision. But American Home wanted more. In response to threats from American Home, Johnson & Johnson modified its ads to clarify the parity claim. The modified ads did not satisfy American Home. It sued Johnson & Johnson yet again in July 1987, claiming that Tylenol's claims of parity were leaving impressions of superiority.

Of course, such impressions are the object of parity claims, as everyone in advertising knows. Nonetheless, American Home, like Claude Rains "discovering" the gambling at Rick's Café in *Casablanca*, professed itself shocked—shocked!—that Johnson & Johnson was misleading the public in this manner. The company wanted to force promotion back to the days of Rosser Reeve's Unique Selling Proposition: claims that truly (even if irrelevantly) distinguished one product from its competitors. Given the near-equivalence of over-the-counter analgesics, such a stance was sure to backfire on Anacin. And, perhaps sensing the trap it was laying for itself, American Home quietly dropped Tylenol III in 1988.

The 1980s turned into the 1990s, with the companies continuing to snap at one another. The long-delayed OTC drug review of the FDA, revived in the mid-1980s, has been making its way to a final set of monographs. Still, there has been no peace. Late in 1989, American Home, among other requests too numerous to list, demanded that the labeling for acetaminophen include the following warning: "Do not exceed recommended dose or duration of use because daily use of this product has been associated with an increased risk of kidney damage." Johnson & Johnson attacked Anacin's use of caffeine in its own presentation early in 1990. Meanwhile, Bristol-Myers continued in its years-long quest to get caffeine accepted in the FDA analgesic monograph as an adjuvant—a drug that increases the power of another drug—for acetaminophen. It submitted the results of three clinical trials in support of its contention that acetaminophen plus caffeine was superior to acetaminophen alone. Johnson & Johnson, guardian of analgesic purity, countered with four studies of its own to prove that caffeine had no such effect. Curiously, Bristol-Myers had begun by seeking FDA blessing for the caffeine in Excedrin, a mixture of aspirin, acetaminophen, and caffeine; by 1990 it was seeking the same approval for Aspirin-Free Excedrin, Excedrin without the principal ingredient the firm had hidden for so long. Promised by the FDA for delivery in 1974, the monograph today stands, some seventeen years later, on the verge of completion. There it may always remain.

And what of Bayer? In the High Court of Ireland, ten years before the battle between the small nations of American Home and Johnson & Johnson spilled over to engulf the entire analgesic world, Sterling Drug watched the crumbling of an empire built on wartime xenophobia and a stolen symbol of quality, the Bayer Cross. Since 1955, Sterling had been embroiled in its own world war: Farbenfabriken Bayer AG, one of three companies born from the ashes of I.G. Farben, wanted its name back. The two firms battled in almost every one of the countries where Bayer AG's earlier incarnation had ceded the Bayer Cross to Sterling in 1923. After seven years of fighting, the U.S. wing of the struggle ended in Sterling's favor.

Bayer AG did not care what Sterling marketed under any other name—it was no longer interested in a global aspirin cartel or other secret contracts dividing up the world. It just wanted its name. The two companies dickered for a time, and Bayer AG offered $2.5 million to purchase the rights to the Bayer Cross and Bayer name everywhere outside the United States. Sterling asked for an amount more than three times higher. (To put these figures in perspective, Johnson & Johnson spent $100 million to preserve the Tylenol name during the poisonings eighteen years later.) After Sterling refused to come down, Bayer AG chose Ireland as a test case. It told Sterling in 1965 that it would market products there under the Bayer Cross with a disclaimer that the products were made in Germany. Bayer AG followed through with its threat, and Sterling sued for trademark infringement; Bayer AG countersued to invalidate Sterling's Bayer trademark. The trial dragged on from June 1967 to February 1968; Sterling's opening remarks alone lasted thirty-one days. Overwhelmed by the twenty thousand pages of documents produced by the trial, the presiding justice only rendered his decision in 1976, eight years after the final argument.

Nobody won. Bayer AG ended up still bound by the 1923 contracts. Bayer AG had agreed in one of these documents not to contest Sterling's title to the Bayer Cross—which it was now doing. Unfortunately for Sterling, the justice also decided that its use of the trademark since the end of the Second World War had been based on a deception: that Bayer's Irish (and British) goods were still being provided by the German company. Sterling was living off the reputation the prewar company had built with high-quality German goods. By nurturing this impression—unintentionally, the court decided—Sterling had fallen prey to a trademark evil: deceiving the public as to the source of its goods. The justice proclaimed Sterling's exclusive title to the Bayer Cross invalid. Bayer AG could use the Bayer Cross with "Made in Germany" added, the very situation it had desperately sought to avoid fifty-five years earlier, but one it now welcomed. The justice concluded: "I realise that the use of the simple [Bayer] cross with or without added words by two great firms will cause confusion and difficulty for everyone: the blame, however, for this cannot be imposed on the law but on the Second World War."

In a series of agreements stretching over the next ten years, Sterling retreated into its U.S. shell, and Bayer AG regained control over its own name in all countries and for all products except pharmaceuticals in the United States and Canada. (In the case of Panadol, Sterling did not mind losing the rights to the Bayer name because the company had never used it to promote the brand.) Bayer AG purchased Miles Laboratories, the makers of Alka-Seltzer, in 1977. And in 1986 Bayer AG unveiled the new name for its U.S. business: Bayer USA. After almost seven decades the German firm could now do business in the United States under its own name. But it still couldn't sell Bayer aspirin.

It's not clear this disturbed Bayer AG. Bayer aspirin's share of the U.S. analgesic market had shrunk to about 6 percent in 1986. The brand's stoic suffering at the hands of Bufferin in the 1950s, its touting of the FTC's own study in the 1960s, its battles with the agency in the 1970s, its attempts to stifle the competition by influencing the OTC analgesic monograph in the late 1970s and 1980s, its efforts to keep the Bayer Cross throughout the world— all had come to naught. Its place at the top of the analgesic heap had long been lost, because aspirin's place had long been lost. Surely it would never get it back. After all, aspirin was just aspirin, wasn't it?

PART THREE

"BLUT, BLUT, VERFLUCHTES BLUT"

CHAPTER FIFTEEN

"GIVE NO DEADLY
DRUG TO ANY"

One recent morning a bright red pamphlet sat on the desk of Noel Rabouhans, manager of the Medical Products Division of Nicholas Laboratories, Ltd., a British drug and consumer products company. Its cover por-
trayed a human artery, blood washing through in a scarlet stream. Floating
inside the stream was a scatter of tiny white discs, representing platelets, a
constituent of blood that is of special concern to Rabouhans. When platelets
come close to a damaged blood vessel wall, they suddenly begin sticking to
the wall and one another at a fantastic rate. In a few seconds tens of thousands clump together to form a protective screen over the injured area. Most
of the time, platelet aggregation, as doctors call it, is clearly beneficial.
Without it, people would bleed to death from every scratch. But if the clump
of platelets grows large enough to dam the blood vessel, the resulting lack of
blood can lead to a stroke or heart attack. Rabouhans was in charge of
marketing a drug intended to stop this from happening, and the pamphlet on
his desk was one of his chief sales tools.

Platet Cleartab, as the drug is called, is a "platelet aggregation inhibitor."
As befits a product with such powerful effects, Platet is sold only by prescription in Great Britain, and cannot be advertised to the public. Instead
Rabouhans pleads his case in special brochures given to the medical profession by Nicholas's squad of detailers. Detailers, one recalls, are pharmaceutical salespeople who call on doctors in their offices and present them with
what amounts to personal commercials for their products, in much the same
way that Farbenfabriken Bayer representatives talked up aspirin to turn-of-
the-century physicians. And just as Carl Duisberg supervised the material
provided to his corps of aspirin salesmen, Rabouhans was responsible for the
graphs and charts in the brochure that explain how Platet is, in the technical
language used on its label, a "platelet aggregation inhibitor for use in patients with unstable angina, or at risk of secondary myocardial infarction."
Angina is the pain caused by depriving the heart of oxygen; myocardial

infarction is a Latinate way of saying "the death of the heart tissue"—that is, a heart attack. Platet is thus a high-tech heart attack preventative, one of the latest and most advanced weapons in humankind's war against heart disease.

Heart disease is the leading cause of death in the United Kingdom, taking about 150,000 lives every year. One would therefore expect that the man in charge of selling a new and successful treatment for heart attack would be in the catbird seat. But Rabouhans was able to control his excitement without apparent difficulty. The reason for the absence of enthusiasm was on the back of each package of Platet: a little printed box with the words "contains aspirin." Indeed, Platet not only *contained* aspirin, it was *nothing but* aspirin. It was made on the same assembly line as Nicholas's ordinary aspirin, but each Platet tablet cost 13 percent more.

Located in Slough, a western suburb of London, Nicholas Laboratories, Ltd., is the successor to the oldest surviving aspirin company outside Germany. In 1914 George Nicholas, a pharmacist, and the oddly named Harry Shmith, an industrial experimenter and inventor, founded the original firm, George Nicholas & Company of Australia, after the Australian government suspended Farbenfabriken Bayer's trademark and declared that the first people to produce pure ASA would get both a new patent and the Aspirin trademark.

The two men set to work in the back of Nicholas's pharmacy. Neither was a chemist, and the lack of knowledge showed. Although ASA is not explosive, Nicholas managed to blow up his pharmacy. Although it is not toxic at ordinary doses, he managed nearly to poison himself. But after a year of work, Nicholas and Shmith won the Aspirin race anyway. Lobbying by importers of British ASA led Australia to renege on its promise; it canceled the trademark after two years. By that time, Shmith had left the company, and Nicholas had coined a new name for his product: Aspro.

Between the two world wars the company built up a worldwide Aspro marketing network under the aegis of George T. Davies, a manic, eccentric advertising man from New Zealand whose free-spending campaigns rivaled the best work of Max Wojahn, David Corcoran, and Rosser Reeves. Together with the requisite drive and tenacity, Davies had a nose for intellectual fashion that is not always found in drug marketers. When quantum mechanics exploded on the scene in the 1920s, for instance, Davies and Aspro were there:

> The science of atomic energy is now more than mere anticipation—scientists tell us that we are on the eve of a great discovery. It is found that there is enough atomic energy in the little finger to run all the trains in England several minutes if it could be harnessed. Truly this is progress.

Similar happenings have been demonstrated in the medical world by Aspro.

When Egypt acquired almost complete domestic independence from Britain in 1936, Davies cloaked Aspro in nationalist colors. EGYPT AWAKES! cried advertisements in Cairo. A NEW ERA DAWNS!

All positive truths have the forces of negation to fight. But negative methods defeat themselves, which explains why the victory of "ASPRO" over ill-health, suffering, limitations, false ideas, takes place in minutes—not years. THE WONDERFUL LITTLE "ASPRO" TABLET has stirred the enthusiasm of the people of Egypt—because it is the medicine with FIFTY USES INSTEAD OF ONE. . . .

In what is now Zaïre, Davies sponsored French-language comic strips in the 1950s that featured "The Marvelous Vacation of Mutumbo." Handsome Mutumbo, who has left his native village to become a bigwig in the capital, returns for a vacation. Everyone gets gifts, but the most precious is for *Maman*—a packet of Aspro for her rheumatism! Touring the village, Mutumbo and his wonderful pills help the village win a local soccer game (the star forward's sudden toothache is cured by Aspro) and put out a fire in Elisa's house (Aspro calms her nerves). But Mutumbo's actually come home to propose to his childhood sweetheart, Véronique. Shatteringly, she does not accept. Why? Because she is afraid of the clamor of the big city. Don't worry, Mutumbo promises. Take Aspro, and you'll soon get habituated to the capital. Reassured, Véronique gives her hand. But before the elated Mutumbo can go back to his job, he must settle a squabble. Six boys have tied up and beaten one of their friends. "Aren't you ashamed to be six against one?" Mutumbo asks them. One of the children cries, "Laurent beat my dog until he was almost dead!" Mutumbo renders judgment: "You will be punished for hitting the dog, Laurent. When you have a toothache, I'm not going to give you Aspro. That way, you'll know what pain really is!" Then he leaves. Everybody cries for him to return with more Aspro.

As is the way with modern business, Nicholas spent the 1970s and 1980s struggling through a multitude of mergers and acquisitions. The parent company retreated to Australia, and the London branch, Nicholas Laboratories, Ltd., came under the Douwe Egberts wing of Sara Lee, a $3.5 billion food and consumer products conglomerate based in Chicago. Nicholas Labs became a British version of Bristol-Myers or American Home Products, selling, among other brands, Radox herbal bath salts, Kiwi shoe polish, Louis Marcel eyelash dye, and two brands of aspirin—Aspro for headaches, fever, and inflammation; and Platet, in a 300-mg version for angina and secondary myocardial infarction, and in a 100-mg version for the prevention of blood clots following coronary bypass surgery.

Nicholas was not alone in trying to cope with aspirin's split personality. Few other companies, however, had two brand names for the same product. (British aspirin makers, like their American cousins, cannot put the new uses for aspirin on the label of an over-the-counter product.) The tale of how aspirin came into its second identity is long and as strange as the situation itself. It began two centuries ago, when scientists first realized that clots inside veins and arteries can starve the body of blood, causing strokes, heart attacks, and thrombophlebitis (clots in a vein near the skin, which create painful inflammation). By the end of the nineteenth century, physicians knew that salicylic acid and its chemical cousins seemed to prolong bleeding—to retard clot formation, in other words. Acetylsalicylic acid, one of those cousins, could logically have been tested as an anticlotting agent right then and there. It wasn't. Perhaps scientists didn't notice the evidence. Perhaps they didn't believe it. Or perhaps aspirin was thought to be too common, too popular, too humdrum to be worth the care and attention of a top scientist. Whatever the reason, heart and blood researchers ignored aspirin for all the decades that firms like Nicholas were doing their best to call it to public attention. Eventually, as the world knows, physicians came to regard aspirin as protection against not only heart attacks but also a host of other ailments—a kind of miracle drug.

On a Saturday afternoon in February 1933, Ed Carlson, a dairy farmer in Deer Park, Wisconsin, drove almost two hundred miles through a heavy blizzard to Madison, the capital. In the back of his truck was a dead heifer and a pail of blood. The blood sloshed around in the milk bucket—it wouldn't coagulate, despite the near-arctic cold. Finding the Office of the State Veterinarian closed, Carlson wandered about the nearby campus of the University of Wisconsin, seeking a professor who could help him. Eventually he wound up at the Biochemistry Building, where he came upon Karl Link, a professor in the department, and his senior graduate student, Eugen Schoeffel, a volatile German immigrant who was completing his doctorate after some years of knocking about the Chicago stockyards. The product of a classical education, Schoeffel spoke in a thickly accented potpourri of literary allusions.

Link and Schoeffel took one look at the contents of the farmer's truck—the dead heifer, the pail of blood, and about a hundred pounds of dried sweet clover, the feed on which his cattle were surviving the winter—and realized what the problem was. Carlson's cows were dying of sweet clover disease, a condition that Link later called "without parallel in animal pathology or human medicine." On the skins of healthy cattle suddenly appeared the dark blooms of internal hemorrhages; blood oozed from the nose, the ears, the anus. Within days, cows turned into swollen bags of blood. They bled to death without being cut. The condition, Link and Schoeffel told Carlson, came from eating sweet clover that had spoiled. It could be reversed by changing the cattle's diet. But that did the farmer no good. It was deep winter; he had no other feed. Hearing the scientists diagnose the disease but offer no realistic cure devastated him. It was a death sentence for his animals, and hence, probably, his livelihood—hardly a comforting thought at the nadir of the Great Depression.

Link was no less upset. "I can still see [Carlson] take off for home about 4:00 P.M.," he recalled twenty-five years later. "Those 190 miles of drifted roads between our laboratory and his barn must have appeared to him like a treacherous and somber ocean."

Furious at his own helplessness, Schoeffel stormed about the lab in a cloud of Germanic imprecations. In Link's recollection, Schoeffel plunged his hands repeatedly into the bucket of blood and spluttered, "Dere's no clot in dat blook! *Blut, Blut, verfluchtes Blut. 'Die Menschen dauern mich in ihren Jammertagen.'* * . . . Vat will he find ven he gets home? Sicker cows. And ven he and his good voman go to church tomorrow and pray and pray and pray, vat will dey haf on Monday? MORE DEAD COWS! . . . *Mein Gott!! Mein Gott!!* Vy didn't ve anti-shi-pate dis? Ya, ve should haf anti-shi-pated dis."

The two men examined the blood and cattle feed for a few fruitless and depressing hours. Leaving the laboratory, Link recalled later, Schoeffel grabbed him by the shoulders and snarled into his face, "Before you go let me tell you something. Der is a destiny dat shapes our end, it shapes our ends I tell you! I vill clean up and gif you a document on Monday morning."

With Carlson's cattle vivid in their memories, Link and Schoeffel set to looking for a cure. This necessarily involved first finding whatever was in the spoiled clover that caused the bleeding—or, more precisely, that robbed cattle blood of its ability to solidify. They had little notion of what they were getting into. In search of an agent to increase clotting, they were about to join, all unwittingly, the medical crusade for a drug to *prevent* it. They were also venturing into a scientific frontier, for the work plunged Link and his colleagues deep into the biochemical mysteries of human blood.

Blood, scientists often say, is the last trace of the ancient ocean in which all life evolved. Billions of years ago, our single-celled ancestors swam in this primitive sea, drawing their sustenance from it. As they developed over the millennia into multicelled creatures, warm, nutrient-rich saltwater continued to be the wellspring of their existence. "As we stepwise became more

---

* Blood, blood, damned blood. "I pity human beings in their suffering." (Goethe, *Faust*, Prologue In Heaven).

complex," an eminent hematologist (blood scientist) once noted, "the all-sustaining ocean had to be preserved, until now this precious sea . . . is land-locked, or truly, flesh-locked, within us. Constantly flowing, surging, and ebbing within us, this internal sea of blood must be maintained intact at all costs."

When the sea is not maintained intact—that is, when people cut themselves—bleeding must be stopped easily, or else one would bleed to death. Yet, paradoxically, blood must also *not* clot easily, for otherwise it would plug up blood vessels. Thus the body contains mechanisms both to foster and to prevent coagulation, each ready to operate at the slightest notice. "Throughout his entire existence," wrote Irving S. Wright, a past president of the American Heart Association,

> man is almost constantly hemorrhaging and thrombosing [bleeding and clotting, in lay language]. It is true that the loss of blood is for the most part small and that the thrombuses [clots] are just adequate to close the breaks in the minute vessels, but the neat balance between the extremes of continued massive hemorrhages and universal clotting is worthy of our most careful study. Perhaps the key question . . . is not why thrombuses occur, but rather why blood remains fluid for most of our lives.

Blood consists chiefly of three types of cells—red blood cells, white blood cells, and platelets—suspended in a salty, straw-colored liquid called plasma. Red blood cells carry oxygen from the lungs to the rest of the body, where it is exchanged for carbon dioxide. White blood cells fight infection, sometimes by surrounding and engulfing invading bacteria. Platelets, the smallest type of blood cell, were the last of the three to be discovered; they are the body's first line of defense against bleeding.

Created at special sites within the bone marrow, platelets are flat discs less than five one-thousandths of a millimeter in diameter; millions teem in every drop of blood. They live only nine days and spend that time bobbing passively in the bloodstream like so many microscopic jellyfish—unless they come into contact with broken blood vessel walls, the places where bleeding occurs. Alerted by the biochemical signals of distress emitted by the damaged area, platelets rapidly attach themselves to the site of the damage, massing together to form a shield over the cut.

In addition to covering the wound, the clumped-together platelets instigate a second, slower healing process by releasing biochemically potent substances into the plasma. Blood plasma, like blood itself, is not just a simple liquid: It is a rich organic stew, packed with many types of sugar, fat, mineral, and protein. One of the last is known as prothrombin. The prothrombin in blood plasma reacts with the substances discharged by platelets to create something called thrombin. In turn, thrombin interacts with another material, fibrinogen, to make fibrin, a ropy, fabric-like material that makes a scab on top of the massed, clumped-together platelets. Hematologists refer to the whole complex chain as the "coagulation cascade."

Every shaving nick, pinprick, or scratch thus sets into motion not one but two linked mechanisms: platelet aggregation and the coagulation cascade. The first quickly covers the wound with a thin barrier of stuck-together platelet cells. It also sets into motion the second, which more slowly builds a thick cover (or, as doctors say, forms fibrin) atop the platelets. The bleeding quickly stops, and the wound slowly closes over, forming a scab of the type that adorns the skinned knees and elbows of small children. Plugging up and healing a broken blood vessel is called hemostasis, and orderly hemostasis is essential to human life.

A clot can grow inside an intact blood vessel, however, in which case doctors refer to it as a thrombus, from the Greek word for lump. (The plural form is thrombi.) Thrombi sometimes form in an artery when the vessel wall cracks and exposes the subsurface, which can be caused by atherosclerosis. Or they can appear in a vein when the blood flow loses speed, a condition that occasionally afflicts patients confined to bed following surgery or injury. Like clots, thrombi are created by platelet aggregation and the coagulation cascade. But despite these similarities, thrombi are such distinct creatures, with their own causes and habitual means of appearance, that doctors now like to refer to them only by that term, and reserve the word "clot" for the way blood solidifies outside the body, in a test tube.

Thrombi can disrupt blood flow anywhere in the body, which is why they manifest themselves in such apparently different maladies as strokes, heart attacks, and thrombophlebitis, and why doctors refer to all three as different aspects of a single disease, thrombosis. When scientists looked for a way to prevent thrombosis, they were in essence trying to find a drug capable of doing one (or both) of two things: stop platelets from aggregating in an intact blood vessel or stop the coagulation cascade that follows platelet aggregation. But rather than deciding carefully which possibility to pursue, researchers simply ignored platelets, viewing them, in the words of a modern worker, as "a cell in search of a function." They ended up searching for anticoagulant rather than antiplatelet drugs—a fateful choice, one made by some of the best minds in medicine, and one that was not at all clearly understood by them.

One of the first anticoagulants was discovered in 1916 by a medical student at the Johns Hopkins Medical School in Baltimore, Maryland. Jay McLean spent his first year at Johns Hopkins on research to determine the active agent in cephalin, a compound in the brain that previous researchers had learned was capable of clotting blood. Dropped into a vial of liquid blood, it started coagulation within seconds. McLean passed the year refining the laborious steps needed to obtain samples of cephalin: mashing up bits of animal brain, spreading the mash on a sheet of glass, drying it over a gas flame, immersing the dried matter in a solvent (ether), concentrating the dissolved extract, and treating the concentrated, dissolved extract with a chemical (alcohol) that made it dribble in solid form to the bottom of a test tube. The end product had a powerful clotting effect on test tubes full of blood. (Again, the effect is known as clotting because the blood is in a test tube; if McLean had been able to test his compound in a living vein, he would have been trying to create thrombi.)

McLean decided to extract what he thought was a cephalin mixture from pieces of liver and heart. He found that all three types of extract—brain, liver, and heart—gradually lost their coagulating power when exposed to air. To see if there was any difference among them, he uncovered a test tube containing each one and measured how quickly the extract lost the ability to induce clotting. The liver sample surprised him. Its clotting power fell to zero—and then to less than zero. After contact with air, the liver extract somehow acquired the capacity to *increase* the time blood took to clot.

McLean had discovered the anticoagulant now called heparin, from *hēpar*, the Greek word for liver. Heparin is used so routinely by heart surgeons today that they talk of "heparinizing" patients. At the time, however, W. H. Howell, McLean's research supervisor, did not believe that his student had discovered a kind of cephalin with a reversed clotting effect. He asked McLean pointedly if he had not contaminated his samples of cephalin. To prove his claim, McLean placed a beaker of heparinized blood on Howell's desk. With it were instructions to call McLean when the blood clotted. It never did.

McLean wanted to pursue his discovery of heparin, but after graduating from medical school he was too busy with patients to do so. As often happens, the professor took over his pupil's work and published the first article about heparin. In those innocent days, medical researchers rarely tried to profit financially from their discoveries, and neither man patented the anticoagulant; instead, Howell gave his techniques to a small pharmaceutical company, Hynson, Westcott, & Dunning. But making cephalin was expensive, and the firm never improved on Howell's methods. It limped through almost ten years without making a dime on the drug.

Howell's heparin was not just costly, it was horribly impure—far too toxic to test on people. "The stuff killed every animal we put it in," recalled Wright, who was then a young research physician. "We didn't dare shoot it in anybody." Only in the mid-1930s did Charles Best, a Canadian doctor, produce heparin pure enough to consider trying it on humans. Doctors cautiously administered it to terminal cancer patients with thrombophlebitis. They were going to die anyway, and it seemed worth the risk. Heparin didn't kill them. But researchers still hesitated to heparinize patients who might otherwise survive—the substance had killed too many animals.

Wright was the first in the United States to use Best's heparin on human beings. Born in 1901, Wright graduated from Cornell University Medical College in New York determined to spend his life in research. "I talked with a wise M.D.," Wright said recently. "He said, 'Go into a field nobody knows anything about. In a few years, you'll be the expert.' " Tall, amiable, bespectacled, Wright continues to exude the confidence of a successful doctor at the age of eighty-nine. Retired from Cornell medical school, where he had spent most of his teaching career, Wright's baritone voice still booms commandingly; his Upper East Side apartment is covered with testimonials from colleagues across the world. He had followed the advice of the wise M.D. and done very well.

Wright had directed his attention to the flow of blood in the tiny veins called capillaries. He learned that smoking seemed to plug up these veins, and could even induce a gangrenous condition called Buerger's disease. Exploring Buerger's disease led him eventually to embolisms (the blockage of an artery by a clump of material, often a broken-off piece of thrombus, floating in the bloodstream) and then to thrombosis in general, which at the time was not a particularly important medical specialty. "When I first got to medical school the average span of life was forty-seven," Wright said. "You don't have many people who live long enough to die of a heart attack if half the population dies before forty-seven." (Indeed, the first official identification of coronary heart disease as a specific clinical entity occurred in the 1929 revision of the *International Lists of Diseases and Causes of Death*, a standard medical reference work.) He was working on the wards in Manhattan's Bellevue Hospital, and perhaps two of the sixty beds in each long room would be occupied by somebody with heart disease. (Today, he said, it might be fifteen or twenty.)

Wright's experiments with emboli stopped in the spring of 1938, when he was felled by appendicitis. After the operation, he developed thrombophlebitis in both legs. At first hand, he learned just how painful this condition is. The only treatment was being wrapped in warm towels. He had a 103-degree fever for three months, and lost forty pounds. Most of the time his legs were hoisted above his head. Even when Wright was released, he could barely move. Resting at the beach on Fire Island, he had to crawl into the water. He was lucky to be alive.

Back at the lab that fall, he was visited by a fellow thrombophlebitis sufferer, Arthur Schulte. The scion of a family of cigar store owners, Schulte was the most remarkable case study in thrombophlebitis that Wright ever encountered. The condition was galloping across his body, migrating from vein to vein. Schulte was in agony; it was as if every limb were on fire. He would certainly not survive. Wright called Best, the Canadian heparin researcher. "He came with a little vial that was almost the world's supply of heparin," Wright said. "We gave it drop by drop for sixteen days, and he survived, and was in very good shape for quite a while."

Despite this and other success stories, heparin was at first not a successful therapy. The drug was expensive, with a typical daily dose costing about ten dollars; it could then only be administered intravenously; and its effects did not last long, which meant that patients had to be hooked up every day to the IV stand. Something cheaper and easier to administer would be needed for anticoagulant therapy to prove its worth. "We knew the principle," Wright said. "But we were absolutely without a clue as to what was the right drug."

Without knowing it at the time, Karl Link had joined the quest for the right anticoagulant drug when his interest and pity were engaged by the farmer with the dying cow. Link was not flying blind. Two years before, in 1931, agricultural scientists in North Dakota had demonstrated that the uncontrolled bleeding from sweet clover disease was apparently due to a lack of prothrombin, the initial step in the coagulation cascade. But to cure the prothrombin deficiency, Link needed the ability to measure the problem— that is, he had to be capable of evaluating the amount of prothrombin in a given sample of blood from a given test animal. This was by no means easy. Different animals have different normal levels, and the tests in any case were unreliable. Before beginning the real research, Link and his colleagues ended up working for five years to devise a measurement test that they felt was trustworthy, and breeding a standardized strain of rabbits as laboratory subjects.

Link's research followed two paths: in the first, he tried to find the cause of the disease; in the second, he looked for something to counteract the prothrombin deficiency created by the disease. Oddly, the second journey was finished before the first. At the time, it was known that a diet low in vitamin K, which is made by the liver, reduced the blood's ability to coagulate. Prothrombin also is made by the liver. Increasing the amount of vitamin K in the diet, Link's team conjectured, might counteract the effects of spoiled sweet clover. Early tests on rabbits, however, were disappointing.

Late in January 1939, H. A. ("Campy") Campbell, one of Link's junior researchers, was sent to an upstate farm to look at an outbreak of sweet clover disease. "What Campbell saw and experienced [there]," Link said later, "would stir the heart and mind of any agricultural chemist." An entire herd was dying. The farmer was particularly worried about his bull, which was so sick that it might not survive taking a blood sample. Campbell carried with him the source of vitamin K used in their experiments: green, fragrant, buttery alfalfa extract, stored in crocks during many months of work. Receiving permission from the farmer, he began ladling the stuff into the mouth of the bull. The bull gobbled up the alfalfa extract, and was on its feet late the next day.

Campbell was elated. He had administered what was in effect a massive dose of vitamin K to the bull—and found a cure for sweet clover disease. Even if vitamin K failed to cure rabbits, the researchers had at least found the cure for sick cattle like those of Ed Carlson. (Not until later did they learn the reason for the different results: Vitamin K deficiency does not have a significant effect on rabbit prothrombin.)

Although the search for a cure was over, Link's team continued along the other path, sorting out what was in the spoiled clover. The rotting cattle feed was, in Link's words, "a biochemical grab-bag," filled with scores, if not hundreds, of compounds that had to be individually isolated and catalogued. The evaluation was endless and complex. It was not until the early hours of June 28, 1939, that Campbell at last trained his microscope on the cause of sweet clover disease: 3,3'-methylene bis(4-hydroxycoumarin), or dicumarol, as it was later named. That morning Link entered his office to find Campbell asleep on the couch in his clothes. The door to his lab was guarded by Campbell's assistant, Chet Boyles, a WPA relief case. Link later reported the scene:

> As I walked into the room, Boyles was taking a nip from the contents of a bottle whose bottom layer consisted of carpet tacks, the upper layer of 95 per cent ethanol. Without the flicker of an eyelash Boyles said, "I'm celebrating, Doc. Campy has hit the jack-pot." (As though I didn't know he had been hitting that bottle for months.) . . . Campbell avoided me for 2 days—until the results of the assay were available— and then he came in to report.
>
> There is a bed-rock of matter-of-fact common sense in Campbell's makeup. He was not inclined to show his emotions, but it was apparent that he was secretly as happy as a boy who had just caught his first big fish. He passed the vial to me and said, "This is H.A.!" (H.A. was the laboratory code for hemorrhagic agent.) I did not disclose that Boyles had given me the tip-off. I told Campbell that I knew a couple of lines of German poetry that fitted the occasion, and I recited to him.

> *"So halt' ich's endlich denn in meinem Händen*
> *Und nenn' es in gwissen Sinne mein."**

Nine months later, the team determined the molecular structure of dicumarol, and learned that it was created when coumarin, the compound that gives sweet clover its lovely smell, combines with oxygen and formaldehyde, which occurs when clover spoils. They published their first article in October 1940, six and a half years after Link was forced to tell Carlson to drive back through the blizzard. The search for an antidote to sweet clover disease had

---

* So at last I hold it in my hands/And call it mine.

produced vitamin K, which was soon synthesized and made widely available. But the more important discovery turned out to be not the cure, but the cause: dicumarol.

When word came out of the discovery of a new anticoagulant, medical researchers like Wright practically snatched it from Link's hands. Link himself was not unwilling; he helped sponsor a series of conferences on the new drug. But before dicumarol could be widely employed as a medicine, someone had to make it and someone had to test it. Link handled the first hurdle himself, by quickly giving the right to patent dicumarol to the Wisconsin Alumni Research Foundation, an independent body that funded scientific research at the University of Wisconsin. After applying for a patent in 1941, the foundation licensed three drug companies—Abbott Laboratories, Eli Lilly & Company, and E. R. Squibb and Company—to produce what all sides hoped would be a highly successful drug. (It was.)

By the time dicumarol worked its way through the patent office, tests on humans had already begun. Two questions had to be resolved. First, did dicumarol inhibit coagulation in human beings? Second, if it had that effect, did dicumarol actually help sick people?

Soon after Link's discovery, the initial question was answered. Edgar V. Allen, a physician at the Mayo Clinic in Rochester, Minnesota, and H. R. Butt, an associate at the clinic, were among the first to ask Link for some dicumarol. After receiving a supply in March 1941, a clinic associate tested it on dogs. Encouraged by the results, Allen, Butt, and J. L. Bollman, another clinic staffer, began with what today would be regarded as unseemly haste to shoot it into people. On May 9, no more than ten weeks after first getting a sample in their hands, they administered intravenous dicumarol to a healthy volunteer whom they described as "an organically sound young man who was 19 years old and who weighed 80 kg [176 lbs.]." Normally, his blood took 3.5 minutes to coagulate in the test tube. By the third day of treatment, the time had shot up to more than 11 minutes; after the fifth and final dose, it increased to 13 minutes. The young man showed a near-complete absence of prothrombin. Concerned about the possibility of bleeding, they stopped treatment and protected their volunteer from injury while the dicumarol wore off. After twenty days, his prothrombin level and coagulation time had returned to normal. Allen and his compatriots published their data in June 1941. Other medical reports soon confirmed that dicumarol was an effective anticoagulant, although it was slower acting than heparin. It could be taken orally, unlike heparin, and cost only a few cents a day. Now the second question had to be answered. Would dicumarol help with the myriad ailments caused by thrombi?

One of the first doctors into the fray was Wright. Again, one of Wright's first patients was Schulte, the victim of galloping thrombophlebitis. Wright gave the drug to Schulte at home, and again the results were dramatically positive. Indeed, every time Schulte stopped taking dicumarol, his condition flared up again; in 1991, he was still on the drug, or a chemical relative. "I've never been able to find out what it is in his blood that does this," Wright said. "He's been on anticoagulants longer than anyone else in the entire world." Schulte was lucky, in Wright's opinion. "If that had happened today, I would have had to wait two to three years for approval to give it to him. Meanwhile, he would have been long since dead."

Between 1941 and 1944 dicumarol was not available for general use; nonetheless about fifty papers on its clinical effects were published in that time. The rush of clinical research soon took on the air of a competition. Researchers raced to employ the drug on ever more serious conditions, and each new paper seemed to trumpet the pathbreaking uses to which its authors had put dicumarol. The most dramatic claims came from E. Sterling Nichol, a Florida cardiologist who jumped on the bandwagon in 1942. Nichol proposed giving dicumarol to recent heart attack victims. Giving an anticoagulant in the midst of a heart attack, he argued, would prevent the extension of the initial thrombus; continuing the therapy for several days after the attack subsided would lessen the chance of subsequent thrombi, especially within the heart, where damage to the tissue elevated the chance that another would form. Such a thrombus does not present a grave danger in itself, but it tends to break apart, sending pieces—emboli—into arteries, raising the chance of a second heart attack or a pulmonary embolism (the blockage of an artery in the lungs).

Nichol's proposal raised a furor. Acute heart attacks bring on clammy skin, vomiting, convulsions, and unbearable pain. The standard treatments, often ineffective and never curative, were oxygen, to aid breathing; digitalis, a sometimes toxic preparation of crushed foxglove leaves, to slow the pulse; and medieval-style bleeding, which was thought to reduce the pressure on the heart. Survivors felt somewhat better after a while, but were likely to have a damaged heart. They were, in other words, still very sick. For this long-term damage doctors could do little but recommend bed rest—and prayer. Even if anticoagulants were developed with heart attacks in mind, many cardiologists flinched at the thought of pumping powerful drugs into such desperately sick people. In June 1943, Nichol nonetheless began to use dicumarol in cases of acute heart attack. He reported increased survival rates at a meeting of the Miami Heart Association in October of the following year. Few believed him. Such meddling into crises could not possibly do good. Nichol persisted anyway. In June 1946 he published an account of treating forty-four heart attacks with dicumarol. "The probability is strong," he wrote, "that dicumarol was effective in reducing the immediate mortality rate."

Provoked, more researchers tried dicumarol on heart attacks. Some reports seemed to confirm Nichol's findings; others did not. Wright, for one, was initially skeptical. By October 1945, however, he had given dicumarol to seventy-six patients immediately after a heart attack, and their progress had turned Wright into an enthusiastic proselytizer for the drug, though he was long confused about the dosage. "Edgar Allen and his group at the University of Wisconsin came up with the recommendation that the average dose would be 350 mg a day," Wright said. "We used that. They reported no bleeding. We had quite severe hemorrhages. We couldn't understand why the same dose produced problems. Later we found out they were treating otherwise healthy midwestern farmers, and we were treating alcoholics with liver disease. Well, liver disease interferes with vitamin K [which counteracts dicumarol]. But we didn't figure that out until much later—there were so many sides to the story."

Doctors didn't know what to make of the contradictory findings. Most of the heart attack studies had fewer than one hundred patients, not enough to rule out the uncertainties of diagnosis, let alone the simple play of chance. With a new therapy for preventing some of the worst killers of modern life at stake, it was time to mount a much larger effort to establish, once and for all, whether dicumarol was effective.

When a new drug is discovered in the laboratory, its effects sometimes can be predicted from studies conducted *in vitro:* "in glass," which is to say, in a test tube. But often the effects observable *in vitro* are not the same as the effects *in vivo,* or in a living creature. Then researchers have little recourse but to give the drug to a human being without firmly knowing whether it will cure or kill. For centuries, doctors viewed such experimentation as unethical: the Hippocratic oath enjoins them to "give no deadly drug to any." The injunction did not prevent physicians from trying experimental treatments. But pharmaceutical advances came from the cautious use of new drugs mixed with intense observations of their effects on individual patients. (Of course, some doctors were less cautious, as the rush to test dicumarol slowed.)

This was not enough. As every doctor learns, people differ astonishingly in their reactions to individual diseases and treatments. If Felix Hoffmann, who rediscovered acetylsalicylic acid, had first given ASA to one of the small number of people who are deathly allergic to it, he would likely have stopped immediately, never passing the drug on to his supervisors. Pharmaceutical history might have been changed, and certainly the history of Farbenfabriken Bayer. Responding to such worries, scientists have figured out ways to reduce the likelihood that chance will play such a determinant role. Because human beings cannot be manipulated like test tubes full of chemicals in a laboratory, medical researchers have slowly put together methods to perform clinical trials: experiments that compare a set of patients given an untested treatment with another group given a standard treatment (or no treatment, if that is the standard). The first group is customarily referred to as the treatment group; the second is the control group.

The use of clinical trials goes back at least to the days of James Lind, a Scottish ship's surgeon who investigated possible cures for scurvy in the eighteenth century. At the time, scurvy ravaged the oceans; Lind estimated that in the Seven Years' War, 1,512 seamen had died in actual battle, while 133,708 were lost to desertion or disease, much of which was scurvy. He decided to investigate possible cures.

> On the 20th of May, 1747, I took twelve patients in the scurvy, on board the *Salisbury* at sea. Their cases were as similar as I could have them. They all in general had putrid gums, the spots and lassitude, with weakness of their knees. They lay together in one place, being a proper apartment for the sick in the fore-hold; and had one diet common to all, *viz.*, water-gruel sweetened with sugar in the morning; fresh mutton-broth oftentimes for dinner; at other times pudding, boiled biscuit with sugar, etc.; and for supper, barley and raisins, rice and currants, sago and wine, or the like.

Lind divided the twelve sailors into six groups of two and added different supplements to the diet of each pair: vinegar; seawater; apple cider; "elixir vitriol" (diluted sulfuric acid); garlic, mustard, and horseradish; and citrus fruits. Ten of the twelve men fared no better, but the two who ate oranges and lemons suddenly and visibly improved. After six days, one was well enough to return to duty; the other, Lind wrote, was "the best recovered of any in his condition; and being now deemed pretty well, was appointed nurse to the rest of the sick." Citrus fruits, Lind concluded, cured scurvy.

Lind was right—but he was also lucky. His trial was too small to ensure that the luck of the draw hadn't given him one pair of seamen with unusual inbred resistance to scurvy, or some other quality that would distort the results. In other words, he could not prove that he was right and that the two men's cure was due not to a happy accident, but to the curative powers of oranges and lemons.

Such concerns are by no means pedantic. Captain James Cook, the famous English explorer, conducted experiments on scurvy at about the same time. He examined only one treatment, however, and had a sample not much bigger than Lind's. He gave all of his sick men malt, and they got well. Malt cures scurvy, his ship's doctors proclaimed. But they were sailing in tropical waters, and the men were eating the local fruits—including, of course, oranges and lemons. Because Cook did not have a control group, he had nobody who was *not* eating malt, and thus he missed the chance to observe that the control group too got well, and that therefore malt could not be the answer. Sadly, the renowned Captain Cook prevailed over the unknown

Lind. Malt, not citrus fruit, was made a part of the standard shipboard diet. Many sailors died. The mistake was only corrected fifty years after Lind's experiment. Eventually British sailors were given so much citrus fruit to eat that they acquired the nickname of "limeys."

Clinical trials can only give good answers when there is a clear comparison between two (or more) groups. During the first half of this century, most clinical trials consisted of volunteers taking a new treatment. The results were then compared with patients who did not volunteer for the treatment, or with doctors' records of patients they had treated in the past. But this type of comparison though better than none, can still be unfair. There can be differences between the volunteers and the non-volunteers; people who sign up for an untested treatment might, for example, be more desperately sick than those who do not. Or they might be less sick—it is easy to imagine either scenario. Similarly, the care given to people today might differ from that given in the past. It makes little sense to claim that people suffer fewer infections with a certain drug if they are being compared with patients in hospitals fifty years ago, when sanitary regimes were not as good.

Thus the best way to perform a trial is to have a distinct treatment group and a distinct control group and to ensure that their members are alike in all respects but one: whether they receive the new treatment. The ideal way to achieve this goal is randomization, which involves allocating patients arbitarily to the two groups—the physician has no voice in the matter. Indeed, the physician should not even know which patients are in each group. A simple means of randomization is flipping a coin: heads, the patient is assigned to the treatment group; tails, the patient is assigned to the control group. Differences may still arise between the treatment and control groups, but at least they will be due to chance, not to the influence of a doctor who believes, perhaps mistakenly, that some patients might be better off in one group or the other.

Allowing chance to determine the treatment of a patient seems to deny the *raison d'être* of the medical profession. How can doctors not step in and make decisions when a patient is sick? And, indeed, they fought the notion. Physicians resisted randomization with particular violence, some specialists say, because allowing chance to reign implicitly admits ignorance—and doctors as a rule hate to confess that they don't know what to do.

Tales of medical opposition to adopting strict randomization are legion. One doctor recounts the story of a day in medical school when a visiting surgeon gave a lecture on the successful results coming from his test of an experimental technique. After describing how well the trial was going, the surgeon, a proud and eminent man, entertained questions.

A young student at the back of the room timidly asked, "Do you have any controls?" Well, the great surgeon drew himself up to his full height, hit the desk, and said, "Do you mean did I not operate on half the patients?" The hall grew very quiet then. The voice at the back of the room very hesitantly replied, "Yes, that's what I had in mind." Then the visitor's fist really came down as he thundered, "Of course not. That would have doomed half of them to their death." God, it was quiet then, and one could scarcely hear the small voice ask, "Which half?"

In some cases, such haphazard methodology was acceptable. Penicillin, for example, cures almost all cases of pneumococcal pneumonia within days, if not hours. The effect borders on the miraculous—sick people seem to leap like Lazarus out of their beds. Many years and many false starts were required for penicillin to move from the laboratory bench to the hospital room. But once there, as Richard Peto, a British expert on clinical trials, put it, "No act of genius was required to see that penicillin worked."

Coronary disease is different. Some heart attack victims recover completely. Others appear to recover but months later are felled by another heart attack. Thus if heart patients take a drug and seem to get better, doctors cannot say with certainty that the treatment was effective. Perhaps they might have risen from their beds anyway. Or, worse, perhaps the drug might actually hasten the onset of a second heart attack. When the course of a disease is so variable, the efficacy of a potential cure is not easy to discern— as the first dicumarol researchers discovered.

Most scientists who examined dicumarol gave it to small groups of patients and compared the results with what they had seen in the past. Dicumarol seemed to be a substantial improvement. But they didn't *know*. Treatment for heart disease was in a state of constant change—how could one truly be sure of what was a valid comparison? The American Heart Association decided it was time for a definitive clinical trial. Recently the AHA had changed from a professional society, which it had been since its creation in 1924, to become a voluntary organization that raised funds for research on heart disease. It was looking to make an impact. Anticoagulants seemed an obvious way to do that, and it handed the task of evaluating them to its Committee on Anticoagulants, which was led by Irving Wright, one of dicumarol's greatest advocates.

Asked by the AHA to put together a big clinical trial, Wright moved with dispatch. Encompassing sixteen medical institutions, the AHA experiment enrolled more than a thousand people who entered the hospital with acute heart attacks. Patients admitted on odd-numbered days were assigned to the treatment group, and those admitted on even-numbered days went to the control group. The work began early in 1946.

In December 1947, Wright issued a striking preliminary report. Twenty-four percent of the control group, but only fifteen percent of the treatment group, had died—a reduction of more than one-third. The AHA did not wait for the final results to issue this recommendation: Anticoagulants should be used in all cases of acute heart attack unless there were definite reasons not to. Wright traveled the country, trumpeting the virtues of dicumarol and his study. ("Anticoagulant therapy," he told the New York Academy of Medicine in October 1948, "should be used in all cases of [heart attack] unless a definite contraindication exists.") With the AHA putting pressure on doctors, sales of dicumarol shot upward. In 1952 Wright became president of the American Heart Association, not least because of his performance of the anticoagulant trial.

Wright's glowing evaluation was soon challenged. In 1951, after Wright's committee updated the American Heart Association study, David Rytand, a medical researcher at the Stanford University Medical School, noted a peculiar feature of the sample of patients. There are 186 odd-numbered days and 179 even-numbered days in a 365-day year. If the AHA study had randomly allocated its 1,031 patients, the expected sizes of the treatment group (admitted on odd days) and control group (admitted on even days) would have been 526 and 505, respectively. The numbers in the study, however, were 589 and 442—a discrepancy that could happen by chance, Rytand calculated, less than once in a thousand times. What had happened?

In their final account of the study, a massive eight-hundred-page volume stuffed with charts and tables, Wright and his colleagues admitted that doctors already convinced of the virtues of anticoagulants had insisted on switching some patients from the control group to the treatment group. But the AHA insisted that this practice had not distorted their findings. Yes, they said, the allocation of patients had not been truly random. Yes, doctors had snuck some people into the hospital extra quickly "to bring as many as possible under the odd-day deadline." And yes, members of the treatment group not only were hospitalized earlier but tended to come from wealthier backgrounds, which meant they had more private nurses, and could afford better care. But that made no difference. In fact, Wright argued, only the extreme punctiliousness with which he had worked made it possible to know about these irregularities at all—proof of the soundness of his methodology.

Rytand never disputed the care taken by the AHA committee. He simply said that without randomization at the beginning, all the care in the world could not produce valid data. He had spotted flaws in other studies of anticoagulants too. In one study, heart attack patients given anticoagulants had a 16.7 percent death rate; similar, untreated patients had a 40 percent death rate. Conclusive proof of the power of anticoagulants? Rytand didn't think so. Before the introduction of anticoagulant therapy, patients who entered that same hospital with heart attacks had a death rate of only 26 percent. This meant that whereas the death rate among patients treated with anticoagulants was lower than the past rate, the death rate among patients *not* treated with anticoagulants was *higher* than the past rate. "One might conclude that a new prognostic factor has been found," Rytand wrote sarcastically in the *Annals of Internal Medicine*. "The prognosis for a patient with [a heart attack] is worse when anticoagulants are given to someone else!" Something strange was happening, and Rytand did not think Wright's study was reliable. Others disagreed; a few years later, Wright was awarded the Albert Lasker Award, the highest honor in U.S. medicine, for his role in the spread of anticoagulants.

Rytand's worries gained credibility in 1957 from a devastating analysis from G. E. Honey and S. C. Truelove, two physicians at the Radcliffe Infirmary in Oxford, which was to become a leading center for the study and performance of clinical trials. Reviewing the outcomes for heart attack patients admitted to the infirmary over the previous fifteen years, Honey and Truelove found that the use of anticoagulant therapy had increased dramatically during that time. Between 1940 and 1947, nobody had been given anticoagulants; between 1948 and 1951, a little more than a third of the patients received them; and between 1952 and 1954, this treatment had been given to three out of every four. In those fifteen years, death rate among patients who took anticoagulants (23 percent) was dramatically lower than among patients who did not (48 percent). An extraordinary benefit, or so it seemed.

Honey and Truelove then examined the three periods separately—and found a startlingly different picture. Between 1940 and 1947, when doctors treated almost no one with anticoagulant therapy, the death rate from heart attack was 40 percent. That figure, Honey and Truelove decided, was the normal death rate from untreated heart attack. Between 1948 and 1951, with dicumarol just coming into use, 27 percent of the patients treated with anticoagulants died, a readily apparent improvement. But the death rate for *untreated* patients increased to 45 percent. And in the third period, between 1952 and 1954, with anticoagulant use climbing, the treated death rate fell to 21 percent, while the rate among untreated patients soared to an appalling 66 percent. "The only likely explanation," Honey and Truelove wrote, "is that the patients not given anticoagulants included an increasingly high proportion with a bad prognosis." In other words, those who got dicumarol were those who were likely to survive anyway.* When this predilection was taken into account, the two concluded, "the extensive use of anticoagulant therapy has not made a dramatic difference to the fatality-rate of [heart attack] in this hospital."

---

* Why didn't those doctors give anticoagulants to the seriously ill? It is impossible to say at this distance, although one can speculate that cardiologists felt it not worthwhile to inflict a treatment on people who were soon going to die.

The analysis by Honey and Truelove helped undermine the unquestioned support for anticoagulants, and advocates and critics of their use in heart attack patients battled each other for the next two decades. The clinical evidence gathered from other conditions fueled the debate. In their article, Honey and Truelove noted that the use of anticoagulants did have one unassailable effect: It eliminated all but a few deaths from pulmonary embolisms in patients who had suffered a heart attack. Anticoagulants also reduced the incidence of deep-vein thrombosis—thrombi in deep-lying veins, usually in the legs—in patients following surgery. Yet after early hope had been raised for the use of the drugs in stroke, careful reviews of the clinical trials found grave errors in randomization and other procedures; the few trials that met with approval showed no effect.

It was hard to see why anticoagulants had such wildly varying outcomes. All of the conditions were caused by thrombi. So why shouldn't anticoagulants work against the recurrence of a heart attack or stroke, which was usually brought on by a thrombus? What was the missing step? Why were patients dying from unwanted coagulation when science had uncovered a drug that stopped coagulation in the laboratory time after time?

CHAPTER SIXTEEN

"BREAK YOUR CODE"

In 1950 Lawrence L. Craven, an eye, ear, and nose specialist from Glendale, California, a suburb of Los Angeles, sent a note to the editor of the *Annals of Western Medicine and Surgery*, the sort of minor medical journal that accepted advertisements for "radon ointment." Craven's report was a striking departure from contemporary scientific prose; clear and straightforward, it eschewed the passive voice and revealed its author exactly as he was—a talented family doctor with a shrewd eye and a knack for speculation. Craven was a tall man with slightly thinning hair and steel-rimmed glasses; he wore discreetly patterned bow ties that even then had the air of an earlier time. Raised in a family of devout Episcopalians from Truro, Iowa, he had spent his adult life treating the ailments of affluent, middle-aged Californians and their children. Despite the formal demeanor that ran in the family, he was a curious man, a good listener who actively sought ways to improve the lot of his patients. For several years, Craven wrote, he had prescribed Aspergum, a chewable form of aspirin, to alleviate the pain of tonsillectomies. Several of his patients bled badly a few days after the operation. Some bled very badly—they had to be hospitalized. After further questioning, he learned "that in every instance of severe hemorrhage [bleeding] the patient had not only chewed the four sticks of Aspergum per day as ordered but had purchased an additional supply, consuming up to 20 sticks" a day, the equivalent of fourteen regular-strength tablets of aspirin.

To Craven, this pattern suggested that aspirin reduced the blood's ability to form thrombi. If this was true, he wondered, would aspirin cut the chance for a heart attack? He found suggestive a difference between men, notoriously vulnerable to heart disease, and women, who fell victim much less frequently.

That the coagulation time of the blood may become shorter as certain individuals grow older is suggested by the progressive decrease in nosebleeds as well as in bleeding from shaving wounds which I, and no doubt other men, have experienced between youth and middle age. . . .

However, only a small percentage of the many overweight middle aged and elderly women in the American population die of coronary thrombosis [heart attacks].* A possible explanation of this apparently contradictory evidence is that women frequently use aspirin to relieve minor discomforts while men hesitate to employ such allegedly effeminate methods.

Based on this reasoning, Craven had begun advising middle-aged men to swallow two to six tablets of aspirin a day. "More than 400 have done so," he wrote, "and of these, none has suffered a coronary thrombosis. From past experience, I should have expected at least a few thrombotic episodes among this group."

Craven continued to urge aspirin on his friends and patients, though he dropped the dose to one or two tablets a day. Many of the men were obese, and most were wealthy enough to eat frequently in expensive restaurants. They were, Craven noted, "tailored" for heart disease. "Surely the practice [of taking aspirin] could do no harm," he wrote later in the equally obscure *Mississippi Valley Medical Journal*. "It might even prove lifesaving." Almost nobody but his patients paid attention.

That ASA might affect blood was not new. Even before aspirin was rediscovered by Felix Hoffmann, Carl Binz, director of the Pharmacological Institute at the University of Bonn and the author of a classic textbook on pharmacology, noted reports of excessive bleeding in people who took salicylic acid, aspirin's chemical cousin. Over time other doctors observed the same phenomenon, and a few letters made their way to medical journals, which published them in the small print reserved for such interesting, if apparently useless, observations. Among surgeons, aspirin's ability to stop the thrombi that often appear after an operation grew into medical folklore— "the sort of thing," the stroke specialist William S. Fields said recently, "that old, experienced surgeons told me when I was an intern in the thirties." Patients seemed to prosper after operations when they had aspirin. "You gave them a pill," Fields said, "and things seemed to work out better. In any case, what was the harm?"

Although many practicing doctors knew at least vaguely of aspirin's anticlotting power, their colleagues in research labs, remote from the hurly-burly of patients and appointments, let Binz's remarks grow moldy in his

* A note on terminology. "Coronary thrombosis" is technical language for the formation of thrombi in the blood vessels around the heart (the coronary system, so called because it circles the upper heart like a corona). Coronary thrombosis can cause myocardial infarction (death of heart tissue). Strictly speaking, people die from the latter, rather than the former, and doctors mean tissue death when they speak of a heart attack. In the past this distinction was not always observed, and many doctors used heart attack, coronary thrombosis, and myocardial infarction interchangeably.

collected works. Scientists spend their lives generating knowledge, but are often too busy to learn their predecessors' discoveries; consequently, they are forever reinventing the wheel—unless, as happened this time, chance intervenes. The exception came in the form of a copy of Binz's 1891 lectures on pharmacology that traveled across the Atlantic with Eugen Schoeffel, who subsequently went to work for Karl Link. Link, who was proud of his German, read through the old, stiff pages. Six years later, in 1940, Link and his co-workers completed the chain of coincidence when they found that their newly discovered dicumarol broke down in the test tube to salicylic acid. "I recalled distinctly," Link wrote later,

> that Binz had written that when salicylic acid is given to certain individuals suffering from rheumatic fever, it causes hemorrhage from the mucous membranes. It did not take very long to find this statement again. I then checked the literature from the time of Binz and found an impressive number of entries on salicylate poisoning in which hemorrhage was noted. . . . I reasoned that it is possible that the delayed action of Dicumarol [that is, the relative slowness with which the drug showed its anticoagulatory effect] might be due, in part at least, to its breakdown in the body to salicylic acid.

In January 1941, Link tested both aspirin and sodium salicylate on himself. Both decreased his blood's supply of prothrombin, the initial step in the coagulation cascade, with aspirin having a greater effect than sodium salicylate. That spring one of Link's assistants fed salicylic acid to rats. Again the drug decreased the coagulability of blood. Again, aspirin had a stronger effect than salicylic acid. Indeed, it was a more powerful anticoagulant than any of the sixty other salicylates tested. In the spring of 1943, a spate of papers from Link's group confirmed these results for humans. In each study, big doses of aspirin—twenty or more tablets a day—were needed to alter the blood.

Although Link dropped his research on the salicylates and returned to dicumarol in the mid-1940s, he urged doctors to pay attention to the anticoagulant power of salicylates—not as beneficial therapy, the hope that had been held out for dicumarol, but as something that presented a grave and ever-present danger. As he warned at lectures:

> Almost eight million pounds of acetylsalicylic acid (equivalent to the carrying capacity of 57 standard hopper coal cars) were consumed in the United States in 1943. It would be interesting to know to what extent the use and abuse of this analgesic contributed to hemorrhage not ascribable to the ordinary recognized causes.

Vitamin K, the "antidote" to sweet clover disease, should be considered to counteract this danger, Link proclaimed, although perhaps "the dietary habits of John Doe and bacterial action in his intestines" were already doing the trick.

Link's discoveries provoked alarm in the medical press. "Is Aspirin a Dangerous Drug?" wondered the *Journal of the American Medical Association*. Aspirin's ability to reduce the coagulability of blood, *JAMA* warned, meant that doctors should no longer consider it safe. Incredibly, the next page of the journal contained an editorial that trumpeted the possible benefits of dicumarol—because of its ability to reduce the coagulability of blood.

Focused on the latest anticoagulants from the laboratories, few researchers noticed the possible use of an old therapy. One exception was Paul Gibson, a little-known English physician who in 1948 discussed the need to fight thrombosis in a letter to the *Lancet,* a major British journal. Dicumarol was steadily gaining favor as a treatment for heart attack, Gibson said, "but its dangers are not yet fully understood." After delivering the standard warning about salicylates and increased bleeding, Gibson made a nonstandard recommendation. "We might," he said, "use salicylic acid for the treatment of coronary thrombosis: it could do no harm and might well do good."

Following his own advice, Gibson gave aspirin to two patients with thrombophlebitis. Before taking aspirin, one had hardly been able to leave her room for three months; after a fortnight of large daily doses of ASA, she could walk and felt much less pain. Gibson called for "a more extensive trial of aspirin in coronary disease."

Unknown to Gibson, such a trial was already under way by the time his ideas appeared in print: the work of Lawrence Craven. By 1953, Craven had put almost fifteen hundred male patients on aspirin; three years later, the number had grown to eight thousand. Among those taking aspirin, Craven wrote, "not a single case of detectable coronary or cerebral thrombosis has occurred among patients who faithfully have adhered to this regime." Even the nine men who apparently died from heart attacks, he said, had been found by autopsy to have ruptured arteries, or, more technically, aneurysms. Therefore, Craven proclaimed, "aspirin administration offers a safe and sure method of prophylaxis against thrombosis." In sum: An aspirin a day keeps heart attacks away.

The response to Craven was less than overwhelming—few doctors read the *Annals of Western Medicine and Surgery* or the *Mississippi Valley Medical Journal* with attention. A suburban M.D. writing in unfashionable journals about a field outside his specialty, Craven was not a member of the club. But the rejection was more than simple snobbery. Because Craven had set out to prove what he already believed; because he could offer no reason *why* aspirin stopped thrombosis; because he didn't make sure his patients actually took the aspirin; because he had no control group of patients who didn't take aspirin; because he didn't present his results in a rigorous form; because he made definite conclusions from incomplete data—for all these reasons, researchers pointed out, Craven's work was, scientifically speaking, invalid.*

Craven's ideas sparked brief interest in the cure-of-the-month section of the popular press but were ignored by members of the medical establishment, who were busy jumping on the bandwagon for dicumarol. (When his study was rediscovered thirty years later, one aspirin expert scoffed that it "could scarcely be dignified with the descriptive term 'clinical trial.'") Unable to interest others in advancing his work, Craven devoted hours to giving interviews to newspapers and posing for photographers with his wife, Mabel, and their daily ration of aspirin. The case for aspirin was not helped when the seventy-four-year-old Craven died in 1957. He dropped dead, quite suddenly, while driving back from a visit with his niece. The cause of death was a heart attack.

Given that millions of lives might have been spared if the medical world had heeded Craven and Gibson, it is tempting to believe that the scientists of the day were outright fools. Certainly their reluctance to treat ASA as a serious drug—stop the West's greatest killer with the pain reliever doctors recommend most?—bespeaks a prejudice unbecoming to supposedly objective savants. True, they were preoccupied by the inexplicable discrepancy between the promise of anticoagulant therapy and what it produced in the clinic. Still, one might ask, in all the hullabaloo over anticoagulant therapy, how *could* they have missed aspirin?

The state of cardiovascular knowledge was summarized in 1961 by John C. F. Poole and John E. French, two pathologists at Oxford. Their article in the new *Journal of Atherosclerosis* pulled together the existing research on thrombosis and found good reasons why anticoagulant therapy not only did not but *should not* work against a heart attack. The enthusiasts for dicumarol, Poole and French observed, simply did not understand the most basic facts about blood.

Since the nineteenth century, hematologists had known that blood solidifies into lumps of platelets and fibrin, mixed with the red and white blood cells that got themselves entangled along the way. The way these lumps were built up, they knew, depended on whether they were formed in a blood vessel or in a laboratory test tube. In a test tube, blood hardens into a haphazard mass of fibrin and platelets, trapping a lot of red and white blood cells. The picture changes in living blood vessels. Platelets come first, adhering to the

---

* From today's perspective it seems possible that Craven fudged his data. "Eight thousand men at risk of a heart attack and not *one* got hit with one over a period of many years?" scoffed William Fields, the stroke specialist. "Impossible! No treatment is that good! I think Craven was right, but I also think he fiddled with his results."

wall of the injured vessel at dizzying speed, and are slowly built upon by fibrin. The resulting thrombus has a precise structure. The structures come in two types, Poole and French noted, depending on whether they are formed in veins or formed in arteries. Veins are blood vessels that carry blood from the body to the heart. Blood flows slowly through them, and their thrombi resemble somewhat the clots found in test tubes. In veins, a thrombus first forms a small "white head," consisting of platelets attached to the vessel wall, and then a big "red tail" composed of red cells mixed together with fibrin. These thrombi can be quite painful, but rarely are fatal unless a piece breaks off and ends up blocking an important blood vessel.

Arteries carry blood the other way—from the heart to the rest of the body. Driven by the relentless pump of the heart, blood shoots quickly through these vessels. When a thrombus closes up an artery, the situation may be dire, especially if the thrombus occurs in the arteries that feed the brain or the heart. (The heart has its own arteries because it pumps blood to itself.) If these arteries are plugged, a heart attack or stroke may follow.

The seriousness of arterial thrombi makes them a fit subject of study, and scientists had thoroughly picked them apart before the dawn of the twentieth century. Staring for long hours through microscopes at the translucent-walled arteries of frogs, these long-ago researchers watched platelets aggregate, piling upon themselves like football players after a fumble. The mass of platelets was soft, but often it alone was enough to impede the flow of arterial blood. Sometimes the clump was broken up by the pressure of the blood-stream, the fragments sluicing through the body. Always the downy mass grew again. The cycle might repeat itself three or four times in fifteen minutes, stopping when the damage to the vessel wall was covered adequately—or when the platelets completely obstructed the vessel. Only when the artery was corked did the fibrin begin to build up and the thrombus become hard. Ultimately it had a big "white head" of platelets and a smaller "red tail." But well before the tail was formed, when the thrombus consisted solely of platelets, the damage had already happened.

This fact had profound implications for anticoagulants. When these drugs were first used in acute heart attacks, their supporters believed that lives could be saved by thwarting the growth of the existing thrombus and block-ing the creation of subsequent thrombi. Poole and French thought this was all wrong. "Obviously," they wrote, "interfering with blood coagulation can-not be expected to bring a piece of dead heart muscle back to life." More-over, it was "sheer supposition that the thrombus is still growing after the patient has suffered an infarct [heart attack]."

The only conceivable use for post-attack anticoagulants, they argued, was against subsequent thrombi. Here the difference between arterial and venous thrombi became important. Anticoagulants work by disrupting the coagula-tion cascade, preventing the formation of the cascade's end product, fibrin.

That means they can counteract the buildup of the fibrinous red tail of a thrombus but have little power against the white head of platelets. Thrombi with a higher proportion of platelets, such as arterial thrombi, would therefore be less affected by anticoagulants. Useful against clotting in veins, drugs such as dicumarol would be ineffective against the platelet aggregation that could stop the flow of arterial blood, leading to a heart attack. "From what is known about the mechanism of thrombosis," Poole and French remarked, "it is hardly surprising that measures designed only to attack the fibrin component of a thrombus should be of limited value."*

An obvious alternative, the two authors noted, was to tackle platelets. To some extent this strategy was counterintuitive, for it asked doctors to ignore the hard, lumpy constituent of a thrombus in favor of the part that was soft as yogurt. Yet the difference between a thrombus in a vein and one in an artery led inexorably to that conclusion. To prevent heart attacks, one had to stop the platelet aggregation that initiated them. Here, Poole and French conceded, was a problem: "Therapeutic measures designed to attack the platelet component of a thrombus are not yet available."

The words "not yet available" gave short shrift to a complex situation. Certainly, no drugs were known to interfere safely with platelet aggregation. Bedazzled by anticoagulants, researchers had never considered antiplatelet treatments—and you can't find something you aren't looking for. But there was another, more subtle obstacle. In 1960 laboratories had no reliable technique for measuring platelets' propensity to clump together—their stickiness, so to speak. And without a good method to gauge the effects of a drug on platelets, no one could establish whether an antiplatelet drug actually worked the way it was supposed to.

Just one year after Poole and French published their article, this obstacle was overcome simultaneously and independently by Gustav Born, a hematologist and the son of a Nobel Prize–winning physicist, and John R. O'Brien, a hematologist at Portsmouth, England. Simple and ingenious, the platelet aggregometer, as their device is called, consists in essence of a test tube, a light, and a photoelectric cell much like the one in elevators that registers when passengers have entered. A researcher fills a test tube with anticoagulated blood plasma—that is, blood treated with anticoagulants and purged of red and white cells. (Red and white cells are removed by spinning a test tube full of blood around until the cells migrate to the bottom; the plasma is then

---

* In hindsight, Poole and French went too far in denigrating the effectiveness of anticoagulant therapy following heart attack, but were accurate in their assessment of the clinical trials designed to test this. Between 1948 and 1975, researchers conducted twenty-six nonrandomized and seven randomized trials. (The greater number of nonrandomized trials testifies to the medical reluctance to embrace randomization.) The nonrandomized trials found an average mortality reduction of 53 percent. Randomized trials showed an average reduction in mortality of 20 percent—not a universal panacea but still a useful weapon in the medical arsenal.

poured out into another tube.) The researcher shines the light through the tube and onto the photoelectric cell, which registers the light falling on it. Because the platelets are still in the plasma, they screen some of the light. Next, a chemical is added that induces aggregation. When the platelets stick together, they make soft little lumps that drift to the bottom of the test tube, and more light shines through. Charting the level of the light thus measures the degree of aggregation. With the aggregometer, researchers suddenly had a tool to measure the effect of the body's myriad of effusions on platelets. (Luckily, platelets stick to one another *in vitro* much as they do *in vivo.*)

Among the many researchers who found the device useful was Harvey J. Weiss of the Mt. Sinai Hospital and School of Medicine in New York City. A specialist in bleeding disorders, Weiss used the new device to learn that patients with long bleeding times often had abnormal platelet aggregation as well. "In reading through the literature," he said later, "I found out that normal people who took aspirin often had mild bleeding problems, even in standard doses." The reason wasn't known; it was just another one of medicine's curious facts. Weiss was intrigued. "I thought aspirin might produce the same platelet defects I was looking at. So I did the study, and found that aspirin did similar, though not identical things."

With Louis M. Aledort, Weiss measured platelet aggregation in the blood of men who had taken aspirin. In an experiment of exemplary clarity, Weiss and Aledort found that people who had consumed an aspirin tablet were likely to bleed three minutes longer from a pinprick than people who hadn't eaten one. They had no notion of why aspirin should affect platelets. But they did recognize, in an apparently offhand remark, the possibility inherent in their result: Aspirin, they wrote, "may have antithrombotic properties."

The aspirin-platelet paper, Weiss said dryly, "was apparently not one of those discoveries that get ignored." Within a year, three separate teams of researchers confirmed and expanded it. "People were *fascinated,*" Weiss said. "It seemed incredible that aspirin could have been doing this under their noses for all those years."

The pieces had fallen into place, and researchers were ready to consider the notion that aspirin might be an antithrombotic drug. One of the first such suggestions came from John O'Brien, the co-inventor of the platelet aggregometer, who had independently discovered that aspirin blocks platelet aggregation. O'Brien knew Poole and French; like them, he had become convinced that platelets might be the key to preventing heart attacks. In the early 1960s he tried dozens of chemicals on platelets. "I was looking for an antiadhesive compound with no side effects," he said. "Actually, I was just looking to alter platelet behavior in any way to see if I could learn something." He even ran a small clinical trial—the world's first—on one anti-platelet agent. (The drug had no effect.) Many compounds, including cocaine, could prevent aggregation. But, as with cocaine, there were indications that these compounds might be therapeutically undesirable. When he came across aspirin, he was delighted. More positively than his American colleagues, O'Brien argued that the effects of aspirin "are not only of great academic interest; they could be of therapeutic value since aspirin medication might alter the course of thrombosis."

O'Brien communicated his enthusiasm about aspirin to a researcher named Peter Elwood at a congress in Munich. Tall and craggy with a snub nose and shrewd brown eyes, Elwood was raised in Northern Ireland, and went to Wales after earning his M.D. He was quickly frustrated by the uncertainty of medical practice: It seemed to him that much of what he was doing for patients was ineffective, and that treatments were often used solely because they had been used in the past. "I asked myself," Elwood said not long ago, "did I want to spend forty years of my life on this? Forty years of always working in the fog? Or did I want to tease out a few *certain* things?" A university class in epidemiology had intrigued him, and he elected to look into it further.

An epidemiologist studies the pattern of a disease across groups of people in a hunt for its cause. (In contrast, a clinician studies disease in individuals.) In the past epidemiologists have looked for linkages between, say, cholera and sources of water, smoking and lung cancer, and, more recently, toxic-shock syndrome and the use of tampons. But although epidemiologists continue to seek correlations between matters such as diet and coronary disease, or cancer and exposure to low-level radiation, they have increasingly moved beyond gathering information in such passive ways. Many now spend their time on clinical trials.

Elwood was hired as an epidemiologist in 1963 by the Medical Research Council, which has funded much of British clinical investigation since the 1920s. He was sent to Cardiff, Wales, where the MRC had taken over a rickety dwelling in an old residential area that was owned by a local medical school. There, in offices overlooking a grim stretch of town, Elwood set out to develop a program of study.

A common joke of the time said that all epidemiologists got their start in spit. For years respiratory diseases—tuberculosis, chronic bronchitis, and the ailments caused by smoking—had been the stock-in-trade of the field. "I didn't want to stay in spit too long," Elwood said. "So I became interested in heart disease." Hoping that the composition of individuals' blood might indicate their likelihood of suffering cardiovascular problems, he measured levels of hemoglobin and iron in thousands of Welsh. While examining these questions, he heard about platelets at Munich.

"The thrombus cuts off the blood supply to the heart," Elwood said over the course of a long conversation. "The lack of blood damages the heart tissue—that's why it's called 'myocardial infarction,' which is medical Latin for 'death of heart tissue.' Well, the origin of the clot is almost always pure platelets. That's been known for a very long time. If platelet aggregation is the mechanism, then an epidemiologist immediately asks, What in our diet or behavior affects that? In those early days, the clearest thing known—we'd just found it out—was that aspirin inhibited aggregation. So I picked up aspirin as a tool, not as a prophylactic drug. I wanted to modify the platelet mechanism to see what would happen to the outcome, and then from there I wanted to find the determinants of platelet aggregation, the ultimate dietary and life-style determinants.''

Elwood's interest in aspirin coincided with that of the Medical Research Council. In May 1968, O'Brien spoke about aspirin and platelets to the MRC Committee on General Epidemiology. The MRC formed a subcommittee to investigate the implications of his findings and ways to test these implications. O'Brien's first choice was to look at aspirin's effect on heart attacks. But he could not persuade the MRC to fund such a radical idea, and reluctantly settled for a trial with deep-vein thrombosis. Ultimately, he found aspirin had no impact, which puzzled him; he was sure that aspirin would have "profound implications for the prophylaxis of coronary, cerebral, and peripheral artery disease." Still, he couldn't complain too loudly. The council's refusal to go farther was not simply an example of hidebound thinking. Testing aspirin—or any drug—as a heart attack preventive was exceedingly difficult, and everyone knew it.

On an annual basis, perhaps 1 in 220 people in the Western world suffers a serious heart attack. To get a sample size big enough to evaluate aspirin, the MRC would need to enroll tens of thousands of people in the trial, assuming that a few score would suffer heart attacks. Such an experiment would cost a staggering amount—not a welcome prospect to the perpetually underfunded MRC.

Elwood came up with a simple means to reduce the trial to a manageable size. Older men who have already had a heart attack often fall victim to another. Indeed, according to Elwood, the rate of heart attacks among members of this group—elderly male heart attack survivors—is about fifteen to twenty times the rate of first heart atttacks. A trial using survivors of first heart attacks would still need to be large, but it was doable.

Elwood turned to Nicholas Laboratories, makers of Aspro, for funding. Nicholas was no longer the wild company of the days when it advertised, with happy disregard for the facts, that Aspro was made from "thousands of tiny . . . antiseptic units which cling to the lining of the throat," killing the germs that cause the dreaded "Khamseen throat." Now Nicholas was a much more sober operation. A coldly economic decision would have been to turn Elwood down. "There was no possibility of Nicholas making any money," explained Ross Renton, then group medical director for the firm. "You

couldn't patent aspirin for that indication [heart attacks].'' Any positive findings would perforce apply equally to the products of other aspirin makers.

The company still had a soft spot in its corporate heart for its oldest
product, however. Bernard Martin, then head of the pharmacy section, had
long worked on mathematical models of the body's absorption of aspirin and
other drugs. After work, Martin spent the evening watching television, drinking coffee, and scribbling out complex calculations of pharmaceutical interactions. ''He collected his own urine all the time to see how drugs broke
down in the body,'' Renton said. ''One time he was out trimming his roses
with a timer so he could collect a sample of his urine every hour. When he
went to the garage, the neighbor said, 'Dr. Martin, you must be terribly
disciplined. You've been timing how much of the rose bed you do every
hour!' ''

When the MRC first broached the notion of examining the effects of
aspirin, Martin, Renton, and Sir Richard Nelson, the company medical director, met over coffee to decide whether Nicholas should help out. ''We felt
a moral responsibility to do something about it,'' Renton recalled. ''But we
couldn't spend huge sums of money.'' Little time was required for the three
men to realize that senior management would never approve the huge expense necessary to mount a trial on first heart attacks. Elwood's modest
request for supplies of specially prepared capsules of aspirin and matching
placebo was a different matter. Nicholas approved a small budget without
hesitation. The trial began in February 1971.

Elwood called six local hospital wards every Monday morning to get the
names of recently discharged male heart attack victims, and then visited these
men at home. To his exasperation, many prospective members of the trial
had been exposed to the anti-aspirin campaign of Panadol, Sterling's British
acetaminophen brand, and thought Elwood was trying to foist off a dangerous drug. ''I had difficulty persuading them it was a serious trial,'' Elwood
recalled. ''People would look wide-eyed at me. 'Aspirin? Doesn't that cause
bleeding?' '' Eventually he found enough patients willing to suspend disbelief, and his trial quietly proceeded. The patients took aspirin or a placebo,
one capsule a day.

Elwood's trial was ''double-blind,'' which means that to avoid uncon-
scious bias neither he nor the subjects knew which people were taking aspirin
(the treatment group) and which people were taking a placebo (the control
group). To ensure ignorance, the capsules were identical in size, color, and
taste—not a simple matter, because it called for Nicholas to set up a special
production run to make blank capsules and packages. Independent of Elwood, another researcher kept track of which patient got what, assigning a
number to each packet of capsules, with a code that related a packet to its
identity, aspirin or placebo. Elwood therefore did not know whether aspirin
was working or not. Barred from tracking the central question of interest, he

spent his time exclusively on enrolling patients, collecting data on heart attacks and deaths, and mailing out pills. It was a great deal of not terribly interesting work. In this way a year passed.

A phone call one Saturday morning in the spring of 1972 jolted him out of his routine. Herschel Jick, an American epidemiologist whom Elwood had never met, wanted to know if he was conducting a controlled trial of aspirin. When Elwood said yes, Jick asked in an urgent tone if he could fly to Wales, and have a meeting the next day. Elwood agreed, and Jick hung up without disclosing the reason for his anxiety. The mystified Elwood could do nothing but speculate until Sunday morning, when he picked up Jick, jet-lagged from the overnight flight, at the airport.

Jick had been collecting data on patients admitted to hospitals in Boston, matching their sicknesses to the drugs they used. By comparing sixty drugs and sixty conditions, he hoped to find correlations that would suggest new ties among them. He hit the jackpot. Patients who were diagnosed as having a heart attack had a lower chance of having taken aspirin prior to admission. To Jick, this meant that people who took aspirin might have a lower chance of having a heart attack. Not just a little lower, he told Elwood. An amazing *80 percent* lower. The taking of the drug apparently had a gigantic protective effect against heart attacks.

But there was another, more counterintuitive possibility, one that frightened Jick. The figures would come out exactly the same way if aspirin did not reduce the incidence of heart attacks but instead drastically increased their deadliness when they occurred. The chain of logic was complicated, but could not be ruled out. If aspirin somehow raised the likelihood that heart attacks would be fatal, aspirin-taking victims would be more prone to die quickly. They would thus rarely live long enough to make it to the hospital and be examined by a member of Jick's team. Therefore most heart attack victims who survived a sufficient time to make it into the study would be those who had not taken aspirin. The data fit this scenario, too, because it ensured that patients who had not taken aspirin would be those who ended up in the hospital. Jick could not exclude this second possibility. Asking around if anyone was studying aspirin and heart attacks, he learned from a visiting Englishman about Elwood's trial, the only one in the world. Jick had called Elwood immediately.

That afternoon Jick, Elwood, Peter Sweetnam, the experiment's statistician, and Archie Cochrane, the unit director, met in a state that was almost giddy with excitement and anxiety. If Jick's first hypothesis—aspirin reduces the chance of a heart attack by 80 percent—was correct, Elwood might be in a position to wipe out the most important killer in the Western world. "We seriously discussed what would happen to all the cardiology care units that were springing up," Elwood said. "They would be museum pieces, because [heart attack] would become a thing of the past."

That was one possibility. If Jick's second hypothesis—aspirin was fatal to heart attack victims—was correct, however, Elwood would be helping his experimental subjects into an early grave.

In Cochrane's recollection, the MRC unit asked Jick, "What do you want us to do?"

"Break your code," Jick said.

Breaking the code meant "unblinding" the study: learning whether each patient was taking aspirin or placebo. Because of the many examples of bad, unblinded experiments that had accumulated since the days of the AHA anticoagulant trial, unblinding was a cardinal sin in clinical trials. It would forever cast doubt on the data, and a year of work would be wasted. On the other hand, what if the scientists were murdering people? "It put us in a terrible dilemma," Elwood later recalled. "Should we break the code or just continue?"

In the end, there was no real doubt. They could not continue if there was any chance that they were killing the subjects of their experiment. That same day, the code was broken. The two groups were of roughly equal size, but there had been six deaths in the aspirin group, and eleven deaths in the placebo group.

Under the lens of statistical analysis, these figures appeared in a confused light. The difference was big enough to rule out the possibility that aspirin was a killer. But it was not enough to conclude that Jick's 80 percent benefit was truly present. Not yet having the power to confirm or deny Jick's results, Elwood's now-tainted trial had to continue.

A few weeks later, Elwood, Sweetnam, and Cochrane were summoned to London to meet at MRC headquarters with a contingent from the United States. The secretary of the MRC sat in on the discussion, as did the most eminent epidemiologist in Britain, and possibly the world, Sir Richard Doll. Several dozen people were in the meeting room, recalled Renton, who attended. "The doors were locked," he said. "People were told that this was highly confidential and not to be reported outside the room. They were afraid that leaking [Jick's data] to the press before we had sorted it out would mislead the public dreadfully. And the Americans really were in a quandary."

The Americans had asked for the meeting largely because Jick did not know how to proceed. Elwood's early results had not supported his study unequivocally. That might be because Jick's numbers were a fluke. Or it might be merely that Elwood had not yet collected enough data, and his first few results were unluckily not indicative of the whole. If Jick released his study to the public, headlines would fly all over the world. But what if Elwood eventually found that he was wrong? The Americans proposed a swap: Jick would postpone publishing his work if Elwood would rapidly enlarge his trial and let Doll secretly monitor its results.

After hearing his superiors unanimously recommend the Americans' proposal, Cochrane was told that the final decision was up to him, as the local
MRC director. He recalled:

> I already knew that a decision not to cooperate would be difficult. The
> Americans had argued their case well and, despite a curious gut reaction
> against messing about with Peter Elwood's carefully designed trial,
> somewhere in the back of my mind I could hear that old saying of my
> stepfather's, "You can't fart against thunder."

The test was expanded throughout southwestern Wales and into three English
cities. Doll agreed to monitor the data as they came in, so that the trial could
be stopped if a strong beneficial or negative effect appeared. Ultimately, the
original patients in Cardiff made up just half of the final study. Months passed
while Elwood chewed his fingernails and the evidence slowly piled up.

A constant danger in running a clinical trial or any other experiment is getting
results that are neither good nor bad—numbers that might be the result of
luck and therefore meaningless. Because luck can never be completely excluded, investigators have developed a rule of thumb to establish whether the
probability that the data are due to chance is low enough to make them worth
considering. If this probability is smaller than some arbitrary number, usually
5 percent, the experimental findings are declared to be "statistically significant." Above this level, the likelihood is too great that other, contrary
results could have turned up instead.

The test of statistical significance places tough constraints on researchers.
In effect, it tells scientists that to remove the element of chance they will not
only have to demonstrate whatever effect they seek to prove, but they will
also have to demonstrate it so many times that it is nearly certain that the
results are not due to the duplicitous hand of Dame Fortune.

Such a test will be more easily passed if the number of patients in the trial
is large and if the trial takes place over a long time. If the investigator is
looking for changes in a comparatively rare event, like heart attacks in
previously healthy people, the trial will have to be very large indeed and take
place over many years to have a hope of producing a statistically significant
result. Such gigantic efforts are expensive, and in the past experimenters
have shied away from them—a reaction that many now regard as a mistake.

Elwood was well aware when he planned his aspirin study that he would
have to collect a lot of patients. In retrospect, he didn't know exactly how
many he would have to find. By the time his trial ended in September 1973,
he had recruited 1,239 patients, about one-quarter more than he had initially
intended. In the thirty-one months of the experiment, 108 men died, 61 in the

placebo group and 47 in the aspirin group. The numbers were in aspirin's favor, but unfortunately they were not statistically significant. The trial had not been big enough.

Moreover, there was a bizarre difference between the results from the half of the patients in Cardiff and the half from outside the city. Aspirin takers in Cardiff showed a 35 percent reduction in mortality. But outside Cardiff aspirin slightly increased the death rate. Elwood suspected that many subjects from more distant hospitals hadn't taken their aspirin, confusing the outcome. Suspicions, however, are not proof. His report thus had to conclude with the galling words "The results of this trial were inconclusive." To Elwood's irritation, the *British Medical Journal* published his work, together with Jick's study, under the rubric "for debate."

In a way, Elwood was relieved that the data had *not* been more favorable to aspirin. "If we'd got a statistically significant result," he said, "we would have felt we couldn't set up another trial. Because it was insignificant, we *had* to do another trial."

In the meantime, he basked in the interest provoked by the publication of Jick's study and his own work. "The results got quite a lot of reaction," said Elwood, "mainly surprise that such a simple humble drug might have such an effect." Elwood went to Korea, Mexico, and Germany to talk about aspirin; at home, he began to set up a second trial. It took four dull years. Doing a thing for the second time is no fun, Elwood learned. Alas, this trial too was inconclusive. Aspirin seemed to reduce mortality by 17 percent— important, but not big enough to rule out chance. He tried a third time, varying the mix slightly. Now he contacted doctors and asked them to give sachets of aspirin or placebo to patients who were apparently in the midst of a heart attack. The idea was that aspirin might shrink the clot while it was still growing, and save some lives. "It's cheap, simple, and easy," Elwood said. "And [in that trial] it was totally ineffective. It's a crying shame, and I don't honestly know why not." As far as Elwood was concerned, that was it. He'd tried three times to learn whether aspirin could stop heart attacks. Each time he had failed to produce convincing evidence.

He had also lost his steady source of funds. Around 1975, a worldwide economic downturn occurred, and Nicholas had bad years in many countries. "The yes-men became no-men," Renton said. "They looked at the bottom line." The company no longer had the resources to launch an ethical product, even if aspirin should become one. "The board sat down and closed down all of our ethical research overnight," Renton said. "It was all done in secret behind locked doors in my clinical unit. People came into the conference room, were told what had happened, and as they went out the door were handed an envelope with a pay slip and a notice." Renton resigned; aspirin research at Nicholas was out of the picture for a while.

Others took up the slack. Intrigued by the evidence that aspirin stopped clotting, half a dozen researchers in Europe and the United States got government funding for trials; some went further, boldly declaring that aspirin should be taken daily by "men over the age of twenty and women over the age of forty" in the hope that this would lessen the incidence of heart disease. Those who chose to test this wisdom in a clinical trial found, like Elwood, tantalizing evidence that ASA reduced heart attacks. But, like Elwood, they could not put together data that passed the test of statistical significance. Aspirin seemed to be on the verge of becoming, so to speak, the next dicumarol.

The obvious solution was to conduct a study so big that chance would be relegated to playing a very small role in the results. This strategy produced the Aspirin Myocardial Infarction Study (AMIS), which ultimately examined more than forty-five hundred U.S. patients. Begun in 1975, the three-year, $17 million experiment was sponsored by the U.S. National Heart, Lung, and Blood Institute, a division of the National Institutes of Health, which in turn is a sister agency to the FDA. It included men and women between the ages of thirty and sixty-nine. Those in the treatment group took one gram of aspirin—equivalent to three regular-strength tablets—every day. Patients were asked to report to a clinical center at four-month intervals for the duration of their participation in the experiment. (The trial ended in August 1979.) To determine whether they were complying with their designated treatment, the center performed a platelet-aggregation test and measured the salicylate level in their urine. The results, of course, were kept from the investigators until the end of the trial.

When AMIS published its conclusions in 1980, they produced dismay: In the aspirin group, overall deaths were actually somewhat *higher* than in the placebo group. Aspirin takers had a third fewer nonfatal heart attacks, but the difference was not statistically significant. "The fact remains that in terms of [mortality]," the study reported in the *Journal of the American Medical Association,*

> AMIS found no benefit from aspirin. This trial is the largest completed and published investigation of aspirin [and heart attacks], and more weight must be given to its results. . . . They clearly indicate that the regular administration of aspirin in this dose does not reduce three-year mortality in patients with a history of [myocardial infarction]. In summation, based on AMIS results, aspirin is not recommended for routine use in patients who have survived a [heart attack].

"We were disappointed by the results," Robert I. Levy, director of the National Heart, Lung, and Blood Institute, the trial's sponsor, told a reporter. "We thought we had a potential winner." A few quibbles could be made about whether the aspirin was given to patients soon enough, he admitted, but the conclusions from AMIS were clear. "On the basis of these findings," Levy told the nation, "the National Heart, Lung, and Blood Institute would advise physicians not to give aspirin on a sustained basis to heart attack patients as a means of preventing another [heart attack]."

AMIS, in the view of most researchers, had settled the question. Aspirin did nothing for heart attacks.

CHAPTER SEVENTEEN

"I THINK I KNOW HOW ASPIRIN WORKS. DO YOU?"

Karl Link and his Wisconsin associates discovered dicumarol, but never learned why it slowed coagulation. Harvey Weiss and other hematologists were in much the same position when they found that aspirin inhibits platelet aggregation. Their research answered one question but raised another: *How* did aspirin stop platelets from aggregating, thereby stopping the formation of most thrombi? By the time AMIS revealed its equivocal conclusions, the answer to this question had been found along a line of research wholly independent of that being followed by Weiss and Elwood. Pharmacologists, who study the effects of drugs, at last stepped forward to explain the mystery of aspirin. In the process, their research solved a host of other puzzles: why aspirin and dicumarol have different effects on the blood, how aspirin produces stomach irritation, and why it reduces fever and soothes headache pain. Indeed, some laboratory scientists now believed that aspirin *must* prevent heart attacks, which gave a powerful boost to those few doctors who did not believe the negative words flowing from the National Heart, Lung, and Blood Institute.

On the grand scale, science seems to advance with slow, inexorable logic. But on the level of individual discoveries it is as higgledy-piggledy as running a business, or any other human endeavor. Science moves in fits and starts—a pleasant surprise here, a startling setback there—its discoveries often coming out of the blue, from the most unexpected people. Aspirin is a case in point. Its function in the body was not unraveled by the Baconian progression, observation to hypothesis to experiment to theory, taught in high school textbooks. Nor was the puzzle fit together by physicians, whom one might expect to study the drug used more than any other by their patients. (Indeed, they largely ignored aspirin.) Nor, finally, was it investigated by the companies that profited from its sale, despite what one would imagine to be their desire to mine all knowledge about their own products. Aspirin's primary mode of action was uncovered by someone who had paid almost no previous attention to it. Little wonder that the discovery was a surprise to almost everyone in the drug world, scientist and salesman alike.

In some ways, the seven-decade delay between the discovery of aspirin and the explanation of its workings is unsurprising. Aspirin was a hard problem. Paradoxically, it reduces fevers but has no effect on people with normal temperatures—as if an ice cube chilled your fingers only if your temperature were higher than normal. It relieves pain but, mysteriously, is not an anesthetic. And it soothes inflamed joints but leaves normal joints untouched. How does aspirin "know" how high the body's temperature is, whether pain is already present, or which joints are inflamed? Researchers didn't have a clue. They didn't even know whether aspirin acts peripherally, at the site of an injury, or centrally, blocking the ability of the brain and central nervous system to feel pain. "The Wonder Drug Nobody Understands," the *New York Times Magazine* called it in 1966.

The *Times* was only half right. Nobody understood aspirin then, but the process of unlocking its secrets was well under way. Eight years before, Harry Collier, a pharmacologist at the British subsidiary of Parke, Davis & Company, a drug firm based in Detroit, had quietly begun to examine its effects on guinea pig lungs. Initially an intellectual hobby, aspirin came to preoccupy and even obsess Collier until his death in 1983. Collier was the first scientist of outstanding ability to investigate aspirin's workings. His prescience cost him dearly; the researchers who arrive in a field earliest often appear before the harvest of discovery is ready, and spend much time in arduous work only to see the fruits of their labor plucked by Johnny-come-latelies.

Born in 1912, Henry Oswald Jackson Collier was a dryly witty man with lean, impassive features and one of those astonishingly complete prewar classical educations. He graduated with highest honors in zoology and chemistry at Cambridge, and sprinkled his writings and his speech with literary and historical allusions. He "was interested in hundreds of things," one obituary wryly noted, "science and medicine amongst them." Blessed with an extraordinarily retentive memory, he knew French, Latin, painting, and poetry, and was forever writing scripts about medicine for television and radio. "Harry was meticulous in everything, especially the English language," recalled Priscilla Piper, a former colleague. "If somebody sent him a letter with a grammatical error, he would correct the letter."

After earning his Ph.D., Collier taught at the University of Manchester until 1941, when the need to support a family—his second child, Joseph, was on the way—drove him into the pharmaceutical industry. At the time, scientists regarded going to work for a corporation as a mixture of slumming and prostitution. "If you went into industry," Joe Collier later explained, "you weren't an acceptable human. He may have regretted [his choice], but he didn't tell us about it."

At first Collier did wartime medical research, including the testing of penicillin. (Collier and a collaborator were probably the first to conduct laboratory tests of its effects on syphilis.) After setting up a pharmacology department for the firm of Allen & Hanburys, he moved in 1958 to Parke, Davis and set up another. There he remained until 1969, the year before the firm was acquired by Warner-Lambert, a merger-minded conglomerate. Collier was director of research for the British branch of Miles Laboratories until his retirement in 1980.

Over the years Collier's family grew to include three children, one of whom, Joe, became a pharmacologist and a prominent critic of the British drug and health care industries. Meanwhile, Collier's teams developed drugs, including dequalinium, an antibacterial, and laudexium, a synthetic version of the poison curare, which is used in adapted form as a muscle relaxant. Despite such discoveries, Collier was not a reliable producer for his employers. He never lost the overweening curiosity that is the hallmark of the pure researcher but a potential liability in a commercial setting.

Collier's work on curare led in a roundabout fashion to his fascination with aspirin. In its natural form, curare interferes with a nerve's ability to send messages to the muscles. Neural messages made Collier think of looking into the mysterious phenomenon of pain. His first work on the subject involved quite literally grasping the nettle, that classic image of pain; he isolated the chemical that gives us its sting. At about this time, several compounds called kinins were discovered. When injured, a cell releases kinins into the blood and nearby tissues. Kinins induce the symptoms of inflammation, including pain, by stimulating nearby nerve endings. If kinins create pain, Collier thought, then perhaps analgesics like aspirin have something to do with stopping them. And when he moved to his new laboratory at Parke, Davis he set out to look for himself.

With an assistant, Patricia Shorley, he spent part of 1958 ascertaining the effects of one particular kinin, bradykinin, on the guinea pig. Their experiments did not directly examine pain, but a related phenomenon that was easier to measure. When guinea pigs are injected with bradykinin, the air passages in their lungs close up—the animal has a kind of asthmatic attack. The reaction, Collier wrote later, is "powerful and prolonged." He wondered if analgesics would influence it. He learned that the bradykinin did not trigger asthmatic attacks if guinea pigs were given aspirin beforehand. Aspirin, as scientists say, inhibited the bradykinin. Interestingly, if aspirin was consumed *after* bradykinin, it had no protective capacity, and the guinea pigs wheezed for air.

Next, Collier and Shorley repeated the experiment with one different parameter. They severed the guinea pigs' vagus nerve, which reaches from the heart and lungs to the brain. This cut off communication, so to speak, between the animal's respiratory system and its central nervous system. When Collier and Shorley injected bradykinin, the lungs seized up again, although the brain of the animal could not sense it directly. Again, the two researchers gave the guinea pigs aspirin. And again aspirin inhibited bradykinin. If this occurred when the central nervous system was surgically removed from the picture, then the drug must act locally, in the lungs, rather than centrally, on the brain. Moreover, by comparing the inhibitory effect of aspirin and other analgesics, Collier and Shorley found that aspirin was many times more effective at inhibiting bradykinin than salicylic acid. In learning these facts, the two scientists had at a stroke learned more about aspirin than all their predecessors. Moreover, they had quietly unhorsed beliefs about aspirin that had ridden unchallenged since the drug's introduction by Farbenfabriken Bayer.

The first scientist to examine aspirin's effects was Heinrich Dreser, the head of Bayer's pharmacological research. Chemically, he knew, aspirin is a molecule of salicylic acid, the parent of sodium salicylate, with an acetyl group—a small, hook-shaped clump of carbon and oxygen atoms—attached to one side. The question was what happened to the drug in the body. After taking aspirin, Dreser tested his urine to learn what his digestive system had done to it. It came out as salicylic acid. From this, he concluded that salicylic acid did the work; the acetyl group only made salicylic acid more easily digestible, allowing it to slip through the stomach and into the bloodstream. In the blood, the acetyl group dropped off, and the salicylic acid relieved the pain. To Dreser, aspirin was not really a drug in its own right but what pharmacologists call a "pro-drug," a substance that the body breaks down into a drug, in this case salicylic acid.

Because salicylic acid (and other analgesics) were then thought to work on the nervous system's ability to feel pain rather than directly upon the damaged part of the body, Dreser presumed that aspirin too affected nerves in the brain and spinal cord, not those near the injury. Aspirin was therefore best regarded as a more palatable means of delivering salicylic acid to the central nervous system.

Despite the perfunctory nature of Dreser's research, his conclusions became part of medical culture, passively imbibed by two generations of physicians. (People have griped for a long time about doctors' uncritical embrace of superstition. "Even a superficial study of the history of medicine," historian George Wedekind complained back in 1791, "reveals . . . how small always the number of sages was who acted on the basis of reason which they had thought about themselves.") Now and then, researchers—like those the FTC used to refute Fortunato Diasio, the man who smeared Aspirub on sprained ankles—would be called to testify to their beliefs concerning aspirin, and usually they parroted Dreser's dogma: Aspirin was an effective means to suffuse the central nervous system with salicylic acid.

Collier's experiment with guinea pigs refuted Dreser's beliefs about aspirin. If aspirin inhibited bradykinin more potently than salicylic acid, it followed that aspirin was not a digestible packing for salicylic acid. It was a potent drug in its own right. And if it acted when the vagus nerve was severed, then it must act locally, not centrally. Two generations of physicians had been told the opposite, but they had been misinformed. It was as simple as that.

In the meantime, Collier had to justify his work to his company. "Because aspirin blocked [the asthmatic reaction]," his colleague Piper recalled, "he thought it might be useful for respiratory disease—which would let him justify his work to Parke, Davis." The company did not agree, and Collier couldn't easily continue the search. But he did not give up; he had fallen in love with the problem. "Part of his polymath," his son said, "was his love of nature. He was a botanist, and knew plants inside out. He went for walks, and couldn't go past a flower till he had identified it. Aspirin comes from willow bark—it was nature to him, and it became one of his favorite subjects." He had to sandwich in aspirin among his other responsibilities, conducting experiments when he could find time. "Parke, Davis was reasonably lenient, I suppose," Joe Collier said. "But he still had to do something for the company, and clearly they thought there wasn't going to be much money coming out of aspirin." Collier *père* seems not to have minded the slow pace unduly. Alone in a neglected corner of pharmacology, he did not have to worry about someone snatching a discovery from him.

Collier's thoughts coalesced around a single medical fact. The main conditions for which people take aspirin are pain, fever, and inflammation. All are by-products of the body's defense against sickness or injury, much as a brake produces heat in its fight to slow down a car. Aspirin, Collier reasoned, was an "anti-defensive" drug. "It would appear," he wrote in 1963, "that the human body has an unwieldy defense establishment that aspirin fortunately can help to control." Aspirin might counter such defensive reactions in one of two ways: directly, by stopping the defense itself, or indirectly, by somehow amplifying the body's control of its defenses. But which? Collier didn't have a clue.

Stepping back for the moment, Collier decided to study an assortment of drugs like ASA in a variety of biochemical surroundings. He intended to create a catalogue of their effects on substances that, like bradykinin, elicited harmful reactions. The hope was that along the way he would learn more about how all these drugs acted on pain, fever, and inflammation, and that eventually the added knowledge would lead him back to aspirin.

In each case, the experiment was the same. An assistant put the drugs in separate, coded containers so that Collier would not know which drug he was using. (After all the experiments were finished, the code was broken.) Picking one container at random, he fed the anonymous drug to guinea pigs, injected them with one of the reaction-causing substances, and waited to see if the drug inhibited the guinea pigs' response. If the drug inhibited the response, they tried to overpower the inhibition by giving the animal more of the substance. And then they did the same thing over again with another drug. And then another. And then all over again with another substance, and still more drugs.

After finishing with guinea pigs, they repeated the entire set of experiments on rats and rabbits. Puzzlingly, reactions often varied from species to species. Aspirin in particular worked in a crazy-quilt way—"capricious," Collier termed it—effective on one species against one pain agent, but not on another species with another drug. There seemed to be no pattern. Collier could not even reproduce the same results if he worked on isolated bits of tissue rather than whole animals. For example, he couldn't get aspirin to inhibit bradykinin in severed strips of guinea pig lung, although it unquestionably did just that in the lungs of live guinea pigs. It was maddening.

Despite these frustrations, he gradually developed a picture of how these drugs worked. In general, molecules of compounds like bradykinin float through the body until they come across a receptor—a molecule-sized place on the cell where they can plug in, like a key in a lock. The analogy is surprisingly exact, for the bradykinin molecule is twisted into a shape that snugly slips into the waiting receptor. To block the kinins, Collier thought, a part of the aspirin molecule must be of sufficiently similar shape to fill up the hole if it got there first. That was why aspirin had no effect after bradykinin was injected. The receptors were already occupied by bradykinin.

But the picture was certainly more complex. As researchers had seen with blood coagulation, biochemical processes take place in elaborate sequences, with one compound causing the body to release a second, which reacts with a third, which impedes the action of a fourth, thus activating a fifth, and so on. Probing the unseen choreography of such complex subcellular dances was an agonizingly slow business.

In 1963 Collier began to work with Priscilla Piper, then a doctoral candidate. After being awarded a B.Sc. in physiology at the Royal Free Hospital Medical School at the University of London, Piper decided against going into medicine—she had allergies—and switched to a program in pharmacology, in which she was sent to work at a commercial laboratory: Parke, Davis. At first she was intimidated by the brilliant supervisor who behaved toward her with such cold formality. Then she realized Collier was as scared of her, a woman in a lab at a time when few women entered labs, as she was of him.

Despite their mutual timidity, they began to work together, and in the way of graduate students she was drawn into her supervisor's quest for the secret of aspirin.

Their work, Piper said later, was "very crude." After five years of pushing drugs at guinea pigs, she and Collier realized they were at a near-standstill. They had a general idea of what aspirin did, but were unable to elicit any of the details. One reason for the frustrating failure was that nobody at the Parke, Davis lab knew how to employ the specialized techniques necessary to do the job. Collier and Piper were working with live animals, which meant, of course, that they could not see exactly what was taking place inside. To gauge the course of reactions, they had to kill the guinea pigs, remove the lungs, and grind them up for testing—a procedure that inevitably disturbed the delicate biochemical interactions they wanted to observe, and in addition took so long that some short-lived compounds disintegrated before they could be examined. They needed a better method.

Collier and Piper turned for help in 1968 to John Vane, a pharmacologist who soon came to play a much larger role in the enterprise than anyone anticipated. Bearish, balding, inclined to stoutness, Vane was not, at first, interested in aspirin at all. Born in 1927, he was raised in Worcestershire, England. Like that of many scientists, his interest in research was awakened by the present of a chemistry set from his parents. After many messy experiments he entered the University of Birmingham in 1944. He quickly learned that his interest in chemistry was not so great as he had thought. When one of Vane's professors suggested that he look into pharmacology, the student agreed on the spot. Afterward, Vane recalled, he immediately went to the library to find out what pharmacology was. It sounded interesting, and he got his Ph.D. in the subject in 1953. By 1968 he was running a laboratory at the gray, overcrowded Royal College of Surgeons in London. He had known Collier long enough for the two men to develop a friendly rivalry.

Collier wanted Vane to teach Piper a special version of the bioassay, which is the principal technique of pharmacology. "The pharmacologist," said John Henry Gaddum, one of the founding fathers of the discipline, "has been a 'jack of all trades' borrowing from physiology, biochemistry, pathology, microbiology and statistics—but he has developed one technique of his own, and that is the technique of bioassay." Bioassay—the name is short for "biological assay"—determines the activity or identity of substances by measuring their effects on a biological test system. In simplest form, it consists of exposing a strip of tissue to a chemical compound and waiting to see if the tissue reacts, by flexing, turning color, releasing chemicals, or whatever. Such measurements are of paramount importance in the development of drugs, but the technique is useful in many other areas as well. "With extraordinary simplicity and convenience . . . ," Vane once wrote, "bioassay distinguishes between the important biologically active compounds and their closely related but biologically unimportant [descendants]."

A few years earlier, Vane had developed a novel way of examining exactly the sort of subtle entities that concerned Collier and Piper. He immersed two sets of tissue in a trickling flow of chemicals, one upstream of the other. The flow of chemicals most often was Krebs' solution, a neutral medium, somewhat like blood plasma, named after Sir Hans Adolf Krebs, a Nobel Prize–winning biochemist. The upstream tissue, such as guinea pig lung, was injected with a substance that threw the tissue into anaphylactic shock—a deadly allergic reaction that is a stronger version of an asthmatic attack. (To induce shock, Vane frequently used egg white, to which, as it happens, guinea pigs are allergic.) In shock, the upstream tissue secreted a fluid that, like the sputum from an asthmatic attack, was a biochemical wonderland of hormones, many of which researchers had never identified. This fluid entered into the wash of solution and was carried downstream, where it was channeled into several tubes. At the end of each tube was a second tissue. The downstream tissues—rat stomach, for example, or chicken rectum—were chosen for their previously known properties. A twitch from a particular sample signaled a reaction to the presence of a particular compound in the solution. Because the solution was neutral, the reaction had to come from something synthesized by the upstream tissue. Gradually Vane and his co-workers built up a chemical dictionary of the processes involved in shock. Vane would plan the day's menu of tissues, and his co-workers would prepare them, send the upstream tissue into shock, and record the results.

"Cascade superfusion bioassay," as Vane called his technique, had the advantage of allowing him to see the chemical dance as it happened, substances changing identity from moment to moment, signaled by the shifting pattern of reactions in Vane's strips of tissue. Another advantage, as Vane said, was that the method "gave maximum opportunity for serendipity." If something novel showed up, you had a good chance to grab it.

"If you had told me [at the beginning]," Vane said recently, "that this would lead to a discovery about aspirin, I would have laughed in your face." He was intent only on tracing the tangled interactions that create the biochemical environment inside the body. He was happy to show Piper how his bioassays worked. For several months, she worked part-time with Vane at the Royal College of Surgeons. The idea was that she would learn Vane's techniques and bring them back to Collier, who would use them to work further on aspirin. In addition, it was a good time for Piper to be out of Parke, Davis. The firm, Piper recalled, "was in financial difficulties because the patent had run out on something. They were firing people, so Harry asked John Vane if he would take me full-time as a Ph.D. student." Vane readily agreed. Rather than returning to Collier, Piper continued to work with Vane at the Royal College of Surgeons. It was bad luck for Collier, because Piper and Vane almost immediately found the key to aspirin.

In one set of experiments, they exposed guinea pig lungs to egg white, sending the lungs into shock. The solution passing over the lungs was then pumped over a bank of six tissues, including rat stomach, chicken rectum, guinea pig trachea, and rabbit aorta (the main blood channel from the heart). Using the lore built up from previous experiments, they added chemicals to the solution to bar the effects of every known substance that might be released by the shocked lungs. If the strips of rectum and aorta twitched, Piper and Vane thought, it would probably be a signal of something new. They got what they were looking for. Something made the rabbit aorta contract convulsively, but vanished within minutes.

Piper and Vane called that something "rabbit aorta contracting substance," and they knew right away it was like nothing they had seen before. (Their paper abbreviated the name to RCS, which, Vane noted, also stood for the Royal College of Surgeons, where they worked.) They tested to see if RCS mimicked the behavior of familiar compounds. It didn't. RCS was something qualitatively different.

Excited, Piper suggested to Vane that they try injecting the upstream guinea pig lungs with Collier's obsession—aspirin. Although the two men were friendly and knew each other's work, Vane had never thought of looking at aspirin. Still, he agreed to give it a try. What harm would be done? To Vane's surprise, the aspirin had a powerful effect. The downstream rabbit aorta did not contract at all, which meant that the shocked lungs were no longer producing any RCS. But why? And what was RCS, anyway?

Aspirin, Piper and Vane learned, did not directly counteract RCS. That is, it did not prevent the mysterious substance from making rabbit aortas twitch. But if they added aspirin to the guinea pig lung before throwing it into shock, the drug prevented the *release* of RCS. Building on Collier's suggestion that aspirin helps control the body's defensive network, Piper and Vane hazarded in the British science journal *Nature* that aspirin might indeed work by interfering with some piece of this network, and that the piece could be RCS—whatever that was.

Told by Piper about RCS, Collier was both elated and frustrated. That aspirin stopped the synthesis of this previously unknown substance seemed a fundamental clue, but he couldn't decipher it. The day after Piper and Vane finished their paper, he sent his own article to *Nature*. Published in the same issue as Piper and Vane's, Collier's paper is a curious, even painful document, an exception to the impersonality in which he usually cloaked his writing. Whereas Piper and Vane straightforwardly recounted their experimental findings, Collier had no new work to present. Rather, he reiterated his contention that aspirin is an "anti-defensive" drug, and then complained that its actions are "capricious."

Then, in what is difficult not to read as a plea for his own research, this reserved and dignified man launched into a summation of recent work on aspirin that cited his own articles no fewer than thirty-two times in five short paragraphs. His years of research, he said, had proved that aspirin acts at the site of injury, that it does not block chemicals' actions directly, and that its activity seems to depend on the particular chemical pathways by which a substance came into contact with the tissues. He pointed out that bradykinin too made guinea pig lungs synthesize RCS, and that aspirin's "inhibition of the RCS mechanism" suggested it was obstructing the action of bradykinin. If aspirin stops RCS, Collier argued, the drug's "capriciousness" might be explained—it only stops those pains elicited by RCS. But all the insights were not quite enough. With an almost audible groan of frustration, the paper concludes: "Even where aspirin acts in this way, however, the full steps of the sequence, the exact point at which aspirin blocks it and the means by which the blockade is effected have yet to be determined."

Collier went back to work on aspirin, hopeful that the secret of aspirin was close at hand. The answer would come in a moment of inspiration, but to Collier's regret the inspiration would not be his own.

Among the dozens of substances Collier, Piper, and Vane had studied was a group of several dozen fatty acids—complex loops and chains of carbon, hydrogen, and oxygen that are the building blocks of fats— known as prostaglandins. In many ways prostaglandins are like hormones. But whereas hormones are produced by single glands, organs, or types of tissue, prostaglandins are made by almost every cell in the body. At the time Collier expressed his frustration, it was known that prostaglandins produced the types of noxious effects that were being studied with Vane's bioassay method. Collier had included one (prostaglandin $F_{2\alpha}$) in his earlier experiments. He found that aspirin failed to put an end to the asthmatic effects of $F_{2\alpha}$ in guinea pig lungs, but potently stopped them in strips of human tissue. In the experiment that produced RCS, Piper and Vane found several prostaglandins that had been observed before in different contexts. Collier passed them over; Vane tarried awhile, and the secret of aspirin was his.

The first hints of prostaglandins appeared as far back as the late 1920s, when Raphael Kurzrock, a gynecologist, performed artificial insemination at a small clinic in Brooklyn. He made dozens of attempts, only two of which were greeted with any success. Along the way, however, he began to note something peculiar:

In a number of cases it was observed that when 0.5 cc. of semen was injected into the uterine cavity, the semen was promptly expelled. . . . The patient always gave the same reaction, apparently independent of the phase of the menstrual cycle. These observations led to the following question: What is the action of human semen upon the human uterus?

One patient felt sharp pain in her lower abdomen every time the insemination occurred. After listening to the woman's description of her symptoms, Kurzrock decided that the throbbing seemed much like the pain of childbirth. By this time he was consulting with a pharmacologist, Charles Lieb. It occurred to the two men that something in human semen might make the uterus contract. Having friends who were professional biochemists, they borrowed a laboratory bench and, after what one enjoyable historical essay calls "the usual trials and errors," found that dripping semen on a little strip of human uterus did indeed make the muscle contract—it twitched. Kurzrock and Lieb published an account of their little discovery in 1930. Almost nobody paid any attention.

Four years later, Ulf Svante von Euler, a Nobel Prize–winning Swedish biochemist whose father was a Nobel Prize–winning Swedish biochemist, extracted a similar substance from sheep semen. He called it "prostaglandin" because he extracted it from the prostate gland. In the next few years, von Euler did just enough work on his sheep extracts to find that his name was a mistake—prostaglandins are present throughout the body, not just in the prostate gland. When the Second World War came, he put nonmilitary research aside. At the end of the conflict, when he could think of science again, he concentrated on the isolation of a basic constituent of the nervous system, noradrenaline. (His work on noradrenaline earned him a Nobel Prize in 1970.)

Von Euler passed his carefully preserved sheep semen samples to a younger colleague, Sune K. Bergström of the Karolinska Institute in Stockholm. Bergström proved in 1949 that several types of prostaglandins exist, and that all were a previously unknown type of chemical. But it was hard to go further. Prostaglandins are present in such minute quantities that the analytical techniques for isolating and studying them had not yet been developed—as Bergström found to his cost, when he spent years futilely trying to do just that.

In 1957 he sought support from a friend, David Weisblat, an organic chemist who had become research director of Upjohn, the company that later brought ibuprofen to the United States as Motrin. Seeing the potential for exciting, patentable drugs, Weisblat induced Upjohn to finance Bergström. (At about this time, one recalls, Collier was having trouble justifying his similar work to Parke, Davis.) A grant of $100,000 enabled Bergström to collect prostates from the sheep of four nations. Tons of glands eventually yielded ounces of prostaglandins. With a colleague, Bengt Samuelsson, Bergström determined the chemical structures of two prostaglandins.

In 1964 Bergström, Samuelsson, and others discovered that prostaglandins derive from a little-known constituent of the body called arachidonic acid. Arachidonic acid is a greasy, buttery substance in the walls of cells that makes them flexible. "Without it," John Vane said recently, "you simply couldn't move. You'd be rigid as a candle." When cells are irritated, physically or chemically, the cell walls release tiny amounts of arachidonic acid— and amazing things happen.

"It's as if the body doesn't like having arachidonic acid floating around," Vane said, "because it gets changed into something else as soon as it appears." In the tumble of chemical reactions triggered by arachidonic acid, scientists found whole new families of hormonelike substances— endoperoxides, leukotrienes, thromboxanes—all of which exert powerful effects even in the most microscopic doses. Unlike hormones such as insulin, which are methodically created and stockpiled inside gland and organ cells, the entities made from arachidonic acid are produced outside cells in response to specific stimuli, such as injury. Something happens to a cell, its membrane releases arachidonic acid, and the body transmutes it into prostaglandins.

For scientists, the sudden appearance of an entire system of biochemical regulators was fascinating. They fell on it eagerly, hoping to shake discoveries from arachidonic acid like children shaking apples from a tree. They had the idea that great things could be learned, names and careers established.

Weisblat at Upjohn agreed; prostaglandins, he thought, could make his company a fortune, and he promptly set up a lab to produce them in quantity. (Before that, one researcher joked, a single sneeze "would have wiped out the world supply.") To find out whether prostaglandins had the potential that Weisblat thought, Upjohn boldly offered free samples to any scientist who wanted to study them. Matching a big supply to a pent-up demand, a flurry of scientific papers appeared.

It developed that prostaglandins are the body's way of regulating such essential phenomena as the widening and narrowing of blood vessels, the contraction of muscles, and the development of the inflammation associated with aching joints and arthritis. As the findings came in, Upjohn researchers hoped that their prostaglandins might become treatments for conditions ranging from peptic ulcer (prostaglandin A_2) to high blood pressure (prostaglandins A_1, E_1, and E_2). The potential use with the highest profile, however, was birth control and abortion. Many prostaglandins, $F_{2\alpha}$ among them, interfere with pregnancy. In the early 1970s prostaglandin $F_{2\alpha}$ was approved as a prescription-only abortion injection in the United States and Britain. Prostaglandin E_2 became an abortion suppository. Both are still sold today— quietly.

Like many others, John Vane was intrigued by the family of short-lived biochemical entities that came from the arachidonic acid in the cell wall. "John is unbelievably determined, hardworking, perceptive, and willing to run risks," Joe Collier said. "He worked every weekend, and grabbed everything that came into his hands—no wonder he was successful."

Vane and Piper were enormously excited by finding RCS, the substance that contracted rabbit aortas. "It *disappeared*," Vane said. "It chemically broke down in two to three minutes. It's only because we were using a dynamic method that we were able to detect it at all." But what was it for? What did it do? Where did it live in the biochemical jungle? What did it mean that aspirin prevented it from coming into existence? Vane and Piper worked for another eighteen months, not getting very far. In mid-1971, they decided to write a paper summarizing all the little scraps of knowledge they had accumulated.

Thinking about the paper at home one weekend night, Vane suddenly wondered if RCS might not be some kind of never-before-seen prostaglandin—one that, unlike the others, was not very stable. If that was true, aspirin would be preventing the creation of a prostaglandin in the body. And if *that* was true, aspirin might not prevent the formation of just one prostaglandin. It might stop them all. Indeed, that would be a definition of what aspirin does—preventing the body from synthesizing prostaglandin.

By this time, pharmacologists had synthesized many drugs with effects similar to those of aspirin, ibuprofen being one of the first and most famous. More than forty of these "nonsteroidal anti-inflammatory drugs," or NSAIDs, are on the market today. All of these drugs, like aspirin, reduce pain, fever, and inflammation. But how they worked was a mystery. Indeed, doctors grouped them together largely on the basis of what they *didn't* do. Unlike steroids such as cortisone, they did not mimic the effects of hormones; unlike morphine or codeine, they did not act on the central nervous system; and unlike antihistamines such as promethazine, they did not attack histamines (chemicals released in allergic reactions). Vane suspected that not only aspirin but all the NSAIDs stopped the creation of prostaglandins, and that he had therefore hit upon the mechanism of action for an entire class of drugs. Aspirin, ibuprofen, fenoprofen, indomethacin, phenylbutazone—Vane had explained them all.*

If Vane was right, he knew why aspirin affected only feverish or inflamed tissue. Injury or some other disturbance produced prostaglandins, which in turn fostered fever or inflammation. By preventing the creation of these prostaglandins, aspirin would also avert the resulting fever or inflammation. It would have no effect on normal, untraumatized tissue, where prostaglan-

---

* One drug that Vane did *not* explain was acetaminophen. Acetaminophen has little if any anti-inflammatory power, and hence is not an NSAID. Today, more than a century after its discovery, acetaminophen is the aspirin of our time—a hugely popular drug that nobody completely understands.

dins are absent. Moreover, Vane guessed that prostaglandins must therefore be related to pain—aspirin's analgesic power came from the same ability to block the appearance of prostaglandins that controlled fever and inflammation. It was all very neat. Vane was elated.

"I came in [to the laboratory]," Vane remembered, "called over Priscilla and all my colleagues and said, 'I think I know how aspirin works. Do you?' They all said no. I said, 'I am going off to do an experiment.' "

To the bemusement of his audience, Vane went directly to the laboratory bench and started mixing chemicals, a job normally left to a research assistant. To prove his notion, he would have to turn some arachidonic acid into prostaglandins, and then try to repeat the same process with aspirin in the test tube. If he couldn't get any prostaglandins, he would know that his idea was right.

"We all knew something was up," Piper said. "He *never* worked at the bench like that."

Vane had always detested this type of experiment, which involved grinding up the internal organs of guinea pigs, whirling the mush in a centrifuge to spin away the debris, dividing the remainder into twenty test tubes, adding arachidonic acid, and then measuring by bioassay the amount of prostaglandins he had produced. In fact, he didn't know exactly how to do it. But he had what he thought was an important idea, and he was not going to spread it all over the lab by asking for help from students or junior colleagues. ("That's the scientific *droit du seigneur*," Joe Collier remarked later. "The professor can do that.") Instead, he consulted some papers, and after a few stabs came up at the end of the day with a reasonable setup. He put the mash in twenty test tubes and stimulated it to produce prostaglandins. Then he added aspirin and tried to make the prostaglandins come out again. They didn't show. Eureka, Vane thought. Wherever aspirin was, he found no prostaglandins. "I got very excited," he said. "I spent the next two weeks confirming it."

One of the first calls he made was to Harry Collier, who was devastated to learn that his friend, a man who had hardly worked with aspirin, had answered the question to which he had devoted ten years of his life. "Harry was very green," Vane said, chuckling. "He just never thought about prostaglandins."

Gamely, Collier wrote a commentary lauding the discovery. But he was bitter; the discovery, he thought, was his by right. It could have been his if the lab had supported him. He had been working so long alone. He watched Vane win honors, a knighthood, election as a fellow of the Royal Society, and then a Nobel Prize. "My father went back and tried to say he was there too," Joe Collier said. "But I don't think he was, and I think he knew it. He worked in industry, so he couldn't have done what John did."

In June 1971, Vane published his aspirin paper in *Nature,* along with two other articles discussing further implications and results from his co-workers. Before the *Nature* papers were published, Collier wrote to Vane with the regret and pride of someone who had almost, but not quite, made a major discovery:

> If you prove to be, as probably you will, the Jesus Christ of aspirin, I think I may claim to be its John the Baptist.

Is the mystery of aspirin truly solved? Different scientists give different answers. Many loose ends have been tied up, but some researchers believe that real puzzles remain. According to Gerald Weissmann of the New York University School of Medicine, a past president of the American Rheumatism Association, the drug has three principal modes of action, each corresponding to a particular dosage level. All three modes are at least partly understood, but there is room for disagreement among scientists about the solidity of their theories.

First, as John Vane showed, in ordinary, over-the-counter doses, aspirin prevents the body from turning arachidonic acid into prostaglandins. It does this, we now know, by deactivating another compound, prostaglandin H synthetase, which catalyzes the reaction. Much as Collier had guessed, molecules of arachidonic acid plug into a slot in the PGH synthetase molecule, and are released in altered form as prostaglandin molecules. (The PGH synthetase is left unchanged and ready for the next molecule of arachidonic acid.)

Aspirin disrupts this procedure completely. Acetylsalicylic acid, one recalls, is made by joining two distinct chemical entities, salicylic acid and the acetyl group. After entering the bloodstream, the acetyl group slowly breaks away; what travels through the bloodstream is a mixture of ASA, SA, and A. Floating through the body, either ASA or SA easily slip into the hole in PGH synthetase, plugging it. Jammed, the PGH synthetase molecule can't produce prostaglandins. All non-steroidal anti-inflammatory drugs affect PGH synthetase, but only ASA, which has an acetyl group, has the chemical makeup to cripple PGH synthetase forever—the others, SA among them, just clog it temporarily.

Inhibition of prostaglandin synthesis, as scientists call this process, is the most thoroughly documented of aspirin's effects, and the one that is likely responsible for its most well known use, relieving headaches. Scientists think that most common headaches are linked to muscle contractions on the scalp or the back of the neck. (No one is sure, though.) Migraine headaches, by contrast, may be caused by the dilation of cranial blood vessels. Both muscle contractions and the swelling of veins and arteries are influenced by the arachidonic acid system. Aspirin's potential role is apparent; the remaining mystery is how one would prove it, given the ethical impossibility of opening up living people to study their headaches.

Alas, aspirin's inhibition of prostaglandins, apparently so beneficial for headaches, is also the source of its major side effects. The stomach lining makes prostaglandins, which help maintain the mucus coating that prevents the stomach from being chewed up by its own acids. If aspirin thwarts these protective prostaglandins, the balance is disturbed—and the result can be an upset stomach or even an ulcer.*

A similar mechanism generates allergic reactions to aspirin. When aspirin stops PGH synthetase from converting arachidonic acid into prostaglandins, a competing substance, lipoxygenase, transforms it into a whole host of other chemical entities, chiefly leukotrienes (which, among other things, constrict blood vessels and promote transfer of materials from the air passages of the lungs to the bloodstream). Some people's genetic makeup gives them a violent allergy to their own leukotrienes, and these people should not take aspirin, ibuprofen, or any other NSAID.

In high, prescription doses, aspirin has a second effect: relieving the redness, swelling, heat, and pain of inflammation. Most people take aspirin for minor aches and pains, but most of the drug by weight is actually consumed by victims of arthritis and other inflammatory conditions. These sufferers often have to down enormous doses—more than ten tablets a day—for months and years on end. Vane believes that this anti-inflammatory mode of action too depends on aspirin's inhibition of prostaglandin synthesis. Some prostaglandins promote inflammation, and aspirin presumably stops them. But Weissmann, among others, suggests that this explanation is inadequate: "Aspirin and the other NSAIDs do too many other things," he said recently. Work at Weissmann's laboratory in the late 1980s pointed instead to aspirin's interference with a type of white blood cell called a neutrophil. In certain circumstances neutrophils can be transformed from part of the immune system, the body's first line of defense, into entities that traitorously attack the body's own tissues. Like platelets, the altered neutrophils mass together, releasing chemicals that cause inflammation by breaking up the proteins that comprise human flesh. Neutrophils are intimately bound up with autoim-

---

* One reason the FDA has long been skeptical of products like Bufferin, which claim that their antacids prevent aspirin-induced stomach upset, is that antacids directly neutralize gastric acids, whereas aspirin works its bad effects by blocking prostaglandins from the stomach lining. The firms contend that the neutralized acids cannot take advantage of the damaged lining to attack the stomach, and that antacids therefore impede aspirin's power to cause stomach upset. But the FDA counters that people with preexisting stomach problems may find that the long-term damage from aspirin is not offset by the short-term weakening of the acids. Although the agency grudgingly allows aspirin-antacid combinations to be sold, it refuses to let companies say that they will eliminate gastric problems—one reason the companies advertise them as "easier on the stomach," rather than "easy on the stomach."

mune diseases such as rheumatoid arthritis. Aspirin, Weissmann has shown, dams up the stream here, too. It prevents neutrophils from sticking to each other and to blood vessel walls, he says, and this action has obvious implications for inflammation. Vane, unsurprisingly, disagrees. "There's a controversy," Weissmann said in early 1991, smiling the smile of someone who loves a good intellectual dispute. "I strongly suspect we're going to be looking at aspirin for a good while into the future." Indeed, Weissmann and his collaborators have recently pinpointed the precise site on the neutrophil where aspirin works.

Aspirin's third mode of action, interfering with the clumping-together of platelets, requires only the smallest doses. ("You could almost lick a baby aspirin every other morning," Weissmann said. "That's a little exaggerated, but not much. You certainly don't need a Maximum Strength Anacin every day, or more, which is what they'll try and sell you.") While circulating through the blood in an inactive state, platelets are tiny, idle chemical factories, waiting for a signal to start up. Most often this signal is sent when a platelet encounters certain chemicals created by the arachidonic acid emitted by a damaged blood vessel wall. When this happens, the platelet is, so to speak, switched on. It pumps out chemicals that, chain reaction–style, cause other platelets to activate, adhere, and aggregate.

One of the most important chemicals produced by an activated platelet is a prostaglandin-like substance known technically as "thromboxane A_2." First uncovered in 1975 by a small team led by Bengt Samuelsson, Sune Bergström's former collaborator, thromboxane is the most important cause of platelet aggregation; it is also the major component of the mysterious rabbit aorta contracting substance (RCS) that sent Priscilla Piper and John Vane on the trail of aspirin in 1969. Soon after the identification of thromboxane, researchers discovered that aspirin and the other NSAIDs interfere with its creation—answering, at long last, the question of how aspirin impedes coagulation.

The body makes thromboxane in two steps. First, arachidonic acid is converted by PGH synthetase into prostaglandin G_2. Then another substance, thromboxane synthetase, transforms prostaglandin G_2 into thromboxane. By clogging up the active slot in PGH synthetase, aspirin throws a monkey wrench into this process, just as it blocks the synthesis of prostaglandins. Hindered by a lack of thromboxane, platelets clump into smaller thrombi—or not at all.

Thromboxane is amazingly sensitive to aspirin. One group of scientists has actually suggested that a daily ration of as little as 1 mg—less than one three-hundredth of a strandard tablet—is enough to cut thromboxane production. The difference between the dose required to inhibit thromboxane and that required to inhibit prostaglandins is explained by variations in the way they are produced in the body. Platelets themselves are the major source of thromboxane; when they come into contact with aspirin, they are permanently blocked from producing it. By contrast, other cells in the body can shake off the effects in a few hours. Partly for this reason, levels of aspirin that have no effect on headaches may suffice to reduce platelet aggregation.

The discovery of the aspirin-thromboxane relation reopened the puzzle first hinted at by Karl Link. If the acetyl group in aspirin enables it to block the production of thromboxane permanently, why, then, did Link and many others see that salicylic acid and other salicylates—compounds *without* an acetyl group—also enhance bleeding? One answer is that, as noted before, they temporarily inhibit PGH synthetase, and this of course will impede the formation of thromboxane. But evidence exists that salicylic acid plays another role in platelet aggregation—a smaller, secondary one. Researchers have suggested that somewhere in the biochemical web spun around arachidonic acid is a mechanism, as yet unknown, by which salicylic acid and its cousins stop platelet aggregation without touching PGH synthetase. As one group of Italian doctors concluded recently, "It is best to assume that . . . aspirin acts by at least *two* mechanisms, one of which is the inhibition of platelet cyclo-oxygenase [another name for PGH synthetase]." Until these other mechanisms are understood, Weissmann has commented, "We still can't say we *truly* know how aspirin works."

Despite these theoretical lacunae, pharmacologists were convinced almost from the moment of thromboxane's discovery that aspirin *should* have an effect on heart attack and stroke. The drug's inhibition of thromboxane in the laboratory was so potent that it seemed ridiculous to suppose it would have no impact on patients' health. Yet doctors had painfully learned that the beliefs of academic scientists do not always translate into useful therapies. Indeed, AMIS suggested exactly that. Perhaps aspirin did bottle up thromboxane. And perhaps this prevented platelets from sticking together. And perhaps this did confer some protection. But AMIS appeared to show that the effect wasn't big enough to save lives. And that meant Vane's work, though of the highest interest to laboratory researchers, was of no practical use to doctors with sick people to treat.

In 1982 Vane shared a Nobel Prize with Bergström and Samuelsson. Vane's discovery—that acetylsalicylic acid inhibits prostaglandin synthesis—had been like a sudden tap on the row of dominoes. By the time Vane went to Stockholm, theoretical discoveries about aspirin were pouring out of the labs. Suddenly, two lines of research, one shepherded by Harry Collier for fifteen years, the other fueled by Upjohn's free prostaglandins, had become inseparable. Aspirin's actions on prostaglandins gave researchers a sure method of knocking them out and observing the results. For the same reason, the workings of aspirin could now be explored by looking for prostaglandins and finding out what happens when they are inhibited. Taking a cue from aspirin, other drugs, more powerful at inhibiting prostaglandins, were soon under development in drug company labs.

Vane's colleagues paid his discovery the ultimate professional tribute: They quoted it in their own work. Between its publication and the end of 1988, Vane's aspirin paper was specifically referred to 3,761 times in other scientific articles, making it the seventy-eighth most cited article in postwar science. With papers building on it, Vane became the fourth most often cited scientist in the world. He was quoted more frequently in the literature than Einstein, or than Watson and Crick, the scientists who unraveled the genetic code of DNA.

Collier, for his part, never gave up work on aspirin. He participated in studies of its safety. In 1983, he proposed an experiment based on the observation that prostaglandins leached calcium from the bones, possibly causing senile osteoporosis, a bone-weakening condition that plagues millions of elderly women. If aspirin throttled off prostaglandins, Collier reasoned, it might prevent osteoporosis. He was lobbying for a clinical trial of the matter when he died suddenly on August 29, 1983. (The study has never taken place.) His last project, completed the day before he died, was a scholarly history of aspirin, written partly to rescue his work from the oblivion it was consigned to by what he called the "blaze of light and publicity" given later, more successful researchers such as John Vane.

CHAPTER EIGHTEEN

"WHO <u>IS</u> THIS GUY, ANYWAY?"

Spare, modern, unhandsome Lister Hill Auditorium, at the National Institutes of Health campus in Bethesda, Maryland, is where Food and Drug Administration advisory committees often convene. The FDA has forty boards of independent experts that make recommendations about the sale and use of prescription and over-the-counter drugs. Although the agency has the authority to overrule their objections, in practice it is next to impossible for a firm to market a new drug or suggest a new use for an old drug without the assent of the relevant advisory committee. Given the high potential profits at stake, advisory sessions can be tense. Seldom, however, is Lister Hill Auditorium the site of a confrontation like the one that occurred on Tuesday, March 1, 1983, the fortieth meeting of the Cardiovascular and Renal Drugs Advisory Committee.

That morning, twenty-eight experts met to debate a request by Sterling Drug to change its aspirin label—or, more precisely, the promotional material about aspirin it distributed to health professionals, which the FDA counts as part of the labeling. The company wished to add a sentence to the agency's official description of aspirin. "Aspirin," Sterling wanted to say, "has been shown to be effective in reducing the risk of death or reinfarction of patients who recently have suffered a myocardial infarction." If this description was approved, Sterling would be allowed to claim in at least some of its promotion that aspirin prevented second heart attacks, an assertion that made the agency very nervous.

Undeterred by the negative data from AMIS, Sterling had applied for permission to change its aspirin label in December 1980. In the subsequent two and a half years, the FDA had avoided a decision. A half-dozen talks with the advisory committee had produced nothing. The agency, one Sterling executive complained, was "stalling, plain and simple."

"From their point of view," said William Soller, then Sterling's medical director, "aspirin was a hot potato." A former associate professor at the

University of Pennsylvania School of Pharmacology, Soller was the prime mover behind the petition. ''My dad took an aspirin every night so he could go to sleep,'' Soller said. ''I used to laugh at him. I went to school at Colby, where I did work at Jackson Lab. 'Dad,' I said, 'trust me—it doesn't help you sleep.' Then I did my Ph.D. at Cornell. I'd come home and say, 'Dad, it doesn't work.' Then I went to Penn, teaching. 'Dad, you're not getting any benefit from taking an aspirin.' Then about a month after I come to Sterling [in 1979] I get a phone call from a man named [Peter] Hauri [then at Dartmouth]. 'My trial's done,' he tells me. 'I've found that aspirin reduces sleep latency time in insomniacs!' I go home at Easter vacation. 'Dad, I have an admission to make. It really does reduce sleep latency.' He says, '*I* could've told you that. You might also look at aspirin and heart attack.' ''

Soller had. Trained as a pharmacologist, he had followed the explorations of Vane, Bergström, and Samuelsson with interest. It made him unable to take at face value the results of AMIS, which he doubted had truly randomized its thousands of patients. As the study's authors conceded, ''some imbalance'' had occurred in the randomization, and the aspirin group was, on the whole, sicker to begin with than the control group. More important, Soller was not willing to give credence to any one experiment. ''I plotted the results of all the aspirin trials, and there was AMIS way down below the rest,'' he said. ''I'm not an expert in the mathematics by any means, but, just statistically, you might expect that something would happen. In a bunch of trials, you're going to get one that's off.''

Many doctors tacitly agreed. On a word-of-mouth basis, belief in aspirin was spreading through the medical profession. Sterling, of course, was pleased, because it wanted to sell aspirin. To sell more aspirin, it wanted to promote the aspirin–heart attack connection to doctors. And to do that, Sterling had to get the FDA to change the labeling—and that meant explaining to the agency why it should overlook the negative results from AMIS, the biggest single experiment with aspirin, and the only study funded by the National Institutes of Health, the FDA's sister agency.

The company had a second problem. Sterling had not paid for AMIS or any of the previous aspirin trials. It therefore did not have direct access to their raw data. The reports in medical journals would not be complete enough to satisfy the fastidious reviewers of the Food and Drug Administration. To get the raw data that the agency would demand, Soller would have to ask people like Peter Elwood to spend time and money on putting together an elaborate package. They would hardly be interested in going through such an exercise on the off-chance that an American drug firm could make a few extra dollars.

From Soller's point of view, the situation was changed dramatically by an editorial in the *Lancet* that appeared in May 1980, four months after the publication of AMIS. At the plenary session of the first congress of the

Society for Clinical Trials, the editorial explained, a consensus had emerged on the evidence from the aspirin and heart attack trials. A novel—and, in fact, extremely controversial—mathematical method for viewing the trials collectively demonstrated that AMIS was the misleading result of "chance fluctuations." Even though no single trial had shown a statistically significant benefit for aspirin, this analysis argued, the *overall* picture was clear: the drug prevented heart attacks, at least for people who had already suffered one. So confident was the editorial in the results of this new analysis that it recommended that

> the pharmaceutical companies should now make aspirin available in some practical form of packaging, such as a day-marked calendar pack, which will help patients to remember to take one tablet a day if it is so prescribed.

Sterling made the *Lancet* editorial the basis of its application. Because all six trials had tested the effects of aspirin on second heart attacks, the company applied for permission to describe aspirin not as a preventive for a heart attack (infarction) per se, but for the recurrence of a heart attack (re-infarction). As Soller had expected, the cardiorenal advisory committee asked for more data from the scientists. "That meant that not only we went back to them," he said, "but the FDA was asking them for it [the data] too." Even so, inveigling the scientists to join a presentation was almost as difficult as persuading the advisory committee to listen to them. Elwood balked. "At first it was the last thing I wanted to do," he said. "But [Sterling] kept coming back." Soller managed to lure him in—the potential benefit, he said, would be great, and no other firm would ever push through the application, because they had all been trying to hide their association with aspirin for years. The FDA would never do it on its own.

When Sterling applied, the advisory committee balked. Its members expressed dismay at what they saw as the muddy results of the aspirin trials. In addition, Soller suspected, they were hoping that a new cardiovascular therapy, beta-blocker drugs, would turn out to be such a successful treatment for heart disease that Sterling's request would be moot. (Beta-blockers slow the heart rate and lower blood pressure.) "They turned out to be no panacea," Soller said. "And when the beta-blocker studies started coming in, we were still there." The FDA reluctantly agreed to hear Sterling out in March 1983.

The company's three main witnesses were Elwood, Jack Hirsch, a cardiovascular expert from McMaster University, in Hamilton, Ontario, and Richard Peto of Oxford University, the statistician who had written the *Lancet* editorial and who had performed the unconventional statistical analysis on which it was based. All three were pure scientists and reluctant in the extreme to say or do anything that looked like caving in to commercial pressure from Sterling. Peto refused to let Sterling pay for his hotel and his plane fare, and he was reluctant to go into details with Soller about what he would say. The day before the meeting, Soller had trouble getting his three witnesses together long enough to ensure that they didn't repeat one another's testimony. "Believe me," he said, "these guys were ethically pure."

Hirsch began the meeting by leading the advisory committee through the evidence that thrombi are the principal cause of myocardial infarction. Autopsies usually found them in the arteries of people who died of heart attacks, he said. Angiography—a procedure in which X-rays are enhanced by the injection of special chemicals—showed clearly such arterial thrombi were created by platelets. Aspirin was a thromboxane inhibitor, he said. Thromboxane caused platelets to aggregate. Aspirin thus should stop thrombi, and therefore heart attacks. Q.E.D.

Elwood then ran through the six published clinical trials, including his own. All but one, AMIS, showed positive effects by aspirin. But none of the results were statistically significant. In a sense, the other five trials were in agreement with AMIS, for it too was unable to show statistically significant benefits. But whereas the other trials saw good things, AMIS saw nothing. These findings were, Elwood remarked to the committee, "at odds with other trial results that have been reported."

Hirsch and Elwood were warm-ups for Peto, the third and most important speaker. A rail-thin man with a sheaf of straw-colored hair and sharp, almost hawklike features, Peto explained the statistical tricks he had used to massage the aspirin data—methods on which the Sterling petition depended but which had never before been approved by the FDA. Suspecting his ideas would be opposed, he came out swinging. He had dealt with the National Institutes of Health before, and regarded U.S. agencies as prejudiced against foreign scientists and foreign ideas. ("We have a saying in Britain," he said. "NIH stands for Not Invented Here—if it's not from an American, they don't want to hear it.")

The committee was fascinated, but quite suspicious. Few of its members were statisticians, but all believed that Peto was breaking the rules. You were not supposed to do what he was doing. Quick, crisp, and abrasive, Peto kept dashing off charts in his sketchy handwriting and slapping them on the overhead projector. The FDA staff listened frigidly; in statistical terms, Peto's message was just short of heresy.

That was not the only negative reaction. As Peto spoke, a Sterling executive named Monroe Trout slipped into the auditorium. The formal, conservative Trout was astounded by what he saw: a long-haired, tieless man with a rumpled corduroy jacket slouched above an overhead projector, scribbling away with a brown felt tip pen. It was the antithesis of the usual corporate presentation, with its neatly garbed representatives, its carefully preprinted transparencies. Trout was appalled. He sent a note to Soller, which was silently passed hand to hand across Lister Hill Auditorium as Peto spoke. When Soller opened the note, he saw it contained a single sentence: "Who *is* this guy, anyway?"

"Richard Peto," Charles Hennekens, an epidemiologist at the Harvard School of Public Health, once said, "is the Mozart of the clinical trial. The metaphor is rather exact, both to the quality and quantity of his output, and his willingness to"— he interrupted himself with a laugh —"suffer fools gladly."

A product of the baby boom, Peto completed a mathematics degree at Cambridge amidst the turmoil of the Vietnam era. "When I finished my degree in the sixties," he has explained, "I really wasn't sure if I wanted to work or not." In this skeptical frame of mind, he spoke about a job with Sir Richard Doll, who ran the Medical Research Council's Statistical Research Unit at the University College Hospital in London. The man who had overseen the expansion of Elwood's first trial, Doll was perhaps the most eminent expert on clinical trials in the world. Peto had heard that Doll had helped prove the association between smoking and lung cancer, but otherwise knew little more than that about the man he was seeing, or about epidemiology and clinical trials. In short order, Doll told him the main point of the enterprise: preventing premature death. Cancer, cardiovascular disease, the effects of pollutants—there were dozens of problems crying out to be solved, dozens of places where a thoughtful and intelligent person could make a real difference in the lives of huge numbers of people. Peto took the job. Soon after, Doll was appointed the Regius Professor of Medicine at Oxford. Peto wanted to work with Doll but was reluctant to move from the gritty reality of a city hospital to what he imagined would be the aloof quiet of a university. Eventually he went to Oxford anyway, where his lack of a Ph.D. forced Doll to employ him in the guise of a computer programmer.

In this inauspicious way, Peto joined the third generation of the remarkable group of Oxford statisticians who have more or less invented the rules for clinical trials. The first was Sir Austin Bradford Hill, sometimes called the father of the clinical trial, whose landmark papers from the 1930s through the early 1950s are credited with establishing the methodology for rational and ethical experimentation on human beings. A professor of medical statistics at the London School of Hygiene and Tropical Medicine, Hill came onto the scene in the 1930s, when the stream of new drugs from pharmaceutical companies was beginning. To Hill's mind, the failure to examine potential medical advances properly was every bit as bad as disease. "He was very clear that randomization had to be used," Peto said, in the course of two wide-ranging conversations. "He could make statistics seem like common sense, which it is when it's at its best. I think he's the greatest medical statistician there's ever been."

After the Second World War, the Medical Research Council established committees to test new drugs. The first drug on the list was streptomycin, an antibiotic intended to treat tuberculosis. Because supplies were limited, not all sufferers of the disease could be given the drug. Hill realized that carefully comparing patients who got streptomycin with patients who did not would tell a great deal about the drug, including its side effects. In the past he had met with resistance when he argued for randomized trials. Now, with no question of being able to give streptomycin to all TB patients, the MRC almost had no choice but to make the best of a bad situation and allow Hill to conduct the first large-scale, strictly randomized clinical trial. The results were published in 1948. That year he became the director of the Statistical Research Unit of the MRC.

On the staff of the Statistical Research Unit was a young, mathematically inclined doctor named Richard Doll, with whom Hill began to talk about lung cancer. Once a rare syndrome, lung cancer was rapidly becoming epidemic in England and Wales. In the quarter-century between 1922 and 1947 it jumped by a factor of fifteen—a "phenomenal increase," the two men wrote. In a hunt for the cause, they used the techniques of epidemiology, studying the pattern of the disease across groups of people. They matched 649 male lung cancer patients at twenty London hospitals with noncancerous control patients of the same age and sex. By 1950 they were ready to issue a preliminary report. As the world knows, they found that the overwhelming majority of lung cancer victims were smokers. That alone proved nothing, because most of the male patients without cancer smoked too. However, the proportion of cancer patients who had never smoked (2 of 649, or 0.3 percent) was lower than the corresponding proportion in the control group (27 of 649, or 4.2 percent). Both 0.3 percent and 4.2 percent are small numbers, but the fourteen-fold difference between them was unmistakable. Doll and Hill calculated that it could happen by chance less than one in one million times.

The study caused a huge commotion and began the fight over tobacco use that continues to the present day. Doll and Hill were denounced by the tobacco industry until Hill's retirement in 1964, when Doll—now Sir Richard—took his place as the chief target of opprobrium and as the most prominent epidemiologist in the United Kingdom. Peto worked under him, evaluating treatments for leukemia and other cancers, as well as heart and liver disease. (He finally acquired an important university position in 1975.) It was hard work: Having accepted randomization, doctors were conducting thousands of clinical trials. The results washed across Peto's desk in a stream. All too often they were disappointing, especially for cancer. Year after year, exciting new treatments were tested, and year after year the findings were inconclusive. There might be a flurry of interest when a trial produced hopeful findings, but almost invariably they didn't reappear in a second trial. "Nothing ever produced any important results," Peto said. "Eventually I started wondering why that was. And the reason was that trials were too complicated and, above all, too small."

The basic problem was that all the easy diseases had been used up. Unlike tuberculosis, conditions like cancer and heart disease are not due to a single bacterium, but are created by an array of environmental and genetic mishaps. Diseases with multiple causes are not likely to have a single cure, in the way tuberculosis is cured by streptomycin. If a simple therapy could make them vanish, it would take only a handful of patients or a few trials to find this out; moreover, if there really was such a therapy out there, it would already be known. Therefore, Peto reasoned, doctors should be looking for modest, incremental improvements. "Unfortunately," he said, "almost nothing that was being done put you in a position to observe those benefits reliably."

Moderate benefits can be spotted reliably only in big trials. And the rarer the affliction, the bigger the trial has to be. Suppose that a new treatment is thought to reduce the probability of a second heart attack by one-fourth. One would want to test that treatment in a way that could reliably observe the one-fourth benefit. Because the incidence of second heart attacks in victims of recent heart attacks is around 10 percent a year, a trial that enrolled 2,000 of these patients, dividing them equally between treatment and control groups, would generate an annual total of about 175 deaths: 75 in the treatment group and 100 in the control group.

Of course, one would have to be extremely lucky to obtain a result that so exactly matched the expected situation. More than this, however, one would have to be quite lucky to get any kind of useful data at all. The chance that this trial, with 2,000 subjects, would be left in statistical limbo after a year—as in Elwood's trials, the results declared statistically insignificant— would be more than 70 percent. The total number of deaths (175) and the expected difference between treatment and control groups (25) just aren't big enough. To reduce the chance of missing the one-fourth annual improvement to less than 10 percent, the trial would have to include approximately 10,000 recent heart attack victims—eight times the number Elwood had in his first trial and two times the number in AMIS.

If the treatment was aimed at preventing *first* heart attacks, the trial would need to be even larger, because the incidence of heart attack in the general population is much smaller. To detect that one-fourth benefit in a year, the number of patients in the trial would have to swell to an incredible *133,000*— the size of a small city.

These numbers can be cut substantially by extending trials over several years. Trials can't be stretched out too long, however, because the subjects will age, move away, or die of other causes. The investigators also can't be expected to devote too many years to a single study. Thus it will never be possible to detect that one-fourth difference in heart attack rates without collecting data on thousands upon thousands of people. "It's perfectly clear," Peto said, "that these trials that appear in the newspaper, where they give something to a few dozen cancer patients and announce how many got better—90 percent of them tell you nothing, and are a waste of time. You've got to have trials big enough to detect realistically moderate differences."

Realistically moderate differences. Simple in concept, the idea involved nothing less than a complete re-evaluation of the customary way of doing medical research. As designed, most trials were—and often still are—too small to detect realistically moderate differences. This failure was due not only to the ignorance of the investigators but also to the expense of getting enough people into the trial to give it statistical power. Most trials constantly monitored their subjects, a scrutiny that drove costs up to $10,000 per subject for a two- or three-year experiment. Handling ten thousand subjects in the kind of mega-trial urged by Peto could cost a staggering $100 million. The price was impossible; it simply couldn't be done.

To Peto, the solution was clear: Eliminate the bells and whistles. Cut down the supervision to the necessary minimum. If doctors wanted to learn what treatments gave the modest benefits possible to obtain in complicated diseases like cancer, he said, they were going to have to learn how to run big, simple trials—experiments that asked uncomplicated questions about treating tens of thousands of people. You would lose all the detail; you wouldn't learn much about subgroups within the trial. You wouldn't even know if everyone had taken their medicine. But if the groups were sufficiently large, you would not need to know, for the differences among their members would all come out in the wash. "People thought, if you do a clinical trial, you do it precisely," said Peto, "and you collect an enormous amount of information on every patient. But you don't have to. Really, what's involved? One-half gets A, one-half gets B, and then you count the dead bodies."

Having concluded that things were being done wrongly, Peto argued vehemently against business as usual. Big, simple trials were the logical way to go, he said, and he sometimes grew impatient with those who did not accept his logic. A young man with youthful features, he acquired the reputation of an *enfant terrible*. "Doctors are used to being surrounded by adoring admirers," explained William K. Hass, a stroke specialist who has worked with Peto. "And when Richard gets into his Newtonian mode—well, it gets their attention, but they don't like it."

Because Peto was advocating the opposite of usual practice, reactions were, unsurprisingly, negative. "Having trials of such a huge size—" Peto shrugged —"people thought it was nutty, that it was not a serious idea." For the time being, he was in a world where small, complicated trials were the norm.

The prospect was discouraging. Most small, complicated trials would be unable to detect the moderate benefits he thought it realistic to hope for. On top of that, even those trials that did report benefits were quite likely to be wrong. If trials of those therapies were held to the usual standard of statistical significance—having a less than 5 percent chance of being due to random fluctuations—one out of twenty trials would show statistically significant effects that weren't there. With hundreds of trials taking place all over the world, medical journals were almost certainly filled with false panaceas and passed-over cures. Peto thought the situation scandalous. Millions of dollars were being wasted on experiments that could not do what they needed to do; the cost in needless suffering and death was huge.

It was time to change things, Peto believed. But he needed a way to demonstrate that things could be done differently. As it turned out, the way that presented itself was aspirin.

At Oxford, Peto had kept abreast of the aspirin trials, but he had drawn conclusions contrary to those of the FDA. "By '77 or '78 the evidence seemed to me fairly definite," Peto said. "Aspirin seemed to be getting stronger. But nothing was statistically significant on the level of the individual trial." Clear answers, he was sure, could best come from a truly large trial. He consulted Doll, who suggested that the trial should seek to learn if, as he put it, an aspirin a day would keep doctors alive. One of the more important tobacco studies by Doll and Hill had followed the smoking habits of British doctors, and Doll wanted to repeat that approach. Knowing the magnitude of the job, the two men induced others to join the team, including Rory Collins, a cardiologist, Charles Warlow, a neurologist (specialist in the brain, spinal cord, and nerves), and Charles Hennekens, the Harvard epidemiologist, who was on leave at Oxford at the time. In 1978 and 1979, they wrote to every male physician in Britain who was born after 1900 and still listed in the medical directory. After disqualifying doctors who were already taking aspirin or who had a history of ulcer, stroke, or heart attack, the Oxford team came up with 5,139 subjects. Two-thirds were given aspirin; the remaining third were asked to avoid aspirin and use acetaminophen for headaches. All were asked to fill out a short questionnaire every six months about their health.

Unlike previous studies, the British doctors trial would be measuring aspirin's effects on a healthy population, not on one of heart attack survivors. It was exactly the kind of simple trial Peto had been advocating—but it was not big enough. "We were very, very clearly aware that there simply weren't enough doctors in Britain to do what we wanted to do," Collins said. "We knew it from the day we started. We thought it might be a way to get the ball rolling."

At the same time, Doll, Peto, and Hennekens jointly applied to the National Institutes of Health for the money to conduct a similar but bigger study in the United States. Every male doctor in the nation would be contacted, and their health would be tracked by postcards. The looseness of the monitoring disturbed the NIH, which complained that trial investigators should follow their subjects more closely. Peto's response was that in both experiments they were mainly looking for a reduction in deaths, and that few pathologists were going to introduce bias into a determination of death. ("Stone-dead has no fellow," Sir Austin Bradford Hill wrote in 1952, "and preeminent [in trials], therefore, stands the number of patients who die. No statistician, so far as I know, has in this respect accused the physician of an over-reliance upon the clinical impression.") The proposal was rejected in 1979, not least, Peto believed, because the NIH discriminated against foreign scientists. After huddling together, the three men decided that Hennekens would rewrite the proposal and submit it to the U.S. government on his own.

In the interim, AMIS came out. "It was the definitive, all-American proof that aspirin didn't work," Peto said. "I was desperate to get an American study going, and there seemed to be no way it was going to happen with this study being misinterpreted." *Misinterpreted*—paradoxically, this advocate of big trials found himself arguing against the single biggest trial of aspirin. Peto had two reasons. First, AMIS was big, but still not big enough, in his view, to settle the question. Second, and more important, nobody should look at just one piece of data, no matter how large and expensive. Instead, all six aspirin trials should be looked at collectively, and agencies like the FDA should base their decision on the totality of the evidence. In Peto's view, the AMIS results did not radically affect the big picture. Taken as a whole, the data still backed aspirin.

He presented his views at the Society for Clinical Trials, where they were subjected to what he diplomatically called "a lot of discussion." His conclusions, he conceded, were "a bit risqué."

It is difficult to evoke the alarm caused in some circles of clinical research by Peto's apparently reasonable suggestion that one should look at the totality of the evidence. Having learned the hard way about the problems that creep in when dissimilar groups are compared, it was an article of faith among biostatisticians that one could never, never combine data from one trial with data from another. " 'You can't do it!' they'd say," recalled Hennekens. " 'You're violating the most elementary rules of statistics! You're adding apples and oranges!' "

"I hate it when they talk about adding apples and oranges," Peto groaned. "They always say that, and it's always wrong. We're _not_ adding apples and oranges." It was absolutely true, Peto agreed, patients from one trial cannot be compared with patients from another. You cannot pool the raw data, treating all patients as if they had been in the same trial, with the same procedures and diagnoses, without creating bias. But you can ask the same question of each trial—did the treatment do any good?—and then add up the answers.

A variant of ideas developed years before by other statisticians, Peto's technique for adding together trials is clever, but simple enough to be clear to the nonspecialist. The trick is to start out with the assumption that the treatment does nothing. In that case, the number of people dying in the treatment group should be the same as the number dying in the control group. Of course, in any individual trial the observed difference between the number of deaths in the two groups will rarely be zero because of the play of chance. It will be off a little bit, $+1$ or -2, nudged one way or the other by the accidents of circumstance. But if one adds up the differences from various trials of the same basic treatment, chance should even things out. The various plusses and minuses will tend to cancel each other, making the total close to zero—if the assumption is true that the treatment actually has no use.

A grand total that strays significantly far from zero provides an important message: The treatment does something, even if the individual trials cannot measure it with clarity. The power of the method comes from its ability to amplify a moderate effect many times. Differences seen in the individual trials will sometimes be larger, sometimes smaller, but most of the time they will point in the same direction, and the sum will drift away from zero.

To Peto's annoyance, this technique has acquired the cumbersome moniker of "meta-analysis" (he prefers "overview"). Whatever the name, it was not greeted with universal enthusiasm when he began touting it in the mid-1970s. "At that time," he said, "though it was _obvious_ that trials could be looked at together, people used to take it as axiomatic that you couldn't. They took too formalistic a view of trials, and there were all sorts of absurd conventions." To show the broad applicability of this technique, he needed to resolve a specific medical dispute with it—a case in which meta-analysis would tell scientists something that they did not expect and could not learn in any other way.

When Peto came to Washington, D.C., in March 1983 at the request of William Soller, he had his medical dispute: aspirin. Just as he wanted to use aspirin to establish the need for big trials, he also wanted to use aspirin to establish the utility of his overview method. First, he intended to show that the lack of positive effects in the AMIS trial proved nothing (as scientists say, the absence of evidence is not evidence of absence). Second, he wanted to document that AMIS should be regarded as part of the combined evidence, rather than as a definitive answer.*

In the Lister Hill Auditorium, Soller listened to Peto with mounting anxiety. Whereas the English statistician's concerns were wholly scientific, Soller was preoccupied as well by the commercial implications of his talk. Aspirin had lost market share not least because it had fallen victim to the aura of medical science that glowed about acetaminophen and ibuprofen. If the professional labeling for aspirin could be changed to include its use as a preventive for second heart attacks, the drug might shed its image as an old and uninteresting home remedy. Already Soller was mulling over how to advertise its benefits for heart attack. This would be no easy task. The FDA had never allowed a prescription drug to be plugged on television. But aspirin was not a prescription drug. If Soller could leap the legal hurdles necessary to tout its wonders on the tube, Bayer aspirin might actually be saved.† All Sterling had to do was push the label change through the FDA. He wanted a nice, simple, friendly presentation. He wanted the panel to accept Peto's analysis quickly, and to vote positively soon after that. Instead, Peto spoke in an ironic, informal style that rubbed the panel members the wrong way. Worse, Soller could see that they simply didn't buy it.

Philip L. Dern, an FDA reviewer, hit Peto with a salvo of questions about Elwood's first trial. The code had been broken early, he pointed out, which automatically made the work suspect. In addition, second heart attacks, the subject of the Sterling application, had not been initially tabulated, as they had in the other experiments. (Elwood originally set his sights on all forms of cardiac death, not just heart attack.) Peto said that it would be foolish to discard so many data points when the trial had been carefully conducted. Dern was not satisfied. The evidence in favor of aspirin was bad, he told the committee, and all the mathematical fiddling in the world could not disguise that fact. He demanded that Peto admit that his reasoning depended on "assumptions about the true results in the [Elwood] trial"—that is, his argument was based on a discredited experiment.

"I don't think that is fair . . . ," Peto said. Obviously, he admitted, anyone would rather have a single, perfectly run trial with thousands of

---

* Unfortunately, the two large studies Peto had started—the British doctors trial and the American doctors trial with Charles Hennekens—were years from completion and so could not be considered on their own or as part of an overview.

† Aspirin was beaten to the screen by ibuprofen. Two months after the cardiorenal advisory meeting, Boots advertised on four Florida TV stations that its Rufen brand of ibuprofen was cheaper than Upjohn's Motrin for the treatment of arthritis, the main prescription use of ibuprofen. The FDA complained, and Boots revised the ad to eliminate the mention of arthritis, which the agency thought would encourage consumers to buy ibuprofen to relieve their arthritis. Because ibuprofen is a safe and effective arthritis treatment, some drug company executives found it difficult to grasp the motive for the FDA's desire to eliminate the mention of the disease.

participants. "The larger your numbers are, the more all this kind of play of chance . . . is going to balance out anyway, so you don't need to bother about it. . . . But if you say, okay, we haven't got that, what is the best we can do in terms of making reliable inferences, then you take the best unbiased analysis you can." One had to follow, he said, "a principle of taking all the available unbiased data." And that meant including Elwood's results.

"Dr. Peto," said committee chairman Richard Kronmal, a biostatistician at the University of Washington in Seattle, "I think Phil's point, which may not be in this case really cogent, is . . . whether or not there might have been some possibility of bias that we are unaware of. That is, some failure in the randomization procedures—"

"Oh, no, no," Peto said. "Randomization was invented in Britain, really."

The committee laughed, but Peto's exasperation was real. Not only did the use of aspirin make sense from a pharmacological point of view, but in the overview the benefits fairly leapt from the page. It was impossible to discount: There was less than one chance in ten thousand that the benefits could be due to luck. Considering that the FDA usually regarded a significance of one chance in twenty as a sufficient basis for a decision, Peto thought that the agency should not vacillate about aspirin.

Meta-analysis ran against the grain at the FDA, which had always based its decisions about drugs on the "gold standard" of two well-conducted clinical trials. This standard had stood for so long that the FTC had tried to adopt it during the early 1970s in the Pfizer case; now it was being challenged by Peto, who was arguing that within the contemporary flood of clinical trials it would be possible for drug companies to find two scrupulously run experiments with almost any result, true or not.

His audience did not want to listen. "AMIS was an emotional question" at NIH, Peto said. "They'd spent $17 million on it, and they were bloody well not going to hear that it was misleading." The criticism, he felt, was especially unwelcome coming from foreigners. He didn't like the way FDA reviewers like Dern came after him. Growing testy, Peto did not disguise his exasperation at the committee's refusal to address the issues raised by meta-analysis. In return, the committee members kept badgering Elwood and Peto about whether the trials had been properly randomized—worries, Peto noted later, that seemed to apply only to the three foreign experiments. Tempers rose, and the meeting that Sterling had hoped might decide the future of the Bayer aspirin name degenerated into an inconclusive squabble.

After Peto's talk, Dern announced that the uncertain randomization in the three foreign studies so cast doubt on the results that one should reject the application on those grounds alone. "Fool!" Peto muttered. "Idiot!" Notwithstanding Peto's scorn, Raymond Lipicky, FDA director of Cardiorenal Drug Products, complained that the proposed aspirin label was for reinfarction, fatal or not, whereas Elwood had principally been looking at deaths. Data on second heart attacks had been extracted afterward from the files on each patient, leaving an opening for bias to enter. And there was always the problem that Elwood had broken his code, unblinding the study. The discussion kept circling around bias, angering Elwood, who had been a faithful practitioner of randomization for twenty years. Peto, sitting next to him, uttered imprecations. A bunch of Americans were attacking Elwood for breaking the code when he had done it at the behest of a bunch of Americans. Peto's voice was low, but it was distinctly audible.

"I am curious," Lipicky said, "as to why you are . . . willing to buy this reinfarction data." Nobody had seen anything, he said scornfully, but the sketchy charts drawn by Peto on the overhead projector. "Why do you accept it so readily?"

A second committee member said that acceptance was of course conditional on the data's accuracy.

"Well," Lipicky said, "the question is, How would one know that they are?"

All they needed to know, committee chairman Kronmal pointed out, was if blinding was maintained at the point of diagnosis. If the doctors who had initially reported the second heart attacks had no idea whether they were examining members of the treatment or control group, there was no problem looking at their reports afterward. Was that the case?

"Yes, it was," Elwood said.

The FDA, Kronmal said, wanted "some documentation" that the blinding was maintained, and thought nobody should take a step until this evidence was provided. Peto and Elwood watched as a show of hands ensued. Once again, to Soller's dismay, a final decision was postponed. He had inveigled Peto and Elwood to testify for nothing. Meta-analysis had never been truly addressed. After two hours of wrangling, they had gone nowhere.

Annoyed, Monroe Trout of Sterling spoke. "May I ask when we can expect a decision on the petition? The petition has been at the FDA since 1980."

Lipicky promised that if the data were provided, they would look at it within four or five months.

"Could I ask a question as well, please?" Peto said. "What, exactly, . . . do you want? Do you want a great big list, one bit of paper for each paper, because it won't help you at all. . . . The key point, as the chairman said, [is that] you need evidence of lack of bias. That is what you need."

Lipicky agreed.

"And *that* you have to take, really, on trust from the investigators. You have to do this. These are not investigators paid by the industry. They are people who decided to study it for their own research interests . . . working for the British Medical Research Council." They could easily generate lots of paper, he said loudly, but it wouldn't actually tell the FDA "a darned thing."

"What we need is something in writing," Lipicky said. He suggested that Peto quietly speak with him after the meeting, instead of their shouting at each other through the microphone.

Peto didn't want to settle the dispute quietly. "I would like to know roughly what you are after. Are you after five pages, fifty, or five hundred, because if it is fifty or five hundred—really, I am not being paid for appearing here. I don't really care too much what Americans do to each other. I mean, you know, what do you want?" In effect, he went on to say, the likelihood of the overall benefits' being due to chance was less than one in ten thousand. That was the central fact. No matter what happened to Elwood's data, nothing would change that.

If the data on reinfarction were retrospective, Lipicky said, "I am not sure that would be data that I would even consider. I don't care whether it is a .00000001. It just won't be considered, period."

Peto was incensed. "If the FDA's policy is to wait until one trial taken in isolation suggests something striking, then you will introduce far greater biases than if your policy were to take an overview of all the relevant data. That is bad science."

Bad science was not what anyone at Sterling wanted to accuse the FDA of performing. With Peto's irate words still reverberating in the auditorium, Soller hastily broke in to thank the committee for attending, and to say that the meeting had been an interesting exchange of views. Startled at the hostility it had unleashed, the committee promptly ended the session.

Still seething, Peto and Elwood went up to Lipicky immediately afterward. "I'm telling you that my team did the randomization properly," Elwood said. "Won't you take my word as a gentleman?"

"No," Lipicky said.

Elwood stalked away. After a moment, Peto followed him.

The next meeting was not in four or five months. It was not in twelve months. It did not occur until December 11, 1984—twenty-one months later. All parties had thoroughly prepared. For the past few months, Soller had spent weekends—even, he later complained, his birthday—in Sterling headquarters at 90 Park Avenue to make sure the three fat loose-leaf volumes of his submission would reach the advisory committee in time for the meeting. The reluctant Elwood had penned a description of his randomization methods, including samples of the sheets on which his team did its original calculations. "I consider this adequate evidence to establish that I had no knowledge of the treatment a patient had received when I prepared the list of reinfarctions," he wrote. Peto, for his part, had been goaded by his annoyance with the FDA to assemble, with Sarah Parish of Oxford, an exhaustive and exhausting re-examination of all six trials that included feeding into the Oxford mainframe the information on each and every one of the ten thousand subjects. Twenty hours of computer churning later, he had the raw figures for a complete meta-analysis. It was exactly the sort of five-hundred-page document he had told the advisory commitee he thought it absurd to produce.

The centerpiece of his presentation was a reanalysis of AMIS. Although Peto had been uncharacteristically polite to the advisory committee on this point, he had not thought AMIS was properly run—it seemed too big to be so far off. When its authors admitted that the aspirin group ended up with more sick people than the control group, he was sure that picking through the study would find something wrong with it. To his surprise, he turned over every stone and found nothing amiss. "It was a very well-done study," he said. "They were just incredibly unlucky—the unluckiest trial I've ever heard of. They randomized thousands of people and did a good job of it, and still luck threw them off."

Despite all the work, the advisory committee was far from convinced about meta-analysis. "I am not willing to say that the emperor has no clothes," one member was later to say. "But, in fact, I think the emperor is in a very dark room, and I can't see the situation." At a dinner on December 10, the night before the aspirin meeting, the committee took a straw poll. The count was seven to zero against Sterling.

As before, the committee met the next morning at the Lister Hill Auditorium at NIH. Many more faces were in the crowd, and some of them, to Soller's dismay, belonged to the competition. If Bayer aspirin were able to change its professional labeling, the other aspirin companies would promptly piggyback on Sterling's work.

The first testimony came from H. Daniel Lewis of the Veterans Administration Medical Center in Kansas City, Missouri, who had just completed a big VA study of aspirin. Conducted at twelve VA medical centers, the trial covered 1,266 men hospitalized for unstable angina. All were screened for the experiment, given aspirin or a placebo, and then followed for at least a year. The aspirin group suffered 43 percent fewer deaths during that period, a disparity that could happen randomly less than 1 percent of the time during that period in a group of that size.

After Soller made a few remarks about aspirin's side effects, Peto took the stand. He wore a jacket and tie. This time the presentation was meticulous; he had a tray of neatly drawn slides and a prepared lecture that even today stands as perhaps the best single explanation of both why aspirin should be regarded as a preventative for heart attacks, despite ambiguous results in single experiments, and why the system of testing disease therapies, especially drugs, in the United States and Europe needs to be changed completely.

Over the years I, and various colleagues at Oxford, have become increasingly concerned that humanly worthwhile therapeutic results may be being missed simply because of inadequacies in the conduct or interpretation of clinical trials.

Now, I know that this is happening in breast cancer; I know it is happening in stroke; I know it is happening in heart disease; and I suspect it may be the case in many other conditions as well. And I think aspirin is just one particular example of a rather general phenomenon that a lot of things are being missed because of inadequate trial size or inappropriate interpretation of the material we have available.

He then made a distinction between qualitative interactions, which he defined as the basic effects of a treatment (positive, negative, or nothing), and quantitative interactions, which are the size of the qualitative interactions (a positive effect of 23 percent, say, or a negative effect of 41 percent). As a general rule, Peto said, one would not expect that a therapy that strongly benefited one patient group, such as young women, would be actively harmful to another group, such as older men. One could easily imagine quantitative differences in the impact, with one subgroup deriving greater or lesser gain than another, but it would be surprising if the qualitative impact were reversed. Thus one may easily generalize results across populations—such-and-such a drug will help or hinder everyone—but one cannot easily pinpoint the precise level of advantage or loss. If aspirin helped the middle-aged men in these studies avoid heart attacks, Peto said, it was likely to be useful to everyone in danger of thrombotic disease in general. But it would not be easy to pinpoint exactly *how* useful it would be.

Now, the second point is rather less abstruse. It is just that a moderate reduction in a major endpoint, like death, may well be worth having. . . . The clinical viewpoint on moderate risk reductions [is] that small reductions in the risk of death are not noticeable in ordinary clinical practice. And so these are theoretical but not of any real immediate interest. And that is the common viewpoint. You will hear some doctor saying, well, if it doesn't show up in a trial with a couple of hundred patients, then it can't be big enough to be worth bothering with. This is not medical wisdom but statistical unwisdom.

The public health viewpoint is quite different. It says that worldwide the total effects of quite moderate risk reductions may be substantial. I mean, every year you are going to get about a million or so patients admitted to acute coronary care units around the well-doctored world. . . . About 150,000 of these will be dead within a year. Now, if you can knock about 15 percent down to say, 13.5 percent—this is just a 10 percent risk reduction—you are talking about prevention of 15,000 deaths a year. From 15 down to 12, a 20 percent risk reduction, 30,000 [deaths a year], if you are talking about something that is widely practicable and not very expensive. . . .

Obviously, some of these people will be old, some will be horrible people who would be better dead anyway, but a fair number of these are going to be in middle age with a reasonable chance of enjoying life. So this kind of thing is worth doing. You may not know whom you saved but nevertheless this kind of thing is worth recognizing. *And at the moment we are missing them.*

Aspirin was a case in point. He went through the six heart attack studies, one by one by one. For each trial he had calculated the observed number of patients in the aspirin group that suffered a "cardiac event"—that is, who died or had a heart attack. For each trial he also had calculated the number of patients who would have been expected to have a cardiac event if aspirin had no effect, based on the number of cardiac deaths in the entire trial. If aspirin had any benefit, the observed number would be less than the expected number, and aspirin would be saving lives. And that is exactly what he got for each trial.

That fit in, he noted, with the idea that qualitative interactions, that is, the *direction* of the therapeutic effect, should not vary from trial to trial. But the difference between the observed number of cardiac events and the expected number varied wildly, from -4.3 in AMIS to -26.3 in Elwood's second experiment. This fluctuation fit in with Peto's notion that the quantitative interactions, that is, the *level* of benefit or harm, were hard to pin down.

Next, he added together the differences he had calculated for each trial. If aspirin had no effect, the individual differences should wobble around zero, sometimes positive, sometimes negative, but the grand total should be close to zero. It wasn't. It was -70.7, which meant more than seventy cardiac events too few. Seventy is simply not close to zero. It was extremely unlikely that you would have six trials and that each one of them would point the same way so strongly. Even with every anti-aspirin assumption Peto could think of, there was less than one chance in a thousand that the results were due to luck.

In patients with previous [heart attacks] aspirin . . . definitely reduces the odds of non-fatal reinfarction—I used the word "definitely" there— by about a third. And [it] significantly reduces the odds of vascular death, by about a sixth. So overall it improves the odds of recurrence-free survival [of a heart attack] by about a fifth or a quarter.

The unstable angina trial reported earlier, Peto said, provided a context that demonstrated the reasonability of accepting his meta-analysis. "You know," he told the committee, "you are not committing any kind of . . . ridiculous error of judgment in doing so."

The reception this time was entirely different. The committee was dead silent for a moment, and then Peto was treated to a round of applause. Soller recalled, "Afterwards Joan [Standaert, the executive secretary of the committee] told me it was the best presentation she'd ever seen." All traces of resistance seemed to have vanished.

Part of the reason for the enthusiastic reception of meta-analysis was, paradoxically, that the committee could now ignore it. AMIS had been a big study that, because of the power of chance, showed almost no benefit from aspirin. To assert that benefit existed, the committee would have had to base its favorable response on Peto's work. Now, happily, the Veterans Administration study had arrived. It was a big study that showed a big benefit from aspirin. (Probably too big, Peto would doubtless have remarked, because of the power of chance.) The gold standard was satisfied. Whereas one trial caused the NIH to recommend against the use of aspirin, the second provided a cover to advocate it. People could accept the meta-analysis, but use the Veterans Administration study as justification. ("I find the unstable angina trial pivotal in several respects," said one committee member, "and I think it makes it much easier to make a recommendation than previously.") Within minutes of Peto's presentation, the advisory committee unanimously voted to recommend a change in the labeling. Aspirin was in, but if Peto had hoped that his meta-analysis would convince the FDA to rethink its way of doing business—well, that hadn't happened.

Now that the science had been settled, it was time to think of marketing. Soller stood up. Sterling had worked for years to get this recommendation through, he reminded the FDA. Now he wanted to make sure that the agency would work on changing the label with Sterling, and not with the competing companies whose representatives were in the audience. "I am just trying to raise the issue so that all the manufacturers who are here will get the message," he said.

"We are simply asking," another Sterling executive, George Goldstein, explained, "for consideration of the fact that we went through the time, trouble, effort and expense to present this to you. . . . That is all."

He was asked if Sterling wanted to be the sole company allowed to claim that aspirin prevented second heart attacks.

"I stand on my statement," Goldstein said, to general laughter.

On October 10, 1985, U.S. Secretary of Health and Human Services Margaret Heckler announced before a battery of reporters that an aspirin a day could prevent the recurrence of heart attacks. Dressed in a dark, tuxedo-like suit with a bulky knit tie, Heckler described the new aspirin labeling over the bedlam of flashing lights and whirring television cameras that has become the hallmark of contemporary government ceremonies. It was thirty-five years since Lawrence L. Craven, the eye, ear, and nose specialist in Glendale, California, had begun dosing his patients with aspirin.

Through the news conference, Heckler held up Sterling's reward: a small bottle of Bayer aspirin. The cameras clicked, and hundreds of images of the Bayer logo were sealed into the silver nitrate of the film. One of those cameras belonged to Sterling, which sent out copies of the photograph across the nation. And why not? For the first time since the scandals that deposed William Weiss, Bayer aspirin was on the front page of the morning paper.

Aspirin was almost stopped in its tracks by Dreser's fear that it would damage the heart. In the 1920s, Sterling had felt obliged to proclaim in every advertisement that Bayer aspirin does not affect the heart—attracting the wrath of Howard Ambruster, who waged a campaign to have Congress alert Americans to the terrible danger the drug posed to their circulatory systems. One can only imagine his horror if he had lived to see the day that Sterling had the government's blessing to trumpet the fact that aspirin *helps* the heart.

CHAPTER NINETEEN

"MIRACLE DRUG"

When marketers find they have a successful new product, their natural impulse is to exploit it in every possible form, as the makers of Tylenol did when they created Tylenol-500, Extra-Strength Tylenol, Tylenol capsules, Tylenol suppositories, and no fewer than nine different varieties of Tylenol with Codeine in two heady years during the 1970s. Scientists, all their pretensions to the contrary, are not greatly different. As the realization spread that aspirin blocked platelet aggregation, researchers across Europe and America wondered if this property might have interesting implications for thrombotic maladies other than heart attack. "It prevents platelet aggregation, right?" Massimo Porta, an Italian blood specialist who worked with aspirin in London, asked recently. "Great for heart disease! So everybody turns around and says, What else is linked to blood clots? And the answer is—half the diseases in the world. So aspirin gets tested everywhere on everything."

An obvious candidate was stroke, which is, crudely speaking, a heart attack in the brain. It is usually caused by thrombi in the cerebral arteries, which starve the brain tissue of oxygen in much the same way that heart tissue is starved in a heart attack. (Perhaps one out of four strokes is not due to thrombosis, but to the bursting of a blood vessel in the gray matter. The damage in this case is caused by blood pooling in the brain.) If the blockage is complete and long-lived, the damage can be permanent—or fatal. About one-third of all stroke victims die, which in the United States works out to an annual death toll of almost 150,000; in the United Kingdom, it is about 70,000. Survivors tend to recover if the stroke is their first, but they may be left with blindness, paralysis, memory loss, and the sad inability to speak or comprehend, which goes under the name of aphasia. Luckily, the interruption of the blood flow is often incomplete or short-lived, and in that case the stroke is called a transient ischemic attack, or TIA, with *ischemic* being medical jargon for an insufficient supply of blood to a specific organ or tissue. TIA victims may experience a scary but temporary loss of vision, speech, or movement, with their faculties recovering gradually over the next few days. People who suffer many TIAs have a high chance of having a subsequent major stroke.

The well-known similarities between stroke and heart attack meant that anticoagulants like dicumarol were quickly tested on strokes. But no bell-wether experiment ever appeared; a few positive hints emerged, but mostly from nonrandomized trials. Faced with this unimpressive record, neurologists did not wax enthusiastic over anticoagulant therapy. ("Neurologists are scared by negative studies," one neurologist dryly remarked. "Not cardiologists.")

The first stroke specialist to conduct a proper clinical trial on aspirin and stroke was William S. Fields of the University of Texas in Houston. In the mid-1960s he noticed that his patients who took ASA regularly had fewer problems with thrombosis and other diseases of the blood vessels. A big man with a booming voice and dark-rimmed glasses, Fields spoke to many of his friends about this impression. "They all pooh-poohed it," he said later. In the late sixties, he received a phone call from William K. Hass, a neurologist friend at New York University. Hass asked, in Fields's recollection, "You see that abstract [of a paper] published by Harvey Weiss over here? It says aspirin inhibits platelet aggregation!"

The news was all that Fields needed. With funding from three aspirin firms, Hass and Fields convened a small, closed meeting in 1969 to explore testing aspirin on stroke. Out of the gathering came plans for two clinical trials: one in the United States, which added aspirin to a more general trial on the effects of surgery in stroke patients; and one in Canada, which compared aspirin to another antiplatelet drug, sulfinpyrazone.* Fields and Hass obtained NIH approval to proceed with the U.S. trial, which began at the end of 1971.

The two men asked investigators in hospitals to use aspirin in two groups of patients with a history of TIA or bouts of temporary blindness. Depending on a decision made by the patient's doctor, one group would have surgery to reduce the possibility of a major stroke, while the other group would not. Within each group, patients were randomized between aspirin and placebo.

In the middle of the trial, the NIH reduced its funding because of a mixup in filling out forms. Fields turned to Sterling to make up the difference. With its support, the team was able to stagger through the trial. The findings were like those from Elwood's first trial: Aspirin reduced the probability of death, but the effect was not statistically significant. (The experiment looked at only 178 patients.) Fields saw a significant reduction, however, in the broader category of "unfavorable" outcomes—death, a major stroke, or the frequency of TIAs.

---

* Sulfinpyrazone is a gout medicine. Its ability to inhibit platelet aggregation was accidentally discovered in 1965 by a team of Canadian researchers led by Mustard.

In January 1976, Fields presented his data in preliminary form at a conference in Princeton, and was roundly hooted for his pains. "They called me a charlatan," Fields said angrily. "Clark Millikan, the former chief of neurology at the Mayo Clinic, really let me have it. And then they cut it [Fields's paper] out of the proceedings." In this way Fields learned that his fellow neurologists were more skeptical about the efficacy of aspirin than he had surmised.

Then, Fields said, it got worse. "I received a phone call from a friend. 'The NIH doesn't believe you, Bill! They're going to send a site-visit team to Houston!' " To his shock and anger, Fields was grilled about the integrity of his trial. He had been planning to present a paper at the American Heart Association's stroke conference in Dallas that February. The NIH investigators demanded that he withdraw it. They wanted to send referees to determine if Fields had fudged his data. Fields was stunned; he could not understand the reason for their hostility.

"They came down in March [1976]," Fields recalled. "I was going off to an American Academy of Neurology meeting. The stress was terrible—I was starting a resident training program at Houston, and these people were going over the data. I drove up to St. Louis with my wife. I was passing blood, and then I passed out. Henry Barnett [a neurologist at the University of Western Ontario, and the leader of the Canadian stroke study] came to the hotel and put me in an ambulance." After recovering, Fields flew home. He spent the rest of 1976 satisfying the NIH and writing up the aspirin study.

His results were published in two parts, the first, on the nonsurgical group of patients, appearing in May 1977. He had hoped to publish the second part, with the patients who had surgery, at the same time, but the troubles with the NIH delayed it by a year. The slowdown was infuriating, because aspirin significantly improved post-surgery recovery—big news. But before the second part appeared, Barnett published the Canadian trial. Among patients with a history of TIA, aspirin reduced the chance of death or a major stroke by more than 30 percent, but this figure, too, just barely passed the test of statistical significance. (The other antiplatelet drug, sulfinpyrazone, had almost no effect.) The Canadian trial also found a curious difference between the effects of aspirin on men and on women. For men, aspirin cut the chance of death or a major stroke by almost 50 percent, a very impressive result. On women, however, it had no discernible impact.

Fields was angered that his study had been held up long enough to lose its unquestioned priority. "If the NIH hadn't gone through this, we could have had it in print a year earlier! Never in my life had I been accused of fabricating data!" The reason for the inexplicable hostility of the NIH came out only later, he said, when he learned that the agency had been in the throes of planning AMIS when he first announced his findings. If it had got round that aspirin had already been found to have significant impact on death, a major stroke, or TIA frequency, he said, "they wouldn't have got anybody in that study." It was, he said, "dirty pool all the way around."

Fields may have been disheartened, but Sterling wasn't. The company went to work immediately after the first, inconclusive part of Fields's study was published. Years before, Sterling had trumpeted an FTC study of analgesics that showed Bayer aspirin was better, though not significantly so, than its competitors; now, with a trial that showed that aspirin had positive, though not significantly so, benefits for stroke, the firm employed the same strategy. In October it distributed eighty thousand reprints of the Fields article to doctors throughout the United States. Fields had acknowledged Sterling's contribution to the study—its Glenbrook Laboratories division had packaged the aspirin and placebo—at the end of the article. "Aspirin from Bayer . . . ," the reprint said. "The Bayer Co., Glenbrook Labs, Div. of Sterling Drug."

The FDA decided to step in. It looked to the agency as if Sterling was trying to advertise Bayer aspirin as a treatment for strokes and TIAs, and there was nothing on the label about either condition. In July 1978, the FDA wrote the firm that "the use of aspirin for the treatment of transient ischemic attacks is not generally recognized as safe and effective." One did not need to be especially attuned to the agency to feel the unspoken threat of a misbranding action.

Sterling's response was to submit an application to change the label in 1979. It was almost the first thing William Soller did when he arrived at the company. Backed by Fields's study, he sought to have aspirin approved for the treatment of TIAs and retinal ischemic attacks (bouts of temporary blindness that sometimes precede a major stroke). Unlike heart attacks, these afflictions had no alternative medical treatments.

The application came before the FDA Peripheral and Central Nervous System Advisory Committee in September 1979. The principal researchers for both studies, Fields and Barnett, appeared in support of Sterling's application. Braced for a fight, Soller was stunned to learn that the committee had apparently decided to approve the application before the meeting. "It was the damnedest thing I ever saw," he said. "We finished the testimony, and the chairman said, 'Well, Bill [Fields], can you live with what we've just decided?' Bill said yes, and that was it. The incredible thing is that when you think about it, the evidence for stroke was much weaker than the evidence we later had for heart attack, but this one just sailed through the agency." The reason, Soller said, was that there was no alternative therapy available.

The Canadian study persuaded the committee that the data were insufficient to include women or retinal ischemic attacks; the professional uses for aspirin were expanded to cover TIAs or stroke in men alone. Soller was pleased. Seeing the evidence mount for heart attack as well, he prepared to push another application through a different FDA advisory committee. But even when Soller contacted Richard Peto, he was in no way prepared for the torrent that was soon to engulf aspirin in the United Kingdom.

Fields's study appeared as the Oxford trial group was set to begin an astonishing flurry of activity. Peto had already begun the rudiments of his meta-analysis of the six aspirin trials, and was discussing with Doll the crazy notion of asking every doctor in the United Kingdom to join a clinical trial on the prevention of first heart attacks by aspirin. In addition, Peto was talking about yet another trial with Charles Warlow, the young visiting neurologist at Oxford. A former lecturer at the University of Aberdeen, Warlow had been constantly confronted by patients with TIAs in his practice. Warlow didn't know how to help them. Stroke, he found out, was an unfashionable affliction in British neurology. Almost nobody seemed to be looking at it. He brought his interest to Oxford in 1976, when he became a lecturer in neurology there. The result was a clinical trial of aspirin for the treatment of TIAs.

Having listened to Peto, Warlow was determined not to have his trial suffer from the problem of small numbers. The British TIA trial got under way in 1978, with Peto as its statistician. Cannily, Peto did not fully explain to Warlow just how big he thought the trial would have to be. "He kept on moving the sample size up as the trial continued," Warlow recalled with amusement. Although his initial plan was for 1,000 patients, Peto eventually inveigled him into enrolling more than 2,400. (The number did not have to be as large as for a heart attack study, because one out of every three TIA victims will have another stroke in five years.)

While he waited for the TIA numbers to crawl upward, Peto and another Oxford statistician, Peter Sandercock, assembled a grand meta-analysis of all antiplatelet trials. By combing through journals, hunting through conference proceedings, sending out pleading letters, and listening to the grapevine, they eventually turned up thirty-one randomized trials in which an antiplatelet drug had been tested as a prophylaxis against the recurrence of TIAs, stroke, angina, or heart attack. Altogether they involved some 29,000 patients, of whom 3,000 had done the easily measured thing, and died. After much cajoling, Peto and Sandercock managed to induce investigators to send them the raw data from twenty-five of these trials (the other six were ongoing). They commenced the laborious process of entering all the numbers into the Oxford computer and extracting a single number from all the trials: the difference between the observed number and expected number of what they termed "important vascular events," that is, something bad that happened to the patient's blood vessels, including heart attack, stroke, TIA, thrombophle-bitis, and any of the other mishaps caused by thrombi.

Meanwhile, they had begun the British doctors trial. For six years, Peto,

Doll, Rory Collins, and Charles Hennekens tracked the physicians as they took their aspirin and filled out biannual questionnaires. They had chosen a relatively high dose of aspirin—about one and a half tablets a day—to be sure of disabling the doctors' platelets. As a result, many complained that their stomachs were upset by the regime. The collaborators decided to keep the trial going until, as Peto put it, the physicians "voted with their feet" and refused to play along anymore.

The British doctors' reluctance placed even more importance on the big experiment with American doctors that Peto felt had to accompany his trial. After the first application was turned down by the NIH, Hennekens became the sole principal investigator for a U.S. primary heart attack prevention trial. Associated with Harvard and a former NIH staffer to boot, Hennekens got the Physicians' Health Study approved, though there was still hostility to its simple design. The government kicked in $3.7 million; in return, Hennekens put together a gigantic enterprise. As a first step, he mailed invitations, consent forms, and questionnaires to the 261,248 male physicians between the ages of forty and eighty-four who lived in the United States. By December 31, 1983, 112,528 had responded, of whom about half were willing to participate. The numbers were further winnowed down by excluding doctors who had histories of stroke and cardiovascular disease, or who already took aspirin for arthritis. Eventually 33,233 physicians satisfied the entrance requirements. Half were given aspirin; half got placebo; all received identical-looking calendar packs filled with red and white pills made by a special agreement with Bristol-Myers. (Sterling was contacted first, but ultimately chose not to participate because it could not get a guarantee from the FDA that it could advertise the results.) The white tablets—ASA for the aspirin group, placebo for the control group—were for odd days, the red tablets—all placebo—for even days. The aspirin group thus ate one aspirin every other day; the placebo group, of course, had nothing but placebos. After eighteen weeks, Hennekens sent out more letters to participants, asking if they had changed their minds or forgotten to take their pills. Ultimately, 22,071 physicians finished the trial.

Trained in internal medicine, Hennekens received a Ph.D. in epidemiology from Harvard in 1971. Becoming interested in the determinants of coronary disease, he quite naturally heard the aspirin rumors that were beginning to float about. A Research Cardiology Development Award took him to Oxford, where he spent a year with Doll and Peto. "I'd never heard of Richard [Peto] before," Hennekens remembered years later. "He took off my blinders and gave me a perspective on trials. And he essentially set me on to aspirin." Eager to pull off a big, simple trial, he convinced the NIH that the game was worth the candle. "It helped that it was cheap," he said. "MR. FIT [Multiple Risk Factor Information Trial, a big heart disease study done in a more traditionally complicated way] cost them $120 million, and up to

$15,000 a patient. Ours was $40 a patient—good for the budget deficit.''

One argument against such big trials is that they take a long time to set up and are intended to run over a number of years, and hence that major cures may be unnecessarily postponed. ''Clinicians come to me with the idea of studying a hundred people,'' Hennekens said. '' 'It's really a breakthrough, you'll see! It'll show up instantly on a hundred people!' I say, study a couple thousand people, independently monitor the results, and *stop the trial* if you find that you have a miracle drug. That's what we did in the Physicians' Health Study.''

If a treatment turns out exactly as expected, the length of the trial and the number of patients enrolled will be enough to produce a statistically significant result at the end. But if a treatment is more effective, the result becomes significant *earlier* than planned. This presents an ethical problem: Should a trial that has prematurely demonstrated the superiority of a new treatment over placebo be allowed to continue? If the trial is halted too early, as Elwood's was, the results may be too equivocal to be useful; if stopped too late, patients in the placebo group may die unnecessarily.

The answer is to have a monitoring committee, which independently looks at the data while the trial is progressing. If the uncertainty drops to a predetermined level, the committee shuts down the trial. Thus the Physicians' Health Study was watched over by a team of doctors from NIH, which met twice a year to review the accumulating data. For several years it had little to do, because the trial had excluded so many unhealthy physicians from its sample that very few of the doctors in the study became seriously ill. After four years, fewer than 40 of the 22,071 physicians had died. But during the first months of 1988 the seven-member board began to worry. And by the end of the year it became apparent that something had to be done.

Hennekens was sitting on a bombshell. The control group had experienced 189 heart attacks, but there were only 104 in the aspirin group, a difference of more than 40 percent. A few minutes on a pocket calculator sufficed to show that the numbers had less than one chance in one hundred thousand of being a random fluctuation. The implications were staggering. Nobody had ever developed a medicine that was cheap enough to use widely and continuously against a serious disease. Now, perhaps, there was one. If enough people at risk of heart attacks could be induced to swallow an aspirin every other day, thousands upon thousands of lives would be saved—*if*, of course, they could be induced to swallow an aspirin. Such a program had never been done before; at the very least, the findings would inaugurate a new era in public health. Meanwhile, there was the problem of what to do with the Physicians' Health Study.

Over Peto's vehement objection, the committee stopped the trial. Soon after, it added Hennekens to its number. After phoning the *New England Journal of Medicine,* the most prestigious journal in the country, Hennekens wrote a summary in three days. The *Journal* sped the manuscript through an expedited review, and on January 7 accepted it for publication. The editor, Arnold Relman, wanted to print it on January 21, but Hennekens insisted that the article be delayed a week so that he could send a letter to the participants.

Relman had been anxious to issue the article quickly because he feared that its dramatic results would be splashed over newspapers and the evening news before the *Journal*'s subscribers had a chance to digest the report. (To ensure that this didn't happen, the editors made reporters promise not to describe its contents until the official date of publication.) In mid-January, rumors appeared on business wire services. Then, on January 26, the Reuters news agency released the full story through its wire service. Relman was furious and canceled its subscription to the *Journal*.

As expected, the Hennekens study was greeted by front-page coverage in newspapers across the world. What was not expected was that two days later the *British Medical Journal,* the most prestigious in the United Kingdom, published the results of the three Oxford aspirin studies—the British doctors trial, the TIA trial, and the overview—in a single issue. They appeared together because Peto, mindful of the need to convince skeptics, thought the work would gather more attention as an ensemble than as three separate reports. The British doctors trial had come to an end in November 1984. (Its work were inconclusive—an "implausible lack of effect," Peto said—but a later meta-analysis of the U.S. and U.K. doctors trials showed what he believed to be the "true" effect of aspirin on first heart attacks: a reduction of about a quarter.) The U.K. TIA trial was completed two years later. (Aspirin reduced the chance of subsequent stroke or heart attack by one-fifth.) But publication was delayed by the complexity of passing the anti-platelet meta-analysis through all the coordinators of the thirty-one trials. The entire package had just been run through the final proofs when Peto got word that the Physicians' Health Study had been shut down. He thought the decision wrong, because he suspected that the very high benefit shown for aspirin in the American experiment was a fluke, and with more time the rate would drop to something more realistic. But events had overtaken the slow pace of scientific research, and Peto, like everyone else, was struggling to keep up.

Aspirin was so hot in the spring of 1988 that the unthinkable happened: Anacin admitted it was made from aspirin. In just a few weeks, publicity from the heart attack study convinced American Home to do what decades of FTC pressure had never accomplished. It happened almost magically. All at once, television screens were filled by a square-jawed man of journalistic aspect who stood before a newspaper printing press. "I've been writing a lot of stories about aspirin lately," the man said in a confident voice. "But if you think you've heard all about it, think again." He flourished a newspaper with a story headlined A BETTER ASPIRIN FORMULA. Then came a graph. A white line indicating the "Pain Relief Level" of regular-strength aspirin crawled along the bottom. Then, rising majestically above it, came the yellow line of Anacin. "Anacin," an announcer said, while teletypes clattered in the background. "A better aspirin formula." (The formula, of course, was just aspirin and caffeine—that, at least, had not changed.)

Given this remarkable corporate turnabout, it is little wonder that the FDA feared that frenzied consumers would consume huge quantities of the drug. On March 2, Commissioner Frank Young summoned aspirin makers to the meeting in his office. He told them not to advertise the Physicians' Health Study, though they could still tout aspirin as a preventive for second heart attacks. They did; ad budgets shot up. Drug chains made plans to increase their promotion of aspirin with more advertising, floor displays, and price reductions. Grocery stores stocked up at a pace more than 50 percent faster than the previous year. All the while, competing aspirin commercials blitzed the airwaves. In one set, Bufferin too came out of the closet, using tennis pro Arthur Ashe to tout its "tri-buffered" aspirin formula in commercials. Another had Ecotrin claiming it was "the one heart specialists recommend more than Bayer." Proud fathers in yet a third watched their daughters graduate, thanks to the Bayer aspirin that saved them from second heart attacks. Anacin, disallowed by the FDA from claiming that caffeine contributes to cardiovascular health, had to content itself with muttering about "startling news" about aspirin.

To the makers of acetaminophen and ibuprofen, the boom must have been hard to believe. It was as if a long-vanquished foe suddenly had come back to life, as unable to stay safely dead as the supervillains fought again and again by costumed heroes. (In the tradition of the comic books, the villain returned when the hero was in a weakened condition—a second Tylenol-poisoning scare in February 1987 put a crimp in acetaminophen sales.) Although Wall Street analysts predicted that the U.S. analgesic market would expand beyond $2.2 billion, its 1987 level, they also predicted that Tylenol wouldn't get any of the increase—aspirin would grab it all. True, Tylenol was still the most important individual brand, with 30 percent of the analgesic market. True, too, the combined share of the four leading U.S. brands of aspirin—Anacin, Bayer, Bufferin, and Excedrin—was only 23 percent. But those numbers masked the fact that one of those brands, Bayer, was on a roll. The "Wonder Drug That Works Wonders" had managed to climb back into second place among aspirin brands, an altitude it had not reached for years.

Aspirin, too, was flourishing. In 1987, it had regained its position as the nation's analgesic. After the news about heart attacks broke, demand was so great at one East Coast food chain, Giant Foods, that a six-bottle limit was placed on sales of aspirin. People were hoarding aspirin. *Hoarding aspirin*—could anything have sounded sweeter to an aspirin maker's ears?

The craze was by no means confined to the marketers. Knowing that aspirin blocks prostaglandins, and that prostaglandins inhibit the immune system, some scientists talked of ASA as a short-term booster of such immune agents as interferon and interleukin-2. George Washington University cardiologist Judy Hsia spent part of 1988 and 1989 inveigling college students to take aspirin and then stand in a mist of cold and influenza viruses. The experiments were inconclusive, but Hsia regarded the amplification of the immune system induced by aspirin as sufficiently important that the drug could well become part of the next generation of flu vaccines.

Because people with weakened immune systems are less able to fight off cancer and AIDS, doctors cautiously tested to see if aspirin could play a role in the treatment of these ailments. According to Chicago cancer researcher Donald P. Braun, many types of tumor need prostaglandins to thrive. The obvious implication is that aspirin, which suppresses prostaglandins, may be of some benefit. In the spring of 1991, one study suggested that regular doses of aspirin may reduce the risk of colon and rectal cancer by almost one-half. Similarly, Braun said, it is now "pretty widely appreciated that at certain stages of AIDS infection one sees abnormal monocyte [white blood cell] function, and that can be somewhat relieved with these compounds." All tests so far have been exclusively on the laboratory bench, but Braun thought it possible that aspirin or its cousins might ultimately play a role in fighting AIDS, perhaps by helping people who have the virus but do not yet experience any symptoms.

In Oxford, Rory Collins and another epidemiologist, Ian Chalmers, took aspirin into an arena once considered taboo: pregnancy. Pregnant women have long been told to avoid aspirin, because it induces bleeding and possibly miscarriage. Yet pre-eclampsia, the most common serious complication of pregnancy, seems to be caused by tiny thrombi in the placenta—exactly the sort of condition that might be treated by aspirin. (The thrombi reduce the flow of blood to the fetus; when the mother's body tries to force nutrients through the barrier, she may damage her liver and kidneys even as the fetus starves; bad cases of pre-eclampsia lead to seizure and death for both mother and child.) An Oxford-based study of pre-eclampsia, the Collaborative Low-dose Aspirin Study in Pregnancy (CLASP), is still pending, but the English tabloids have already published articles about "aspirin babies," complete with photos of cooing infants and grinning, tearful mums saved by aspirin.

Just as dramatic may be aspirin's ability to ameliorate senility. Coming without pain or sudden warning, senility gradually steals away cherished recollections, the ability to take care of oneself, and then even one's own personality. Recently it has become possible to distinguish between two principal causes of senility: Alzheimer's disease and what is called "multi-infarct dementia." (Infarct, again, is medical jargon for the death of tissue.) Multi-infarct dementia is the loss of mental ability caused by many small strokes in the tiny blood vessels of the brain, each destroying a bit of tissue, each pushing the victim gently down the slope of forgetting. The cost of caring for multi-infarct dementia patients has been estimated at $13 billion a year; the personal cost to the victim is, of course, incalculable.

John Stirling Meyer, director of the Cerebral Blood Flow Laboratory at the Houston Veterans Administration Medical Center, has been trying to cut down that cost—with aspirin. The author of more than 750 scientific papers, Meyer studied stroke for three decades. Because strokes occur mostly among the elderly, his interests widened to include other diseases of older people, especially senile dementia. In a pilot study, Meyer assembled seventy people with multi-infarct dementia. To half he administered an aspirin a day; to the rest he gave no aspirin. He watched both groups for three years. "The patients who received aspirin showed an increase in cerebral blood flow and cognition," he said later. "From the practical point of view, that meant that some could return to work, and many no longer needed supervision by their spouses and families." More and bigger experiments are needed, he cautioned. But if aspirin becomes a weapon against senility, the implications are startling: The generation of babies that survive pre-eclampsia thanks to aspirin may postpone senility with the same drug.

Even that was not the end of the good news. In March 1988, rumors circulated of aspirin's unexpected ability not only to prevent heart attacks but also to treat them while they occur. Several treatments for acute heart attack existed, but doctors did not agree on their merits. In 1980 an international group of scientists decided to evaluate them collaboratively. Coordinated by Rory Collins, the International Study of Infarct Survival (ISIS) selected beta-blockers, which reduce blood pressure, for its first trial. Twenty-three previous clinical trials had failed to establish whether administering intravenous beta-blockers during the early hours of a heart attack was a good idea. After three and one half years, 245 coronary care centers in fourteen nations, and 16,027 patients, ISIS found a 15 percent reduction in mortality—small, but definitely worthwhile.

ISIS went so smoothly that ISIS-2 began just two months after the first study had ended. The treatment chosen for the second go-round was streptokinase, manufactured primarily by Behringwerke AG, a German pharmaceutical firm, under the brand name Streptase. Streptokinase is one of a class of drugs called thrombolytics: drugs that dissolve ("lyse," in medical terminology) the fibrin in a thrombus. Until the late 1970s, Behringwerke considered streptokinase to be almost worthless; a string of trials had been inconclusive, and the drug was off patent in any case. The company agreed to support the trial only as a favor to streptokinase's inventor, who sat on the board and was about to retire. Peto, Collins, and Salim Yusuf, a visiting statistician from the National Heart, Lung, and Blood Institute, and others performed the by now familiar technique of viewing these past trials collectively rather than individually. Streptokinase was effective, they found, in dissolving thrombi and reducing mortality if administered shortly after the onset of a heart attack. At the last moment, they decided to include an antiplatelet drug in the trial. Aspirin was the cheapest. "It was a bit of a shot in the dark," Collins admitted. "It appeared to be a whim, and most people expected no effect."

Reasonably so, for ISIS-2 would give half a tablet of aspirin to patients no later than twenty-four hours after the onset of a heart attack and continue for just one month thereafter. Arriving at a coronary care center, patients would randomly receive placebo, aspirin alone, streptokinase alone, or aspirin and streptokinase. Begun in 1985, the trial eventually enlisted more than seventeen thousand patients in four hundred hospitals. As announced at the annual American College of Cardiology meeting on March 29, 1988, the results were astounding. Both drugs were very effective for surviving an acute heart attack. But the combination of aspirin and streptokinase slashed mortality by up to 50 percent—nearly twice as potent as either drug alone, and far better than anyone had guessed. "I was as amazed as anyone else," Peto said. "I couldn't believe what was coming out." Streptokinase, a cheap drug, and aspirin, the cheapest drug, cut deaths from acute heart attack in half. This was no statistical artefact—it was, at least in potential number of lives saved, one of the greatest advances in medicine since the development of the smallpox vaccine.

By the summer of 1988, the National Institutes of Health was sponsoring at least thirty-five investigations of aspirin for conditions running the gamut of medical disciplines. The companies had barraged consumers with publicity, and acetaminophen and ibuprofen were running scared. American Home was rumored to be planning a pure-aspirin product that it could plug for heart conditions, and Ecotrin was chortling over the success of its ad campaign. Polls showed that nine out of ten Americans knew the news about aspirin, a level so high that Sterling, in a perverse sign of triumph, cut its ad budget for Bayer aspirin—there was nobody left to inform.

Newsweek neatly captured the ambiance in the drug world when it put a big white aspirin tablet on its cover in August 1988, two weeks after the publication of ISIS-2. The headline was simple:

Miracle Drug

The wheel had turned full circle. Decades after the death of Carl Duisberg, aspirin firms no longer had to advertise. They merely had to remind doctors of their existence, which the old man had always thought was best. That didn't stop the laboratory lights from burning late, of course. Indeed, the pharmacologists at places like Sterling were busier than ever. What were they looking for? Robin Mills, president of Sterling, explained it with a trace of a smile. "New aspirins, of course," he said. "This one's been good for a while, but we'd really make some money if we could find another one."

E P I L O G U E

"THE ECONOMIC INCENTIVES"

The doctors were being treated well. The long tables in the great dining hall of Christ Church College were laden with trout and rabbit, and waiters stood by through the evening with bottles of Chablis and Côtes du Rhône. No students marred the festivities with their presence—the second quinquennial meeting of the Antiplatelet Trialists Collaboration had been planned to take advantage of spring recess. Two hundred strong, the scientists had made the trip through rain and fog to Oxford to celebrate the latest accomplishments of what was surely the biggest medical research project ever undertaken. It was the last weekend of March 1990, and the Oxford computers, whirring into the early hours of Saturday morning, had tabulated a staggering 115,701 patients in 207 completed trials, of whom some 6,011 had died from "vascular events" such as heart attack.

Practicing what they preached, most of the M.D.'s and Ph.D.'s spurned the eggs and bacon for their breakfast on Saturday; selections ran to yogurt and cereal, accompanied by coffee that was most often black. All part of the global sodality of science, the collaborators knew one another well from previous meetings; they drifted in conversational knots of threes and fours across the empty campus.

They regrouped in a medium-sized auditorium in the University Chaplaincy. At the head of the room sat that universal feature of scientific congresses, an overhead projector. It showed the first of what was to become a numbing series of transparencies. The man explaining what the slide meant was Richard Peto, the animating spirit—he resisted terms like "leader" as insufficiently recognizing the efforts of others—of the huge enterprise. Pacing around the projector, Peto ran through what had become a polished performance on the need for and principles of meta-analysis: bigger studies; the need to emphasize overall results, rather than looking at subgroups of the population; the avoidance of moderate biases; the appreciation of moderate benefits. "If I ever hear about mixing apples and oranges again I'm going to scream,'' he said, not for the first time. And he led his audience through a sample overview, taking the observed vascular events in the treatment group (O) and subtracting them from the vascular events that would be expected with no treatment (E), then adding up a column of the results:

$$[(O - E)_1 + (O - E)_2 + \ldots + (O - E)_n].$$

It was the sort of calculation, he joked, that most people learned when they were ten or eleven and then promptly forgot. If each quantity $(O - E)$ differs randomly from zero, he said, then the grand total should be zero. But if they all drift the same way, the summing-up amplifies the positive result. This is what he had done with the 207 trials.

Throughout his presentation, Peto spoke of ''antiplatelet drugs,'' but he was principally talking about aspirin. Twenty antiplatelet drugs had been tested by the collaboration, but the overwhelming majority of the trials examined aspirin—part of the transformation of aspirin into a sizable scholarly industry.

With the sea of data generated by the collaboration, Peto said, science was at last in a position to understand the benefits of the most widely used drug in the world. Aspirin had benefits that could be characterized paradoxically as modest and enormous. It was by no means a cure-all. ''The ten-ton truck rule applies,'' he said. ''No pill can protect you against an oncoming ten-ton truck.'' But across the board aspirin in particular and antiplatelet therapy in general had significant benefits for every type of thrombotic condition. Stroke, heart attack, transient ischemic attacks, pulmonary embolism, deep-vein thrombosis, peripheral vascular disease, renal hemodialysis fistulas, coronary artery bypass graft complications—aspirin worked on the whole dreadful list. ''The world is getting simpler,'' Peto said, closing his speech. ''There are very few times in medical research when this can be said.''

His collaborators stood behind the projector to deliver the latest entries in the list of almost monotonously successful results. Sometimes the benefits were extraordinary. Antiplatelet therapies prevented a startling 60 to 70 percent of pulmonary embolisms and 30 to 40 percent of deep-vein thrombosis, a common post–heart attack and post-surgery syndrome in which thrombi form in veins deep within the body. In both conditions the odds were less than one in one hundred thousand that the results were due to chance. After placing these results on the screen, a rather gleeful Rory Collins quoted prominent experts' past claims that aspirin was useless for this condition. Although the NIH had once recommended the use of aspirin for deep-vein thrombosis in 1975, he informed the audience, it had reversed itself and disparaged aspirin in March 1986. ''Perhaps 1 percent of all general surgery patients die because of pulmonary embolism,'' he said. ''Aspirin can cut that dramatically.''

"It's more than that," Peto said, interrupting. "There's been a serious medical mistake over the last ten years that has resulted in very large numbers of people not being protected. In developed countries alone, there's millions of patients this has immediate relevance to. It couldn't be clearer—give these people aspirin and you'll be saving lives."

Peter Sandercock of Edinburgh listed the results from the stroke studies. The overall reduction from antiplatelet therapy was a good 18 to 26 percent. Again, the chance of being wrong was less than one in one hundred thousand. Aspirin apparently produced a slight excess of one type of stroke, hemorrhagic stroke (burst blood vessels in the brain), but this was vastly counterbalanced by the "very important" improvement in the more common occlusive stroke (blocked blood vessels in the brain).

Did it matter, he was asked, that many of the stroke results came from studies on doctors? Didn't they have access to much better medical care than most others?

It doesn't matter, Peto said, jumping to his feet. If anything, it was good, because doctors were accurately diagnosed when they got sick. That, he said dryly, "was one reason that it's much better to study doctors than human beings."

The representative from the FDA rose. He was wearing a blue suit and a white shirt, an exception in the roomful of slacks and sweaters. He was extremely skeptical. He asked about side effects (the reports in clinical trials are higher than the real situation, Peto said, because patients are encouraged to report them). He asked about dosage (nobody yet knows the optimal dosage for aspirin, Peto said, but one tablet will certainly do the trick, especially if it is enteric-coated, that is, covered with a thin, gelatinlike film that makes the pill easier to digest). He asked about hemorrhagic stroke (aspirin will make you bleed, but it is extremely unlikely to kill you). He asked about the size of the change in mortality with aspirin (bigger even than it seems, Peto said, because so many people do not take their medicine).

A few minutes later, a break was called. The assembled researchers filed out for tea and biscuits. It seemed as if the entire world of aspirin stood in one room. William Fields waited behind Charles Warlow, and Rory Collins filled his coffee ahead of J. A. Schoenberger from Chicago, a member of the unlucky AMIS trial, which was included in the overview. (Charles Hennekens was among the few who were absent; he got sick at the last moment.) Peto stood talking with the skeptical man from the FDA and Earle Lockhart, Sterling's new medical director. Peto had been up until five that morning working out computer glitches, but his pleasure and excitement were evident from across the room. He was seeing the validation of beliefs he had nurtured for years. He had coordinated a big, simple trial, and got a big, simple result: Antiplatelet therapy worked across the board.

"There have been hypotheses about all these subgroups," Peto was say-

ing. He was looking at Lockhart, but an outside observer might have been
excused for imagining that the vehemence of his tone was reserved for the
man from the FDA. "That aspirin works for males but not females, that it
works for middle-aged but not for the old, that it would be dangerous for
hypertensives but work particularly well for diabetics. Male-female, diabetic-
nondiabetic, old-young, high blood pressure–low blood pressure—it's all the
same. The idea that antiplatelet therapy should focus on men should be
absolutely and totally abandoned." He waved the sheaf of charts in his hand.
"You'll see it in the afternoon session," he said. "We're ending that question as of 3:00 P.M. There can be no more reasonable discussion of it."

If aspirin was beneficial to everyone, Peto was asked by a listener, did that
mean everyone should take it?

"Dr. Lockhart here would like that," he said.

Lockhart, a wiry, bearded man with owlish glasses, spread his hands in a
gesture of "What can I say?"

"It's an extremely interesting situation," Peto said. "Normally, I believe
that one should separate the theoretical analysis of a public health problem
from the decision as to what, if any, action to take about it. For instance, it
is absolutely clear that high cholesterol levels contribute to heart disease, and
that reducing them would save lives. But one shies away from making the
recommendation that the nation should go on a cholesterol-reducing program, if that involves giving millions of people unpleasant drugs that they
can't afford, and telling them to change their diets so drastically that for all
we know the agricultural system may capsize, and with it, of course, the
economy. That's for a government to decide.

"Aspirin may be another matter. The number of people who are going to
suffer serious side effects from one 325-milligram tablet of enteric-coated
aspirin is small indeed, and the majority of them can quickly recover by
stopping the treatment. You find yourself asking, Why *shouldn't* we push all
the adults in high-risk categories to take it? It's safe, it's quite effective, and
it's so cheap that it would have next to no financial impact on people's lives.

"It not only would not capsize the economy"—he glanced at Lockhart and
laughed—"it apparently would not even have much effect on the analgesic
companies."

As the ripples of the multiple new uses for aspirin spread across the world,
they lapped up against Nicholas Laboratories, the makers of Aspro and the
second-oldest aspirin company in the world. Like Sterling, Nicholas believed
that the new scientific aura around aspirin might lead consumers to regard it
with greater respect and possibly buy it instead of acetaminophen for their
headaches and fever. Encouraged by the FDA's decision to accept aspirin as
a preventive for second heart attacks, Nicholas put together a similar appli-

cation to the Department of Health and Social Services, the British equivalent of the U.S. Department of Health and Human Services.

The department rejected the application, partly because the agency was not yet prepared to accept Peto's brand of medical evidence, and partly because the optimal dose of aspirin for these new uses had never been established. Nicholas was dismayed: The aspirin clinical trials being conducted used all sorts of dose levels, with no standard yet to emerge. (This was because different doses are standard in different countries.) Until the medical community pronounced with any certainty what the best dose should be, the message from the Department of Health and Social Services was that no new uses would be forthcoming.

In 1987 Nicholas tried again. This time the company decided to find a new use for aspirin where a single study produced a significant result. This would avoid the problem of combining results and doses of aspirin. It would also raise the problem of basing a drug therapy on what might be a flukishly positive result, but the Department of Health and Social Services could hardly complain about that. The company found what it was looking for in a paper that had been published three years earlier in the *Lancet*. Conducted by a team of cardiologists in Munich and partly funded by Bayer AG, the trial had found that one hundred milligrams of aspirin significantly decreased the chance that a thrombus would form in a grafted blood vessel following coronary bypass surgery. (One hundred milligrams is standard for children's aspirin in Germany.) Nicholas submitted the results of the trial and got the department's approval. The result was Platet 100, first marketed in a calendar pack in July 1988. Only ten thousand coronary bypass surgeries are performed in Britain every year, and Nicholas knew that the market for Platet was therefore limited. Nonetheless, Nicholas thought of it as a chink in the armor of the Department of Health and Social Services. Shortly thereafter, based on ISIS-2 and the results of the Veterans Administration trial for unstable angina, Nicholas applied for and was granted two more new uses, secondary myocardial infarction and unstable angina. Platet 300 became the first aspirin to be marketed in the United Kingdom for heart attack prevention.

Nicholas charged Noel Rabouhans, the manager of their Medical Products Division, with marketing Platet. It was clear he didn't have high hopes. Nor was he interested in sponsoring pathbreaking research such as that of the Antiplatelet Trialists Collaboration. "You'd have to sell a hell of a lot of aspirin to get your money back from a clinical trial," he recently explained. Something in his tone suggested that he didn't think that would happen. Indeed, something in his tone suggested that he regarded Platet as a kind of good-news/bad-news joke. The good news was that his employer, Nicholas International, had a major new prescription drug for heart attacks. The bad news was that Nicholas Labs had already been selling it for seven decades.

*   *   *

A few people at the antiplatelet meeting were as glum as Rabouhans. They were the representatives of the drug companies whose products were under scrutiny. They were anxious about the second part of the presentation, in which the merits of the various drugs would be compared one against another. Some of these treatments were highly profitable; others were the object of much hope. Their makers had voluntarily produced information from proprietary studies; now they were about to learn if their efforts would be rewarded. They were waiting, in short, to see if the other shoe would drop.

No one doubted that the data being flashed on the screen could have commercial impact. They had seen what happened after ISIS-2, the big clinical trial that showed that aspirin and streptokinase could sharply cut mortality in acute heart attacks. Even at two hundred dollars a shot, the going price, streptokinase sales had shot up after ISIS-2. That was good news for Behringwerke, its chief manufacturer—but terrible news for the competition, Activase.

Activase is a trade name for tissue plasminogen activator (TPA). Like streptokinase, TPA works by activating the blood's own chemical system for dissolving a thrombus. The difference is that TPA is made by genetic engineering, and costs more than two thousand dollars a dose—so much that alarmed legislators in several nations had considered refusing to allow government health plans, like Medicare, to pay for it. Discovered, patented, and manufactured by Genentech, of South San Francisco, California, one of the first biotechnology firms, TPA was initially hailed (by Genentech's corporate officers, at least) as a panacea for acute heart attacks. And despite the shock over the incredible price, TPA made more money upon its introduction in 1987 than any drug ever.

The release of data from ISIS-2 at the end of March 1988 put a damper on Genentech's spirits, and a dent in its stock. Whereas the doctors in the study focused on the unexpected power of aspirin, Wall Street focused on the fact that streptokinase and aspirin were just as good as Activase. Genentech's stock lost almost 25 percent of its value in the next two months. By the time ISIS-2 was formally published in the *Lancet* the following August, Genentech stock valued at $52 per share in 1987 was selling for little more than $20—which meant, at least in theory, that the company had lost more than half of its value to one clinical study. At the time of the antiplatelet meeting, it had crept back up to $25⅜, in part, analysts said, because the firm had announced on February 2 that it would merge with Roche Holding, a big Swiss drug company.

Genentech was unlikely to be disturbed further by the antiplatelet collaboration, because TPA was not intended for the same uses as antiplatelet drugs. But that was not true of the makers of the nineteen non-aspirin anti-platelet drugs, which were distinctly vulnerable. The most notable of these therapies were sulfinpyrazone, sold mostly under the name Anturane by Ciba-Geigy, of Summit, New Jersey; ticlopidine hydrochloride, a relatively recent entry made in North America by Syntex, of Palo Alto, California, but not yet approved by the FDA; and dipyridamole, sold as Persantine by Boehringer Ingelheim, of Germany.

The question was whether aspirin was going to reach out and drag them down to its commercial level. Unlike their cousins in the over-the-counter field, these drug firms rarely compared their products with one another; it was too hard and too expensive to establish definite claims of superiority. More than likely, one drug would only be slightly different from the other, and, as Peto had shown, a huge trial would be needed to establish the difference clearly. The Antiplatelet Trialists Collaboration had provided that unwelcome opportunity. Little wonder that the company representatives pulled out their notebooks and jotted furious notes when Peto placed his transparencies on the overhead projector.

Knowing that firms like Syntex, Ciba-Geigy, and Boehringer Ingelheim were major funders of research, some anxious collaboration members had insisted that the meeting be closed to the daily press. The decision was perhaps wise, for Peto gave little satisfaction to the antiplatelet drug makers. "No significant difference," he kept saying. "No significant difference." On the big screen the slides kept flashing, and always aspirin was too close in effect to its competitors to say which was better. "There may be important differences between these agents," Peto said, "but we're a hundred miles away from demonstrating [them]. As of now, there is absolutely nothing to prove there is any difference between the therapeutic effects of these drugs." It was unnecessary to add that when there is no known difference between two drugs, doctors are supposed to prescribe the cheapest and safest, that in this case that would certainly be aspirin, and that if this sentiment got around the result would be painful to people whose fortunes were tied to the other antiplatelet drugs.

A distinct element of unease settled over the gathering. In the ensuing debate, Garrett Fitzgerald of Vanderbilt University raised his hand. He had two worries, he said. The first was that they would send out an overconfident message about aspirin. And the second, he said sharply, "is that we don't discourage the drug industry" with these findings.

"One gains by these side-to-side comparisons," Peto said.

"As far as I can see from this," Fitzgerald said, "what we have here is that ticlopidine is in the ballpark with aspirin, sulfinpyrazone is somewhat less, and dipyridamole has no effect at all. That's fine. *But where are we going to go in the future?*"

Heads nodded across the assembly. Fitzgerald was pointing to an enormous roadblock to progress in the treatment of heart disease, and everyone
knew it. The problem was aspirin.

In terms of cost per life saved, aspirin was likely the greatest medical
miracle ever discovered. But it also put researchers in a peculiar bind. Imagine that in 1995 some brilliant drug company researcher developed a therapy
that prevented 33 percent of heart attacks. To prove the new drug's efficacy
it would be matched up not against a placebo but against aspirin, because
researchers could not ethically give the control group anything less than the
best known treatment, which is aspirin. The 33 percent benefit of the new
drug is better than the 30 percent of aspirin, and would translate into saving
thousands of lives around the world each year. But the improvement is small
in statistical terms and discerning it from random chance would require a trial
of several hundred thousand people. Not many private entities can gamble on
such costly experiments. Even if the treatment is somehow tested, M.D.'s
may well counsel their patients to take aspirin anyway because it has few side
effects and because the disparity in therapeutic effectiveness is not enough to
overcome the disparity in price. "It will be very, very difficult to beat
aspirin," Lockhart said. "No matter what they come up with, Bayer aspirin
will still cost three dollars for a bottle of one hundred."

To Peto, these worries seemed far in the future. His more immediate
concern was the article eventually to be published by the huge collaboration.
Simply circulating drafts among hundreds of scientists at dozens of institutions would be a logistical nightmare. Each person in the room being an
expert, there would be an inevitable divergence of opinions. And then, he
said, there was the pressing matter of the future of the team itself. Hands
raised; people rose to make points. Peto stood up front, nodding, the overhead projector making his pale features seem even more pale. In a few
minutes it was clear that most people thought enough mysteries remained to
keep things interesting. They would keep working; there would be another
meeting in 1995. "Good," Peto said, smiling. "We'll see you in five years.
By then we should have some *data*. The trial will be getting into some real
numbers."

It was late in the afternoon. Physicians are busy souls; many were already
late for other engagements. The discussion continued, numbers being traded
about aspirin, the FDA man raising his cautious objections. One by one the
people quietly left, drifting into the rain and back to work. Many of them
would return in five years, and the list of ailments under Peto's scrutiny
would grow longer.

Six months before, on August 18, 1989, John Stirling Meyer, the neurologist
who treated multi-infarct dementia with aspirin, had arrived in a cab at the

Park Avenue headquarters of Sterling Drug. He had entered the white lobby and rode the elevator up to the seventh floor. His hat, so to speak, was in his hand: He was there to ask Sterling for money.

Glenbrook Laboratories, the Sterling subsidiary that was Meyer's destination, has its medical offices on the seventh floor of 90 Park Avenue. The rooms are pleasant, quiet, and anonymous, neither shabby enough to seem out of place in a big profitable company nor lavishly enough appointed to offend shareholders. Secretaries tap on computer keyboards beneath fluorescent lighting; fax machines spring into unexpected life at the command of distant callers. After telling Sterling about his research, Meyer had been asked to come here, and it was here that Meyer presented his data to Steven Weisman, Glenbrook's deputy medical director, and several members of its marketing department.

Meyer had published his work in the June issue of the *Journal of the American Geriatrics Society,* which treated the work with the medical journal's inverse mark of respect—it ran an editorial chiding readers who might place too much faith in the results. Part of the reason for the caution was that Meyer's experiment was not a randomized, double-blind, placebo-controlled clinical trial. The reason he had not done the study that way was because he didn't have enough money to order three years' worth of placebo tablets, and had decided to do the best he could with the resources he had. Now Meyer was in New York to see if Sterling would support a second experiment, which would be randomized, double-blind, and placebo-controlled.

Using charts and slides, Meyer told the aspirin executives that perhaps one out of every twenty elderly people in the United States suffers from multi-infarct dementia; that the figure rises to one in twelve for those over 85; and that in the next century this single condition would lay waste to the lives of more than two million older men and women. It was fantastic to think that a drug so cheap and safe—even the carping *Journal* editorial called it "ubiquitous and apparently benign"—could help hundreds of thousands live better lives. As a man who had devoted years of his life to fighting stroke, Meyer found the prospect exhilarating.

After the presentation, Weisman was encouraging but said he would have to talk it over with his superior, Earle Lockhart. (Lockhart was at his father's funeral.) Meyer left with some satisfaction. From Weisman's interested reaction, he thought he might be able to keep going. Some money might come his way, and he would be able to go on.

At first glance, it would appear that a scientist like Meyer would have no trouble obtaining funds from a company to pursue a treatment that not only is important but also will provide a new use for that company's product. If most of the older people with multi-infarct dementia took an aspirin a day, someone would sell a lot of aspirin. Moreover, the extra sales and publicity—

Aspirin Conquers Senility!—would be particularly opportune for Sterling, which was desirous of avoiding another aspirin sales slump.

The marketing people took a different view. When all was said and done, Meyer was asking for a quarter of a million dollars. With aspirin costing somewhere in the realm of a tenth of a penny per pill, Sterling would have to sell millions upon millions of extra tablets to break even. Even that grossly underestimated the company's risk. If Meyer's experiments were wildly successful, somebody—more exactly, some company, and most likely Sterling—would have to shell out the millions necessary to shove the new use through the Food and Drug Administration. Once the FDA approved aspirin as a senility drug, moreover, the approval applied not just to Bayer aspirin, but to every other variety, which would mean that Sterling and Glenbrook Laboratories would have paid for their competitors to gain access to a new market. "The economic incentives for a company to push aspirin through are not there," Steve Weisman said afterward, "whereas the economic incentives are all there to develop a cherry-flavored nose drop."

Unlike some aspirin makers, Sterling had paid its public dues, sponsoring the labeling changes for stroke and heart attacks. In addition, it was committed to paying more than half a million dollars for other research projects, including three big tests with thousands of patients, one on aspirin and heart attacks, and two others using aspirin to treat pre-eclampsia. The firm was supplying thousands of specially manufactured calendar packs of aspirin and placebo, both being flavored and dyed to researchers' particular specifications. At some point the bottom line had to be considered. "It's expensive getting a factory to produce these materials," Lockhart said. "You can't just make this stuff up."

Bearing all these factors in mind, Sterling decided not to fund Meyer's research. There were just too many other revolutionary new uses for aspirin being discovered, and one aspirin company couldn't deal with them all.

In many ways, aspirin is the drug of doctors' dreams. It is hugely effective: One aspirin a day, or every other day, will save hundreds of thousands of lives a year. It can be taken safely by more people than almost any other drug. And it costs next to nothing to the consumer, because it is unpatented, and competition for sales is fierce. Some drugs more effectively attack pain, fever, inflammation, or blood clots, but no other drug is as safe or cheap. It is likely to remain the only heart attack preventive sold in grocery stores for years to come. For all its wondrous abilities, though, marketing this miracle is a nightmare: There's not enough easy money in it. Carl Duisberg, the great industrialist, brought aspirin to the world; but without Ernst Möller, William Weiss, William Laporte, Rosser Reeves, and George Davies—connivers and hucksters all—the drug would never have achieved its monumental success.

These men endeavored to grow ''rich beyond the dreams of avarice'' by staking claim to the public's desire to relieve the aches and pains of everyday life. They differed from their predecessors, the magnetic healers and the cancer treaters, in an important respect: The miracle cure they extolled actually worked. As it now turns out, it works in more ways than they imagined. But without a quick buck to squeeze from the new uses for aspirin, one wonders whether these benefits, discovered after so much effort by so many talented scientists, will ever reach the people most in need of them. Indeed, doctors like Hennekens are convinced that the great majority of people who could benefit from aspirin are not taking it, and that even those people who have been ordered by doctors to use it mostly forget.

Given the opportunity, a present-day Rosser Reeves could get people to take their aspirin. He would give it the old hard sell. Imagine the three Anacin boxes reincarnated, the shrieking announcer returned: ''Stops blood clots! Fights heart attacks!! Wipes out stroke!!!'' Imagine the airwaves filled with a jumble of shrill pitches for serious medicine. It would work; in a sense, it would be a testament to the free-market system, unshackled from the constricting oversight of the FDA and FTC. This way of doing things is dismaying to imagine; its only virtue seems to be that it can get things done faster and more thoroughly than the others.

Such musings are not just philosophical. By the time of Meyer's visit to Sterling, the aspirin bubble of 1988 had well and truly burst. The spurt of aspirin orders after the Physicians' Health Study had proved to be just that—a spurt of orders, not sales. In the wake of the study, U.S. aspirin advertising jumped 22 percent, to $102.7 million. It was all very cautiously worded, of course. It was low-key enough to satisfy doctors. And, unsurprisingly, it didn't work. Hordes of anxious, heart attack–fearing consumers failed to buy aspirin. The dollar volume of ASA sales was absolutely flat in 1988; aspirin's percentage of the analgesic market actually fell. Meanwhile, the market shares of acetaminophen and ibuprofen climbed, bringing grief to any Wall Street analysts who had bet on their own advice from the previous year.

Although its aspirin brand, Bufferin, was used in the Physicians' Health Study, Bristol-Myers abandoned hope in aspirin enough to bring out a new brand, Aspirin-Free Excedrin, in August 1990. It is made from acetaminophen and caffeine, a combination the company said in its advertisements was superior to acetaminophen alone—and hence better than Tylenol. (The evidence for these claims has yet to be accepted by the FDA.) To the surprise of nobody, Johnson & Johnson sued Bristol-Myers for false advertising one week after the commercials began. A judge granted an injunction; Bristol-Myers appealed. In early October, Johnson & Johnson hit the airwaves with a new round of Tylenol ads, urging consumers to ''check the label'' of their pain reliever for the presence of caffeine because ''you certainly don't want to find it in unexpected places.'' Meanwhile, the tension headache lived again in the guise of the "stress" headache, reincarnated by American Home Products in commercials for both Anacin (aspirin and caffeine) and Anacin-3 (acetaminophen). For its part, Sterling broadcast a new slogan: "The wonder drug doctors themselves take more often for pain."*

Aspirin is once again a mere analgesic, back in the trenches fighting the advertising wars with acetaminophen and ibuprofen. These wars have steadily driven up the retail sales of analgesics as a whole: Dollar sales went up 9.5 percent in 1990 to a new height of $2.668 billion. "If that isn't soothing enough," wrote Packaged Facts, a New York–based market research company, the next few years will be "even cushier." Packaged Facts predicted in a special analgesic market study in February 1991 that the year's sales would rise 15 percent. "By 1995," it said, "annual sales growth will stand at 19 percent and the market will reach $5,846 million"—almost $6 billion. The reason for this amazing growth? According to Packaged Facts president David A. Weiss, the 1990s are a "reality decade," an unpleasant time of reckoning that will cause a nationwide wave of stress, which in turn will lead to a boom in headaches.

Unfortunately, Packaged Facts said, aspirin will not share many of these benefits. Aspirin's market share, standing at 42 percent in 1991, will be nibbled away further by ibuprofen. Companies like Sterling may fight back with innovations such as time-release aspirin, Packaged Facts said, but they are doomed. One of the few things that could upset this picture is the discovery of new side effects. With all the screaming press attention paid to minor medical problems, any analgesic that got the rap for a dangerous side effect would be in trouble.

The companies are fully aware of this, of course. Research attention has, in fact, turned from the miracle powers of analgesics to their darker side. Part of this attention comes from the National Toxicology Program, which coordinates federal government research on the toxic effects of chemicals. Although analgesics have not been singled out for special attention, they are included in a number of ongoing NTP studies. When over-the-counter ibuprofen was approved in 1984, public interest groups demanded that the labeling warn about the possibility of kidney damage from constant use of the drug. (Because animal studies have shown the possibility of such damage, the labeling on high-dose, prescription ibuprofen includes such a notification.) Although no evidence has been found that kidney damage can occur in humans, the drug is part of an NTP study for a broader range of toxicological effects.

Late in 1990, the NTP drafted a report on the toxicology and carcinogen-

---

* In the spring of 1990, the company also renewed its decades-old battle with Bayer AG, suing the German company for misusing the Bayer name and Bayer Cross in the United States. Meanwhile, the two companies continued, through the summer of 1991, negotiations toward bringing the Bayer name back to its original owner.

esis of acetaminophen. After a two-year study of male and female rats and mice, there was no evidence of carcinogenic effects of the drug in male rats and in male and female mice; in female rats, there was what the program calls "equivocal" evidence of carcinogenic effects. ("Equivocal" evidence describes study results that show a marginal increase in carcinogenic effects but that fail to establish with any confidence either the presence or absence of such effects.) The results leave the question of a link between acetaminophen and cancer in the same state as before the study: There is no reason yet to believe that the relation exists, but neither is there evidence to rule it out.

Aspirin has not been immune. In an article published in the *British Medical Journal* in November 1989, researchers from the University of Southern California School of Medicine found an elevated risk of kidney cancer in elderly aspirin users. Their conclusions raised a storm of protest from British aspirin manufacturers and other researchers, including a denunciation of the experiment's methodology signed by Rory Collins, Sir Richard Doll, Charles Hennekens, Richard Peto, and Peter Sandercock, among others. As is the case for acetaminophen, the question of aspirin and cancer has now been raised, but science has yet to provide any definite answer to confirm or rule out such a link.

With the issue broached, however, one wonders how long the analgesic companies can afford to leave it alone. Just as Claude Hopkins knew that the product first associated with a simple fact could nevertheless receive "an exclusive and lasting prestige," so the companies know that the first analgesic to be tarred with even a speculative link to a serious affliction will be saddled with "an exclusive and lasting" cloud over its safety.

Some months before, another day had drawn to a close above the Bayer AG factory in Leverkusen. In an office in a high floor of the company headquarters, Jürgen Hohmann was showing a visitor pictures of Bayer Aspirin advertisements. The huge circular BAYER sign, disassembled during the war but remounted in a somewhat less grandiose manner in 1958, is unlighted and barely visible against the gray clouds. "Obviously," he said, "we are delighted by all the news about Aspirin." The man in charge of selling Aspirin, the most famous brand of ASA in the world, Hohmann was explaining his marketing strategy. "And, of course, we have been doing everything we can to make doctors and the public aware that Aspirin is not something old, but a new drug, an exciting drug." The company headquarters is a modern skyscraper that looks out of place next to the older buildings on the campus, which otherwise seems much as William Weiss saw them seventy years ago. Not a trace remains of Duisberg's villa, where he and Carl Bosch argued over the formation of I.G. Farben. The new Bayer AG headquarters is built on top of it.

A few hundred yards away from Hohmann's office is the plant where Aspirin powder is mixed up and put into tablets. The factory is the exact opposite of anything Upton Sinclair ever wrote about. Everything is clean, and almost everything is quiet. The corridors are almost empty; the few people on the assembly lines wear surgical masks and hair nets. A machine pops open the boxes; another stuffs in a bottle of Aspirin. A third drops the packages into a bigger box. Then the boxes are loaded into trucks and ships and trains, and sent out into the world.

A small amount of this Aspirin is put into unmarked cartons and given to laboratories and hospitals for use in clinical trials. Bayer AG, like other ASA manufacturers, sponsors research into the drug; Hohmann said that new requests come to Leverkusen every day, and new suggestions for possible uses. "I can't believe the interest there is in this," he admitted. "We followed the heart attack research closely, but I must tell you truthfully that nobody here ever dreamed of how much bigger it would get." Bayer AG's famously well stocked scientific library was filled to bursting with new reports. Clotting diseases, of course. Influenza. Cancer. Osteoporosis. Even AIDS. Like Sterling, its former partner, then antagonist, now competitor, Bayer AG can't fund more than a tiny fraction of the necessary research, as company representatives acknowledge. It would be economically foolish. The company would never recoup its costs.

There was hope for new consumption, Hohmann said. Few of the people who should be taking Aspirin were actually doing so. Such preventive campaigns had rarely worked in the past; they foundered on the human inability to remember to eat a pill every day unless the consequences were imminent and dire. (Even that may not be enough; look at the figures for unwanted pregnancy.) For most people heart attacks are not imminent, and so they don't take seriously the idea of preventing them. Continued aggressive advertising for Aspirin on television might convince them otherwise, but it was almost never allowed. German television permits commercials to appear only in two blocks during the evening. Hohmann smiled apologetically. It was doubtful in any case that the company could make back the investment, even should such a campaign be permitted.

It was close to night now in Leverkusen. Hohmann was looking through the graphs on his desk, charting the rise and fall of ASA sales. In a few hours, the BAYER sign would come on, all at once, a huge electric Aspirin tablet in the heavens. Until dawn every night, it shines its message—the Bayer name, and with it, the silent command to buy.

A NOTE ON SOURCES

ABBREVIATIONS

NOTES

BIBLIOGRAPHY

ACKNOWLEDGMENTS

INDEX

A NOTE ON SOURCES

This book is built upon archival material and interviews with dozens of scientists, businesspeople, and government officials. Often during the research we were asked if drug companies sponsored our work. They didn't. Except for Bayer AG, Sterling Products, and Nicholas International, every firm mentioned in this book rejected our repeated requests for interviews, assistance, and comment. Indeed, American Home Products refused to let us speak with its public relations staff; the one "interview" with one of its executives—William Laporte—consisted of one off-color characterization of the press and lasted less than thirty seconds. Even Sterling, generous with its help in the early stages of our research, changed its behavior as publication neared. After we sought permission to quote from internal memoranda we had discovered in archives open to the public, Sterling announced that it could "neither confirm nor deny" the accuracy of the quotes and was unable to assist us any further.

Part One is chiefly constructed from documents in archival collections. The history of Farbenfabriken Bayer in the United States before the First World War is taken from Bayer AG's archives in Leverkusen. The takeover of Farbenfabriken Bayer's U.S. operations is covered in the Alien Property Custodian archives in the National Records Center, Suitland, Maryland. Background on the treatment of enemy property during war came from Gathings's *International Law and American Treatment of Alien Enemy Property*. The saga of Sterling and I.G. Farben comes chiefly from three sources: the massive collection of photocopied business documents in the Department of Justice Central Files under Case 60-21-56 (Sterling Products); the smaller but equally important collection of Thomas Corcoran's papers in the Library of Congress; and the company archives of Bayer AG. (Other archival sources are cited in the Notes.) Although we relied on these primary sources, we must acknowledge Howard Ambruster's *Treason's Peace*. We were often stunned by Ambruster's wild, even loony interpretations, but we found not a single instance where his facts were wrong. Finally, the late David Corcoran provided us with a wealth of information on Sterling's activities in South America and the personalities of many of the individuals who populate Part One.

In Part Two, the early history of drug advertising and regulation in the United States owes much to articles and books by David Cavers, who helped write the 1938 Food, Drug, and Cosmetics Act, and James Harvey Young, whose *Medical Messiahs* inspired us to use the Harper trial to open this section. Our discussion of the Federal Trade Commission era is based on FTC records, the coverage in *Food, Drug and Cosmetic Reports* (the ''Pink Sheet'') and *Advertising Age,* and interviews with many of the lawyers involved in the analgesic proceedings. The story of acetaminophen and ibuprofen is based on interviews with the businesspeople and scientists involved, especially Laurie Spalton and Gordon Fryers (for the early days of Panadol); Wayne Nelson and William Lynch (the rise of Tylenol); and Stewart Adams (the discovery, with John Nicholson, of ibuprofen). Also important were contemporary accounts in *Advertising Age* and Celeste Aaron's paper on the Institute for the Study of Analgesic and Sedative Drugs. The attempts by the analgesic companies to saddle one another with label warnings and other regulatory shenanigans are derived from the tons (literally) of paper in the FDA records for the internal analgesic monograph. Finally, the tales of analgesic warfare come from the court records and decisions for the numerous lawsuits that have spanned the past three decades. Our thanks to Judge William Conner and to a Johnson & Johnson lawyer and two drug company executives, the last three of whom wished not to be named, for frank views of the proceedings.

Part Three is based on a stack of medical papers several feet tall and interviews with the medical researchers who have been investigating aspirin for the past twenty years. For the early history of anticoagulants, the works of Karl Link, Irving S. Wright, and John Poole and John French were most useful. The 1971 book by William Fields and William Hass introduced us to Lawrence Craven. Peter Elwood cheerfully gave us an account of his early trials. The unwitting race between Harry Collier and Sir John Vane is covered in Collier's article, ''The Story of Aspirin,'' finished just before his death. Joe Collier also provided us with details of his father's search for aspirin's secrets. Sterling's effort to get aspirin approved as a heart attack treatment comes from FDA documents and interviews with Richard Peto, Peter Elwood, William Soller, Earle Lockhart, and Peter Rheinstein. The renaissance of aspirin is based on surveys of the current scientific literature and interviews with the scientists mentioned above and, among many others, Erik Änggård, Rory Collins, William Fields, Charles Hennekens, John Stirling Meyer, Noel Rabouhans, Peter Sandercock, Charles Warlow, and Gerald Weissmann.

Finally, the equivocal profitability of this renaissance was apparent from the media coverage of aspirin since 1988, interviews with marketers at Sterling, Nicholas Laboratories, and Bayer AG, and our own observation of the analgesic market in the three years that followed the publication of the Physicians' Health Study. Other evidence can be construed from Sara Lee's decision, in June 1991, to sell the Nicholas nonprescription line, including Aspro, to Roche Holding, the Swiss pharmaceutical giant.

ABBREVIATIONS

PERIODICALS

AA	Advertising Age
BMJ	British Medical Journal
BW	Business Week
CR	Congressional Record
DM	Drug Markets
FDC	Food, Drug, and Cosmetics Report
JAMA	Journal of the American Medical Association
NEJM	New England Journal of Medicine
NYT	New York Times
OPDR	Oil, Paint & Drug Reporter
WSJ	Wall Street Journal

LEGAL SOURCES

Atl.	Atlantic Reporter
Ch.	Chancery Reports (United Kingdom)
Civ.	Civil case
D.L.R.	Dominion Law Reports (Canada)
Ex.C.R.	Exchequer Court Reports (Canada)
Fed.	Federal Reporter
F.2d	Federal Reporter, Second Series
F.R.D.	Federal Rules Decisions

F.Supp.	*Federal Supplement*
FTC	*Federal Trade Commission Decisions*
F.S.R.	*Fleet Street Intellectual Property Reports* (United Kingdom)
N.E.	*North Eastern Reporter*
R.P.C.	*Reports of Patent Cases* (United Kingdom)
S.W.	*South Western Reporter*
S.C.R.	*Supreme Court of Canada Reports*
Stat.	*U.S. Statutes at Large*
U.S.	*United States Reports*

OTHER ABBREVIATIONS

(A)	A copy of this source is in the authors' possession.
(I)	Interview (see Section V of the bibliography)
. . .	Title is abbreviated
Doc.	Document
Ltr.	Letter

We have abbreviated the citations to five archival sources. The full citations are the following:

APC	Records of the Office of Alien Property, Record Group 131, U.S. National Archives, Washington, D.C.
CORC	Thomas G. Corcoran Papers, U.S. Library of Congress, Manuscript Division, Washington, D.C.
DOJ	Department of Justice Central Files, Classified Subject Files, Case 60-21-56 (Sterling Products, Inc.), Record Group 60, U.S. National Archives, Washington, D.C. In the Notes, the number following *DOJ* (e.g., 1301) is the document number.
DOS	General Records of the Department of State, Decimal File, Record Group 59, U.S. National Archives, Washington, D.C.
FDA	Food and Drug Administration, General Records, Rockville, Md. In the Notes, NDA refers to the New Drug Application files.
LEV	Bayer AG, Company Archives, Leverkusen, Germany. In the Notes, the number following *LEV* is the record group within the archives.

Finally, we have abbreviated sources that are frequently cited in the Notes. A list of the full citations for these abbreviated sources, which are not repeated in the Bibliography, follows:

AHP v. *J&J* (*1*): *American Home Products* v. *Johnson & Johnson,* 77 Civ. 1363, Southern District of New York (*Docket*); and *American Home Products* v. *Johnson & Johnson,* 436 *F.Supp.* 785 (1977) (*Decision*).

AHP v. *J&J* (*2*): *American Home Products* v. *Johnson & Johnson,* 85 Civ. 4858, Southern District of New York (*Docket*); *American Home Products* v. *Johnson & Johnson,* 654 *F.Supp.* 568 (1987) (*Decision (A)*); and *American Home Products* v. *Johnson & Johnson,* 672 *F.Supp.* 135 (1987) (*Decision (B)*).

AHP v. *J&J* (*3*): *American Home Products* v. *Johnson & Johnson,* 671 *F.Supp.* 316 (1987) (*Decision*).

APC-Bayer: APC, Entry 155, Bayer Company, CM201.

Basic Information: Basic Information on I.G. Farbenindustrie AG by Defense. Records of *U.S.* v. *Carl Krauch et al.* Microfilm M892, Reel 98, U.S. National Archives, Washington, D.C.

Bayer v. *United Drug: The Bayer Company* v. *The United Drug Company,* Docket E14-180, Southern District of New York, Federal Records Center, Bayonne, N.J. (*Docket*); and *The Bayer Company* v. *The United Drug Company,* 272 *Fed.* 505 (1921) (*Decision*).

Besprechung: Wiederschrift über die Besprechung am Montag, den 22. September 1919 mit William Weiss et al., *LEV,* 9/A.7, 1955 + .

FDA Meeting: U.S. Food and Drug Administration. Minutes and Transcript, Cardiovascular and Renal Drugs Advisory Committee, *FDA.*

FEA Memorandum: U.S. Federal Economic Administration, Economics Organization Staff. "Sterling, I.G., and the Nazi Government" (*Part III*) and "Patents in the Drive Toward Monopoly" (*Part IV*). N.d., Cartel Files, Entry 210, Box 1111, Record Group 169, U.S. National Archives, Washington, D.C.

FTC-AHP: In the Matter of American Home Products, FTC Docket 8918, Federal Records Center, Suitland, Md. (*Docket*); and *In the Matter of American Home Products,* 98 *FTC* 136 (1981) (*Decision*).

FTC-BM: In the Matter of Bristol-Meyers, FTC Docket 8917, Federal Records Center, Suitland, Md. (*Docket*); and *In the Matter of Bristol-Meyers,* 102 *FTC* 21 (1983) (*Decision*).

FTC-Haynes: In the Matter of Justin Haynes & Company, Inc., FTC Docket 2743, Federal Records Center, Suitland, Md. (*Docket*); and *In the Matter of Justin Haynes & Company, Inc.,* 26 *FTC* 1147 (1938) (*Decision*).

FTC-Sterling: In the Matter of Sterling Drug, FTC Docket 8919, Federal Records Center, Suitland, Md. (*Docket*); and *In the Matter of Sterling Drug,* 102 *FTC* 395 (1983) (*Decision*).

Hill Deposition: Hill, J., Deposition, *Farbenfabriken Bayer AG* v. *Sterling Drug,* Civ. 908–55/909–55, District Court of New Jersey, Dec. 3–5, 1957.

Konferenz: Bericht über die Konferenz mit Herrn Weiss aus New York vom
8 April 1920. *LEV,* 9/A.7, 1955+.

Korthaus: Korthaus, W., Pharmazeutische Geschäft in Südamerika währen
des Krieges. N.d., *LEV,* 9/A.7, 1955+.

Kronstein Affidavit: Kronstein, W., Supplemental Affidavit, *Farbenfabriken
Bayer AG* v. *Sterling Drug, Inc.* Civ. 909–55, District Court of New
Jersey, Feb. 18, 1960.

Littell Memorandum: Littell, N., "Memorandum Submitted to Senate Committee," Jan. 8, 1945. Reproduced in *Congressional Record,* vol. 91(1),
79th Congress, 1st session, Jan. 22, 1945, 426.

McNeil v. *AHP: McNeil* v. *American Home Products,* 79 Civ. 3973, Southern District of New York (*Docket*); and *McNeil* v. *American Home
Products,* 501 *F.Supp.* 517 (1980) (*Decision*).

N.Y. Minutes: Minutes of the New York Pharmazeutische Konferenz, *LEV,*
9/K.1.

OTC Analgesic Docket: U.S. Food and Drug Administration. Over-the-
Counter Drugs, Monograph for OTC Internal Analgesic, Antipyretic,
and Antirheumatic Products. FDA Docket 77N-0094, FDA Archives,
Rockville, Md.

OTC Analgesic Report: U.S. Food and Drug Administration. "Over-the-
Counter Drugs: Establishment of a Monograph for OTC Internal Analgesic, Antipyretic, and Antirheumatic Products." *Federal Register,* July
8, 1977, 35346.

OTC Drugs: U.S. Food and Drug Administration. "Over-the-Counter Drugs:
Proposal Establishing Rule Making Procedures for Classification." *Federal Register,* Jan. 5, 1972, 85.

Reynolds Deposition: Reynolds, F. J., Deposition, *William S. Merrell* v.
Anacin Company. U.S. Court of Customs and Patent Appeals, Patent
Appeal Docket No. 4133, Opposition 15,051, 1938.

Simon Deposition: Simon, G., Deposition. *APC,* Entry 199, Heyden Chemical Company, Case File 131.

Stamm Deposition: Stamm, C., Deposition. July 17, 1918, *APC,* Entry 7,
Box 7.

Sterling Aspirin Analysis: Sterling Drug. "Aspirin in Cardiovascular Disease." Doc. SUP026, Dec. 1, 1983, *OTC Analgesic Docket.*

U.S. v. *Alba:* Complaint and Consent Decree, Sept. 5, 1941, *United States
v. Alba Pharmaceutical Company et al.* Civ. 15–363, Southern District
of New York (*Docket*).

U.S. v. *Bayer:* Complaint and Consent Decree, Sept. 5, 1941, *United States
v. The Bayer Company et al.* Civ. 15–364, Southern District of New
York (*Docket*).

U.S. v. *Harper: United States* v. *Harper.* Police Court, Washington, D.C.,
Mar. 12, 1908 (*Decision*).

N O T E S

The Notes list all sources for facts and quotations in the text, with a few exceptions. Unless indicated otherwise, quotes from individuals are drawn from the interviews listed in the Bibliography, and figures for advertising expenditures are from *National Advertising Investments* for the relevant years. When a published article is identified by author and date in the text, the article is listed in the Bibliography but not in the Notes. To save space, we have frequently abbreviated names.

PROLOGUE

3, 10–12 Description of the meeting: Freisham (I), Israel (I), Rheinstein (I), Young (I), and Nychis (1988).

4 Heart attacks and AIDS: American Heart Association (1989), p. 2; and *NYT*, Jan. 25, 1991, p. A3.

5 Aspirin "repositioned": Mills (I).

5 $600 million increase: Mellow (1989).

5–6 Sterling's heart attack campaigns: *AA*, June 1, 1987, p. 64; Bayer press releases (A), Jan. 27, 1988.

6 "One aspirin every other" and subsequent NBC quotes: Transcript, *NBC Nightly News*, Jan. 27, 1988, NBC News Archives.

6 "every male": Transcript, *Today*, Jan. 28, 1988, NBC News Archives.

6 Extra Bayer commercials: *AA*, Feb. 1, 1988, p. 1.

6 "Good News for Heart Health in America": *NYT*, Jan. 29, 1988, p. 26.

7 FDA calls Sterling: Rheinstein (I).

7 1990 analgesic sales: Press release, Packaged Facts, Feb. 1991. We thank Patricia Winter for sending us a copy of the press release.

7 Analgesic costs and prices: *Chemical Marketing Reporter*, July 18, 1988, p. 40; and *Consumer Reports*, Feb. 1987, p. 85.

8 Rorer dispute: *AA*, Feb. 8, 1988, p. 3; *id.*, Feb. 15, 1988, p. 1; *NYT*, Feb.

10, 1988, p. B28 (Ascriptin ad); and Ltr. (A), Mindell and Gardner to Smith, Feb. 11, 1988, courtesy H. Israel.

8   "the nastiest four-letter word": F. Young, press conference, Dec. 6, 1990, Seattle.

10–11   "considerable press interest" and quotes from meeting: Nychis (1988).

CHAPTER ONE

15, 30   Duisberg's visit to Rensselaer: Flechtner (1959), Chapter 11; and Duisberg (1933), pp. 85–88.

16–25   Duisberg's career: Armstrong (1935), p. 1021; Beer (1959), pp. 80–93; Duisberg (1933), pp. 85–89; Flechtner (1959), pp. 169–187; and Verg et al. (1988), pp. 68–83, 90–93.

16   "the greatest industrialist": Quoted in Verg et al. (1988), p. 68.

18   Eleven graduate students: Haber (1958), p. 78.

18–21   Early history of German dyestuffs industry and Farbenfabriken Bayer: Beer (1959), pp. 49–56, 70–93.

20   Footnote source: Verg et al. (1988), p. 78.

21   Discovery of acetanilid: Schweitzer (1906).

21   Three antipyretics: Binz (1897), vol. 2, chap. 24.

21–22   Early uses of salicin and salicylic acid: Weissmann (1991).

22–23   Antipyrine and Antifebrin: McTavish (1986), pp. 33–40.

23   Duisberg's search for new drug: Eichengrün (1918), p. 409.

23   Side effects of acetanilid and acetophenetidin: Gross (1946), pp. 25–37.

23   Phenacetin's worldwide use: Smith (1958), p. 1.

24   Duisberg's research staff: Beer (1959), pp. 79–88.

24   Workers' footsteps: Verg et al. (1988), p. 95.

24   Purchase of Leverkusen site: Stokes (1988), p. 71.

24   Drug research center: Eichengrün (1949), p. 582.

25   Duisberg's additional check on drugs: Pinnow (1938), p. 93, cited in McTavish (1986), p. 44.

25–27   Discovery of Aspirin: Eichengrün (1918) and Eichengrün (1949). These are the only two principal accounts of the discovery of ASA by a primary source. Although both are by the same person, they differ greatly in their version of events. We place more trust in the second. The first was written while Eichengrün was still at Bayer, and is from an unpublished corporate history; the second, which is less laudatory of the firm, was written much later, when Eichengrün was 81, retired from Bayer, and, as it happens, freshly released from a concentration camp.

25 "enfeebling action on the heart": Binz (1897), vol. 2, pp. 262–3.

25 Footnote source: Weissmann (I).

26 History of Heroin: *Bulletin of Narcotics,* Apr.–June 1953, p. 3; and Morgan (1981), pp. 94–97.

26 "death sentence": Eichengrün (1949), p. 583.

26 "This is the usual": Eichengrün (1949), p. 583.

27 Medical-journal ads: *Bulletin of Narcotics,* Apr.–June 1953, pp. 4–5.

27 "a literature . . . so voluminous": Wohr (1902), p. 274, cited in McTavish (1986), p. 52.

27 Aspirin treatment for diabetes: Williamson (1902).

28 Aspirin and German patent office: McTavish (1986), pp. 50, 64–65.

28 Earnings from Aspirin patent: Collier (1984), p. 568.

28 "Aspirin has in the decade": Quoted in McTavish (1986), p. 56.

28–31 Early years of Bayer in America: Verg et al. (1988), pp. 47, 50–51; Hendrick (1924).

28 "old-fashioned" Schieffelins: Ltr., Muurling to Duisberg, Feb. 23, 1897, *LEV,* 9/A.1, 1909–1954.

28 "Farbenfabriken is making progress": Quoted in Flechtner (1959), p. 169.

28 U.S. market for Bayer dye products: *id.,* p. 170.

29 "For God's sake": ibid.

30 "The longer I think": Quoted in *id.,* p. 183.

30 Duisberg's cost cutting: Cited in Verg et al. (1988), p. 156.

30 Aspirin foundry: E. von Salis, Testimony, May 17, 1920, *Bayer* v. *United Drug, Docket,* Trial Transcript, p. 415.

30 "heart neurosis": Quoted in Flechtner (1959), p. 185.

31 "one of the mightiest": Quoted in Verg et al. (1988), p. 69.

31 Duisberg's speech: Flechtner (1959), pp. 185–187.

31 "Americans are not yet" and "my scolding": Quoted in *id.,* p. 187.

CHAPTER TWO

33 "We are not here": *Boswell's Life of Johnson,* G. B. Hill, ed. (New York: Harper & Brothers, 1891), vol. 4, pp. 100–101.

33 Footnote source: Young (1967), p. 14.

35   U.S. Aspirin sales: *N.Y. Minutes,* Mar. 1, 1911.

35–36   English ASA patent trial and "none of the experienced": *Farbenfabriken vormals Friedrich Bayer & Co.* v. *Chemische Fabrik von Heyden,* 22 *R.P.C.* 501 (1905), quote p. 516; and *Pharmaceutical Journal,* May 6, 1905, p. 672.

36   "only a possibility": Ltr., Gifford to Gref, July 28, 1905, *APC,* Entry 274, Box 1.

36   U.S. patent upheld: *Farbenfabriken of Elberfeld Co.* v. *Kuehmsted,* 171 *Fed.* 887 (1909); *Kuehmsted* v. *Farbenfabriken of Elberfeld Co.,* 179, *Fed.* 701 (1910).

36   Market share of counterfeit Aspirin: *N.Y. Minutes,* Mar. 7, 1910.

36   Letter to druggist associations: *id.,* Oct. 4, 1910.

36   "Frauds are practiced": Quoted in *Pharmaceutical Era,* Sept. 1912, p. 602.

36   Squad of detectives: *Druggists Circular,* Sept. 1912, p. 585.

36   Extent of bogus Aspirin: *N.Y. Minutes,* Feb. 26, 1914.

36   International prices of Aspirin: *JAMA,* Jan. 20, 1917, p. 201.

37   Aspirin labeling: N. A. Buttle, Testimony, May 17, 1920, *Bayer* v. *United Drug, Docket,* Trial Transcript, p. 354.

37   AMA and fans: *N.Y. Minutes,* Apr. 19, 1910.

37   Debate on Aspirin advertising: *id.,* May 28, 1913.

37   Switchover to Aspirin tablets: *id.,* Oct. 30, 1908, Oct. 4, 1910, and Feb. 14, 1914.

37   First Bayer Aspirin ad: *NYT,* Oct. 2, 1916, p. 18.

38   "Not a sentence": *Printers' Ink,* June 29, 1916, p. 189.

38   "For seventeen years": *JAMA,* Jan. 20, 1917, pp. 201–2.

39–40   German activities in U.S.: Witcover (1989), pp. 39–41, 89–93; and *Brewing and Liquor Interests . . .* (1919), vol. 1, pp. ix–x.

39   Schweitzer's background: Dr. Hugo Schweitzer, *APC,* Entry 195; F. Haynes, "Doctor Hugo Schweitzer," *APC,* Entry 199, Dr. Hugo Schweitzer, Case File 4062; and H. Schweitzer, Testimony, *Farbenfabriken of Elberfeld* v. *Louisville Inventors Association,* U.S. Patent Office, Opposition no. 473, Mar. 12, 1908.

39   Duisberg's comment about Schweitzer: Ltr., Muurling to Duisberg, Feb. 23, 1897, *LEV,* 9/A.1, 1909–54.

39   German Secret Service Code No. 963192637: J. Choate, Testimony, *Dyestuffs* (1919), pp. 134–35.

40   "committed suicide outright": Quoted in *NYT,* Nov. 1, 1917, p. 1.

40–42 Great Phenol Plot: *Simon Deposition*, May 25, 1918, pp. 27–28, *id.*, July 26, 1918, pp. 6–14; and *id.*, Sept. 16, 1918, p. 5.

40 Phenol prices: Jones and Cassebeer (1919).

40 Aspirin plant almost shut down: Leverkusen Pharmazeutische Konferenz, *LEV*, 169/5, vol. 3, April 11, 1915.

40 Edison's phenol: Dyer and Martin (1929), pp. 792–94.

41 Footnote source: *Simon Deposition*, May 25, 1918, p. 33 (Simon quote); and Dyer and Martin (1929), pp. 793–94 (Army and Navy contracts).

41 Three long freight trains' worth of explosives: *NYT*, Apr. 25, 1919, p. 1, citing a letter from Albert to Schweitzer.

41 Albert's papers: Landau (1937), p. 100.

41 "The entire output": Quoted in *New York World*, Aug. 19, 1915, p. 2.

42 240,000 pounds of disinfectant: *NYT*, Aug. 20, 1915, p. 7.

42 Loving cup: *NYT*, Oct. 19, 1918, p. 9.

42 Schweitzer's death: F. Haynes, *op. cit.*

43–47 Story of Williams & Crowell and all quotes: Report for Mr. Francis P. Garvan from Louis F. Muccino, Re: The Bayer Company, Inc.—Williams & Crowell Color Company, Inc., *APC*, Entry 199, Bayer Company, Case File 1048.

44 German investment in the U.S.: Wilkins (1989), p. 169.

45 Seebohm and Hardy's promise to Lynch: Ltr., Hardy to Palmer, Aug. 1, 1918, *APC*, Entry 155, Synthetic Patents Co., Inc. CM1909.

45 APC takes over Bayer: Order of Sale, The Bayer Company, Inc., and Synthetic Patents Company, Inc., Nov. 1918, *APC*, Entry 216.

45 Hardy's scheme: *OPDR*, Aug. 26, 1918, p. 27.

45 "A machine that is oiled well": *Stamm Deposition*.

45–46 Bayer's corporate restructuring: Emory, Booth, Janney, and Varney, Patent and Trade Mark Report: The Bayer Company, Inc., *APC-Bayer; NYT*, Nov. 19, 1915, p. 18.

46 Footnote source: *Druggists Circular*, Oct. 1912, p. 629; J. Choate, Testimony, *Dyestuffs* (1919), pp. 103–105 ("It's no use, boys"); Ambruster (1947), pp. 1–14; Ltr., Hardy to Palmer, Aug. 1, 1918, *APC*, Entry 155, Synthetic Patents, Inc., CM1909; *Dobson* v. *Farbenfabriken of Elberfeld Co. et al.*, 206 *Fed.* 125 (1913).

47 "dangerous germs": Ltr., Weston to Department of Justice, Apr. 29, 1918, *APC*, Entry 7, Box 7.

47 Stamm's arrest and stay in jail: *Stamm Deposition*.

47 Hardy quits board: Ltr., Hardy to Lynch, July 16, 1918, *APC-Bayer*.

47 Seebohm and von Salis resign: Ltr., von Salis to Lynch, July 18, 1918, and Ltr., Seebohm to Lynch, July 18, 1918, *APC-Bayer.*

47 Arrests of officials: *OPDR,* Aug. 26, 1918, p. 27.

47–48 Ernst Möller's tale: *DOJ* 2495 and *Korthaus.*

48 Möller purchases export business: A copy of the contract is in *LEV,* 9/A.1, 1909–1954.

48 Möller runs Aspirin business outside the United States and Europe: Minutes, Bayer Company, Inc., Nov. 19, 1918, *APC-Bayer.*

48 "Made by Americans": Cited in Ltr., FTC to Palmer, Sept. 18, 1918, *APC-Bayer,* Correspondence.

48 Bayer can barely operate: Ltr., Lynch to Heald, Sept. 30, 1918, *APC-Bayer,* Correspondence.

48 Rumors about poison Aspirin: Ltr., Trumbull to Palmer, Oct. 3, 1918, *APC-Bayer,* Correspondence.

CHAPTER THREE

50–51 Sterling history: Hiebert (1963); and *Drug and Chemical Markets,* Dec. 18, 1918, p. 5.

50–51 Patent medicine examples and quotes: Young (1967), pp. 25–29, 44, 49, 74–81.

50 "Have you a friend": *id.,* p. 204 (photo).

51 Sterling and Grasselli: *DOJ* 2911.

51 "It is the object": *DOJ* 3310.

52 New board: Minutes, Bayer Company, Inc., Feb. 4, 1919, *APC-Bayer.*

52 McClintock's role: E. McClintock, Deposition, *Farbenfabriken Bayer AG* v. *Sterling Drug,* Civ. 908-55/909-55, U.S. District Court of New Jersey, Dec. 5, 1957, pp. 226–249.

52 Bifurcation of Bayer Company: *DOJ* 3257.

52 Reason for Winthrop creation: *DOJ* 1883 and 4204.

52 Winthrop name: Mahoney (1959), p. 213.

52 Sterling attacks title to Bayer Cross: Statement by Dr. Richard C. Hennings, May 1, 1925, on Sterling-Farben contracts of April 9, 1923, *LEV,* 19/A.395.

52–53 Vagueness of patents: *Aktennotiz über eine Besprechung mit Herrn Dr. W. H. Duisberg in New York am 18. Marz 1955, LEV,* 19/A.394.4; and *DOJ* 1883 and 4204.

53 Möller's desire to work with Sterling: *Korthaus.*

53   Möller urges Weiss to meet Duisberg: *Besprechung.*

53   McClintock goes to Holland: Telegram to secretary of state from Mr. Garrett, American Legation, The Hague, May 14, 1919, *DOS,* 1910–29, 311.625 B34/1; and Ltr., [Unknown] to A. Mothwurf, Sept. 3, 1919, *APC,* Entry 199, A. Mothwurf, Case File 1376.

53   "100 percent American": *DOJ* 3261.

53   Trading with Germany illegal: U.S. Tariff Commission (1918), p. 74.

53–55   Duisberg tries to combine German coal-tar industry: Beer (1959), pp. 124–25; and Haber (1971), p. 279.

54   Production of wartime chemicals: Haber (1971), p. 198.

55   Troops from New Zealand and British officers: Verg et al. (1988), p. 207.

55   I.G. production falls: Haber (1971), p. 247.

55   Creation of British Dyestuffs Corporation, Ltd.: Miall (1931), pp. 93–94.

55   French dye combine: Beer (1959), p. 141.

55–56   German delegation at Versailles: Luckau (1941), pp. 59–62, 84–89, 110–112; and Borkin (1978), p. 29.

56   Germany required to surrender stocks: Haber (1971), p. 248.

56   "serious menace": Lefebure (1923), p. 18.

57   Möller's meeting with Korthaus: *Korthaus.*

57–58   Ltrs. from Möller to Mann: Ltr., Möller to Mann, Aug. 15, 1919, *LEV,* 9/A.7, 1955 + ("after the catastrophe"); and *DOJ* 2495 ("swindler" and other descriptions).

58   Weiss's meeting with Rudolf Mann and all quotes: *Besprechung.*

59   Duisberg's deal with Weiss: *DOJ* 1499.

59   Gifford reviews pact and recommends changes: *DOJ* 3283.

59   "When you, a stranger": *DOJ* 3290.

59   Weiss travels to Leverkusen in 1920: *DOJ* 1499.

59   "fed up on Europe": *DOJ* 3795.

59   Duisberg's achievement: Plumpe (I); Göb (I); Beer (1959), p. 90.

59–62   Second round of negotiations: *DOJ* 1499 and *Konferenz* (all quotes).

60   APC still seizing enemy assets: It continued seizing "enemy" property until May 27, 1921. Gathings (1940), p. 84.

60   Leverkusen's proposals to Grasselli: The nature of the "proposals" is unclear. On May 12, 1924, Grasselli and Farbenfabriken Bayer agreed to create a new company, Grasselli Dyestuff, to make and sell dyes in the United States. Pack (1943), p. 505.

61 "The absolute condition": *Konferenz,* emphasis in original (*"rechte Bayer"* and *"falsche Bayer"*). This quotes the meeting transcript, and so is probably a paraphrase of Duisberg's statement.

62 April 22 meeting: *DOJ* 1499, Supplement.

62 Mann reneges again: *DOJ* 3271.

62 Weiss sends Rowles and Möller to Europe: *DOJ* 3280.

62 "a proposal so liberal" and Weiss's offer: Ltr., Weiss to Rowles, June 17, 1920, *LEV,* 9/A.7, 1955+.

62 "make greater demands": *DOJ* 3280.

62–63 Möller's final meetings and all quotes: *DOJ* 3282.

63 1920 contract: Agreement between The Bayer Company . . . and Farbenfabriken . . . , Oct. 28, 1920, Exhibit B, *U.S.* v. *Alba, Docket.*

CHAPTER FOUR

64–65 ASA in Mexico: *DOJ* 3277, 3281, and 3285.

64 "absolute demoralization": *DOJ* 6524.

65–66 Loss of U.S. Aspirin trademark: Bill of Complaint, and Testimonies of A. Matthews and E. Kelley, *Bayer* v. *United Drug, Docket; Bayer* v. *United Drug, Decision;* and *United Drug* v. *Farbenfabriken of Elberfeld,* U.S. Patent Office Cancellation no. 424.

67 Farbenfabriken Bayer in England: In re Badische Company, Ltd., 2 *Ch.* 331 (1921); In re "Aspirin," American Druggists Syndicate, Ltd. (Petitioner), and Bayer Company, Ltd. (Objecting Party), 1923 *Ex.C.R.* 65 (1923); and *Sterling-Winthrop Group Ltd.* v. *Farbenfabriken Bayer AG,* 1976 *R.P.C.* 469 (1976).

67 British sell Aspirin and "The large army": *The Prescriber,* Mar. 1915, p. 41.

67 "After eight months" and following quotes: *id.,* May 1915, p. 89.

67–68 Sterling buys Farbenfabriken Bayer's U.K. rights: *Sterling-Winthrop Group Ltd.* v. *Farbenfabriken Bayer AG,* 1976 *R.P.C.* 469 (1976), p. 478.

68 Leverkusen violates Sterling's U.K. rights: *Die mit Herrn W. E. Weiss . . . unter dem 9 April 1923 abgeschlossenen Vertrage, LEV,* 19/A.395.

68 Sterling threatens legal action: Letters between McKenna & Co. and Doermer written in December 1920 are in *LEV,* 9/A.7, 1955+, and *DOJ* 3791.

68 "You can sympathize": *DOJ* 1504.

68 Weiss's response and "to eliminate from all": *DOJ* 349.

68–69 1923 negotiations: *Amerika Besprechung*, Leverkusen, Mar. 1923, *LEV*, 19/A.394.4.

69–70 1923 contracts: Contract between Farbenfabriken Bayer and Winthrop Chemical Co., Apr. 9, 1923, Exhibit A, Schedule A, *U.S.* v. *Alba, Docket;* Contract between Farbenfabriken Bayer and the Bayer Company, Apr. 9, 1923, Exhibit A, Schedule A, *U.S.* v. *Bayer, Docket;* and Undertaking from Sterling Company, Inc., re Bayer trademarks, Apr. 9, 1923, Exhibit C, *U.S.* v. *Alba, Docket.*

69–70 Proposal to establish U.K. company and footnote source: Proposed Contract between Farbenfabriken Bayer and Bayer Products, Ltd., Exhibit A, Schedule A (supplement), *U.S.* v. *Bayer, Docket.*; In the Matter of the Trusts . . . , 58 *R.P.C.* 31 (1940); *Sterling-Winthrop Group Ltd.* v. *Farbenfabriken Bayer AG*, 1976 *R.P.C.* 469 (1976); and *DOJ* 3303 ("soon as circumstances. . . .").

70–71 1920–21 depression: Friedman and Schwarz (1963), pp. 231–39; and Holtfrerich (1986), pp. 208–11.

71–72 German cost of living: Holtfrerich (1986), p. 33.

71 "made it almost impossible": *Die mit Herrn W. E. Weiss . . . , op. cit.*

72 Private scrips: Bresciani-Turroni (1937), pp. 341–43.

72 Government money presses and other hyperinflation tales: *NYT,* July 17, 1923, p. 3; *id.*, Sept. 20, 1923, p. 1; *id.*, Sept. 18, 1923, p. 5; *id.*, Oct. 8, 1923, p. 3; *id.*, Oct. 13, 1923, p. 3; *id.*, Nov. 11, 1923, II, p. 1 ("Thank you").

72 Trillion-mark notes: Bresciani-Turroni (1937), pp. 24–25.

72 Abandonment of mark and return to normality: Holtfrerich (1986), p. 316.

72–73 Creation of I.G. Farben: Hayes (1987), pp. 13–15; Haber (1971), pp. 283–84; Verg et al. (1988), p. 225; Michels (1928), p. 143.

73 Footnote source: Verg et al. (1988), p. 232.

73 Size of I.G. Farben: Liefmann (1932), p. 318; and E. Piwowarczyk, Affidavit, *Basic Information*, Vol. 2, Doc. 17, p. 43.

73–75 Weiss's surprise: *DOJ* 148.

75 "Was it [what] in the United States": *DOJ* 4217.

75–76 1926 negotiations: *DOJ* 4211, 4214, and 4925.

75 Stroehmer's opinion: *DOJ* 4216.

75–76 "It seemed to us": *DOJ* 4211.

76 Mann informs Weiss: *DOJ* 4220.

76 "As far as aspirin": *DOJ* 4816.

76 1926 contracts: Contract between I.G. and Winthrop Chemical Co.,

Nov. 15, 1926, Exhibit A, *U.S.* v. *Alba, Docket;* Contract between I.G. and The Bayer Company, Inc., New York, Nov. 15, 1926, Exhibit A, *U.S.* v. *Bayer, Docket;* Supplemental Agreement between I.G. and Winthrop, Nov. 15, 1926, *CORC,* File no. 521.

76 "He was always": D. Corcoran (I).

77 Only Mann and a few others could sign by themselves: Owen (I) and Göb (I).

77 Diebold worked separately: *Hill Deposition,* vol. 2, p. 187.

77 "Certainly she didn't": D. Corcoran (I).

77 Elaborate ceremony for Weiss: Ambruster (1947), pp. 99–100.

77 "Doctor Weiss": D. Corcoran (I).

77–78 Wojahn's map of Latin America: ibid.

78 "aspirin and a little caffeine": J. Corcoran (I).

78 "Even the illiterates": *DOJ* 643.

78–79 Cafiaspirina sales and tablet prices: *DOJ* 51 ("an almost miraculous"), 643, 1792, 4499, and 5073.

79 I.G. profits and footnote source: I.G. Handbuch, 1939, p. 70, *Basic Information,* vol. 1 (I.G. profits); and *Aufstellungen über an I.G. und GAW ausgeschütte Gewinne,* 1919–37, *LEV,* 9/A.3 (Aspirin and Sterling contract profits).

79 "show[ing] as often as possible": *DOJ* 168.

79 "the correspondence be conducted": *DOJ* 18.

79 "absolutely wrong in attempting" and subsequent quotes from Leverkusen conference: *DOJ* 21.

80 "make the mistake": *DOJ* 4992.

CHAPTER FIVE

81 "As the Southern Cross": Verg et al. (1988), p. 268.

81–82 Meeting with Hitler: *Trials of the War Criminals . . .* (1953), vol. 7, pp. 555–64; Hayes (1987), pp. 83–86.

82 "a glance": Hayes (1987), pp. 71–72.

83 "calmly contemplate the prospect": *id.,* p. 90.

83–84 I.G.'s Leuna plant: Hughes (1969).

83–84 I.G. contributions, 1933–39: H. Walter, Affidavit, *Basic Information,* vol. 2, Doc. 4, p. 6.

83 Footnote source: *FEA Memorandum, Part III,* p. 4.

84 Bosch's protection of Jewish employees and other actions: Hayes (1987), p. 109.

84 "communicates abroad an invention": *Trials of the War Criminals . . .* (1953), vol. 7, p. 1268.

84 Wilhelm Mann's background: *id.,* vol. 7, pp. 331–37, 703–24; vol. 8, p. 1371; and Hayes (1987), p. 101.

84–85 "one of the quietest" and subsequent quotes from Mann's letter to Wojahn: *DOJ* 5914, emphasis in original.

85 "was a clearly noticeable": Ltr., Mann to Weiss, Mar. 23, 1933, quoted in *FEA Memorandum, Part III,* p. 4.

85 Arrangement with American I.G.: *id.,* pp. 5–8.

85 Fall in Latin American sales: *DOJ* 1792.

85–86 Sales force in the hinterlands: Minutes of Directors' Conference, Oct. 19, 1936, in Exhibit M, *Kronstein Affidavit;* and J. Corcoran (I).

86 Bayer headquarters in Brazil and "the Latin Americans are": *DOJ* 752. Wojahn's claim seems exaggerated but no official statistics are available.

86–89 Bohle and Nazi expatriates: McKale (1977), pp. 11–65, 126–27, quote p. 11.

87 "We camouflaged" and other Ilgner quotes: Quoted in *Trials of the War Criminals . . .* (1953), vol. 7, pp. 725–26.

88 German embassy's request: Hayes (1987), p. 106.

88 Brazilian party's and Bohle's demands: *Trials of the War Criminals . . .* (1953), vol. 7, pp. 655–57.

88 Advertising in anti-Nazi papers, and quotes from Wojahn and I.G.: *FEA Memorandum, Part III,* pp. 26–28.

88 "Weiss informs Mann": *DOJ* 6246.

89 "the party in Germany": *FEA Memorandum, Part III,* p. 28.

89 Nazis politicize I.G. advertising: *Trials of the War Criminals . . .* (1953), vol. 7, pp. 126–27.

89 Salesman's pitch: J. Corcoran (I).

89 "unequivocal adjustment": and subsequent Mann quotes: *Trials of the War Criminals . . .* (1953), vol. 7, pp. 666–68.

89 "Germany is deprived": Armstrong (1935), p. 1021.

90 Schmitz's motto and "carried reticence beyond": Hayes (1987), p. 26. The British historian was D. Warriner.

90 Geniol and Instantin: *FEA Memorandum, Part IV,* pp. 82–85; and Exhibits P, Q, R, *Kronstein Affidavit.*

90 "a cheap, small packet": *DOJ* 28.

90   "the fruits": Quoted in *FEA Memorandum, Part IV*, p. 84.

90   Sterling and I.G. take over Laboratorios Suarry: Minutes of a Private
      Discussion, Oct. 22, 1937, Exhibit R, *Kronstein Affidavit; FEA Memo-
      randum, Part III*, pp. 14–15.

90   Sterling buys more stock: *DOJ* 752 and 3528.

91   "was trying to dictate": Quoted in *FEA Memorandum, Part III*, p. 15.

91   McClintock's visit to Leverkusen: *id.*, pp. 19–20; and *DOJ* 6283.

91   McClintock's meeting with Gwatkin and "that the directors of Winthrop":
      FEA Memorandum, Part III, pp. 19–20.

92   "as there was no permission": *id.*, pp. 14–15.

92   Weiss gives in to I.G. on Suarry business: *id.*, pp. 16–17.

92   NSDAP announcement: Hayes (1987), p. 170.

92   New Year's Eve phone call and "I am, in spirit": *DOJ* 6434.

                              CHAPTER SIX

93–95 Ambruster and ergot: *DM*, June 1930, p. 569 ("After the market posi-
       tion," p. 569); *id.*, Sept. 6, 1927, p. 255; *JAMA*, Jan. 14, 1928, p. 121;
       and Jackson (1970), pp. 9–11.

93   Uses for ergot: *Ambruster v. Mellon et al.*, 41 *Fed.2d* 430 (1930).

94–95 Ambruster's background: Ambruster (1947), pp. 31, 36, 91, 117, 232–37
       (quotes from pp. 1, 416); Ambruster and Ambruster (1935); *Ambruster v.
       National Bank of Westfield*, 182 *Atl.* 613 (1930), and *id.*, 198 *Atl.* 843
       (1930); and Jackson (1970), p. 9.

95   "The only thing": Quoted in *JAMA*, Sept. 6, 1930, at p. 724.

95   Wheeler's magazine article: Described in Jackson (1970), pp. 11–13.

95   Senate FDA hearings: Abstracted in *OPDR*, June 9, 16, 23, and 30, and
       July 7, 1930.

95   "These men can't conceive": Quoted in *DM*, June 1930, p. 569.

95–96 Ambruster's campaign against Bayer aspirin: Ambruster (1947), pp. 229–
       39.

96   Bayer aspirin slogans: In the Matter of Bayer Company, 19 *FTC* 229
       (1934), p. 231.

96   FTC order against Sterling: ibid.

96   "Sterling did not give": Ambruster (1947), p. 239.

96   Ambruster and Cummings: *id.*, p. 158.

96   Justice Department subpoenas Sterling's records: *id.*, pp. 179–80.

97 Weiss's background: *Wheeling News-Register,* Sept. 3, 1942, p. 1.

97 Wojahn and Hill's trip to Latin America: *DOJ* 585; and M. Wojahn, "Business Conferences in Rio" (A), n.d., *DOJ,* Box 1361.

97 Inquiries on Sterling's business in Latin America: *DOJ* 592, 1939, 4652, 4654, and 6145.

97 English request for sample Sterling labels: *DOJ* 590.

98 Two sets of negotiations: "Appendix I. The Sterling and I.G. Negotiations in 1940," Federal Economic Administration Economics Programs— Economic Organization Staff, Cartel Files, Entry 210, Box 1109, "Sterling-General" folder, RG 169, National Archives, Washington, D.C.

98 Ownership of Bayer Products, Ltd.: *Sterling-Winthrop Group Ltd.* v. *Farbenfabriken Bayer AG,* 1976 *R.P.C.* 469 (1976), at pp. 491–93.

98 "neither controlled by": *The Chemist and Druggist,* Sept. 9, 1939 (A); a copy of the ad is in *DOJ,* Box 1366.

98 Weiss's plan for separation of aspirin and ethical businesses: *DOJ* 6059.

98 Footnote source: The negotiations between the three companies are discussed at length in *FEA Memorandum,* Part IV.

98 Mann's rejection and "goods as American property": *DOJ* 6106.

98 Doubling of ocean freight rates: *DOJ* 4659.

98–99 I.G.'s plan for repacking ASA and Wojahn's response: *DOJ* 4658 and 4659.

99 Cost of ASA powder: *DOJ* 5073 and 5074.

99 Weiss and Mann cables: *DOJ* 6063, 6065, 6066, and 6112.

99 British blacklist of firms with German connections: *NYT,* Oct. 26, 1939; *DOJ* 4661.

99 Weiss's two telegrams: Telegrams, Weiss to Mann, Oct. 30–31, 1939, *LEV,* 9/A.7, 1955+; and *DOJ* 5327 and 6068.

99 Mann's reply: Untitled DOJ memorandum (A), Aug. 19, 1941, *DOJ,* Box 1371.

99 Weiss telephones Mann: Described in *DOJ* 695; Ltr., Brüggemann and Mentzel to Weiss, Nov. 30, 1939, *LEV,* 9/A.7, 1955+.

99 Mann refuses to surrender trademarks: Untitled DOJ memorandum (A), n.d., *DOJ,* Box 1370.

99–100 Weiss's *quid pro quo: DOJ* 1373 and 1853; Ltr., Mann to Weiss, Nov. 30, 1939, *LEV,* 9/A.7, 1955+; and memo of transatlantic telephone conversation between Weiss and Mentzel, Dec. 5, 1939, *CORC,* Box 523.

100 "very gratifying to me": *DOJ* 3114.

100   Winthrop's poor preparedness: *DOJ* 439; and transcript of telephone conversation, Weiss and Mentzel, Jan. 9, 1940, *CORC,* Box 523.

100   I.G. Farben and Sterling capital: *Moody's Manual of Investments* (1939).

100   "Syntent" and "Richter": *DOJ* 1162.

100–101   Florence meeting: *DOJ* 1172, 2663, 3101, and 3104.

100   McClintock's belief that Hitler would win: Landreth (I).

101   Formulae brought back by McClintock: *DOJ* 1515, 1516, and 2638–42.

101   Winthrop's production increases: *DOJ* 1209.

101   Wojahn asserts control: *DOJ* 3803.

101   Wojahn severs I.G.'s connection to Quimicas: *DOJ* 470.

101   Establishment of Farma Continental companies: Hill, McClintock, and Wojahn, memorandum to Weiss, Sept. 17, 1940, cited in "Memorandum to Edward P. Hodges, Esq." (A), n.d., *DOJ,* Box 1370; *Hill Deposition,* vol. 2, pp. 87–90; and M. Wojahn, "Legal Status of Aspirin and Tonico Business-Reorganization," Nov. 30, 1940, cited in untitled memorandum (A), n.d., *DOJ,* Box 1370.

102   Conversation between Kaelble and Mentzel (all quotes): Telefongespräch, Kaelble and Mentzel, Oct. 30, 1940, *LEV,* 19/A.396.2.

102–103   Quotes from Wojahn and Kaelble: *DOJ* 1905, which quotes an earlier letter from Kaelble to Wojahn.

102   Footnote source and quotes: H. Conover, "Memorandum for Mr. Cox—Subject: I.G.-Sterling Bank Loans" (A), Aug. 20, 1941, *DOJ,* Box 1329.

103   Rockefeller committee begins collecting information: J. Stanley, "Axis-Sympathizing Representatives of United States Firms in Latin America," War Department memorandum, Apr. 30, 1941, *DOS,* 1940–44, 862.20211 Bayer Aspirin Company/18.

103   Senate announces plans to investigate German patents. *NYT,* Jan. 4, 1941, p. 4.

104   Price-fixing indictments: *NYT,* Jan. 31, 1941, p. 1.

104   FBI reports: "Memorandum on Bayer Co., Inc.," Federal Bureau of Investigation, May 3, 1941, *DOS,* 1940–44, 862.20211 Bayer Aspirin Company/20.

104   Thomas Corcoran's background: Lash (1988).

104   Background on Sydney Ross Company: D. Corcoran (I).

104–105   Meeting between David and Tom Corcoran, and quotes: T. Corcoran, with P. Kopper, Rendezvous with Democracy, The Memoirs of "Tommy the Cork," *CORC,* unpub. ms., chapter 10, p. 27.

105   Cahill joins Tom Corcoran: *CR,* Jan. 22, 1945, p. 424.

105   McClintock's February trip to South America: B. Long, "Memorandum

of Telephone Conversation," Department of State, Feb. 18, 1941, *DOS*, 1940–44, 164.12 Bayer Co.

105 Kaelble's huge portrait of the führer: D. Corcoran (I).

105 Telephone conference between McClintock, Kaelble, and Mann: Telfongespräch, Kaelble and Mann, Feb. 12, 1941, *LEV*, 19/A.396.2.

106 Grand jury looks at pharmaceuticals: *NYT*, Feb. 13, 1941, p. 13.

106 Weiss demands transfer of trademarks: *DOJ* 4934.

106 Weiss about to get trademarks: *DOJ* 380–429, and 6467.

106 "the South American market": *NYT*, Apr. 10, 1941, p. 1.

106 Justice Department subpoenas: *NYT*, Apr. 11, 1941, p. 1.

106 Weiss tells Wojahn to cancel ethical shipments to South America: *DOJ* 1860.

CHAPTER SEVEN

107 Weiss and McClintock meet with Arnold: T. Corcoran, untitled memorandum, May 4, 1941, *CORC*, Box 523.

107 "redoubled their efforts": *Littell Memorandum*, p. 428.

107–108 Corcoran's actions: T. Corcoran, untitled memorandum, Apr. 30, 1941, *CORC*, Box 523; C. Guthrie(?), untitled memorandum, May 1941, *CORC*, Box 523.

108 Jackson does not mention Sterling: *NYT*, May 10, 1941, p. 1; *New York Herald-Tribune*, May 10, 1941, p. 1.

108 Conversation between Kaelble and Mentzel (all quotes): Telefongespräch, Kaelble and Mentzel, May 13, 1941, *LEV*, 19/A.396.2.

108 Corcoran asks McClintock about new schemes: Ltr., Corcoran to McClintock, May 16, 1941, *CORC*, Box 523.

108 Corcoran's plan and "danger that this money": T. Corcoran, "Setting Off Aspirin Profits against I.G.'s Debt," n.d., *CORC*, Box 521.

108–109 Sterling's treasurer in Kaelble's office: Telefongespräch, Kaelble and Mentzel, May 29, 1941, *LEV*, 19/A.396.2.

109 "That is the time": Ltr., Corcoran to Cahill, May 27, 1941, *CORC*, Box 521.

109 Account of Latin American drug trade: *New York Herald-Tribune*, May 29, 1941, p. 1; *id.*, May 30, 1941, p. 6.

109 "Listening on the radio": *Graphic Picture Newsmagazine*, Jan. 1942, p. 6, emphasis in original.

109 "These Firms Earn Money": *PM*, June 1, 1941, p. 1.

109 Second *PM* article: *PM*, June 6, 1941, p. 14.

110 Corcoran considers giving up Latin American aspirin: T. Corcoran, "Setting Off Aspirin Profits against I.G.'s Debt," n.d., *CORC*, Box 521.

110 Sterling statement: "Statement Concerning Relations with I.G. Farben," June 6, 1941, *CORC*, Box 521.

110 Biddle appointed acting attorney general: Lash (1988), p. 59.

110 Arnold staff's worries about Corcoran: *Littell Memorandum*, pp. 428–29.

110 Winthrop transactions covered by Roosevelt's order: *Hill Deposition*, vol. 2, p. 179.

110–111 Hill's background: *id.* and Landreth (I) ("a truck-driver type").

111 Conversation between Hill and Mulhern: *Hill Deposition*, vol. 2, p. 179.

111–112 Conference at Treasury Department: *id.*, vol. 1, pp. 292–314.

111 Weiss's brother and daughter sick: *Wheeling News-Register*, Sept. 2, 1942, p. 1.

111 Six prosecutors investigating Sterling: H. Conover, "Sterling Products Inc. File Assignments" (A), June 27, 1941, *DOJ*, Box 1370.

111 Justice Department lawyers talking to Ambruster: Ambruster (1947), pp. 179–80.

112 "declared Sterling": Ltr., Hill and Guthrie to Foley, June 21, 1941, *CORC*, Box 522.

112 Hill and Corcoran meet with government people and "They wanted to know": *Hill Deposition*, vol. 1, p. 331.

112 Corcoran thinking about replacing Winthrop management: T. Corcoran, Untitled memorandum, June 30, 1941, *CORC*, Box 523; and T. Corcoran, "Notes for meeting of July 7 in N.Y.," July 1941, *CORC*, Box 523.

112 Transfer of Winthrop's export business to Sydney Ross: T. Corcoran, Untitled memorandum, July 12, 1941, *CORC*, Box 523.

113 "getting the problems": Ltr., Corcoran to Cahill, July 15, 1941, *CORC*, Box 521.

113 Corcoran's meeting with Arnold and trip to Biddle's house: T. Corcoran, proposed memos, July 18, 1941, *CORC*, Box 522; F. Biddle, Testimony, *Nomination of Ugo Carusi* . . . (1944), pp. 80–82; *Littell Memorandum*, p. 428; and Johnston (1945).

113 Footnote source: "Memorandum for the Secretary's Files," Diary of Henry Morgenthau, Jr., July 18, 1941, vol. 422, pp. 204–205, National Archives, Hyde Park, N.Y.

113 Justice Department staff's desires and "Sterling Products had in fact": *Littell Memorandum*, p. 429.

114 Value of Sterling's trademarks and goodwill: *The Commercial and Financial Chronicle,* Mar. 8, 1941, p. 1606.

114 Corcoran pushes consent decree: Ltr., Guthrie to Corcoran, July 26, 1941, *CORC,* Box 521.

114 Meeting before Interdepartmental Committee and quotes: D. Corcoran (I) and J. Corcoran (I). A reproduction of the map used by David Corcoran is in *Sterling Newsreel,* Special DMC Issue, 1973, courtesy Sterling Drug.

114–115 Corcorans' request and quotes: C. Guthrie, untitled draft memoranda, July 30, 1941, *CORC,* Box 522.

115 Hill and Corcoran negotiate with Biddle: *Littell Memorandum,* p. 429.

115 "insurrection" at the Justice Department: *Hill Deposition,* vol. 1, p. 353.

115 Arnold's staff threatens to quit: Stokes (1941).

115 Corcoran and Hill meet with Arnold: Ltr., (Arnold?) to Hills, Aug. 12, 1941, *CORC,* Box 522.

115 "Mr. Arnold, it's understood" and subsequent quotes: *Hill Deposition,* vol. 1, pp. 332, 351.

115 Hill and Corcoran meet with the Interdepartmental Committee, and quotes: *id.,* pp. 316–17.

115 Sterling's representations: "Sterling Products (Incorporated) Representations to Interdepartmental Committee" (A), Aug. 15, 1941, *DOJ,* Box 1329.

116 Sterling's board accepts representations: Ltr., Weiss to Foley, Aug. 15, 1941, *CORC,* Box 525.

116 Weiss sends cable to Leverkusen: *Hill Deposition,* vol. 1, p. 345.

116 "THE AIM AND PURPOSE": Cable, Weiss to Mann, Aug. 15, 1941, *LEV,* 9/A.7, 1955+.

116 "Doubtless Weiss made this proposal": Wentzel, "Remarks on a Cable by Dr. Weiss from Washington on 15 August 1941," Aug. 19, 1941, *LEV,* 19/A.396.2.

116 "AFTER CAREFUL CONSIDERATIONS": Cable, Mann to Weiss, Aug. 21, 1941, *LEV,* 19/A.396.2.

116 "WE HAVE NO ALTERNATIVE": Cable, Weiss to Mann, Aug. 22, 1941, *LEV,* 9/A.7, 1955+.

116–117 Justice Department staff's opinion of consent decree: H. Conover, "Memorandum for Mr. Cox—Subject: I.G.-Sterling Bank Loans" (A), Aug. 20, 1941, *DOJ,* Box 1359; and untitled memorandum (A), Aug. 19, 1941, *DOJ,* Box 1359.

117 APC seizes I.G. property: *BW,* July 8, 1944, p. 54.

117   One investigator's opinion: E. Levi, "Memorandum for Hugh Cox" (A), Aug. 19, 1941, *DOJ,* Box 1329.

117   Interdepartmental Committee's meeting of August 19: "Memorandum for the Secretary's Files," diary of Henry Morgenthau, Jr., Aug. 19, 1941, vol. 434, pp. 93–94, National Archives, Hyde Park, N.Y.; *Hill Deposition,* vol. 1, pp. 338–39.

117–118   Justice Department's demand for resignations and quotes: *id.,* pp. 335–39.

118   Rogers replaces Weiss: *id.,* pp. 335–36.

118   Final I.G. cable: Telegram, Vorstand Farbenindustrie to Weiss, Aug. 26, 1941, *LEV,* 19/A.396.2

119   "Hitler still has his": Ambruster (1941), p. 17.

119   Weiss resists resigning: D. Corcoran (I); and "Agenda for Sterling Products Meeting," Department of Treasury, Dec. 2, 1941, Records of the Treasury Department, Office of the General Counsel, General Correspondence, Box 45, Record Group 56, National Archives, Washington, D.C.

119   Weiss refuses to clear out office: Higham (1983), pp. 147–48. We have not been able to verify this story from Higham's cited sources.

119   Weiss's last year and death: *Wheeling News-Register,* Sept. 2–5, 1942.

120   I.G. executives tried as war criminals: *Trials of the War Criminals . . .* (1953), vol. 7.

CHAPTER EIGHT

123–124   Harper's background: *Washington Herald,* Mar. 17, 1908, p. 2 ("one of Washington's"); and *OPDR,* Mar. 16, 1908, p. 9.

124   Acetanilid and antipyrine lose favor: Gathercoal (1933), pp. 28–29.

125   Quotes from Judge Kimball's instructions: Charge to the jury, *U.S.* v. *Harper, Decision.*

125–126   Early history of patent medicines: Young (1961), pp. 3–30. We owe a great debt to the works of Young for the material in this chapter.

125   Bilious Pills: Young (1967), pp. 16–17.

126   Patent medicine sales: Young (1961), pp. 93–110.

126   "were schooled": Hopkins (1927), p. 73.

126   "an evil": *Patent Medicines,* Report no. 52, U.S. House of Representatives, 30th Congress, 2nd session, Feb. 6, 1849, p. 32.

126–137   Story of Wiley: Anderson, Jr. (1958); Young (1961), chapter 14; Young (1967), pp. 13–53; and Young (1989).

126   "His hair never stays": Björkman (1910), p. 12443.

127   Wiley's bicycle: Wiley (1930), p. 156.

127   "Wiley had the knack": Young (1967), p. 33.

127–128   "We sit at a table": Quoted in Anderson, Jr. (1958), p. 124.

128   "It is not for me": Quoted in Anderson, Jr. (1958), p. 127.

129   "would practically destroy": Young (1961), p. 226.

129   Magnetic Healing story and footnote source: *American School of Magnetic Healing* v. *McAnnulty*, 187 *U.S.* 94 (1902); and *Weltmer et al.* v. *Bishop*, 71 *S.W.* 167 (1902).

129   "only to a limited degree": *id.*, pp. 168–69.

129   "be proved as a fact" and "still in the empirical stage": *American School of Magnetic Healing* v. *McAnnulty*, 187 *U.S.* 94 (1902), pp. 104–105.

130   "shameful trade" and "Acetanilid will": Adams (1905b), p. 16.

130   "If the Federal Government": Young (1961), pp. 236–37.

131   "[Washington, D.C.] has been full": Ltr., Wiley to Frear, Apr. 7, 1906, quoted in Young (1989), p. 220.

131   "Where liberty reigns": Quoted in Anderson, Jr. (1958), p. 175.

131   "How does a general": Wiley (1930), p. 231.

131   "which shall be false": Federal Food and Drug Act of 1906, 34 Stat. 768 (1906), Sections 7 & 8.

132 133   Trial of Harper: *OPDR*, Feb. 24, 1908, p. 40 ("There is no food" and subsequent quotes from trial); *id.*, Mar. 2, 1908, p. 28D; *id.*, Mar. 9, 1908, p. 9; *id.*, Mar. 16, 1908, p. 9; *id.*, Mar. 23, 1908, p. 7 ("A class of men"); *Washington Evening Star*, Mar. 16, 1908, p. 2; *id.*, Mar. 17, 1908, p. 12; *Washington Herald*, Mar. 17, 1908, p. 2; *id.*, Mar. 19, 1908, p. 2; *Washington Post*, Mar. 6, 1908, p. 14; *id.*, Mar. 13, 1908, p. 2; and *U.S.* v. *Harper, Decision*.

133   Judge Kimball's instructions and quotes: Charge to the jury, *U.S.* v. *Harper, Decision*.

133–134   Sentencing of Harper: *OPDR*, Mar. 23, 1908, p. 28B; *id.*, Apr. 20, 1908, p. 15; *Washington Evening Star*, Mar. 16, 1908, p. 2; *Washington Herald*, Mar. 17, 1908, p. 2; *id.*, Mar. 19, 1908, p. 2; *id.*, Apr. 16, 1908, p. 12; and *U.S.* v. *Harper, Decision*.

134   "It is your duty": Quoted in *Washington Herald*, Mar. 17, 1908, p. 2.

134   "I am not": *Washington Evening Star*, Mar. 17, 1908, p. 12.

134   Footnote source: *NYT*, Sept. 24, 1940, p. 23 (Harper's obituary).

135   Bureau of Chemistry report: Kebler (1909).

135   Acetophenetidin substituted for acetanilid: Adams (1907).

135   Acetanilid brands: Bureau of Chemistry, Notices of Judgment nos. 260, 392, 418, 568, and 919, respectively, U.S. Department of Agriculture, Washington, D.C.

135 "increasing daily": U.S. Department of Agriculture (1909), pp. 434–35.

135 1910 survey: U.S. Department of Agriculture (1910), p. 19.

135 "This is an effective tonic": *U.S.* v. *Johnson*, 221 *U.S.* 488 (1911), p. 490.

135 Johnson court decisions: *U.S.* v. *Johnson*, 177 *Fed.* 313 (1910); *U.S.* v. *Johnson*, 221 *U.S.* 488 (1911), p. 490.

136 "I don't" and "joker": Quoted in Young (1967), p. 47.

136 "actually the result": Quoted in Anderson, Jr. (1958), pp. 232–33.

136 "Dear Madam": Ltr., Wiley to Clark, Oct. 10, 1916, Harvey H. Wiley Papers, Container 163, Manuscript Division, Library of Congress, Washington, D.C.

137 "I am a very ill man": Quoted in *NYT*, July 1, 1930, p. 29.

CHAPTER NINE

138 Creel's later fame and "the people's": Knightley (1975), pp. 122–23, quote p. 122.

138 "its teeth drawn": Creel (1915c), p. 4.

138 "The ultimate goal": Creel (1915a), p. 112.

138–139 "What proportion" and "grown old and decrepit": Creel (1915b), p. 136.

140 "unfair methods": U.S. Code, 1982 ed., Title 15, Sec. 45(a)(1).

140–141 Background on the FTC Act: Rublee (1926).

141 Rublee's interpretation of "unfair methods": *id.*, p. 118.

141 Early fight against false advertising: Kenner (1936), pp. 27–32, 49; Pope (1983), pp. 202–12; and Cole (1921).

141 Associated Advertising Clubs and FTC: Kenner (1936), p. 65; and Kintner (1960).

142 "a very stupid person": *John C. Winston Co.* v. *FTC*, 3 *F.2d* 961 (1925), p. 962.

142 "seriously the suggestion": *FTC* v. *Standard Educational Society et al.*, 86 *F.2d* 692 (1936), pp. 693–94.

142 "Laws are made": *FTC* v. *Standard Educational Society et al.*, 302 *U.S.* 112 (1937), p. 116.

142 FTC sues facial cream maker: 34 *FTC* 1203 (1942).

142 "perpetual fountain of youth": *Charles of the Ritz Distributors Corp.* v. *FTC*, 143 *F.2d* 676 (1944), p. 679.

142 "seems scarcely possible": *Gelb* v. *FTC*, 144 *F.2d* 580 (1944), p. 582.

142 "clear enough so that": ibid, quoting *General Motors Corp.* v. *FTC,* 114 *F.2d* 33 (1940), p. 36.

143 FTC misrepresentation complaints: *Public Regulation of Competitive Practices* (1929), pp. 271–78.

143 "colds, pain, toothache": *Delineator,* Dec. 1921, p. 81.

143 "Warning! Say 'Bayer' ": *id.,* May 1922, p. 98.

143 Bayer competition: *Daily News,* Mar. 6, 1929, p. 35 ("No waiting"); 24 *FTC* 1128 (1937) ("Registered"); 21 *FTC* 1009 (1935), ("the lower"); and Brief of Counsel to Commission, Jan. 21, 1938, *FTC-Haynes, Docket,* p. 17 (thousand brands of aspirin).

143–144 Alka-Seltzer story: Yates (1986). We thank Dr. Yates for sending us this account.

144 NBC early history and ad figures: *Fortune,* Sept. 1932, p. 41.

144 Two-thirds radio programming had no sponsorship: *id.,* p. 37.

144 "to speak, think": Quoted in Barnouw (1966), vol. 1, p. 30.

144 National radio drug and cosmetic advertising: Hettinger (1933), p. 123.

144 Sterling's early radio programs: Hughes (1943).

144 "Take Care!": Paragraph Six, Complaint, In the Matter of Bayer Company, FTC Docket 2192, Federal Records Center, Suitland, Md.

145 Sterling and Bayer aspirin advertising: *AA,* Jan. 25, 1937, p. 38; and *AA,* Jan. 18, 1937, p. 36.

145 Advertising by Bayer's competitors: 21 *FTC* 924 (1935) ("All competitors"); 22 *FTC* 921 (1936) ("Nauseate"); and 22 *FTC* 210 (1936) ("Fresher").

145 FTC sues thirteen aspirin companies: 19 *FTC* 229 (1934); 20 *FTC* 695 (1935) and 24 *FTC* 115 (1936) (same company); 21 *FTC* 924 (1935); 21 *FTC* 1009 (1935); 21 *FTC* 1087 (1935); 22 *FTC* 921 (1936); 22 *FTC* 89 (1936); 22 *FTC* 210 (1936); 23 *FTC* 1116 (1936); 23 *FTC* 1124 (1936); 23 *FTC* 1126 (1936); 24 *FTC* 1128 (1937); and 26 *FTC* 1147 (1938).

145–147 Story of Aspirub and Justin Haynes: *FTC-Haynes, Docket* and *Decision.*

145 "Get a jar": *FTC-Haynes, Decision,* p. 1152.

146 "hurried to all parts": Answer to Complaint, Mar. 30, 1936, *FTC-Haynes, Docket,* p. 3.

146 Footnote source: *FTC* v. *Raladam,* 283 *U.S.* 643 (1931).

146 Diasio's clinical trial: Clinical Test on Aromatic Ointment, Apr. 5, 1937, Respondent's Exhibit 1-A-F, *FTC-Haynes, Docket.*

146 Justin Haynes loses appeal: *Justin Haynes & Co.* v. *FTC,* 105 *F.2d* 988 (1939).

147–150 Story of 1938 Food, Drug, and Cosmetic Act: Cavers (1939).

147   1906 act cannot ban ingredients: U.S. Department of Agriculture (1932), p. 11.

147   FDA prohibited from lobbying Congress: Cavers (1939), p. 5.

147   Death of Pittsburgh businessman: Pais (1986), p. 100.

148   FTC allowed to lobby Congress: *Printers' Ink*, Jan. 14, 1937, p. 20.

148   Davis and Ambruster testify, Summer 1935: *Food, Drugs, and Cosmetics* (1935).

148   "If you want to place" and "Are you not tired": *CR*, June 20, 1936, p. 10677.

148   Compromise rejected in House, June 1936: *CR*, June 20, 1936, p. 10679.

149   "not the practical": *CR*, Jan. 12, 1938, p. 406.

149   Elixir Sulfanilamide story: Jackson (1970), pp. 151–64; and Cavers (1939), pp. 20–21.

150   "Despite the apparent stringency": *BW*, Mar. 19, 1938, p. 42.

CHAPTER TEN

151   Mejoral in Mexico and quotes: This section is a paraphrase of an unusual document. In June 1942, *Fortune* published an article ("Popguns on the Southern Frontier") covering Sterling's economic war with I.G. Farben in South America. The opening section and quotes are from a draft of that article, which is in the "Fortune article" folder, *CORC*, Box 523.

151   Bayer Cross placard: J. Corcoran (I).

151–154   Mejoral campaign in South America: D. Corcoran (I), J. Corcoran (I), and Landreth (I); *Fortune*, June 1942, p. 90; Cathcart (1943a 1943b, ["making headaches"], 1943c); Hughes (1943); and *Printers' Ink*, Feb. 13, 1942, p. 13.

152–153   "The peons of Colombia" and "The point can't be missed": Cathcart (1943c).

154–155   Anacin history: *Reynolds Deposition*, pp. 13–15; and 44 *FTC* 1130 (1944).

155   "twenty cents' worth": Quoted in *Journal of the American Dental Association*, June 1929, p. 1121.

155   "simply a mixture": ibid.

155   Anacin sales: *Reynolds Deposition*, p. 17.

155   Diebold sets up American Home: *Fortune*, Apr. 1958, p. 141.

155–156   Brush's background: *NYT*, Apr. 25, 1965, p. 87; Ida (I) and Weinstein (I).

156   Anacin and Bayer spending, 1935: *AA*, Jan. 18, 1937, p. 36; and *id.*, Jan. 25, 1937, p. 38.

156 "Ambitious Smith" ad: *Boston Post,* Nov. 14, 1933, p. 8.

157 Anacin spending quadruples: *AA,* Jan. 22, 1940, p. 31.

157 Sixty-five thousand monthly samples: *Reynolds Deposition,* p. 16.

157 1941 Anacin and Bayer radio advertising: *AA,* Feb. 2, 1942, p. 20.

157 Laporte's background: *BW,* Oct. 20, 1980, p. 80; *Fortune,* July 25, 1983, p. 59; and Shapiro (I).

157 Laporte's credo: *BW,* Mar. 21, 1970, p. 76.

157 "Anacin is compounded": 44 *FTC* 1130 (1944), p. 1132.

157 Anacin's changing ingredients: *WSJ,* Mar. 14, 1963, p. 11.

158–160 Story of Reeves and quotes: Whiteside (1969).

158–159 Growth of television: Barnouw (1975) and Smith (1990), pp. 185ff.

159 Invention of the commercial: Whiteside (1954).

160 "Pounding Hammers" one of the worst ads: *BW,* Oct. 10, 1959, p. 56.

160 Story of Drug, Inc.: *Fortune,* Oct. 1930, p. 42; Merwin (1935); *Sales Management,* Feb. 16, 1929, p. 373; *Pharmaceutical Era,* Aug. 1930, p. 233; and *DOJ* 6717.

160 "Acts twice as fast": *Life,* Jan. 17, 1949, p. 13.

160 "Headache throbbing like a drum?": Bufferin ad (A).

161–162 1950s market shares: *FTC-Sterling, Decision,* p. 417.

162 "more about proprietary medicine": *DOJ* 3310.

162 "Tense nervous headaches": *Saturday Evening Post,* Jan. 12, 1957, p. 66.

162 "Don't pay twice": *id.,* Jan. 5, 1957, p. 36.

162 Graham's complaints to the FTC: RX156A,B, RX156L-N, RX156P, and CX371-2045, in *FTC-Sterling, Docket.*

162–163 Meeting between Sterling and Dobbs: RX407A-H, *id.*

163 1957 FTC budget figures: S. Anderson, Testimony, *False and Misleading Advertising . . .* (1957), p. 113.

163 "could not and would not": RX407A-H, *FTC-Sterling, Docket,* p. 8.

163 FTC contacts NIH and VA: A. Egendorf, Testimony, *Establish a Department . . .* (1969), p. 284.

163–164 Lasagna and DeKornfeld study: DeKornfeld et al. (1962).

164 Suspension of aspirin cases and FTC investigation: *FDC,* July 2, 1963, p. 33.

164 Permission to publish mistakenly given: P. Dixon, Testimony, *Frauds and Quackery . . .* (1963), p. 282.

164   Sterling uses study in radio and print ads: *FDC*, Jan. 14, 1963, p. 20. An example of the ad can be found in *Life*, Jan. 25, 1963, p. 95.

164–165   Commission's reaction to *JAMA* article: *FDC*, Jan. 7, 1963, p. 2. The FTC was described as "teed off."

164–167   Sterling complaint and subsequent FTC decisions: 64 *FTC* 898 (1964).

165   FTC files for preliminary injunction: *FDC*, Jan. 21, 1963, p. 3.

165   FTC asks for and is refused a temporary restraining order: *FDC*, Feb. 11, 1963, p. 5.

165   "picking at a fly": *FDC*, Feb. 25, 1963, p. 16.

165–166   Denial of preliminary injunction and "The advertisement is definite": *FTC* v. *Sterling Drug*, 215 *F.Supp.* 327 (1963), quote p. 332.

166   Appellate court upholds decision: *FTC* v. *Sterling Drug*, 317 *F.2d* 669 (1963).

166   "She Learned about Bayer" ad: *FDC*, May 13, 1963, p. 3.

166–167   Story of consumer testimony, "Pink Sheet" interviews, and witness quotes: *FDC*, Apr. 29, 1963, pp. 16–19.

167   Sterling urges commission to dismiss case: *FDC*, Feb. 10, 1964, p. 21.

167   Commission continues investigation of aspirin industry: *FDC*, Sept. 14, 1964, p. 2.

167   Companies demand dismissal of original complaints: *FDC*, Jan. 18, 1965, p. 3; and *id.*, Feb. 8, 1965, p. T&G–4.

167   FTC dismisses original complaints: 67 *FTC* 430 (1965).

CHAPTER ELEVEN

168   Background of Nader report: A. Egendorf, Testimony, *Establish a Department* . . . (1969), pp. 85–88.

168   Quotes from Nader report: *FDC*, Jan. 6, 1969, p. 30.

169   Dixon's response and Nader group's rebuttal: *FDC*, Jan. 13, 1969, p. 12.

169   "a glut of information": W. Taft IV, Testimony, *Establish a Department* . . . (1969), p. 84.

169   "Somebody must be lying": A. Egendorf, Testimony, *Establish a Department* . . . (1969), p. 85.

169   "We are going to have": Quoted in *FDC*, June 2, 1969, p. T&G-8.

169   "The agency's performance": *Report of the ABA Commission* (1969), p. 35.

169   Footnote source: "Separate Statement of Richard Posner," *id.*, p. 119.

169   Weinberger studies history of FTC: *FDC*, Oct. 6, 1969, p. 11.

170   "put down the shotgun": Quoted in *FDC*, Feb. 9, 1970, p. 8.

170   Analgesic advertising themes: Taken from *FTC-AHP, Decision; FTC-BM, Decision;* and *FTC-Sterling, Decision.*

170   Commission orders lawyers to gather evidence: G. Thain, Testimony, *Advertising of Proprietary Medicines* (1971), p. 137.

171–172   Pfizer case and adequate substantiation doctrine: 81 *FTC* 23 (1972); and Pitofsky (1977).

171   Footnote source: 81 *FTC* 23 (1972), pp. 44–50, 67–68.

171–172   "Weinberger and Kirkpatrick": Weil (I).

172   Bickart's background: Bickart (I).

172   "Substantial question" approach: *AA*, Dec. 28, 1970, p. 1; and *FDC*, Jan. 4, 1971, p. 16.

173   FTC intends to file charges: *WSJ*, Apr. 10, 1972, p. 26.

173–174   Contents of proposed complaints: *FTC-AHP, Decision*, pp. 136–45; *FTC-BM, Decision*, pp. 21–34 ("New Housing," p. 26); *FTC-Sterling, Decision*, pp. 395–405; and Bickart (I).

173   Excedrin's beginnings: *WSJ*, Sept. 20, 1961, p. 8.

173   Excedrin and Anacin remove acetophenetidin: *WSJ*, Mar. 14, 1963, p. 11.

174–175   Negotiations between FTC and companies: Bickart (I) and Sterling lawyer (confidential interview).

175   FTC analgesic trade regulation rule and "marked by industry opposition": P. Dixon, Testimony, Exhibit 48, n.d., *Establish a Department . . .* (1969), p. 676.

175   Bristol-Myers sues FTC: *BNA Antitrust and Trade Regulation Reporter*, Nov. 21, 1967, p. A20.

175   FTC stops work on rule: P. Dixon, Testimony, Exhibit 48, n.d., *Establish a Department . . .* (1969), p. 676.

176   Appellate court grants Bristol-Myers's request: *Bristol-Myers* v. *FTC*, 424 *F.2d* 935 (1970).

176   Analgesic trade regulation rule dropped: *FDC*, Jan. 4, 1971, p. 16.

176   1972 Bristol-Myers's case: Memorandum Dismissing Request for Injunction, *Bristol-Myers* v. *FTC*, 72 Civ. 2794, Aug. 25, 1972, District Court of District of Columbia.

176   Formal complaints issued and other background on aspirin cases: *FTC-AHP, Decision; FTC-BM, Decision; FTC-Sterling, Decision;* and Bickart (I), FTC lawyers (confidential interviews), and Sterling lawyer (confidential interview).

176   Reputation of Judge Jackson: *FDC*, Mar. 19, 1973, p. 7.

176   Eleven of thirty-two lawyers on aspirin cases: *FDC*, May 28, 1973, p. 13.

177   "I have no yardstick" and subsequent quotes from hearing: Transcript, Pre-trial Hearing, June 26, 1973, *FTC-BM, Docket*, pp. 20–21.

178   Details from American Home trial: *FTC-AHP, Decision*, pp. 206–16, 227–29, 243.

179   "If we go out there" and American Home considers dropping regular Anacin: *AA*, Nov. 5, 1979, p. 1, quoting D. McClain, former vice-president of marketing, AHP.

179–181   Details from Bristol-Myers trial: *FTC-BM, Decision*, pp. 162–82.

179   "In this study": *id.*, p. 28.

180   "reject the hypothesis": *id.*, p. 170.

180   "It is quite true": *id.*, p. 182, quoting from CX508.

181–182   Details from Sterling trial: *FTC-Sterling, Decision*, pp. 501–611.

182   Appearance of Sterling witness canceled by Congress: Sterling lawyer, confidential interview.

182   "Aspirin: homey, familiar": Opinion, Sept. 9, 1981, *FTC-AHP, Decision*, p. 362.

182–183   Commission retreats from American Home principle: Opinion, July 5, 1983, *FTC-BM, Decision*, p. 383.

183   Three modifications to AHP order: 101 *FTC* 698 (1983), 103 *FTC* 57 (1984), and 103 *FTC* 528 (1984).

183   "Developments in the [over-the-counter]": Memorandum of American Home Products Corporation in Support of Its Request for Reopening of the Proceedings and Modification of the Order, Apr. 15, 1983, *FTC-AHP, Docket*, p. 5.

CHAPTER TWELVE

184   Hopkins and Liquozone: Fox (1984), p. 54; and Adams (1905a).

184–185   "They put the word" and Hopkins quotes: Hopkins (1927), pp. 79–81.

185   First synthesis of acetaminophen (APAP): Morse (1878).

185   von Mering's analysis: von Mering (1893).

185   1894 study of APAP: Hinsburg and Treupel (1894).

186   Founding of institute and "These old drugs": Ringuette (1986), quote at p. 4. We thank C. Aaron (formerly C. Ringuette) for sending us this paper.

186   FDA's action against bromide: *BW*, Oct. 31, 1942, p. 22.

187   Research on APAP: Brodie and Axelrod (1948, 1949); Flinn and Brodie

(1948); Greenberg and Lester (1946); and Lester and Greenberg (1947).

187 Sumner Chemical Company makes APAP: *Chemical Week,* Jan. 20, 1951, p. 19.

187 Trigesic: Spooner and Harvey (1976), p. 3.

187 *Chemical Week* report and "will never threaten": *Chemical Week,* Jan. 20, 1951, p. 19.

187–188 Institute symposium: *Symposium on N-Acetyl p-aminophenol* (1951).

188–191 Story of Bayer Products, Ltd., and Panadol: Spalton (I), Fryers (I), Landreth (I), and Baruch (I).

189 "swimming pools of blood": Fryers (I).

190 Consumption of ASA and APAP: Spooner and Harvey (1976), p. 5.

191–192 Background on McNeil Laboratories and Johnson & Johnson: Foster (1986).

191 "the analgesic of choice": Boréus and Sandberg (1953), p. 264.

191 Approval for Tylenol: Ltr., Smith to McNeil Laboratories, June 3, 1955, *FDA,* NDA 9927, Tylenol elixir.

191 McNeil bought by Johnson & Johnson: *WSJ,* Jan. 16, 1959, p. 10.

192 Approval for adult Tylenol: Ltrs., DeFelice to McNeil Laboratories, Apr. 24, 1959, and Sept. 12, 1960, *FDA,* NDA 11630, Tylenol Tablet.

192 Tylenol one of two hundred most frequently prescribed drugs: *FDC,* May 17, 1965, p. 5.

192 "out in front" and aspirin's cost advantage: *OPDR,* Jan. 17, 1966, p. 4.

193 "The name Truce": Quoted in *Forbes,* June 26, 1978, p. 97.

193 Introduction of Neotrend and quotes from Neotrend ads: *AA,* Oct. 21, 1968, p. 1; and *FDC,* Oct. 28, 1968, p. T&G–1.

193 "Many doctors have": Quoted in *AA,* Nov. 25, 1968, at p. 37.

193 Analgesic market shares and sales: RX291, *FTC-Sterling, Docket.*

193 Doctor analgesic recommendations: W. Nelson, Testimony, *AHP* v. *J&J* (*1*), *Docket,* p. 371.

193–197 Story of Datril v. Tylenol and quotes from Datril ads: *AA,* Oct. 28, 1974, p. 3; Mar. 29, 1976, p. 1; June 16, 1975, p. 6; July 14, 1975, p. 1; July 28, 1975, p. 1; Aug. 8, 1975, p. 1; Oct. 20, 1975, p. 4; Mar. 29, 1976, p. 1; July 28, 1975, p. 1; Oct. 20, 1975, p. 4; Mar. 22, 1976, p. 1; Apr. 26, 1976, p. 1; and Nov. 1, 1976, p. 3.

194 Burke calls Gelb: *BW,* Oct. 6, 1975, p. 78.

194–197 Background on Nelson and Tylenol marketing: Nelson (I).

195 "Let your rivals": *Printers' Ink,* Apr. 21, 1897, p. 32, quoted in Pope (1983), p. 200.

195   Clinical trial comparing Darvon and APAP: W. Nelson, Testimony, May 11, 1977, *AHP* v. *J&J* (*1*), *Docket*, pp. 138, 142.

195   Approval of prescription Extra-Strength Tylenol: Ltr., Crowt to McNeil Laboratories, June 26, 1973, *FDA*, NDA 17552, Extra-Strength Tylenol.

195   Approval of OTC Extra-Strength Tylenol: Ltr., Finkel to McNeil Laboratories, July 22, 1975, *id.*

196   "attempts to take advantage": U.S. pharmaceutical executive (confidential interview).

197   Tylenol passes Anacin: *AA*, Nov. 1, 1976, p. 3.

CHAPTER THIRTEEN

198   Bayer's market share: Market Shares of Selected Analgesics, 1968–79, Doc. RX291, *FTC-Sterling, Docket.*

198   Hiebert and Wescoe: Landreth (I); D. Corcoran (I); Spalton (I).

198   Sterling brings out Bayer Non-Aspirin: Nelson (I); and *AA*, Aug. 8, 1975, p. 1.

198–199   Bayer's 1976–77 campaign and quote, McNeil's complaint, and NAD decision: *AA*, Apr. 18, 1977, p. 1.

199   McNeil ad, Bayer response, and quotes from ads: *Time*, June 27, 1977, p. 1.

199   McNeil letter to Sterling: *AA*, Aug. 15, 1977, p. 1.

200   More people take aspirin than APAP: Ltr., A. K. Done, Feb. 1, 1978, RC009, *OTC Analgesic Docket.*

200   Tylenol's market share: *AA*, Aug. 15, 1977, p. 1.

200   "range[d] from 100,000": FDA press release, Jan. 4, 1972, quoted in *FDC*, Jan. 10, 1972, p. 41.

200   More than eight thousand antacids: *FDA*, "Progress Report: OTC Drug Review" (A), n.d., p. 1.

200–201   NAS and NRC reports issued in May 1969: *FDC*, May 19, 1969, p. 3.

201   Three-quarters of OTC drugs ineffective: *OTC Drugs*, p. 85.

201   FDA plan for OTC monographs: *OTC Drugs.*

202   First draft monograph by May 1972: C. Edwards, Jan. 4, 1972, quoted in *FDC*, Jan. 10, 1972, p. 38.

202   Bristol-Myers and FDA advisory panel: *FDC*, Nov. 26, 1973, p. 10; and *id.*, Dec. 3, 1973, p. 5.

202–203   American Home and FDA advisory panel, and Grollman and Kushner quotes: Transcript, FDA Arthritis Advisory Committee, pp. 299–305, in vol. 6, appendix 5, C00043, *OTC Analgesic Docket.*

203   "hours of gentle relief": Quoted in *FDC,* Oct. 29, 1973, at p. 10.

204   OTC Analgesic Panel's report: *OTC Analgesic Report.*

204   Sterling's arguments on APAP claims: *AA,* Nov. 29, 1976, p. 1.

205   "considered to be equivalent": *OTC Analgesic Report,* p. 35413.

205   "Do not exceed recommended dosage": *id.,* p. 35416.

205   Johnson & Johnson press conference: Press release, McNeil Laboratories, July 7, 1977, copied in RC0010, *OTC Analgesic Docket.*

205–206   Weil's attack and quotes: C00060, Dec. 2, 1977, *OTC Analgesic Docket.*

206   Bayer ad, Kennedy's letters, and "we will find it": *AA,* Dec. 19, 1977, p. 2.

206   "DO NOT TAKE THIS PRODUCT": C00040, vol. 6, Dec. 2, 1977, *OTC Analgesic Docket.*

206–207   "specific consequence" and Johnson & Johnson's proposed warnings for ASA and APAP: Introduction, C00044, Dec. 5, 1977, *OTC Analgesic Docket.*

207   Moriarty's letter and quotes from letter: Ltr., R. Moriarty, RC002, Jan. 30, 1978, *OTC Analgesic Docket.*

207   Panadol brochure and quotes: Winthrop Laboratories, Paracetamol-Containing Products, Exhibit IV, p. 32, in RC0005, Feb. 6, 1978, *OTC Analgesic Docket.*

208   "Your body knows": Quoted in *AHP* v. *J&J (1), Decision,* p. 788.

208   Nelson protests: Nelson (I); and *id.,* p. 789.

208   American Home sues McNeil: *id., Docket.*

209   Trilium and Extranol: *AA,* Sept. 1, 1975, p. 3.

209   Johnson & Johnson sues American Home over Extranol: *McNeil* v. *American Home Products,* 416 *F.Supp.* 804 (1976).

209   "special Anacin ingredient" and introduction of Anacin-3: *AA,* May 23, 1977, p. 1, quote at 99.

209   "its right to broadcast": Complaint, Apr. 22, 1977, *AHP* v. *J&J (1), Docket.*

210   "Any person who shall": 60 Stat. 427, Section 43(a). In November 1988, Congress amended the Lanham Act, changing Section 43(a). All the Lanham Act trials discussed in this book, however, were brought under the version of Section 43(a) quoted here.

210   "calculated to deceive": Answer and Counterclaim, Apr. 22, 1977, *AHP* v. *J&J (1), Docket.*

210   "prime example of adapting": Appeal Brief for Johnson & Johnson, *American Home Products* v. *Johnson & Johnson,* 77 Civ. 7503, U.S. Court of Appeals, 2nd Circuit.

210 Tylenol's share drops: T. Gardner, Testimony, Apr. 26, 1977, Motion for Preliminary Injunction, *AHP* v. *J&J* (*1*), *Docket*, p. 464.

210 American Home to spend additional $5 million: ibid, and *AA*, May 9, 1977, p. 3.

211 "The question in such cases": *American Brands, Inc.*, v. *R. J. Reynolds Tobacco Co.*, 413 *F.Supp.* 1352 (1976), p. 1357.

211–212 Consumer surveys and footnote source: D. Payne, Testimony, June 20, 1977, Trial transcript, *AHP* v. *J&J* (*1*), *Docket*, pp. 777–80; *id.*, *Decision*, p. 793.

212 "by triggering the viewer's": *id.*, p. 794.

213 "Anacin is a superior": *id.*, p. 804.

213 Johnson & Johnson considers using decision: *AA*, Aug. 29, 1977, p. 8.

213 Appellate court establishes precedent: *American Home Products* v. *Johnson & Johnson*, 577 *F.2d* 160 (1978).

214 American Home back in court: Complaint, *McNeilab* v. *American Home Products*, 78 *Civ.* 562, Southern District of New York, Jan. 31, 1978.

214 Judge Stewart refuses to dismiss charges: Memorandum Decision, *id.*, July 10, 1979.

214 Anacin II settlement: Affidavit of David F. Dobbins in Opposition to Motion to Strike or Sever, *AHP* v. *J&J* (2), *Docket*, July 7, 1986.

214 "New Maximum Strength Anacin is here": quoted in McNeil's Post Trial Brief, *McNeil* v. *AHP*, *Docket*, pp. 23–24, Oct. 12, 1979.

215 American Home changes ads: *id.*, *Decision*, p. 523.

215 "the latest in a series": McNeil Post Trial Brief, Oct. 12, 1979, *McNeil* v. *AHP*, *Docket*, pp. 23–24.

215 Consumer surveys: *McNeil* v. *AHP*, *Decision*, p. 529.

215 "I can't remember": Quoted in McNeil Post Trial Brief, Oct. 12, 1979, *McNeil* v. *AHP*, *Docket*, at p. 79.

215 "terribly poor" commercial: *McNeil* v. *AHP*, *Decision*, p. 527.

216 Footnote source: *McNeil* v. *Sterling Drug*, 81 Civ. 6714, Southern District of New York.

216 Extra-Strength Tylenol capsules, and 1981 market shares and advertising campaigns: *AA*, Feb. 2, 1981, p. 1.

CHAPTER FOURTEEN

217–219 Tylenol poisonings: *BW*, Oct. 18, 1982, p. 151 ("McNeil will definitely"); *id.*, Nov. 29, 1982, p. 37; and Moore (1982) (Tylenol 8 percent of sales and more than 15 percent of profits).

217 Tylenol's market share: *AA*, Oct. 4, 1982, p. 1.

218 $2 billion loss: Mitchell (1989).

218 Competing APAP brands and "ghoulish": *AA*, Oct. 11, 1982, p. 1.

218 Sterling to introduce Panadol: *Barron's*, Sept. 12, 1983, p. 13.

218 Footnote source: Shapiro (I).

219 Coupons: *BW*, Nov. 29, 1982, p. 37.

219–221 Discovery of ibuprofen: Adams (I); Adams (1987); and Nicholson (1982).

219 Boots and Drug, Inc.: Merwin (1935).

222 Upjohn and ibuprofen, and "Boots will get": *BW*, Feb. 1, 1982, p. 55.

222 "65 percent rule": Nelson (I).

223–225 American Home and Upjohn race to market ibuprofen: *FDC*, July 25, 1983, p. 1; and *id.*, Aug. 22, 1983, p. 11.

223–224 Details of arthritis committee meeting and all quotes: FDA Arthritis Advisory Committee, Transcript of Hearings, Aug. 18, 1983, pp. 175–219.

224 "we have to": Quoted in *AA*, Aug. 22, 1983, at p. 2.

224 Upjohn licenses ibuprofen to Bristol-Myers: *AA*, Apr. 2, 1984, p. 1.

225 FDA approves ibuprofen for OTC use: *FDC*, May 21, 1984, p. 3.

225 Johnson & Johnson sues FDA and quotes: *FDC*, May 28, 1984, p. 4.

225 "It's so effective": Quoted in *Upjohn v. American Home Products*, 598 *F.Supp.* 550 (1984), p. 553.

225 Upjohn sues American Home: *Upjohn v. American Home Products*, 598 *F.Supp.* 550 (1984).

226 1984 amendments: *FDC*, Sept. 10, 1984, pp. S1–S16.

226 Sales of sixty million dollars: *FDC*, June 10, 1985, p. 3.

226 Analgesic market shares: Total Analgesic Market Sales and Share Trend Report, Exhibit 5, W. T. Eldridge, Affidavit in Opposition to Motion to Strike or Sever, July 8, 1986, *AHP v. J&J* (2), *Docket*.

226–227 Johnson & Johnson mailing and quotes: Exhibit 1, G. Diskant, Affidavit in Support of McNeil's Motion for Leave to Amend Answer and Counterclaims, Jan. 9, 1986, *id.*

227 "tar ibuprofen products" and "McNeil never informs consumers": Quoted in *FDC*, July 1, 1985, at p. T&G–2.

227–228 Rotten-apple ad and quotes: *AHP v. J&J* (2), *Decision* (A), pp. 580–81.

228 American Home claims $167 million in damages: Ltr., Land to Diskant, June 3, 1986, *AHP v. J&J* (2), *Docket*.

228 Johnson & Johnson counterclaims: Amended Answer and Counterclaims of McNeilab, Inc., to the First Amended Complaint, June 12, 1986, *id.*

228   Drug interaction claim: *AHP* v. *J&J* (2), *Decision* (A), p. 589.

228   Children's analgesic market shares: Total Analgesic Market Sales and Share Trend Report, Exhibit 5, W. T. Eldridge, Affidavit in Opposition to Motion to Strike or Sever, July 8, 1986, *AHP* v. *J&J* (2), *Docket.*

228   $1.1 billion in lost profits: Ltr., McGrew to Diskant, July 2, 1986, *AHP* v. *J&J* (2), *Docket.*

228   Conner splits trial in three: *American Home Products* v. *Johnson & Johnson,* 111 *F.R.D.* 448 (1986).

228   Footnote source: *McNeil* v. *Bristol-Myers,* 656 *F.Supp.* 88 (1986), quote p. 89.

229   Conner's first decision and "Small nations": *AHP* v. *J&J* (2), *Decision* (A), quote pp. 571–72.

229   "mild-to-moderate" pain": *id.,* p. 591.

229   Conner dismisses second suit: *AHP* v. *J&J* (2), *Decision* (B).

229   "philosophical grounds": *AHP* v. *J&J* (2), *Decision* (B), p. 142.

229   Conner's warning to American Home: *id.,* p. 146.

230   Tylenol II: *McNeil* v. *American Home Products,* 675 *F.Supp.* 819 (1987); and *McNeil* v. *American Home Products,* 848 *F.2d* 34 (1988).

230   Tylenol III and "the latest skirmish": *AHP* v. *J&J* (3), *Decision,* quote at p. 317.

230   "apparently attempting" and "the largest headache study": ibid.

230   American Home's APAP warning: *FDC,* Dec. 4, 1989, p. T&G–15.

230   Caffeine as an adjuvant: *FDC,* Dec. 18, 1989, p. T&G–5–7; *AA,* Aug. 13, 1990, p. 3; and *FDC,* Sept. 10, 1990, p. T&G–12.

231   Ireland case and "I realise": *Sterling-Winthrop Group Ltd.* v. *Farbenfabriken Bayer AG,* 1976 *R.P.C.* 469 (1976), quote p. 509.

231   Offer of $2.5 million: Negotiations with Sterling towards a settlement in the countries outside the United States, Oct. 16 and 17, 1964, *LEV,* 9/A.4.

232   Bayer AG returns to U.S.A.: *AA,* Oct. 3, 1977, p. 1; and *Chemical Week,* Apr. 30, 1986, p. 9.

232   Bayer's 1986 market share: *AA,* June 1, 1987, p. 64.

CHAPTER FIFTEEN

235–236   Platet Cleartab: Rabouhans (I).

236   U.K. heart attack deaths: *1988 Demographic Yearbook,* New York: United Nations, 1990, p. 516.

236–238 Background on Nicholas Laboratories, Ltd.: Smith and Barrie (1976); Morgan (1959), pp. 21–22; and Dick (I).

236–237 "The science of atomic energy": Smith and Barrie (1976), p. 30, emphasis in original.

237 Examples of Nicholas ads, Egypt and Zaïre: Nicholas International files, courtesy J. N. Dick.

238 Physicians knew that salicylates prolong bleeding: Binz (1897), p. 272; and Bousser (1974).

238–246 Link, Schoeffel, the pail of blood, and all quotes: Link (1959).

239–240 "As we stepwise became": Alexander (1963), p. 6.

240 "Throughout his entire existence": Wright (1952), p. 1.

241 "a cell in search": Mielke (1975), p. 8.

241–242 McLean and heparin: McLean (1959) and Best (1959).

242 Pure heparin available in mid-1930s: Murray et al. (1937) and Jorpes (1963).

243 Wright's background: Wright (I).

243 First identification of coronary heart disease in 1929: Gordon (1988).

244 Sweet clover disease and lack of prothrombin: Link (1945), p. 370.

244–246 Link, Campbell, the discovery of dicumarol, and all quotes: Link (1945).

245 "a biochemical grab-bag": Link (1959), p. 105.

246 Link sponsors series of conferences on dicumarol: Wright (I).

246 Link and Wisconsin Alumni Research Foundation: Ross and Schoenfield (1948), Link (1945), and Wright (1959).

246 Allen and Butt test dicumarol and "an organically sound": Allen (1959), quote p. 118.

247 Early clinical use of dicumarol: Wright (1959), p. 112.

247 Nichol on using dicumarol after heart attack and "The probability": Nichol and Page (1946), quote p. 370; and Nichol (1959).

247 Standard treatments for heart attack: Thomas (1983), p. 45, describing treatments used by an intern in 1937.

247–248 Wright's initial skepticism: Wright (1959), p. 111.

248 Other heart attack studies: Wright (1946) and Peters, Guyther, and Brambel (1946).

249 Lind's study of scurvy: Lind (1753), quotes pp. 191, 193.

249 Cook's study of scurvy: Lloyd (1961).

250–251 "A young student": Dr. E. Peacock, Jr., in *Medical World News,* Sept. 1, 1972, p. 45.

251   AHA begins funding of research: American Heart Association, *AHA Heart Facts*, n.d.

251–252   Wright's trial: Wright et al. (1948).

252   "Anticoagulant therapy should be used": Wright (1948).

252   AHA pressures doctors: Rytand (1951), p. 207; and Wright (1959), p. 112.

252–253   Rytand's analysis and "One might conclude": Rytand (1951), quote p. 210.

252   Wright's final account: Wright et al. (1954), pp. 8–10, and chapter 3.

253–254   Honey and Truelove's analysis: Honey and Truelove (1957), quotes pp. 1158, 1160.

254   Reduction in pulmonary embolism deaths: *id.*, p. 1161.

254   Effect on deep-vein thrombosis: See citations in Poole and French (1961), p. 274.

254   Conflicting evidence on strokes: See, e.g., Marshall and Shaw (1959, 1960); Millikan, Siekert, and Whisnant (1958); V.A. Cooperative Study of Atherosclerosis (1961); and Pearce, Gubbay, and Walton (1965).

CHAPTER SIXTEEN

255–256   Craven's note and quotes: Craven (1950). The radon ad is on p. 99 of the journal.

255   Craven's background: Mosey (I); *Los Angeles Times*, Aug. 19, 1957 (obituary, L. Craven); and *Los Angeles Times*, Jan. 10, 1956 (obituary, E. Craven). We are grateful to C. Mosey for sending us these obituaries.

256   "Surely the practice": Craven (1956), p. 215.

256   Binz notes reports of bleeding and salicylic acid: Binz (1897), p. 272.

257–258   Link on salicylates and "I recalled distinctly": Link (1945), quote p. 380.

257   Link tests aspirin and sodium salicylate: Link et al. (1943).

257–258   "Almost eight million" and "the dietary habits": Link (1943–44).

258   Alarm in the medical press: *Lancet*, Oct. 2, 1943, p. 419; *BMJ*, Nov. 13, 1943, p. 615; and *BMJ*, July 7, 1945, p. 19.

258   "Is Aspirin a Dangerous Drug?": *JAMA*, Mar. 18, 1944, p. 777.

258   Gibson's letter to *Lancet* and quotes: Gibson (1948).

258   Gibson's aspirin treatment and "a more extensive trial": ibid.

258   "Not a single case": Craven (1956).

259   "could scarcely be dignified": Barnett (1982), p. 190.

259   Craven publicizes his work: Parcher (I); *Los Angeles Times*, Aug. 19,

1957 (obituary); C. Parcher, "Local Doctor Who First Learned About Aspirin" (A), *Glendale News Press,* date unknown.

259–261   Poole and French article and all quotes: Poole and French (1961).

261   Footnote source: Peto (1978).

261   Discoveries by Born and O'Brien: Born (1962) and O'Brien (1962).

262   Weiss uses platelet aggregometer: Weiss (I).

262   Weiss and Aledort, and "may have antithrombotic properties": Weiss and Aledort (1967), quote p. 497.

262   Weiss and Aledort's work confirmed and expanded: Evans et al. (1968), Zucker and Peterson (1968), and O'Brien (1968).

262–263   O'Brien investigates aspirin: O'Brien (I).

263   "are not only": O'Brien (1968), p. 779.

263–269   Elwood's clinical trials with aspirin: Elwood (I), Renton (I), and Cochrane (1989), pp. 248–51.

263   Elwood's background: Elwood (I).

264   O'Brien speaks to MRC committee about aspirin and platelets and "profound implications": Steering Committee of a Trial of Aspirin and Deep-Vein Thrombosis (1972), quote p. 445.

264   O'Brien investigation of aspirin for deep-vein thrombosis: ibid, and O'Brien (1973).

264–265   Elwood and Nicholas Laboratories: Elwood (I) and Renton (I).

264   Aspro advertisements: Nicholas International files, courtesy J. N. Dick.

267   "What do you want": Cochrane (1989), p. 249.

268   "I already knew that": *id.,* p. 250.

269   *British Medical Journal* publishes Elwood and Jick: Elwood, Cochrane, and Burr (1974), Elwood (1981), and Boston Collaborative Drug Surveillance Group (1974).

269   Elwood's second and third trial: Elwood and Sweetnam (1979) and Elwood (1979).

270   "men over the age": Wood (1972).

270   AMIS trial: *Science,* Feb. 22, 1980, p. 859; and AMIS Research Group (1975).

270–271   AMIS results and "The fact remains": AMIS Research Group (1980), p. 667, quote p. 669.

270   "We were disappointed": *Science,* Feb. 22, 1980, p. 859.

CHAPTER SEVENTEEN

273 "The Wonder Drug Nobody Understands": *New York Times Magazine,* Sept. 11, 1966, p. 56.

273–274 Collier's background: J. Collier (I), Piper (I), and Vane (I); we have also been given access by J. Collier to some of his father's papers.

273 "was interested in hundreds": Born (1983), p. 750.

274–278 Collier's experiments: Collier and Shorley (1960), Collier (1963b), Collier and Sweatman (1968), and Collier (1969).

274 "powerful and prolonged": Collier (1984), p. 570.

275 Dreser's aspirin research: *id.,* 567–69.

275 "Even a superficial study": Quoted in Ackerknecht (1973), pp. 123–24.

276 "It would appear": Collier (1963a), p. 108.

277 Piper's background and work with Collier: Piper (I).

278 Vane's background: Vane (I).

278 "The pharmacologist has been": Quoted in Vane (1983), p. 743.

278 "With extraordinary simplicity": ibid.

279 Vane's method of examining tissue reactions: Vane (1983).

279 "gave maximum opportunity": *id.,* p. 744.

280 Piper and Vane's experiments: Piper and Vane (1969).

280–281 Collier's paper and quotes: Collier (1969).

281–282 "In a number of cases": Kurzrock and Lieb (1930), p. 268.

282 "the usual trials and errors": Weissmann (1987), p. 74.

282–283 Upjohn's support of prostaglandins research and "would have wiped out": Bylinsky (1972), quote p. 98.

283 Prostaglandin $F_{2\alpha}$ approved as abortion injection: *FDC,* Dec. 10, 1973, p. 14.

284–286 Vane's discovery of aspirin's effect on prostaglandins: Vane (I), Piper (I), and Collier (1984), pp. 560–61.

286 "If you prove to be": Quoted in Collier (1984), p. 576.

286–289 Three modes of action: Weissmann (I).

286 ASA, SA, and A: Lester et al. (1946).

287 Footnote source: *OTC Analgesic Report,* pp. 35471–79; and Proposed Rule, *Federal Register,* Nov. 16, 1988, p. 46220.

287 Allergic reaction to aspirin: Abramson et al. (1985).

287 Aspirin and neutrophils: Abramson and Weissmann (1989) and Weissmann (1991).

288   Samuelsson's team identifies thromboxane: Hamberg et al. (1975).

288–289 Aspirin interferes with thromboxane: Roth and Majerus (1975).

288   One milligram: Toivanen et al. (1984).

288–289 Thromboxane and platelets: Moncada and Vane (1979).

289   "It is best to assume": de Gaetano et al. (1985), emphasis added.

290   Citations to Vane's article: Institute for Scientific Information (1990). We thank David Pendlebury of ISI for amplification.

290   Collier's later work: Collier (1982) and Collier (1983), both courtesy J. Collier.

290   "blaze of light and publicity": Collier (1984), p. 557.

CHAPTER EIGHTEEN

291–305 Account of Cardiovascular and Renal Drugs Advisory Committee meeting, Mar. 1, 1983: *FDA Meeting,* Mar. 1, 1983 (quotes from meeting); and Elwood (I), Lockhart (I), Peto (I), and Soller (I).

291   Sterling asks FDA to change aspirin labeling: *FDC,* Mar. 7, 1983, p. 5.

292   "some imbalance": AMIS Research Group (1980), pp. 667.

292–293 Editorial in *Lancet* and quotes: *Lancet,* May 31, 1980, quote pp. 1172–73.

295   Peto's background and "When I finished": Ferry (1989), quote p. 18.

295–296 Hill's background: Himsworth (1982) and Doll (1982).

296   Streptomycin study: Medical Research Council (1948).

296   "phenomenal increase" and lung cancer preliminary report: Doll and Hill (1950), quote p. 730.

297   133,000 needed for trial: This calculation is based on the following parameters: two-sided significance level, .01; power of test, .90; control group event rate, 1 in 160; and expected relative risk of experimental treatment, .75. Donner (1984), using the relative risk formula on p. 202.

298   Cost of clinical trial: E. Goldensohn (I).

300   "Stone-dead has no fellow": Hill (1952), p. 117.

301   Peto's technique for adding trial results together: Mantel and Haenszel (1959) and Peto et al. (1976b).

302   Footnote source: *FDC,* May 23, 1983, p. 3; and *id.,* May 30, 1983, p. 11.

305–309 Cardiovascular and Renal Drugs Advisory Committee meeting, Dec. 11, 1984: *FDA Meeting,* Dec. 11, 1984 (all quotes from meeting); and Peto (I) and Soller (I).

305 "I consider this adequate": Ltr., Elwood to Cardiorenal Advisory Committee, Nov. 28, 1983, in *Sterling Aspirin Analysis,* Appendix I.

306 Meta-analysis of six aspirin trials: R. Peto and S. Parish, A Detailed Overview of the Six Randomised Trials of the Effects of Aspirin on the Odds of Reinfarction and/or Deaths Among MI Patients, in *id.,* volume 1, pp. 11–33.

306 Re-analysis of AMIS: R. Peto and S. Parish, Re-Analysis of "AMIS" Results Allowing for Prognostic Features, in *id.,* Appendix I.

306 "I am not willing": I. Fisher, *FDA Meeting,* Dec. 11, 1984, p. 188.

306 Veterans Administration aspirin study: Lewis et al. (1983).

309 "I find the unstable": R. Goldstein, *id.,* pp. 190–91.

309–310 Heckler's press conference: Sterling Drug, press release (A), n.d.

CHAPTER NINETEEN

311 Tylenol products: U.S. Food and Drug Administration (1987), p. 382.

312 Anticoagulants and stroke: For a history of anticoagulant stroke trials, see Fields and Lemak (1989), pp. 104–115.

312 "Neurologists are scared": Fields (I).

312–313 Fields's clinical trial: Fields (1983) and Fields (I).

313 Fields's first article: Fields et al. (1977).

313 Barnett's Canadian trial and Fields's second article: Canadian Cooperative Study Group (1978) and Fields et al. (1978).

314 Sterling, reprints of Fields's article, and the FDA: *FDC,* July 31, 1978, p. T&G–1, quotes at p. T&G–2.

314 Sterling's stroke application: Soller (I).

315 Warlow's background and TIA trial: Warlow (I).

315 TIA and stroke: Millikan and McDowell (1978), p. 301.

315–317 Story of British doctors trial and Physicians' Health Study: Steering Committee of the Physicians' Health Study Research Group (1988), Peto (I), and Hennekens (I).

317–318 Physicians' Health Study stopped: Relman (1988a).

318 Meta-analysis of U.S. and U.K. doctors trials: Hennekens, Peto, and Hutchinson (1988).

318–319 Anacin commercial: Transcript (A).

319 Stores stock up on aspirin: *AA,* Mar. 28, 1988, p. 3.

319 Aspirin commercials: Mellow (1989).

319 Second Tylenol scare: *AA,* Feb. 17, 1986, p. 1.

319   Predictions of U.S. analgesic market expansion: *AA*, Feb. 1, 1988, p. 1.

319   Analgesic market shares: ibid.

319   Aspirin leading analgesic in 1987: We thank Patricia Winter for supplying us with this information.

319   Six-bottle limit on sales of aspirin: *AA*, Mar. 28, 1988, p. 3.

320   Aspirin and colds: Hsia (I).

320   Aspirin and cancer: Braun (I).

320   Aspirin and pregnancy: Collins (I).

321   Cost of multi-infarct dementia: Meyer (I).

321   Meyer's study: Meyer et al. (1989) and Cebul (1989).

321–322   ISIS and ISIS-2: Collins (I).

321   ISIS results: International Study of Infarct Survival (1986).

321–322   Overview of streptokinase trials: Yusuf et al. (1985).

322   ISIS-2 results: ISIS-2 (Second International Study of Infarct Survival) Collaborative Group (1988).

322   Aspirin polls: Mellow (1989).

EPILOGUE

325–332   Anti-Platelet Trialists Collaboration meeting: Anti-Platelet Trialists Collaboration (1990); all quotes from meeting are from authors' notes.

326   Experts' past claims: E.g., Hull, Raskob, and Hirsh (1986) state (p. 377S) that "aspirin prophylaxis . . . has limited application, if any, because of its relative inefficiency."

328–329   Nicholas pushes aspirin for second heart attacks: Rabouhans (I).

330   Article in *Lancet*: Lovenz (1984).

330   Genentech stock prices and proposed merger: We thank Maggie Mahar, then at *Barron's*, for providing us with stock price quotations; and *WSJ*, Feb. 5, 1990, p. A3 (proposed merger).

332–334   Meyer and Sterling: Kelley (I), Lockhart (I), Meyer (I), and Weisman (I).

335   1988 U.S. aspirin advertising: *AA*, July 24, 1989, p. 80.

335   1988 market share, 1989 advertising figures: We thank Patricia Winter for supplying us with this information.

335   "check the label": Transcript (A).

336   "The wonder drug doctors": Quoted in *WSJ*, Nov. 19, 1989, p. B1.

336   Footnote source: complaint, May 21, 1990, *Sterling Drug, Inc.* v. *Bayer AG*, 90 Civ. 3460.

336   Packaged Facts study: Press release, Packaged Facts, Feb. 1991. We thank Patricia Winter for sending us a copy of the press release.

336   Ibuprofen and kidney damage: Ltr., Wolfe and LaCheen to Novitch, June
      13, 1984, in Motion for Discovery, *McNeilab* v. *Heckler,* Civ. 84-1617,
      June 21, 1984.

336   Ibuprofen under study: Case No. 15687-27-1, National Toxicology Pro-
      gram, Review of Current DHHS, DOE and EPA Research Related to
      Toxicology, NTP-89-168, Washington, D.C.: National Toxicology Pro-
      gram, Nov. 1989.

336–337   Acetaminophen NTP study: Toxicology and Carcinogenesis Studies of
      Acetaminophen (Case No. 103-90-2) in F344/N Rats and B6C3F1 Mice,
      NTP Technical Report, NTP Publication 90-2849, Washington, D.C.:
      NTP, 1991.

337   ASA and kidney cancer: Paganini-Hill et al. (1989); and correspondence,
      "Aspirin Use and Chronic Diseases," *BMJ,* Jan. 13, 1990, pp. 116–18.

337–338   Visit to Leverkusen: Hohmann (I).

BIBLIOGRAPHY

I. *Books and Articles*

Abramson, S., and G. Weissmann. "The Mechanisms of Action. . . ." *Arthritis and Rheumatism,* Jan. 1989, 1.

Abramson, S., et al. "Modes of Action of. . . ." *Proceedings of the National Academy of Sciences,* Nov. 1985, 7227.

Ackerknecht, E. H. *Therapeutics: From the Primitives to the 20th Century.* New York: Hafner Press, 1973.

Adams, S. "The Discovery of Brufen." *Chemistry in Britain,* Dec. 1987, 1193.

Adams, S. H. "Liquozone." *Collier's Weekly,* Nov. 18, 1905a, 20.

———. "Patent Medicines under the. . . ." *Collier's Weekly,* June 8, 1907, 11.

———. "The Subtle Poisons." *Collier's Weekly,* Dec. 2, 1905b, 16.

Alexander, B. "Some Perspectives on Coagulation. . . ." *Thrombosis et Diathesis Haemorrhagica* 9, supp. 11 (1963), 6.

Allen, E. V. "My Early Experience with. . . ." *Circulation,* Jan. 1959, 118.

Allen, E. V., N. W. Barker, and J. M. Waugh. "A Preparation from Spoiled. . . ." *JAMA,* Nov. 28, 1942, 1009.

Ambruster, H. W. "Hitler's Lobby Is Still. . . ." *Dan Gillmor's Scoop,* Nov. 1941, 17.

———. *Treason's Peace: German Dyes & American Dupes.* New York: The Beechhurst Press, 1947.

Ambruster, H.W., and U. Ambruster. *Why Not Enforce the Laws We Already Have? How and Why Industries' Outlaws Are Crucifying Harvey Wiley's Pure Food and Drug Law.* Westfield, N.J.: Ursula Ambruster, 1935.

American Heart Association. *1990 Heart and Stroke Facts*. Dallas: American Heart Association, 1989.

AMIS Research Group. "Aspirin and Myocardial Infarction: . . ." *JAMA*, June 30, 1975, 1359.

———. "A Randomized, Controlled Trial. . . ." *JAMA*, Feb. 15, 1980, 661.

Anderson, Jr., O. E. *The Health of a Nation*. Chicago: University of Chicago Press, 1958.

Antiplatelet Trialists' Collaboration. "Secondary Prevention of Vascular. . . ." *BMJ*, Jan. 30, 1988, 320.

Armstrong, H. E. "Chemical Industry and Carl Duisberg." *Nature*, June 22, 1935, 1021.

Barnett, H. J. M. "Platelet Antiaggregants in Stroke. . . ." In H. J. M. Barnett et al., eds., *Acetylsalicylic Acid: New Uses for an Old Drug*. New York: Raven Press, 1982.

Barnett, H. J. M., J. Hirsh, and J. F. Mustard, eds. *Acetylsalicylic Acid: New Uses for an Old Drug*. New York: Raven Press, 1982.

Barnett, H. J. M., J. W. D. McDonald, and D. L. Sackett. "Aspirin—Effective in. . . ." *Stroke*, July–Aug. 1978, 295.

Barnouw, E. *History of Broadcasting in the United States*. Vol. 1. New York: Oxford University Press, 1966.

———. *The Sponsor*. New York: Oxford University Press, 1978.

———. *Tube of Plenty*. New York: Oxford University Press, 1975.

Beer J. J. "Coal Tar Dye Manufacture. . . ." *Isis*, June 1958, 123.

———. *The Emergence of the German Dye Industry*. Illinois Studies in the Social Sciences, vol. 44. Urbana: University of Illinois Press, 1959.

Benigni, A., et al. "Effect of Low-Dose Aspirin. . . ." *NEJM*, Aug. 10, 1989, 357.

Bergström, S., L. A. Carlson, and J. R. Weeks. "The Prostaglandins: A Family. . . ." *Pharmacological Reviews*, Mar. 1968, 1.

Best, C. H. "Preparation of Heparin and. . . ." *Circulation*, Jan. 1959, 79.

Bingham, J. B., O. O. Meyer, and F. J. Poole. "Studies on the Hemorrhagic. . . ." *American Journal of the Medical Sciences*, Oct. 1941, 563.

Binz, C. *Lectures on Pharmacology for Practitioners and Students*, vol. 2. London: New Sydenham Society, 1897.

Björkman, E. "Our Debt to Doctor Wiley." *World's Work*, Jan. 1910, 12443.

Boréus, L., and F. Sandberg. "The Analgesic Action of. . . ." *Acta Physiologica Scandinavica*, 1953, 266.

———. "A Comparison of Some. . . ." *Acta Physiologica Scandinavica*, 1953, 261.

Borkin, J. *The Crime and Punishment of I.G. Farben*. New York: The Free Press, 1978, 29.

Borkin J., and C. A. Welsh. *Germany's Master Plan*. New York: Duell, Sloan, and Pearce, 1943.

Born, G. V. R. "Aggregation of Blood Platelets. . . ." *Nature*, 1962, 927.

———. "Henry Oswald Jackson Collier," *Lancet*, Sept. 24, 1983, 750.

Boston Collaborative Drug Surveillance Group. "Aspirin Use in Patients. . . ." *NEJM*, May 23, 1974, 1158.

————. "Regular Aspirin Intake and. . . ." *BMJ*, Mar. 9, 1974, 440.

Bousser, M. G. "Aspirine et plaquettes." *La Revue de Médecine*, Apr. 22, 1974, 1039.

————. *Contribution à l'étude des thromboses artérielles expérimentales, Effet préventif de l'aspirine et de la prostaglandine* E_1. Ph.D. Thesis, Paris: Impressions C.L.J., 1972.

Bousser, M. G., et al. "AICLA Controlled Trial of. . . ." *Stroke*, Jan.–Feb. 1983, 5.

Breddin, K., et al. "Secondary Prevention of Myocardial. . . ." *Haemostasis*, 1980, 325.

Bresciani-Turroni, C. *The Economics of Inflation*. London: George Allen & Unwin, Ltd., 1937.

Brodie, B. B., and J. Axelrod. "The Fate of Acetanilide. . . ." *Journal of Pharmacology and Experimental Therapeutics*, 1948, 29.

————. "The Fate of Acetophenetidin. . . ." *Journal of Pharmacology and Experimental Therapeutics*, 1949, 58.

Buchanan, M. R., et al. "Aspirin Inhibits Platelet Function. . . ." *Thrombosis Research*, 1982, 363.

Butt, H. R., E. V. Allen, and J. L. Bollman. "A Preparation from Spoiled. . . ." *Proceedings of the Staff Meetings of the Mayo Clinic*, June 18, 1941, 388.

Bylinsky, G. "Upjohn Puts the Cell's. . . ." *Fortune*, June 1972, 96.

Campbell, H. A., et al. "Studies on the Hemorrhagic. . . ." *Journal of Biological Chemistry*, Oct. 1940, 47.

Canadian Cooperative Study Group. "A Randomized Trial of. . . ." *NEJM*, July 13, 1978, 53.

Cathcart, J. D. "It's Still Sales Promotion. . . ." *Sales Management*, June 1, 1943c, 22.

————. "Radio Advertising as a. . . ." *Sales Management*, Mar. 1, 1943a, 32.

————. "With Sound Truck and. . . ." *Sales Management*, Apr. 1, 1943b, 68.

Cavers, D. F. "The Food, Drug, and. . . ." *Law and Contemporary Problems*, Winter 1939, 12.

Cebul, R. D. "Aspirin and MID: Notes. . . ." *Journal of the American Geriatrics Society*, June 1989, 573.

Chalmers, I., et al., eds. *Effective Care in Pregnancy and Childbirth*. Vol. 1, *Pregnancy*. Oxford: Oxford University Press, 1989.

Chalmers, T. C. "Evidence Favoring the Use. . . ." *NEJM*, Nov. 17, 1977, 1091.

Cochrane, A., with M. Blythe. *One Man's Medicine*. London: The Memoir Club, 1989.

Cole, R. "Review of the Ten. . . ." *Printers' Ink*, Mar. 3, 1921, 122.

Colgan, M. T., and A. A. Mintz. "The Comparative Antipyretic Effect. . . ." *Journal of Pediatrics*, May 1957, 552.

Collier, H. O. J. "Aspirin." *Scientific American*, Nov. 1963a, 108.

————. "Effects of Salicylates on. . . ." in A. St.J. Dixon, et al., eds., *Salicylates: An International Symposium*. Boston: Little, Brown, 1963b, 120.

————. "New Light on How. . . ." *Nature*, July 5, 1969, 35.

————. "The Story of Aspirin." In M. J. Parnham and J. Bruinvels, eds., *Discov-

eries in Pharmacology. Vol. 2, *Haemodynamics, Hormones & Inflammation.* New York: Elsevier, 1984, 555.

Collier, H. O. J., and P. G. Shorley. "Analgesic Antipyretic Drugs as. . . ." *British Journal of Pharmacology,* 1960, 601.

Collier, H. O. J., and W. J. F. Sweatman. "Antagonism by Fenamates of. . . ." *Nature,* Aug. 24, 1968, 864.

Cornely, D. A., and J. A. Ritter. "N-Acetyl-Para-Aminophenol (Tylenol Elixir) as. . . ." *JAMA,* Apr. 7, 1956, 1219.

Craven, L. L. "Acetylsalicylic Acid, Possible Preventive. . . ." *Annals of Western Medicine and Surgery,* Feb. 1950, 95.

———. "Prevention of Coronary and. . . ." *Mississippi Valley Medical Journal,* May 1956, 213.

Creel, G. "How the Drug Dopers Fight," *Harper's Weekly,* Jan. 30, 1915b, 112.

———. "The Law and the Drug Sharks," *Harper's Weekly,* Feb. 6, 1915c, 136.

———. "Poisoners of Public Health," *Harper's Weekly,* Jan. 2, 1915a, 4.

———. "The Press and Patent Medicines," *Harper's Weekly,* Feb. 13, 1915, 155.

de Gaetano, G., et al. "Pharmacology of Platelet Inhibition. . . ." *Circulation,* Dec. 1985, 1192.

DeKornfeld, T. J., L. Lasagna, and T. M. Frazier. "A Comparative Study of Five. . . ." *JAMA,* Dec. 29, 1962, 1315.

Directory for the Year 1903 of the Cities of Albany and Rensselaer. Albany: Sampson, Murdock, 1903.

Doll, R. "Clinical Trials: Retrospect and Prospect." *Statistics in Medicine,* 1982, 337.

Doll, R., and A. B. Hill. "The Mortality of Doctors. . . ." *BMJ,* June 26, 1954, 1451.

———. "Smoking and Carcinoma of. . . ." *BMJ,* Sept. 30, 1950, 730.

Donner, A. "Approaches to Sample Size. . . ." *Statistics in Medicine,* 1984, 199.

Dreser, H. "Pharmakologisches über Aspirin (Acetylsalicylsäure)," *Archiv für die Gesammte Physiologie,* 1899, 306.

Duisberg, C. "The Influence of Liebig. . . ." *Popular Science Monthly,* Apr. 1904, 533.

———. *Meine Lebenserinnerungen.* Leipzig: P. Reclam, Jr., 1933.

Dyer, F. L., and T. C. Martin. *Edison: His Life and Inventions.* New York: Harper & Brothers, 1929.

Dyken, M. L. "Transient Ischemic Attacks and. . . ." *Stroke,* Jan.–Feb. 1983, 2.

Eichengrün, A. "50 Jahre Aspirin." *Pharmazie,* 1949, 582.

———. "Pharmazeutische-Wissenschaftliche Abteilung." In *Geschichte und Entwicklung der Farbenfabriken vorm. Friedrich Bayer & Co. Elberfeld in den ersten 50 Jahren.* Leverkusen, 1918 (unpublished), 409.

Elwood, P. C. "British Studies of Aspirin. . . ." *American Journal of Medicine,* 1983, 50.

———. Letter, *BMJ,* Feb. 7, 1981, 481.

———. "A Randomized Controlled Trial. . . ." *Journal of the Royal College of General Practitioners,* July 1979, 413.

Elwood, P. C., A. L. Cochrane, and M. L. Burr. "A Randomized Controlled Trial. . . ." *BMJ*, Mar. 9, 1974, 436.

Elwood, P. C., and P. M. Sweetnam. "Aspirin and Secondary Mortality. . . ." *Lancet*, Dec. 22, 1979, 1313.

Evans, G., et al. "The Effect of Acetylsalicylic. . . ." *Journal of Experimental Medicine*, Nov. 1, 1968, 877.

Ferreira, S. H., S. Moncada, and J. R. Vane. "Indomethacin and Aspirin Abolish. . . ." *Nature New Biology*, June 23, 1971, 237.

Ferry, G. "A Passion for Numbers," *Oxford Today*, 1989, 18.

Fields, W. S. "Aspirin for the Prevention. . . ." *American Journal of Medicine*, June 14, 1983, 61.

Fields, W., and W. Hass. *Aspirin, Platelets, and Stroke: Background for a Clinical Trial*. St. Louis: Warren H. Green, Inc., 1971.

Fields, W., and N. Lemak. *A History of Stroke*. New York: Oxford University Press, 1989.

Fields, W. S., et al. "Controlled Trial of Aspirin. . . ." *Stroke*, May–June 1977, 301.

———. "Controlled Trial of Aspirin . . . II. . . ." *Stroke*, July–Aug. 1978, 309.

Flechtner, H. *Carl Duisberg: vom Chemiker zum Wirtschaftsführer*. Düsseldorf: Econ, 1959.

Fleming, H. M. "Holding Hands with Hitler." *Nation's Business*, June 1942, 17.

Flinn, F. B., and B. B. Brodie. "The Effect on the. . . ." *Journal of Pharmacology and Experimental Therapeutics*, 1948, 76.

Foster, L. G. *A Company That Cares*. New Brunswick, N.J.: Johnson & Johnson, 1986.

Fox, S. *The Mirror Makers*. New York: William Morrow and Company, Inc., 1984.

Friedman, M., and A. Schwarz. *A Monetary History of the United States, 1867–1960*. Princeton, N.J.: Princeton University Press, 1963.

Gathercoal, E. N. *The Prescription Ingredient Survey*. Chicago: American Pharmaceutical Association, 1933.

Gathings, J. A. *International Law and American Treatment of Alien Enemy Property*. Washington, D.C.: American Council on Public Affairs, 1940.

Gerhardt, C. "Recherches sur les acides. . . ." *Annales de Chimie*, 1853, 285.

Gibson, P. "Aspirin in the Treatment. . . ." *Lancet*, Dec. 24, 1949, 1172.

———. "Salicylic Acid for Coronary Thrombosis?" *Lancet*, June 19, 1948, 965.

Glass, G. V. "Primary, Secondary, and Meta-Analysis. . . ." *Educational Researcher*, Jan. 1976, 3.

Gordon, T. "The Diet-Heart Idea: Outline. . . ." *American Journal of Epidemiology*, Feb. 2, 1988, 220.

Greenberg, L. A., and D. Lester. "The Metabolic Fate of Acetanilid . . . I. . . ." *Journal of Pharmacology and Experimental Therapeutics*, 1946, 87.

Gross, M. *Acetanilid: A Critical Bibliographic Review*. New Haven, Conn.: Hillhouse Press, 1946.

Haber, L. F. *The Chemical Industry during the 19th Century*. Oxford: Clarendon Press, 1958.

———. *The Chemical Industry 1900–1930*. Oxford: Clarendon Press, 1971.

Hamberg, M., et al. "Thromboxanes: A New Group. . . ." *Proceedings of the National Academy of Sciences USA,* Aug. 1975, 2994.

Hamilton, W. "The Strange Case of. . . ." *Harper's Magazine,* Jan. 1943, 123.

Hammond, E. C., and L. Garfinkel. "Aspirin and Coronary Heart. . . ." *BMJ,* May 3, 1975, 269.

Handler, J. "Pfizer Revisited: From 'Reasonable. . . .' " *Food, Drug, Cosmetic Law Journal,* 1983, 325.

Harris, S. C., and L. S. Fosdick. *Northwestern University Bulletin,* 1952, 6.

Harrison, M. J. G., et al. "Effect of Aspirin in. . . ." *Lancet,* Oct. 2, 1971, 743.

Hass, W. K. "Aspirin for the Limping Brain." *Stroke,* May–June 1977, 299.

Hauri, P. J., and P. M. Silberfarb. "Effects of Aspirin on. . . ." *Current Therapeutic Research,* Dec. 1980, 867.

Hayes, P. *Industry and Ideology: I.G. Farben in the Nazi Era.* Cambridge: Cambridge University Press, 1987.

Haynes, W. *American Chemical Industry,* vols. 1–6. New York: Van Nostrand Company, Inc., 1954.

Hedges, L. V., and I. Olkin. *Statistical Methods for Meta-analysis.* London: Academic Press, 1985.

Hendrick, E. "Records of the Coal-Tar. . . ." *Journal of Industrial and Engineering Chemistry,* Apr. 1924, 411.

Hennekens, C. H., and J. E. Buring. "Aspirin and Cardiovascular Disease." *Bulletin of the New York Academy of Medicine,* Jan. 1989, 57.

———. *Epidemiology in Medicine.* Boston: Little, Brown, 1987.

Hennekens, C. H., R. Peto, and G. B. Hutchinson. "An Overview of the. . . ." *NEJM,* Apr. 7, 1988, 923.

Hettinger, H. S. *A Decade of Radio Advertising.* Chicago: University of Chicago Press, 1933.

Hiebert, J. M. *Our Policy Is People: Their Health Our Business.* New York: The Newcomers Society, 1963.

Higham, C. *Trading With the Enemy: An Exposé of the Nazi-American Money Plot 1933–1949.* New York: Delacorte Press, 1983.

Hill, A. B. "The Clinical Trial." *NEJM,* July 24, 1952, 113.

———. "Observation and Experiment." *NEJM,* June 11, 1953, 995.

———. *Statistical Methods in Clinical and Preventive Medicine.* London: E. & S. Livingstone, 1962.

Himsworth, H. "Bradford Hill and Statistics. . . ." *Statistics in Medicine,* 1982, 301.

Hinsburg, O., and G. Treupel. "Ueber die physiologische Wirkung. . . ." *Archiv für experimentelle Pathologie und Pharmakologie,* 1894, 216.

Holtfrerich, C. *The German Inflation 1914–1923.* Berlin: Walter de Gruyter, 1986.

Honey, G. E., and S. C. Truelove. "Prognostic Factors in Myocardial Infarction," *Lancet,* June 8, 1957, 1155.

Hopkins, C. *My Life in Advertising.* New York, Harper & Brothers, 1927.

Howell, W. H., and E. Holt. "Two New Factors in. . . ." *American Journal of Physiology,* 1918, 328.

Hughes, L. M. "Sterling Streamlines Corporate Setup. . . ." *Sales Management*, Apr. 15, 1943, 32.

Hughes, T. P. "Technological Momentum in History. . . ." *Past and Present*, 1969, 106.

Hull, R., G. E. Raskob, and J. Hirsh. "Prophylaxis of Venous Thromboembolism." *Chest*, May 1986 (suppl.), 374S.

Institute for Scientific Information. "Citation Superstars." *The Scientist*, Feb. 19, 1990, 22.

International Study of Infarct Survival. "Randomised Trial of Intravenous. . . ." *Lancet*, July 12, 1986, 57.

ISIS-2 (Second International Study of Infarct Survival) Collaborative Group. "Randomised Trial of Intravenous. . . ." *Lancet*, Aug. 13, 1988, 349.

Jackson, C. O. *Food and Drug Legislation in the New Deal*. Princeton, N.J.: Princeton University Press, 1970.

Johnston, A. "The Saga of Tommy. . . ." *Saturday Evening Post*, Oct. 13, 1945, 9; Oct. 20, 1945, 24; and Oct. 27, 1945, 34.

———. "White House Tommy." *Saturday Evening Post*, July 31, 1937, 5.

Jordan, H. W. "The Development in the. . . ." *Transactions of the American Institute of Chemical Engineers*, 1915, 209.

Jorpes, E. "First Steps with Heparin." *Thrombosis et Diathesis Haemorrhagica* 9, supp. 11 (1963): 23.

Kenner, H. J. *The Fight for Truth in Advertising*. New York: Round Table Press, Inc., 1936.

Kintner, E. W. "Federal Trade Commission Regulation. . . ." *The Business Lawyer*, Nov. 1960, 84.

Knightley, P. *The First Casualty: From the Crimea to Vietnam—The War Correspondent as Hero, Propagandist, and Myth Maker*. New York: Harcourt Brace Jovanovich, 1975.

Kolbe, A. "Über eine neue Darstellungsmethode. . . ." *Journal für Praktische Chemie*, 1874, 89.

Kraut, K. "Über Salicylverbindung." *Annalen der Chemie*, 1869, 1.

Kurzrock, R., and C. Lieb. "Biochemical Studies of Human. . . ." *Proceedings of the Society of Experimental Biology and Medicine*, 1930, 268.

Landau, H. *The Enemy Within*. New York: G. P. Putnam's Sons, 1937.

Lash, J. *Dealers and Dreamers: A New Look at the New Deal*. New York: Doubleday, 1988.

Lefebure, V. *The Riddle of the Rhine*. New York: The Chemical Foundation, 1923.

Lester, D., and L. A. Greenberg. "The Metabolic Fate of Acetanilid . . . II. . . ." *Journal of Pharmacology and Experimental Therapeutics*, 1947, 68.

Lester, D., et al. "The Fate of Acetylsalicylic Acid." *Journal of Pharmacology and Experimental Therapeutics*, 1946, 329.

Lewis, H. D., et al. "Protective Effects of Aspirin. . . ." *NEJM*, Aug. 18, 1983, 396.

Liebenau, J. "Ethical Business: The Formation. . . ." *Business History*, Jan. 1988, 116.

———. "Industrial R&D in Pharmaceutical. . . ." *Business History*, Nov. 1984, 329.

Liefmann, R. *Cartels, Concerns and Trusts*. London: Methuen & Company, Ltd., 1932.

Light, R. J., and D. B. Pillemer. *Summing Up: The Science of Reviewing Research*. Cambridge: Harvard University Press, 1984.

Lim, R. K. S., et al. "Site of Action of. . . ." *Archives Internationales de Pharmacodynamie et de Thérapie*, Jan. 1964, 25.

Lind, J. *A Treatise of the Scurvy*. Edinburgh: Sands, Murray, and Cochran, 1753.

Link, K. P. "The Anticoagulant Dicumarol." *Proceedings of the Institute of Medicine of Chicago*, Oct. 15, 1945, 370.

———. "The Anticoagulant from Spoiled. . . ." *The Harvey Lectures*. New York: Academic Press, Series 39, 1943–44, 162.

———. "The Discovery of Dicumarol. . . ." *Circulation*, Jan. 1959, 97.

Link, K. P., et al. "Studies in Hemorrhagic Sweet . . . XI. . . ." *Journal of Biological Chemistry*, 1943, 463.

Lloyd, C. "The Introduction of Lemon. . . ." *Bulletin of the History of Medicine*, 1961, 123.

Luckau, A. M. *The German Delegation at the Paris Peace Conference*. New York: Columbia University Press, 1941.

Mahoney, T. *The Merchants of Life*. New York: Harper & Brothers, 1959.

Mantel, N., and W. Haenszel. "Statistical Aspects of the. . . ." *Journal of the National Cancer Institute*, Sept. 1959, 719.

Marcus, A. J. "Aspirin and Thromboembolism. . . ." *NEJM*, Dec. 8, 1977, 1284.

Marshall, J., and D. A. Shaw. "Anticoagulant Therapy in Cerebrovascular Disease." *Proceedings of the Royal Society of Medicine*, 1959, 547.

———. "Anticoagulant Therapy in Cerebrovascular Disease." In W. Walker, ed. *Thrombosis and Anticoagulant Therapy*. St. Andrews, Scotland: University of St. Andrews, 1960, 65.

McKale, D. M. *The Swastika Outside Germany*. Kent, Ohio: Kent State University Press, 1977.

McKenzie, J. R. P. *Weimar Germany, 1918–1933*. London: Blandford Press, 1971.

McLean, J. "The Discovery of Heparin." *Circulation*, Jan. 1959, 75.

McTavish, J. "What's in a Name? . . ." *Bulletin of the History of Medicine*, Fall 1987, 343.

Medical Research Council. "Streptomycin Treatment of Pulmonary Tuberculosis." *BMJ*, Oct. 30, 1948, 769.

Mellow, C. "Winning Hearts and Minds. . . ." *Across the Board*, Oct. 1989, 21.

Merwin, S. *Rise and Fight Again: The Story of a Life-Long Friend (Louis K. Liggett)*. New York: Albert & Chas. Boni, 1935.

Meyer, J. S., et al. "Randomized Clinical Trial of. . . ." *Journal of the American Geriatrics Society*, June 1989, 549.

Meyer, O. O., J. B. Bingham, and V. H. Axelrod. "Studies on the Hemorrhagic . . . I. . . ." *American Journal of the Medical Sciences*, July 1942, 11.

Meyer, O. O., and B. Howard. "Production of Hypoprothrombinemia and. . . ." *Proceedings of the Society for Experimental Biology and Medicine*, June 1943, 234.

Miall, S. *A History of the British Chemical Industry.* London: Ernest Bouverie Ltd., 1931.

Michels, R. K. *Cartels, Combines and Trusts in Post-War Germany.* New York: Columbia University Press, 1928.

Mileke, C. H. "Platelets: The Last Hundred Years." *Series Haematologica,* 1976, 8.

Millikan, C. H., R. G. Siekert, and J. P. Whisnant. "Anticoagulant Therapy in Cerebral. . . ." *JAMA,* Feb. 8, 1958, 587.

Millstein, I. M. "The Federal Trade Commission. . . ." *Columbia Law Review,* 1964, 458.

Mitchell, M. "The Impact of External. . . ." *Economic Inquiry,* Oct. 1989, 601.

Moncada, S., and J. R. Vane. "Mode of Action of. . . ." *Advances in Internal Medicine,* 1979, 1.

Moody's Manual of Investments. New York: Moody's Investor Service, 1939.

Moore, T. "The Fight to Save Tylenol." *Fortune,* Nov. 29, 1982, 45.

Morgan, B. *Apothecary's Venture: The Scientific Quest of the International Nicholas Organisation.* Melbourne: Nicholas Kiwi, 1959.

Morgan, H. W. *Drugs in America.* Syracuse, N.Y.: Syracuse University Press, 1981.

Morse, H. N. "Darstellungsmethode der Acetylamidophenole." *Berichte der Deutschen chemischen Gesellschaft,* 1878, 232.

Munroe, C. E., and A. M. Doyle. "Washington's Relation to the. . . ." *Industrial and Engineering Chemistry,* Apr. 1924, 417.

Murray, D., et al. "Heparin and the Thrombosis. . . ." *Surgery,* Aug. 1937, 163.

Mustard, J. F. "Prostaglandins in Disease: Modification. . . ." In H. J. M. Barnett, J. Hirsh, and J. F. Mustard, eds. *Acetylsalicylic Acid: New Uses for an Old Drug.* New York: Raven Press, 1982, 1.

Mustard, J. F., and M. Packham. "The Reaction of Blood. . . ." In H. Movat, ed. *Inflammation, Immunity and Hypersensitivity.* New York: Harper & Row, 1978, 557.

National Advertising Investments. New York: Leading National Advertisers, 1945–89.

Newton, D. R. L., and J. M. Tanner. "N-Acetyl-para-Aminophenol as an Analgesic." *BMJ,* Nov. 10, 1956, 1096.

Nichol, E. S. "Personal Experiences with Anticoagulants. . . ." *Circulation,* Jan. 1959, 129.

Nichol, E. S., and S. W. Page. "Dicumarol Therapy in Acute. . . ." *Journal of the Florida Medical Association,* Jan. 1946, 370.

Nichols, G. A. "U.S. Company Wages All-Out. . . ." *Printers' Ink,* Feb. 13, 1942, 13.

Nicholson, J. "Ibuprofen." In J. S. Bindra and D. Lednicer, eds. *Chronicles of Drug Discovery.* New York: John Wiley & Sons, 1982, 149.

O'Brien, J. R. "The Adhesiveness of. . . ." *Journal of Clinical Pathology,* Jan. 1961, 140.

———. "Effects of Salicylates on. . . ." *Lancet,* Apr. 13, 1968, 779.

———. "Platelet Aggregation: II. Some. . . ." *Journal of Clinical Pathology,* 1962, 452.

———. "A Trial of Aspirin. . . ." In K. M. Brinkhous et al., eds. *Thrombosis: Mechanisms and Control.* Stuttgart: Schauttauer Verlag, 1973, 345.

O'Brien, J. R., et al. "Two In-vivo Studies. . . ." *Lancet,* Sept. 2, 1972, 441.

Orme, M. "Aspirin All Around?" *BMJ,* Jan. 30, 1988, 307.

Paganini-Hill, A., et al. "Aspirin Use and Chronic Disease. . . ." *BMJ,* Nov. 18, 1989, 1247.

Pais, A. *Inward Bound.* New York: Oxford University Press, 1986.

Palmer, A. M. *Aims and Purposes of the Chemical Foundation.* New York: Chemical Foundation, 1919.

Parcher, C. "Local Doctor Who First. . . ." (A). *Glendale News Press,* date unknown.

Peacock, Jr., E. *Medical World News,* Sept. 1, 1974, 45.

Pearce, J. M. S., S. S. Gubbay, and J. W. Walton. "Long-Term Anticoagulation Therapy in. . . ." *Lancet,* Jan. 2, 1965, 6.

Peters, H. R., J. R. Guyther, and C. E. Brambel. "Dicumarol in Acute Coronary Thrombosis." *JAMA,* Feb. 16, 1946, 398.

Peto, R. "Clinical Trial Methodology." *Biomédicine* (Special Issue), 1978, 24.

Peto, R., et al. "Design and Analysis of . . . I. . . ." *British Journal of Cancer,* 1976, 585.

———. "Design and Analysis of . . . II. . . ." *British Journal of Cancer,* 1976, 1.

———. "Randomised Trial of Prophylactic. . . ." *BMJ,* Jan. 30, 1988, 313.

Pinnow, H. *Werksgeschichte der Gefolgschaft der Werke Leverkusen, Elberfeld und Dormagen zur Erinnerung an die 75 Wiederkehr des Gründungstages der Farbenfabriken vormals Friedrich Bayer & Co.* Munich: I.G. Farbenindustrie, 1938.

Piper, P., and J. R. Vane. "Release of Additional Factors. . . ." *Nature,* July 5, 1969, 29.

Pitofsky, R. "Beyond Nader: Consumer Protection. . . ." *Harvard Law Review,* 1977, 661.

Poole, J. D. F., and J. E. French. "Thrombosis." *Journal of Atherosclerosis,* Aug. 1961, 251.

Pope, D. *The Making of Modern Advertising.* New York: Basic Books, 1983.

Presbrey, F. *The History and Development of Advertising.* New York: Doubleday, Doran & Company, Inc., 1929.

Public Regulation of Competitive Practices. New York: National Industrial Conference Board, Inc., 1929.

Quick, A. J. "Salicylates and Bleeding: The. . . ." *American Journal of the Medical Sciences,* Sept. 1966, 265.

Rapoport, S., M. Wing, and G. M. Guest. "Hypoprothrombinemia after Salicylate Administration. . . ." *Proceedings of the Society for Experimental Biology and Medicine,* May 1943, 40.

Rapp, G. W. "A Cause of Delayed. . . ." *Journal of the American Dental Association,* Apr. 1, 1947, 484.

Relman, A. S. "Aspirin for the Primary. . . ." *NEJM,* Jan. 28, 1988, 245.

———. "Reporting the Aspirin Study." *NEJM,* Apr. 7, 1988, 918.

Remsen, D. "The Use of N-Acetyl p-Aminophenol." In *Symposium on N-Acetyl p-Aminophenol.* Elkhart, Ind.: Institute for the Study of Analgesic and Sedative Drugs, 1952, 59.

Report of the ABA Commission to Study the Federal Trade Commission. Chicago: American Bar Association, Sept. 15, 1969.

Ross, W., and C. Schoenfield. "W.A.R.F. Report." *Wisconsin Alumnus,* June 1948, 21.

Roth, G. J., and P. W. Majerus. "The Mechanism of the . . . I. . . ." *Journal of Clinical Investigation,* Sept. 1975, 624.

Rublee, G. "The Original Plan and. . . ." *Proceedings of the Academy of Political Science,* Jan. 1926, 114.

Rytand, D. A. "Anticoagulants in Coronary Thrombosis. . . ." *Archives of Internal Medicine,* Aug. 1951, 210.

Sandercock, P. "Aspirin for Strokes and. . . ." *BMJ,* Oct. 22, 1988, 995.

Schacht, H. *The Stabilization of the Mark.* New York: Adelphi Company, 1927.

Schiff, E., et al. "The Use of Aspirin. . . ." *NEJM,* Aug. 10, 1989, 351.

Schröter, V. "Participation in Market Control. . . ." In A. Teichova, M. Lévy-Leboyer, and H. Nussbaum, eds. *Multinational Enterprise in Historical Perspective,* 1986, 171.

Schweitzer, H. "The Chemist's Side of. . . ." *Review of Reviews,* Aug. 1915, 207.

———. "German Militarism and Its. . . ." *Popular Science,* Dec. 1914, 581.

———. "The Influence of Sir. . . ." *Science,* Oct. 19, 1906, 481.

Shapiro, S., M. H. Redish, and H. A. Campbell. "Studies on Prothrombin: IV. . . ." *Proceedings of the Society for Experimental Biology and Medicine,* June 1943, 251.

Singer, R. "Acetylsalicylic Acid, A Probable. . . ." *Archives of Otolaryngology,* 1945, 19.

Smith, J. B., and A. L. Willis. "Aspirin Selectively Inhibits Prostaglandin. . . ." *Nature New Biology,* June 23, 1971, 235.

Smith, P. K. *Acetophenetidin: A Critical Bibliographic Review.* New York: Interscience Publishers, 1958.

Smith, R. G., and A. Barrie. *Aspro—How a Family Business Grew Up.* Melbourne, Nicholas International, Ltd., 1976.

Smith, S. B. *In All His Glory: The Life of William S. Paley, the Legendary Tycoon and His Brilliant Circle.* New York: Simon and Schuster, 1990.

Spooner, J. B., and J. G. Harvey. "The History and Usage. . . ." *Journal of International Medical Research,* 1976, 1.

Steering Committee of a Trial on Deep-Vein Thrombosis. Committee on General Epidemiology, Medical Research Council. "Effect of Aspirin. . . ." *Lancet,* Sept. 2, 1972, 441.

Steering Committee of the Physicians' Health Study Research Group. "Preliminary Report: Findings from. . . ." *NEJM,* Jan. 28, 1988, 262.

———. "Final Report on the. . . ." *NEJM,* July 20, 1989, 129.

The Sterling Story. New York: Sterling Drug Co., 1947.

Stokes, R. G. *Divide and Prosper: The Heirs of I.G. Farben Under Allied Authority 1945–51.* Berkeley: University of California Press, 1988.

Stokes, T. "Articles on Corcoran by. . . ." *New York World-Telegram,* Sept. 26, 1941, 9.

———. "Link Tommy the Cork. . . ." *Washington Daily News,* Sept. 15, 1941, 1.

Stone, E. "Account of the Success. . . ." *Philosophical Transactions of the Royal Society*, 1753, 195.

Symposium on N-acetyl p-aminophenol. Elkhart, Ind.: Institute for the Study of Analgesic and Sedative Drugs, 1951.

Temple, H. C. "Has the Use of. . . ." *Ohio State Medical Journal*, May 1936, 429.

Terkel, S. *"The Good War."* New York: Pantheon, 1984.

Thomas, L. *The Youngest Science*. New York: Viking, 1983.

Tilly, R. "Germany: 1815–1870." In R. Cameron, ed. *Banking in the Early Stages of Development*. New York: Oxford University Press, 1967, 151.

UK-TIA Study Group. "United Kingdom Transient Ischaemic. . . ." *BMJ*, Jan. 30, 1988, 316.

Vane, J. R. "Adventures and Excursions in. . . ." *Postgraduate Medical Journal*, Dec. 1983, 743.

———. "Inhibition of Prostaglandin Synthesis. . . ." *Nature New Biology*, June 23, 1971, 232.

———. "Prostaglandins and the Aspirin-Like Drugs." *Hospital Practice*, Mar. 1972, 61.

Vane, J. R., and R. Botting. "Inflammation and the Mechanism. . . ." *F.A.S.E.B. Journal*, 1987, 89.

Verg, E., et al. *Milestones*. Leverkusen: Bayer AG, 1988.

Veterans Administration Cooperative Study of Atherosclerosis, Neurology Section. "An Evaluation of Anticoagulant. . . ." *Neurology*, 1961, 132.

von Euler, U. S. "Zur Kenntnik der pharmakologischen. . . ." *Archiv für Experimentelle Pathologie und Pharmakologie*, 1934, 78.

von Mering, J. "Beitrage zur Kenntniss der Antipyretics." *Therapeutische Monatshefte*, 1893, 577.

Wehler, H. *The German Empire: 1871–1918*. Leamington Spa: Berg Publishers, 1985.

Weiss, H. J. "Aspirin—A Dangerous Drug?" *JAMA*, Aug. 26, 1974, 1221.

———. *Platelets*. New York: Alan R. Liss, Inc., 1982.

Weiss, H. J., and L. M. Aledort. "Impaired Platelet/Connective Tissue Reaction. . . ." *Lancet*, Sept. 2, 1967, 495.

Weiss, H. J., L. M. Aledort, and S. Kochwa. "The Effect of Salicylates. . . ." *Journal of Clinical Investigation*, 1968, 2169.

Weissmann, G. *They All Laughed at Christopher Columbus*. New York: Times Books, 1987.

———. "Aspirin." *Scientific American*, Jan. 1991, 60.

Whiteside, T. "The Communicator." *New Yorker*, Oct. 16, 1954, 37, and Oct. 23, 1954, 43.

———. "The Man from Iron City." *New Yorker*, Sept. 27, 1969, 47.

Wiley, H. W. *Harvey W. Wiley—An Autobiography*. Indianapolis: Bobbs-Merrill Co., 1930.

Wilkins, M. *The History of Foreign Investment in the United States to 1914*. Cambridge: Harvard University Press, 1989.

Williamson, R. T. "On the Treatment of. . . ." *BMJ*, Dec. 27, 1902, 1946.

Witcover, J. *Sabotage at Black Tom: Imperial Germany's Secret War in America, 1914–1917.* Chapel Hill, N.C.: Algonquin Books, 1989.

Wohr, F. "Observations of Three Hundred. . . ." *Medical Bulletin (Philadelphia)*, 1902, 274.

Wood, L. "Aspirin and Myocardial Infarction." *Lancet*, Nov. 11, 1972, 1021.

———. "Treatment of Atherosclerosis and. . . ." *Lancet*, Sept. 9, 1972, 532.

Wood, P. H. N. "The Man Who Invented Aspirin." *Medical News (London)*, Nov. 9, 1962, 20.

Wright, I. S. "Experience with Anticoagulants." *Circulation*, Jan. 1959, 112.

———. "Experiences with Dicumarol. . . ." *American Heart Journal*, 1946, 20.

———. *The Pathogenesis and Treatment of Thrombosis.* Modern Medical Monographs, No. 1. New York: Grune & Stratton, 1952.

Wright, I. S., et al. *Myocardial Infarction: Its Clinical Manifestations and Treatments with Anticoagulants.* New York: Grune & Stratton, 1954.

———. "Report of the Committee. . . ." *American Heart Journal*, Dec. 1948, 801.

Young, F. E., S. L. Nightingale, and R. A. Temple. "The Preliminary Report of. . . ." *JAMA*, June 3, 1988, 3158.

Young, J. H. *The Medical Messiahs.* Princeton, N.J.: Princeton University Press, 1967.

———. *Pure Food.* Princeton, N.J.: Princeton University Press, 1989.

———. *The Toadstool Millionaires.* Princeton, N.J.: Princeton University Press, 1961.

Yusuf, S., et al. "Beta Blockade During and. . . ." *Progress in Cardiovascular Diseases*, Mar.–Apr. 1985, 335.

———. "Intravenous and Intracoronary Fibrinolytic. . . ." *European Heart Journal*, 1985, 556.

Yusuf, S., R. Collins, and R. Peto. "Why Do We Need. . . ." *Statistics in Medicine*, 1984, 409.

Zucker, M. B., and J. Peterson. "Inhibition of Adenosine Diphosphate-Induced. . . ." *Proceedings of the Society for Experimental Biology and Medicine*, Feb. 1968, 547.

II. Government Publications

Advertising of Proprietary Medicines. Hearings, June 17, 1971, Subcommittee on Monopoly, Select Committee on Small Business. U.S. Senate, 92nd Congress, 1st session.

Brewing and Liquor Interests and German and Bolshevik Propaganda. Doc. no. 62, vols. 1 and 2, U.S. Senate, 66th Congress, 1st session, 1919.

Delahanty, T. W. *The German Dyestuffs Industry.* Department of Commerce, Bureau of Foreign and Domestic Commerce. Miscellaneous Series, no. 126, 1924.

Dyestuffs. Hearings, June 18, 1919, Committee on Ways and Means. U.S. House of Representatives, 66th Congress, 1st session.

Economic and Political Aspects of International Cartels. Monograph no. 1, Subcommittee on War Mobilization, Committee on Military Affairs. U.S. Senate, 78th Congress, 2d session, 1944.

Establish a Department of Consumer Affairs. Hearings, Apr. 24, 1969, Subcommittee on Executive Reorganization, Committee on Government Operations. U.S. Senate, 91st Congress, 1st session.

False and Misleading Advertising (Weight-Reducing Preparations). Hearings, Aug. 7, 1957, Committee on Government Operations. U.S. House of Representatives, 85th Congress, 1st session.

Food, Drugs, and Cosmetics. Hearings, Aug. 9–10, 1935, Committee on Interstate and Foreign Commerce. U.S. House of Representatives, 74th Congress, 1st session.

Frauds and Quackery Affecting the Older Citizen. Hearings, part 3, Jan. 17, 1963, Special Committee on the Aging. U.S. Senate, 88th Congress, 1st session.

Independent Offices Appropriations for 1962: Federal Trade Commission. Hearings, Apr. 20, 1961, Subcommittee on Independent Offices, Committee on Appropriations. U.S. Senate, 87th Congress, 1st session.

Jones, W. N., and F. W. Cassebeer. *Prices of Coal-Tar Crudes, Intermediates, and Dyes.* War Industries Board, Price Bulletin no. 53, 1919.

Kebler, L. F. *The Harmful Effects of Acetanilid, Antipyrin, and Phenacetin.* U.S. Department of Agriculture, Bureau of Chemistry, Bulletin no. 126, 1909.

Kronstein, Heinrich. "German Cartels." Exhibit no. 132, *Scientific and Technical Mobilization.* Hearings, part 4 (Patents), June 4, 1943, Subcommittee of the Committee on Military Affairs. U.S. Senate, 78th Congress, 1st session, 409–445.

Nomination of Ugo Carusi as Commissioner of Immigration and Naturalization. Hearings, Dec. 9, 1944, Committee on Immigration. U.S. Senate, 78th Congress, 2nd session.

Norton, T. H. *Dyestuffs for American Textile and Other Industries.* Department of Commerce, Bureau of Foreign and Domestic Commerce, Special Agent Series no. 96, 1915, 30.

———. "Dyestuff Situation in the United States." *Commerce Reports,* May 17, 1915, Department of Commerce, Bureau of Foreign and Domestic Commerce.

———. *Dyestuff Situation in the United States, November, 1915.* Department of Commerce, Bureau of Foreign and Domestic Commerce, Special Agents Series no. 111, 1916.

Pack, C. D. "The Dyestuffs Cartel." Exhibit no. 136, *Scientific and Technical Mobilization, Part 4 [Patents].* Hearings, June 4, 1943, Subcommittee on War Mobilization, Committee on Military Affairs. U.S. Senate, 78th Congress, 1st session.

Patent Medicines. Report no. 52, U.S. House of Representatives. 30th Congress, 2nd session, Feb. 6, 1849, 32.

Porter, H. C. "Coal-Tar Products." Department of the Interior, Bureau of Mines, Technical Paper 89, Feb. 1915.

Sanger, J. W. *Advertising Methods in Argentina, Uruguay, and Brazil.* Department of Commerce, Special Agents Series no. 190, 1920.

Trials of the War Criminals Before the Nuremberg Military Tribunals under Control Council Law No. 10. Washington: Government Printing Office, 1953.

U.S. Department of Agriculture, Bureau of Chemistry. *Report.* Washington, D.C.: Government Printing Office, 1909, 1910, and 1932.

U.S. Department of Commerce. *Foreign Commerce and Navigation of the United States.* Washington, D.C.: Government Printing Office, 1915.

U.S. Food and Drug Administration. "List of All Currently Marketed Products." FDA Archives, unpub. MS., Oct. 20, 1987.

———. "Over-the-Counter Drugs: Internal Analgesic, Antipyretic, and Antirheumatic Drug Products for Over-the-Counter Human Use, Tentative Final Monograph." *Federal Register,* Nov. 16, 1988, 46204.

———. "Over-the-Counter Internal Analgesic and Antirheumatic Drug Products, Safety and Efficacy Review, Request for Data and Information." *Federal Register,* July 21, 1972, 14633.

———. *Progress Report: The OTC Drug Review,* n.d.

———. *Summary of the Report of the Advisory Review Panel on OTC Internal Analgesic, Antipyretic, and Antirheumatic Products,* n.d.

U.S. Office of the Alien Property Custodian. *Annual Report of the Alien Property Custodian, 1918–February 15, 1919,* 1919.

U.S. Tariff Commission. *Census of Dyes and Coal-Tar Chemicals.* 1918–29, Tariff Information Series, nos. 11, 22, 23, 26, 31–35, 37–39.

III.   *Legal Proceedings*

Ambruster v. *Mellon et al.* 41 *F.2d* 430 (1930).

Ambruster v. *National Bank of Westfield.* 182 *Atl.* 613 (1930), 198 *Atl.* 843 (1930).

American Brands, Inc. v. *R. J. Reynolds Tobacco Co.* 413 *F.Supp.* 1352 (1976).

American Home Products v. *FTC.* 695 *F.2d* 681 (1982).

American Home Products v. *Johnson & Johnson.* 77 Civ. 7503, U.S. Court of Appeals, 2nd Circuit.

American Home Products v. *Johnson & Johnson.* 87 Civ. 4097, Eastern District of Pennsylvania.

American Home Products v. *Johnson & Johnson.* 111 *F.R.D.* 448 (1986).

American Home Products v. *Johnson & Johnson.* 682 *F.Supp.* 769 (1988).

American Home Products v. *Johnson & Johnson.* 577 *F.2d* 160 (1978).

American School of Magnetic Healing v. *McAnnulty.* 187 *U.S.* 94 (1902).

Anacin Company. 44 *FTC* 1130 (1944).

Bayer Company, Ltd. v. *American Druggists Syndicate, Ltd.* 1924 *S.C.R.* 558 (1924).

Bayer Company, Ltd. v. *Farbenfabriken vorm. Bayer & Co. et al.* 2 *D.L.R.* 616 (1944).

Bayer Company v. *United Drug Company.* 272 *Fed.* 505 (1921).

Bayer Company v. *United Drug Company.* Docket E14-180, Southern District of New York, Federal Records Center, Bayonne, N.J.

Bayer Pharma Pty. Ltd. v. *Henry York & Co. Ltd.* 1964 *F.S.R.* 143 (1964).

"Bayer" Trademark (Australia). 1965 *F.S.R.* 261 (1965).

"Bayer" Trademark (England). 1965 *F.S.R.* 354 (1965).

Bristol-Myers v. *FTC.* 284 *F.Supp.* 745 (1968).

Case nos. 2452, 2466, 2504, 2508, 2564, 2566, 2568, 2570, 2572, 2574, 2576, 2578. U.S. District Court, E.D. of Pennsylvania.

Charles of the Ritz Distributors Corp. v. *FTC.* 143 *F.2d* 676 (1944).

Dobson v. *Farbenfabriken of Elberfeld Co. et al.* 206 *Fed.* 125 (1913).

Farbenfabriken Bayer AG v. *Sterling Drug.* Civ. 908–55/909–55, District Court of New Jersey.

Farbenfabriken Bayer AG v. *Sterling Drug.* 148 *F.Supp.* 733 (1957).

Farbenfabriken Bayer AG v. *Sterling Drug.* 148 *F.Supp.* 738 (1957).

Farbenfabriken Bayer AG v. *Sterling Drug.* 153 *F.Supp.* 589 (1957).

Farbenfabriken Bayer AG v. *Sterling Drug.* 197 *F.Supp.* 613 (1961).

Farbenfabriken Bayer AG v. *Sterling Drug.* 197 *F.Supp.* 627 (1961).

Farbenfabriken Bayer AG v. *Sterling Drug.* 307 *F.2d* 207 (1962).

Farbenfabriken Bayer AG v. *Sterling Drug.* 307 *F.2d* 210 (1962).

Farbenfabriken of Elberfeld Co. v. *Kuehmsted.* 171 *Fed.* 887 (1909).

Farbenfabriken vormals Friedrich Bayer & Co. v. *Chemische Fabrik von Heyden.* 22 *R.P.C.* 501 (1905).

FTC v. *Raladam.* 283 *U.S.* 643 (1931).

FTC v. *Standard Educational Society et al.* 86 *F.2d* 692 (1936).

FTC v. *Standard Educational Society et al.* 302 *U.S.* 112 (1937).

FTC v. *Sterling Drug.* 215 *F.Supp.* 327 (1963).

FTC v. *Sterling Drug.* 317 *F.2d* 669 (1963).

General Aniline & Film v. *Bayer Co.* 113 *N.E.* 2d 844 (1953).

In re "Aspirin." American Druggists Syndicate, Ltd. (Petitioner), and Bayer Company, Ltd. (Objecting Party). 1923 *Ex.C.R.* 65 (1923).

In re Badische Company, Ltd. 2 *Ch.* 331 (1921).

In the Matter of American Home Products, Bristol-Myers, Plough, and Sterling Drug. 67 *FTC* 430 (1965).

In the Matter of the Anacin Co., *FTC* Docket 5213, Federal Records Center, Suitland, Md.

In the Matter of Bayer Company. 19 *FTC* 229 (1934).

In the Matter of Bayer Company. *FTC* Docket 2192, Federal Records Center, Suitland, Md.

In the Matter of Cal-Aspirin. 22 *FTC* 89 (1936).

In the Matter of Charles of the Ritz Distributors Corp. 34 *FTC* 1203 (1942).

In the Matter of Pfizer. 81 *FTC* 23 (1972).

In the Matter of Plough. 24 *FTC* 115 (1936).

In the Matter of Plough. 65 *FTC* 583 (1964).

In the Matter of Raladam Company. 12 *FTC* 363 (1929).

In the Matter of Sterling Drug. 64 *FTC* 898 (1964).

In the Matter of the Trusts of an Agreement Dated the 15th November, 1926, and Made between I.G. Farbenindustrie Aktiengesellschaft and Bayer Products Limited, etc. 58 *R.P.C.* 31 (1940).

In the Matter of the Trusts of an Agreement Made between I.G. Farbenindustrie Aktiengesellschaft and Bayer Products Ltd., etc. 60 *R.P.C.* 193 (1943).

Indo-Pharma Pharmaceutical Works Pvt. Ltd. v. *Farbenfabriken Bayer AG.* 1975 *R.P.C.* 545 (1975).

James Dobson, surviving co-partner, etc., trading as John and James Dobson, v. *Farben (NY) & Farben (Lev).* No. 2466, March session 1913, Eastern District Court of Pennsylvania, June 3, 1913.

John C. Winston Co. v. *FTC.* 3 *F.2d* 961 (1925).

Justin Haynes & Co. v. *FTC.* 105 *F.2d* 988 (1939).

Kuehmsted v. *Farbenfabriken of Elberfeld Co.* 179 *Fed.* 701 (1910).

McNeil v. *American Home Products.* 78 *Civ.* 562, Southern District of New York.

McNeil v. *American Home Products.* 416 *F.Supp.* 804 (1976).

McNeil v. *American Home Products.* 675 *F.Supp.* 819 (1987).

McNeil v. *American Home Products.* 848 *F.2d* 34 (1988).

McNeil v. *Bristol-Myers.* 656 *F.Supp.* 88 (1986).

McNeil v. *Margaret M. Heckler.* 84 *Civ.* 1617, District Court for District of Columbia.

McNeil v. *Sterling Drug.* 81 *Civ.* 6714, Southern District of New York.

Raladam Co. v. *FTC.* 42 *F.2d* 430 (1930).

Sterling Drug v. *FTC.* 741 *F.2d* 1146 (1984).

Sterling Drug, Inc. v. *Bayer AG et al.,* 90 Civ. 3460, Southern District of New York.

Sterling-Winthrop Group Ltd. v. *Farbenfabriken Bayer AG & F.B.A. Pharmaceuticals Ltd.* 1966 *R.P.C.* 477 (1966).

Sterling-Winthrop Group Ltd. v. *Farbenfabriken Bayer AG & F.B.A. Pharmaceuticals Ltd.* 1967 *R.P.C.* 326 (1967).

Sterling-Winthrop Group Ltd. v. *Farbenfabriken Bayer AG & F.B.A. Pharmaceuticals Ltd.* 1969 *R.P.C.* 274 (1969).

Sterling-Winthrop Group Ltd. v. *Farbenfabriken Bayer AG* 1976 *R.P.C.* 469 (1976).

The King v. *The Comptroller-General of Patents, etc.,* Ex parte *Bayer Products, Ltd.* 58 *R.P.C.* 251 (1941).

U.S. v. *Alba Pharmaceutical Company et al.* 1941 *Trade Cases* 56,151 (1941).

U.S. v. *Johnson.* 177 *Fed.* 313 (1910).

U.S. v. *Johnson.* 221 *U.S.* 488 (1911).

U.S. v. *The Bayer Company et al.* 1941 *Trade Cases* 56,151 (1941).

U.S. v. *The Bayer Company et al.* 105 *F.Supp.* 955 (1952).

U.S. v. *The Bayer Company et al.* 135 *F.Supp.* 65 (1955).

United Drug Company v. *Farbenfabriken of Elberfeld Co.* U.S. Patent Office Cancellation no. 424.

Upjohn v. *American Home Products.* 598 *F.Supp.* 550 (1984).

Weltmer et al. v. *Bishop.* 71 *S.W.* 167 (1902).

William S. Merrell v. *Anacin Company.* U.S. Court of Customs and Patent Appeals, Patent Appeal Docket no. 4133, Opposition 15,051, 1938.

IV. *Miscellaneous Sources*

Anti-Platelet Trialists Collaboration. "Methods and Results" (A). Unpub. MS., Mar. 23–25, 1990.

Collier, H. O. J. "Aspirin and the Prevention of Senile Osteoporosis" (A). Unpub. MS., H. O. J. Collier's files, Mar. 4, 1983.

———. "Notes on the Safety of Aspirin and Paracetamol" (A). Unpub. rept., Aspirin Foundation, Mar. 15, 1982.

McTavish, J. *The German Pharmaceutical Industry 1880–1920: A Case Study of Aspirin.* M.A. thesis. University of Minnesota, 1986, 50.

Nychis, W. Memorandum of Meeting (A). Mar. 2, 1988, FDA, courtesy P. Rheinstein.

Ringuette, C. A. "Proprietary Medicines in an Age of Transition" (A). Paper presented at the Annual Meeting of the Indiana Historical Society, Nov. 1, 1986.

Wright, I. S. "The Use and Abuse of Anticoagulants." Abstract of Address Delivered to New York Academy of Medicine, Oct. 5, 1948. NYAM Medical Information Bureau press release.

Yates, D. N. "Origin of Alka-Seltzer" (A). Paper presented at the Annual Meeting of the Indiana Historical Society, Nov. 1, 1986.

V. *Interviews*

Stewart Adams, Erik Änggåard, John Baruch, David Bickart, Donald Braun, Joe Collier, Rory Collins, David Corcoran, Joan Corcoran, Jonathan Dick, Peter Elwood, Federal Trade Commission lawyers (confidential interviews), William Fields, Ray Freisham, Gordon Fryers, Peter Göb, Eli Goldensohn, Richard Gryglewski, William Hass, Peter Hauri, Charles Hennekens, Jürgen Hohmann, Judy Hsia, Knox Ide, Herbert Israel, Johnson & Johnson lawyer (confidential interview), Jack Jordan, Terry Kelley, Ed Landreth, William Laporte, Earle Lockhart, William Lynch, John Stirling Meyer, Robin Mills, Charles Mosey, Wayne Nelson, John O'Brien, Barbara Owen, Carrol Parcher, Richard Peto, Priscilla Piper, Robert Pitofsky, Massimo Porta, Noel Rabouhans, Ross Renton, Peter Rheinstein, Peter Sandercock, Jack Shapiro, William Soller, Laurie Spalton, Sterling lawyer (confidential interview), U.S. pharmaceutical executives (confidential interviews), Sir John Vane, Charles Warlow, Gilbert Weil, Aaron Weinstein, Steve Weisman, Harvey Weiss, Gerald Weissmann, Irving Wright, Frank Young.

ACKNOWLEDGMENTS

No book is solely written by its authors, and this one is a testament to that fact. Our debts are manifold, because many people and institutions helped us write this history. Archival material came from the British Library; Bayer AG Archives (Leverkusen); the Library of Congress; the National Archives in Washington, D.C., and the associated archives of the Federal Trade Commission, the Food and Drug Administration, and the Department of Justice; the Federal Record Centers in Suitland, Maryland, Bayonne, New Jersey, and Philadelphia, Pennsylvania; and the University of Washington library system. Of the many archivists and agency employees who devoted their time to what they must have considered our peculiar requests, we would like to especially thank Ken Williams of the Department of Justice and Bruce Ashkenas of the Suitland record center.

Special gratitude is owed to Peter Göb, Thomas Reinert, Christina Sehnert, Kurt Sappert, Ingeborg Fabri, and Gottfried Plumpe of Bayer AG, who patiently put up with many importuning faxes and requests for clarification. Of course, our conclusions about Bayer in no way reflect their opinions. We have fewer debts to other aspirin companies, but we are delighted to acknowledge help from Sterling, where Terry Kelley answered repeated phone calls; Nicholas, where Jonathan Dick spent hours showing us through his company's history; and Miles (now a Bayer subsidiary), where Celeste Aaron and Donald Yates provided much helpful material.

In our various travels, we were given hospitality by, among others, Steve Suffern, Amanda Spake, Danielle Drevet, John and Terry Wallis, and, especially, Newell and Greta Blair. It is a pleasure to remember their kindness. Ellen Goldensohn and June Kinoshita tolerated repeated requests for the use of fax machines. Karin Richards and Susan Booker performed long-distance research assistance with care. Some journalists shared their expertise, including Craig Mellow, Patricia Winters, and Thomas Whitesides.

We would like to tip our hats in special appreciation to Peter Rheinstein, Peter Hayes, Pauline Ippolito, Peter Elwood, Peter Mann, Ed Zuckerman, Alan Levy, Gerald Weissmann, John O' Brien, and Steve Hall, who commented on early drafts of the manuscript. We owe further debts to Ray Kinoshita, Gerry Butters, Alan Mathios, Gordon Fryers, Stewart Adams, Ken Plevan, Howard Adler, Morris Blatman, Steve Salant, Susan Landau, Laurie Spalton, Gordon Phillips, Richard Kronmal, Barbara McKnight, Ira Gallen, Brian Wolff, Lawrence Plummer, Gerri Hurlbutt, and Ray Freisham.

This book was shaped with the counsel of a brace of brave and talented editors: William Whitworth and Corby Kummer at *The Atlantic*, who first accepted the notion that examining the history of a commodity might be worthwhile, and Jonathan Segal, Sonny Mehta, and Ida Giragossian at Knopf. In a thousand ways they have pushed and prodded this sometimes reluctant material (and its authors) into shape. Here we must also note our special thanks to Jane Amsterdam, who initially acquired this project but left for greater things. Rick Balkin walked the contract tightrope with his usual grouchy aplomb. Bayer AG and Thomas G. Corcoran, Jr., responded quickly to our requests for permission to quote material, for which we are grateful. Along the way, our families put up in reasonably graceful style with much talk of aspirin and many late hours, as well as considerable travel. Thank you, Newell and Sasha, Robert and Elizabeth, Gwenda and Cassie (with love). And, of course, each of us, in a gesture made awkward by the constraints of the English language, thanks the other for the wonderful time we had writing this book.

INDEX

Index

PERMISSIONS
ACKNOWLEDGMENTS

Grateful acknowledgment is made to the following for permission to reprint previously published material:

Chemical Engineering CEEBG: Modification of "Colossal Structure and Ramifications of the Great German Chemical Combine" diagram, published in *Swensk Kemisk Tidskrift,* June 1927. *Chemical and Metallurgical Engineering,* January 1928, p. 6. Reprinted by permission.

Circulation: Excerpts from "The Discovery of Dicumarol" by K. P. Link. *Circulation,* January 1959, vol. 19, no. 1, p. 97. Reprinted by permission of the American Heart Association Scientific Publications Department.

Elsevier Scientific Publishers Ireland Ltd.: Excerpts from "Thrombosis" by J. D. F. Poole and J. E. French. *Journal of Atherosclerosis,* August 1961, p. 251. Reprinted by permission.

The Harvey Society: Excerpt from article by K. P. Link. *The Harvey Lectures,* Series 39, 1943–44, p. 162, Academic Press. Reprinted by permission of The Harvey Society.

Institute of Medicine of Chicago: Excerpts from "The Anticoagulant Dicumarol" by K. P. Link. *The Proceedings of the Institute of Medicine of Chicago,* October 15, 1945, p. 370. Reprinted by permission.

Journal of the American Medical Association: Excerpt from an editorial. *Journal of the American Medical Association,* January 20, 1917, vol. 68, pp. 201–202. Copyright 1917 by American Medical Association. Reprinted by permission.

Los Angeles County Medical Association: Excerpts from "Acetylsalicylic Acid, Possible Preventive of Coronary Thrombosis" (Letter to the Editor) by L. L. Craven. *Annals of Western Medicine and Surgery,* February 1950, p. 95. Reprinted by permission.

The Macmillan Press Ltd.: Excerpt from "Design and Analysis of Randomized Clinical Trials Requiring Prolonged Observation of Each Patient" by Peto et al. *British Journal of Cancer,* December 1976, vol. 34, p. 594. Reprinted by permission.

Medical World News: Excerpt from article by E. Peacock, Jr. *Medical World News,* September 1972, p. 45. Reprinted by permission.

Sales & Marketing Management: Excerpt from article by J. D. Cathcart. *Sales Management,* April 1, 1943, p. 68. Copyright 1943 by *Sales Management.* Reprinted by permission.

Society of Experimental Biology and Medicine: Excerpt from "Biochemical Studies of Human Semen. II. The Action of Semen on the Human Uterus" by R. Kurzrock and C. Lieb. *Proceedings of the Society of Experimental Biology and Medicine,* 1930, pp. 268–272. Reprinted by permission.

A NOTE ON THE TYPE

The text of this book was set in a face called Times Roman, designed by Stanley Morison (1889–1967) for *The Times* (London), and first introduced by that newspaper in 1932.

Among typographers and designers of the twentieth century, Stanley Morison was a strong forming influence, as typographical adviser to the English Monotype Corporation, as a director of two distinguished English publishing houses, and as a writer of sensibility, erudition, and keen practical sense.

In 1930 Morison wrote: "Type design moves at the pace of the most conservative reader. The good type-designer therefore realises that, for a new fount to be successful, it has to be so good that only very few recognise its novelty. If readers do not notice the consummate reticence and rare discipline of a new type, it is probably a good letter." It is now generally recognized that in the creation of Times Roman, Morison successfully met the qualifications of this theoretical doctrine.

Composed by American–Stratford Graphic Services, Inc.,
Brattleboro, Vermont
Printed and bound by Halliday Lithographers,
West Hanover, Massachusetts
Designed by Virginia Tan